Constitutionalism and the Economy in Africa

STELLENBOSCH HANDBOOKS IN AFRICAN CONSTITUTIONAL LAW

Series Editors

Professor Charles Manga Fombad

Director, Institute for International and Comparative Law in Africa (ICLA), Faculty of Law, University of Pretoria, South Africa

Professor Nico Steytler

South African Research Chair in Multilevel Government, Law and Development
Dullah Omar Institute of Constitutional Law, Governance and Human Rights
University of the Western Cape, South Africa

Constitutionalism and the Economy in Africa

Edited by

CHARLES M FOMBAD

and

NICO STEYTLER

OXFORD
UNIVERSITY PRESS

Great Clarendon Street, Oxford, OX2 6DP,
United Kingdom

Oxford University Press is a department of the University of Oxford.
It furthers the University's objective of excellence in research, scholarship,
and education by publishing worldwide. Oxford is a registered trade mark of
Oxford University Press in the UK and in certain other countries

First Edition published in 2022

Impression: 1

Published in the United States of America by Oxford University Press
198 Madison Avenue, New York, NY 10016, United States of America

British Library Cataloguing in Publication Data

Data available

Library of Congress Control Number: 2022941526

ISBN 978–0–19–288643–9

DOI: 10.1093/oso/9780192886439.001.0001

Printed and bound in the UK by
TJ Books Limited

Preface

This sixth book in our *Stellenbosch Handbooks in African Constitutional Law* series is the outcome of the seventh Stellenbosch Annual Seminar on Constitutionalism in Africa (SASCA). As in the past, it was organized by the Institute for International and Comparative Law in Africa (ICLA) of the Faculty of Law, University of Pretoria, the South African Research Chair in Multilevel Government, Law and Development (SARChI) at the Dullah Omar Institute, University of the Western Cape, and the Stellenbosch Institute for Advanced Study (STIAS). This was done in partnership with the Konrad Adenauer Stiftung (KAS) Rule of Law Programme for Anglophone Sub-Saharan Africa, Nairobi, Kenya. The seminar took place from 18 to 20 September 2019.

The theme for the seventh SASCA conference, 'Constitutionalism and the Economy in Africa', was largely informed by the fact that the economic benefits that were supposed to accrue from the constitutional reforms of the last three decades in Africa have not materialized. Most African economies remain weak, with some of them floundering. The participants examined a number of questions with regard to the nature of the economy, the nature of the state, the relationship between them, as well as the global economic order within which they operate. Some of the issues looked at included how the relationship between the state and the economy is structured and managed through the constitution. This raised a number of important questions. To what extent do constitutions determine the nature of the economy? How do they express different economic models? How does the notion of limited government play out in the economy? Overall, the participants tried to see to what extent the economic constitution not only protects economic interests but also ensures that all the fundamental principles of constitutionalism as well as the political system itself are protected.

As in previous years, the seminar attracted eminent and emerging young constitutional scholars from across Africa and abroad. A key objective of these seminars continues to be our desire to encourage and mentor up-and-coming scholars concerned with constitutional law and its practice in Africa. This important goal is reflected in the inclusion of papers in this volume written by young scholars who participated in the seminar. We have also endeavoured, in line with the fundamental objective of this series, to secure papers that would cover a cross-section of the continent's regions and legal traditions.

We would like to acknowledge and thank a number of persons and institutions that made this book possible. First, the seminar would not have taken place without the financial support provided by Swedish Riksbankens Jubileumsfond to STIAS to fund the SASCA programme. We would like to thank in particular the director of STIAS, Professor Edward Kirumira, and his predecessor, Professor Hendrik Geyer, and the Coordinator of Strategic Initiatives, Professor Johann Groenewald, for their enthusiasm and guidance. We would also like to acknowledge the assistance of the very able Mrs Nel-Mari Loock for all the practical arrangements. Secondly, we are grateful to Dr Lukman Abdulrauf of the Faculty of Law, University of Ilorin, Nigeria and Dr Michelle Maziwisa, postdoctoral fellow at the South African Research Chair in Multilevel Government, Law and Development (SARChI) at the Dullah Omar Institute, who also provided excellent assistance in the management of the papers as well as casting a critical eye on their content. Thirdly, we would like to acknowledge support provided by the South African Research Chairs Initiative of the Department of Science and Technology and National Research Foundation, through the South African Research Chair in Multilevel Government, Law and Development. Fourthly, we much appreciate the financial and advisory support provided by KAS. Fifthly, thank you to all the peer-reviewers who helped in ensuring the quality of the end product. Sixthly, we would also wish to thank Andre Wiesner for his incisive editorial eye. Finally, special thanks go to OUP staff, especially Mr Alex Flach, Ms Paulina dos Santos Major, and Mr Ashirvad Moses.

Charles M Fombad and Nico Steytler

Pretoria and Cape Town
May 2022

Contents

IV. THE CONSTITUTIONAL FRAMEWORK FOR THE STATE'S ROLE IN THE ECONOMY

V. IMPACT OF GLOBALIZATION ON THE ECONOMY AND CONSTITUTIONALISM

VI. GENERAL CONCLUSION

Table of Cases

INTERNATIONAL AND REGIONAL COURTS

NATIONAL JURISDICTIONS

Table of Legislation

List of Abbreviations

ACHPR	African Charter/Commission/Court on Human and Peoples' Rights
AfCFTA	African Continental Free Trade Area
AFEA	Armed Forces Engineering Authority
AHRLR	African Human Rights Law Reports
ANC	African National Congress
AOI	Arab Organization for Industrialization
AU	African Union
AUC	African Union Commission
BCLR	Butterworths Constitutional Law Reports
BEE	Black Economic Empowerment
BIPPA	Bilateral Investment Protection and Promotion agreement
BIT	Bilateral Investment Treaty
BRICS	Brazil, Russia, India, China and South Africa
BSAC	British South African Company
BVerfGE	Bundesverfassungsgericht
CC	Close Corporation
CC	Constitutional Court
CFA	Communauté Financière Africaine
COMESA	Common Market for Eastern and Southern Africa
Cosatu	Congress of South African Trade Unions
CPA	Comprehensive Peace Accord
CTA	Civil Transactions Act
DRC	Democratic Republic of the Congo
DSU	Dispute Settlement Understanding
EAC	East Africa Community
ECB	European Central Bank
ECC	Environmental Clearance Certificate
ECHR	European Convention on Human Rights
ECOWAS	Economic Community of West African States
EFF	Economic Freedom Fighters
EGP	Egyptian pound
EIA	Environmental Investigation Agency
EITI	Extractive Industries Transparency Initiative
EJIL	European Journal of International Law
EPRDF	Ethiopian People's Revolutionary Democratic Front
EPZ	Export Processing Zone
ETB	Ethiopian birr
EU	European Union
FAO	Food and Agriculture Organization of the United Nations
FDI	foreign direct investment
FDRE	Federal Democratic Republic of Ethiopia

FTLRP	Fast-track Land Reform Programme
GATS	General Agreement on Trade in Services
GATT	General Agreement on Tariffs and Trade
GDP	gross domestic product
GEAR	Growth, Employment, and Redistribution
GLR	Ghana Law Review
GNI	gross national income
GNP	Gauteng North Pretoria
GTP	Growth and Transformation Plan
HDI	Human Development Index
HH	Harare High Court
HoF	House of Federation
ICMM	International Council on Mining & Metals
ICSID	International Centre for Settlement of Investment Disputes
IGR	intergovernmental relations
ILO	International Labour Organization
IMF	International Monetary Fund
ITO	International Trade Organization
JSAL	Journal of South African Law
LDC	least-developed country
MAWF	Ministry of Agriculture, Water and Forestry
MDG	Millennium Development Goal
MET	Ministry of Environment and Tourism
MoFED	Ministry of Finance and Economic Development
MPRA	Munich Personal RePEc Archive
MPRDA	Mineral and Petroleum Resources Development Act 28 of 2002
NAD	Namibian dollar
NAHC	Namibia High Court
NAHCMD	Namibia High Court Main Division
NASC	Namibia Supreme Court
NBER	National Bureau of Economic Research
NDP	National Development Plan
NMP	Namibian Marine Phosphate (Pty) Ltd
NNP	nations, nationalities, and peoples
NOMP	National Organization for Military Production
NP	National Party
NPA	National Prosecuting Authority
NPC	National Planning Commission
NRGI	Natural Resource Governance Index
NSPO	National Service Projects Organization
ODA	official development aid
ODI	Open Data Institute
PELJ	Potschefstroom Electronic Law Journal
PER	Potschefstroomse Elektroniese Regsblad
PPP	purchasing power parity
PSNR	Permanent Sovereignty of Natural Resources
RDP	Reconstruction and Development Programme
SA	South Africa

SABC	South African Broadcasting Corporation
SACP	South African Communist Party
SACU	Southern Africa Customs Union
SADC	Southern African Development Community
SADCT	SADC Tribunal
SAP	structural adjustment programme
SARB	South African Reserve Bank
SBEC	Sustainable Blue Economy Conference
SCA	Supreme Court of Appeal
SCAF	Supreme Council of Armed Forces
SCGLR	Supreme Court of Ghana Law Reports
SCR	Supreme Court of India
SDGs	Sustainable Development Goals
SNNP	Southern Nations, Nationalities, and Peoples
SOE	state-owned enterprise
SPLA	Sudan People's Liberation Army
SSA	Sub-Saharan Africa
SWAPO	South West Africa People's Organization
TFA	Trade Facilitation Agreement
TPLF	Tigray People's Liberation Front
TRIPS	Trade-Related Aspects of International Property Rights
TSAL	Tydskrif vir die Suid-Afrikaanse Reg
ULA	Unregistered Land Act
UNCTAD	United Nations Conference on Trade and Development
UNDP	United Nations Development Programme
UNGA	United Nations General Assembly
USD	US dollars
VAT	value-added tax
VCLT	Vienna Convention on the Law of Treaties
WP	Working Paper
WTO	World Trade Organization
WUA	Water User Association
ZACC	Constitutional Court of South Africa
ZAFSHC	South Africa Free-State High Court
ZAGPPHC	South Africa North Gauteng Pretoria High Court
ZANU-PF	Zimbabwe African National Union—Patriotic Front
ZLR	Zimbabwe Law Review
ZWL	Zimbabwean dollar

List of Contributors

Adem Kassie Abebe
Senior Program Officer, International IDEA; Extraordinary Lecturer, Centre for Human Rights, University of Pretoria, South Africa.

Eva Maria Belser
Chair of Constitutional and Administrative Law, University of Fribourg and UNESCO Chair in Human Rights and Democracy; co-director of the Institute of Federalism, University of Fribourg, Fribourg, Switzerland.

Sherif Elgebeily
Director, Centre for the Study of International Peace and Security, London, United Kingdom

Charles M Fombad
Director, Institute for International and Comparative Law in Africa (ICLA) of the Faculty of Law, University of Pretoria, Pretoria, South Africa

John Hursh
Director of Research, Stockton Center for International Law, US Naval War College, New Port, Rhode Island, United States; Editor-in-Chief, *International Law Studies*

Heinz Klug
Evjue-Bascom Professor of Law, University of Wisconsin, Madison, Wisconsin, United States

Ramos Emmanuel Mabugu
Professor of Economics at Sol Plaatje University, Kimberly; former director of research, Financial and Fiscal Commission, South Africa

Makanatsa Makonese
Deputy Chief of Party, Advancing Rights in Southern Africa, American Bar Association, Johannesburg, South Africa

Trevor Manuel
Chairperson of the Board of Old Mutual Ltd; former Minister of Finance; former Chairperson of the National Planning Commission, South Africa

Henning Melber
Extraordinary Professor, Department of Political Science, University of Pretoria and Extraordinary Professor, Centre for Gender and African Studies, University of the Free State, Bloemfontein, South Africa

Hanri Mostert
NRF/DST Research Chair in Mineral Law in Africa, Faculty of Law, University of Cape Town, Cape Town, South Africa

Solomon Negussie
Associate Professor of Law and former Dean, College of Law and Governance Studies, University of Addis Ababa, Addis Ababa, Ethiopia

Stephan FH Ollick
Country Manager (Afghanistan) and
Research Fellow (Asia), Max Planck Foundation for International Peace and the Rule of Law, Heidelberg, Germany

Nico Steytler
South African Research Chair in Multilevel Government, Law and Development (SARChI Chair), at the Dullah Omar Institute, University of the Western Cape, Cape Town, South Africa

Keynote Address

Trevor Manuel

One of the distinct privileges I have enjoyed in life was to be amongst the 490 women and men who, as a group of public representatives, adopted the South African Constitution as the supreme law of our country on 8 May 1996. The date marked the culmination of a process that began in 1991, led to the adoption of an Interim Constitution in 1993, and saw the first cadre of public representative assume the responsibility of the Constitutional Assembly.

We adopted the Constitution as the supreme law so as to

Heal the divisions of the past and establish a society based on democratic values, social justice and fundamental human rights;

Lay the foundations for a democratic and open society in which government is based on the will of the people and every citizen is equally protected by law;

Improve the quality of life of all citizens and free the potential of each person; and

Build a united and democratic South Africa able to take its rightful place as a sovereign state in the family of nations.[1]

It should thus not surprise anybody that I am biased towards the values articulated in our Constitution. Underpinning that approach is an acknowledgement that the supreme law acquires its status as such from the values embodied in it and acquires its operationality from its durability. In the context of South Africa, and probably of most jurisdictions across the African continent, political plurality is an operational principle.

The shift to values, rights, economic choice, and political plurality is a fundamental shift away from the political-economy, big-systemic arguments about 'free market', 'mixed', or 'market' economies, 'command of the controlling heights', or 'Marxist-Leninism'. Having perused a few constitutions (read with the eye of a non-expert, of course), I am encouraged by the fact that these 'big systemic arguments' appear to be largely absent in South Africa's Constitution.

By way of example, the excellent 2004 Constitution of Mozambique (as revised in 2007) retains the principle that '[a]ll ownership of land shall vest in the State'.[2] It also expresses a view on sectors of ownership that includes the public sector, the private sectors, and the 'co-operative and social sector', and it allows for the right of inheritance.[3] All of this speaks to a profound modernization that includes a raft of socio-economic rights.

Similarly, the 2013 Constitution of the Republic of Zimbabwe describes its commitment to national development as follows:

---

[1] Constitution of the Republic of South Africa of 1996, preamble.
[2] Constitution of the Republic of Mozambique of 2007, art 109.
[3] Constitution of the Republic of Mozambique of 2007, art 83.

Trevor Manuel, *Keynote Address* In: *Constitutionalism and the Economy in Africa*. Edited by: Charles M Fombad and Nico Steytler, Oxford University Press. © Trevor Manuel 2022. DOI: 10.1093/oso/9780192886439.003.0001

The state and all institutions and agencies of government at every level must endeavour to facilitate rapid and equitable development, and in particular must take measures to—

a) Promote private initiative and self-reliance;

b) Foster agricultural, commercial, industrial, technological and scientific development;

c) Foster the development of industrial and commercial enterprises in order to empower Zimbabwean citizens; and

d) Bring about balanced development in the different areas of Zimbabwe, in particular a proper balance in the development of rural and urban areas.[4]

I have no doubt that there are still a few countries whose constitutions place a strong emphasis on centralized control, but these are a small minority, with most countries having modernized their approach.

The approach in South Africa as well as Mozambique and Zimbabwe, as evidenced above, has a focus on socio-economic rights. As Christof Heyns and Danie Brand observe in a seminal paper of theirs, '[B]ills of rights invariably emanate from periods of struggle and represent a collective commitment to ensure that the conditions which led to the conflict from which the society in question is emerging, are not allowed to develop again in the future'.[5] Their paper offers a useful overview of the threads of the debate that eventually knotted together in the South African Bill of Rights. They also explain the modus of a progressive realization of rights—a rising floor of rights, dependent on, among other features, that their realization is 'subject to available resources'.[6]

Let me briefly digress and note that the question of affordability of aspects of the South African Bill of Rights has been tested in our Constitutional Court on a number of occasions. The first of these, *Soobramoney v The Minister of Health*,[7] related to the right of the applicant to specialized health treatment, namely dialysis. The court in that instance held that the need for dialysis was not an emergency and that the right not to be refused emergency medical treatment was independent of the right to life and had to be interpreted in the context of the availability of health services generally. The second case, *Grootboom*, related to the need for access to housing.[8] The court then held that whilst access to housing is a matter of human dignity, this does not oblige the state to go beyond its available resources. The third case was brought by the Treatment Action Campaign on appeal to the Constitutional Court.[9] The application related to the availing of nevirapine to pregnant mothers to prevent mother-to-child transmission of HIV. In this instance, the court ordered the government to avail nevirapine in public health facilities.

In 'Constitutions, Politics and Economics: A Review Essay on Persson and Tabellini', Daron Açemoglu uses Persson and Tabellini's Policy Process Framework to construct an understanding of how policies differ over time and how polities make choices.[10] The

---

[4] Constitution of Zimbabwe Amendment Act 20 of 2013, s 13(1)(a)–(d).

[5] C Heyns and D Brand, 'Introduction to Socio-Economic Rights in the South African Constitution' (1998) 2(2) Law, Democracy & Development 153.

[6] ibid 159–60.

[7] *Soobramoney v Minister of Health (KwaZulu-Natal)* [1997] ZACC 17.

[8] *Government of the Republic of South Africa and Others v Grootboom and Others* [2000] ZACC 19.

[9] *Minister of Health and Others v Treatment Action Campaign and Others (No 2)* [2002] ZACC 15.

[10] D Acemoglu, 'Constitutions, Politics, and Economics: A Review Essay on Persson and Tabellini's *The Economic Effects of Constitutions*' (2005) 43(4) Journal of Economic Literature 1025.

key challenge is how to ensure that constitutional objectives are realized, how adequate resources are generated, and how the resources are utilized. According to Persson and Tabellini, the debate shifts to the authority of institutions created by democracy, their functioning, power, and the political consequences thereof.

Essentially, the authors' seminal work inserted the issue of public choice strongly into the discourse. In the policy-making process, the cross-country outcomes of policies and implementation join together: the cycle of markets that leads to consideration of economic outcomes; the policy preferences that the economic outcomes afford; and the constitutional rules, leading to political outcomes. Both the economic choices and political outcomes in turn influence policy decisions. The available resources are not a given. They arise through what is actually a cyclical process in which policy choices are translated into legislation and then into programmes of implementation, with accountability exercised by legislatures. It is this interrelationship that provides the resources to deliver public social goods.

There are a number of factors to be considered in this delivery model. These include:

- The nature of the political system. Presidential systems tend to be more majoritarian, have smaller governments, and have smaller welfare-state spending. Conversely, countries with parliamentary systems tend to have more persistent fiscal outcomes.
- The degree of control that a government can exercise over fiscal and monetary policy.
- The extent of accountability exercised by core components of the state, such as its parliament.
- The operation of governance across the various tiers or spheres, and the competence of the public administration.
- The quality of the institutions that support democracy (in South Africa, this includes the State Institutions Supporting Democracy (Chapter 9 Institutions), including the Public Protector, the Human Rights Commission, the Commission of Gender Equality, the Auditor General and the Electoral Commission).
- Other external agencies, such as donors, the World Bank, and International Monetary Fund (IMF), which continue to play important roles in many countries in Africa.
- How the entire political-economy machinery articulates across the three arms of government.

Let us briefly examine the potential impact on each of these factors.

1. The Nature of the Political System

This is frequently a given in the endeavour to optimize the functioning of a democracy. In South Africa, we have adopted the Westminster system in which Parliament is elected by proportional representation, and the President is elected from the ranks of parliamentarians. The President appoints the cabinet from Parliament, but has two 'wild cards' that he or she may use from outside Parliament. These processes are set out in the Constitution and its rules. However, what history teaches us is that the qualities and attributes of leaders matter. So, where a president is interventionist, especially through the party, Parliament is weakened. In such instances, there is the risk that rent-seeking and the desire to be appointed may occur, as a result of which the system is weakened.

2. Fiscal and Monetary Policy

Fiscal policy is the expression of the will of the majority party, if we accept that budgets are the most pivotal expression of cabinet collective decision-making. The choice of which programmes get funded at what level, and the metrics announced for measuring outcomes, are key to the success or otherwise of constitutional values. The appropriations are actually laws passed by Parliament—this gives the legislature purchase over decisions, even though it is frequently an underutilized power. Similarly, revenue laws raise the taxes to ensure adequate resource availability.

In respect of monetary policy, the institutional arrangements are important. In South Africa, we have a constitutionally independent central bank. The independence of the South African Reserve Bank (SARB) is carefully and clearly crafted 'to protect the value of the currency in the interest of balanced and sustainable growth in the Republic'.[11] The SARB is protected from political interference, but there is a requirement for regular consultation between it and the cabinet member responsible for national financial matters. The legal structure of the institutions is important, as noted, but equally important is agency over policy choices. In the midst of intense economic distress, Zimbabwe decided some years ago to adopt the US dollar as its local currency. The impact of that decision not only exacerbated the crisis in the medium term but poses huge challenges for the country now.

3. Accountability to Parliament

In South Africa, our Constitution articulates clearly and extensively the roles and responsibilities of Parliament, its operational structures, powers and functions, roles and responsibilities of elected members, office bearers, President, national executive, provinces and local government. Yet if Parliament is weak, the constitutional values will not be attained because if measurement and accountability are not required by Parliament, the project derails. I have encountered situations where the tabling of a budget is celebrated but there is no inquiry or debate into how the resources were actually utilized, apart from a perfunctory post-audit report. For the sake of a well-functioning developmental state, what is required are ongoing engagement and continuous building of institutional knowledge, data, analytical capabilities, and policy deliberation.

4. Cooperation across Tiers of Government

Frequently, an elected government is required to operate at national, state/county, and local levels. Each tier is usually assigned powers and functions, and acts within the dictates of its own mandate. However, a number of countries have services, such as education, health, and social services, that are split across the three tiers, so dissonance is a key risk. For example, if primary health care operating at a local level is under-resourced, it puts stress on the entire

---

[11] Constitution 1996, s 224(1).

health system up to the tertiary level. Focusing on powers and functions, as well as the planning and execution of service delivery, is obviously a critical function.

5. The Quality of Institutions Supporting Democracy

Many countries have included institutions supporting democracy in their constitutions. These institutions include a variety of ombuds, permanent commissions representing particular interests, broadcasters, auditors-general, and the like. Ensuring that such institutions play the role they were intended to play and that they are not weakened as a consequence of what Açemoglu, Johnson, and Robinson refer to as the 'institutionalized polities'[12] is an essential task. The authors make the point that much more work is required on how changes in formal political institutions affect policy and economic outcomes in weakly institutionalized polities.

6. The Articulation of the Entire Political System

The organism of the state is a complex enterprise. The executive, the legislature, and the courts each have their own distinct roles. Political management is necessary to allow each organ to flourish, yet to hold all of them in the same orbit. Anger and cross-purposes appear to be what cause the system to come unstuck.

7. External Agencies

Donors and lenders also insist on voice. Donors occasionally push for their aid to be tied to contractors from their countries, thus weakening economic potential in recipient countries. Alternatively, donors might insist on particular measurable services only—so in terms of the Sustainable Development Goals (SDGs) donors might push very hard for these, disallowing the necessary spending on, say, infrastructure roll-out and maintenance. Across the African continent, lenders are also loosely termed 'donors' and we should all be aware of the swathe of destruction cut by the implementation of programmes such as the Structural Adjustment Programmes driven by the Bretton Woods institutions.

So, the realization of constitutional objectives is far more complex than the mere pronouncements of the ends. Far beyond a constitutional declaration of the style of government is the recognition that economic systems are, by their very nature, complex and multidimensional. If the practice is to focus on systems, the question arises of definition, or of what happens when there is a change of voter preferences? Then there are questions such as 'What precisely is socialism?' or 'what is the free market?' It appears far better to focus on the efficient operations of the institutions responsible for the outcomes of particular aspects of economic delivery. Even then, the situation is not without its complexities.

---

[12] Daron Açemoglu, Simon Johnson, and James A Robinson, 'Institutions as a Fundamental Cause of Long-Run Growth' in Philippe Aghion and Steven N Durlauf (eds), *Handbook of Economic Growth*, Volume IA (Elsevier 2005).

Permit me to again dig into a bit of recent South African history. In early 1994, the African National Congress (ANC) and its alliance partners adopted a far-reaching Reconstruction and Development Programme (RDP). Given the combination of the constraints of time and lack of experience, scant attention was paid to affordability—the court judgments on resource adequacy were still some way off. By mid-1996, the government had to adopt a macroeconomic stabilization programme called Growth, Employment, and Redistribution (GEAR). This unleashed a major debate, one which is still unresolved in the minds of some. It gave rise to intense discussions at an ANC Conference eighteen months later. There was a resolution at this conference that read:

> The emphasis in the RDP on macro-economic balance has been a consistent part of ANC policy and has been mentioned in every policy document since 1990. The strategy for Growth, Employment and Redistribution (GEAR) aims at creating the environment of macro-economic balances required for the realisation of the RDP. In this therefore, the GEAR does not seek to displace the RDP.[13]

Notwithstanding this resolution, adopted to acclaim, the debate continues within the same organization twenty-two years later. These matters are fairly complex.

What appears important is that in each country we should move beyond the epithets, whether big or small, and try and focus on how we need to act to ensure that we attain the desired socio-economic outcomes. It bears repeating that their attainment will not be possible without skilfully crafted constitutions. I make this point to suggest that it has near-universal application across the continent because the intent of our constitutions is now so similar. So the question of what we want our successes to be measured by is pertinent. Would it be the number of millionaires we create, or the opportunities for the poor to lift themselves out of poverty sustainably? Would it be in the number of indigenous people who drive large German sedans or occupy estates valued at many millions of dollars, or would it be a transformed built environment and an efficient, safe, affordable, and reliable public transport system in every town and city? These appear to be the pertinent choices that the socio-economic aspirations of our constitutions require us to turn our gaze towards, yet we seem to give them scant attention.

From about 2010, I was privileged to lead the National Planning Commission (NPC) that sought to re-energize our Constitution. The starting point for the NPC was the preamble to the Constitution, and we made that the object of our work. Among the key issues we dealt with was a body of work we called 'The Elements of a Decent Standard of Living'. It comprises a mere nine elements that, when realized, will fundamentally start the journey to improving the quality of life of all citizens. These elements are:

- nutrition;
- housing, water, sanitation, and electricity;
- transport;
- education and skills;

---

[13] ANC's 50th National Conference, 22 December 1997, Resolutions Economic Transformation, para 3.2.2, <https://www.anc1912.org.za/50th-national-conference-resolutions-economic-transformation-2/> accessed 18 August 2020.

- safety and security;
- health care;
- employment;
- recreation and leisure; and
- a clean environment.

I realize that this extends the raft of socio-economic rights provided for in our Bill of Rights. This is not, however, a case of moving the goalposts; rather, it is refocusing the attention of all. We realized that these rights and values would not emerge automatically.

We need to pay attention to yet another aspect of democracy, namely building a capable and developmental state. For this, we articulated a set of very basic objectives:

- a state that is capable of playing a developmental and transformative role;
- a public service immersed in the development agenda but insulated from undue political interference;
- staff at all levels with the authority, experience, competence, and support they need to do their jobs;
- improving relations between the national, provincial, and local government through a proactive approach to managing the intergovernmental system; and
- clear governance structures and stable leadership to enable state-owned enterprises (SOEs) to achieve their developmental potential.

The matters raised by giving nuance to debate about the implementation of our Constitution and energizing it through, for example, the National Development Plan,[14] are part of a vital discourse to advance the same objectives as contained in the preamble to the Constitution. Policy-makers are obliged to ensure that the values are not tarnished by age or desuetude.

The issues that I raise are not uniquely South African. We must commit to them finding application everywhere. We have transcended the battle for democracy. Most of us live in countries that have the accoutrements of functioning democracies. We have regular elections, dynamic parliaments, independent central banks, and a range of other matters. But notwithstanding these achievements—and they are not to be sneered at—our democracies will be counted out 'on their feet' if all we have is democracy in form.

The Brazilian philosopher Roberto Mangabeira Unger invokes the concept of 'high-energy democracy'.[15] He calls for a set of institutional arrangements that ensure a continuing high level of organized popular engagement in politics. He goes on to say that

a cold, demobilised politics cannot serve as a means to reorganise society. A hot, mobilised politics is compatible with democracy only when institutions channel its energies. It is a goal that can be achieved as the cumulative and combined effect of many devices.[16]

---

[14] National Planning Commission, *National Development Plan: Vision for 2030*, RP270/2011 (National Planning Commission 2011).

[15] RM Unger, *The Left Alternative* (Verso 2009) 22.

[16] Unger (n 15) 78–79.

The alternative is to have constitutions. The adoption of a constitution cannot be an end-point: it has to be the beginning of a platform to reorganize society.

Bibliography

Acemoglu D, 'Constitutions, Politics, and Economics: A Review Essay on Persson and Tabellini's *The Economic Effects of Constitutions*' (2005) 43(4) Journal of Economic Literature 1025

Açemoglu D, Johnson S, and Robinson J, 'Institutions as a Fundamental Cause of Long-Run Growth', in Aghion P and Durlauf SN (eds), *Handbook of Economic Growth* Volume IA (Elsevier 2005)

ANC, 50th National Conference, 22 December 1997, Resolutions Economic Transformation, para 3.2.2, <https://www.anc1912.org.za/50th-national-conference-resolutions-economic-transformation-2/> accessed 18 August 2020

Heyns C and Brand D, 'Introduction to Socio-Economic Rights in the South African Constitution' (1998) 2(2) Law, Democracy & Development 153

National Planning Commission, *National Development Plan: Vision for 2030*, RP270/2011 (National Planning Commission 2011)

Unger RM, *The Left Alternative* (Verso 2009)

Overview

Nico Steytler and Charles M Fombad

Despite expectations that its celebrated second wave of democracy would facilitate economic development, Africa remains the continent with the highest level of poverty in the world. There is no denying that it has seen economic growth, but poverty is still rampant and inequality is ever-increasing, with more than half of its population lacking access to the basic amenities of nutrition, water, shelter, and health care. The fight against poverty hinges on a vibrant economy that creates jobs and income and generates enough revenue to enable the state to take anti-poverty measures. A strong economy is central to the well-being of a country and its ability to exercise its sovereignty. However, in spite of the economic benefits that were supposed to accrue from the constitutional reforms of the last three decades, African economies remain weak, with some of them floundering. Since 2020, this plight has been aggravated by among others the impact of COVID-19 and the policy responses to it such as the lockdown measures taken globally and in Africa to control the spread of the coronavirus.

The focus of this volume of the *Stellenbosch Handbooks in African Constitutional Law* series—constitutionalism and the economy in Africa—thus could not have been more timely. It flows ineluctably from the last three volumes in the series and draws attention to the single greatest entanglement of challenges facing the continent today.

In *Decentralisation and Constitutionalism in Africa*,[1] we decried the superficiality of decentralization in Africa, which, inter alia, aims to promote economic development. While there is no scarcity of policy declarations, laws, and public utterances, decentralization at the state or provincial and local level is stymied by a lack of political will among governments, which by and large still cling to centralized control. The tenets of constitutionalism are simply ignored. One aspect of this problem is that the breadth and depth of corruption in Africa hampers not only local development but so too national economic progress. Hence, the volume *Corruption and Constitutionalism: Revisiting Control Measures and Strategies*[2] sought to understand this phenomenon in all its complexity. Again, while the legal framework for combating corruption is more or less in place, the patrimonial state is so pervasive that this framework has had little traction. The main reason for the pervasiveness of patrimonialism is that the state remains the central vehicle for self-enrichment.

What, then, is to be done? How can governments be held accountable when they appropriate state money for private purposes? In *Democracy, Elections and Constitutionalism in Africa*,[3] we considered whether accountability could be enhanced through democratic governance. The findings were bleak despite the optimism that has accompanied Africa's era

---

[1] Charles M Fombad and Nico Steytler (eds), *Decentralisation and Constitutionalism in Africa* (OUP 2019).

[2] Charles M Fombad and Nico Steytler (eds), *Corruption and Constitutionalism in Africa: Revisiting Control Measures and Strategies* (OUP 2020).

[3] Charles M Fombad and Nico Steytler (eds), *Democracy, Elections and Constitutionalism in Africa* (OUP 2021).

Nico Steytler and Charles M Fombad, *Overview* In: *Constitutionalism and the Economy in Africa*. Edited by: Charles M Fombad and Nico Steytler, Oxford University Press. © Nico Steytler and Charles M Fombad 2022. DOI: 10.1093/oso/9780192886439.003.0002

of post-Cold War democratization. Although elections are held and regime changes have taken place by way of the ballot box, there has been a pronounced slide into 'authoritarian democracy'. Again, a principal reason for the failure to establish democracy through free and fair elections is that ruling elites continue to cling to power, as part of which they maintain their vice-like grip on the economy.

This volume underlines a cardinal fact: there can be little prospect of entrenching a culture of constitutionalism and respect for the rule of law when millions of Africans lack the basic necessities of life. At the end of the 1980s, the continent's economies were in poor shape under socialist, statist, and corrupt, non-democratic regimes. With the populace taking to the streets and without the backing of superpowers, one-party states reluctantly made way for multiparty democracy, by the same token often also shifting from command to market economies. This included protecting private property in bills of rights and attempting to reduce the state's role in the economy. It is in this context that our attention now focuses on constitutions, constitutionalism, and the economy in Africa. What, indeed, has happened on this score in the past thirty years, and what does it betoken for the future?

Answering this in turn raises questions about the nature of the economy and the state, the relationship between them, and the nature of the global economic order in which they operate. Given that constitutions are an element in this mix, how is the relationship between the state and economy structured or managed through a constitution? Put differently, to what extent, if at all, do constitutions influence the nature of economies?

These and other questions about African economies in the era of constitutionalism are addressed in the six parts into which the volume is divided. The foundation is laid in the first part, which examines the basic concepts and main questions at issue. Thereafter, Part II reviews various attempts to constitutionalize the economy in modern African constitutions, while Part III examines selected constitutional frameworks for dealing with land and natural resources. This is followed, in Part IV, by a discussion of the state's role in the economy. Part V assesses the impact of globalization on constitutionalism. In concluding the volume, Part VI draws together and articulates its key findings and emergent themes.

This volume commences with the keynote address by Trevor Manuel, a former Minister of Finance in South Africa and chair of its National Planning Commission. A struggle-era activist, he was closely involved in South Africa's transition to democracy and the shaping of its economic direction. Manuel notes that, constitutionally, South Africa made 'a fundamental shift away from the political-economy big-systemic arguments' about a free market, command economy, or mixed economy. This shift, he points out, is evident in other African countries, notably in the constitutional modernization of the previously 'socialist' states of Mozambique and Zimbabwe. Another element of modernization was the inclusion of justiciable socio-economic rights in South Africa's Constitution, the implementation of which is dependent on the availability of state resources. The big challenge is thus 'how to ensure that constitutional objectives are realized, how adequate resources are generated, and how the resources are utilized'.

Manuel argues that available resources are not a given: they are a product of a number of factors that influence the delivery of these social goods. The first of these, among others, is the impact of either a presidential or parliamentary system; a second is the degree of control a government can exercise over fiscal and monetary policy and the role of a central bank in managing the value of a currency. A third factor is the role that a parliament plays in holding the executive to account, a role which is often weak when the executive dominates the legislature.

Other crucial factors are the prominence of multilevel government and the competence of public servants across different levels of government; the ability of constitutional institutions, such as ombudsmen, to perform their oversight role; the role that external agencies, including donors, the World Bank and International Monetary Fund (IMF), play in providing financial support as well as intruding in the policy space; and finally, the manner and extent to which the three branches of government—parliament, the executive and the judiciary—work in an independent yet coordinated way.

As chairperson of the National Planning Commission and architect-in-chief of South Africa's National Development Plan, Manuel sought to carve out a clear set of strategies for achieving the constitutional objectives of socio-economic rights. To channel the collective energy of a nation towards these goals, he concludes, is to see a constitution not as an end point but as the starting point of a platform by which to reorganize society to those ends.

In the first part of the volume, Nico Steytler, in Chapter 1, 'Constitutionalism and the Economy: Concepts and Questions', elaborates on the five crucial questions that the chapters in this collection seek to address. The first is the question of why and how democracy and the market were coupled in the wave of democratization of the 1990s. Were the liberal concepts of multiparty democracy and open markets included due to the influence of the West? How did constitutions reflect the shift towards a market economy? In those countries where a market economy was established, how is it reflected in their constitutions? Are the protection of property and the enforcement of contracts in a bill of rights key elements of a market economy? Secondly, given that agriculture and the extractive industries are the main components of many of Africa's economies, how are land and other natural resources dealt with constitutionally? Thirdly, in capturing the market economy in a constitution, how is the state's relationship to the economy formulated—is it interventionist, *laissez-faire*, or somewhere in between? In cases of multilevel government, how has a regulatory role been apportioned between different levels of government? In addition to a market economy, have constitutions institutionalized the 'social' state providing the basic elements of a dignified life? Fourthly, in the process of constitution-making and implementation in regard to the economy, what impact has globalization, in particular trade liberalization, had on constitutionalism and economies? Finally, how has the relationship between constitutionalism (ie implementation of the normative framework of the constitution) and economic growth played out in practice?

In examining the linkage between constitutions and the economy, Ramos Mabugu, in Chapter 2, 'Relationships between the Economy and Constitution in Sub-Saharan Africa', sets the economic context for the discussions that follow. He points out that during the 1980s there was a decline in African economies, during which real income per capita fell by about a quarter due to external and domestic factors. Internationally, global markets in raw commodities fluctuated significantly, with devastating consequences for states reliant on one or two export commodities; domestically, the crisis was caused, inter alia, by poor economic policies, mounting budgetary deficits, loss-making public enterprises, and deterioration in governance, as exemplified by corruption.

According to Mabugu, during the wave of democratization over the past three decades there has been significant economic improvement, but that, too, has declined in recent years due, again, to fluctuations in export commodity prices. The decline has been amplified by the COVID-19 pandemic and its aftermath. Globally, Africa south of the Sahara is one of the poorest and most unequal regions in the world, facing seemingly intractable problems of unemployment, poverty, and inequality.

Mabugu proceeds to indicate how various sectors of the economy relate to constitutional issues. Agriculture is still an important sector albeit that its contribution has declined on average by 20 percentage points between 2000 and 2015. However, it accounts for the majority of livelihoods, as nearly two-thirds of the population live in rural areas. Dependent as they are on land for agricultural purposes, the right and access to land remain vital to the rural population. Mining and oil extraction, along with industry and manufacturing, are also in decline, but are the main source of revenue for the state and are responsible for most of Africa's exports.

This brings control of natural resources to the fore. With agriculture, manufacturing, mining, and industry in decline, more than half of national gross domestic product (GDP) is now produced by services, which are provided mainly by the state or informal sector. In most countries the latter is large, and given that it falls outside formal state regulation, the upshot is that, irrespective of whatever labour rights are enshrined in a constitution, they have little traction in practice.

According to Mabugu, states' financial and fiscal policies also impact on constitutionalism. Revenue-raising efforts focus on trade taxes, commodity royalties, foreign aid and borrowing, rather than on personal income tax and other direct taxes, which would strengthen the link of democratic accountability between the state and citizens. Where that link is tenuous or absent, it is not surprising that government expenditure is skewed towards servicing loans and paying public sector salaries—that is, when it is not being syphoned off by corruption.

The promise of the 'social' state thus remains hollow, while reliance on borrowing ultimately compromises a country's sovereignty since debt default places countries under the dictates of the lenders. Mabugu observes that governments face the triple challenge of unemployment, poverty, and increasing inequality—a formidable task. His challenge to lawyers, then, is: can the constitution in any way bend governmental action towards better socio-economic outcomes?

In addressing the question, Stephan Ollick, in Chapter 3, 'Constitutional Law and the Economy: Comparing Liberal Market Orders', notes that constitutions at times are conspicuous in setting out a country's macroeconomic approach (usually when it concerns a command economy), while on other occasions they are more restrained (usually when a free market underpins the economic system). He considers four Western countries: France, the United Kingdom, United States, and Germany. In these countries, not only is the market economy indirectly constitutionalized, but their constitutional paradigm has influenced the constitutional orders in Africa over the past thirty years.

Ollick identifies points of contact between constitutional law and the economy—although many aspects of a constitution may have economic implications, his focus is on those provisions intended to have a direct impact on macroeconomic policy-making. The four countries, known for their market economies, do not impose constitutional obligations on governments to intervene in the economy or, for that matter, abstain from it. By and large, in the US and United Kingdom the market is preserved by omission rather than direct provisions. Constitutions are, however, explicit in the case of the two federal countries—the US and Germany; they leave the protection of economic unity exclusively in the hands of the federal government. Ollick also notes that since states have an interest in controlling inflation and deflation, such monetary policy is vested in central banks to shield it from the interference of governments. This approach is, however, constitutionalized only in Germany, in the form of the European Central Bank.

Ollick points out that a number of individual rights may also have a macroeconomic impact, most notably the protection of private property (which does not preclude expropriation against compensation), contracting, occupation, enterprise, and association. According to him, this may have a steering effect on the economy by inspiring specific forms of market-oriented behaviour. The protection of labour rights may result in better wages and working conditions for individual labourers, it could also affect macroeconomic policies on investment and reduction of unemployment. In the US, the commitment to social welfare policies is unsteady and often minimal. In spite of the extensive welfare schemes in the United Kingdom, it is only France and Germany that have elevated the model of the social state to constitutional rank. Although state-owned enterprises play an important role worldwide, this is only formally recognized in Germany and France; in the US and United Kingdom, Ollick asserts, a constitution is neither a guide nor an obstacle with respect to these enterprises.

He concludes that, driven not least by the liberal underpinnings of the European Union, the three European states have emerged as free market-driven economic orders reluctant to entertain state interference; the US, for its part, draws on an even longer and more deep-rooted history of economic liberalism. In spite of this, Ollick notes that there are some differences between the countries that hold the potential for the state to play a large role in economic affairs, an example of which is Germany's establishment of the 'social' state.

The second part of this volume consists of two chapters that look at the way the constitutional relationship between the state and the economy has evolved and the manner in which this is reflected in modern African constitutions. Charles Fombad, in Chapter 4, 'Comparative Overview of Measures and Devices to Shape the Economy in Some Modern African Constitutions', provides a bird's-eye view of the economic doctrines, principles, measures, and devices that have been incorporated, explicitly or implicitly, in African constitutions to guide governmental action and promote development. The chapter considers how these 'economic constitutions' pave the way for consolidating constitutionalism and respect for the rule of law.

In reviewing the manner in which the economy is covered in these constitutions, a number of questions arise. Do these constitutions mark a break from the post-independence constitutions that were easily distorted to create a large gap between the 'haves' and the 'have nots' and that left few avenues for accountability and for the voice of the ordinary citizen to be heard? Are the constitutions able to deal with the increasing risk of debt distress associated with the debt-trap diplomacy of certain countries and prevent predatory foreign investment and loan agreements from becoming a form of state capture and recolonization?

In pursuit of answers, Fombad examines the types and levels of economic rights recognized and protected in the constitutions of selected countries. He then discusses the role of institutions for economic management and considers whether the relevant provisions are strong enough to promote proper economic management. This is followed by an analysis of the interplay between the constitution, the economy, and constitutionalism. It is shown that there is close interdependence between the mechanisms designed to promote a sound economic constitution and those that promote constitutionalism, respect for the rule of law, and good governance. The chapter ends by suggesting some ways in which constitutionalism in general and economic constitutionalism in particular can be promoted to protect a country's economic and political sovereignty as well as its ability to pursue economic growth and development.

In the second chapter in this part, Nico Steytler focuses in Chapter 5 on 'The Unravelling of the Constitution, the Economy, and Constitutionalism in South Africa'. In the country's transition to democracy in 1994, part of the compromise was that the African National Congress (ANC) relinquished its commitment to a socialist future (in essence, no more than a 'social' state) in favour of a more market-driven economy. Steytler hence argues that because of the collapse of the East Bloc economies and the stridency of the free-market West, local and international pressures led to the ANC's abandoning its yearning for a state that would play a strongly interventionist role in the economy.

In the 1996 Constitution this was achieved by protecting the basic elements of a market economy in the Bill of Rights—the right to property, the freedom of association both of workers and employers, contractual freedom derived from the constitutional values of 'freedom and dignity', and the right to choose one's own occupation. While these elements of the free market economy were entrenched in the Bill of Rights, the establishment of a 'social' state through enforceable socio-economic rights was also envisaged; given the historical legacy of land dispossession and inequality, land reform to rectify the injustices of the past was an important constitutional matter. Accordingly, although the Bill of Rights protects the market from unreasonable state action, the Constitution does not prevent a regulatory role for the state. In regard to monetary policy, the national government is constrained by the constitutionalization of a central bank with the mandate to protect the value of the currency.

Yet even having the most secure constitutional state on the continent has not led inevitably to a productive economy: the South African economy has long been stagnant, and, thanks to the COVID-19 pandemic, has slumped into a deep recession. This has paved the way for critical questioning of the market economy and the country's limited economic transformation. A softening of the Constitution's property clause is already in the pipeline, with the means of effecting changes to the ownership of wealth a subject of contestation. Steytler thus argues that, after more than twenty-seven years, the economic compact underpinning the Constitution is slowly unravelling. This brings the economy to the fore as *the* central issue confronting South Africa today, a country where more than half of the population lives in poverty and the bulk of land and wealth is still in white hands.

The five essays in Part III examine the constitutional framework for land and natural resources, which in most African countries are the pillars of the economy—access to land is the basis of agriculture, while the extractive industries rely either on non-renewable resources (minerals, oil, and gas) or natural resources (forestry and fisheries) that are renewable in theory but which could be depleted entirely in practice.

In Chapter 6 John Hursh focuses on 'Protecting the Land, Protecting the Resources: A Comparative Assessment of Constitutional Protections in Kenya, Sudan, and South Sudan'. He starts by pointing out that few regions of Africa are as resource-rich yet as conflict-prone as East Africa. Several states in this region also face alarming rates of corruption, as well as correspondingly low levels of transparency and checks on executive power. According to Hursh, states in this region have seen repressive governance, over-concentration of executive power, and rampant misuse of natural-resource wealth—a concatenation of affairs that has resulted in personal enrichment for a few and poverty for the vast majority.

In the chapter, Hursh addresses constitutional efforts to protect land and natural resources, particularly as these protections relate to economic development. He does so by comparing how the constitutions of Kenya, Sudan, and South Sudan safeguard land and natural resources for their citizens. These states allow for a useful comparison of three distinct legal traditions in an important region of Africa; moreover, their constitutions emerged from armed conflict and have contributed to the growing study of constitutional reform in post-conflict settings. Hursh provides a detailed examination of constitutional provisions and supporting legislation of the countries from independence to the present day. He notes that while all three suffered from poor governance and authoritarian and semi-authoritarian rule, jurists, scholars, and members of civil society continue to push for strong constitutional safeguards to advance equitable and sustainable use of natural resources. Hursh concludes by recognizing the link between resource use of this kind—especially in relation to land—and strengthened economic development, a linkage that stands to benefit all citizens in these states.

Also on the land question, Heinz Klug's chapter, 'The Political Economy of Post-Colonial Constitutionalism in Southern Africa', begins with an examination of theories pertaining to the economic analysis of constitutions. He argues that to understand the relationship between a constitution and the economy, it is necessary to identify that constitution's political economy—a rigorous and critically engaged undertaking which, he suggests, is to be distinguished from the technicist neutrality of a purely economic analysis. The elements Klug selects for the purposes of his comparative study are economic rights, democratic participation, fiscal policy, corruption, the rule of law, and judicial authority. The specific constitutional clauses related to these issues include rights to property; electoral systems; the status of central banks; anti-corruption or integrity institutions; and the status and role of the judiciary, including the nature of the constitutional review established in the constitution.

Klug contends that the institution of property rights in land is the most significant constitutional element shaping the political economy of southern Africa. Agriculture is a core pillar of the countries selected for study, namely Botswana, Mozambique, South Africa, and Zimbabwe. As they did under colonialism, control of and access to land remain burning issues in the post-independence era. The land tenure systems in these countries are very different but also evince certain similarities. In South Africa, as in Botswana, there is both freehold and communal property, while in Zimbabwe the state is accorded a strong role in controlling land; in Mozambique, by contrast, all land belongs to the state. In each country land is a contested issue, but the nature of that contestation is profoundly influenced by each country's history.

In view of these case studies, Klug concludes that economic development depends less on the nature of land tenure per se than on the stability afforded by a constitutional order's recognition of property rights and by a functioning set of institutions that uphold the rule of law. While some of the elements relevant in this regard are long-standing features of constitutionalism—for example constitutional rights and judicial or constitutional review—the recent inclusion of fiscal institutions such as central banks and the constitutionalization of integrity institutions reflect a post-Cold War or neoliberal form of constitutionalism.

In Chapter 8, Makanatsa Makonese's essay, 'Land, Conflict, and the Economy: The Role of the Constitution in Addressing the Land Issue in Post-Independence Zimbabwe', examines that country's widely publicized land issues. She begins by observing that although the economy of Zimbabwe is built around the three mainstays of land, minerals, and manufacturing, it is the land question that has dominated public, political, and economic discourse since colonial times—indeed, it was the impetus for two wars of liberation (1896–97 and 1966–80), with the black majority resisting frequently violent expropriation of their land by white colonial settlers. At independence in 1980, Zimbabwe sought to address the question since the new government had, whilst still a liberation movement, promised it would do so. The first port of call was the constitution as negotiated at the Lancaster House independence conference and supported by various enabling legislative instruments. Subsequent constitutional amendments were made in regard to the land question, culminating in the adoption of the Constitution of 2013 that extensively addresses the land rights of Zimbabweans.

Makonese reviews the evolution of the constitutional protection of land and related rights from independence in 1980 and through the course of successive constitutional amendments and implementing laws aimed at advancing economic development. Zimbabwe's government at one point coined the slogan, 'Land is the economy and the economy is the land'; as Makonese observes, it was also the mishandling of the land question that destroyed the country's once-vibrant economy and saw it reduced from 'bread basket' to 'basket case'. The central role of land in the economy led to its contestation on multiple fronts, including in courts of law at home and abroad. She concludes that the failure by the government to find a constitutional balance between protecting acquired land rights and correcting the historical land grabs of the colonial period has diminished any prospect of constitutionalism and respect for the rule of law emerging under the ostensibly transformative 2013 Constitution.

In Chapter 9, 'Custodial Resource Holding as an Expression of Constitutional and Economic Intent in Africa', Hanri Mostert conducts a review of the extractive regimes across Africa. She argues that understanding the interdependency between Africa and the rest of the world in relation to natural resources—minerals, oil, and gas in particular—requires scrutiny of how accountability for mineral resource exploitation is envisioned and managed through the constitutions of African countries.

The potential fault lines in the relationship between a state's constitution and its economic approach usually show up clearly in the context of resources, all the more so in the context of resource dependency. Where there is resource dependency, the relationship between a state's economic policies and its extractives sector often finds expression in constitutional provisions relating to property and constitutional commitments to transformation and social justice. These elements combine to indicate a state's resource-holding model. As articulated in the legal framework, a country's resource-holding model requires particular types of response in terms of governance to give effect to the ideologies underlying a state's economic choices.

Poverty, inequality, underdevelopment, and lack of productivity are more than just the by-products of these systemic and ideological failures: they have become the tragic constraints to Africa's future prosperity. Mostert cites examples from a cross-section of African jurisdictions (Botswana, Kenya, Nigeria, South Africa, Tanzania, Uganda, Zambia, and Zimbabwe) to show how inherently contradictory narratives about economic policy and the extractives sectors impact on the optimal and sustainable exploitation of resources. In turn, the impairment of such exploitation affects an extractive sector's potential to contribute to the eradication of poverty in countries plagued by underdevelopment and lack of productivity.

To examine various models for holding mineral resources and the legal frameworks expressing these models, the chapter relies on country examples to illustrate its three lines of inquiry. First, it establishes how a state's constitutional framework articulates its particular take on state sovereignty over natural resources, with the focus specifically on mineral resources. Secondly, it identifies the main political concerns that drive the development of mineral law and policy and shows as well how the applicable law responds to those concerns. Thirdly, the study links governance practices to a country's choice of resource-holding model or paradigm, thereby highlighting the nature of the concomitant commitment to a particular economic path.

In Chapter 10, 'Namibia's Resource-Based Economy: Protection versus Exploitation of Nature', Henning Melber considers extractive industries from an environmental perspective, with the focus placed on three industries: fisheries, phosphate mining, and timber and agriculture. Melber examines Namibia's apparent constitutional commitment to the protection of the environment against its needs for economic growth. Deep-sea mining of phosphate is exhausting a non-renewable resource, in the process laying waste to what was once one of the world's richest marine areas, while the over-exploitation of fisheries and timber may have the same effect—the depletion of a resource and its consequent long-term destruction. Vast amounts of hardwoods found only in a small part of the country are being decimated by Chinese companies with little or no beneficiation of the wood locally; elsewhere, forests are being cleared for tobacco cultivation—a case where the destruction of a national resource is all the more egregious for leading to the production of an injurious substance.

In Namibia, Melber notes, legislation on the environment is strong and sets out appropriate principles and measures for protecting it, but implementation thereof is incomplete, with the granting of permits and sanctioning of non-compliance often mired in corruption. He shows that the tension between the economy and the ecology scarcely features in any of the ruling party's strategies or programmes, as a result of which the lofty ideals espoused in laws and policies remain just that. Melber argues that while an independent judiciary is essential for upholding the rule of law, the decisive element in enforcement rests with the government and civil society. Nevertheless, the Namibian government faces a dilemma it shares with numerous other African states: as Melber puts it, it has 'a rich country with poor people'. In a country with one of the highest levels of inequality on the continent, the majority of people are poor and demand an improvement in their lives. The exploitation of resources for short-term gain is all too attractive. The medium-term policy requires, however, a balancing of the protection of public goods—the environment—and the extraction of non-renewable resources for gain.

The two contributions in Part IV examine constitutional frameworks governing the state's role in the economy. These case studies, of Egypt and Ethiopia, illustrate the contrasting ways in which two countries in Africa have sought, over several decades, to engineer a constitutional framework to guide national economic development; they also demonstrate the impact this has had on the furtherance of constitutionalism.

Sherif Elgebeily's chapter, 'The New Economic Empire of the Egyptian Military: A Lesson in Blurred Lines and Constitutional Transgression', describes the paramount role which the state, in the form of the military, plays in the economy. He shows how state-owned enterprises are owned by the military, a circumstance that adds a significant layer of unaccountability to such enterprises—there is no transparency, the military draws on a conscripted work-force, and it enjoys a special dispensation. The role of the military in the economy is as long-standing as the nexus between the military and government is tight: from the time that Abdul Nassar rose to power in 1956, the armed forces received special exemptions from ci-vilian oversight and payments to the state, an arrangement that has remained in place in the present day.

While the Arab Spring in 2011 brought hope not only of democracy but of an opening up of the economy, this has not come to pass. The military first supported the ousting of Hosni Mubarak, helping the Morsi regime to come to power, but when its position was threatened by the latter, it staged the second revolution to bring the El-Sisi regime to power, and, at the same time, seized the opportunity to cement its control of the economy. Elgebeily asserts that 'the creation of a new economic empire under the control of the military, coupled with the political controls that President Sisi has assumed as head of state, places at his discretion control over both the economic and political levers of Egypt'.

Elgebeily argues that the favoured position accorded by law to the military and its economic activities has had an immensely damaging impact on the constitutional pro-tections of private business. The military benefits from the following: their factories and companies are exempted from taxes and customs duties; they may procure goods and services without resort to a tender process; military companies receive secret subsidies that lie beyond budgetary oversight or constraint under Egypt's Constitution; and they deploy conscripted soldiers to work in their factories, bakeries, night clubs, and a myriad other locales—the reach of military companies extends into consumer goods including cement, steel, marble, pasta, and tourism. Furthermore, the extent of the military's hold-ings, its involvement in the private sector, and its procurement methods are opaque, making the full relationship between the military and economy unclear. Elgebeily con-cludes that the principles of constitutionalism in Egypt with respect to economic protec-tions have been undermined by a private military sector that blurs the line between public provision and private gain.

The situation in Ethiopia—a constitutional federation based on the principle of non-centralism—is examined by Solomon Negussie in Chapter 12, 'Determining the Jurisdiction of Regional States in Promoting Investment in Ethiopia: A Constitutional and Practical Inventory'. The question he addresses is whether, in view of the division of powers between the federal government and regional states, the latter have a voice in determining invest-ment decisions. Although the federal constitution provides that the regions are authorized to administer land and other natural resources, in practice that is not the case. The federal government plays the dominant role, doing so under a constitutional provision that enables it to formulate policies on social and economic development matters. In its thoroughgoing employment of this provision, the federal government crafts highly detailed policies and strategies that leave little room for regional initiative.

Negussie argues, however, that constructive federal–state relations are important. Although investment, which is vital to economic development, is governed primarily by federal laws, its implementation in the areas of mining, large-scale agricultural investment, and manufacturing is carried out by the regions—for example, regions have to ensure the timely allocation of land as well as monitor and supervise investment activities. He points out that these federal–state relations are conducted against the doctrine of the 'democratic developmental state' which the state, spurred on by the success of the Asian Tigers, has adhered to since 2002 as the regnant model by which it understands itself. Accordingly, the federal government has become the driver of economic development through major investment in infrastructure that consumes half of the national budget.

The notion of the developmental state, Negussie argues, has injected tension into the federal nature of the country inasmuch as regional governments also wish to make decisions about investment. Moreover, despite the impressive economic growth Ethiopia has recorded over the last two decades, its political instability since 2018 can be linked to the deficits of the developmental-state approach adopted by the ruling party. He also notes that 'one of the major factors in political unrest in Ethiopia is the lack of proportionality in the benefits that have accrued to local people from investment taxation'. Negussie argues for a fuller implementation of the federal model in which regions also play a role in investment decisions.

The two chapters in Part V underscore the fact that globalization has had a profound effect on the economies of African countries and trade relations between them. From a historical perspective, international economic agendas have made, and continue to make, a significant impact on constitutional sovereignty and to influence the economic models and policies which African countries adopt.

In Chapter 13, entitled 'Taming the Spectre of Unsustainable Public Debt in Africa: A Heightened Role for Constitutions', Adam Abebe explores a crucial aspect of the impact of global economic trends on constitutionalism in Africa. He notes that public (or sovereign) debt makes up a significant portion of the regular budget of African countries and is central to the management of their economies. Such public debt, he argues, involves decisions about the distribution (including across generations) of societal benefits and burdens—issues that lie at the heart of democratic theory. Given its significance for the economy and democracy, Abebe believes it is critical to assess the extent to which African constitutions regulate public debt. This is particularly important today, a time when there are growing and, in cases, unsustainable debt levels and reports abound of 'debt traps' in which governments are at risk of being forced to hand over key infrastructure to foreign states to settle odious debts.

The chapter discusses the potential role of constitutions in the proper management and control of public debt. Noting that there is little literature on constitutions and public debt in Africa, the chapter provides an important basis for conversation at the political and scholarly level on the role of constitutions in regulating public debt and ensuring transparency and accountability in its mobilization and use. Abebe argues that this is an issue to which the African Union and the continent's regional economic communities need to give urgent focus.

In Chapter 14, Eva Maria Belser focuses on 'The Turn to Global Constitutionalism at the WTO and Its Impact on African Constitutionalism'. She engages with the global 'constitutionalist question' and examines the claim that the global trade regime fulfils, or ought to fulfil, the functions of a constitutionalized order. Belser considers what this turn to constitutionalism at the WTO signifies for its African member states and their constitutional law and practice, in particular their aim of constituting state authorities as active actors of human rights fulfilment and development.

Her first contention is that international trade rules lack procedural legitimacy because most states in the South contributed only marginally to their making, after which she demonstrates that the flawed 'constitution-making' process had an independent outcome on the rules themselves: they favour those who negotiated them. Although global trade rules have changed over time, their bias has remained: they limit the regulatory leeway of member states when it comes to liberalizing trade, but fail to do the same when special and differential treatment for developing states is at issue.

Belser's argument is that the constitutionalization of global trade rules is worrisome from an African perspective. The elevation of global trade rules to constitutional rules implies a priority of free trade over international and constitutional non-trade rules. In such a system, concerns such as human rights and development—ranked highly by most African constitutions—lose out when they clash with obligations to liberalize trade. By way of a number of examples, Belser demonstrates that the risk of clashes between the global trade regime and domestic constitutional values is both real and potentially harmful. Hence, the way forward cannot lie in a schematic hierarchy of international trade rules over international human rights or domestic constitutions; it lies instead in a pluralistic understanding of global constitutionalism in which trade is one value among others and can be challenged by national constitutions.

In the concluding Part VI, Nico Steytler seek to answer the questions posed in Chapter 1. Chapter 15, entitled 'Constitutionalizing the Market Economy and the Quest for Constitutionalism', shows that the move towards multiparty democracy that began in the 1990s was often accompanied by an ostensible embrace of the market; thirty years later, though, the economy is not an open market: it is still largely statist, is controlled by the state, typically with corrupt purposes, and shows increasing inequality.

Steytler argues, first, that after the end of the Cold War and the dismal state of the continent's command economies, the liberal precepts of democracy and free markets were firmly coupled together. Constitutional reforms that entrenched multiparty democracy also protected the basic elements of a market economy, among them the protection of property rights and freedom of contract. Secondly, given that agriculture and extractive industries are the main components of the economy and sources of state revenue in many countries, natural resources, both non-renewable and sustainable, are inadequately managed constitutionally. The state often has a controlling hand in their exploitation, but not always to the benefit of the majority of the people.

Thirdly, in the attempts to embody the market economy in constitutions, the state's relationship to the economy has ranged from interventionist to *laissez-faire*, but generally lies somewhere in between. Under the paradigm of the developmental state, state-owned enterprises still have a significant presence in most economies, though with modest contributions (at best) towards development. A number of constitutions institutionalized the 'social' state as a corrective to the poor resource-distribution capacity of the market by providing for the basic rights of a dignified life. However, the chasm between constitutional promises and the grinding reality of poverty is as deep and wide as ever.

Fourthly, the relation between the local economy and the constitution must be viewed in the context of globalization in general and trade in particular. Given the dominance of the international trade regime, it impacts negatively on state sovereignty as a key element of constitutionalism.

Finally, the relationship between constitutionalism and economic growth remains inconclusive. No direct correlation between constitutionalism and economic growth can be firmly established: many of Africa's high-growth countries, such as Ethiopia and Rwanda, are characterized by authoritarian regimes. However, in countries such as South Africa, corruption—the very negation of the rule of law—has had disastrous economic consequences.

PART I
CONCEPTS AND CONTEXT

1

Constitutionalism and the Economy

Concepts and Questions

Nico Steytler

1. Introduction

Newly independent African states in the 1960s and 1970s sought to bring about economic and social progress by controlling the levers of economic power and nationalizing the economy. Unshackled from colonialism and market economies skewed in favour of the colonial masters, leaders such as Nkrumah and Nyerere developed forms of African socialism that entailed state ownership and control of land and natural resources. These endeavours were supported during the Cold War by the Soviet Union or communist China. The state became the rower of the economic boat, but rather than reaping the rewards of a Marxist utopia, citizens were met with a whirlwind of conflict, corruption, ineptitude, and economic collapse.

By the 1980s, many of these states had tasted the bitter fruits of deep indebtedness and were left with little choice but to bow to the structural adjustment programmes of the World Bank and International Monetary Fund (IMF), measures that required privatization of key industries and the reduction of bloated civil services. With the end of the Cold War marking the demise of the Soviet command economy model, a new wave of constitutions in Africa ushered in not only multiparty democracy but, concomitantly, a free-market economy, both of which were extolled by a triumphalist West.

The state had to relinquish its role as rower of the economic boat and take charge only of the tiller, its job being to steer the economy towards growth. Constitutional principles were incorporated that provide for the protection of private property and the autonomy of the private sector. Of course, there were countries where no such shift took place—in Botswana and Mauritius, for example, democracy and the market economy had been embedded in their constitutions since independence.

Africa's new wave of constitutions sets lofty goals for promoting constitutionalism, but the actualization of constitutionalism over the three decades since the 1990s has proven to be highly uneven. The decentralization that accompanied democratization generally remains an unfulfilled policy goal; the rule of law, too, has been a mirage in the face of rampant corruption by the patrimonial state. Even the foundation of constitutionalism—competitive democracy—is being eroded by what is termed 'authoritarian democracy'.

In the same period, the African economy, at least on the face of it, has grown at a rapid pace, albeit from a low base. A study by the United Nations Development Programme (UNDP) shows that economic progress in Africa over the last twenty-five years has been propelled by annual gross domestic product (GDP) growth of about 5 per cent,[1] although

---

[1] UNDP, *Income Inequality Trends in Sub-Saharan Africa: Divergence, Determinants and Consequences* (United Nations Development Programme: Regional Bureau for Africa 2017).

Nico Steytler, *Constitutionalism and the Economy* In: *Constitutionalism and the Economy in Africa*. Edited by: Charles M Fombad and Nico Steytler, Oxford University Press. © Nico Steytler 2022. DOI: 10.1093/oso/9780192886439.003.0003

this has eased off in the last three years and the trend is likely to worsen due to the COVID-19 crisis of 2020–21. Significant progress has been made in meeting the Sustainable Development Goals.[2]

Despite this growth, many economies in Africa are underdeveloped, unproductive, and marred by high levels of poverty and inequality—indeed, Africa is the continent with the highest level of poverty in the world. Half of its population lives in poverty and goes without access to basic amenities of life such as nutrition, water, and shelter.[3] The resultant food in-security is often the result of conflict and violence as well as poor governance; for the same reasons, millions die or suffer from preventable diseases. Where countries fail to meet basic needs with their own revenue, they are obliged to take out the begging bowl and, with that, compromise their sovereignty. A large number of African countries are consequently de-pendent on foreign aid to support their budgets and provide basic services. Moreover, in-equality is high in sub-Saharan Africa—it is, collectively, one of the most unequal regions in the world, and, individually, ten of its countries are among the nineteen most unequal in the world.

The state has played no small role in these levels of both poverty and inequality. In African countries that adopted a command economy, the results have been disastrous; in those with a market economy, the impact of state corruption and mismanagement on pov-erty is demonstrable. The fusion of the ruling party and the state leads to an entity that controls or captures the economy, which in turns leads to 'crony capitalism' and slow and skewed growth.

A further characteristic of the continent's economies is that although free-market the-ories of economic growth are predominant, some of the most prosperous economies are ones that function under autocratic regimes seeking to emulate the success of China and the Asian Tigers of the 1980s. Ethiopia is an example of a country that has seen high growth rates and reduction of poverty under the helmsmanship of an autocratic, hege-monic party. In a similar vein, African governments often champion the virtues of the free market yet continue to run state-owned enterprises; most states also keep an iron grip on resources through their ownership and/or control of land transfers and natural resources.

In the past three decades, Africa has been exposed increasingly to globalization, in-cluding trade liberalization and the investment interests of the West and China, a reality with a direct bearing on countries' economies and the health of their constitutionalism. In a time of robust globalization under the World Trade Organization, African states often appear to watch from the sidelines as global market forces dictate their domestic economic policy. In some countries the state has, in order to boost foreign investment, alienated land to foreign companies to the detriment of the subsistence tillers of the soil, leading to out-cries of 'land grabbing'. Due to their indebtedness for foreign-built infrastructure, even more countries are selling off the family silver to China.

---

[2] See Ramos Mabugu, 'Relationships between the Economy and Constitution in Sub-Saharan Africa' (Chapter 2 of this volume).

[3] World Bank, *Poverty and Shared Prosperity: Piecing Together the Poverty Puzzle* (World Bank 2018).

2. Research Questions

In view of the scenario above and given the focus of this book series—*Constitutionalism in Africa*—the present volume addresses five crucial questions:

1. In the constitutional reforms of the 1990s and thereafter, how did constitutions reflect the shift towards a market economy? Do constitutions envisage a market economy, and if so, how is it spelt out? As for countries where the market economy has been long established (as noted, Botswana and Mauritius are examples), how is this reflected in their constitutions? Are the protection of property and the enforcement of contract in a bill of rights key prerequisites for a market economy?

2. Given that agriculture and extractive industries are the main source of state revenue in many an African economy, how are matters of land and other natural resources dealt with constitutionally?

3. In capturing the market economy in a constitution, how is the state's relationship to the economy formulated—interventionist or *laissez-faire*, or somewhere in between? In cases of multilevel government, has a regulatory role been apportioned between the different levels of government? In addition to institutionalizing a market economy, have constitutions done the same in establishing a 'social' state that provides the basic elements of a dignified life?

4. In the process of constitution-making and implementation with regard to the economy, what impact has globalization had on constitutionalism and economic life in Africa?

5. How has the relationship between constitutionalism (briefly, the implementation of the normative framework of the constitution) and economic growth played out in practice? Is there a symbiotic relationship?

This volume is concerned primarily with the question of what constitutions have to say about the economy; a second concern is whether constitutionalism affects the economy. The volume is not about *how* to make the economy grow—for instance, about which stimulus packages work the best. The focus is also not on the economic impact that certain constitutional institutions and processes can have, such as the effects associated with this or that electoral system or the choice of a presidential versus parliamentary system.[4] The task instead is to understand the link between constitutions and economies and examine the dynamics between constitutionalism and the economy. Our concern is with the constitutional framework in which economic growth is pursued. A growth strategy cannot be made without a development strategy—and the latter must be democratically legitimate and thus constitutional.

Before proceeding to unpack these relationships, it is useful to consider the basic concepts of constitutions, constitutionalism, and the economy.

---

[4] There is a voluminous literature on the latter topic, with this line of enquiry led by the work of Persson and Tabellini; see Torsten Persson and Guidio Tabellini, *The Economic Effects of Constitutions* (MIT Press 2005). These studies can be taken to extremes: it has been claimed that the longer a constitution, the lower is the per-capita GDP; see Alvaro A Montenegro, 'Constitutional Design and Economic Performance' (1995) 6 Constitutional Political Economy 161.

3. Conceptual Clarification

The concepts of constitutions, constitutionalism, and the economy lie at the core of this research project. As they do not have universally accepted meanings, a discussion is necessary of some of the different ways in which they are understood in the literature.

3.1   Constitutions

The primary function of constitutions is to regulate state power. This may entail the formal essentials of constitutionalism: the democratic process of law-making, an accountable executive implementing law, and a judiciary interpreting and enforcing that law. Among the other matters that are regulated are the security forces, the management of public finances, and international relations. A constitution may embed a system of multilevel government that involves a division of powers and functions between different levels of government.

It may also operate at a normative level, setting goals and principles in regard to how the state should be governed. Justice Ismael Mohammed famously said that a constitution represents the 'soul of the nation' in that it expresses the aspirations and normative values by which the state and citizens should be guided in their conduct.[5] A bill of rights may express those aspirations and impose limitations on the reach of governmental powers.

Many constitutions of democracies are given a special legal status: first, they are the supreme law in that all other legislation must conform to them, and secondly, they may be amended only with a super majority in parliament and, in some countries, with popular approval through referenda. These qualities, along with constitutions' normative dimensions, are captured in the concept of constitutionalism.

3.2   Constitutionalism

Constitutionalism is, as the 'ism' suggests, a set of liberal political values finding expression in legal form and practice. Its first component is the grounding of these values in a constitution, while the second is concerned with whether those constitutional provisions are a lived reality and a part of the dominant political culture.

The Western notion of constitutionalism is essentially one of limited government, with at least three basic elements being enshrined in a constitution that itself is not readily amendable.[6] The first is democracy—the establishment of accountable government both in terms of representative and participatory mechanisms. The second element is limited government: this entails the separation of powers, which provides checks and balances, and an enforceable bill of rights. The third is the rule of law—governance under rules and not by arbitrary discretion—which includes the supremacy of the constitution and its justiciability by an independent judiciary.

---

[5] *S v Acheson* 1991 (2) SA 805 (Nm) 813.
[6] See Nico Steytler, 'The Relationship between Decentralisation and Constitutionalism in Africa: Concepts, Conflicts, and Hypotheses' in Charles M Fombad (ed), *Decentralisation and Constitutionalism in Africa* (OUP 2019)and authorities cited therein.

In the literature on the relationship between law and the economy, the concept most often used is that of 'the rule of law', which may be either narrower than the concept of constitutionalism or coincident with it.[7] The World Bank, which has assiduously advanced the principle that the rule of law is critical to economic development, illustrates the conceptual differences. In an analysis of the Bank's policy statements, Alvaro Santos shows how it moved from a narrow conception of the rule of law to a conception in which the latter is equivalent to constitutionalism.[8] The Bank's structural adjustment policies of the 1980s adopted a narrow institutional concept focusing on clear and efficacious rules regardless of their content.[9] The next addition was a substantive element: the content of the rules should enshrine at least the protection of property rights and enforcement of contracts. The final addition, emerging post-2000 as part of 'comprehensive development', was an 'intrinsic' concept of the rule of law that enshrines the greatest values of a society such as democracy, justice, and freedom,[10] and thus suggests the equivalent of constitutionalism.

In Africa, the second wave of democratization saw components of constitutionalism formally embedded in most constitutions. However, a fourth element of constitutionalism was also emerging: state power should be directed towards development.[11] The new constitutional enterprise in Africa envisages a larger role for the state—a transformative or developmental one—where equal citizenship is the goal and is pursued through, among other legal measures, enforceable socio-economic rights and substantive equality.[12] The state is not merely a passive regulator of a free-market economy but plays an active role in ensuring effective distribution of resources to the entire population.

The grounding of constitutionalism in a constitution is but the first step; equally important, if not more, are observing and advancing those provisions in practice. Democracy requires free and fair elections and the practice of participatory democracy. The legislature is the main lawmaker distinct from the executive and provides oversight of the latter, with the bill of rights constraining the exercise of state power. Constitutional provisions and legislation are enforced by a judiciary which is independent and impartial. Finally, the state fulfils its developmental duties by providing the basic amenities of education, health services, food and water, and social security.

[7] See CI Ten, 'Constitutionalism and the Rule of Law' in Robert E Goodin, Philip Pettit, and Thomas Pogge (eds), *A Companion to Contemporary Political Economy* (Wiley 2017).

[8] Alvaro Santos, 'The World Bank's Uses of the "Rule of Law" Promise in Economic Development' in David Trubek and Alvaro Santos (eds), *The New Law and Economic Development: A Critical Appraisal* (Cambridge University Press 2006). Ramanujam describes this definition as the 'thin' approach, one in which the core elements are 'legitimacy, predictability, and [the] uniformity [with] which laws are created, applied and enforced'; see Nadini Ramanujam, 'A Comparative Analysis of the Approaches to Economic Development across BRIC Countries' (2012) Rule of Law and Economic Development Research Group, McGill University.

[9] This was also the original linkage that Adam Smith drew: 'Commerce and manufactures can seldom flourish long in any state which does not enjoy a regular administration of justice, in which the people do not feel themselves secure in the possession of their property, in which the faith of contracts is not supported by law, and in which the authority of the state is not supposed to be regularly employed in enforcing the payment of debts from all those who are able to pay. Commerce and manufactures, in short, can seldom flourish in any state in which there is not a certain degree of confidence in the justice of government.' (*An Inquiry into the Nature and Causes of the Wealth of Nations* (1776) (Soares Salvio ed, modern edn, Metalibri Digital Library 2007) 710).

[10] Santos (n 8) 259–67. Ramanujam (n 8) refers to this definition as the 'thick' approach to the rule of law, one focusing on broader concerns than the economy.

[11] See Yash Ghai, 'Chimera of Constitutionalism: State, Economy, and Society in Africa' (unpublished paper, University of Pretoria 2011) <http://www.up.ac.za/media/shared/Legacy/sitefiles/file/47/15338/chimera_of_constitutionalism_yg1.pdf> accessed 30 November 2020.

[12] Karl Klare, 'Legal Culture and Transformative Constitutionalism' (1998) 14 South African Journal on Human Rights 146; Pius Langa, 'Transformative Constitutionalism' (2006) 17 Stellenbosch Law Review 351.

3.3   Economy

A national economy may be defined as a country's system of producing and consuming goods and services and determining how they are distributed among the population. The products and services can be few or many. In pre-industrial societies, the economy was largely agriculturally based, but as societies developed, different sectors of the economy emerged: an industrial economy (the manufacturing of goods), a service economy (the provision of services), and an extractive economy (the exploitation of natural resources).

The role of the state in the economy varies. In a market economy, conventional wisdom holds that the state mainly plays a regulatory role, leaving the ownership of the means of production in private hands and with goods and services produced on the basis of supply and demand. Adam Smith believed that competition in the marketplace secures the effective distribution of goods and services to all and that the state's role should be that of a distant regulator of fair play. The forces of supply and demand determine the prices and quantities for most goods and services available in the market. Apart from its role of policing the rules of the market, state interference is tolerated only when it is necessary to provide stability.

By contrast, Karl Marx, witnessing the poor distributive efficiency of the capitalist market economy of the nineteenth century, predicted that its inherent contradictions would lead to its self-destruction, and he thus advocated for the socialization of the means of production. The Russian and Chinese revolutions pursued the goals of ownership by 'the people' and a command economy in which the state controls the means of production as well as the distribution of products and services.

In the mid-twentieth century, John Maynard Keynes, recognizing that the market does not automatically allocate resources to the poor, maintained that the state should play a far more interventionist role in the economy through fiscal and monetary policies. After the Second World War, the 'social' state emerged—here, on the back of a market economy, the state is responsible for the equitable distribution of resources to all.

Although there are still voices today proclaiming the virtues and viability of socialism, a strong consensus has emerged, particularly after the collapse of Soviet socialism, that a market economy is the only one that generates wealth. The social democrat Paul Collier argues that capitalism, with market-based competition as its vital core, is 'the only economic system that has proved to be capable of generating prosperity'.[13] This result, he argues, flows from the fact that capitalism 'spawns and disciplines firms, [which are] organisations that enable people to harness the productivity potential of scale and specialisation'.[14]

While Collier enthuses about social democratic government of the post-war years, he bemoans the loss of communitarian ideals in the twenty-first century. Capitalism has the potential to lift societies to 'unprecedented levels of prosperity', he contends, but this has not come about because modern capitalism is not being harnessed for social-democratic ends.

---

[13]   Paul Collier, *The Future of Capitalism: Facing New Anxieties* (Allen Lane 2018) 181.

[14]   ibid 17. Likewise, Thomas Piketty (*Capital in the Twenty-First Century* (Belknap Press of Harvard University Press 2014)) is equally convinced of the productive energy of capitalism, but warns of the emerging crisis in capitalism where inequality increases unchecked. This occurs when income from capital exceeds the growth rate of the economy, that is, the income from investments (mostly inherited) exceeds income from labour. This results in extremely high levels of inequality, which is incompatible with a society based on meritocracy and principles of social justice (ibid 26).

3.4 The Relationship between Constitutions and the Economy

The notion that there is no relationship between the economy and the constitution is now only an amusing historical footnote attributed to Oliver Wendell Holmes.[15] It is evident, even in the United States Constitution written in 1789,[16] that a relationship obtains between the two, albeit not always directly and explicitly articulated. Broadly speaking, there are three kinds of intersection between a constitution and a country's economy. In the first, the constitution gives expression to a pre-existing economic structure, be it a private property-based market economy or system of communal ownership. In the second, the constitution heralds a revolutionary change in property relations, while in the third, the constitution provides for some balance between the state and the market.

The classic Marxist analysis posits that a society's legal order, along with its constitutional pinnacle, is part of a superstructure determined by its economic base.[17] In a capitalist society, and hence one founded on private property, the law and the constitution reflect these underlying economic relations and seek to ensure their furtherance. Moreover, according to this analysis, the rise of constitutionalism was a direct product of the development of capitalism.[18] Socialism, by contrast, as brought about by revolution, would base the new economic order on the founding constituent document, namely the revolutionary declaration (or proto-constitution) nationalizing all property. In such a case, the constitution is a political document aiming to reshape society into a socialist one. There may be shades in between these two extremes, for example where the state nationalizes only a certain class of property, such as mines and banks. The constitution, in short, can serve the function of reflecting an existing economic order, heralding a new one, or doing a bit of both.

Africa offers examples of these various intersections between constitutions and economies. With the onset of colonialism, the private ownership of land only partially replaced communal ownership. Constitutions that expressed mainly parliamentary sovereignty implicitly reflected such an economy. Examples of such implicit embrace of a market economy are found in the constitutions of South Africa (1910, 1961, 1983), Botswana (1966), and Mauritius (1968). It was only in the independence constitutions that the protection of private ownership featured in these colonial legacies, for example in Nigeria (1960), Senegal (1960), and Kenya (1963).

In contrast to the 'reflective' constitutions, a significant number of countries imposed radical change on the economy. The constitutions of Angola, Benin, Burkina Faso, Congo, Ethiopia, Ghana, Guinea, Madagascar, Mozambique, and Somalia at various times proclaimed commitments to a socialist state.[19] While the Constitution of Benin of 1977, for example, expressed a commitment to socialism, in Zambia only the property clause in the

---

[15] In his dissenting opinion, Holmes wrote that 'a constitution is not intended to embody a particular economic theory, whether of paternalism and the organic relation of the citizen to the State or of laissez faire' (*Lochner v New York* [1905] 198 US 45, 75–76).

[16] Subsequent commentaries have pointed out that the framers of the US Constitution sought to entrench a market economy through the high value they placed on the right to property and freedom of contract (see eg James W Ely, 'The Constitution and Economic Liberty' (2011) 35 Harvard Journal of Law and Public Policy 27).

[17] Jonathan R Macey, 'Competing Economic Views of the Constitution' (1987) Faculty Scholarship Series. Paper 1732 <https://digitalcommons.law.yale.edu/fss_papers/1732/> accessed 30 November 2020.

[18] Ghai (n 11).

[19] See Victor T Le Vine, 'The Fall and Rise of Constitutionalism in West Africa' (1997) 35(2) Journal of Modern African Studies 181.

Constitution was deleted to allow for legislation nationalizing the mines.[20] Negotiations about democracy in South Africa in the early 1990s engaged with the nature of the economy and whether it would be socialist, free-market, or mixed.

How linkages are drawn between constitutions and economies and what their likely impact is on each other are the focus of this volume. These linkages and impacts, once identified and examined, are then analysed in the context of constitutionalism.

4. Constitutionalizing a Market Economy

The first line of enquiry is whether (and if so, how) the second wave of democratization and constitutional reform of the 1990s and thereafter impacted on the constitutional framework of the state's relationship to the economy. More particularly, was a market economy constitutionalized, and if so, how? This enquiry raises a number of questions. First, was there an envisioning of the market economy? Secondly, if so, was the market economy constitutionally protected from state intervention, and if so, how?

4.1 The Constitutional Envisioning of the Economy

In the case of proclaimed African socialist economies, this vision was explicitly captured in constitutional instruments.[21] Socialism was put upfront in bold letters in either the preamble or the founding principles of the state. The Benin Constitution of 1977, for example, reads: 'In the People's Republic of Benin the development path is socialism. Its foundation is Marxism-Leninism, which should be applied in a living and creative way to Beninois realities.'[22] This was not an operative provision in a legalistic sense but worked at a normative level.

In contrast to socialist exhibitionism, constitutions premised on an underlying market economy seldom make direct reference to it, albeit that their fundamental concepts and institutions reflect it.[23] At a superficial glance, then, the constitutions of the second democratic era do not proclaim the market-economy model, but in the small print there are ample provisions to secure this particular economic model, which is usually entrenched most powerfully in a core component of the constitution—the bill of rights.

4.2 Protecting the Basics of the Market Economy from State Intervention

While the main purpose of a bill of rights can be said to be limiting state action vis-à-vis individuals, in the West it has served primarily to protect the market economy by limiting

---

[20] Rukudzo Murapa, 'Nationalization of the Zambian Mining Industry' (1976) 7 The Review of Black Political Economy 47; Muna Ndulo, 'Mining Legislation and Mineral Development in Zambia' (1986) 19 Cornell International Law Journal 11.

[21] Yash Pal Ghai, 'The Constitution and the Economy' (2002) Institute of Economic Affairs (IEA).

[22] Art 4, which was omitted in the Constitution of the People's Republic of Benin of 1990.

[23] Ghai (n 21).

the extent of state regulation of its essential elements—property ownership and freedom of contract; the relationship between the economy and the state is then couched in terms of individual freedoms from state interference,[24] noting that economic enterprises (juristic persons) may lay claim, even under South Africa's Constitution of 1996, to the same rights as natural persons.[25] A number of different rights and freedoms thus give effect to the market economy and institutionalize its distinctiveness from the state.

First, ever since the emergence of the market economy, private property has been regarded as its institutional foundation and as encompassing ownership of the means of production, including land and its products, and the retention of profit.[26] Private property has thus been included in a bill of rights to afford protection against arbitrary deprivation of property by the state. Property rights have extended beyond material commodities to include the protection of intellectual property rights, which are regarded as incentives to invention and innovation.[27] The economist Justus Haucap argues that the emergence of a market economy necessitates a property-rights regime comprising clearly defined rights that are as secure and stable as possible.[28] He cautions, however, that protection of a property right (as a counter-majoritarian measure) nevertheless must be socially sustainable and acceptable to the majority of the population lest it become a source of instability that upsets the constitutionally ordained property regime.[29]

Secondly, the freedom of contract is, along with the right to property, regarded as an essential element underpinning the individualism and competitiveness that are characteristic of a market economy. This element per se is rarely protected directly by the constitution unless it is seen as an inherent part of the right to freedom. What constitutions do more usually is protect the enforceability of contracts by providing for the right to access courts to settle legal disputes.[30] The state thus may not deny the sanctity of contract, which imposes an obligation on it (the state) to institute a functioning judicial system and, among other things, respect the independence of the judiciary.

Thirdly, although competition lies at the basis of the market economy, it often does not find direct articulation in bills of rights, as it is regarded as inherent to the freedom of contract. In more recent constitutions, such as South Africa's, the foundation of such competition is weakly entrenched in the rights of individuals to 'choose their trade, occupation or profession', subject to state regulation.[31] Provisions of this kind stress the individualistic nature of an open, competitive economy: any person (or company) may enter the economy in whatever way desired, this by virtue of curtailment of the power of the government to prevent or unreasonably restrict open competition.

---

[24] See László Bruszt, 'Market Making as State Making: Constitutions and Economic Development in Post-Communist Eastern Europe' (2002) 13 Constitutional Political Economy 53; John Harrison, 'The Constitution of Economic Liberty' (2008) 45 San Diego Law Review 709.

[25] South African Constitution of 1996, s 8(2).

[26] Viktor J Vanberg, *The Constitution of Markets: Essays in Political Economy* (Routledge 2001) 23.

[27] Ceyhun Haydaroğlu, 'The Relationship between Property Rights and Economic Growth: An Analysis of OECD and EU Countries' (2015) 6(4) Danube: Law and Economics Review 217, 222. Section 40(5) of the Kenyan Constitution of 2010, for example, obliges the state to 'support, promote and protect the intellectual property rights of the people of Kenya'.

[28] Justus Haucap, 'The Rule of Law and the Emergence of Market Exchange: A New Institutional Economic Perspective' in U von Alemann, D Briesen, and LQ Khanh (eds), *The State of Law: Comparative Perspectives on the Rule of Law* (Düsseldorf University Press 2017).

[29] ibid 144.

[30] See eg South African Constitution of 1996, s 33.

[31] ibid s 22.

Fourth, of even more recent vintage is the protection of consumers as the ultimate benefi-ciaries of a competitive market economy.[32] The Kenyan Constitution of 2010 sports a clause in the Bill of Rights that seeks to protect consumer rights from an imperious market:[33]

> Every consumer has the right—
>   (a) To goods and services of reasonable quality;
>   (b) To the information necessary for them to gain full benefit from goods and services;
>   (c) To the protection of their health, safety, and economic interests; and
>   (d) To compensation for loss or injury arising from defects in goods and services.
> The state is then given the duty ensure the realisation of these rights.[34]

Fifth, while the protection of the collective rights of workers has its origins in the first part of the twentieth century, the collective rights of employers are another newer development. Such rights are established either directly or indirectly (through the right of assembly) and give recognition to the two components of a market economy—labour and owners of the means of production. South Africa's Bill of Rights, for instance, protects the rights both of workers and employers, the two parties to the production of wealth.[35] The recognition of labour rights—principally the right to strike—limits the power of the government to let a free market reign unencumbered in the interests solely of owners.

Thus, when individual rights are transposed as obligations of restraint (and fulfilment) im-posed on the state, the resultant delineation of what the state may not do offers a clear picture of how the inner core of the economy is defined. As with all other rights, these rights may be limited by state action, of course, but such limitations cannot extinguish the core of those rights or, in regard to the economy, the basics of a market economy.

5. The Constitutional Framework for Land and Other Natural Resources

While economic activity on communal lands forms part of Africa's agricultural economy, the value that agriculture adds to GDP has declined over the past fifteen years, decreasing between 2003 and 2015 from nearly 23 per cent to 17.3 per cent.[36] Farmland remains an important component of capital, yet is likely to follow the pattern seen in Europe over the last two centuries in which land, once the primary form of capital, was replaced by housing, industry, and finance.[37] In addition, in several African countries the source of economic growth is not agriculture but extractive industries,[38] which constitute 26 per cent of GDP albeit that most mining assets are foreign owned.[39] It is reported that, in 2012, minerals

---

[32] For Adam Smith, the virtue of the market is precisely that the consumer benefits from competition. Collier (n 13) argues more than 200 years later that a healthy, sustainable market must place the public ahead of individual owners' accumulation of capital.
[33] Kenyan Constitution of 2010, art 46(1).
[34] ibid art 46(2).
[35] South African Constitution of 1996, s 23.
[36] Mabugu (n 2).
[37] See Piketty (n 14) 119 et seq.
[38] Greg Mills and others, *Making Africa Work: A Handbook for Economic Success* (Tafelberg 2017) 4.
[39] Mabugu (n 2).

and oil contributed to 77 per cent of total exports and 42 per cent of all government revenue.[40]

One of the reasons advanced for the stagnation of the agricultural sector is uncertainty of land title.[41] The constitutional regulation of land and natural resources is thus of crucial importance. As both communal land and private ownership are present, however, the protection of property in a constitution is not as straightforward as it is in some Western bills of rights, where the safe assumption is that private property is the dominant form of ownership. Moreover, a number of African constitutions also lay claim to state ownership of land on behalf of the nation. The latter claim is of particular importance with respect to natural resources: given that agricultural and extractive industries are the main components of many developing economies, the state often has an overriding interest in their ownership, control, and products.

In short, land and natural resources are important in Africa and feature prominently in certain constitutions. A second line of enquiry is hence concerned with the nature of the constitutional frameworks in this regard. Who 'owns' such wealth and how is the revenue derived from it distributed among the inhabitants of a country?

6. The Constitutional Framework for the State's Role in a Market Economy

The third line of enquiry focuses on the state's role in a market economy. The following are the pertinent considerations. First, in African constitutions, has a trend developed with regard to the state's regulatory role in the market? Is there any constitutional regulation of the state's active participation in the market? Conversely, how does the state protect itself from the predations of the market, in particular from capture by market forces and players? Secondly, where the state comprises multilevel government, how does that shape such a regulatory role? Thirdly, how have central banks, as constitutional institutions, imposed a substantive limit on states' regulatory roles in respect of monetary policy? Finally, where the market does not adequately distribute the benefits of the economy to all sectors of society, are there constitutional obligations on the state to do so?

6.1 The State's Power to Regulate the Economy

In entrenching a market economy in a constitution, what regulatory role is accorded to the government—interventionist, *laissez-faire*, or, again, something in between? Although this is not often expressed directly, constitutions empower the state, both through legislation and policy, to regulate the economy inasmuch as it (the state) may regulate any other aspect of societal life. In unitary states, this proposition is so obvious that it is seldom mentioned. The government of the day may thus legislate on the main sectors of the economy. Such regulation may include development programmes, stimulation packages, and other measures the government deems fit for growing the economy.

---

[40] Mills and others (n 38) 113.
[41] ibid 91.

A central question for market economists is the protection and fostering of competition and avoidance of monopolies, all of which is putatively geared towards the interests of consumers. As Vanberg notes, '[C]ompetition is clearly desirable for those who are competed for; it is less desirable for those who have to compete.'[42] How could it be otherwise? 'Competition in ordinary markets is there to benefit consumers, not to please businessmen.'[43] The simplicity of the proposition belies the complexity that arises when state-owned enterprises enter the picture, often as monopolies in the provision of key goods such as energy, water, and transport. Likewise, where the economy is based on agriculture and the exploitation of natural resources, and it is the case that land and such resources are constitutionally vested in the state, where does the dimension of competition come into play?

For many African leaders, the authoritarian governments of the Asian Tigers are an attractive model for enhancing economic growth,[44] but there have only been occasional successes; the result more usually is just a heavy governmental hand on the economy. Mills and others argue that there are crucial differences between countries in the two regions. While the private sector in the Southeast Asian countries was distinct from government (and enjoyed its support), in Africa a separate private sector is anathema for governments—instead ruling elites typically seek to extend their monopoly of power to the market as well and absorb it into the patrimonial state.[45]

Ghai thus describes the post-colonial economy as an 'administered economy';[46] the state has a heavy hand in all aspects of the economy, from controlling mineral wealth and issuing business licences to awarding state contracts and owning or managing key sectors. Crucially, the economy, as with the state, must be subordinate to politics and the ruling elite. For Ghai, '[t]he link between the state and economy is corruption.'[47] Moreover, without an 'independent' private sector to act as a counterweight to the government, there is no limited government.

Economists are quick to point out as well that the state, apart from trying to ensure a competitive market, needs to protect itself in turn from market forces that could compromise the competitiveness of that market.[48] The focus hence shifts to the institutional structures that a constitution provides for ensuring accountability and combating corruption. By implication, what developing countries require is not a weak state where the market is the dominant actor, but a strong state which can ensure that the market functions to the benefit of the population as a whole.[49]

---

[42] Vanberg (n 26) 4.

[43] ibid 13.

[44] Uche Ewelukwa Ofodile, 'Trade, Empires, and Subjects—China–Africa Trade: A New Fair Trade Arrangement, or the Third Scramble for Africa?' (2008) 41 Vanderbilt Journal of Transnational Law 505, 537–38.

[45] Mills and others (n 38) 19–20.

[46] Ghai (n 11) 9.

[47] ibid.

[48] Vanberg (n 26) 3. Haggard, MacIntyre, and Tiede note the following consequences: the market has no confidence in the formal judicial system for the enforcement of contract; corruption raises costs for producers and consumers; and it induces distortions in the market through 'monopolies, restrictions on entry, protectionism, misallocation of government spending, and private expropriation of assets through managerial malfeasance' (Stephan Haggard, Andrew MacIntyre, and Lydia Tiede, 'The Rule of Law and Economic Development' (2008) 11 Annual Review of Political Science 205, 211).

[49] Hilton L Root, 'Do Strong Governments Produce Strong Economies?' (2001) 5(4) The Independent Review 565; Guido Tabellini, 'The Role of the State in Economic Development' (2005) 58(2) KYKLOS 283, 292.

6.2 Multilevel Governments

In the case of countries whose constitutions entrench multilevel government (be it a federation or a system decentralizing power to local government), two distinct issues come to the fore. The first has to do with the value-add that subnational government brings to the economy, while the second, flowing from the first, is about how regulatory functions should be divided among the levels of government.

The literature on the value that non-centralism has for economic growth is considerable. The economist Anwar Shah is at the forefront in arguing that, for the sake of allocative efficiency, decisions should be made at the lowest level of government—that is, local government.[50] Of particular relevance to economic development in Africa is the World Bank's investment in decentralization and local economic development;[51] billions of dollars have been devoted to decentralization projects.[52] A key underlying idea is that subnational governments could make growth more sustainable and responsive to the needs and priorities of the locality by preventing an over-concentration of growth and wealth at the centre.

Given the beneficial role that subnational governments could play, the question, then, is: what is their reach in regard to economic regulation and policy development? In the case of the world's first modern federation, the US Constitution reserves for the federal government the power to control interstate commerce. The constitutional vision of the economy is that it is singular and indivisible and that subnational governments should not be entitled to fracture it by imposing restrictions on the free movement of goods, capital, and labour. The economic assumption is that, for the market to function effectively and efficiently, it must operate in a unitary fashion, with capital, goods, and labour circulating freely and unhampered by internal imposition of duties and taxes. The same argument applies, of course, in magnified form to the regional and global levels, a matter to which we shall return.

In Africa, the growth of federal-based systems in the Comoros, Democratic Republic of the Congo (DRC), Ethiopia, Kenya, Nigeria, and South Africa, and anticipated in other countries (Somalia, South Sudan, and Sudan), is motivated in part by the promise of developmental returns.[53] Federalism has been touted as being good for economic growth in Ethiopia,[54] for instance; likewise, in a number of African countries where decentralization appears in the form of constitutionalized local government,[55] local economic development is an important object and function associated with it.

The next questions that arise are about how economic development forms part of the functions of subnational government and how the regulatory role has been apportioned between different levels of government.

---

[50] Anwar Shah, 'On the Design of Economic Constitutions' (1996) 29 Canadian Journal of Economics 614. In general, see Anwar Shah (ed), *The Practice of Fiscal Federalism: Comparative Perspectives* (McGill-Queen's University Press 2007).

[51] World Bank, 'Decentralization in Client Countries: An Evaluation of World Bank Support, 1990–2007' (2008) 1–59.

[52] ibid 7.

[53] See Charles M Fombad and Nico Steytler (eds), *Decentralisation and Constitutionalism in Africa* (OUP 2019).

[54] Assefa Fiseha, 'Federalism, Development and the Changing Political Dynamics in Ethiopia' (2019) 17(1) I•CON 151.

[55] See Charles M Fombad, 'Constitutional Entrenchment of Decentralisation in Africa: An Overview of Trends and Tendencies' (2018) 62(2) Journal of African Law 175.

6.3 Central Banks and Monetary Policy

While the central government may have to share some regulatory powers with subnational governments, there is an aspect of regulation—price stability—that has increasingly been taken out of the hands of the central government and entrusted to an independent central bank. Such independence often finds expression in constitutions that allocate to central banks the mandate of protecting the currency and ensuring price stability. The orthodoxy is that a market requires a stable and predictable currency for its proper functioning.[56] Price stability benefits not only a market economy but so too the purchasers of products and services. A central bank is also the lender of last resort, which makes it the only institution capable of preventing the collapse of a financial system.[57] Long-term monetary stability is something that a government, subject to the exigencies of the next election, usually cannot deliver successfully. In Africa, central banks are making increasing appearance in constitutions and slowly consolidating their independent space notwithstanding strong governmental resistance.[58]

6.4 The Developmental State and the 'Social' State

Apart from being a regulator, the state may itself be a strong player in the economy. The concept of the developmental state posits that the state should be at the forefront in leading economic development through infrastructural investment and by itself owning the means of production in the form of state-owned enterprises. A constitution may expressly empower a state to be an active economic player, or it may say nothing. Arguments are made for and against a strong developmental state, with aspects of the debate turning around whether constitutionalism is essential or inessential (even a hindrance) to economic growth, a topic discussed below. Strong states, it has been pointed out, 'often ended up pursing power for the sake of its own leaders, and elitism, corruption, and misallocation of resources have resulted'.[59]

A notion central to arguments extolling capitalism's ability to create prosperity is Adam Smith's belief that, through its 'invisible hand', the market is capable of distributing resources in a way that meets everyone's basic needs. A century later Karl Marx asserted the very opposite—that the market is not effective at all at this—and saw class warfare as inevitable. In response, the 'social' state emerged in the twentieth century, beginning in the US with Roosevelt's New Deal in the 1930s and followed by the social democracies of post-war Europe. These attempted to harness capitalism as an engine for creating the revenue needed in order to provide education, health, housing, and security for all.[60]

As Piketty notes, the 'social' state was built on a framework of rights derived from the principle of equal access to those goods and services regarded as fundamental.[61] Where the

---

[56] Christopher Crowe and Ellen E Meade, 'The Evolution of Central Bank Governance around the World' (2007) 24(4) Journal of Economic Perspectives 69; Alex Cukierman, 'Central Bank Independence and Monetary Control' (1994) 104 The Economic Journal 1437; Harrison (n 24) 716.

[57] Piketty (n 14) 473.

[58] Nico Steytler, '"Financial Constitutions" to Prevent Corruption' in Charles M Fombad and Nico Steytler (eds), *Corruption and Constitutionalism in Africa: Revisiting Control Measures and Strategies* (OUP 2020) 398.

[59] Root (n 49) 565.

[60] See Collier (n 13) 48.

[61] Piketty (n 14) 479.

market does not distribute resources effectively to all citizens through jobs and livelihoods, a constitution may impose positive duties on the state to do so. Reflecting the 'second generation' of rights, the International Covenant on Social, Economic, and Cultural Rights contains the rights to education, health, food and water, housing, and social security. These were given effect to largely through policies rather than constitutions, and were key to the 'social' states established in Europe from the 1950s onwards. It was only much later, in the context of developing countries, that they began to be crystallized as enforceable obligations on the state to fulfil them. In India, the Supreme Court found that the right to life was a broad concept that included a 'decent' life requiring adequate housing.[62] In South Africa, the Constitutional Court has endeavoured to give effect to socio-economic rights in the Bill of Rights of the 1996 Constitution, nonetheless shying away from finding that the core content of the rights entails the delivery of actual commodities.[63]

Actualizing such rights is no mean feat. Piketty records that in the 'social' states of the West, taxes make up 40–45 per cent of national income and can be used to fund social commitments; in developing countries, by contrast, the percentage is only between 10 and 15, and since this does not enable the state to fulfil a 'social' role, the latter can do no more than stick to its traditional regulatory role.[64]

7. Globalization, Economies, Constitutions, and Constitutionalism

It would be naive to assume that the dynamic relations between constitutions, constitutionalism, and the economy are purely a domestic affair—that 'the people' draft their constitution, that the institutions of democracy make, implement, and oversee local economic policy choices, and that all this plays out within a homemade constitutional framework.

In the age of globalization, national sovereignty has weakened. International human rights law and its institutions bind governments in their conduct and affect the formulation of bills of rights. It is, moreover, in the area of the economy that the influence of globalization has been felt with particular acuteness. As already noted, in Africa's second wave of democracy, the return to multiparty democracy was closely associated with the institutionalization of a market economy.[65] A further, related, and crucial factor is the growing power of the international trade regime, which includes real sanctions and has become so extensive as to inspire the notion of a 'global trade constitutionalism'.

How economic integration affects developing countries has been the subject of much controversy.[66] In Africa, international economic agendas impact on democratic sovereignty, with trade agreements said to be profoundly 'non-African' because African countries had little substantive participation in the design of the global trading system. The question arises of whether (and how) the dominance of developed nations' economic interests in the trade regime embodied in the World Trade Organization (WTO) serves to impinge on democratic sovereignty as well as prioritize trade over human rights.

[62] *Francis Coralie Mullin v The Administrator, Union Territory of Delhi* (1981) 2 SCR 516.
[63] Sandra Liebenberg, *Socio-Economic Rights: Adjudication under a Transformative Constitution* (Juta 2010).
[64] Piketty (n 14) 491.
[65] See Haggard, MacIntyre, and Tiede (n 48) 205.
[66] See eg Joseph E Stiglitz, *Globalisation and its Discontent* (Penguin 2002).

A related question is whether African economic integration can help cure these ills. Such integration is high on the agenda of the African Union (AU) as well as regional cooperation blocs, which see integrated markets as an opportunity to boost collective growth. Several often overlapping trading blocs already exist at the regional level and seek to open markets among their member states: the Common Market for Eastern and Southern Africa (COMESA), East Africa Community (EAC), Economic Community of West African States (ECOWAS), Southern African Customs Union (SACU), Southern African Development Community (SADC), and West African Economic and Monetary Union (WAEMU). At the AU level, the agreement creating the African Continental Free Trade Area was launched in Niger in 2019 after seventeen years of negotiation and signed by fifty-four AU members, with Eritrea the only outsider. It is predicted that this continental initiative will increase intra-African trade from the current 16 per cent to 60 per cent by 2022.[67]

Economic integration necessarily entails voluntary surrender of a sliver of sovereignty, given that enforcement of the relevant agreement by definition limits domestic policy freedom. One of the issues that arise here is the question, then, of how closely or not trade agreements align with a country's domestic constitutional commitments.

8. The Relationship between Constitutionalism and the Economy

Where the basic elements of constitutionalism—the practice of democracy, limited government, and the rule of law—are present, what impact, if any, do they have on the economy? Do they help or hinder it, or are they neutral in regard to economic growth?[68]

8.1 The Correlation between Constitutionalism and Economic Growth

A strong correlation between 'the rule of law' and economic growth has proven to be elusive. Studies show that the impact of the rule of law on economic growth varies from positive to neutral and even negative; conversely, in countries operating outside of the rule-of-law paradigm, economies have flourished.

On the positive side, the 'pro-democracy' school of thought has argued persistently that the presence of the rule of law (principally the protection of private property and the enforcement of freedom of contract) results in positive economic results because the market flourishes in an environment of certainty and predictability.[69] Private capital is invested if there is security of ownership and if individual enterprise is protected through the enforcement of contracts by independent courts. The World Bank, for example, was convinced for decades that the supremacy of the constitution, the rule of law, and an independent judiciary were essential for a thriving market, and by 2012 had supported 330 'rule-of-law' projects dealing with legal and judicial reform in more than a hundred countries.[70]

---

[67] Agence France-Presse, 'Applause as African Leaders Finally Launch Landmark Free-trade Deal' *Business Day* (8 July 2019) 11.

[68] As mentioned, the literature on this topic usually refers to 'the rule of law' rather than 'constitutionalism'. See Santos (n 8).

[69] Santos (n 8). See Adam Smith (n 9), as quoted there.

[70] Santos (n 8) 253.

Indeed, a study of 71 countries found that while *de jure* judicial independence has no impact on economic growth, de facto independence was positively correlated to real GDP per capita growth in 57 countries.[71] Although the standard view is that democracy per se has no statistically significant effect on economic growth, it at least does not reduce economic growth;[72] moreover, democracy has an indirect impact on the economy through enhancement of human capital.

By contrast, the link between authoritarianism and economic growth seems strong. The robust growth of the Asian Tigers, and subsequently China, showed that market economies bloomed under authoritarian regimes in Singapore, South Korea, and Malaysia, while China's economy flourished in the absence of democracy, privatization, and liberalization. Then again, a 2012 study of the then BRIC countries with vibrant economies—be they democracies (Brazil and India), authoritarian democracies (Russia), or one-party states (China)—found no clear correlation between the rule of law and economic development.[73] Since South Africa joined BRICS, the growth rate in Brazil, Russia, and South Africa has shrunk or faltered, with only China and India still posting positive growth rates.[74]

To explain this enigma, scholars argue that the critical factor for growth is stability, as a market flourishes in an environment of predictability.[75] Stability can be provided by either authoritarian or democratic regimes. Scholars on the democratic side of the fence maintain, though, that authoritarian regimes provide a flawed sense of stability. Douglass North, for example, posits that economies based on authoritarian rule are not sustainable in the long run.[76] Although economic growth without the rule of law is possible in the short term (the government's legitimacy lies in producing prosperity), long-term development requires capital investment based on the certainty of protection of property rights.[77] With stability taken as the key factor, regime types are viewed through a historical lens and the argument then made that long-term democracy (providing better stability) is positively linked to economic growth.[78]

8.2 Constitutionalism and Economic Growth in Africa

Does the practice of constitutionalism (or its absence) in Africa reflect the same patterns as elsewhere in the world? Are constitutional democracies faring better economically than authoritarian countries? In answering this question, an initial problem is that it presupposes

---

[71] Lars P Feld and Stefan Voigt, 'Economic Growth and Judicial Independence: Cross-country Evidence Using a New Set of Indicators' (2003) CESIFO Working Paper No 906. See also Cass R Sunstein, 'On Property and Constitutionalism Comparative Constitutionalism: Theoretical Perspectives on the Role of Constitutions in the Interplay between Identity and Diversity' (1992) 14 Cardozo Law Review 907, 908.

[72] Amartya Sen, *Development as Freedom* (Alfred Knopf 1999) 149; Carl Henrik Knutsen, 'Democracy and Economic Growth: A Survey of Arguments and Results' (2012) 15(4) International Area Studies Review 393.

[73] Ramanujam (n 8) 231.

[74] See Nico Steytler (ed), *The BRICS Partnership: Challenges and Prospects for Multilevel Government* (Juta 2018).

[75] Haggard, Macintyre, and Tiede (n 48) 212.

[76] Douglass North, *Institutions, Institutional Change, and Economic Performance* (Cambridge University Press 1992).

[77] ibid.

[78] John Gerring and others, 'Democracy and Economic Growth: A Historical Perspective' (2005) 57(3) World Politics 323.

that constitutionalism is enough of an actuality in some African countries for it to be regarded as an independent variable. In many, if not most, of them, it is not the case.

First, as the previous volumes in this series attest, the basic elements of constitutionalism are at best unevenly captured in Africa's constitutions. The separation of powers between the three branches of government tends to be weak,[79] which has disastrous consequences for combating corruption.[80] Constitutional adjudication is also thinly spread across the continent.[81] Secondly, even where constitutions espouse the principles of constitutionalism, it is the exception rather than the rule for them to be implemented. The absence of constitutionalism has hampered decentralization,[82] and despite the numerous constitutional institutions designed for combating corruption, high levels of corruption attest to the absence of rule enforcement;[83] furthermore, 'authoritarian' democracies are a widespread phenomenon.[84]

In this context, the available evidence does indeed suggest that patterns in Africa are similar to those seen elsewhere: as yet there is no conclusive evidence that constitutionalism inevitably leads to economic growth and that its absence does not. The democratic rule-of-law countries of Botswana, Mauritius, and South Africa (in 2000–08) have posted consistent positive growth rates. Moreover, the absence of constitutionalism has been linked to negative growth. In South Africa, for instance, rampant corruption under the Zuma presidency both undermined constitutionalism and crippled economic growth; in Zimbabwe, the implosion of its economy since 2000 stems in good part from the negation of property rights.[85] On the other hand, the strict protection of intellectual property rights is said to have a negative impact on growth in sub-Saharan Africa in that it protects foreign firms at the expense of local enterprises.[86]

The liberal refrain nevertheless continues to be '[that] Rule of Law, by providing the framework for protecting private property and individual freedom, creates the stability and predictability in economic affairs necessary to promote entrepreneurship, saving and investment, and capital formation.'[87]

There is also strong evidence that authoritarian regimes, by definition operating outside the purview of constitutionalism, can enjoy impressive economic growth. Ethiopia is a prime example of where steady growth, at times in double figures, occurred over two decades under an authoritarian government that took a firmly interventionist stance and had scant regard for constitutionalism.[88] Where corruption is one of the main scourges

---

[79] Charles M Fombad (ed), *Separation of Powers in African Constitutionalism* (OUP 2015).
[80] Charles M Fombad and Nico Steytler (eds), *Corruption and Constitutionalism in Africa: Revisiting Control Measures and Strategies* (OUP 2020).
[81] Charles M Fombad (ed), *Constitutional Adjudication in Africa* (OUP 2016).
[82] Fombad and Steytler (n 53).
[83] Fombad and Steytler (n 80).
[84] Charles M Fombad and Nico Steytler (eds), *Democracy, Elections and Constitutionalism in Africa* (OUP 2021).
[85] Craig J Richardson, 'The Loss of Property Rights and the Collapse of Zimbabwe' (2005) 25(3) Cato Journal 541.
[86] A Samuel, 'Intellectual Property Rights, Innovations, and Economic Growth in Sub-Saharan Africa' (2011) 28 Journal of Third World Studies 231, referred to by Haydaroğlu (n 27) 227.
[87] NA Curott, 'Foreign Aid, the Rule of Law, and Economic Development in Africa' (2010) 11 University of Botswana Law Journal 3, 14, quoted in Joseph Isanga, 'Rule of Law and African Development' (2016) 42 North Carolina Journal of International Law and Commercial Regulation 2, 2.
[88] Assefa Fiseha and Fiseha H Gebresilassie, 'The Interface between Federalism and Development in Ethiopia' in Fantu Cheru, Christopher Cramer, and Arkebe Oqubay (eds), *The Oxford Handbook of the Ethiopian Economy* (OUP 2019) 86. Rwanda may be a further example.

of economic development, the fact that authoritarian states are often better than others at combating it, as for example in Singapore, might explain why authoritarian states sometimes fare better in terms of advancing economic growth.

As mentioned, many an African leader sees the success of the Asian Tigers as lying in their authoritarianism, a mode of government that consequently looks appealing as a way '[to] get things done'.[89] However, Mills and others point out that the legitimacy of the Asian 'soft' authoritarian governments rested on the ability of their economic performance to bring benefit to the general population, with the resultant legitimacy then supporting political stability. In contrast, few benign autocrats are to be found in Africa: the fruits of economic growth wind up in the pockets of ruling elites. Ethiopia illustrates this point. Assefa Fiseha argues that strong economic growth and meeting the Sustainable Development Goals seemingly did not cement the legitimacy of the authoritarian Ethiopian People's Revolutionary Democratic Front (EPRDF) government, as evidenced by the country's recent years of protests and conflict.[90] Indeed, the unravelling of the once-hegemonic EPRDF is attributable to its unwillingness to accommodate democracy at the level of subnational government.[91]

Central to the explanation of different growth paths is, again, political stability or its absence. Approaching the lack of economic growth from an investment perspective, Piketty argues that Africa is not developing partly due to chronic political instability.[92] One of the reasons for instability, he posits, is that when a country's wealth is owned largely by foreigners, 'there is a recurrent and almost irrepressible demand for expropriation';[93] such instability makes further investment risky. Contrariwise, some political actors believe that investment and development are possible only if existing property rights are unconditionally protected; but a country is then caught in endless alternation between revolutionary governments and governments dedicated to preserving property, whereas the real problem lies with the ownership of resources.[94] The more extreme example is the disastrous effect of civil conflict on the economy: it leads to the diversion of public and private resources from productive purposes to the use of violence, the destruction of infrastructure, criminal activities, and the loss of human capital.[95]

One argument that emerges is that democracy can provide stability in the long term and thus help ensure sustainable development.[96] Therefore, Mills and others also argue that democracy and economic development go hand in hand as mutually reinforcing—as such, long-term economic success in Africa depends on more democracy, not less.[97] The importance of democracy is also stressed by commentators on the left. For Piketty, democratic control of capitalism is essential for ensuring that 'the general interest takes precedence over private interests, while preserving economic openness and avoiding protectionist and nationalist reactions'.[98]

[89] Ofodile (n 44); Mills and others (n 38) 19.
[90] Fiseha (n 54).
[91] ibid.
[92] Piketty (n 14) 70.
[93] ibid.
[94] ibid.
[95] Paul Collier, 'On the Economic Consequences of Civil War' (1999) 51 Oxford Economic Papers 168; Haggard, Macintyre, and Tiede (n 48) 209.
[96] Isanga (n 87).
[97] Mills and others (n 38) 19.
[98] Piketty (n 14) 1.

Given the rather inconclusive link between economic growth and constitutionalism, the question that needs to be addressed is this: is a developmental (and intrusive) state possible without its being authoritarian? Can a democratic state which is constitutionally mandated to be developmental in direction and action secure economic growth within the broader political parameters of constitutionalism? Does the practice in Africa suggest that it is likely? Is the fundamental problem that the dominant political culture of centralism militates against it? Is it that the overwhelming thrust of centralist rule includes capturing and controlling the market, thereby not releasing its productive energy?

9. Summary

In summary, this volume seeks to understand the relationship between constitutions, constitutionalism, and the economy. Its guiding questions cover a broad area and not all of them may be answered by the contributions to this book. To reiterate them, the questions are as follows:

- The first line of enquiry is whether (and if so, how) a market economy has been constitutionalized across Africa since the second wave of democratization. How has the market influenced the constitution and vice versa?
- The second line of enquiry focuses on a specific constitutional issue: the governance of land and other natural resources. Given their centrality to many African economies, what is the constitutional framework for determining who 'owns' such wealth and how the revenue derived from such wealth is distributed among the inhabitants of a country?
- The third line of enquiry is the constitutional scope for the state to intervene in the economy.
  - First, is there a clear framework for state regulation and intervention? Conversely, how does the state protect itself from the predations of the market and being captured by some market forces?
  - Secondly, where the state comprises multilevel government, how does that shape such a regulatory role?
  - Thirdly, how have central banks, as constitutional institutions, imposed a substantive limit on the state's regulatory role in monetary policy?
  - Finally, where the market does not adequately distribute the benefits of the economy to all sectors of society, are there constitutional obligations on the state to do so?
- The fourth line of enquiry concerns the impact that global economic integration may have on constitutionalism in Africa. What is the impact of international trade liberalization on democratic sovereignty, and does it make a difference when home-grown trade agreements seek a similar objective of lowering trade barriers?
- Finally, the largest, hardest questions are about the dynamic between constitutionalism and economic growth. Where the basic elements of constitutionalism—the practice of democracy, limited government, and the rule of law—are present, what impact, if any, do they have on the economy: do they enhance or hinder it, or are they neutral to economic growth?

These questions are of importance for constitutional lawyers and economists. For constitutional lawyers, the question is how constitutionalism, which they advance as the superior way of governing and advancing social justice, can impact on the economy. A growing economy is, after all, necessary for providing the state with sufficient revenue for it to comply with its constitutional mandate of securing social justice. This issue also preoccupies economists: how to obtain economic growth within the political paradigm of constitutionalism. Viewing authoritarianism as the better way of 'getting things done' is no longer an option. Although there is a growing literature on some aspects of the questions that are posed here, it is still underdeveloped in respect of Africa. It is in this area that the present volume makes its main contribution.

Bibliography

Agence France-Presse, 'Applause as African Leaders Finally Launch Landmark Free-Trade Deal' *Business Day* (8 July 2019) 11

Bruszt L, 'Market Making as State Making: Constitutions and Economic Development in Post-Communist Eastern Europe' (2002) 13 Constitutional Political Economy 53

Collier P, 'On the Economic Consequences of Civil War' (1999) 51 Oxford Economic Papers 168

Collier P, *The Future of Capitalism: Facing New Anxieties* (Allen Lane 2018)

Crowe C and Meade EE, 'The Evolution of Central Bank Governance around the World' (2007) 24(4) Journal of Economic Perspectives 69

Cukierman A, 'Central Bank Independence and Monetary Control' (1994) 104 The Economic Journal 1437

Curott NA, 'Foreign Aid, the Rule of Law, and Economic Development in Africa' (2010) 11 University of Botswana Law Journal 3

Ely JW, 'The Constitution and Economic Liberty' (2011) 35 Harvard Journal of Law and Public Policy 27

Feld LP and Voigt S, 'Economic Growth and Judicial Independence: Cross-Country Evidence Using a New Set of Indicators' (2003) CESIFO Working Paper No 906

Fiseha A and Gebresilassie FH, 'The Interface between Federalism and Development in Ethiopia' in Cheru F, Cramer C, and Oqubay A (eds), *The Oxford Handbook of the Ethiopian Economy* (OUP 2019)

Fiseha A, 'Federalism, Development and the Changing Political Dynamics in Ethiopia' (2019) 17(1) I•CON 151

Fombad C (ed), *Separation of Powers in African Constitutionalism* (OUP 2015)

Fombad C *Constitutional Adjudication in Africa* (OUP 2016)

Fombad C, 'Constitutional Entrenchment of Decentralisation in Africa: An Overview of Trends and Tendencies' (2018) 62(2) Journal of African Law 175

Fombad C and Steytler N (eds), *Decentralisation and Constitutionalism in Africa* (OUP 2019)

Fombad C and Steytler N (eds), *Corruption and Constitutionalism in Africa: Revisiting Control Measures and Strategies* (OUP 2020)

Fombad C and Steytler N (eds), *Democracy, Elections and Constitutionalism in Africa* (OUP 2021)

Gerring J and others, 'Democracy and Economic Growth: A Historical Perspective' (2005) 57(3) *World Politics* 323

Ghai Y, 'The Constitution and the Economy' (2002) Institute of Economic Affairs (IEA)

Ghai Y, 'Chimera of Constitutionalism: State, Economy, and Society in Africa' (unpublished paper, University of Pretoria 2011) <http:// www. up. ac. za/media/shared/Legacy/sitefiles/file/47/15338/ chimera_of_constitutionalism_ yg1. pdf> accessed 30 November 2020

Haggard S, MacIntyre A, and Tiede L, 'The Rule of Law and Economic Development' (2008) 11 Annual Review of Political Science 205

Harrison J, 'The Constitution of Economic Liberty' (2008) 45 San Diego Law Review 709

Haucap J, 'The Rule of Law and the Emergence of Market Exchange: A New Institutional Economic Perspective' in Von Alemann U, Briesen D, and Khanh LQ (eds), *The State of Law: Comparative Perspectives on the Rule of Law* (Düsseldorf University Press 2017)

Haydaroğlu C, 'The Relationship between Property Rights and Economic Growth: An Analysis of OECD and EU Countries' (2015) 6(4) Danube: Law and Economics Review 217

Isanga J, 'Rule of Law and African Development' (2016) 42 North Carolina Journal of International Law and Commercial Regulation 2

Klare K, 'Legal Culture and Transformative Constitutionalism' (1998) 14 South African Journal on Human Rights 146

Knutsen CH, 'Democracy and Economic Growth: A Survey of Arguments and Results' (2012) 15(4) International Area Studies Review 393

Langa P, 'Transformative Constitutionalism' (2006) 17 Stellenbosch Law Review 351

Le Vine VT, 'The Fall and Rise of Constitutionalism in West Africa' (1997) 35(2) Journal of Modern African Studies 181

Liebenberg S, *Socio-Economic Rights: Adjudication under a Transformative Constitution* (Juta 2010)

Macey JR, 'Competing Economic Views of the Constitution' (1987) Faculty Scholarship Series. Paper 1732 <https://digitalcommons. law. yale. edu/fss_papers/1732/> accessed 30 November 2020

Mills G and others, *Making Africa Work: A Handbook for Economic Success* (Tafelberg 2017)

Montenegro AA, 'Constitutional Design and Economic Performance' (1995) 6 Constitutional Political Economy 161

Murapa R, 'Nationalization of the Zambian Mining Industry' (1976) 7 The Review of Black Political Economy 47

Ndulo M, 'Mining Legislation and Mineral Development in Zambia' (1986) 19 Cornell International Law Journal 11

North D, *Institutions, Institutional Change, and Economic Performance* (Cambridge University Press 1992)

Ofodile UE, 'Trade, Empires, and Subjects—China–Africa Trade: A New Fair Trade Arrangement, or the Third Scramble for Africa?' (2008) 41 Vanderbilt Journal of Transnational Law 505

Persson T and Tabellini G, *The Economic Effects of Constitutions* (MIT Press 2005)

Piketty T, *Capital in the Twenty-First Century* (Belknap Press of Harvard University Press 2014)

Ramanujam N, 'A Comparative Analysis of the Approaches to Economic Development across BRIC Countries' (2012) Rule of Law and Economic Development Research Group, McGill University

Richardson CJ, 'The Loss of Property Rights and the Collapse of Zimbabwe' (2005) 25(3) Cato Journal 541

Root HL, 'Do Strong Governments Produce Strong Economies?' (2001) 5(4) The Independent Review 565

Samuel A, 'Intellectual Property Rights, Innovations, and Economic Growth in Sub-Saharan Africa' (2011) 28 Journal of Third World Studies 231

Santos A, 'The World Bank's Uses of the "Rule of Law" Promise in Economic Development' in Trubek D and Santos A (eds), *The New Law and Economic Development: A Critical Appraisal* (Cambridge University Press 2006)

Sen A, *Development as Freedom* (Alfred Knopf 1999)

Shah A (ed), *The Practice of Fiscal Federalism: Comparative Perspectives* (McGill-Queen's University Press 2007)

Shah A, 'On the Design of Economic Constitutions' (1996) 29 Canadian Journal of Economics 614

Smith A, *An Inquiry into the Nature and Causes of the Wealth of Nations* (1776) (Soares Salvio (ed), modern edn, Metalibri Digital Library 2007)

Steytler N (ed), *The BRICS Partnership: Challenges and Prospects for Multilevel Government* (Juta 2018)

Steytler N, 'The Relationship between Decentralisation and Constitutionalism in Africa: Concepts, Conflicts, and Hypotheses' in Fombad CM (ed), *Decentralisation and Constitutionalism in Africa* (OUP 2019)

Steytler N, '"Financial Constitutions" to Prevent Corruption' in Fombad CM and Steytler N (eds), *Corruption and Constitutionalism in Africa: Revisiting Control Measures and Strategies* (OUP 2020)

Stiglitz JE, *Globalisation and Its Discontent* (Penguin 2002)

Sunstein CR, 'On Property and Constitutionalism Comparative Constitutionalism: Theoretical Perspectives on the Role of Constitutions in the Interplay between Identity and Diversity' (1992) 14 Cardozo Law Review 907

Tabellini G, 'The Role of the State in Economic Development' (2005) 58(2) KYKLOS 283

Ten CI, 'Constitutionalism and the Rule of Law' in Goodin RE, Pettit P, and Pogge T (eds), *A Companion to Contemporary Political Economy* (Wiley 2017)

UNDP, Income Inequality Trends in Sub-Saharan Africa: Divergence, Determinants and Consequences (United Nations Development Programme: Regional Bureau for Africa 2017)

Vanberg VJ, *The Constitution of Markets: Essays in Political Economy* (Routledge 2001)

World Bank, 'Decentralization in Client Countries: An Evaluation of World Bank Support, 1990–2007' (World Bank 2008)

World Bank, *Poverty and Shared Prosperity: Piecing Together the Poverty Puzzle* (World Bank 2018)

2

Relationships between the Economy and Constitutionalism in Sub-Saharan Africa

Ramos Emmanuel Mabugu

1. Introduction

This chapter examines features of sub-Saharan African (SSA)[1] economies that influence the relationship between a country's economy and its constitution.[2] After a slump in the 1980s, SSA economies recovered gradually from the mid-1990s for the next two decades before going back into a decline that has been further exacerbated by the onset of the COVID-19 pandemic. Despite its economic growth, sub-Saharan Africa is one of the poorest and most unequal regions in the world, with unemployment, poverty, and inequality remaining stubbornly high and on the increase.[3] The structural shifts witnessed in SSA economies pose challenges not only for future growth and development but the prospects for constitutionalism.

A first issue in this regard is that the sustained high share of agriculture in gross domestic product (GDP)[4] has implications for the right to property (and land). Another is that control of natural resources, an important constitutional issue, is related to the role of mining and minerals in the economy. Mining is embedded in an industry which is declining in its contribution to the economy, albeit that, through exports, it remains a key source of foreign currency.

Thirdly, the boom in services, coupled with the importance of the agricultural sector, points to an imbalance in the SSA economic structure, where manufacturing can be seen as the missing link between agriculture and services. This often results in strong external dependence on manufactured imports, leading to a trade imbalance that ultimately could invite foreign influence, which in turn impacts directly on the core constitutional value of state sovereignty. A stronger manufacturing base would make these economies less vulnerable to volatility in commodity prices as well as generating important spillovers from

---

[1] As the term implies, SSA countries are partly or wholly located south of the Sahara Desert—forty-three are in mainland Africa and six are island nations. In land area, the region is larger than China, India, and the United States combined. The population is growing rapidly and currently stands at more than 930 million, roughly twice the number of people in the European Union. Despite increasing urbanization, SSA economies remain predominantly rural-based and are consequently highly dependent on agriculture and primary commodities.

[2] The analysis in this chapter was undertaken prior to the COVID-19 pandemic and the unprecedented economic crisis it has caused. The reported projections are thus to be viewed as indicative upper-bound estimates that should be updated as the pandemic unfolds and the nature of its economic fallout becomes clearer.

[3] LF Jirasavetakul and C Lakner, 'Distribution of Consumption Expenditure in Sub-Saharan Africa: The Inequality among all Africans' (2020) 29(1) Journal of African Economies 1.

[4] GDP is defined as the market value of final goods and services produced in an economy over a certain period, typically a quarter or a year.

Ramos Emmanuel Mabugu, *Relationships between the Economy and Constitutionalism in Sub-Saharan Africa* In: *Constitutionalism and the Economy in Africa*. Edited by: Charles M Fombad and Nico Steytler, Oxford University Press. © Ramos Emmanuel Mabugu 2022.
DOI: 10.1093/oso/9780192886439.003.0004

industrial development, such as job and enterprise creation, increased foreign investment, transformation of the informal sector, technology dissemination, and increased exports.

Fourthly, in regard to the informal sector and social protection, earning distributions are gaining increased attention in sub-Saharan Africa. Income inequality is heterogeneous across Africa, with southern Africa seeing the highest levels of it. Given that inequality has been identified as one of the biggest challenges the world is facing today[5] and that labour markets, with high shares of informality in Africa, play a crucial role in shaping inequality, analysing the link between the informal sector and economic inequality is highly relevant. This is all the more critical for Africa in that the world is entering the so-called 'Fourth Industrial Revolution', which is characterized by knowledge-intensive value creation and whose compatibility with informality is an open question.[6] Increasing informality coupled with deindustrialization affects the usefulness of a constitution's labour rights, which tend to focus on the formal economy.

The skewed SSA economic structure is compounded by the state's poor economic policy and public finances. SSA state actions have had a profoundly negative impact on public finances in three crucial ways. First, states have been reluctant to mobilize personal taxes and other direct taxes that build the link between government and citizens, instead placing heavy reliance on indirect sources such as trade taxes, commodity royalties, foreign aid, and borrowing. Secondly, government expenditure is, to varying degrees, skewed predominantly towards salaries and servicing loans, while corruption and looting of state coffers have been rampant.

Thirdly, with economic growth stagnating, there has been a significant slump in public revenue through taxation. With expenditure continuing to increase, this has driven up debt levels. The coming debt crisis differs from that experienced in the 1980s in that a substantial portion of debt is owed to China and private sector creditors rather than international financial institutions and the Paris Club, which could put state sovereignty at risk. SSA countries would need to implement politically difficult policies to unlock their revenue potential and improve spending quality.

The consequences of these trends in economic policy and public finances (and lack of inclusive growth) are poor socio-economic outcomes. While there have been massive strides in education, many of the countries remain off track in achieving the Sustainable Development Goals (SDGs) to which they are all signatories. With the urgent need to mobilize additional revenues to finance the SDGs and restructure the economies, the recent COVID-19 crisis has complicated matters not only by bringing in a new set of expenditure requirements for dealing with the health crisis, but also by negatively affecting economic growth and lowering revenue collection. An important question, then, is: in what ways can the constitution shape government actions in any manner?

This is a large subject addressed by other chapters in the volume; the present chapter sets out to give economic context to them by examining key features of SSA economic performance. These include demographic structure, economic structure (agriculture, industry, services, and the like), fiscal dynamics, and socio-economic outcomes. For consistency, data from the International Monetary Fund (IMF) and the World Bank are used wherever available.

[5] World Economic Forum, *The Global Risks Report 2017* (WEF 2017).
[6] Karl Schwab, *The Fourth Industrial Revolution* (Currency 2017).

The rest of this chapter is structured as follows. Section 2 reviews recent macroeconomic developments, focusing on economic growth, both in level and on a per capita basis, as well as on high birth rates, inflation,[7] unemployment, and aid. Section 3 looks more closely at evolving trends in expenditure and touches on issues of globalization and government size relative to demand. Section 4 considers fiscal trends, highlighting revenue mobilization, expenditure, overall fiscal balance, and government debt. Section 5 looks at socio-economic outcomes, particularly in regard to poverty and the likelihood of sub-Saharan Africa's meeting the SDGs. Section 6 provides a summary and draws out key policy implications.

2. General Macroeconomic Background

The membership of SSA countries in the major regional cooperation bodies is summarized in Box 2.1 and accords with information from the IMF and World Bank.

The rest of this section provides an overview of the economic performance and outlook of sub-Saharan Africa, with specific reference to the region's economic stagnation in the 1980s and early 1990s and its rebound in the last two decades. Most SSA countries attained independence between 1957 and 1965 and inherited economies with structural weaknesses.[8] Political independence coincided with worldwide policies to boost aggregate demand, the establishment of the Bretton Woods institutions (the World Bank, IMF, and World Trade Organization (WTO)), and state intervention and planning of the economy (the Soviet Union).

During the early post-independence years, the structural weaknesses of sub-Saharan Africa's economic position were generally perceived as reflecting a low-level equilibrium caused by low savings, high population growth, and market failures due to scale economies and externalities. Given the prevailing development thinking, most countries opted for active state intervention in the belief that this would be necessary to overcome these factors. Although Africa would still be expected to earn its way by playing its traditional role of primary-product exporter, the 'developmental state' was to accumulate surpluses from the agricultural sector and apply them to the infrastructural and other requirements of industrialization driven by import substitution. Taking advantage of goodwill and generally cheap finance, many SSA governments borrowed heavily to invest in public infrastructure and meet other demands.

Subsequently, a combination of colonial-legacy structural problems, declining commodity prices, unbridled government borrowing, and weak economic management led to protracted poor economic performance. The significant increase in crude oil prices by the Organization of Petroleum Exporting Countries (OPEC) in 1973 was a major turning point. Many SSA countries had borrowed heavily, but their economies suffered a series of external shocks that left governments unable to repay their loans, triggering a severe debt crisis.

---

[7] Inflation refers to a sustained increase in the general price level.

[8] Structural weaknesses refer to 'flaws' on the supply side. The structure and relative underdevelopment of SSA economies have their roots in colonialism, a result of which is that many are in effect monoculture (mineral or commodity) exporters. Economic dualism is common—in other words, traditional activities with low productivity and slow productivity growth (eg traditional agriculture and small, informal firms) coexist with modern activities with high productivity and rapid growth (eg manufacturing and high-tech mining). The economies are also dependent on imports for equipment, capital goods, and most of their consumer goods, expertise, and technology. Primary production still predominates in SSA exports, making the region's economies more susceptible to capricious world price changes and other external shocks than more diversified economies.

Box 2.1 *SSA member-country groupings*

The CFA franc zone comprises the West African Economic and Monetary Union (WAEMU) (Benin, Burkina Faso, Côte d'Ivoire, Guinea-Bissau, Mali, Niger, Senegal, and Togo) and the Economic and Monetary Community of Central African States (CEMAC) (Cameroon, Central African Republic, Chad, Congo, Republic of Equatorial Guinea, and Gabon).

The Common Market for Eastern and Southern Africa (COMESA): Burundi, Comoros, Congo, Democratic Republic of Congo, Eritrea, Eswatini, Ethiopia, Kenya, Madagascar, Malawi, Mauritius, Rwanda, Seychelles, Uganda, Zambia, and Zimbabwe.

The East Africa Community (EAC-5): EAC-5 aggregates include data for Rwanda and Burundi, which joined the group of Kenya, Tanzania, and Uganda only in 2007.

The Economic Community of West African States (ECOWAS): Benin, Burkina Faso, Cabo Verde, Côte d'Ivoire, The Gambia, Ghana, Guinea, Guinea-Bissau, Liberia, Mali, Niger, Nigeria, Senegal, Sierra Leone, and Togo.

The Southern African Development Community (SADC): Angola, Botswana, Congo, Democratic Republic of Congo, Eswatini, Lesotho, Madagascar, Malawi, Mauritius, Mozambique, Namibia, Seychelles, South Africa, Tanzania, Zambia, and Zimbabwe.

The Southern Africa Customs Union (SACU): Botswana, Eswatini, Lesotho, Namibia, and South Africa.

The oil exporters are countries where net oil exports make up 30 per cent or more of total exports. These are Angola, Cameroon, Chad, Congo, Equatorial Guinea, Gabon, Nigeria, and South Sudan.

Middle-income countries consist of Angola, Botswana, Cabo Verde, Cameroon, Congo, Republic of Côte d'Ivoire, Equatorial Guinea, Eswatini, Gabon, Ghana, Kenya, Lesotho, Mauritius, Namibia, Nigeria, São Tomé & Príncipe, Senegal, Seychelles, South Africa, and Zambia.

Low-income countries include Benin, Burkina Faso, Burundi, Central African Republic, Chad, Comoros, Congo, Democratic Republic of Congo, Eritrea, Ethiopia, Gambia, The Guinea, Guinea-Bissau, Liberia, Madagascar, Malawi, Mali, Mozambique, Niger, Rwanda, Sierra Leone, South Sudan, Tanzania, Togo, Uganda, and Zimbabwe.

Countries in fragile situations are Burundi, Central African Republic, Chad, Comoros, Congo, Democratic Republic of Congo, Republic of Côte d'Ivoire, Eritrea, The Gambia, Guinea, Guinea-Bissau, Liberia, Malawi, Mali, São Tomé & Príncipe, South Sudan, Togo and Zimbabwe.

Source: Adapted from IMF (2019)

SSA countries then underwent a number of structural adjustment programmes (SAPs) in the 1980s and 1990s aimed at restoring economic growth and equilibrium. The major thrust of the reforms was to reduce state involvement in the economy and remove restrictions on imports, banking, and exchange controls. The countries relied heavily on external development aid while undergoing these structural and institutional reforms. They achieved a measure of economic stabilization with improvements in terms of budget balance, monetary policy control, and a liberalization of the foreign exchange market, and implemented a range of structural reforms, such as privatization of state-owned firms. Following a slump in the 1980s, economies gradually began recovering from about 1995 and onwards. However, the recovery has been driven largely by commodity exports, with structural transformation remaining low while population growth rate soared.

To put numbers and context to this discussion, the key measure to gauge the state of the economy used in the analysis that follows is GDP, as defined earlier. Beyond GDP, the section also looks at demographics, inflation, unemployment, debt, and trade. Focusing on this broad range of outcomes is important from a governance perspective for at least two reasons. First, they affect living standards. Constitutions are about organizing state power and how it relates to societies; ultimately, they are about the people and improving their standards of living. Secondly, the measures speak to issues of economics and price stability, which can be important governance imperatives.

2.1 Economic Stagnation in SSA in the 1980s and 1990s

The discussion starts with an overview of economic development in the 1980s using the GDP growth rates of SSA countries. GDP growth rate is an indicator of economic progress from one year to another. Figure 2.1 plots average GDP growth by country during the 1980s, that is, an average of economic performance between 1980 and 1990.

As Figure 2.1 shows, the 1980s were essentially a lost decade for SSA economies in that growth virtually collapsed, with only a handful of countries experiencing positive economic growth from very low initial bases (eg Malawi). Between 1980 and 1987, real income per capita in sub-Saharan Africa fell by about a quarter.

It is fair to say that both external and domestic factors contributed to the poor overall performance during this period. Many countries were hit hard by rising import prices, declining export prices, and severe droughts. The deterioration was also due largely to inappropriate economic policies, poor investment choices, increasing budgetary deficits,[9] increases in loss-making public enterprises, growing inflationary pressures, and a loss of international competitiveness.

There was also serious deterioration in governance, which was characterized by a weakening of the legal framework and judicial system, as well as by corruption in the management of public resources, particularly resources involved in the marketing of key crops and minerals. These problems were compounded by rapid population growth, neglect of human resource development, deteriorating infrastructure, and outbreaks of ethnic conflict and political instability. Five political variables are often cited as having been crucial for the political instability: democracy, strikes, demonstrations, coups, and guerrilla wars.[10]

Thus, in the 1980s sub-Saharan Africa faced a triple whammy of declining terms of trade, increased interest rates on existing debts, and lack of access to further loans. This was aggravated by the deep factors of rising population growth, deterioration in governance, and geography. The impact of worsening economic conditions, increased rates of interest, and

---

[9] Budget deficits occur when governmental expenses exceed revenues.
[10] Macartan Humphreys and Robert Bates, 'Political Institutions and Economic Policies: Lessons from Africa' (2005) 35(3) British Journal of Political Science 403.

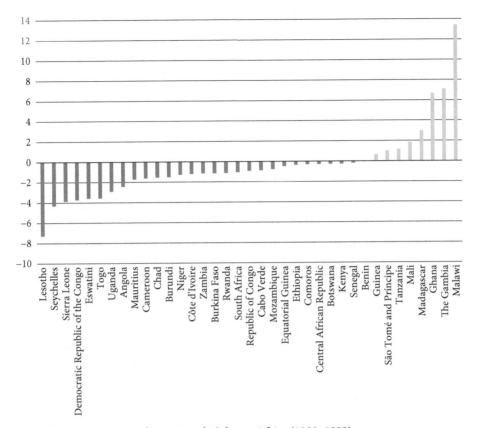

Figure 2.1 Economic growth rates in sub-Saharan Africa (1980–1990)
Source: Author's computations based on IMF data for 2019

the imposition of penalties for failure to repay loans on time meant that African debt soared, resulting in a debt crisis with defaults and debt rescheduling.

SSA countries were left with no option but to implement SAPs-inspired policies involving budget cuts, trade liberalization, deregulation, and privatization. By the mid-1980s most of the government debt in SSA was owed to the World Bank and IMF, severely comprom-ising state sovereignty in the process. Indeed, adjustment has become a perennial feature of developing countries, extending beyond SAPs to areas such as terms-of-trade shocks (eg the recent commodity super-cycle associated with the rise and deceleration of China), or rapid changes in technology (eg the Fourth Industrial Revolution). In these cases, national governments are forced to impose adjustment on domestic constituencies in response to external imbalances, which erodes the legitimacy of the state and undermines attempts to embed constitutionalism rooted in domestic political-economy factors.

The lost decade of economic crisis extended into the 1990s as the decline in terms of trade continued and was worsened by capital flight, brain drain, and the devastating effect of HIV/AIDs. Although the AIDS pandemic is now coming under control in most coun-tries, about two-thirds of people with HIV/AIDS globally are living in Africa, with half of them found in ten countries: Angola, Botswana, Eswatini, Lesotho, Malawi, Mozambique, Namibia, South Africa, Zambia, and Zimbabwe.

2.2 Economic Growth Returns for the Twenty-First Century

SSA economies finally managed to achieve reasonable economic growth in the early years of the twenty-first century. Table 2.1 shows sub-Saharan Africa's macroeconomic development in the last two decades to 2015, based on calculations using the World Bank's World Development Indicators. Wherever possible, the analysis takes the years 2000–03 as the reference period and 2010–14 as the current period; it does not account for uneven performance triggered by the global financial crisis in 2008 and 2009.

Table 2.1 reveals several notable trends. First, GDP per capita (USD PPP) rose from USD 2,442.80 per year on average during 2000–03 to USD 3,377.10 per year on average during the period 2014–17, an increase of 36.6 per cent between the periods. Growth in real GDP per capita accelerated from 1.1 per cent to 1.8 per cent between the two periods, an increase of 0.6 percentage points during the 2014–17 period compared to the 2000–03 period. A similar accelerating trend is visible in real GDP growth, rising from 3.8 per cent per year during 2000–03 to 4.6 per cent during the 2014–17 period (an increase of 0.7 percentage points over the two periods).

In a similar fashion, unemployment as a percentage of total labour force declined from 8.9 per cent per year during 2000–03 to 8.0 per cent during 2010–14, or a decline of 0.9 percentage points over the two periods. Even the youth unemployment situation improved moderately by 1.0 percentage points over the 2014–17 period compared to the 2000–03 period, that is, it fell from 15.4 per cent to 14.4 per cent before and during the 2014–17 period. As will be discussed in the next section, this unemployment outcome is, however, dominated by informal employment, which in turn affects the usefulness of labour rights in the constitution to the extent that they are confined to the formal economy.

The SSA population has grown from an average of 695 million over 2000–03 to 923 million people over 2010–14, that is, a growth rate of about 32.9 per cent over a decade. Sub-Saharan Africa has the fastest population growth in the world. To compound the problem, the proportion of people living in rural areas has fallen from 68.6 per cent to 63.8 per cent, a decline of 4.8 percentage points between the two periods, implying an urbanizing region. This demographic transition has negative implications for economic growth and development in general, as the rate of job creation is insufficient to support the increasing population, while demand for public services (eg education, health care, skills development) by a rapidly urbanizing and young population exerts serious pressure on an already constrained fiscus.

Secondly, focusing on price stability as proxied by inflation is of interest because controlling inflation could be enshrined directly or indirectly in a constitution. For example, in South Africa the inflation mandate is given to a central bank the independence of which potentially shields it from governmental and political interference. According to Table 2.1, sub-Saharan Africa has maintained a reasonable degree of price stability. The low inflation rate of 5.5 per cent on average during the 2000–03 period was reduced during the 2014–17 period to 5.1 per cent, a decline of 0.4 percentage points over the two periods.

Thirdly, aid could also invite foreign influence (which, as noted, directly impacts on the core constitutional value of state sovereignty). Sub-Saharan Africa has consistently received high official development aid (ODA), particularly so during the SAPs period. Table 2.1 shows that in recent years ODA as a percentage of gross national income declined by 1.7 percentage points from 4.8 per cent during 2000–03 to 3.1 per cent during 2014–17. This

Table 2.1 Macroeconomic indicators: Sub-Saharan Africa

Metrics	Reference period Average 2000–2003	Economic crisis period 2008	Economic crisis period 2009	Recent period Average 2010–2014	Change between period (averages 2000–2003 vs 2010–2014)	Unit
GDP growth (annual %)	3.8	5.3	2.8	4.6	0.7	pp
GDP per capita growth (annual %)	1.1	2.5	0.1	1.8	0.6	pp
GDP per capita, PPP (constant 2011 international $)	2,442.8	3,122.7	3,138.7	3,337.1	36.6	%
Gross savings (% of GDP)	16.5	19.5	15.0	18.5	1.9	pp
Inflation, consumer prices (annual %)	5.5	10.4	7.1	5.1	–0.4	pp
Net ODA received (% of GNI)	4.8	4.1	4.6	3.1	–1.7	pp
Population, total	695,093,421.3	827,239,670.6	850,190,285.5	923,465,615.6	32.9	%
Rural population (% of total population)	68.6	65.7	65.3	63.8	–4.8	pp
Total debt service (% of GNI)	3.8	2.0	1.6	1.6	–2.2	pp
Trade (% of GDP)	69.3	74.6	65.1	63.1	–6.2	pp
Unemployment, total (% of total labour force)	8.9	8.1	8.1	8.0	–0.9	pp
Unemployment, youth total (% of total labour force ages 15–24)	15.4	14.4	14.5	14.4	–1.0	pp

Source and legends: WDI: World Development Indicators; author's computations based on WDI database; pp: percentage point

is a significant reduction in ODA of earlier years, and is due to the fact that aid inflows from donors have been drying up rather than that SSA countries have made a conscious decision to reduce their dependency on aid. The trajectory does indicate, though, that the region's dependency on ODA decreased over time and that ODA resources are now directed mostly to financing development budgets.

Table 2.2 provides deeper insight into economic growth. It uses recent data from the IMF to compute GDP growth for sub-Saharan Africa, its sub-regions and selected countries;

Table 2.2 Real GDP (annual percentage change)

	2010–15	2016–18	2019	2020	Change (2016–18 vs 2010–15)
Sub-Saharan Africa	5.1	2.4	3.5	3.7	–2.7
Oil-exporting countries	5.3	0.0	2.2	2.7	–5.3
Oil-importing countries	4.9	4.0	4.3	4.3	–0.9
Middle-income countries	4.7	1.5	2.9	3.1	–3.2
Low-income countries	6.5	5.3	5.3	5.5	–1.2
Countries in fragile situations	5.5	3.5	4.6	5.1	–2.0
CFA franc zone	4.6	3.9	5.2	5.2	–0.7
COMESA (SSA members)	6.8	5.4	5.3	5.7	–1.4
EAC-5	6.1	5.8	5.3	5.4	–0.3
ECOWAS	5.9	2.2	3.8	3.8	–3.7
SACU	2.6	1.0	1.3	1.6	–1.6
SADC	3.9	1.8	1.9	2.6	–2.1
Angola	4.6	-1.5	0.4	2.9	–6.1
Ethiopia	10.2	8.6	7.7	7.5	–1.6
Nigeria	5.8	0.4	2.1	2.5	–5.4
South Africa	2.3	0.9	1.2	1.5	–1.4
Zambia	6.0	3.6	3.1	2.9	–2.4
Zimbabwe	9.4	2.9	-5.2	3.3	–6.5

Source and legends: 2019 and 2020 are IMF estimates; author's computations are based on IMF World Economic Outlook database; see Box 2.1 for a table of country groupings

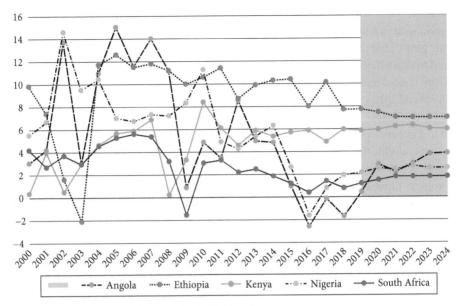

Figure 2.2 Economic growth rates of Africa's 'Big 5'
Source: Author's computations based on IMF data (2019)

unlike Table 2.1, it takes 2010–15 as the reference period and 2016–18 as the current period, and has a projection for 2019 and 2020,[11] choices determined largely by data availability. Growth in real GDP decelerated from 5.1 per cent to 2.4 per cent between the two periods, a deceleration of 2.7 percentage points. However, drilling down shows that these aggregate figures mask considerable heterogeneity across countries and resource intensities.

While growth is lower across the board when one compares 2016–18 to 2010–15, it is striking that growth deceleration was worse in oil-exporting and middle-income countries than in countries in fragile situations and that they saw the greatest decline.[12] When it comes to regional economic communities, ECOWAS experienced the sharpest deceleration, followed by SADC, with EAC-5 experiencing the lowest deceleration. Of the selected countries, the oil-exporting countries of Angola and Nigeria took a massive knock in GDP growth, faring better only than Zimbabwe. South Africa has the best overall performance, largely because the preceding years' performance against which current GDP is compared had been very poor; nevertheless, its overall growth in 2016–18 was worse than that of Zimbabwe, Zambia, and Ethiopia.

Before concluding this discussion of the macroeconomy, it is useful to gain an idea of the difference in sizes of the various economies. The five biggest countries in terms of size of GDP are, in descending order, Nigeria, South Africa, Angola, Ethiopia, and Kenya, and together they account for more than 75 per cent of SSA economic activity. Figure 2.2 plots their economic growth rates over the past two decades, showing that growth rates

---

[11] Zimbabwe has adopted a new local currency unit, the RTGS dollar, which became the official unit of account in February 2019. Efforts are under way to update all national accounts series to the RTGS dollar. Current data are based on IMF staff estimates of price and exchange rate developments in US (and RTGS) dollars, so there may be some discrepancies between IMF staff estimates and government estimates.

[12] The best explanation is that this is due to the low export commodity prices experienced during the period.

in Nigeria, South Africa, and Angola lag behind those in Kenya and Ethiopia. Given that Angola, Nigeria, and South Africa account for nearly 60 per cent of SSA GDP, their low economic growth has dire consequences for overall growth in the region as a whole and make it hard to attain the SDGs.

There is no doubt that sub-Saharan Africa did well during 2000–15. However, between 2016–18 and 2010–15 the average GDP growth rate of the region and the largest three countries (South Africa, Nigeria, and Angola) decelerated. In the same period, the region exhibited improved positive macroeconomic indicators, including a low inflation rate and substantial decline in aid dependence. Although annual GDP growth of late has been impressive, it has been powered by commodities and natural resources and has not created the volume of jobs required, leaving an increasing share of sub-Saharan Africa's rapidly expanding population either unemployed or underemployed in the low-productivity informal sector.

3. Economic Structure and Expenditure on GDP

'Economic structure' refers to an average of activities relating to the production, distribution, and consumption of scarce resources and implies a changing balance of production, trade, incomes, and employment drawn from the different sectors that make up an economy. Economic structure is important when considering how to manage economic growth and transform an economy's absorptive capacity (eg can sub-Saharan Africa absorb aid and foreign investment?), diversify an economy (eg how can one transition from the primary sectors into a diversified productive economy?), or sustain urbanization (eg how can one generate the revenue necessary to provide the infrastructure and social services required by a rapidly growing urban population?). This section briefly discusses these issues and teases out certain of their implications for constitutionalism.

3.1 Expenditure on GDP Trends

The well-known basic equation for GDP, often referred to as the National Income Identity, states that GDP = consumption + investment + government spending + (exports–imports). This equation is important because it gives us a measure of economic-growth components. It also allows us to gauge the size of state participation in the formal economy (government spending) or the size of the private sector.

Table 2.3 presents growth-component computations for sub-Saharan Africa based on this identity, and shows that GDP at purchasers' prices increased by 3.3 percentage points in 2012–15 when compared to 2000–03. Private consumption constitutes about 65 per cent of GDP, followed by investment, at about 19 per cent, and then government expenditure at 15 per cent.

Growth in GDP over the two periods is undergirded by sustained investment in infrastructure, with a growth of 4.4 percentage points over the two periods, strong governmental spending on infrastructure, and an increase in domestic demand. Increase in private

Table 2.3 Expenditure on GDP: Sub-Saharan Africa

Metrics	Reference period	Economic crisis period		Recent period	Change between period (averages 2000–03 vs 2012–15)		Average 2000–15
	Average 2000–03	2008	2009	Average 2012–15	Value	Unit	
General government final consumption expenditure (% of GDP)	14.9	14.8	15.8	15.4	3.2	%	14.9
Household final consumption expenditure, etc (% of GDP)	65.8	63.7	68.2	66.3	0.6	pp	65.4
Gross capital formation (% of GDP)	16.4	18.8	19.2	20.8	4.4	pp	18.6
Exports of goods and services (% of GDP)	35.6	38.4	31.0	29.8	–5.8	pp	33.4
Less imports of goods and services (% of GDP)	33.7	36.2	34.1	32.7	–1.0	pp	33.1
GDP at purchasers' values (%)	100	100	100	100			100

Source and legends: WDI: World Development Indicators; pp: percentage point; author's computations based on WDI database

consumption has continued to underpin GDP growth, despite the tightening of monetary policies, trade protectionist policies in some developed economies, and the decline in demand in China. Strong global growth and public investment in infrastructure, especially in East and West Africa, have also underpinned growth. For example, growth in non-resource rich countries such as Senegal, Côte d'Ivoire, Ethiopia, and Kenya remained strong, driven in large part by high public investments, especially in infrastructure.

In regard to public infrastructure, two points indirectly relevant to constitutional issues are worth highlighting. First, the growth in public infrastructure spending witnessed in sub-Saharan Africa is financed mainly by concessional loans or project finance by development partners—of late, this has increasingly been China. The 'China effect' raises complex issues of state sovereignty. Secondly, many SSA countries have placed state-owned enterprises (SOEs) at the centre of their national development strategies.

This resurgence of SOEs is in part a response to the perceived failures of the privatization and SAPs of the 1990s. As in the 1950s and 1960s, it is believed that SOEs can remedy market failures and remove obstacles to development. SOEs operate in virtually all areas of activity, including infrastructure, oil, agriculture, transport, public utilities, telecommunications, finance and insurance, health, and training and education. Although their economic contribution varies in size from country to country, data collected several years ago by the World Bank suggest that, in an average low-income developing country, they account for about 20 per cent of all non-agricultural economic activity. For example, in Mauritius

SOEs account for 15 per cent of GDP; in South Africa, as at 2012, about 27 per cent; in Eswatini, as at 2011, 8 per cent; in Tanzania, 30 per cent; and, in Zimbabwe, 40 per cent.[13]

The final demand-side factor contributing to output is international trade. Table 2.3 shows that exports inject about 36 per cent into the economy, whereas imports syphon off 35 per cent. More than 50 per cent of economic growth in sub-Saharan Africa in the twenty-first century has been due to increased commodity revenue, which is due in turn to higher demand, particularly among the emerging economies, such as India and China, into which SSA exports have been diversified. The proportion of exports to the BRICS countries (Brazil, Russia, India, China, and South Africa) increased from less than a tenth in 2002 to more than a third in 2012,[14] which is comparable to exports to the European Union and United States combined. China is now the largest destination for African exports, taking nearly a quarter of the total (having increased from only 5 per cent in 2000).[15] It has also become the single largest trading partner for the region, as well as a key investor and provider of aid.[16]

Other significant trade-related factors in the region's growth include huge inflows of foreign direct investment, mainly in extractive industries; development aid; and increased remittances from nationals working abroad—remittances from Africans working outside Africa exceeded foreign direct investment from 2007 and overtook development aid from 2010.[17]

The dynamics of globalization described above are likely to impact on state sovereignty in a variety of ways. First, sub-Saharan Africa's export destinations are now more broad-based, with the monopsony[18] previously enjoyed by the European Union and US having been diluted by BRICS and China in particular. In addition, intra-African exports have grown rapidly, albeit from a low base—this augurs well for sub-Saharan Africa, if only in terms of increased legitimacy and state sovereignty.

Secondly, and less encouragingly for the region, the liberal world order that benefited SSA commodity exports appears to be at risk, given the evolving trade relations between the US and China and the ramifications of Britain's exit from the European Union. This has the potential to compromise large markets for SSA exports, a situation that would have dire consequences. Thirdly, there has been increasing resistance in the North to globalization. This threatens the future of remittances from Africans in the diaspora working abroad.

Fourth, as happened in the late 1990s, sub-Saharan Africa today faces a bleak external environment where a strong US dollar, combined with a slowdown and rebalancing of the Chinese economy, lower commodity prices, and strains between large market economies (notably the tariff wars between the US and China), weakens the prospects for further high growth.[19] The impact on sub-Saharan Africa of these global developments is hard to quantify, but is likely to be negative and include concentration of production in large firms (economies of scale), tax evasion, higher tariffs in the North, and outsourcing, with sub-Saharan

---

[13] Sara Sultan Balbuena, 'State-owned Enterprises in Southern Africa: A Stocktaking of Reforms and Challenges' (2014) OECD Corporate Governance Working Papers No 13.

[14] International Monetary Fund, *Sub-Saharan Africa Regional Economic Outlook: Recovery Amid Elevated Uncertainty* (IMF 2019).

[15] ibid.

[16] ibid.

[17] ibid.

[18] Monopsony is a market structure in which one buyer controls a significant portion of the market.

[19] IMF (n 14).

Table 2.4 Economic structure and evolution

Metrics	Reference period	Economic crisis period		Recent period	Change between period (averages 2000–03 vs 2012–15)		Average 2000–15
	Average 2000–03	2008	2009	Average 2012–15	Value	Unit	
Agriculture, value added (% of GDP)	22.7	20.5	21.5	17.3	–5.4	pp	20.0
Industry, value added (% of GDP)	31.8	31.7	28.7	26.4	–5.4	pp	29.5
Manufacturing, value added (% of GDP)	11.8	10.2	9.9	10.4	–1.3	pp	10.8
Services, etc, value added (% of GDP)	45.4	47.8	49.8	56.2	10.8	pp	50.4
TOTAL	100.0	100.0	100.0	100.0			

Source and legends: WDI: World Development Indicators; pp: percentage point; author's computations based on WDI database

Africa not featuring in supply chains. The impact of the COVID-19 pandemic on output and public finances will exacerbate these negative effects. The World Bank has estimated that in 2020 SSA economies will have contracted by between 2.1 and 5.1 per cent due to the pandemic.[20]

3.2 Economic Structure and Trends

Table 2.4 presents broad trends in the evolution of the structure of SSA economies.

According to the table, there has been a gradual but steady structural shift in the SSA economy from manufacturing, industry, mining, and agriculture to service sectors. The latter are now predominant, accounting on average for more than 50 per cent of GDP in 2000–15, followed by agriculture (20 per cent) and manufacturing (10.8 per cent). The share of the services sector is higher than that seen in other developing regions, taking into account differences in per capita income.

While growth of the services sector has been driven to some extent by recent dynamism in finance, telecommunications, and tourism, the dominant trend has been the growth of the informal economy. The agricultural sector declined from more than 22.7 per cent of total output to just over 17 per cent of the economy's GDP in the 2012–15 period. Manufacturing and industry (which include mining) also experienced a decline in GDP share during the

---

[20] AG Zeufack and others, 'An Analysis of Issues Shaping Africa's Economic Future' [2020] 21 Africa's Pulse <https://openknowledge.worldbank.org/handle/10986/33541> accessed 30 November 2020.

recent periods. In the industrial sector, with a few exceptions there has been weak within-sector productivity growth in industry, with both manufacturing and mining being lethargic.[21] A major concern is that while manufacturing employment has grown, informal manufacturing is dominating such growth.

Thus, while sub-Saharan Africa succeeded with structural adjustment, the deindustrialization being witnessed suggests that so far it has failed with structural change. With the exception of Botswana, Ghana, and, to some extent, Mauritius, all SSA countries have deindustrialized, leading some to suggest that industrialization plateaued in the heyday of post-independence import-substitution-induced industrialization.

Viewed through an economics lens, it would appear that the main cause of deindustrialization in the 1980s and 1990s lies in the choice of macroeconomic and financial policies in the aftermath of the debt crises of the early 1980s. In the context of SAPs, sub-Saharan Africa undertook financial liberalization in parallel with trade liberalization, the latter accompanied by high domestic interest rates to curb high inflation rates or attract foreign capital. Often, this led to currency overvaluation, loss of competitiveness by domestic producers, and decline in industrial production and fixed investment even when domestic producers tried to respond to the pressure on prices by wage compression or lay-offs.

There was hence not only a bad choice of policy mix but a problematic sequencing of these policies, resulting in widespread deindustrialization and unemployment. For those still able to keep their jobs in industry, this meant a sharp fall in real wages—on average, a 30 per cent decline between 1980 and 1986, while in several countries the average rate dropped 10 per cent every year from 1980.

These structural shifts in SSA economies pose challenges not only for future growth and development but for constitutionalism as well, seeing that the structure of these economies is unlikely to sustain a trajectory of inclusive growth. For example, recent economic growth has been driven largely by commodity exports (which do not absorb labour) and subject to world markets (which make control and access to natural resources a government function). Compounding this is the fact that the majority of the poor in sub-Saharan Africa reside in rural areas and earn a living from agriculture, which has been on the decline. Though declining in its share of total output, agriculture remains highly relevant in these economies, given the low urbanization level (control of access to land). Within urban areas, the formal labour market is unable to absorb most citizens, a situation linked to underlying economic structures (such as the absence of a strong manufacturing base and/or a declining one) and long-term developments. This means that informality, defined as livelihood strategies external to the formal institutions of law, is widespread.

4. Revenue, Expenditure, Fiscal Balance, and Government Debt

This section outlines developments in revenue and expenditure in SSA countries since 2000 and discusses their implications for public debt. On the revenue side, countries have relied disproportionately on indirect sources of revenue instead of direct sources, which are deemed important for fostering strong links between citizens and the mobilization

---

[21] Margaret McMillan, Dani Rodrik, and Claudia Sepúlveda, *Structural Change, Fundamentals, and Growth: A Framework and Case Studies* (International Food Policy Research Institute 2016).

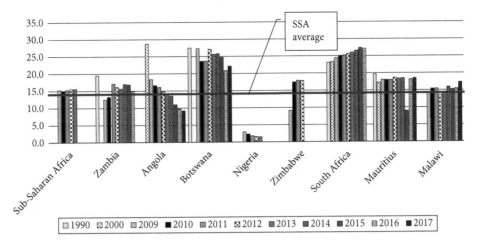

Figure 2.3 Tax revenue as a percentage of GDP
Source: IMF data and author's calculations

of revenue. Similarly, on the expenditure side, government expenditure has been poor in quality in that it is skewed towards salaries and debt repayment. This mismatch between revenue mobilization and expenditure has led to rising indebtedness (discussed in the final part of the section).

4.1 Developments in Revenue and Expenditure

Taxation is a strategic tool for a variety of reasons, which explains why SSA constitutions focus on it to such an extent that the phrase 'fiscal constitutions' is commonplace. Raising tax revenue enhances the legitimacy of governments by enabling them to function and pay for goods and services such as infrastructure (water, sanitation, electricity, roads, bridges, and the like), education, health, justice, and defence, all of which are essential for economic growth. Over and above enabling the provision of public goods, taxation affects crucial decisions such as how much to save and invest. What affects these decisions is not only the level of taxation but its structure, that is, the way in which different fiscal instruments are designed and combined to generate governmental revenue.

Figure 2.3 plots sub-Saharan Africa's tax-to-GDP ratio. The average is hovering around 15 per cent. This ratio is on par with benchmark figures requisite for sustained economic growth—it has been found empirically that countries which reach this 15 per cent threshold of the tax-to-GDP ratio tend to experience higher growth.[22] Tax collection is relatively higher in Botswana, Malawi, and Zimbabwe than elsewhere in the region, while South Africa's tax-to-GDP ratio is getting close to the average of high-income OECD countries.

What is concerning is that Nigeria is at the bottom of the selected economies, with a tax-to-GDP ratio of about 2 per cent. This is lower than the average tax-to-GDP ratio of about 10–15 per cent in the low-income countries. For example, Burkina Faso (15.3 per

---

[22] Vito Gaspar, Laura Jaramillo, and Philippe Wingender, 'Tax Capacity and Growth: Is There a Tipping Point?' (2016) 17(4) IMF Research Bulletin.

cent), Côte D'Ivoire (14 per cent), Ghana (14.9 per cent), and Mali (13.5 per cent) all have far higher tax-to-GDP ratios than Nigeria. This below-par tax revenue mobilization has impeded economic growth and social development in Nigeria. Given that it is the largest economy in sub-Saharan Africa, its low tax effort not only significantly limits its capacity to implement the onerous development agenda but also threatens the region's prospects of reaching tax-revenue targets to address developmental goals.

Since 2000 to the present, tax revenues have risen on average from 12 per cent to about 15 per cent. The main driver of the increase has been increases in consumption taxes following the adoption of value-added tax (VAT) and improvements in direct taxes. In regard to direct taxes, corporate taxes have stagnated at about 4 per cent of GDP. Trade taxes performed poorly, as was expected in view of trade liberalization's reduction of tariffs. With regional integration and the African Free Trade Area gaining momentum, the contribution of trade taxes to total revenue will continue to decline due to gradual reduction of trade tariffs.[23]

As one would expect, tax evolution has not been uniform across the region. For example, countries rich in natural resources have mobilized far less non-resourced tax revenues than their counterparts poorly endowed with natural resources.[24] The share of indirect tax revenues is higher in resource-poor countries.[25] Conversely, the share of direct taxes in revenues has been higher in resource-rich countries, with personal and corporate taxes making up, respectively, 15.6 per cent and 13 per cent of revenue in resource-rich countries compared to 12 per cent and 11.7 per cent in resource-poor ones.[26]

Now we shift focus to expenditure. The overall size of governments in sub-Saharan Africa, measured by the ratio of expenditure to GDP, is relatively high—on average, it is 25 per cent, ranging between 10 per cent in Equatorial Guinea to 37 per cent in Lesotho in 2015.[27] Although all the SSA governments wish to increase their size in the economy, they are constrained by the failure to raise higher levels of revenue relative to GDP. Government spending is divided into two areas, namely current spending and capital spending. Current spending is the state's allocation of resources in providing public services; capital spending relates to allocations for new public infrastructure.

The majority of the recurrent governmental budget is directed towards salaries, allowances, and social benefits for government employees. For example, within SACU countries, Lesotho and Namibia have the highest percentage of expenditure on compensation of employees, according to the World Bank and IMF data. Namibia, for the period of analysis, paid its public servants about 47.8 per cent (using the median) of total governmental expenditure, followed by Lesotho, which paid its public official 40.8 per cent. South Africa has the lowest expenditure on compensation of employees relative to total governmental expenditure. Notably, the country spends half (ie 18.5 per cent) in comparison to Botswana, Namibia, and Lesotho. After compensation, governments spend on interest payments,

---

[23] C Adam, *The Fiscal Foundations of Deep Regional Integration: From Customs Unions to Economic and Monetary Union* (African Economic Research Consortium 2018).

[24] Andre Gbato, 'Impact of Taxation on Growth in Sub-Saharan Africa: New Evidence Based on a New Data Set' (2017) MPRA Paper No 80903 <https://mpra.ub.uni-muenchen.de/80903/ accessed 7 September 2019.

[25] ibid.

[26] ibid.

[27] International Monetary Fund Government Finance Statistics; World Bank and OECD GDP estimates.

subsidies, goods, and services. Interest payments have been on the increase in several countries due to rising public debt, subsequently crowding out goods and services.

To turn to sectoral expenditure, the trends highlight SSA governments' focus on development. Most spending is on education, health, and social development—military expenditure (defence) is small nowadays and has declined marginally as a percentage both of the economy in general and governmental spend in particular. This would suggest that the era of civil conflicts is well and truly over, with the spending patterns of that era having shifted to a focus on addressing the triple challenge of growth, poverty, and inequality. Indeed, education spend in sub-Saharan Africa is now comparable to that of other regions in the world; however, health status is poor, the cost of doing business remains high, and the region's basic infrastructure is poorer than that of other regions.

The region's low collection of revenue from citizens and direct taxes in general has important constitutional implications. It weakens the accountability link, as reliance on indirect taxes such as trade taxes, commodity royalties, aid, and borrowing generally makes governments impervious to citizens, an orientation which is at odds with the basic accountability structures inscribed in constitutions; moreover, the focus of government expenditure is on sustaining government, with expenditures skewed towards salaries rather than serving the people.

4.2 Fiscal Balance and Public Debt Trends

Table 2.5 shows that, owing to sustained fiscal consolidation, sub-Saharan Africa's fiscal deficit has narrowed considerably since 2000.

Sub-Saharan Africa had a primary surplus averaging 1.7 per cent during the 2010–15 period. High oil prices and increased oil production (Angola, Chad, Nigeria, and Ghana) meant that oil-exporting countries recorded the largest surplus, that of 5.3 per cent. The CFA franc zone recorded the second highest surplus, driven by sustained fiscal consolidation. Across several other SSA countries, a widening tax base and automation of tax administration (Congo, Lesotho, Malawi, and Nigeria) led to narrowing deficits. The only country groups that still ran a deficit in this period were oil-importing, low-income countries and those in COMESA and EAC-5. Largely driven by upswings in infrastructural spending, fiscal deficits were observed in Ethiopia, while in Zimbabwe the deficit was due to economic meltdown and fiscal indiscipline.

The rosy picture changed for the worse in the period 2016–18 when all country groups and countries experienced fiscal deficits. The main reason was terms-of-trade shocks, in particular those emanating from commodity prices. Fiscal deficits on average converged on a trend towards a 5 per cent level among all economic groups. Commitment to continued investment in infrastructure development is expected to weigh on the fiscal deficits' positive performance going forward, which suggests that the quality of public investments will become central.

Sub-Saharan Africa has a curious, if not notorious, history when it comes to sovereign debt crisis. As recently as the 1990s, twenty-nine SSA countries benefited from the Highly Indebted Poor Countries (HIPC) and Multilateral Debt Relief initiatives (MDRI) that left the countries almost debt-free in the mid-2000s. Thanks to these initiatives, general

Table 2.5 Overall fiscal balance, including grants (percentage of GDP)

	2010–15	2016–18	2019	2020	Change (2016–18 vs 2010–15)
Sub-Saharan Africa	1.7	−4.3	−4.0	−3.3	−6.0
Oil-exporting countries	5.3	−4.1	−3.5	−3.3	−9.4
Oil-importing countries	−0.5	−4.4	−4.3	−4.1	−3.9
Middle-income countries	2.2	−4.6	−4.3	−4	−6.8
Low-income countries	−1.3	−3.4	−3	−3.4	−2.1
Countries in fragile situations	0.6	−3.9	−1.9	−1.9	−4.5
CFA franc zone	4.7	−3.9	−1.7	−1.3	−8.6
COMESA (SSA members)	−1.6	−4.8	−3.9	−3.9	−3.2
EAC-5	−1.9	−5.1	−4.6	−4.5	−3.2
ECOWAS	2.8	−4.7	−4.7	−4.2	−7.5
SACU	0.3	−4.3	−5.1	−5	−4.6
SADC	0.3	−3.8	−3.7	−3.8	−4.1
Angola	1.1	−2.8	0.1	−0.1	−3.9
Ethiopia	−3.4	−2.9	−3	−3	0.5
Nigeria	4.7	−4.6	−5.1	−4.6	−9.3
South Africa	0.1	−4.3	−5.1	−5.1	−4.4
Zambia	2.1	−6.7	−5.0	−5.9	−8.8
Zimbabwe	−3.0	−6.2	−2.0	−2.5	−3.2

Source and legends: 2019 and 2020 are IMF estimates; author's computations based on IMF World Economic Outlook database; see Box 2.1 for country groupings table

government debt as a percentage of GDP fell substantially from 110 per cent in 2001, to 32 per cent over 2010–15, as shown in Table 2.6.

Until recently, public debt management had been prudent, particularly with respect to reliance on external debt. In the last two to three years, sub-Saharan Africa has been relying on non-concessional foreign borrowing to finance many large infrastructure projects, which is likely to contribute to faster debt build-up and debt-service payments in the coming years and is not reflected in the data for debt and debt-service obligations until now. During 2016–18, the debt-to-GDP ratio increased by more than 14 percentage points in SSA countries, by 17 per cent in oil-importing countries and CFA franc zone countries, and by a whopping 40.2 per cent and 33.5 per cent, respectively, in Angola and Zambia.

There are hence increasing concerns about the prospect of a new sovereign debt crisis in countries across sub-Saharan Africa. Again, debt build-up invites foreign influence, which impacts directly on the constitutional value of state sovereignty.

Table 2.6 Government debt (percentage of GDP)

	2010–15	2016–18	2019	2020	Change (2016–18 vs 2010–15)
Sub-Saharan Africa	31.9	46.7	49.2	48.9	14.8
Oil exporting countries	21.7	39.1	41.6	40.6	17.4
Oil importing countries	40.0	51.3	53.7	53.7	11.3
Middle-income countries	31.1	46.4	49.9	49.5	15.3
Low-income countries	35.7	47.4	47.2	46.8	11.7
Countries in fragile situations	40.1	47.9	43	41.5	7.8
CFA franc zone	32.9	50.8	50.4	48.6	17.9
COMESA (SSA members)	39.3	50.5	50.6	50	11.2
EAC-5	35.9	45.9	48.1	47.7	10.0
ECOWAS	23.0	34.6	38.6	38.8	11.6
SACU	40.6	51.2	55.1	57.1	10.6
SADC	38.8	53.8	56.7	56.5	15.0
Angola	37.2	77.4	90.5	82.8	40.2
Ethiopia	46.3	58.7	57.4	56.3	12.4
Nigeria	16.9	25.7	30.1	31.4	8.8
South Africa	42.4	53.7	57.8	59.8	11.3
Zambia	31.8	65.3	80.5	83.5	33.5
Zimbabwe	41.5	45.6	21.0	20.5	4.1

Source and legends: 2019 and 2020 are IMF estimates; Author's computations based on IMF World Economic Outlook database; See Box 2.1 for country groupings table

5. Recent Socio-economic Developments

Socio-economic developments in sub-Saharan Africa reflect the role of socio-economic rights in bills of rights and the creation of the 'social' state. In 2000, world leaders committed to a global vision to 'spare no effort to free our fellow men, women and children from abject and dehumanizing conditions of extreme poverty'. The global mobilization, known as the Millennium Development Goals (MDGs), comprised eight goals targeted at eradicating poverty by 2015. Although all the world's countries embraced this vision and governments made concerted efforts to achieve the targets, it was apparent by the end of 2015 that developing regions such as sub-Saharan Africa were experiencing delays in poverty reduction.

The UN post-2015 agenda continues to seek to improve the quality of life globally through the SDGs. SSA countries are signatories to the SDGs that replaced the MDGs, the objective being to achieve, by 2030, a set of common goals that meet urgent global environmental, economic, and political challenges. As is evident in the SDGs, growth, poverty, and income distribution are increasingly issues of global concern.[28] Three of the seventeen SDGs focus directly on the nexus of growth, poverty, inequality, and redistribution: SDG 1 (no poverty), SDG 8 (decent work and economic growth), and SDG 10 (reduced inequalities).

Also relevant for sub-Saharan Africa is Agenda 2063, which the African Union Commission (AUC) adopted in 2013 as a strategic framework for the continent's socio-economic transformation over the next fifty years. It seeks to accelerate implementation of past and existing continental initiatives for growth and sustainable development, with its main goals including equitable and people-centred growth and development; the eradication of poverty; and internal coherence and coordination in continental, regional, and national frameworks and plans adopted by the AUC, regional economic communities, and member states of the African Union.

In regard to the MDGs, a UN report summarized the successes and remaining challenges, which are set out in Table 2.7.[29]

The poverty headcount ratio in Africa dropped from 54.3 per cent in 1990 to 41 per cent in 2013 and to 36 per cent in 2016.[30] Because the population is increasing, the reduction in poverty was insufficient to reduce significantly the number of people in absolute poverty, which remained at 390 million.[31] The poverty gap in Africa stands at 15.2 per cent, compared to 8.8 per cent globally. In regard to ending extreme poverty, major advancements have been made.[32] The rate of extreme poverty decreased by approximately a third between 1990 and 2013; nevertheless, 11 per cent of the world population still lives in extreme poverty.[33]

Although it is declining, income inequality on the continent remains extremely high, with a Gini coefficient of 0.44. Nine African countries, all situated in southern Africa, experienced increasing Gini coefficients in the period 1993–2008.[34] West Africa experienced a decline in its inequality levels in seven out of twelve (mostly agrarian) countries, while a slow decline is observable in some countries in East Africa. Around the globe, labour productivity has increased and the unemployment rate decreased, leading to progress towards promoting sustained, inclusive, and sustainable economic growth.[35]

Sub-Saharan Africa recorded the world's fastest growth in primary school enrolment rates, which rose from 52 per cent in 1999 to 80 per cent in 2015 (an increase of 48 percentage points). Despite this significant stride in access to primary education, the continent still lags behind other developing regions. The pace of progress was also insufficient to

---

[28] United Nations, *Transforming Our World: The 2030 Agenda for Sustainable Development* (UN 2015).

[29] ibid.

[30] UNDP, *Income Inequality Trends in Sub-Saharan Africa: Divergence, Determinants and Consequences* (United Nations Development Programme: Regional Bureau for Africa 2017). United Nations Economic Commission for Africa, African Union, African Development Bank and United Nations Development, *MDG Report 2015: Assessing Progress in Africa toward the Millennium Development Goals* (United Nations 2015).

[31] United Nations Economic Commission for Africa, *Agenda 2063/ SDGs Progress Report 2017: Assessing Africa's Domestication and Implementation of Agenda 2063 and the SDGs* (United Nations 2017).

[32] UNDP (n 30).

[33] ibid.

[34] GA Cornia, 'An Econometric Analysis of the Bifurcation of Within-Country Inequality Trends in Sub-Saharan Africa Other than North Africa, 1990–2011' (2016) Inequality Project, UNDP RBA Working Paper Series.

[35] UNDP (n 30).

Table 2.7 Africa's MDG progress (1990–2015)

MDG Goals	1990	2015
Goal 1: Eradicate extreme poverty % of people living in extreme poverty	57	36
Goal 2: Achieve universal primary education % enrolment in primary education	52	80
Goal 3: Promote gender equality and empower women % of women in wage employment	14	21
Goal 4: Reduce child mortality Number of deaths for children aged under-5 (per 1,000 live births)	179	86
Goal 5: Improve maternal health Number of maternal deaths per 100,000 live births	990	510
Goal 6: Combat HIV/AIDS, Malaria, and other diseases % of HIV prevalence between 2005 and 2013 (million)	5.6	4.7
Goal 7: Ensure environmental sustainability % of population with access to improved sanitation between 1990 and 2012	24	30
Goal 8: Develop a global partnership for development Number of mobile subscriptions between 1990 and 2013 (per 100 inhabitants)	0.005	80.20

Source: United Nations (2015)

ensure that by 2015 all girls and boys are able to complete full primary schooling. In 2008, 33 million of the 69 million children out of school worldwide were in sub-Saharan Africa.[36]

Similar progress is seen in the reduction in deaths of children under the age of 5. The annual rate of under-5 mortality has declined significantly by 52 per cent since 1990, a trend in keeping with the decline in all developing regions.[37] The challenge remains that the highest rates of child mortality persist in sub-Saharan Africa, which also continues to make progress in combating diseases such as HIV/AIDS, malaria, and tuberculosis. The decline in people with new HIV infections has seen the prevalence of the disease decrease moderately over the period 2005–13.

The same cannot be said, however, for changes in maternity health, gender equality, and access to drinking water. Sub-Saharan Africa and Southern Asia accounted for 86 per cent of maternal mortality rates globally in 2015.[38] The decline in gender inequality also continued to lag behind other developing regions, with only 21 per cent of African women in wage employment in 2015, compared to 41 per cent globally. Similarly, the ratio of boys to girls in colleges and universities continues to favour the male child in sub-Saharan Africa.[39] As of 2012, only 36 per cent of the population had access to improved drinking water.[40]

---

[36] Africa Renewal, 'Africa's Hard Road to the Millennium Development Goals' *Africa Renewal* (August 2010) <https://bit.ly/36sgudC> accessed 30 November 2020.
[37] UN (n 28).
[38] United Nations, *The Millennium Development Goals Report 2015* (UN 2015).
[39] Africa Renewal (n 36).
[40] United Nations Economic Commission for Africa (n 30).

To reach the first SDG's target of ending extreme poverty at USD 1 a day PPP and halving poverty at the national poverty line by 2030, policy-makers need to understand the inequality–economic growth–poverty nexus. This will enable them to plan better to meet the 2030 targets. The consequences of economic policy and public finances (and lack of inclusive growth) are poor socio-economic outcomes. All these challenges are symptoms of economic growth which is not inclusive. As such, the high growth that sub-Saharan Africa experienced between 1990 and 2015 failed to contribute to reduced inequality and poverty rates, which translated into poor quality of life for the population. Many of the countries now face unprecedented economic recession induced by COVID-19, with poor people everywhere hit the hardest.

6. Conclusion

Economic growth in sub-Saharan Africa has been at its strongest over the last two decades. Most countries have achieved substantial structural adjustment and a measure of economic stabilization (ie inflation and debt are under control), and have seen improvements in terms of budget balance, monetary policy control, liberalization of the foreign exchange market, and implementation of structural reforms such as the privatization of state-owned firms. However, there is little structural change in productive sectors, where the trend instead is towards deindustrialization and increased informalization of the economy.

The region's economic growth has thus been driven not by fundamental structural change but growth in demand due to high export prices. The latter typically results in stop-and-start spurts of growth that come about more from luck than anything else, whereas the former leads to sustainable growth. Moreover, the region's population growth is now amongst the highest in the world and has diluted the potential benefits of this economic growth. For most SSA countries, revenue generation is still below the levels necessary for meeting the SDGs.

As sub-Saharan Africa struggles with inadequate albeit positive economic growth, incomes are not rising as fast as anticipated, high population growth is a major challenge, and unemployment remains a concern, as does dissatisfaction with the pace of progress in addressing long-standing problems of high poverty and inequality. This has intensified pressures to identify additional interventions that could support national development goals, foster sustained economic growth, generate employment, and increase domestic revenue mobilization so as to expand the fiscal space for addressing poverty and inequality. Against this backdrop, can constitutions shape governmental action in ways that lead to better socio-economic outcomes? This is a question that will be addressed in the rest of the chapters.

Bibliography

'Africa's Hopeful Economies: The Sun Shines Bright' *The Economist* (3 December 2011)

Adam C, *The Fiscal Foundations of Deep Regional Integration: From Customs Unions to Economic and Monetary Union* (African Economic Research Consortium 2018)

Africa Renewal, 'Africa's Hard Road to the Millennium Development Goals' *Africa Renewal* (August 2010) <https://www.un.org/africarenewal/magazine/august-2010/africa%E2%80%99s-hard-road-millennium-development-goals> accessed 30 November 2020

AUC and OECD, *Africa's Growth Dynamics: Growth, Jobs and Inequality* (AUC and OECD 2018)

Balbuena SS, 'State-owned Enterprises in Southern Africa: A Stocktaking of Reforms and Challenges' (2014) OECD Corporate Governance Working Papers No 13

Charmes J, 'The Informal Economy Worldwide: Trends and Characteristics' (2012) 6(2) Journal of Applied Economic Research 103

Chitiga-Mabugu M, Mabugu R, and Fofana I, *Ending Poverty by 2030: Is Africa on Track?* (Mimeo 2019)

Cho Y and Tien B, 'Sub-Saharan Africa's Recent Growth Spurt: An Analysis of the Sources of Growth' (2014) World Bank Human Development Network Social Protection and Labor Unit Policy Research Working Paper 6862

Cornia GA, 'An Econometric Analysis of the Bifurcation of Within-Country Inequality Trends in Sub-Saharan Africa Other than North Africa, 1990–2011' (2016) Inequality Project, UNDP RBA Working Paper Series

Coulibaly BS, Ghandi D, and Senbet LW, 'Is Sub-Saharan Africa Facing Another Systemic Sovereign Debt Crisis?' (2019) Policy Brief: Africa Growth Initiative, Brookings Institution

Crivelli E and Gupta S, *Resource Blessing, Revenue Curse? Domestic Revenue Effort in Resource-Rich Countries* (International Monetary Fund 2014)

Diao X and McMillan M, 'Toward an Understanding of Economic Growth in Africa: A Re-Interpretation of the Lewis Model' (March 2015) National Bureau of Economic Research Working Paper Series

Gaspar V, Jaramillo L, and Wingender P, 'Tax Capacity and Growth: Is There a Tipping Point?' (2016) 17(4) IMF Research Bulletin

Gbato A, 'Impact of Taxation on Growth in Sub-Saharan Africa: New Evidence Based on a New Data Set' (2017) MPRA Paper No 80903 <https://mpra.ub.uni-muenchen.de/80903/> accessed 7 September 2019

Humphreys M and Bates R, 'Political Institutions and Economic Policies: Lessons from Africa' (2005) 35(3) British Journal of Political Science 403

International Monetary Fund, *Sub-Saharan Africa Regional Economic Outlook: Recovery Amid Elevated Uncertainty* (IMF 2019)

Jirasavetakul LF and Lakner C, 'Distribution of Consumption Expenditure in Sub-Saharan Africa: The Inequality among all Africans' (2020) 29(1) Journal of African Economies 1

McMillan M, Rodrik D, and Sepúlveda, C, *Structural Change, Fundamentals, and Growth: A Framework and Case Studies* (International Food Policy Research Institute 2016).

McMillan M, Rodrik D, and Verduzco-Gallo, IG, 'Globalization, Structural Change, and Productivity Growth, with an Update on Africa' (2014) 63 World Development 11

Meagher K, 'The Scramble for Africans: Demography, Globalisation and Africa's Informal Labour Markets' (2016) 52(4) Journal of Development Studies 483

Radelet S, *Emerging Africa: How 17 Countries are Leading the Way* (Center for Global Development 2010)

Radelet S, *The Great Surge: The Ascent of the Developing World* (Simon and Schuster 2015)

Sachs J, 'Government, Geography, and Growth: The True Drivers of Economic Development' (2012) 91(5) Foreign Affairs 142

Schwab K, *The Fourth Industrial Revolution* (Currency 2017)

Shehu E and Nilsson B, *Informal Employment among Youth: Evidence from 20 School-to-Work Transition Surveys* (ILO 2014)

UNDP, *Income Inequality Trends in Sub-Saharan Africa: Divergence, Determinants and Consequences* (United Nations Development Programme: Regional Bureau for Africa 2017)

United Nations, *Transforming Our World: The 2030 Agenda for Sustainable Development* (UN 2015)

United Nations, *The Millennium Development Goals Report 2015* (UN 2015)

United Nations Economic Commission for Africa, African Union, African Development Bank and United Nations Development, *MDG Report 2015: Assessing Progress in Africa toward the Millennium Development Goals* (United Nations 2015)

United Nations Economic Commission for Africa, *Agenda 2063/ SDGs Progress Report 2017: Assessing Africa's Domestication and Implementation of Agenda 2063 and the SDGs* (United Nations 2017)

World Economic Forum, *The Global Risks Report 2017* (WEF 2017)

Young A, *The African Growth Miracle* (National Bureau of Economic Research 2012)

Zeufack AG and others, 'An Analysis of Issues Shaping Africa's Economic Future' [2020] 21 Africa's Pulse <https://openknowledge.worldbank.org/handle/10986/33541> accessed 30 November 2020

3

Constitutional Law and the Economy

Comparing Liberal Market Orders

Stephan FH Ollick

1. Introduction

Many constitutions across the globe advocate, or at least presuppose, distinct economic theories for the polities they govern. Provisions in this regard differ markedly in style and content. Some constitutions are outspoken about economic approach, while others are subtle, though not silent; in form, they range from the express proclamation of one or another system to a quiet privileging of selected individual or collective rights that either encourage or stifle economically relevant patterns of behaviour. Similarly, in substance, these clauses could support ideas across the board from liberal *laissez-faire* economics to the prescription of planning and regulation by governmental command.

Constitutions and the economic models exist along a continuum. Some states may largely permit the play of forces of the free market, yet allow for state-led intervention in certain situations or within designated economic domains; others presume the state's centralized ownership of productive assets, while nonetheless recognizing private property and corporate ownership even if this sharply contradicts their long-standing and vigorous political rhetoric.

In the context of the present volume, the approaches taken by France, the United Kingdom, the United States, and Germany are of particular interest, as their systems have influenced each other as well as constitutional orders elsewhere, not least in Africa. All of them subscribe to a significant degree to the ideal of a free market, albeit again that they differ in style and content.

2. Constitutional Law and the Economy

Historically, *laissez-faire* and planned economies have both had their triumphs. Both have also related their economic agendas to the legal order of the polity, even citing those agendas—if only in retrospect—as the key to the polity's success. A first question is how they relate such outcomes to constitutional law. In this respect, constitutions can be distinguished in terms not only of the macroeconomic approach they adopt but their style.

As noted, some are vociferous about the economic order they aim to establish or preserve, especially where it is ideologically relevant to the state. An example is the 1982 Constitution of the People's Republic of China, which declares in its opening lines that '[t]he People's Republic of China is a socialist state under the people's democratic dictatorship

Stephan FH Ollick, *Constitutional Law and the Economy.* In: *Constitutionalism and the Economy in Africa.* Edited by: Charles M Fombad and Nico Steytler, Oxford University Press. © Stephan FH Ollick 2022. DOI: 10.1093/oso/9780192886439.003.0005

led by the working class and based on the alliance of workers and peasants'.[1] Direct references to the economic order abound, for instance in the provision that '[t]he basis of the socialist economic system of the People's Republic of China is socialist public ownership of the means of production, namely, ownership by the whole people and collective ownership by the working people' in terms of which '[t]he system of socialist ownership supersedes the system of exploitation of man by man'.[2] Other constitutions, including those of greater concern in this survey, proceed more inconspicuously in framing the economic underpinnings of the polity, for example by hedging against political interference in the market or privileging certain rights.

A different, though equally relevant, question concerns the efficacy of constitutional pronouncements on the economy, regardless of their stylistic guise. To pursue the example of China, one may question how strictly the contemporary Chinese economy still follows socialist lines as they were understood in the middle of the twentieth century. In the late 1970s, the ruling Communist Party of China led by Deng Xiaoping oversaw the abolition in effect of the centrally planned economy, henceforth reframed as a 'socialist market economy'.[3] Shifts like these in the face of economic expediency find their legal grounding in the preamble of the Constitution, which provides that 'China will stay in the primary stage of socialism for a long time'. The state shall adhere to the basic economic system with the public ownership remaining dominant and diverse sectors of the economy, developing side by side, and to the distribution system with the 'distribution according to work' remaining dominant and the coexistence of a variety of modes of distribution.[4]

This should not be taken to mean that strong constitutional formulations of economic principle amount to lip service alone. Observers of China can point to the fact that, to this day, the Chinese state retains majority ownership of most companies and that the commitment to socialism continues to be relevant,[5] especially outside constitutional legal discourse *stricto sensu*.[6] In other words, constitutional prescriptions for the economic system ought not to be dismissed merely for taking the form of broad ideological labels: many an important constitutional principle will appear in ceremonial guise, with its concretization left to the legislature and judiciary. Meanwhile, economically liberal states have on occasion altered their economic approaches, taking on interventionist trappings and dispensing state subsidies and public welfare; few would deny that such state orders are still essentially market based.

Despite these ambiguities that arise where political and economic commitments converge and the constitution enshrines policy in complex terms, the search for congruence between the constitution's substance and the political realities of the state is a tempting exercise. The task is not an easy one: critical observers have problematized the extent to which

---

[1]   Constitution of the People's Republic of China of 1982, art 1.
[2]   ibid art 6.
[3]   Chao Xi, 'Transforming Chinese Enterprises: Ideology, Efficiency and Instrumentalism in the Process of Reform' in John Gillespie and Pip Nicholson (eds), *Asian Socialism and Legal Change: The Dynamics of Vietnamese and Chinese Reform* (Asia Pacific Press 2005) 92.
[4]   Constitution of the People's Republic of China 1982, art 6.
[5]   Xi (n 3) 96.
[6]   cf Michael Dowdle, 'Of "Socialism" and "Socialist" Legal Transformations in China and Vietnam' in John Gillespie and Pip Nicholson (eds), *Asian Socialism and Legal Change: The Dynamics of Vietnamese and Chinese Reform* (Asia Pacific Press 2005) 36.

our understanding of constitutional cause and economic effect is limited.[7] Some notable accounts deserve our attention.

In one now-classic study, Douglass North and Barry Weingast traced the impact of strong rights and parliamentary control over the executive on economic growth in the context of the 1688 Glorious Revolution in Stuart Britain.[8] They argued that the extent to which the sovereign monarch became subordinate to the rules governing economic exchange proved decisive in stimulating growth.[9] The ever-increasing fiscal needs of the Stuart rulers were met unsustainably through the imposition of customs, sale of monopolies, and extraction of 'forced loans' from subjects by the monarchs, the full repayment of which was uncertain at the best of times. Property would be seized even more directly for 'public purposes', and in desperate moves, hereditary titles put up for sale.[10]

A grim picture of the larger economy emerged, with returns on private investments being greatly diminished by the cost of monopolies, expropriation disguised as loans or forced sale, and productive engagement in markets stifled by lack of incentive or means.[11] Unsurprisingly, the resulting failures of the economy ran counter to the interests of the monarchs themselves. In their own interests, they subjected themselves to parliamentary oversight that would limit state intervention in the economy and guarantee private rights as well as the free play of market forces, thus providing security, building trust, and incentivizing investment.[12]

The historical case appears in line with more contemporary ones. Jon Elster advanced the argument that constitutions can influence economic performance by providing the stability, accountability, and credibility on which non-state actors in the economy thrive.[13] Richard Posner pointed out the cost of substituting enforceable rights with alternatives such as violence, alliances, and self-protection;[14] at the same time, he observed that while the rule of law may be a contributory factor to economic growth, it is certainly not its necessary precondition. East Asian states, including former British colonies, have at times economically outperformed the United Kingdom despite their more tenuous commitments to formal legal procedures.[15]

Any economic approach may in principle be implemented simply as a matter of policy without constitutional anchoring. Nonetheless, constitution-makers often choose to consider the economy. Given that constitutional norms tend to be significantly more difficult to change than policies, economic choices embedded in constitutions may be more likely than otherwise to survive the governments that wished to see to their implementation.[16] It is

---

[7] Jon Elster, 'The Impact of Constitutions on Economic Performance' (1994) 8 The World Bank Economic Review 209.

[8] Douglass C North and Barry R Weingast, 'Constitutions and Commitment: The Evolution of Institutions Governing Public Choice in Seventeenth-Century England' (1989) 49 The Journal of Economic History 803.

[9] ibid 803.

[10] ibid 811.

[11] ibid 810–11.

[12] ibid 808.

[13] Elster (n 7) 210.

[14] Richard A Posner, 'Creating a Legal Framework for Economic Development' (1998) 13 The World Bank Research Observer 1, 3.

[15] ibid 2.

[16] This follows the logic of insurance. cf Ran Hirschl, *Towards Juristocracy: The Origins and Consequences of the New Constitutionalism* (Harvard University Press 2009); Rosalind Dixon and Tom Ginsburg, 'Constitutions as Political Insurance: Variants and Limits' in Erin F Delaney and Rosalind Dixon (eds), *Comparative Judicial Review* (Edward Elgar 2018).

not unusual for supermajority requirements to be imposed on constitutional amendment, thereby enabling former ruling parties to block departures from their preferred economic model even when they find themselves in an opposition role.

Even when regime change is not imminent, constitutions and their promise of endurance play a foundational role in encouraging economic activity by instilling trust. Such trust will grow where the rules of the game are predictable in their content and enforcement and binding on all actors. As constitutions can limit government power, they can respond to economic concerns to protect unimpeded market-based activity. Today, economic prescriptions feature in many constitutions. Even articles which are not directly economic in nature often respond to ills and imbalances that befall the polity and produce adverse effects that are not least economic in nature.

3. Constitutional Law and the Economy: Points of Contact

In their study of Stuart Britain, North and Weingast highlighted the importance of committing the state to economic fair play. Since then, states have taken on added responsibilities for providing a level playing field between private actors as well. Given the general tendency in constitution-making towards an ever-widening scope, many modern constitutions now have distinctly economic dimensions. The example of China illustrated how colourful ideological terms blend economic approaches together with constitutional law. The constitutions to be discussed here largely refrain from prescribing in any programmatic fashion the workings that are to sustain the national economy; even less so do they condense them into emotive language. In fact, in the case of Germany, the Federal Constitutional Court has gone so far as to emphasize the 'economic policy neutrality of the Basic Law'.[17] Nevertheless, the implications of the Basic Law for economic policy are far reaching.

The same is true for the other constitutional orders under consideration. Their economic dimension is manifested not in broad pronouncements on the polity's system but in the inhibition of particular market constellations and in the protection afforded to select rights; and although they might not be outspoken about economic principle, they may yet include provisions situated squarely where constitutional law and macroeconomic policy intersect.

While nearly every constitutional provision may be said to have some economic effect, however indirect, some of them can be construed as an intentional act of macroeconomic policy-making, expressing choices of economic approach that were deemed foundational, durable, and thus duly placed atop the hierarchy of norms. This cannot necessarily be said of clauses with only indirect economic import or of general provisions from which judges, largely through their own exertions, have derived substantive economic criteria for legislation and governance.

Some constitutional texts provide detailed rules, whereas in other orders their functional equivalents have grown out of ordinary legislation, court rulings, or unguided practice: the case of Hong Kong in the nineteenth century exemplifies how deeply rooted commercial traditions both preceded and imposed themselves on the formalization of economic ordering after the handover to the People's Republic of China in 1997.[18] In cases where the

---

[17]   BVerfGE 4, 7/17, BVerfGE 7, 377/400, BVerfGE 50, 290/336.

[18]   cf EC Ip, 'The Constitution of Economic Liberty in Hong Kong' (2015) 26 Constitutional Political Economy 307, 311.

constitutional text is terse, as with the US Constitution, the economic significance of the constitution is attenuated. More readily distinguishable from dynamic economic governance are provisions with an economic dimension that was known to the framers and intended by them at the time. These rules may be understood as conscious acts of constitutional and macroeconomic design.

Constitution drafters rely in some instances on courts to tackle difficult questions in their stead. This is notably prevalent in the realm of 'mega-politics' which specifically includes constitutional dicta informing later economic policy.[19] Contrariwise, the inclusion of economic ideals in formal constitution-making attests strongly to the special conviction of the drafters that the model in question would stand the test of time. Rules that are largely the product of the judiciary's engagement with the constitution are less likely to be, or intended to be, enduring. Courts generally can overturn their previous interpretations more quickly and at lower political cost than is the case in constitutional amendments. In the context of a dynamic economic environment, judicial pronouncements are closer in nature to quotidian economic governance than fundamental commitment to specific economic concepts and approaches.

3.1 Positive Intervention or Non-intervention

When governments intervene in liberal economies, they often seek to avert acute crises. These usually cannot be anticipated in their concrete form at the time when a constitution is drafted, but there are longer-term economic targets which constitutions can feasibly anticipate and include as enduring commitments. An example is the general desire to foster and sustain economic growth. In Germany, for instance, the Basic Law demands 'due regard to the requirements of overall economic equilibrium'.[20] This somewhat elusive directive was subsequently concretized as consisting of those measures within a free-market framework that favour economic growth as well as price stability, high employment, and balance of payments.[21]

Constitutions may then prescribe state intervention in the economy ranging in level from comprehensive command economies to a positive commitment to non-intervention. In Germany, the constitutional mandate to intervene actively in the economy has been and continues to be put to significant use.[22] For instance, the German state responded to the 2008 financial crisis with a series of state-led investments supported by newly created funds intended to stimulate growth and stability at all levels of governance down to the municipalities. The German Basic Law also permits active federal measures even within the realm of state-level governance where the improvement of the regional economic structure and agrarian orders is concerned.[23] This provision gained particular relevance after reunification with the German Democratic Republic (GDR) in 1990, which required the integration of two territories that had pursued very different macroeconomic pathways in the second

---

[19] Ran Hirschl, 'The Judicialization of Politics' in Keith E Whittington, Daniel R Kelemen, and Gregory A Caldeira (eds), *The Oxford Handbook of Law and Politics* (OUP 2008) 123.

[20] German Basic Law, art 109(2).

[21] Law for the Advancement of Economic Stability and Growth 1967, § 1.

[22] cf Peter Badura, *Staatsrecht: Systematische Erläuterung Des Grundgesetzes* (5th edn, CH Beck 2012) 891–92.

[23] German Basic Law, art 91(a)(1).

half of the twentieth century. The displacement of the socialist structures in the new *Länder* led to the eastward extension of this constitutionally mandated government task to cover the new constituent states.

At the same time, the constitutional orders considered here by and large do not expressly commit governments to a general level of intervention or abstention therefrom, aside from the more specific target of some to be a 'social' state.[24] In particular, the United Kingdom and US arrived at predominantly liberal orders by way of constitutional omission rather than express stipulation. The few mechanisms that facilitate state intervention administer it only in low dosages. For example, the US Constitution envisaged only a narrow scope for national provision of public goods, in particular those of national security and unhindered domestic trade between the states,[25] though the latter provided a significant safeguard against political intervention at the state level of governance, where hindrances to trade were most likely to occur.[26] In France and the United Kingdom, state intervention is not prescribed by higher-order law, though in what follows we consider individual provisions that effectuate state restraint in matters of economic import.

3.2 Economic Unity in Federalism

Of the four states under consideration, Germany and the US are two that govern their territories in a federal framework. Given that federated states retain qualities of individual statehood,[27] they are theoretically in a position to fragment the domestic economic area into a multitude of smaller, protected markets. Federations thus face the additional question of where to allocate the competence to shape economic ordering. If the power to determine policy in this regard is anchored at the state level, disparities may spring up. They may hinder growth and interstate investment or trade, but at the same time offer test sites for economic competition and experimentation.[28]

By the letter of the US Constitution, economic order would be determined by and large at state level. However, in the pursuit of what has been termed a 'market-preserving federalism'[29] that counteracts restrictions to trade among the several states, the US Constitution divests the states wholesale of their competence in interstate economic affairs. The Commerce Clause stipulates that '[t]he Congress shall have Power to ... regulate Commerce with foreign Nations, and among the several States, and with the Indian Tribes'.[30] Such measures against state-level restrictions to trade between them were no mere theoretical concern at a time when tolls and tariffs were widely imposed.[31] Consequently, imports and

---

[24] Constitution of France, art 1(1); German Basic Law, arts 20(1) and 28(1).

[25] Douglass C North, William Summerhill, and Barry R Weingast, 'Order, Disorder, and Economic Change: Latin America Versus North America' in Bruce Bueno de Mesquita and Hilton L Root (eds), *Governing for Prosperity* (Yale University Press 2000) 37.

[26] ibid.

[27] cf Basic Law of Germany, art 30.

[28] cf AM Sbragia, 'American Federalism and Intergovernmental Institutions' in RAW Rhodes, Sarah A Binder, and Bert A Rockman (eds), *The Oxford Handbook of Political Institutions* (OUP 2006) 247; but see also LR Basta Fleiner and J-F Gaudreault-DesBiens, 'Federalism and Autonomy' in Mark Tushnet, Thomas Fleiner, and Cheryl Saunders (eds), *Routledge Handbook of Constitutional Law* (Routledge 2013) 154.

[29] North, Summerhill, and Weingast (n 25) 37.

[30] US Constitution, art 1 s 8 cl 3.

[31] Forrest McDonald, *Novus Ordo Seclorum: The Intellectual Origins of the Constitution* (University Press of Kansas 1985) 102–06.

duties on imports and exports by states without approval by the US Congress are unconstitutional.[32] The Contract Clause,[33] despite its more general wording, likewise has a distinct interstate dimension. Its drafting was motivated in part by the fear of debt-relief laws that states might issue at their convenience to rid themselves of obligations.[34]

The framers of the US Constitution also anticipated state obstructions to trade by other than formal legal means. More specifically, there were concerns that out-of-state or foreign merchants might reconsider engaging in trade where disadvantage and prejudice could threaten their interests in state courts.[35] Trade among the several states was hence thought better protected by the Interstate and Alien Diversity Clause, which provides that

> [t]he judicial Power shall extend to all Cases, in law and Equity ... between a State and Citizens of another State; between Citizens of different States; between Citizens of the same State claiming Lands under Grants of different States, and between a State or the Citizens thereof, and foreign States, Citizens or Subjects.[36]

In Germany, the Basic Law likewise allocates competences of economic import largely to federal decision-makers in the name of legal and economic unity.[37] Laws touching on industry, business, mining, trade, banking, labour, vocational training, expropriation, socialization, and many other areas are the prerogative of federal legislation, with state-level laws filling only the gaps in a manner that avoids contradiction.[38] An important feature in this regard is the allocation of competence to the federal legislature where this is required for homogeneity of living conditions and economic ordering.[39] This concerns a wide range of legislative fields far beyond those of immediate economic import, such as laws pertaining to training and research.[40] Even more stringently anchored at the federal level is the imposition or omission of tolls and customs, on which no subsidiary state legislation is permitted.[41] Further limitations arise in relation to other member states of the European Union (EU) on whom no customs duties may be imposed.[42]

In the two federal states, therefore, the constitutions respond to the economic implications of the federal arrangement with differing foci. In the case of the US, the power of the Union is used to inhibit potentially destructive state behaviour that could lower overall wealth, regardless of its distribution. In Germany, the state is called upon to balance the economic conditions for all its citizens and work towards the public good. Both orders draw on the power of the federation to perform an ordering function, but each expresses a distinct understanding of its union's nature.

---

[32] US Constitution, art 1 s 10 cl 2.

[33] US Constitution, art 1 s 10 cl 1.

[34] cf F Petrie, 'The Contracts Clause and the Constitutionality of a Model Law Approach to Sovereign Debt Restructuring' (2017) 19 Journal of Constitutional Law 1207, 1222.

[35] cf Renée Lettow Lerner, 'Enlightenment Economics and the Framing of the U.S. Constitution' (2012) 35 Harvard Journal of Law & Public Policy 1.

[36] US Constitution, art 3 s 3.

[37] Badura (n 22) 358.

[38] cf German Basic Law, art 74(1).

[39] ibid art 72(2).

[40] cf ibid art 74(1)(13).

[41] ibid art 105(1).

[42] Treaty on the Functioning of the European Union, art 28.

3.3 Price Stability

Since states have an interest in controlling inflation and deflation, it seems conceivable that such powers and targets could be enshrined not least in the constitution. In the legal orders under scrutiny here, monetary policy is vested in central banks, thus shielding it from the interference of the governments to whom the constitution is primarily addressed. The United Kingdom and US look to the Bank of England and the Federal Reserve Bank, respectively; France and Germany have vested the making of monetary policy in the European Central Bank (ECB), which was expressly tasked with guarding price stability.[43]

The German Basic Law now makes particular reference to price stability. An earlier clause merely tasked the state to 'establish a note-issuing and currency bank as the Federal Bank', and was thus silent on its orientation in monetary policy. At the end of the twentieth century, however, an amendment responding to greater European integration and the 1992 Maastricht Treaty not only permitted the Bundesbank to delegate powers to the ECB but also qualified this power by characterizing the ECB as 'independent and committed to the overriding goal of assuring price stability'.[44]

Although it is worded as a description, this borders on a prescription to a supra-state entity beyond the Basic Law's remit. The policy-dependent limit to delegation reflects the strength of a constitutional orientation towards price stability through an independent central bank that had not been expressed previously in the Basic Law itself. This commitment is singular in the current analysis, and arguably reflects Germany's historical experience of inflations following the two world wars, subsequent to which price stability was considered fundamental to the new social market order.[45] Constitutional law in France, by comparison, is silent on the policies that EU institutions will pursue. The US Constitution, for its part, does not afford the Federal Reserve an anchor in the text.

3.4 Employment and Working Conditions

Constitutional law can touch on the dynamics of the labour market in a variety of ways. However, in none of the legal orders surveyed here do provisions of constitutional rank directly address unemployment or working conditions as a macroeconomic issue.

Binding quotas and privileges, welfare policies that open up opportunities or steer incentives, anti-discrimination guarantees in employment, and the opening or restriction of access to the labour market for non-citizens take little account of those disfavoured by their outcomes, doing more to guide the allocation of jobs than to create them. Freedom of occupation, where expressly granted, offers no positive entitlement detached from the vagaries of the labour market, and labour policies are left broadly to the discretion of the legislative and executive branches.

However, associative rights that explicitly or implicitly guarantee the formation of labour unions may not only alleviate the working conditions of individual labourers or the wages

---

[43] ibid art 141(2).
[44] German Basic Law, art 88.
[45] cf L Erhard, *Wohlstand Für Alle* (8th edn, Econ-Verlag 1964) 15.

they are paid, but also affect investment patterns through raising the price of labour. This may in turn have ramifications for state targets of low unemployment.

3.5 Subsidies and Taxes

Subsidies to private enterprise express the relative importance governments attach to selected branches of the national economy. They feature most prominently in times of sector-specific crises, which suggests a closer alignment with the realm of dynamic and acute intervention than with the enduring letter of the constitution. Even where they do not take the form of monetary transfers, subsidies have obvious repercussions for competing market actors, both domestically and internationally. This is of particular relevance in member states of the EU, where Germany and France may issue subsidies only in forms that do not affect the market of the EU or otherwise in predetermined exceptional cases.[46] The departing United Kingdom, on the other hand, is set to escape these particular restraints, although other international trade agreements remain in place. Other challenges in the formulation of a consistent framework for subsidies may result from further devolution to Scotland, Wales, and Northern Ireland.[47]

Perhaps surprising is the lack of doctrinal clarity with regard to state-level subsidies in the US. Despite the relative stringency with which the Commerce Clause has been applied to level the playing field for in- and out-of-state enterprises,[48] direct payment of subsidies by states was not held to run against constitutional dictum or purpose.[49] The Supreme Court eventually created an opening to address the seeming incongruence when it denied that the matter of subsidies had been critically assessed so far.[50] However, such clarification has not yet been forthcoming.

Tax policy can invite or discourage investment more generally, and can be used indirectly to steer the economic opportunities that subjects to taxation will seek to exploit, for instance by privileging a particular sector. Even in radically free market orders, stringent taxation would factor into entrepreneurial decision-making as a pervasive externality.[51] Codified constitutions differ in the extent to which they touch on tax, typically anchoring a general power to tax in the text but leaving the intricacies, including its precise assignment, to statutory legislation.[52] The US Constitution does so much as vest a general power to tax in Congress while guiding the apportionment of direct taxes among the several states with specificity sufficient to have necessitated an amended mandate to impose an income tax.[53]

The German Basic Law stands out by making provision for raising and distributing taxes in a rather more comprehensive manner[54] that at times obscures the formal fiscal separation between the federation and the *Länder*.[55] Particular sources of tax revenue are

---

[46] Treaty on the Functioning of the European Union, art 107(1).

[47] cf M Sandford and C Gormley-Heenan, '"Taking Back Control", the UK's Constitutional Narrative and Schrodinger's Devolution' (2020) 73 Parliamentary Affairs 108, 119.

[48] cf DT Coenen, 'Business Subsidies and the Dormant Commerce Clause' (1998) 107 Yale Law Journal 965, 967.

[49] *New Energy Co v Limbach* [1988] 486 US 269, 278.

[50] *West Lynn Creamery, Inc v Healy* [1994] 512 US 186, 199.

[51] Badura (n 22) 880.

[52] cf Constitution of France, art 34(1); Declaration of Human and Civic Rights of 26 August 1789, art 14.

[53] cf US Constitution, art 1 s 8 cl 1 and art 1 s 2 cl 3; Amend XVI; cf also *Pollock v Farmers' Loan & Trust Co* [1895] 157 US 429.

[54] cf German Basic Law, arts 105–07.

[55] cf ibid arts 109(1) and 104(a)(1).

assigned separately to either one of the two, with customs duties income tax accruing to the federation and property and inheritance taxes to the constituent states, to name only a few.[56] The level of detail has enabled constitutional amendments to be passed in relatively short intervals; for instance, article 106 governing the above allocations has been modified six times so far.

3.6 Individual Rights of Macroeconomic Import

In the opening passages of this chapter, the rights-based approach to economic development was highlighted as essentially undergirding the four legal orders discussed here. Even if the economic approach that is furthered or presupposed by the constitution is not expressly labelled as liberal, individual and collective rights can have a steering effect on the economy by inspiring specific forms of market-oriented behaviour. Central in this regard are protections of private property, contracting, occupation, enterprise, and association.

3.6.1 Private property and expropriation

Without a guaranteed right to property, the incentive to engage individually in economically productive activity is greatly diminished. In the array of sources that form the Constitution of the United Kingdom, an early formulation on the protection of property can be found in the Magna Carta of 1297, promising its select beneficiaries that '[n]o Freeman shall be ... disseised of his Freehold'.[57] More recently, the European Convention on Human Rights (ECHR) has come to serve in effect as a bill of rights in the United Kingdom. The 1998 Human Rights Act renders its provisions applicable as domestic human rights law.[58] This extends to the ECHR's additional 1952 Protocol to the Convention for the Protection of Human Rights and Fundamental Freedoms, which entitles natural and legal persons to the enjoyment of their possessions and limits the deprivation thereof to procedures guided strictly by domestic law.[59]

France, like the United Kingdom, has ratified the ECHR and its 1952 Protocol, thus introducing an express clause on the protection of property to its domestic rights guarantees. Although the 1958 Constitution of France does assign international treaties a higher rank than domestic Acts of Parliament,[60] French courts have on previous occasions shown reluctance to treat them as standards of higher-law review.[61] In practice, they can derive safeguards for private property more directly from domestic sources. French constitutional law is understood to comprise more than the Constitution of 1958, with the Declaration of Human and Civic Rights of 26 August 1789 and the Preamble to the Constitution of 1946 forming a wider *bloc de constitutionnalité*.[62] The former commands that the right to property be 'inviolable and sacred'.[63]

---

[56] cf ibid art 106.
[57] Magna Carta of 1297, art 29.
[58] Human Rights Act of 1998, art 1(1).
[59] 1952 Protocol to the Convention for the Protection of Human Rights and Fundamental Freedoms, art 1(1).
[60] Constitution of France, art 55.
[61] cf Catherine Dupré, 'France' in Robert Blackburn and Jörg Polakiewicz (eds), *Fundamental Rights in Europe: The ECHR and Its Member States, 1950–2000* (OUP 2001).
[62] Constitution of France, preamble.
[63] Declaration of Human and Civic Rights of 26 August 1789, art 17.

However, expropriation may go ahead as of public necessity and against compensation.[64] The French Constitution itself provides a separate basis for the nationalization of companies.[65] The still-valid preamble to the older 1946 Constitution stipulates more specifically that property and enterprises which acquire the character of a public service or virtual monopoly become the property of society.[66] In the 1958 Constitution of France, security of property receives another mention in the context of obligations that may be imposed for purposes of national defence by subsequent legislation.[67]

In the US, property is guaranteed by the Fifth and Fourteenth Amendments, which provide that no one may be 'deprived of life, liberty, or property, without due process of law' and likewise prohibit that 'private property be taken for public use, without just compensation'.[68] The two clauses provide the indispensable material and procedural guarantees that sustain both the institution of private property itself and the political legitimacy of dealings between state and citizen where property is involved.[69] Of significance is the narrower scope of the latter amendment, deriving from the specific meaning of property 'taken' and excluding other forms of interference with property from compensatory liability.[70] 'Taking' is distinguished in particular from 'regulation' by its displacement of the previous owner from key legal positions in relation to the property; this entails a conception of property which sets the safeguards found in the US Constitution apart from those of the European orders considered here, where ownership is indivisible and compensation for acts approximating 'regulation' is accorded greater recognition.[71]

In Germany, private property is generally guaranteed[72] and its economic dimension highlighted by the extensive scope of the protection of property, understood to encompass many legal positions that typically sustain modern market transactions, such as outstanding debts, intellectual property, and even rights of first refusal.[73] As in France, the Basic Law is quick to add that limits will be imposed by subsequent legislation.[74] Somewhat ominously, the Basic Law itself stipulates that the owner of property shall be committed to use it to further the public good.[75] The Basic Law also contains a more express provision on expropriation, conditioning it on the public good and requiring an express basis in law and just compensation in view of all circumstances.[76]

Quite apart from cases that necessitate expropriation, the German Basic Law stands out among the orders considered here by its ambiguous stance on private property. In a noteworthy departure from the guarantees dispensed by the aforementioned provisions, the

---

[64] United States Constitution, Amend V and XIV s 1.

[65] Constitution of France, art 34(2).

[66] Constitution of 27 October 1946, preamble.

[67] Constitution of France, art 34(1).

[68] US Constitution, Amend V and XIV s 1; on their overlapping motivations, see J Nedelsky, *Private Property and the Limits of American Constitutionalism: The Madisonian Framework and Its Legacy* (University of Chicago Press 1990) 96–97; CR Sunstein, 'Constitutionalism and Secession' (1991) 58 University of Chicago Law Review 633, 639.

[69] CR Sunstein, 'On Property and Constitutionalism' (1993) 14 Cardozo Law Review 907, 923–24.

[70] T Allen, 'The Right to Property' in Tom Ginsburg and Rosalind Dixon (eds), *Comparative Constitutional Law* (Edward Elgar 2011) 507.

[71] ibid 508–09.

[72] German Basic Law, art 14(1).

[73] BVerfGE 83, 201.

[74] German Basic Law, art 14(1).

[75] ibid art 14(2).

[76] ibid art 14(3).

Basic Law's extant 'socialization clause' envisages an agenda of socialist nationalization of the forces of production.[77] This differs markedly in character from the acquisition of private property for a pressing public interest in cases where it cannot otherwise be obtained. Socialization implies a constitutional economic transformation of private productive assets into public property as part of a larger and ideologically driven process of 'overcoming' capitalism.[78] While the socialization clause of the Basic Law itself falls short of requiring socialization, it does empower the state to embark on such a course through its recognition of socialization as a legitimate purpose of later legislation.[79]

We thus find that the protection of property is granted rather uniformly across the four orders and is likewise open to expropriation against compensation as a last resort. The German Basic Law differs by qualifying the right to property rather more sharply, emphasizing the responsibilities of individual owners to the community and maintaining socialization as a potential state target.

3.6.2 Freedom of contract

Without freedom of contract, the play of market forces cannot develop properly; at the same time, if unrestrained, it can have adverse effects on individual welfare by perpetuating power asymmetries and causing problems for collective action.[80] Despite its apparently overwhelming economic relevance, freedom of contract does not feature very prominently in the constitutions under investigation here.

In the case-law of the United Kingdom, freedom of contract is simply recognized as a foundational principle in the common law.[81] The German Basic Law makes no express mention of the principle: freedom of contract was affirmed by the Federal Constitutional Court as flowing only from freedom of action as protected more generally.[82] The case of France is similar, with neither the Constitution nor other texts of constitutional rank specifically including freedom of contract among their enumerations of rights. Instead, this freedom finds concrete expression in the civil code, which allows contracts to be formed without any restraint that is not required by the public order.[83] Approximating the German variant more closely still, the French Constitutional Council reasoned that limitations on contracting capacity can contravene other guarantees as explicitly granted by the Constitution.[84] In a later decision, the Council derived contractual freedom from article 4 of the Declaration of Human and Civic Rights of 26 August 1789.[85] This protects in very general terms any behaviour that does not harm others.

The US Constitution takes a different approach. The Contract Clause does not so much protect the freedom to form contracts as recognize contracts that have indeed been formed.[86] While this has shifted the protection of creating contracts without undue

---

[77] ibid art 15.
[78] Badura (n 22) 273.
[79] ibid 274.
[80] Michael J Trebilcock, *The Limits of Freedom of Contract* (Harvard University Press 1997).
[81] cf *Printing and Numerical Registering Co v Sampson* [1875] 19 Eq 462.
[82] German Basic Law, art 2(1); BVerfGE 8, 274/328.
[83] Code Civil, art 1102.
[84] 97–388 DC, 31.
[85] 2000-47 DC, 190, 2006-535 DC, 50.
[86] US Constitution, art 1 s 10 cl 2; cf JW Ely, Jr, *The Contract Clause: A Constitutional History* (University Press of Kansas 2016) 189–90.

hindrance to judges who in turn derived it from due process guarantees,[87] the Contract Clause nonetheless protects an economically crucial interest in the stability of contractual relations. Yet, owing in part to the condensed style of the text, this fundamental guarantee appears only towards the end of a convoluted enumeration of other constitutional commands concerning international relations, minting and legal tender, and retroactive laws, and is followed only by an unrelated prohibition of the granting of noble titles.

All four orders tend to presuppose, rather than stipulate, freedom of contract as following from freedom of action more generally. Whereas judges have developed and entrenched the right, legislators have done more to limit it through consumer protection provisions[88] and specialized laws for guiding particular kinds of contractual relationship.[89]

3.6.3 Freedom of occupation and enterprise

Freedom of occupation leaves to individual private actors the decisions on how to invest their productive energies. It consequently reduces the planning capacity of economic policy-makers, who may well have an interest in channelling labour into particular sectors and regions at particular times—thus setting its price—and may be understood either as expressing faith in the individual to maximize overall economic gain through market-oriented choices or as prioritizing the fulfilment of individual aspirations over considerations of productivity.

The German Basic Law expressly provides for the right of the individual citizen to freely choose his or her occupation or training path;[90] corporate entities have a corresponding entitlement.[91] Foreign nationals do not automatically benefit from this protection, thus allowing the state to render migrant labour subject to permission and regulation. While the freedom to embark on an occupational path of choice is guaranteed, there is no promise that its economic viability will not be undermined by regular competition in the free market, which notably includes participation by actors from the state sector.[92]

In France, a right to employment is similarly part of the *bloc de constitutionnalité*.[93] The preamble to the 1946 Constitution, still valid as constitutional law, stipulates not only a right but notably also a duty to work, coupled with protections against discrimination in the workplace.[94] The US Constitution does not mention freedom of occupation. The Bill of Rights touches on the matter of work only with different thrust that responds to its historical context by stressing that slavery and involuntary labour shall generally not exist in the US.[95] However, observers have long noted the viability of and practical demand for developing judicial responses to modern occupational questions at the level of constitutional law.[96]

Freedom of enterprise broadly entails the right to conduct the affairs of one's professional ventures freely and without state direction. In Germany, such a right has been found to derive likewise from protected general freedom of action.[97] Private corporations are generally

---

[87] AF McEvoy, 'Freedom of Contact, Labor, and the Administrative State' in Harry N Scheiber (ed), *The State and Freedom of Contract* (Stanford University Press 1998) 212.
[88] Eg German Civil Code, ss 134, 138, 242, 305–10; Consumer Rights Act of 2015 (United Kingdom).
[89] Eg Sale of Goods Act of 1979 (United Kingdom).
[90] German Basic Law, art 12(1).
[91] ibid art 19(3).
[92] BVerfGE 98, 218/259; 105, 252/265.
[93] cf Constitution of France, preamble.
[94] Constitution of 27 October 1946, preamble.
[95] US Constitution, Amend XIII s 1.
[96] Fraley N Weidner, 'Freedom of Occupation' (1940) 25 The Marquette Law Review 8, 12.
[97] German Basic Law, art 2(1).

free to organize their material and human resources, decide on investments, and devise their own strategies in the market.[98] As for the US, its Constitution does not expressly mention freedom of enterprise. However, other rights and mechanisms it provides for contribute significantly to its realization, and the framers themselves were known to hold it in high regard as the basis of prosperity.[99] The Constitution of France likewise does not mention freedom of enterprise. Such a right was expressly confirmed by the French Constitutional Council only more recently to strike down as unconstitutional statutes that would interfere with staff dismissals and increase permit requirements.[100]

3.6.4 Freedom of association

Freedom of association has significant import for the political process in that it allows people to assemble publicly to present their grievances to power-holders with amplification through numbers, or privately to coordinate the pursuit of their interests. The same two mechanisms operate in the economic realm, in one respect as collective action in the form of workers' strikes that increase bargaining power vis-à-vis employers, and in another, as coordinated individual effort in cooperative ventures undertaken for greater economic gain. Constitutional doctrines that recognize freedom of association in its economic dimension tend to be relatively new, deriving from more general rules on the relations prevailing between state and citizen.

The Constitution of France makes specific mention of protected collective action, particularly in the private sector, through its link to the preamble of the Constitution of 1946. The latter expressly entitles citizens to pursue union action and freely join unions,[101] go on strike,[102] and engage in collective bargaining.[103] In the United Kingdom, freedom of association and assembly are granted expressly through the application of the ECHR, which likewise alludes to the economic context of association by granting an express right to form and join trade unions.[104]

In Germany, the Basic Law's guarantee of freedom of association[105] situates it less clearly in the context of private relations, though it has been understood to include specifically economic dimensions beyond the formation of unions, such as the freedom to form joint-stock and trading companies.[106] In the US, on the other hand, freedom of association is derived from the First Amendment, which recognizes a general 'right of the people peacefully to assemble'.[107] The remainder of the clause suggests the extent to which this right had been envisaged with the political citizen–state relationship in mind, with pronouncements on freedom of speech, of the press, and petitions to the government framing it on either side; however, no right to strike follows from the Constitution itself.

---

[98] Badura (n 22) 259.

[99] National Center for Constitutional Studies, 'Freedom of Individual Enterprise' (*Our Ageless Constitution*) <https://nccs.net/blogs/our-ageless-constitution/freedom-of-individual-enterprise> accessed 26 May 2019.

[100] cf Roger Errera, 'The Right of Property and Freedom of Enterprise in French Constitutional Law' (2009) Institute of Law and Public Policy 22 with further references.

[101] Constitution of 27 October 1946, preamble s 6.

[102] ibid s 7.

[103] ibid s 8.

[104] Human Rights Act of 1998, art 1(1); ECHR, art 11.

[105] German Basic Law, art 9(1).

[106] Badura (n 22) 276.

[107] US Constitution, Amend I.

A systematic reading thus shows that the French Constitution from the outset enshrined associative guarantees for distinctly economic purposes; the protections afforded only later by the ECHR in the United Kingdom have a similar thrust. By contrast, the First Amendment to the US Constitution and the German Basic Law emphasize only the political nature of free association, leaving it to the courts to clarify the applicability of this right between private actors.

3.7 The Social State

Several of the constitutions examined here characterize the state as 'social'. The term is used in a material sense to imply a more equitable distribution of goods, albeit without giving any immediate indication as to the extent of the change or the nature of the standards aspired to.

The French Constitution is a case in point, stipulating that France be a social Republic.[108] More specific in this regard than the operative clause in the 1958 Constitution is the still-applicable preamble to the 1946 Constitution, which prescribes that the state shall provide individuals and families with 'conditions necessary to their development', understood as 'health, material security, rest and leisure' as well as unemployment benefits.[109] In Germany, equitable distribution is likewise pursued under the label of the social justice dispensed by the *Sozialstaat*.[110] This task of the state is enshrined in the Constitution and protected from amendment by means of an eternity clause.[111] For the legislator, it produces a perpetual tension between economic liberties, on the one hand, and its fulfilment of its social mandate, on the other.[112] As for the United Kingdom, despite an extensive public welfare apparatus, there is no such foundational commitment anchored in the country's fundamental laws; instead, political and social factors preserve a broad spectrum of legislative choice.

In the US, the capacity or obligation of the state to order social affairs in the name of public welfare was not conclusively decided on during the constitutional drafting process—or at any moment thereafter. Largely free from constitutional constraints, governments and interest groups have engaged in debating and shaping the scope of state intervention for social ends as a matter of policy alone. Public support for public welfare measures has likewise waxed and waned in the course of the twentieth century, endorsing them only in the wake of acute crises.[113] Debates are thus framed as matters of economic and social expediency with little import from the more durable maxims of constitutional law.

We thus find the expected difference in approach between the US and western Europe. Whereas in the former the commitment to social welfare policies is unsteady and often minimal with no anchoring in lasting legal dicta, two out of three European nations surveyed here have elevated the social state model to constitutional rank.

---

[108] Constitution of France, art 1(1).
[109] Constitution of 27 October 1946, preamble, s 11.
[110] German Basic Law, arts 20(1) and 28(1).
[111] ibid art 79(3).
[112] Badura (n 22) 355.
[113] cf Georg Schild, 'Der Amerikanische "Wohlfahrtsstaat" von Roosevelt Bis Clinton' (1998) 46 Vierteljahrshefte für Zeitgeschichte 579.

3.8 State-Owned Enterprises

State-owned enterprises, both wholly owned by governments or listed for partial private ownership, still feature prominently on the world economic stage, accounting for one-fifth of world market capitalization.[114] Whereas some legal orders make constitutional arrangements for state-owned enterprises as the norm,[115] the question of public ownership is visibly relegated to more dynamic realms of legislation and governance in the systems considered here.

France looks back on a long tradition of state-led enterprise, although the practice only took on modern forms in the twentieth century.[116] Since then, France has seen both nationalization and privatization drives, as well as deliberate abstention from interfering in the public-private balance ('*ni privatisation, ni nationalisation*' or '*ni-ni*').[117] In Germany, state-owned enterprises exist in substantial numbers. However, privatization drives have been ongoing to unlock competition in further sectors and reduce the workload of the state.[118] This is based on domestic policy considerations. Despite the liberal ideals advocated by the EU, its laws place no immediate demands on states to privatize their assets.[119]

The US, on the other hand, is generally seen as being openly opposed to state ownership. Not one state-owned enterprise is currently listed for trading at US stock exchanges.[120] However, it has also been noted that a tradition of public ownership has not been alien to the US experience, especially during its earlier years, and that is has involved key entities such as the partially public First Bank of the US of 1791.[121] This was no isolated historical aberration; the eighteenth and nineteenth centuries would see the US government partake in joint ventures of finance and infrastructure.[122] The twentieth century saw the emergence of hybrid government-sponsored enterprises (GSEs) with largely formal ties to the state through appointment procedures that nonetheless fulfilled public tasks, such as Federal National Mortgage Association (Fannie Mae) and Federal Home Loan Mortgage Corporation (Freddie Mac).[123] In yet another shift in gear, the US government would bail out large corporations in the wake of the 2008 financial crisis through a large-scale purchase of shares.[124]

In the US, all of this went ahead unimpeded by constitutional constraints. Governments and legislators have brought about changes to the public-private balance as a matter of policy quite separate from constitutional law. The stances on state-owned enterprises taken

---

[114] 'China Buys up the World' *The Economist* (11 November 2011) <http://www.economist.com/leaders/2010/11/11/china-buys-up-the-world> accessed 30 November 2020.

[115] Eg Constitution of the People's Republic of China, art 6(1).

[116] Curtis J Milhaupt and Mariana Pargendler, 'Governance Challenges of Listed State-Owned Enterprises Around the World: National Experiences and a Framework for Reform' (2017) 50 Cornell International Law Journal 473, 480.

[117] ibid 481.

[118] Badura (n 22) 911.

[119] cf Treaty on the Functioning of the European Union, art 345.

[120] Milhaupt and Pargendler (n 116) 487.

[121] Mariana Pargendler, 'State Ownership and Corporate Governance' (2012) 80 Fordham Law Review 2917, 2927.

[122] Lloyd D Musolf, 'American Mixed Enterprise and Government Responsibility' (1971) 24 Western Political Quarterly 789.

[123] Milhaupt and Pargendler (n 116) 490.

[124] ibid 491.

by governments in the US and western Europe, though visibly different, are in all cases informed by political expedience. Constitutional law here is neither guide nor obstacle.

4. Country Perspectives

The previous section provided a description of the most notable constitutional devices that link constitutional law, ordinary legislation, and policy-making in the economic realm. It is important to note that in most respects, whether in isolation or in concert, they fall short of producing fully determinate outcomes. Instead, these provisions guide subsequent processes by raising the political costs of departures from economic ideals that constitutional interpretation had yielded until then. The following discussion frames the four constitutional orders in a more holistic manner that reflects on how they took broadly similar cues from their respective fundamental laws, disparities in form notwithstanding. In terms of substance, it is apparent that idiosyncrasies in the relevant constitutional law are not only few in number but have failed to translate into more starkly diverging policies.

4.1 United Kingdom

Constitutional law in the United Kingdom is commonly described as 'unwritten'. In the absence of a consolidated document that claims for itself the position atop the legal order, what amounts to the British Constitution is the sum of statutes, conventions, court decisions, and treaties, making 'uncodified' a perhaps more accurate characterization.[125] Another characteristic of this constitutional arrangement is the principle of parliamentary sovereignty, which does not generally acknowledge higher-order obstacles to its legislature composed of Lords, Commons, and Crown in the passage of acts. While enforceable individual guarantees existed in substance, they hardly appeared in the typical guise of a modern bill of rights before the passage of the 1998 Human Rights Act which directs courts towards the ECHR. However, given that review procedures are not 'strong', inasmuch as laws infringing upon ECHR guarantees are merely declared incompatible instead of nullified, it is unsurprising that some observers have come to regard the United Kingdom as protecting economically relevant rights without constitutional backing.[126]

In terms of substance, the British model of constitutional law and the economy lends credibility to the liberal rights hypothesis which identifies individual rights protecting property, contractual capacity, and legal certainty and predictability as conditions for economic growth.[127] No general level of state intervention is envisaged in the constitution and foundational guarantees of private property and associations are in place. Other freedoms, such as that of contract, are understood as so foundational that they scarcely merit mention.

---

[125] UCL Constitution Unit, 'What Is the UK Constitution?' <http://www.ucl.ac.uk/constitution-unit/what-uk-constitution/what-uk-constitution> accessed 15 May 2019; but see also T Gyorfi, 'The Supreme Court (House of Lords) of the United Kingdom' in András Jakab, Arthur Dyevre, and Giulio Itzcovich (eds), *Comparative Constitutional Reasoning* (Cambridge University Press 2017) 683.

[126] T Daintith, 'The Constitutional Protection of Economic Rights' (2004) 2 International Journal of Constitutional Law 56, 88; see also M Tushnet, 'The Rise of Weak-Form Judicial Review' in Tom Ginsburg and Rosalind Dixon (eds), *Comparative Constitutional Law* (Edward Elgar 2011).

[127] cf North and Weingast (n 8) 803.

In the tradition of English common law, freedom of contract has simply been presupposed, albeit that the twentieth century witnessed the emergence of countervailing trends.[128]

Economic mechanisms thus exist without codified constitutional guarantees of durability, allowing governments to respond with greater flexibility to the demands of their time and perpetuating a dynamic of incremental change. Formulation of coherent policy may in the future be hindered more by the 'quasi-federalism' currently taking shape in the United Kingdom.[129] Powers of not least economic relevance were continually devolved to regional bodies in Scotland, Wales, and Northern Ireland in a series of parliamentary acts. A reduced gravitational pull towards constitution-level economic dicta may be more acutely felt where such centrifugal tendencies prevail.

However, the consistently liberal ordering of the economy has not so far suffered from any lack of anchoring in higher law. Widely shared understandings, manifest in case-law, statute, and public opinion, are capable of reliably subjecting government policy to the same limitations and inertia that constitutions are expected to impose. It remains to be seen whether the departure from the EU will have significant repercussions at the intersection of constitutional law and the economy.

4.2 France

In France, governments are likewise free to deploy a wide range of economic approaches that would not be resisted by the existing constitutional framework, but relative to the United Kingdom, the framework includes a broader and codified set of devices that are expressive of tendencies relevant for economic ordering. It provides the building blocks of a liberal market economy with guarantees of property, freedom of contract, and right to work, but likewise evinces a legacy of more interventionist times. It was noted that the protection of private property not only allows for expropriation more generally but also makes specific arrangements for the nationalization of private monopolists.[130] The right to work is accompanied not least by a duty to do so.[131] Like Germany, France is constitutionally characterized as a 'social' state and enumerates particular benefits that the state is liable to provide.[132]

Apart from this, the French economy is largely independent of constitutional constraints. As the most unified of the four states, with neither federalism nor devolution dividing the Republic, economic policies can be pursued with firmness from the centre, which has resulted in alternating waves of nationalization and privatization. Today, France is more firmly than ever on the path of non-statist, liberal economic ordering, fully in line with the demands levelled at French governments by the EU. As a result, the cost of policy shifts is more likely to accrue at the European level rather than in the realm of domestic constitutional law.

---

[128] cf *Printing and Numerical Registering Co v Sampson* [1875] 19 Eq 462; JN Adams and R Brownsword, 'The Ideologies of Contract' (1987) 7 Legal Studies 205.

[129] cf M Goodwin, M Jones, and R Jones, 'Devolution, Constitutional Change and Economic Development: Explaining and Understanding the New Institutional Geographies of the British State' (2005) 39 Regional Studies 421, 422.

[130] Constitution of France, art 34(2).

[131] Constitution of 27 October 1946, preamble.

[132] Constitution of France, art 1(1); Constitution of 27 October 1946, preamble, s 11.

4.3 The United States

The US Constitution would appear to afford significant leeway to government policy, despite many historical arguments to the effect that the liberal tenets of Enlightenment-age economic thought were in fact accepted by the framers and likewise found their way into the constitutional text.[133] Lockean thought and the importance it accorded to safeguarding private property are often seen as having pervaded the intellectual climate of the time.[134]

While no formula in the US Constitution prescribes and labels its vision for the economy, the text does reflect a primacy of free trade and a pointed aversion to rent-seeking and monopolies. It provides only a limited number of public goods, and makes it the government's role to sustain the free flow of market operations amongst private actors. Relevant safeguards include the protection of private property and the protection of contracts,[135] as well as the aforementioned measures to inhibit economic obstacles that could spring from federalism.[136]

The US Constitution further eschews any pronouncements on wholly or partially state-owned enterprises. It has been argued that the general rejection of public ownership, deeply felt both in the early stages of the US and in the Cold War years, even then did not impede public participation in enterprise where momentary demands required it.

In terms of style, the US Constitution is often noted for its brevity, a feature reflecting its framing at a time before constitutions grew wordier. This manner of drafting opens up a broad spectrum of options for governments and legislators. No initiative to narrow their scope of action has succeeded in the economic realm where disputes of approach continue to play out as policy debates. For example, social policy in the US has not been shaped by demands made on governments by the Constitution, with governments thus free to pursue a stance on welfare provision that would be politically opportune or in alignment with their ideological convictions.

Of the four orders, the US most closely resembles the United Kingdom in the degree to which justifications for economic policy choices remain largely separate from the constitutional realm. Critical economic readings of the US Constitution have achieved popularity as well as attracted controversy.[137] The view of the courts may not be altogether accurately represented by the remark of Justice Holmes that 'a constitution is not intended to embody a particular economic theory'.[138] However, it does evince a conviction that the battle over economic policy plays out elsewhere. The constitutional text has not been a significant factor in determining state abstention or large-scale involvement. From the founding of the First Bank of the US to the major acquisitions of stocks in the wake of the 2008 financial crisis, economic needs were discussed and responded to without requiring much guidance or sanction of the Constitution. On the whole, while the liberal economic approach

---

[133] cf Isaac Kramnick, *Republicanism and Bourgeois Radicalism: Political Ideology in Late Eighteenth-Century England and America* (Cornell University Press 1990) 289; Kermit L Hall and Peter Karsten, *The Magic Mirror: Law in American History* (OUP 2009) 72.

[134] cf James W Ely, *The Guardian of Every Other Right: A Constitutional History of Property Rights* (OUP 2008) 42–43.

[135] US Constitution, art 1 s 10 cl 1.

[136] ibid art 3 s 3, art 1 s 8 cl 3.

[137] See eg CA Beard, *An Economic Interpretation of the Constitution of the United States* (Macmillan 1913).

[138] *Lochner v New York* [1905] 198 US 45.

can be plausibly discerned from the Constitution, the spectrum of permissible policy remains wide.

4.4 Germany

The German Basic Law, unlike its predecessor, the Weimar Constitution, does not contain a dedicated chapter on the economic order.[139] Nevertheless, the makers of law and policy in Germany must observe constitutional dicta on federalism, the *Sozialstaat*, balance of payments,[140] and individual rights of economic import.[141] Further pointers to the envisaged economic order can be discerned from the foundational 1990 Treaty Establishing a Monetary, Economic, and Social Union.[142] The continuing economic integration of Europe spells an end to the remains of formal constitutional neutrality on economic matters: it is a potent bulwark of free market principles and unhindered competition.[143] In the context of this survey, the German model is distinguished by its relatively high demands of the state in pursuing *Ordnungspolitik*.

The degree to which the Basic Law enshrines specificities of policy in enduring, fundamental dicta attests to a remarkable conviction of the correctness and sustainability of its economic assumptions. This is striking with regard to the creation of a social state, which enjoys protection from constitutional amendment by virtue of an eternity clause,[144] thus putting the state under some pressure to perform economically so that meaningful sums can go towards constitutional redistributive commitments as they have come to be understood.

The specificity of the Basic Law's economically relevant provisions stands out particularly when compared with the other orders surveyed here, but begging the question how to correct conceivable flaws in its tenets and how to accommodate future postulates of economic orthodoxy. The answer would seem to lie in amendments, which have indeed not been infrequent—the more pronounced economic dimension of the Basic Law does much to render it more malleable. Moreover, while being actively committed to promoting a united Europe[145] and open the German legal order to European influence,[146] the Basic Law speaks back to Europe by requiring that the European Central Bank be independent and committed to price stability.[147]

For the time being, the ambitions and values of the Basic Law appear justified by economic performance, the provision of welfare continues without impediment, and the EU, for its part, is wary of the preferences of its economically most powerful member state.[148]

---

[139] cf Weimar Constitution, art 151–65.
[140] cf German Basic Law, art 109(2).
[141] Badura (n 22) 279.
[142] 1990 Treaty Establishing a Monetary, Economic and Social Union; see also Badura (n 22) 279.
[143] Badura (n 22) 279–80.
[144] German Basic Law, art 79(3).
[145] ibid art 23(1).
[146] ibid art 24(1).
[147] ibid art 88.
[148] C Joerges, 'Europe's Economic Constitution in Crisis and the Emergence of a New Constitutional Constellation' (2014) 15 German Law Journal 985, 1004.

4.5 EU Economic and Monetary Policy

Pursuant to reforms introduced by the Maastricht Treaty, the EU assumed the mandate of monetary policy among the euro states.[149] Economic and fiscal policy-making remains the preserve of the Union's member states, although they are formally called to coordinate their decisions and adhere to competitive open market principles.[150]

In fact, EU law itself provides a whole set of principles to guide economic policy. For instance, the Treaty on the Functioning of the European Union under Title VIII ('Economic and Monetary Policy') stipulates that the economic policies of members states be adopted in close cooperation while nonetheless requiring that the general outcome of such deliberation align 'with the principle of an open market economy with free competition'[151] and the principles of 'stable prices, sound public finances and monetary conditions and a sustainable balance of payments'.[152] The efficacy of such stipulations is in question, leading some observers to doubt that effective coordination would ever take place and likewise to caution against the destabilizing effects of separating monetary from larger economic policy and the displacement of hard law by executive governance.[153]

5. Conclusion

Constitutions are intended as economic documents, whether expressly or implicitly. This chapter has shown the constitutional devices working towards converging economic ideals in France, the United Kingdom, the US, and Germany. Few disparities emerge in the kind of ordering that these states envisage as sustaining their polity. Driven not least by the liberal underpinnings of the EU, the three European states have emerged as free market-driven economic orders with only reluctant state interference. The US draws on an even longer and more sustained history of economic liberalism, despite episodic pursuits of welfare policies based on the socio-political challenges of the day and the ebb and flow of popular support. The US Constitution is commonly portrayed as firmly rooted in Enlightenment-age economic thought based on free trade unimpeded either by customs or by monopolies and a tendentially minimal state.

At the margins of the four orders remain idiosyncrasies in substance. The French Constitution hands down not only a right but also a duty to work,[154] while the German Basic Law circumscribes the right to property, subjecting it to expropriation and demanding that its use benefit the community.[155] Still more curious for what is in effect a liberal order is the Basic Law's socialization clause,[156] which could be relied upon to legitimize the nationalization of the means of production without immediate need and which hence, if not requiring it, certainly permits the state to impinge on private capitalist ventures.

---

[149] Treaty on the Functioning of the European Union, art 3(1)(c).
[150] ibid art 119(1).
[151] ibid.
[152] ibid art 119(3).
[153] cf Joerges (n 148).
[154] Constitution of 27 October 1946, preamble.
[155] German Basic Law, art 14.
[156] ibid art 15.

Striking disparities emerge in the degree to which economic tenets are either enshrined in durable constitutional documents or left to legislatures, governments, and courts to determine based on expediency. In this respect, there is no correlation of form and substance. Concise constitutions may yet reflect important assumptions of economic ordering, as in the US; more expansive constitutions may do the same, though with differences in substance, as in Germany—or open up space for both étatism and liberal economics according to policy choice, as in France.

The US Constitution, despite its relative brevity, makes available a significant repertoire of devices which can be used to shore up liberal economic policies. The examples of the Commerce Clause and Interstate and Alien Diversity Clause illustrate the liberal tendencies to which governments have proven very receptive. These principles must now be regarded as deeply entrenched. The much lengthier French Constitution of 1958 and the other documents that form the *bloc de constitutionnalité* do not inform economic policy to the same degree. They generally permit both governmental interference and abstention therefrom based on political and economic convenience. At the same time, they include the familiar armoury of liberal economics, such as enumerations of rights that strengthen and predictably motivate individuals inclined toward market-based pursuits. More recently, restraints on French étatism have been imposed by the growing influence of EU law and its liberal economic precepts.[157]

The United Kingdom and the supremacy of its parliament reflect the possibility of achieving high levels of economic performance based on faith in enforceable rights and restraint of the state as well as institutionalizing the security of social welfare without compact enshrinement in higher law. This affords ample space for policy-making. The departure of the United Kingdom from the EU may bring with it a disentanglement from its economic ideals as restraints to policy-making are loosened. Meanwhile, coherence may be challenged by the increasing devolution of economic governance to the various regions.

The German Basic Law is rich in both words and economic dicta. However, beyond the earlier examples of anti-capitalist remnants and its general leaning towards the common weal, there remains the question of the extent to which policy-makers will find themselves constrained by the word of the law. While both the Basic Law and EU law evince great confidence that liberal fundamentals will continue to bolster the success of the German social market economy, this reading is premised on the current levels of economic performance.

At a broader level, this is true for all four orders. As national economies are subjected to the waxing and waning of global market forces, national constitutional commitments might come to mean little when flexibility is key. Just as the EU's principled economic approach sits uneasily with extra-legal measures,[158] national governments may come to seek similar relief from once-hallowed readings of constitutional maxims. Given the questionable import of durably codified principles for economic growth, not to mention the creativity of policy-makers in exploiting the level of abstraction that is characteristic of constitutional law, constitutions that limit their scope by not subscribing to particular economic theories may in the long run render a greater service to the credibility and success of constitutionalism as such.

---

[157] cf Treaty on the Functioning of the European Union, Title VIII.
[158] Joerges (n 148) 991.

Bibliography

'China Buys up the World' *The Economist* (11 November 2011) <http:// www.economist.com/leaders/ 2010/11/11/china-buys-up-the-world> accessed 30 November 2020

Adams JN and Brownsword R, 'The Ideologies of Contract' (1987) 7 Legal Studies 205

Allen T, 'The Right to Property' in Ginsburg T and Dixon R (eds), *Comparative Constitutional Law* (Edward Elgar 2011)

Badura P, *Staatsrecht: Systematische Erläuterung des Grundgesetzes* (5th edn, CH Beck 2012)

Basta Fleiner LR and Gaudreault-DesBiens J-F, 'Federalism and Autonomy' in Tushnet M, Fleiner T, and Saunders C (eds), *Routledge Handbook of Constitutional Law* (Routledge 2013)

Beard CA, *An Economic Interpretation of the Constitution of the United States* (Macmillan 1913)

Coenen DT, 'Business Subsidies and the Dormant Commerce Clause' (1998) 107 Yale Law Journal 965

Daintith T, 'The Constitutional Protection of Economic Rights' (2004) 2 International Journal of Constitutional Law 56

Dixon R and Ginsburg T, 'Constitutions as Political Insurance: Variants and Limits' in Delaney E and Dixon R (eds), *Comparative Judicial Review* (Edward Elgar 2018)

Dowdle M, 'Of "Socialism" and "Socialist" Legal Transformations in China and Vietnam' in Gillespie J and Nicholson P (eds), *Asian Socialism and Legal Change: The Dynamics of Vietnamese and Chinese Reform* (Asia Pacific Press 2005)

Dupré C, 'France' in Blackburn R and Polakiewicz J (eds), *Fundamental Rights in Europe: The ECHR and Its Member States, 1950–2000* (OUP 2001)

Elster J, 'The Impact of Constitutions on Economic Performance' (1994) 8 The World Bank Economic Review 209

Ely Jr JW, *The Guardian of Every Other Right: A Constitutional History of Property Rights* (OUP 2008)

Ely Jr JW, 'The Constitution and Economic Liberty' (2012) 35 Harvard Journal of Law & Public Policy 27

Ely Jr JW, *The Contract Clause: A Constitutional History* (University Press of Kansas 2016)

Erhard L, *Wohlstand für Alle* (8th edn, Econ-Verlag 1964)

Errera R, 'The Right of Property and Freedom of Enterprise in French Constitutional Law' (2009) Institute of Law and Public Policy 22

Goodwin M, Jones M, and Jones R, 'Devolution, Constitutional Change and Economic Development: Explaining and Understanding the New Institutional Geographies of the British State' (2005) 39 Regional Studies 421

Gyorfi T, 'The Supreme Court (House of Lords) of the United Kingdom' in Jakab A, Dyevre A, and Itzcovich G (eds), *Comparative Constitutional Reasoning* (Cambridge University Press 2017)

Hall KL and Karsten P, *The Magic Mirror: Law in American History* (OUP 2009)

Hirschl R, 'The Judicialization of Politics' in Whittington KE, Kelemen DR, and Caldeira GA (eds), *The Oxford Handbook of Law and Politics* (OUP 2008)

Hirschl R, *Towards Juristocracy: The Origins and Consequences of the New Constitutionalism* (Harvard University Press 2009)

Ip EC, 'The Constitution of Economic Liberty in Hong Kong' (2015) 26 Constitutional Political Economy 307

Joerges C, 'Europe's Economic Constitution in Crisis and the Emergence of a New Constitutional Constellation' (2014) 15 German Law Journal 985

Kramnick I, *Republicanism and Bourgeois Radicalism: Political Ideology in Late Eighteenth-Century England and America* (Cornell University Press 1990)

Lerner RL, 'Enlightenment Economics and the Framing of the U.S. Constitution' (2012) 35 Harvard Journal of Law & Public Policy 1

McEvoy AF, 'Freedom of Contact, Labor, and the Administrative State' in Scheiber HN (ed), *The State and Freedom of Contract* (Stanford University Press 1998)

Milhaupt CJ and Pargendler M, 'Governance Challenges of Listed State-Owned Enterprises Around the World: National Experiences and a Framework for Reform' (2017) 50 Cornell International Law Journal 473

National Center for Constitutional Studies, 'Freedom of Individual Enterprise' *Our Ageless Constitution* <https://nccs.net/blogs/our-ageless-constitution/freedom-of-individual-enterprise> accessed 26 May 2019

Nedelsky J, *Private Property and the Limits of American Constitutionalism: The Madisonian Framework and Its Legacy* (University of Chicago Press 1990)

North DC and Weingast BR, 'Constitutions and Commitment: The Evolution of Institutions Governing Public Choice in Seventeenth-Century England' (1989) 49 The Journal of Economic History 803

North DC, Summerhill W, and Weingast BR, 'Order, Disorder, and Economic Change: Latin America Versus North America' in de Mesquita BB and Root HL (eds), *Governing for Prosperity* (Yale University Press 2000)

Petrie F, 'The Contracts Clause and the Constitutionality of a Model Law Approach to Sovereign Debt Restructuring' (2017) 19 Journal of Constitutional Law 1207

Posner RA, 'Creating a Legal Framework for Economic Development' (1998) 13 The World Bank Research Observer 1

Sandford M and Gormley-Heenan C, ' "Taking Back Control", the UK's Constitutional Narrative and Schrodinger's Devolution' (2020) 73 Parliamentary Affairs 108

Sbragia AM, 'American Federalism and Intergovernmental Institutions' in Rhodes RAW, Binder S, and Rockman B (eds), *The Oxford Handbook of Political Institutions* (OUP 2006)

Schild G, 'Der Amerikanische "Wohlfahrtsstaat" von Roosevelt Bis Clinton' (1998) 46 Vierteljahrshefte für Zeitgeschichte 579

Sunstein CR, 'Constitutionalism and Secession' (1991) 58 University of Chicago Law Review 633

Sunstein CR, 'On Property and Constitutionalism' (1993) 14 Cardozo Law Review 907

Trebilcock MJ, *The Limits of Freedom of Contract* (Harvard University Press 1997)

Tushnet M, 'The Rise of Weak-Form Judicial Review' in Ginsburg T and Dixon R (eds), *Comparative Constitutional Law* (Edward Elgar 2011)

UCL Constitution Unit, 'What Is the UK Constitution?' <http://www.ucl.ac.uk/constitution-unit/what-uk-constitution/what-uk-constitution> accessed 15 May 2019

Weidner FN, 'Freedom of Occupation' (1940) 25 The Marquette Law Review 8

Xi C, 'Transforming Chinese Enterprises: Ideology, Efficiency and Instrumentalism in the Process of Reform' in Gillespie J and Nicholson P (eds), *Asian Socialism and Legal Change: The Dynamics of Vietnamese and Chinese Reform* (Asia Pacific Press 2005)

PART II
CONSTITUTIONALIZING A MARKET ECONOMY

4

Comparative Overview of Measures and Devices to Shape the Economy in Some Modern African Constitutions

Charles M Fombad

1. Introduction

Most studies of the profound constitutional renewal Africa has undergone in the past three decades have focused on its political dimensions. Although this is unsurprising, given that the dictatorships that emerged after independence in the 1960s restricted ordinary citizens' civil and political rights, the result is that little attention is paid to the economic aspects of the revised constitutions. It was, however, not only a lack of political participation that made protesters take to the streets in the 1990s. They were also motivated by an economic crisis afflicting most of the continent, one that was caused in large part by corruption, mismanagement, and bad governance and that saw rising poverty and unemployment, a widening gap between the ruling elites and the masses, and the collapse of health care and basic education. They were thus demanding not only political rights but also freedom from poverty, prosperity, and economic security.

The purpose of this chapter is hence to provide an overview of the economic doctrines, principles, measures, and devices that have been incorporated, explicitly or implicitly, in modern African constitutions to guide government action and promote development. In so doing, the chapter considers how these 'economic constitutions' pave the way for consolidating constitutionalism and respect for the rule of law.

As Steytler points out in Chapter 1, in the immediate post-independence period during the Cold War, African countries flirted with a range of economic models, the main ones being the free market, the socialist or command model, and the mixed economic model, and gave them constitutional expression in various ways. Regarding the new generation of constitutions, the critical issue is whether they introduced effective principles, measures, and devices for addressing present and future economic challenges. In other words, do modern African constitutions provide an economic framework for shaping and directing national policies in such a manner that their implementation facilitates economic development through wealth creation and sharing and ensures proper management of the economic lives and well-being of all citizens rather than a privileged elite?

An economic constitution entails that a rule-based approach is taken to economic policy. Such a constitution establishes a framework that seeks to guide government action and ensure that the government's management of the economy not only promotes growth and development but protects the country's economic and political sovereignty. Indeed, in the last

Charles M Fombad, *Comparative Overview of Measures and Devices to Shape the Economy in Some Modern African Constitutions*
In: *Constitutionalism and the Economy in Africa*. Edited by: Charles M Fombad and Nico Steytler, Oxford University Press. © Charles M Fombad
2022. DOI: 10.1093/oso/9780192886439.003.0006

few years there have been numerous reports about the risk that various African countries face of losing their sovereignty over strategic national assets—including land, mineral resources, and state-owned enterprises (SOEs) such as their national broadcasters and power utilities—due to predatory debt linked to infrastructure.[1]

For many an African country, one of the biggest dangers to sovereignty is the threat of the capture, control, and possible perpetual ownership of strategic national assets.[2] In looking at the manner in which the economy is covered in modern African constitutions, a number of key questions arise. Do these constitutions mark a break from the post-independence constitutions that were easily distorted to create a large gap between the 'haves' and the 'have nots', and left few avenues for accountability and for the voice of the ordinary citizens to be heard? Are the constitutions able to deal with the increasing risk of debt distress associated with the debt-trap diplomacy of certain foreign countries, such as China's Belt Road Initiative (BRI),[3] and prevent predatory foreign investments and loan agreements becoming a form of state capture and recolonization? In short, do these constitutions protect the economic and political sovereignty of African countries?

In pursuit of answers, this chapter undertakes a comparative examination of the economic constitutions of selected African countries, the aim being to obtain an overview of the degree to which the constitutional recognition and protection of core economic principles shape contemporary African practice. The choice of countries for purposes of illustrating contemporary trends takes into account the variety of constitutional traditions in Africa, as well as other factors such as differences in post-colonial historical and political evolution, the extent of a country's endowment of natural resources, its geographical location, and its population size and diversity. Accordingly, the focus is on the following ten countries: Angola, Benin, Botswana, Cameroon, Ghana, Mozambique, Niger, Nigeria, South Africa, and Tunisia.

Angola and Mozambique afford examples of the approach taken in two lusophone countries that have civilian-style constitutions and which, prior to the 1990s, were self-proclaimed Marxist-Leninist states. Benin, Cameroon, and Gabon are francophone countries that have also adopted civilian-style constitutions based on the 1958 Gaullist constitution of France's Fifth Republic. More specifically, Benin is an example of a country with a progressive Gaullist constitutional model, whilst Cameroon is an example of a typical conservative model; the Gabonese Constitution sits somewhere between the two extremes.

Turning to anglophone Africa, four countries have been selected. The first is Botswana, which (apart from Mauritius) is the only country still operating under its independence constitution, based on the so-called Westminster constitutions that the British designed in Whitehall for their former colonies. Ghana adopted a revised form of this British constitutional model in 1992, as did Nigeria in 1999. South Africa, however, is the country with the

---

[1] See eg 'China to Take over ZESCO—Africa Confidential' <https://bit.ly/2oMtTXy> accessed July 2019. According to this report, due to default in the payment of its debts, the Zambian state-owned television and radio news channel ZNBC is now run by a Chinese-owned company. The Zambian electricity company ZESCO is in talks about a takeover by another Chinese company. Similar events are happening in many other African countries. See further AM Larrarte and G Claudio-Quiroga, 'The DRC and China's Sicomines: Why Future Deals Should be Different' <https://bit.ly/2yI4piQ> accessed 1 July 2019.

[2] For detailed discussion, see M Meirotti and G Masterson, 'State Capture in Africa: Old Threats, New Packaging?' <www.eisa.org.za/pdf/sym2017papers.pdf> accessed 1 July 2019. See also Adem Abebe in Chapter 13 of this volume.

[3] See 'African Countries at Highest Risk of Debt Distress: EXX Africa Exclusive' <https://bit.ly/2M5ri8G> accessed 1 July 2019.

most modern constitution on the continent and has significantly influenced the Kenyan and Zimbabwean constitutions of 2010 and 2013, respectively. Finally, Tunisia also has a civilian-style constitution and illustrates to some extent the approach of northern African Arab constitutions.

Taken as whole, a textual analysis of the constitutions of these ten countries can provide an indication of the state of the economic constitution in African practice.[4] This is subject, though, to three caveats. First, the non-implementation of constitutions is a serious problem and one the post-1990 reforms failed to address, barring a timid effort by Kenya's Constitution of 2010.[5] By implication, few of the progressive provisions in Africa's revised constitutions have been implemented fully. There is thus no guarantee that the entrenchment of sound economic principles and measures in a constitution will translate into change on the ground.[6]

Secondly, while constitutional entrenchment of this kind is desirable for the purposes of policy certainty and predictability in government action, its absence does not necessarily mean that the relevant principles and measures are not present at all, seeing as they may well be introduced through ordinary legislation. In jurisdictions where the rule of law is strictly respected, such legislation can make up for a lack of constitutional entrenchment; however, in those jurisdictions where there is little respect for it—the case in many African states—the adoption of sound economic principles in ordinary legislation is no guarantee that these principles will be implemented.[7]

Thirdly, as we will see, in this era of globalization and regional integration, many important economic principles, such as those regulating transnational trade and investment, have their source outside the constitution itself.[8] These raise issues of transnational economic constitutionalism that have a significant impact on the way national economic constitutions operate.

The discussion proceeds in section 2 with a comparative analysis of the types and levels of economic rights recognized and protected in the various constitutions. The objective is to assess the scope of economic rights protection. In section 3 we look at the role of institutions for economic management and consider whether the relevant provisions are strong enough to promote proper economic management. In section 4, the focus is on the interplay between the constitution, the economy, and constitutionalism. It is shown that there is close interdependence between the measures and mechanisms designed to promote a sound economic constitution and those that promote constitutionalism, respect for the rule of law, and good governance. The chapter ends by suggesting some ways in which constitutionalism in general and economic constitutionalism in particular can be promoted to protect a country's economic and political sovereignty as well as its ability to pursue economic growth and development.

---

[4] It should be noted that although the year-date supplied with a constitution indicates the year it was adopted as a new or substantially revised document; this study uses only its latest amendments.

[5] Kenya's Constitution sought to address this but by using what proved to be a short-lived commission. The latter accomplished much during its five-year lifespan, but became a victim of its own success when Parliament refused to extend its mandate. See in general CM Fombad (ed), *The Implementation of Modern African Constitutions: Challenges and Prospects* (PULP 2016).

[6] ibid.

[7] For the state of the rule of law in Africa, see CM Fombad, 'An Overview of the Crisis of the Rule of Law in Africa' (2018) 18(1) African Human Rights Law Journal 213.

[8] See Terence Daintith, 'The Constitutional Protection of Economic Rights' (2004) 2(1) I.CON 66.

2. Types and Levels of Economic Rights Recognized and Protected

There is no general agreement on the exact meaning of the concept of the economic consti-tution, nor on its constitutive elements.[9] Nevertheless, in a broad sense, one can say that the structural elements of the economic constitution consist of laws, policies, and institutional arrangements designed to regulate economic activity in the country.[10] As Linck notes, what are at issue are the constitutional and other legal norms and rules on the basis of which the state defines the scope of economic freedoms and conducts monitoring or economic regulation.[11]

This section examines the types of economic rights that are recognized and protected and the level of protection which is provided. The aim is to determine how the constitu-tions selected for study recognize and protect economic interests to ensure that all citi-zens benefit rather than just a privileged minority. From this perspective, the comparative textual analysis of the constitutions engages with five main rights or clusters of rights that can be considered as expressive of the economic orientation of the constitution: property rights; freedom of enterprise; consumer protection; the right to work and workers' rights; and control of national assets and resources.

Before we proceed, an initial point needs to be made. In a sense, all the rights recognized and protected in the constitution, particularly in the bill of rights, have a bearing on the economic interests of individuals and groups in the society concerned. For example, the violation of the prohibition against discrimination may result in a person losing his job be-cause of his race or even in his being denied an opportunity to work and earn a living for this same reason. Be that as it may, our focus here is on those constitutional provisions dealing strictly with economic relations as distinct from civil, social, and political relations. Although socio-economic rights are also not covered in this discussion, it is worthwhile pointing out that these are now incorporated in most modern African constitutions and have become a key aspect of the modern economic constitution.[12]

A second point to note is that not all economic rights are stated in the constitution. For example, most constitutions hardly mention the freedom of contract, albeit that it is gen-erally understood as the 'building block of the market economy'; in this regard, it has been argued that the framers of a constitution, by recognizing the right to property and freedom of enterprise, necessarily recognize the freedom of contract.[13]

---

[9] For some of these divergent views, see Franz Böhm, 'Rule of Law in a Market Economy' in Alan Peacock and Hans Willgerodt (eds), *Germany's Social Market Economy: Origins and Evolution* (Macmillan 1989); Knut Wolfgang Nörr, 'On the Concept of the "Economic Constitution" and the Importance of Franz Böhm from the Viewpoint of Legal History' (1996) European Journal of Law and Economics 345; Knut Wolfgang Nörr, ' "Economic Constitution": On the Roots of a Legal Concept' (1994) 11(1) Journal of Law and Religion 343; and T Prosser, *The Economic Constitution* (OUP 2014).

[10] RA Posner, 'The Constitution as an Economic Document' (1987) 56 George Washington Law Review 4–5 suggests that no fewer than eight distinct, and sometimes overlapping, issues are associated with the economic constitution. See also Prosser (n 9) 7–11.

[11] Cited in L Jingkun, 'The Development of European Economic Constitution and Its Roles in Regulating the Common Market—with Free Competition and Free Movements as an Example' (2007) 1(21) Working Paper Series on European Studies, Institute of European Studies, Chinese Academy of Social Sciences, 1 <http://ies.cass. cn/webpic/web/ies2/en/UploadFiles_8765/201209/2012092508352997.pdf> accessed 1 July 2019.

[12] For some of the prodigious literature on socio-economic rights, see eg John Mubangizi, 'The Constitutional Protection of Socio-Economic Rights in Selected African Countries: A Comparative Evaluation' (2006) 2(1) African Journal of Legal Studies 1; Sandra Freedman and Meghan Campbell, *Social and Economic Rights and Constitutional Law* (Edward Elgar 2016); Sandra Liebenberg, *Socio-Economic Rights: Adjudication under a Transformative Constitution* (Juta 2010).

[13] Daintith (n 8) 64.

2.1 Economic Orientation of the Constitutions

In considering the economic orientation of modern African constitutions, a brief excursus is necessary for historical context. On gaining independence, many African countries either adopted constitutions declaring the state to be socialist[14] or, following military coups, adopted socialism or, in some instances, 'African socialism'.[15] For example, after seizing power in 1968, the Congolese military regime of Marien Ngouabi adopted a new constitution in 1969, article 35 of which promised a transformed society built upon 'scientific socialism, basing its thoughts and actions upon Marxism-Leninism'.

Mathieu Kérékou took a similar ideological line when he assumed power in Dahomey in 1972, underscoring this by changing the name of the country to the People's Republic of Benin. In Ghana, Kwame Nkrumah, regarded as 'the father of African socialism', exhorted fellow African leaders to reject as imperialist dogma the idea that '[W]estern democracy and the parliamentary system are the only valid ways of governing; [and] that capitalism, free enterprise, free competition, etc. are the only economic systems capable of promoting development'.[16] Drawing on African tradition, Julius Nyerere of Tanzania instituted his own version of socialism, called *Ujamaa*,[17] while in Zambia, Kenneth Kaunda called his version 'humanism'.

At one stage or another, numerous other African countries adhered to Marxism-Leninism or scientific socialism, whether superficially or authentically.[18] A critical examination of their constitutions nevertheless reveals a confused, sometimes contradictory mix of economic approaches made up of ideas borrowed from liberalism and collectivism as well as western European and Soviet constitutionalism.[19] As such, some authors argue that support for socialism had more to do with populism than adherence to orthodox socialism.[20] As Ottaway puts it, '[T]he choice of socialism [was] not based on a rational analysis of costs and benefits or on a strict evaluation of the probability of success ...'. Conversely, most of the countries that did not adopt socialism were silent on the economic orientation of the constitution.

During the 1990s, then, Africa's abandonment of socialism after the collapse of the Berlin Wall was made easy by the fact that in many countries its adoption had been more symbolic than substantive.[21] In spite of the continent's traditional communitarian approach to life, the core principles of Marxist-Leninism had never penetrated deeply and could be

---

[14] All the former Portuguese colonies (Angola, Cape Verde, Guinea-Bissau, Mozambique, and São Tomé) adopted independence constitutions that were influenced by socialist ideologies. The same is true of Algeria. What these countries share is a common history of bloody resistance, as a result of which they gained independence only through protracted violent conflict in which they benefited from the military support of former Eastern Bloc countries, notably the Union of Soviet Socialist Republics. See further S Onésimo, *Africa South of the Sahara: Party Systems and Ideologies of Socialism* (Rabén & Sjögren 1976).

[15] President Nyerere of Tanzania was one of the foremost promoters of 'African socialism', a vision he shared with others such as Leopold Sedar Senghor, the former president of Senegal.

[16] Quoted in George BN Ayittey, 'The End of African Socialism?' <http://www.heritage.org/africa/report/the-end-african-socialism> accessed 1 July 2019.

[17] This was the name of a socialist system of village cooperatives based on the principles of self-help and equality that Nyerere established in the 1960s.

[18] Eg Egypt, Guinea, Mali, Togo, and Seychelles.

[19] See Filip Reyntjens, 'Recent Developments in the Public Law of Francophone African States' (1986) 30(2) Journal of African Law 87.

[20] ibid 84–87.

[21] See Marina S Ottaway, 'The Crisis of the Socialist State in Africa' in Zaki Ergas (ed), *The African State in Transition* (Palgrave Macmillan 1987).

discarded at the least opportunity. Socialism, moreover, had led only to near economic collapse, political chaos, and institutional and social decay.

It was against this background of socialist experimentation and ensuing economic crisis that the new generation of post-1990 constitutions were crafted and need to be understood. Generally, the constitutions differ from each other in terms of whether the country's economic orientation is stated explicitly or implicitly. An analysis of the diverse approaches they take brings to light a number of trends and patterns.

In the case of the anglophone countries, the 1966 Botswana Constitution is silent on the general economic orientation of the government, whilst the pro-market orientation of the South African Constitution of 1996 is implicit in the provisions in chapter 2, sections 7–39 on the bill of rights and in chapter 13, sections 213–30, which deal with general financial matters. Botswana's approach is typical of the independence constitutions the British prepared for their former colonies, whereas the South African approach reflects a modern trend which has been replicated in many progressive anglophone constitutions, such as the Kenyan and Zimbabwean constitutions of 2010 and 2013, respectively.[22] By contrast, both Ghana and Nigeria take a different approach: the economic model is spelt out in elaborate provisions that define the economic objectives of the state in a chapter containing the directive principles of state policy.[23] Subject to what is said below about the status of these principles, the provisions usually require the government, inter alia, to foster an enabling environment for the private sector to play a pronounced role in the economy.[24]

As regards constitutions in francophone Africa, unlike in recent progressive anglophone ones, very few provisions deal with the country's economic orientation and, when they do, usually only in a vague and indirect manner. This is true not only of countries which, like Benin, have gone some way in modernizing their inherited Fifth French Republic Constitution of 1958, but also of those which, like Cameroon and Gabon, retained this constitutional model in more or less its original, fairly ineffective form. These constitutions provide for an economic and social council, an institution which, depending on the scope of powers conferred upon it, is usually indicative of a pro-market orientation.[25]

Angola and Mozambique, previously socialist regimes par excellence, take a distinctive approach. Unlike other civilian-style constitutions, they have elaborate provisions setting out the economic orientation and policies to be adopted by the government.[26] Whilst many provisions in these two constitutions are a legacy of the recent socialist past,[27] the economic

---

[22] In Kenya, this is covered by ch 4, arts 19–59, which deal with the bill of rights, and ch 12, arts 201–31, dealing with public finance. In Zimbabwe, this appears in ch 4, ss 44–87 of the Bill of Rights, and ch 17, ss 298–317, dealing with finance.

[23] See ch 6, art 36 of Ghana's Constitution of 1992 and ch 2, s 16 of Nigeria's Constitution of 1999.

[24] See eg Ghana's Constitution of 1992, in particular ch 5, arts 12–33 on the Bill of Rights, and ch 6, arts 34–41 on the directive principles of state policy, especially art 36; see also Nigeria's Constitution of 1999, in particular ch 4, ss 33–46, especially s 16.

[25] See eg arts 139–40 of the 1990 Benin Constitution, art 54 of the Cameroon Constitution of 1996, arts 94–102 of Gabon's Constitution of 1991, and arts 146–55 of Niger's Constitution of 2010. These economic and social councils are supposed to, inter alia, advise the government on economic and social policies but it is doubtful whether they ever do this.

[26] In the Angolan Constitution of 2010, see title III, arts 89–104, on economic, financial, and fiscal organization; in Mozambique's Constitution of 1990, see title IV, arts 96–132, on economic, social, financial, and fiscal organization.

[27] See eg arts 90–91 of the Angolan Constitution of 2010, which refers to issues of social justice and planning. In the case of Mozambique's Constitution of 1990, traces of its Marxist-Leninist past can be found in art 87, which underlines the fundamental principles that govern economic policy.

model to be pursued is articulated clearly to leave no room for doubt about where the countries stand now. For example, article 89(1)(c) of the Angolan Constitution states as a fundamental principle that there shall be 'a market economy based on the principles and values of healthy competition, morality and ethics, as prescribed and ensured by law'. As regards Mozambique, article 97(b) makes it clear that 'market forces' shall dictate the country's economic policy.

However, the two countries' socialist past remains salient, and it is apparent from a reading of the economic principles that what is contemplated is a mixed economy. In this regard, it is worth noting that one of Africa's most elaborate formulations of a mixed economy is found in article 95 of the 1990 Namibian Constitution.[28]

Having examined the economic philosophy of the constitutions, we next examine the manner in which specific economic rights are recognized and protected. We begin with property rights.

2.2 Property Rights Recognition and Protection

The right to property is without doubt one of the most important economic rights, so it is no surprise that all the constitutions under study recognize and protect it. Indeed, classical systems guaranteed such rights as a matter of foremost principle, with the United States' Constitution of 1787 being the harbinger and pre-eminent example. Property rights are interpreted from a broad perspective as including the right to use, possess, exchange, and otherwise dispose of property.[29]

In general, because security of property rights reduces uncertainty and stabilizes expectations, there is likely to be long-term investment. In the absence of secure property rights, investors invest only in projects with a short time horizon, or even refrain from investing altogether. The nature and scope of such protection is therefore important.

The level of protection provided in the African constitutions reviewed in this chapter varies. Generally, the level is weak in the francophone and lusophone constitutions.[30] The weakest formulation of this appears in the preamble to the 1996 Cameroonian Constitution, where the recognition of the right to property is superficially stated in the preamble.[31] By contrast, the anglophone constitutions have elaborate provisions that recognize and protect property rights.[32] Perhaps the strongest protection of this right is provided for in section 8(2) of the Botswana Constitution. In allowing for the expropriation of private property subject to adequate and prompt payment of compensation, it states:

---

[28] It states: '(1) The economic order of Namibia shall be based on the principles of a mixed economy with the objective of securing economic growth, prosperity and a life of human dignity for all Namibians. (2) The Namibian economy shall be based, inter alia, on the following forms of ownership: (a) public; (b) private; (c) joint public–private; (d) co-operative; (e) co-ownership; (f) small-scale family.'

[29] See Ellen Frankel Paul, Fred D Miller Jr, and Jeffrey Paul (eds), *Economic Rights* (Cambridge University Press 1992) vii.

[30] See art 14 of the 2010 Angolan Constitution, art 19 of the Benin Constitution, art 1(10) of the 1991 Gabonese Constitution, art 82 of the 1990 Mozambican Constitution, art 33 of the 2010 Niger Constitution, and art 41 of the 2014 Tunisian Constitution.

[31] Its art 65 states that 'the preamble shall be part and parcel' of the constitution, but given the hortatory language of the constitution, this does not give it the same legal status as that of substantive provisions.

[32] See s 8 of the 1996 Botswana Constitution, arts 18–20 of the 1992 Ghanaian Constitution, and ss 25 and 43–44 of the 1996 South African Constitution.

> No person who is entitled to compensation under this section shall be prevented from re-
> mitting, within a reasonable time after he has received any amount of that compensation,
> the whole of that amount (free from any deduction, charge or tax made or levied in respect
> of its remission) to any country of his choice outside Botswana.

Unlike the situation in most other countries, in Botswana investors know their property is
protected from arbitrary seizure and safe from expropriation for a public purpose without
'prompt and adequate compensation'; they also know that in the event that it is lawfully expropriated, they will be able to repatriate the proceeds from the expropriation.

The importance of clear provisions protecting property rights has recently been underscored by the challenges that South Africa faces in trying to amend section 25 of its 1996
Constitution to provide for expropriation of land without compensation. Department of
Trade and Industry officials, during a briefing of a National Assembly ad hoc Committee,
have warned parliamentarians that amending the constitution to allow for wholesale expropriation of land without compensation is likely to discourage investment, threaten food
security, and harm economic activity and job creation.[33]

Although it is clear that all African constitutions today provide for security of private
ownership of property, there is considerable variation in the scope of that protection and of
the unavoidable restrictions and limitations regarding the individual and collective exercise
of these property rights (a matter to which we return in section 4 below).

2.3   Freedom of Commerce or Enterprise

The primary objective of the freedom of commerce or enterprise is to free economic activity
from arbitrary public and private regulation. There is, however, a general reticence by states
to allow an unqualified *laissez-faire* economic order. In France, for example, freedom of
commerce has never received express constitutional formulation, and until recently was regarded only as a general principle of law of uncertain constitutional status.[34] Daintith notes
that the incorporation of freedom of commerce in modern constitutions rarely predates the
end of the Second World War.[35] In his study of eighteen European constitutions, he found,
moreover, that only ten of them contain a provision guaranteeing freedom of commerce.[36]
Freedom of commerce is, as a result, subject to a variety of concerns and values, such as the
health and safety of consumers, stable employment, and national economic stability and
development.[37]

It is against this background that the approach adopted in the constitutions under study
must be understood. Whilst the often obscure or laconic language of most of the constitutions could be interpreted as betokening implicit recognition of the freedom of commerce,
it is only in the Angolan Constitution of 2010 where this recognition is given in clear, unambiguous terms: article 38, dealing with the right to free economic initiative, states, inter

---

[33] See 'Legislation: MPs Told of Legal Snag in Expropriating Foreign-Owned Land' *Legalbrief Today*, Issue No
4835 (28 November 2019).

[34] See Francoise Dreyfus, *La liberté du commerce et de l'industrie* (Berger-Levrault 1973).

[35] Daintith (n 8) 80.

[36] ibid 82.

[37] ibid 83.

alia, that 'everyone shall have the right to engage in free business and cooperative initiatives, to be exercised under the terms of the law'. As with property rights, the scope of the express or implicit recognition of the freedom of commerce and of the associated restrictions and limitations varies from one constitution to another.

2.4 Consumer Protection

Protecting consumers in today's globalized world is an issue of increasing domestic and international importance. This is especially true of Africa, which is being flooded with cheap goods of dubious quality from countries in the Far East, China in particular.[38] Thus, among the many constraints on freedom of commerce and other economic rights are those based on values and concerns to do with protecting consumers. Given the inherent tension between the freedom of commerce and consumer protection, there is a need to provide clear guidance to the courts on the standards to use in balancing these two potentially conflicting interests; ideally, this guidance should be provided by entrenching the scope of each of the rights in the constitution.

Although nearly all the constitutions under study contain provisions couched in language that may be interpreted as protecting consumers, only two constitutions do so explicitly. The 2010 Angolan Constitution devotes the whole of article 78 to consumer rights. It provides, inter alia, that 'consumers shall have the right to good quality goods and services, information and clarification, guarantees for products and protection with regard to consumer relations'.[39] The article also provides for the protection of consumers against the manufacture and supply of goods and services that are harmful to health and life and for compensation for any harm caused. The other country with a constitutionally entrenched framework for consumer protection is Niger: the entirety of article 92 of the 1990 Constitution is devoted to the rights of consumers, and is as elaborate as its Angolan counterpart.

2.5 The Right to Work and Workers' Rights

As noted, unemployment and poverty were among the major causes of the 1990s revolution that overturned many of the continent's dictators. There was hence an expectation that drafters would make a concerted effort to address the problem in the new or revised constitutions, but, surprisingly, little in this vein is evident in those under study in this chapter.

With regard to the right to work, there are, on the one hand, constitutions that are silent about it (eg the Botswana Constitution), gloss over it in the preamble (eg the Cameroon Constitution), or accord it weak and superficial recognition.[40] On the other hand, strong

---

[38] For example, the South African Revenue Services (SARS), in 2,500 raids conducted between July and September 2019, seized counterfeit goods including clothing, textiles, footwear, and leather worth more than ZAR 1 billion (USD 70 million). According to a *Business Day* report, these counterfeit goods, all of which come from China, are strangling an embattled South African economy and led to the government holding meetings with Chinese officials. See 'Trade: Counterfeit Goods Cost SAR 1bn—Ramaphosa' *Legalbrief Today*, Issue No 4748 (17 September 2019).

[39] See art 78(1) of the 2010 Angolan Constitution.

[40] For examples of the latter, see art 30 of Benin's Constitution of 1990, art 1(7) of Gabon's Constitution of 1991, and s 17 of the 1999 Nigerian Constitution, where this appears in provisions dealing with directive principles of

provisions define the right to work and security of work in detail in article 76 of the 2010 Angolan Constitution and article 84 of the 1990 Mozambican Constitution.[41] In fact, article 76 of the former not only makes work a right and duty, but imposes a duty on the state to adopt and implement policies that generate work.[42]

It is not by coincidence that the Angolan and Mozambican approach differs from that of the other countries. The constitutions of these two countries make a greater attempt than others to balance an orientation towards a new economic order (with the recognition of property rights and freedom of enterprise) with some collectivist and socially protective measures. The reality is that, by contrast, most African constitutions have opted for a middle ground in seeking, explicitly or implicitly, to balance these potentially conflicting tendencies. This is the reason they are ambivalent when it comes to guaranteeing the security of work[43] or recognizing the right to strike.[44] Section 23 of the South African Constitution of 1996, probably because of the legacy of apartheid and its impact on workers, has elaborate provisions on labour relations. This evinces a strong commitment to the protection of work and workers.

2.6 Control over National Assets and Natural Resources

Until the 1990s, few constitutions offered any guidance on how national assets or economic activities of a specially sensitive nature were to be regulated. The result was that governments had a free hand in dealing with national assets such as land, natural resources, energy resources, essential public services, and goods, services, and enterprises whose exploitation necessitates public or private monopolies. Has anything changed since the 1990s, and if so, what?

The critical issue is not just recognizing national assets,[45] something many of the constitutions do, but ensuring that the constitution constrains the way the government manages them in advancement of the national interest. However, only a few constitutions provide

---

state policy, which are not justiciable. Another example of a weak framework is s 22 of the 1996 Constitution of South Africa.

[41] A similar approach appears in art 24 of Ghana's Constitution of 1992.
[42] This provision is worth quoting in its entirety:
  (1) Work shall be the right and duty of all.
  (2) Every worker shall have the right to vocational training, fair pay, rest days, holidays, protection, and workplace health and safety, in accordance with the law.
  (3) In order to ensure the right to work, the state shall be charged with promoting:
    (a) The implementation of policies to generate work.
    (b) Equal opportunities in the choice of profession or type of work and conditions which prevent preclusion or limitation due to any form of discrimination.
    (c) Academic training and scientific and technological development, as well as vocational development for workers.
  (4) Dismissal without fair cause shall be illegal and employers shall be obliged to pay just compensation for workers who have been dismissed, under the terms of the law.
[43] The best example of this is found in art 76(4) of the 2010 Angolan Constitution.
[44] The right to strike is recognized in art 51 of the 2010 Angolan Constitution of 2010, art 31 of the 1990 Benin Constitution, art 87 of the 1990 Mozambican Constitution, and art 34 of the 2010 Niger Constitution.
[45] See eg arts 15–16 of the 2010 Angolan Constitution, arts 257–66 of the 1992 Ghanaian Constitution, and arts 99 and 101–04 of the 1990 Mozambican Constitution.

for measures to guard against the abuse or misuse of national assets. This is done in various ways. For example, article 268(1) of the 1992 Ghanaian Constitution states:

> Any transaction, contract or undertaking involving the grant of a right of concession by or on behalf of any person including the Government of Ghana, to any other person or body of persons however described, for the exploitation of any mineral, water or other natural resources of Ghana made or entered into after the coming into force of this constitution shall be *subject to ratification by Parliament*.[46]

In other words, Parliament is required to ratify agreements relating to the exploitation of the country's natural resources. This is reinforced by article 269, which provides for the establishment, within six months of the first parliamentary sitting, of a number of natural resources commissions, such as a minerals, a forestry, and a fisheries commission, to regulate and manage the exploitation of these resources.[47] The Gabonese Constitution requires Parliament to ratify, inter alia, all commercial treaties that engage the finances of the state.[48] Article 150 of the 2010 Constitution of Niger affords rather weak protection against abuse, requiring simply that all contracts for the exploitation and management of natural and subsoil resources be transparent and published in the official gazette. Surprisingly, only Ghana's Constitution of 1992 has anything to say about SOEs; even then, the relevant provision, article 192, states merely that public corporations may be established only by an Act of Parliament.

Parliamentary ratification of economic agreements is of particular importance. This is so because the increasing pace of globalization, the moves being made towards economic integration, and the interconnectedness of national economies through transnational trade and investment entail that economic policy is no longer dictated only by the constitution. The impact of these agreements, whether in directing how national resources are exploited or in setting international standards for protecting domestic consumers, depends on their status in domestic law. More generally, it depends on two important considerations. The first is the role played by institutions established in the constitution for managing the economy, an issue to which we now turn, and, secondly, the legal impact of the economic rights recognized and protected by the different constitutional provisions, which is addressed thereafter.

3. The Role of Institutions for Economic Management

One of the major objectives of the economic constitution is to protect the state and its institutions from being captured by interest groups. This entails that the economic policies and measures entrenched in the constitution should be supported by institutions capable of ensuring their full implementation in a transparent and accountable manner. In all the constitutions under review there has been some attempt to put in place measures to protect the country's economic interests and promote economic development for the benefit of all.

---

[46] Emphasis added.
[47] To a similar effect, see art 13 of the 2014 Tunisian Constitution.
[48] See art 107 of Gabon's Constitution of 1991.

These measures consist of the establishment of institutions to promote sound economic management and others to promote financial legitimacy and accountability.

3.1 Institutions for Sound Economic Management

A wide range of institutions exist to ensure the proper functioning of the economy, with many of them constitutionally mandated to do so, but they vary in number from one country and constitutional tradition to another. Whilst the key institutions are the treasury or ministry of finance and the central bank, other important actors include the government (both central and devolved government) and executive agencies. A full comparative examination of the workings of these institutions would require extensive empirical research that is beyond the scope of this chapter; we therefore focus briefly on the treasury and the central bank.

The treasury, or what is referred to in most countries as the ministry of finance, is at the heart of the economic management system, yet in spite of its importance is hardly mentioned in African constitutions. An exception is South Africa, where the treasury, headed by the Minister of Finance, is the only government department specifically mentioned in the Constitution. To underscore the importance of this ministry, the Constitution also defines its powers in respect of government transactions and plans in such a way that they are tantamount to a veto.[49] In fact, section 216(2) of the Constitution gives the South African Minister of Finance powers to intervene that could be exercised even in disregard of advice or instructions by the President and not be dismissed on that basis alone. In an economy such as South Africa's which is heavily reliant on investment, the country's economic stability and growth depend to a large extent on the credibility of the person appointed as finance minister.[50]

The second of the major economic institutions that are critical to the proper management of the economy is the central bank. In what is probably an important indicator of national sovereignty, most African countries have their own national central banks. However, there are some exceptions. The two blocs of mainly francophone countries in West and Central Africa that still use the CFA franc (African Financial Community franc) have a single central bank. The first bloc is the West African Economic and Monetary Union (BCEAO), made up of eight countries whose central bank is based in Dakar, Senegal;[51] the second is the Economic and Monetary Union of Central African States (BCEAC), made up of six member states with a central bank based in Yaoundé, Cameroon.[52] Regarding the countries covered in this study, all have a central bank, but its mandate is defined in the constitutions of only three of them, namely, Angola, Ghana, and South Africa.[53] The question, then,

---

[49] See s 216 of the South African Constitution of 1996.

[50] It was thus no surprise that the value of the currency fell dramatically in 2015 and again in 2017 when the President arbitrarily dismissed two highly respected finance ministers. As regards the removal, first, of Minister Nhlanhla Nene, see 'South Africa Finance Minister's Departure Drives Rand down to All-Time Low' <https://bit.ly/2KxVIhT> accessed 1 July 2019; as regards the removal, secondly, of Minister Pravin Gordhan, see Mullen and Petroff, 'South Africa's Currency Plummets after Finance Minister Fired' <https://cnn.it/2KtG6Me> accessed 1 July 2019.

[51] The member states are Benin, Burkina Faso, Côte d'Ivoire, Guinea Bissau, Mali, Niger, Senegal, and Togo.

[52] The member states are Cameroon, Central African Republic, Chad, Congo Republic, Gabon, and Equatorial Guinea.

[53] Art 132 of the Mozambican Constitution of 1990 covers the central bank, but it is not legally significant as it merely states that the bank's operations shall be determined by parliamentary legislation.

is: what role does the central bank play in promoting economic growth and prosperity? It is necessary here to make a distinction between the francophone countries that have a common central bank and the other three countries whose constitutions define the role of the central bank.

According to article 100 of the 2010 Angolan Constitution, the role of the central bank is to preserve the value of the currency by 'defining monetary, financial and exchange rate policies'. In Ghana, article 183 of the 1992 Constitution requires the central bank '[to] promote and maintain the stability of the currency' in the interests of economic progress. The bank is also required to promote economic development and the efficient utilization of national resources through the effective and efficient operation of the country's banking and credit system. The South African central bank, otherwise known as the South African Reserve Bank (SARB), is regulated by two brief provisions in the 1996 Constitution. Section 224(1) states that its primary function is to protect the value of the currency in the interests of balanced and sustainable growth. This has been understood to mean that the SARB is responsible for monetary policy through ensuring the achievement and maintenance of price stability, whilst the treasury is responsible for fiscal policy.[54]

The CFA franc zone, by contrast, emerged from colonial arrangements. Although there are two central banks, each in Cameroon and Senegal, respectively, that are supposed to oversee the zone's operations, the monetary policy of the member countries is set in effect by the French treasury. The currency is pegged at a fixed rate to the euro, with convertibility guaranteed by the French treasury. Until recently, this was done on conditions that include covering 20 per cent of sight liabilities by foreign exchange reserves and depositing 50 per cent of the foreign reserves of the countries in an operations account in the French treasury.

While the use of the CFA franc and its control by the French treasury have brought benefits to the countries,[55] serious disadvantages increasingly outweigh them.[56] These include the fact that member countries cannot change monetary policy to respond to their particular macroeconomic needs and that the currency is exposed to extraneous volatility due to fluctuations in the euro. These countries have consequently lost the ability to adjust to export shocks and are vulnerable to imported inflation. The monetary and exchange rate policies of the franc zone countries are essentially dictated by the European Central Bank; the latter's monetary orthodoxy has an anti-inflation bias detrimental to growth and has encouraged massive capital outflows from the CFA franc zone countries. As a result of the continued use of the CFA in francophone Africa, France retains and exercises as much control over the financial policies of these countries as it did during the colonial period.

---

[54] See 'Finance: No Attempt to Influence the Reserve Bank, says Masondo' *Legalbrief Today*, Issue 4733 (5 July 2019). More recently, Masondo, the Deputy Finance Minister, was rebuked by the Governor of the SARB when he suggested that, instead of buying government securities in the secondary market in order to boost liquidity problems caused by the COVID-19 pandemic, SARB should buy government bonds directly from the Treasury. See Paul Richardson, 'Masondo: No "Pressure" for Reserve Bank to Purchase Govt Bonds' *Fin24.com* (3 May 2020) <http://www.fin24.com/Economy/masondos-call-for-reserve-bank-to-purchase-govt-bonds-directly-is-dangerous-analyst-20200503-2> accessed May 2020; 'Finance: Reserve Bank Governor Rebukes David Masondo' *Legalbrief Today* Issue 4931 (7 May 2020).

[55] Proponents of the CFA franc argue that it provides macroeconomic stability in a region which is politically unstable due to weak governance in checking against inflation, reducing uncertainty, promoting economic growth and development, and facilitating international trade.

[56] See Issiaka Coulibaly, 'Costs and Benefits of the CFA Franc' <https://worldpolicy.org/2017/02/28/costs-and-benefits-of-the-cfa-franc/> accessed 1 July 2019; Ndongo Samba Sylla, 'The CFA Franc: French Monetary Imperialism in Africa' <https://bit.ly/2KGMHBR> accessed 1 July 2019.

The key issue with regard to central banks is that they ought to be able to act independently in implementing monetary policy free from political manipulation for short-term gain. However, the rise of central bank independence around the world in the last three decades has come under threat, largely from populism and nationalism, as many politicians want to manipulate interest rates to boost their popularity.[57] An independent central bank with powers to influence monetary policy has never been a feature of francophone Africa. In June 2019, the Economic Community of West African States (ECOWAS) agreed to launch a new common currency, the ECO, by 2020. Many felt this signalled the death knell for the increasingly anomalous CFA franc in Africa and removed one of the root causes of the slow growth rate in francophone Africa. However, all these plans were thrown into doubt a few months later when, in late December 2019, Ivory Coast President Alassane Ouattara announced that the West African CFA franc would be retired sometime in 2020 and replaced with a new currency also called the ECO.[58]

Research consistently shows that economies perform better when their central banks are independent and make difficult decisions that have the long-term interests of the economy in mind and do not merely pander to the wishes of self-serving politicians.[59] Therefore, because of the critical role that central banks play in the economy, it is desirable that their structure, mandate, and relationship with national government be clearly defined in the constitution in a manner that guarantees their independence from governmental interference. Furthermore, allowing foreign bodies, such as the French Treasury or the EU Central Bank, to play such a role is not only an anachronistic anomaly but seriously compromises a country's sovereignty.

3.2 Institutions for Financial Legitimacy and Accountability

Having a variety of forms of legal, political, and administrative oversight is essential in holding together the different parts of the constitution generally and the economic constitution in particular. For example, the objectives and tools of monetary policy (usually set by central banks) and financial policy (usually set by the government) should be subject to democratic scrutiny and accountability. The institutions that undertake this task differ in nature and the scope of their scrutiny. Although their mandate is often broad, the focus in this discussion is on their role in ensuring that the economic aspects of the constitution are

---

[57] See 'The Independence of Central Banks is under Threat from Politics: That is Bad News for the World' *The Economist* (13 April 2019).

[58] In a statement thereafter, the Nigerian Finance Minister Zainab Ahmed said the December announcement was 'inconsistent with the decision of the Authority of the Heads of State and Government of ECOWAS for the adoption of the Eco as the name of an independent ECOWAS single currency'. See 'West African States Mired in Controversy over "Eco" Currency' <http://www.dw.com/en/west-african-states-mired-in-controversy-over-eco-currency/a-52045052> accessed May 2020. By the end of July 2020, the ECO was supposed to replace the CFA franc in the West African zone. However, as Michael Schmidt, 'The End of the West African CFA' *Business Live* <http://www.businesslive.co.za/fm/features/africa/2020-07-02-the-end-of-the-west-african-cfa-franc/> accessed August 2020, points out, the move is merely symbolic. The new currency will remain pegged to the euro, with France guaranteeing its convertibility. The only apparent advantage is that the reserves of these countries will no longer be kept at the French Treasury but pooled collectively. French influence on monetary policy is barely diminished.

[59] See Michael Klein, 'Why Federal Reserve Independence Matters' <http://www.salon.com/2019/07/01/why-federal-reserve-independence-matters_partner/> accessed 1 July 2019.

implemented effectively. The main institutions are parliament, specialized institutions, and the courts.

3.2.1 Parliament

Because parliament has major powers in terms of approving the budget, raising taxes and spending public funds, as a matter of constitutional principle it is the most important institution in scrutinizing the management of public funds. However, in reality its powers of advance scrutiny are usually minimal and what is of greater importance is its power to scrutinize spending *ex post facto* and draw future lessons from its findings.

Generally, parliament's dominance in almost all African countries by the ruling party has limited its ability to call government to order. The enlarged scope of governmental economic management at both the central and local level is another impediment to effective scrutiny. However, all modern African constitutions make provision for the establishment of several oversight committees.[60] It is these committees that are supposed to scrutinize and hold the government departments accountable.

There are two points to note. First, the dominant-party phenomenon ensures that ruling parties have a majority in these committees, a factor that limits the ability of the committees to hold the government accountable. Secondly, following an old tradition in common law, one of the most important committees, the public accounts committee, is usually chaired by a member of an opposition party. In many anglophone countries, this has enabled the committee, through its meetings and reports, to make a positive impact in holding the government to account.[61] This is just one of several committees. For example, in South Africa other committees within Parliament that scrutinize government management of public funds are the committee on the Auditor-General, the Joint Standing Committee on the Financial Management of Parliament (convened jointly with the National Council of Provinces, the second house of Parliament); the select committee on finance, the Standing Committee on Finance; and various portfolio committees responsible for examining the expenditure, administration, and policy of government departments and public bodies. These committees play an important role in scrutinizing decisions relating to economic management and the extent to which these decisions are implemented.

3.2.2 Specialized institutions

A number of specialized institutions have been given the mandate to, amongst other things, ensure financial legitimacy and accountability. The most innovative, and probably the most effective, of them in the countries under study are those appearing in chapter 9 of the South African Constitution of 1996 under the heading 'state institutions supporting constitutional democracy'.[62] Two of the six institutions are of particular relevance.

---

[60] See eg arts 156 and 160(a) of the Angolan Constitution of 2010; art 89 of the Benin Constitution of 1990; ss 63 and 103 of the Nigerian Constitution of 1999; and s 57(2)(a) of the South African Constitution of 1996. The rather flimsy Cameroonian Constitution of 1996 has no provision in this regard.

[61] See R Pelizzo, 'Public Accounts Committees in the Commonwealth: Oversight, Effectiveness, and Governance' (2011) 49(4) Journal of Commonwealth and Comparative Politics 528.

[62] For further discussion, see CM Fombad, 'The Role of Emerging Hybrid Institutions of Accountability in the Separation of Powers Scheme in Africa' in Charles Manga Fombad (ed), *Separation of Powers in African Constitutionalism* (OUP 2016); and, for the spread of this into other African countries, CM Fombad, 'The Diffusion of South African-style Institutions? A Study of Comparative Constitutionalism' in R Dixon and T Roux (eds), *Constitutional Triumphs, Constitutional Disappointments: A Critical Assessment of the 1996 South African Constitution's Local and International Influence* (Cambridge University Press 2018).

The first is the Public Protector, who has the powers under section 182(1)(a) of the Constitution 'to investigate any conduct in state affairs, or in the public administration in any sphere of government, that is alleged or suspected to be improper or to result in any impropriety or prejudice'. Since 1996, especially during the tenure of the former Public Protector (Advocate Thuli Madonsela), this institution has been at the forefront of the fight against corruption and abuse of powers in the country. Some of its famous reports are those on the misuse of state funds to renovate the private home in Nkandla of former President Jacob Zuma under the pretext of security upgrades, and the 2016 state capture report on the influence of an Indian family, the Guptas, on government appointments.[63]

The second key institution is the Auditor-General, who under section 188 of the Constitution has the responsibility for regularly monitoring the management of public funds. The Auditor-General's reports have contributed substantially to enhancing accountability and transparency in the use of government resources.[64]

Similar institutions are found in some of the constitutions reviewed in this study.[65] What perhaps make the South African ones distinct are the special establishment principles provided for in section 181 of the Constitution to insulate these institutions from political interference. As we will see, francophone African countries rely on courts, particularly audit courts.[66]

3.2.3 Courts and administrative justice

Three observations can be made about the role of the courts in promoting transparency and accountability with regard to the economic aspects of the constitution. First, the courts are regularly approached when there is abuse of power, corruption, or misuse of public funds. States usually enact several pieces of legislation to deal with this. Most anglophone constitutions confer on the attorney-general or director of public prosecutions the powers to institute criminal proceedings on behalf of the state against anybody who has committed a crime.[67] In the civil law jurisdictions, the power to prosecute is usually conferred by ordinary legislation.

Secondly, disputes about the interpretation and application of constitutional provisions dealing with the economy or finance are dealt with by the special procedure the constitutions provide for the purpose. This raises complex issues, but here it suffices to point out that in the civil law jurisdictions such disputes are decided by specialized courts, whereas in the anglophone countries they are usually dealt with by ordinary courts, but with the high court having original jurisdiction.[68]

Thirdly, the courts may also intervene by way of judicial review when there are challenges to any of the reports issued by institutions created by the constitution to regulate or monitor

---

[63]   Fombad 2016 (n 62); Fombad 2018 (n 62)

[64]   See eg Auditor-General of South Africa, 'Auditor-General Reports an Overall Deterioration in the Audit Results of National and Provincial Government Departments and Their Entities' <https://bit.ly/2H3p4CO> accessed July 2019.

[65]   For example, the office of the auditor-general is provided in s 124 of the Botswana Constitution of 1966; art 187 of the Ghanaian Constitution of 1992; and s 127 of the Nigerian Constitution of 1999. The Angolan Constitution of 2010 provides for an ombudsman in art 192.

[66]   For a detailed discussion of these principles, see the papers referred to in n 62.

[67]   See eg ss 113–14 of the Botswana Constitution of 1966; s 174 of the Nigerian Constitution of 1999; and s 179(2) of the South African Constitution of 1996.

[68]   For a full discussion, see CM Fombad (ed), *Constitutional Adjudication in Africa* (OUP 2017).

financial matters, such as a report by the auditor-general. However, the courts often defer to public authorities on matters of economic policy and detailed management of resources.[69]

It is also important to note that in francophone and other civil law jurisdictions there are audit courts that specialize in auditing the accounts of government and SOEs to ensure that they conform to the economic principles laid down in the constitution, legislation, and in government policy.[70]

Another innovation by the South African Constitution is the right to just administrative action provided for in section 33. This gives every ordinary citizen the right to expect that any administrative action taken with respect to any matter, including one of an economic nature, such as the decision to expropriate land or refusal to grant a trading licence, is lawful, reasonable, and procedurally fair. Although the right to just administrative action is a well-established common law principle, and is also provided for in article 23 of the Ghanaian Constitution, the South African Constitution gives greater clarity and certainty as to its scope.[71]

From a practical standpoint, and in the light of the enormous economic challenges today, the role of courts in promoting economic constitutionalism will be determined by the way they are able to provide a proper balance between, for example, protecting property entitlements and promoting property redistribution. The broader issue that this raises is the extent to which the economic rights can effectively benefit the ordinary citizens and in this way enhance the prospects for constitutionalism.

4. The Interplay between the Constitution, Economy, and Constitutionalism

The constitutional entrenchment of principles to guide or control government economic action improves their chances of being implemented effectively. This depends, however, on a range of factors, including the extent of the protection of economic rights and, more importantly, whether the constitution promotes constitutionalism. In other words, the interaction between the economy, the state, and individuals must be consistent with principles of constitutionalism such as the recognition and protection of fundamental rights (including economic rights), separation of powers, an independent judiciary, and respect for the rule of law. Economic constitutionalism necessitates that economic policies and action are constrained by the constitution, and it takes it as axiomatic that only state interventions defined and established by an economic democratic mechanism can avoid or limit the risks of economic autocracy.[72] In fact, the early German ordoliberals argued that a proper economic constitution protects not only economic and other freedoms but the political system itself.[73]

---

[69] See T Prosser, *The Economic Constitution* (OUP 2014) 53.

[70] See eg art 183 of the Angolan Constitution of 2010; arts 37–42 of the Cameroon Constitution of 1996; art 67 of the Gabonese Constitution of 1991; and art 117 of the Tunisian Constitution of 2014. For insight to their operationalization, see MB Akakpo, 'Démocratie financière en Afrique Occidentale francophone' <https://library.fes.de/pdf-files/bueros/benin/12070.pdf> accessed July 2019.

[71] See CRM Dlamini, 'The Right to Administrative Justice in South Africa: Creating an Open and Accountable Democracy' (2000) JSAL 53. This right is now also entrenched in the Kenyan and Zimbabwean constitutions. See art 47 and s 68, respectively.

[72] See eg S Feiyue, 'Economic Constitutionalism: Path for State to Intervene in the Economy' (2003) 1(3) Frontiers of Law in China 372.

[73] See K Tuori, 'Tony Prosser: The Economic Constitution' (2014) 12 ICON 1075.

From the preceding analysis, it is clear that almost all the constitutions examined have made strides in promoting economic constitutionalism in formal terms. However, there are considerable differences in the nature and scope of the rights they purportedly confer, differences that may limit the substance of these rights in practice. In other words, the constitutional recognition and protection of, for example, the right to property, does not necessarily guarantee such a right. This is because Africa's strides towards economic constitutionalism are subject to several constraining factors at both the national and international level.

4.1 Constraints at the National Level

At the national level, a key problem is the limited nature and scope of the economic rights that are recognized and protected. For example, while the constitutions of Ghana and South Africa, and to some extent Angola and Mozambique, have detailed provisions conferring several economic rights, these matters are dealt with superficially in most francophone constitutions, particularly those of Benin and Cameroon. This weakness is compounded in many cases by the extensive use of either vague language or claw-back clauses.[74]

As an example of the former, article 89(1)(c) of the 2010 Angolan Constitution provides for a 'market economy based on the principles and values of healthy competition, morality and ethics, as prescribed and ensured by law'. While it is possible to say what is or is not 'healthy competition', that is not so with 'morality and ethics'. As for claw-back clauses, an example is found in article 148 of the Niger Constitution of 2010. In trying to regulate the exploitation and management of natural resources, it states, inter alia, that 'the law determines the conditions for their prospection, exploitation and management'. Subjecting this to subsequent legislative intervention without giving any guidelines on the nature and scope of this framework means the lawmaker has the right to determine not only when, if at all, such a law is adopted but its content. The implication of such unchecked power of discretionary action is that a government with the slightest parliamentary majority is free to dictate what exactly the law is.

Closely linked to this is the fact that some constitutions, in purporting to recognize and protect economic rights, subject them to diverse limitations, some so broad as to leave the government with the discretion to legislate in a manner that undermines the very rights the constitutions are meant to promote and protect. Granted, limitations on the exercise of all rights, including economic rights, are necessary and inevitable,[75] but their scope determines the quality and extent of the economic rights protection enjoyed in a particular country. As noted, constitutions with extensive claw-back clauses, such as those of Benin and Cameroon, provide the executive and legislature with a potent weapon for restricting the benefits of economic rights at their pleasure.

An example of limitations that could easily be abused appears in section 8(1)(a) of the 1966 Constitution of Botswana. The section protects individuals from arbitrary acquisition of their property, except where it is necessary or expedient 'in the interests of defence,

---

[74] For further examples of claw-back clauses, see arts 37, 42(2), 49(2), 50(2), 51(2), and 77(3) of the 2010 Angolan Constitution.

[75] See generally Charles M Fombad, 'African Bill of Rights in a Comparative Perspective' (2011) 17(1) Fundamina 33.

public safety, public order, public morality, public health, town and country planning or land settlement'. The list ostensibly tries to limit the arbitrary actions a repressive government might want to take, but is formulated in language that is so vague that it could be used to cover virtually every conceivable contingency the legislature and/or executive may wish to cite as grounds for limiting the right in question and proceeding to do whatever it wishes.

A better approach is taken in the South African Constitution, which sets out a general limitation clause to check against legislation that could undermine rights conferred in the bill of rights.[76] This provision lays down strict, objective conditions against which any legislation attempting to limit these rights must be tested. Article 24(1) of Kenya's Constitution is similarly worded, but has other clauses that erect even greater restrictions in this regard. For example, clause 2 states that in spite of what is provided for in clause 1, a provision in legislation limiting a right or fundamental freedom shall not do so to the extent of 'derogat[ing] from its core or essential content'. It can be said that the Kenyan and South African bills of rights provide the greatest protection, while the Cameroonian constitution provides the least. More generally, the Gaullist constitutional model allows considerable scope for legislative and executive enactments[77] that are likely to undermine the economic constitution.

Another point to note is that in some of these constitutions the important economic principles appear under sections headed 'directive principles of state policy'. In certain cases, such as the Nigerian Constitutions, these principles are explicitly or implicitly non-justiciable.[78] Moreover, unlike in India,[79] in some African jurisdictions the courts too have held that such directive principles are non-justiciable.[80]

In other constitutions, the status of these principles is obscure. An example is found in chapter 6 of the 1992 Ghanaian Constitution, article 34 of which has the heading, 'Implementation of directive principles'. The article states that the principles act as a 'guide' to 'all citizens, Parliament, the President, the judiciary, the Council of State, the cabinet, political parties and other bodies and persons in applying or interpreting this Constitution or any other law and in taking and implementing any policy decisions . . .' It imposes on the President a duty to report to Parliament at least once a year on all the steps he or she has taken to realize the policy objectives contained in the chapter. In the Ghanaian Supreme Court case of *New Patriotic Party v Attorney-General (31st December Case)*,[81] Bamford-Addo JSC was of the view that chapter 6 is not justiciable, but his colleague, Adade JSC, thought otherwise:

---

[76] It states: '(1) The rights in the Bill of Rights may be limited only in terms of law of general application to the extent that the limitation is reasonable and justifiable in an open and democratic society based on human dignity, equality and freedom taking into account all relevant factors, including (a) the nature of the right; (b) the importance of the purpose of the limitation; (c) the nature and extent of the limitation; (d) the relation between the limitation and its purpose; and (e) less restrictive means to achieve the purpose. (2) Except as provided in subsection (1) or in any other provision of the Constitution, no law may limit any right entrenched in the Bill of Rights.'

[77] In the Gaullist system the executive is responsible for making most of the laws. In fact, it has what is termed an 'exclusive executive law-making domain', one that goes beyond the normal delegated legislation. These laws can take the form of presidential ordinances and decrees as well as ministerial orders and regulations.

[78] See similar principles in ch 2, ss 16–17 of the Nigerian Constitution of 1999 and the preamble to the Ugandan Constitution of 1995.

[79] See Gautam Bhatia, 'Directive Principles of State Policy' in Sujit Choudhry, Madhav Khosla, and Pratap Bhanu Mehta (eds), *The Oxford Handbook of the Indian Constitution* (OUP 2016).

[80] See Eje Adakole Odike, Hemen Philip Faga, and Iruka Wilfred Nwakpu, 'Incorporation of Fundamental Objectives and Directive Principles of State Policy in the Constitutions of Emerging Democracies: A Beneficial Wrongdoing or a Democratic Demagoguery?' (2016) 7(4) Beijing Law Review <http://file.scirp.org/Html/1-3300458_71212.htm> accessed July 2019.

[81] [1993–94] 2 GLR.

I do not subscribe to the view that chapter 6 of the Constitution, 1992 is not justiciable; it is. First, the Constitution, 1992 as a whole is a justiciable document. If any part is to be non-justiciable, the Constitution, 1992 itself must say so. I have not seen anything in chapter 6 or in the Constitution, 1992 generally, which tells me that chapter 6 is not justiciable. The evidence to establish the non-justiciability must be internal to the Constitution of 1992, not otherwise, for the simple reason that if the proffered proof is external to the Constitution, 1992, it must of necessity conflict with it, and be void and inadmissible; we cannot add words to the Constitution in order to change its meaning.[82]

In the subsequent case of *Ghana Lotto Operators Association & Others v National Lottery Authority*,[83] the Supreme Court, per Justice Date-Bah, reiterated the position of Justice Adade that '[t]here is no language in the Constitution stating that the principles are not of and by themselves legally enforceable by any court'.[84] However, taking the specific nature of the matters contained in chapter 6 into account, Justice Date-Bah further explained that

> there may be particular provisions in chapter 6 which do not lend themselves to enforcement by a court. The very nature of such a particular provision would rebut the presumption of justiciability in relation to it. In the absence of a demonstration that a particular provision does not lend itself to enforcement by courts, however, the enforcement by this court of the obligations imposed in chapter 6 should be insisted upon and would be a way of deepening our democracy and the liberty under law that it entails.[85]

Whilst this may clear up the ambiguity about the justiciability of chapter 6, it raises the question of how to determine which aspects lend themselves to judicial enforcement and which aspects do not. Ultimately, taking key economic principles that need constitutional recognition and protection and incorporating them in the so-called directive principles of state policy is not particularly helpful given the uncertainty this creates about their legal enforceability.

Perhaps a more serious problem is that in some jurisdictions, especially in francophone and lusophone Africa, the economic rights and protection ostensibly conferred by the constitution are negated by the absence of an effective mechanism for challenging violations of the constitution. This occurs mainly when individuals have no *locus standi* to challenge the government over any action or omission that breaches the constitution, a deficiency found in the Gaullist model of constitutional review that was adopted in the post-independence constitutions of francophone Africa. The issue has been addressed in a number of countries, among them Benin, but other countries, such as Cameroon, continue to deprive citizens of the fundamental right of vindicating violations of the constitution.[86] A constitution's influence in encouraging investment and promoting economic development necessitates a speedy and reliable system for resolving disputes, especially economic ones. What is required in particular is that there is confidence that constitutional commitments will be enforced by competent and independent judges—an all-important consideration that

---

[82] [1993–94] 2 GLR 35.
[83] [2007–08] SCGLR 1088.
[84] ibid 1101–02.
[85] ibid 1106.
[86] For a synopsis of constitutional review in Africa, see Fombad 2016 (n 62).

underscores the link between the constitution, constitutionalism, and economic constitutionalism. Without a clear, certain, and predetermined mechanism for dealing with violations of constitutional rights, one of the pillars of constitutionalism is missing.

4.2 Constraints at the International Level

Bilateral economic agreements—such as the trade agreements between China and Chinese companies, on the one hand, and African countries, on the other, as well as international agreements such as those under the World Trade Organization (WTO) and, more recently, the African Continental Free Trade Area (AfCFTA)—pose a potential risk to the national economic constitution. Are these different components of what may be called transnational economic constitutionalism reconcilable with national economic constitutionalism?

It can be said that African constitutions do not usually provide adequate safeguards to ensure that the economic principles they state are not contradicted by transnational economic agreements. This is all the more problematic because many of them, particularly in francophone and lusophone Africa, provide that an international agreement takes precedence over national legislation once it is ratified.[87] However, a few of these constitutions provide for some degree of transparency and accountability in commercial and related treaties. For example, article 67 of the Tunisian 2014 Constitution provides, inter alia, that all commercial treaties and international agreements imposing a financial obligation on the state are subject to ratification by parliament.[88] In some cases, parliamentary review is allowed only in the case of treaties on matters falling within the exclusive parliamentary legislative domain.[89] A weaker regime of parliamentary scrutiny is provided for in the case of '[an] international agreement of a technical, administrative or executive nature, or an agreement which does not require either ratification or accession, entered into by the national executive': these are binding on condition that they are tabled in the assembly and the council within a reasonable time.[90]

International economic agreements of a global dimension, such as WTO agreements, or of a broad regional nature, such as AfCFTA and other agreements within regional economic communities, are usually tabled before and ratified by parliament. By contrast, most of the bilateral trade agreements that African countries have entered into, which are often to the massive detriment of their economies, were concluded and signed in secret. For example, the Mozambican economy is in dire straits after the country borrowed USD 760 million in 2014 supposedly to invest in a tuna-fishing fleet, a loan which was illegal because it was obtained without parliamentary approval. Not only has the money disappeared, but today the country is struggling to pay between USD 1.7 billion and 2.2 billion for a USD 760 million loan from which it has received no benefit.[91]

The Mozambican crisis is probably just the tip of the iceberg of the debt situation in which many African governments find themselves. It is estimated, indeed, that more than 40 per

---

[87] See eg art 147 of the Benin Constitution of 1990 and art 45 of the Cameroonian Constitution of 1996.
[88] See also art 114 of the 1990 Constitution of Gabon.
[89] See eg art 43 of the Cameroon Constitution of 1996 and art 179(2)(e) of the 1990 Mozambican Constitution.
[90] See s 231(3) of the South African Constitution of 1996.
[91] See T Jones, '"Outrageous" Mozambique Debt Deal Could Make 270% Profit for Speculators'<http://www.cadtm.org/spip.php?page=imprimer&id_article=16793> accessed July 2019.

cent of countries in sub-Saharan Africa are at a high risk of debt distress.[92] One reason for this is that most of their constitutions fail to provide a comprehensive system for managing the economy, monitoring public finances, and managing public debt. An effective framework for economic constitutionalism is one that provides economic guidelines to ensure accountability, transparency, and due process when governments sign international commercial agreements. Sometimes, even where the constitution provides for parliamentary oversight over these agreements, this is ignored.[93]

In spite of the comparatively liberal constitutions that are in operation and the great strides taken towards democratic and accountable governance, most African states have never faced a graver threat to their independence and sovereignty than they do today. Whilst the move from the centralized planned economies of the past to market or mixed economies that emphasize the freedom to own property and freedom of enterprise may have been designed to restrain the state's regulation and control of major sectors of the economy, weak constitutional constraints remain a problem.

Although many international commercial treaties are subject to ratification and domestication, the reality is that once the procedural aspects of domestication are taken care of, and in spite of the supposed supremacy of the constitution, the enforcement mechanisms of these treaties usually ensure that the transnational economic legal order takes priority in many areas over the national constitutional legal order. For example, South African officials in the Department of Trade and Industry warned parliamentarians against the expropriation of land owned by foreign nationals. They pointed out that this will violate existing bilateral treaties and may attract sanctions from some key trading partners such as the US. The officials pointed out that even if some of these treaties were terminated, there are often 'survival clauses' that guarantee and protect the investments for between ten to twenty years.[94]

Besides the snags that may be encountered in termination of some of these agreements, some analysts argue that, at the beginning, many international economic institutions, such as the WTO, tried to accommodate a variety of economic models and social policies. Since the collapse of communism in eastern Europe, however, there is open, undisguised bias in favour of untrammelled private competition in the neoliberal ideal-typical market.[95] Neoliberal market liberalization has virtually become an international or regional standard, and has eventuated in transnational economic constitutions that often operate side by side with national economic constitutions.

For example, core ideas of the African Union integration project and its agenda for promoting constitutionalism are constructed around an integrated common market based on the market economy, free competition, and voluntary contracts, all of which accentuates the tendency towards privatization and against public property. When AfCFTA, which came into force on 30 May 2019, becomes fully operational, it may signal the emergence

---

[92] See S Mustapha and A Prizzon, 'Africa's Rising Debt: How to Avoid a New Crisis' <http://www.odi.org/sites/odi.org.uk/files/resource-documents/12491.pdf> accessed July 2019.

[93] See 'China Accuses Zimbabwe of Understating Financial Support' News24 (19 November 2019) <http://www.news24.com/Africa/Zimbabwe/china-accuses-zimbabwe-of-understating-financial-support-20191119> accessed December 2019, where it is noted that the 'Zimbabwean authorities have a history of quietly racking up foreign debt without the approval of parliament ...'

[94] See further, 'Legislation: MPs Told of Legal Snag in Expropriating Foreign-Owned Land' Legalbrief Today Issue No. 4835 (28 November 2019).

[95] See David Harvey, A Brief History of Neoliberalism (Oxford University Press 2007)

of an African economic constitution with the potential to harness the enormous benefits of enhanced intra-African trade.[96] The progressive spread of transnational economic constitutionalism through the WTO and AfCFTA membership is likely to push many African countries towards market-oriented economic reforms that neither the constitution nor the government desires. Commenting on the Brexit crisis in Britain, *The Economist* opines that it illustrates the difficulties that any country would face if it tried to 'take back control' (ie withdraw) in today's globalized and interconnected world:

> If you take back the right to set your own rules and standards, it will by definition become harder to do business with countries that use different ones. If you want to trade, you will probably end up following the rules of a more powerful partner—which for Britain means the EU or America—only without a say in setting them. Brexit thus amounts to taking back control in a literal sense, but losing control in a meaningful one.[97]

Thus, in many respects, global constitutionalism makes domestic choice less and less possible by entrenching and imposing one ideological model from above on the domestic legal framework. The national and international dimensions of the economic constitution could be mutually reinforcing. This, however, will require greater awareness of the importance of clearly articulating and defining the scope of constraints within which all matters affecting the national economy will operate.

5. Conclusion

The dominant paradigms that influenced economic policies in Africa until the 1990s have changed. In the redesign of constitutions after 1990, the assumption was that the mistakes of the past were going to be corrected. Uppermost was the goal of promoting constitutionalism, yet while major strides have been taken in promoting political constitutionalism, the same cannot be said of economic constitutionalism.

This chapter focused on ten countries, but the representative nature of these countries is such that many of the main conclusions that can be drawn will apply to most other African countries. It can be said that one of the constitution's main goals should be to promote investor confidence in the country. The starting point for this is the manner in which the fundamental principles that guide and orient the economy are spelt out in the constitution and implemented in practice. This is particularly important in view of the opaque bilateral and international commercial agreements that various African governments have signed. These agreements pose a serious existential risk to national sovereignty because most of them involve the disposal of strategic national assets and resources.

---

[96] AfCFTA will bring together all fifty-five members of the African Union and a market of 1.2 billion people, making it potentially the largest free-trade area in the world since the formation of the WTO. It also has the potential to boost intra-African trade by 52.3 per cent. Some of the principal elements of the African economic constitution that the AfCFTA espouses include open markets, the protection of economic freedoms, the guaranteeing of undistorted competition, and the construction and maintenance of the market economic order by law. See in particular art 3 of AfCFTA, available at <https://bit.ly/31yVi0n> accessed July 2019.

[97] See 'Britain's Crisis: Brexit, Mother of All Messes' *The Economist* (17 January 2019) <http://www.economist.com/leaders/2019/01/17/brexit-mother-of-all-messes> accessed 1 January 2019.

Although some attempts have been made to constitutionally entrench a framework for regulating the economy and to provide mechanisms and measures to promote transparency and accountability, there are many challenges preventing them from operating in a manner that will promote constitutionalism, good governance, and the rule of law. At a formal level, many of the provisions that purport to provide the framework for regulating and managing the economy are not well thought out and are often couched in obscure language that leaves too much discretionary power to the government. At a substantive level, there is a low level of implementation of constitutions, which combines with creeping authoritarianism, corruption, and the increasing influence of the transnational economic order to undermine effective national economic constitutionalism.

Nevertheless, most African constitutions now show an inclination towards the mixed economic model that balances some of the prescripts of central planning with those of the free market. The impact of transnational economic influence—through the WTO at international level and the AfCFTA and similar instruments at regional level—has ensured the prevalence of these more market-oriented economic approaches in Africa.

Looking to the future, if the strides towards economic constitutionalism are to succeed in complementing, reinforcing, and consolidating Africa's faltering steps made towards political constitutionalism, far more needs to be done in terms of design. So far, the efforts to reconcile oligarchic authoritarianism with democracy, individual opportunity with community interest, free enterprise with equity, growth with stability, competition with cooperation, and freedom with responsibility has yielded mixed results. Economic constitutionalism presupposes a heightened level of transparency, accountability, and freedom from arbitrary state action in the economic sector. This has not happened, mainly because of the continuous surge in the scale of endemic corruption.

Three areas deserve priority in both the medium and long term. First, there is the need, in constitutional design, to entrench fundamental economic principles and key institutions for implementing them to ensure that government economic policy operates within clear constraints. Secondly, to protect society from the capture of the economy by interest groups, whether foreign or national, all commercial agreements involving the use or disposal of national assets and resources must be scrutinized by parliament and made public to ensure that national interests and sovereignty are never put at risk by self-seeking politicians.

Finally, there is need for national constitutions to expressly prohibit any international agreements that are inimical to the national interest, especially those that concern sovereign ownership and control over national assets. The crux of the economic constitution in Africa today is to ensure that Africans do not become strangers in their own countries, tenants on their own land, and outsiders to their own national economy.

Bibliography

'Britain's Crisis: Brexit, Mother of All Messes' *The Economist* (17 January 2019) <http://www.econom ist.com/leaders/2019/01/17/brexit-mother-of-all-messes> accessed 1 January 2019

'China Accuses Zimbabwe of Understating Financial Support' *News24* (19 November 2019) <http:// www.news24.com/Africa/Zimbabwe/china-accuses-zimbabwe-of-understating-financial-supp ort-20191119> accessed 1 December 2019

'China to Take over ZESCO—Africa Confidential' (4 September 2018) <https://bit.ly/2oMtTXy> accessed 1 July 2019

'Finance: No Attempt to Influence the Reserve Bank, says Masondo' *Legalbrief Today*, Issue 4733 (5 July 2019)

'The Independence of Central Banks is under Threat from Politics: That is Bad News for the World' *The Economist* (13 April 2019)

'Legislation: MPs Told of Legal Snag in Expropriating Foreign-Owned Land' *Legalbrief Today*, Issue No 4835 (28 November 2019)

'South Africa Finance Minister's Departure Drives Rand down to All-Time Low' (10 December 2015) <https://bit.ly/2KxVIhT> accessed 1 July 2019

'Trade: Counterfeit Goods Cost SA R 1bn—Ramaphosa' *Legalbrief Today*, Issue No 4748 (17 September 2019)

Auditor-General of South Africa, 'Auditor-General Reports an Overall Deterioration in the Audit Results of National and Provincial Government Departments and Their Entities' (21 November 2018) <https://bit.ly/2H3p4CO> accessed 1 July 2019

Ayittey GBN, 'The End of African Socialism?' (1 May 1990) <http:// www.heritage.org/africa/report/the-end-african-socialism> accessed 1 July 2019

Besseling, Robert, 'African Countries at Highest Risk of Debt Distress: EXX Africa Exclusive' (31 May 2019) <https://bit.ly/2M5ri8G> accessed 1 July 2019

Bhatia G, 'Directive Principles of State Policy' in Choudhry S, Khosla M, and Mehta PB (eds), *The Oxford Handbook of the Indian Constitution* (OUP 2016)

Coulibaly I, 'Costs and Benefits of the CFA Franc' (28 February 2017) <https://worldpolicy.org/2017/02/28/costs-and-benefits-of-the-cfa-franc/> accessed July 2019

Daintith T, 'The Constitutional Protection of Economic Rights' (2004) 2(1) I.CON 66

Dlamini CRM, 'The Right to Administrative Justice in South Africa: Creating an Open and Accountable Democracy' (2000) 2000(1) JSAL 797

Dreyfus F, *La liberté du commerce et de l'industrie* (Berger-Levrault 1973)

Feiyue S, 'Economic Constitutionalism: Path for State to Intervene in the Economy' (2003) 1(3) Frontiers of Law in China 372

Fombad CM (ed), *The Implementation of Modern African Constitutions: Challenges and Prospects* (PULP 2016)

Fombad CM *Constitutional Adjudication in Africa* (OUP 2017)

Fombad CM, 'African Bill of Rights in a Comparative Perspective' (2011) 17(1) Fundamina 33

Fombad CM, 'The Role of Emerging Hybrid Institutions of Accountability in the Separation of Powers Scheme in Africa' in Fombad CM (ed), *Separation of Powers in African Constitutionalism* (OUP 2016)

Fombad CM 'The Diffusion of South African-style Institutions? A Study of Comparative Constitutionalism' in Dixon R and Roux T (eds), *Constitutional Triumphs, Constitutional Disappointments: A Critical Assessment of the 1996 South African Constitution's Local and International Influence* (Cambridge University Press 2018)

Harvey D *A Brief History of Neoliberalism* (Oxford University Press 2007)

Jingkun L, 'The Development of European Economic Constitution and Its Roles in Regulating the Common Market—with Free Competition and Free Movements as an Example' (2007) 1(21) Working Paper Series on European Studies, Institute of European Studies, Chinese Academy of Social Sciences, 1 <http://ies.cass.cn/webpic/web/ies2/en/UploadFiles_8765/201209/2012092508352997.pdf> accessed 1 July 2019

Jones T, '"Outrageous" Mozambique Debt Deal Could Make 270% Profit for Speculators' (8 November 2018) <http://www.cadtm.org/spip.php?page=imprimer&id_article=16793> accessed 1 July 2019

Klein M, 'Why Federal Reserve Independence Matters' (1 July 2019) <http://www.salon.com/2019/07/01/why-federal-reserve-independence-matters_partner/> accessed 1 July 2019

Larrarte AM and Claudio-Quiroga G, 'The DRC and China's Sicomines: Why Future Deals Should be Different' (3 April 2019) <https://bit.ly/2yI4piQ> accessed 1 July 2019

Meirotti M and Masterson G, 'State Capture in Africa: Old Threats, New Packaging?' (2018) <http://www.eisa.org.za/pdf/sym2017papers.pdf> accessed 1 July 2019

Mullen and Petroff, 'South Africa's Currency Plummets after Finance Minister Fired' (1 April 2017) <https://cnn.it/2KtG6Me> accessed 1 July 2019

Mustapha S and Prizzon A, 'Africa's Rising Debt: How to Avoid a New Crisis' (1 November 2018) <http://www.odi.org/sites/odi.org.uk/files/resource-documents/12491.pdf> accessed July 2019

Odike EA, Faga HP, and Nwakpu IW, 'Incorporation of Fundamental Objectives and Directive Principles of State Policy in the Constitutions of Emerging Democracies: A Beneficial Wrongdoing or a Democratic Demagoguery?' (2016) 7(4) Beijing Law Review <http://file.scirp.org/Html/1-3300458_71212.htm> accessed July 2019

Onésimo S, Africa South of the Sahara: Party Systems and Ideologies of Socialism (Rabén & Sjögren 1976)

Ottaway MS, 'The Crisis of the Socialist State in Africa' in Ergas Z (ed), The African State in Transition (Palgrave Macmillan 1987)

Paul EF, Miller Jr FD, and Paul J.(eds), Economic Rights (Cambridge University Press 1992)

Pelizzo R, 'Public Accounts Committees in the Commonwealth: Oversight, Effectiveness, and Governance' (2011) 49(4) Journal of Commonwealth and Comparative Politics 528

Posner RA, 'The Constitution as an Economic Document' (1987) 56 George Washington Law Review 4

Prosser T, The Economic Constitution (OUP 2014)

Reyntjens F, 'Recent Developments in the Public Law of Francophone African States' (1986) 30(2) Journal of African Law 87

Schmidt M, 'The End of the West African CFA,' (2 July 2020) <http://www.businesslive.co.za/fm/features/africa/2020-07-02-the-end-of-the-west-african-cfa-franc/> accessed August 2020

Sylla NS, 'The CFA Franc: French Monetary Imperialism in Africa' (12 July 2017) <https://bit.ly/2KGMHBR> accessed 1 July 2019

Tuori K, 'Tony Prosser: The Economic Constitution' (2014) 12 ICON 1075

5

The Unravelling of the Constitution, Economy, and Constitutionalism in South Africa

*Nico Steytler**

1. Introduction

In March 1993, the African National Congress (ANC) produced a 'draft Bill of Rights' shortly before the final round of negotiations with the white minority regime began in earnest. It contained an article that sought to protect property from confiscation without just compensation (which would be justiciable), and, along with it, the following paragraph: 'The above provisions shall not be interpreted as impeding legislation such as might be deemed necessary in a democratic society with a mixed economy...'[1] The provision was followed immediately by a cautionary 'note' which read:

> Reference to a mixed economy may be unnecessarily provocative both to those in favour of an extensive free market and those who wish for considerable state intervention. It is not normal to have any constitutional prescription on either issue.[2]

In these two quotes lie the history and possible future of the link between the constitution and the economy in South Africa. The economic system was a key issue in the negotiations between the ANC, supporting socialism, and the white minority regime, advocating a market economy and the protection of acquired wealth. It was not *the* key issue, though, as many in the ANC envisaged a two-stage revolution: the first was the 'National Democratic Revolution' capturing political power, the second, an economic revolution.[3] At the time, a 'provocative' stance on a 'mixed economy' was to be avoided (as if a constitution could be neutral about economic policy). In the end, the constitutional compromises of 1993 and 1996 followed the dominant economic model of the post-Cold War era and enshrined the basics of a free market but with a few openings made for the transformation of the economy.

After twenty-seven years of democracy, the economic compact underpinning the two constitutions is slowly unravelling. This brings the economy to the fore as *the* central issue confronting South Africa today, with more than half of the population in poverty, and the bulk of land and wealth still in white hands.

* I wish to acknowledge the research assistance of Dr Michelle Maziwisa, a postdoctoral fellow, and Curtly Stevens, a SARChI Chair doctoral research fellow, at the Dullah Omar Institute of the University of the Western Cape.

[1] ANC, *Bill of Rights: Policy Guide* (ANC Department of Information and Publicity March 1993), art 13(8).
[2] ibid.
[3] Mcebisi Jonas, *After Dawn: Hope after State Capture* (Picador Africa 2019) 37.

Nico Steytler, *The Unravelling of the Constitution, Economy, and Constitutionalism in South Africa* In: *Constitutionalism and the Economy in Africa*. Edited by: Charles M Fombad and Nico Steytler, Oxford University Press. © Nico Steytler 2022. DOI: 10.1093/oso/9780192886439.003.0007

The focus of this chapter is on the following questions. First, why did the negotiations produce a constitutional framework friendlier towards a market economy rather than a mixed one? Secondly, how was this negotiated result cemented in the 1993 and 1996 constitutions? Thirdly, after more than twenty-five years, why is the economic compact being questioned, and what are the constitutional implications of such an unravelling?

It will be argued, first, that due to the collapse of the East Bloc economies and the stridency of the free-market West, the resultant local and international pressures led the ANC to abandon its yearning for a strong interventionist state in the economy.

Secondly, while the basic elements of the free-market economy were firmly entrenched in the Bill of Rights, the establishment of a 'social' state through enforceable socio-economic rights was also envisaged. Although a quasi-federal system was adopted, the Constitution posits a single national economy under the regulation of the national government.

Thirdly, having the most secure constitutional state on the continent has not led inevitably to a productive economy. The South African economy is stagnating, and, under the pressure of the COVID-19 pandemic, threatening to implode, all of which has prepared the ground for questioning of both the market economy and its lack of transformation. A softening of the Constitution's property clause is already in the pipeline, albeit that the means of effecting changes to the ownership of wealth are a subject of contestation.

The chapter begins by describing how South Africa's constitutional negotiations resulted in a reasonably free-market economy, after which it dissects the latter's concretization in the 1993 and 1996 constitutions, with specific attention paid to the issue of land and natural resources. It goes on to outline the constitutional framework for the state's role in the economy, before discussing the broader issue of constitutionalism and economic growth.

2. Negotiating a Market Economy

The debate in South Africa about the place of the state in the market economy began as long as seventy years ago when the National Party (NP) was voted into office and used its political power to entrench apartheid and advance whites (Afrikaners in particular) economically through state institutions and interventions in the economy.[4] The private sector, almost exclusively in white hands, was left to thrive, however; indeed, the mainstay of the economy, the mining industry, benefited from apartheid through the supply of cheap labour.[5]

It was only in the late 1980s that the white government fully embraced the free market. Following its 1987 *White Paper on Privatization and Deregulation*, it sought to open up the market, privatized the major state industries—the Iron and Steel Corporation (South Africa) (Iscor), and Suid-Afrikaanse Steenkool (Sasol), a company producing oil from coal—and commercialized the Post Office, Telecommunications (Telkom), and the Electricity Supply Commission (Eskom).[6] With majority rule in the country imminent, the overall objective was to reduce the state's role in the economy—a preventative strategy for

---

[4] See Roger Southall, 'The ANC, Black Economic Empowerment and State-Owned Enterprises: A Recycling of History' in Sakhela Buhlungu and others (eds), *State of the Nation: South Africa 2007* (HSRC Press 2007) 201.

[5] See Steven Friedman, *Race, Class and Power: Harold Wolpe and the Radical Critique of Apartheid* (UKZN Press 2015).

[6] David Lazar, 'Competing Economic Ideologies in South Africa's Economic Debate' (1996) 47(4) British Journal of Sociology 599, 617.

the coming democratic transition, which would see these state institutions falling under majority control.[7]

In the same period, African nationalists and communists articulated an opposing vision, crying out against the injustices of apartheid and the economic system that bolstered it. In the Freedom Charter, adopted by the Congress of the People in 1956,[8] the economic demand was that '[t]he people shall share in the country's wealth'. The Charter declared:

> The mineral wealth beneath the soil, the banks and monopoly industry shall be transferred to the ownership of the people as a whole.
>
> All other industries and trade shall be controlled to assist the well-being of the people.
>
> All people shall have equal rights to trade where they choose to manufacture and to enter all trades, crafts and professions.

The NP government charged the drafters with the crime of treason and furthering the aims of communism, contending that the Charter could be implemented only through the overthrow of the state in a socialist revolution. After a marathon trial, the court dismissed the charges, finding no such socialist intent.[9] The document was, according to commentators, no more than a social democratic programme of action similar to many European welfare states;[10] in the view of Dennis Davis, though, 'one of the most indigenous aspects of the Freedom Charter [was] the inclusion of social and economic rights'.[11]

Despite the banning and persecution of the ANC, the Freedom Charter resurfaced in the 1980s and became the rallying point for the United Democratic Front, a mass democratic movement aligned to the ANC. As the ANC and NP clandestinely edged towards a negotiated deal, the ANC set about giving meat to the Charter's bones. In the ANC's Constitutional Principles of 1988, the language is still that of the state dominating the economy: 'The state shall have the right to determine the general context in which economic life takes place and defines the limits to the rights and obligations attaching to the ownership and use of productive capacity'.[12] There is no more talk of nationalization of industry and mines, though, but rather of a 'mixed' economy[13] in which only '[p]roperty for personal use and consumption shall be constitutionally protected'.[14] Significantly, aversion to 'the rule of law' is evident:[15] rights were to be enforced by 'appropriate mechanisms', not the courts.[16]

---

[7] James Jude Hentz, 'The Two Faces of Privatisation: Political and Economic Logics in Transitional South Africa' (2000) 38(2) Journal of Modern African Studies 203.

[8] The Congress of the People comprised the ANC, South African Indian Congress, South African Congress of Democrats (consisting mainly of former members of the banned South African Communist Party), and the South African Coloured People's Organization. See Dennis Davis, 'The Freedom Charter: A Challenge and Bequest' in Nico Steytler (ed), *The Freedom Charter and Beyond: Founding Principles for a Democratic South African Legal Order* (Wyvern 1992) 2.

[9] Kumi Naidoo and Dan Pillay, 'The Freedom Charter in the 1956 Treason Trial' in Nico Steytler (ed), *The Freedom Charter and Beyond: Founding Principles for a Democratic South African Legal Order* (Wyvern 1992).

[10] Pieter le Roux, 'The Social Democratic Nature of the Charterist Economic Vision' in Nico Steytler (ed), *The Freedom Charter and Beyond: Founding Principles for a Democratic South African Legal Order* (Wyvern 1992) 125.

[11] Davis (n 8) 10.

[12] ANC, Constitutional Guidelines for a Democratic South Africa: African National Congress Proposals— 1955 & 1988 (1988) para o.

[13] ibid para q.

[14] ibid para t.

[15] Davis (n 8) 14.

[16] Constitutional Guidelines (1988), para h.

When the ANC was unbanned in 1990, its socialist orientation soon withered away under internal and external pressure. In a working draft for consultation, its Bill of Rights for a Democratic South Africa of 1990 was a different kettle of fish from its Constitutional Principles. The state no longer commands the economy but seeks collaboration with the private sector;[17] the right to property is recognized, as is expropriation with just compensation. However, it is also declared that '[a]ll natural resources below and above the surface areas of the land ... shall belong to the state', and that the state has the right to regulate the exploitation of such resources.[18] Labour and socio-economic rights are included, while a constitutional court is the ultimate enforcer, albeit that the grounds of judicial review are weak.[19]

The ANC draft policy on the economy of 1991 also reflected the shift away from the command economy. In adopting a mixed economy model, the party explained that '[w]e are convinced that neither a commandist central planning nor an unfettered free market system can provide adequate solutions to the problems confronting us'.[20] What was required was a 'developmental state' that would 'lead, coordinate and dynamise a national economic strategy'.[21] Central to the strategy were state-owned enterprises in transport, housing, electricity, water, and telecommunications that would provide the infrastructural base for development. Instead of commanding the economy, the state should encourage and support 'a more dynamic and efficient private sector'.[22] The document ends with the double-exclamation-mark rallying cry, 'Forward to a democratic mixed economy!!'[23]

As the negotiations inched closer, the ANC in March 1993 produced a further draft Bill of Rights with several major differences to the 1990 version. The state itself no longer has ownership of natural resources: land, waters, and natural resources 'are the common heritage of the people of South Africa who are equally entitled to their enjoyment and responsible for their conservation'.[24] However, the state retains its right to regulate the exploitation of all natural resources, with such regulation 'subject to payment of just compensation in the event of interference with any existing title, mining right or concession'.[25] By then the game was over, or for time being anyway: existing property rights were sacrosanct.

Explaining the dramatic shift, David Lazar argues that, as democratic victory drew nearer, there was growing realism within the ANC about the economic options open to it, particularly in the face of white resistance and intense pressure from both internal and foreign business interests.[26] For Lazar, the most potent factor, though, was 'the humiliating collapse of state-run repressive "planned" (in reality often chaotic) economies of East-Central Europe'.[27] The ANC had also started to see some positive value in the market, separating capitalism from apartheid. Lazar remarks that by 1994 the difference in economic policy

---

[17]   ANC, ANC's Bill of Rights for a Democratic South Africa of 1990, art 11(1).

[18]   ibid art 11(3) and (4).

[19]   Davis (n 8) 18.

[20]   ANC, Draft Resolution on ANC Economic Policy for National Conference (Centre for Development Studies, UWC 1991) 3.

[21]   ibid.

[22]   ibid 4.

[23]   ibid 12.

[24]   ANC, *Bill of Rights* (1993), art 12(1).

[25]   ibid art 12(13).

[26]   David Lazar, 'Competing Economic Ideologies in South Africa's Economic Debate' (1996) 47(4) British Journal of Sociology 599, 614.

[27]   ibid 612.

between the ANC and the NP was a matter of emphasis: the ANC wanted more interventionism by the state, while the NP sought to reduce it.[28]

The grand compromise reached by the end of 1993 was twofold: political power shifted to the black majority, in return for which white economic power was preserved more or less intact—this thanks to the entrenchment of the market economy through the protection of private property. For some in the ANC, it was the first phase in the two-phase transition: after the National Democratic Revolution comes the economic revolution that focuses on transforming property relations.

From a broader perspective, Mcebisi Jonas, a former Deputy Minister of Finance,[29] argues that the constitutional consensus was built on four pillars.[30] First, an established elite (white) was accommodated by providing financial continuity and the protection of property; secondly, a new (black) elite was accommodated by public sector employment, state-business patronage, and black economic empowerment (BEE); thirdly, organized labour was accommodated by labour rights; and, finally, the poor and unemployed were accommodated through the roll-out of the welfare state. It is this consensus that was given constitutional expression in the 1993 and 1996 constitutions.

3. Protecting a Market Economy

The interim Constitution of 1993,[31] which shepherded in the first democratic elections in April 1994, reflected the basics of a market economy and provided the national government with limited scope to command the economy. It also contained a set of Constitutional Principles to which the new Parliament was bound in its drafting of a final constitution; however, the Principles did not say much about the economic model for the future. The focus of this chapter thus falls on the provisions of the 1996 Constitution.[32]

3.1 Interim 1993 Constitution

The 1993 Constitution was a typical liberal constitution protecting the basic elements of a market economy. First, in reaction to the exclusivity of the business environment under apartheid and in reflection of the Freedom Charter, it proclaimed 'the right freely to engage in economic activity and to pursue a livelihood anywhere in the national territory'.[33] Great caution was then shown in preventing this right from entrenching a *laissez-faire* economic policy. Thus, it did not

> preclude measures designed to promote the protection or the improvement of the quality of life, economic growth, human development, social justice, basic conditions of

---

[28] ibid 620.
[29] He was fired by President Zuma, along with the then Minister of Finance, Pravin Gordhan, for resisting state capture.
[30] Jonas (n 3) 2, figure 1.
[31] Constitution of the Republic of South Africa Act 200 of 1993 (hereafter interim Constitution).
[32] Constitution of the Republic of South Africa of 1996 (hereafter 1996 Constitution).
[33] Interim Constitution, s 26(1).

employment, fair labour practices or equal opportunity for all, provided such measures are justified in an open and democratic society based on freedom and equality.[34]

By virtue of this claw-back clause, an open—that is to say, competitive—economy was placed firmly placed under government regulation, pre-emptively ensuring that the United States Supreme Court's restrictive jurisprudence on regulating labour relations[35] during the *Lochner* era could not find traction before a conservative South African court. The right of workers to unionize and take strike action was protected, on the one hand, as, on the other, was the employer's right of lockout.[36] Central to this market system was that private property was protected from expropriation without fair compensation (with the fairness of such compensation determinable by reference to a number of factors, including the property's history of acquisition and its market value).[37] Specific provision was made, however, for the restitution of land where there had been dispossession on racial grounds.[38] No reference was made to socio-economic rights.

The multilevel structure of the state, another key aspect of the negotiations, was in the end no more than a flirtation with federalism.[39] Provinces were given no independent taxing powers, and those they received by the grace of the national parliament could not be exercised in a way 'detrimentally affecting economic policies, inter-provincial commerce or the national mobility of goods services, capital and labour';[40] their borrowing powers were also highly restricted. Although provinces enjoyed concurrent powers in matters such as 'trade and industrial promotion',[41] the economy was seen as indivisible and allowing for only limited provincial regulation. Moreover, in the event of a clash between a concurrent national and provincial power, the national law would prevail if this were necessary, inter alia, for 'national economic policies [and] the maintenance of economic unity'.[42]

As the 1993 Constitution was only an interim measure and the 'final' constitution the mandate of a democratically elected parliament, the outgoing white government sought to entrench a set of principles with which that future constitution would have to comply. These 'Constitutional Principles' were remarkably low-key when it came to the economy. There was no reference to the right to property, for example, merely the stipulation that fundamental rights should be universal and enforceable and that, in the drafting of these fundamental rights, those rights in the interim Constitution should be 'given due consideration'.[43]

---

[34] ibid s 26(2).
[35] In *Lochner v New York*, 198 US 45 (1905), the majority held that the imposition of minimum conditions of service violated the 14th Amendment 'freedom of contract'.
[36] Interim Constitution, s 27.
[37] ibid s 28.
[38] ibid s 119.
[39] Nico Steytler, 'The Withering Away of Politically Salient Territorial Cleavages in South Africa and the Emergence of Watermark Ethnic Federalism' in George Anderson and Sujit Chowdry (eds), *Territory and Power in Constitutional Transitions* (OUP 2019).
[40] Interim Constitution, s 156(2).
[41] ibid sch 6.
[42] ibid s 126(3)(d).
[43] ibid sch 4, Constitutional Principle II.

3.2 1996 Constitution

The Bill of Rights protected the basic elements of a market economy, securing the right to property, the freedom of trade, occupation, and profession, and, implicitly, contractual freedom. As a corrective to a 'free' market, it entrenched workers' rights and a range of socio-economic rights in setting the broad parameters of a social state. Section 25 establishes a system of property rights (movable and immovable) that takes the two-pronged approach of protecting private property while permitting the transformation of property holdings in the interests of historically disadvantaged persons.[44] Similarly, the courts have tried to strike a balance between the ownership claims of those who have property and those who do not.[45]

As the ANC was not keen at all on a property clause, the right to property, expressed in the interim Constitution as a positive right, is expressed in the negative:[46] section 25(1) allows for the deprivation of property in terms of a law of general application provided that such deprivation is not arbitrary. In terms of section 25(3), expropriation, a special type of deprivation that negates ownership, is permitted for a public purpose or in the public interest, provided there is compensation for the property so expropriated. Unlike section 12(a)(i) of the Expropriation Act,[47] which required compensation at market value based on a willing buyer and willing seller, section 25(3) lists various factors that should be considered when determining compensation, with market value being only one of them:

a) the current use of the property;
b) the history of the acquisition of the property and use of the property;
c) the market value of the property;
d) the extent of direct state investment and subsidy in the acquisition and beneficial capital improvement of the property; and
e) the purpose of the expropriation.

The second ingredient of a market economy—open competition—is implicitly recognized in section 22, which guarantees the right of everyone to choose his or her 'trade, occupation or profession freely'. This right is weakly protected, though, in that '[t]he practice of a trade, occupation or profession may be regulated by law'; since no qualification is attached to the regulation, the state has a more or less free hand.[48]

The third ingredient of a free market is the protection of freedom of contract. As in most constitutions, freedom of contract is not explicitly provided for in the Bill of Rights. However, the common law principle of *pacta sunt servanda* (the freedom of contract and the enforceability of such) finds a new constitutional basis. Such freedom, the Constitutional

---

[44] Jackie Dugard, 'Unpacking Section 25: Is South Africa's Property Clause an Obstacle or Engine for Socio-Economic Transformation?' (2018) 4 <https://bit.ly/37ouvZh> accessed 30 November 2020.

[45] In *Port Elizabeth Municipality v Various Occupiers* 2005 (1) SA 217 (CC) [15], the Constitutional Court (Sachs J) noted: 'The blatant disregard manifested by racist statutes for property rights in the past makes it all the more important that property rights be fully respected in the new dispensation, both by the state and private persons. Yet such rights have to be understood in the context of the need for the orderly opening-up or restoration of secure property rights for those denied access to or deprived of them in the past.'

[46] Mohamed Ever Surty, *In Pursuit of Dignity* (Awqaf South Africa 2019) 181.

[47] Act 63 of 1975.

[48] See Dennis Davis, 'Freedom of Trade, Occupation and Profession' in Stuart Woolman and others (eds), *Constitutional Law of South Africa* vol 4 (Juta 2014) ch 54.

Court held, is now derived from the constitutional values of 'freedom and dignity'.[49] The principle is supported by the constitutional value in section 1(c) of the Constitution, the rule of law, of which legality (and legal certainty) is a key component.[50] The law of contract has also been infused by other values in the new constitutional era, including that of *ubuntu*. In seeking to develop the common law of contract in a more communitarian direction, Moseneke DCJ noted:

> Had the case been properly pleaded, a number of interlinking constitutional values would inform the development of the common law. Indeed, it is highly desirable and in fact necessary to infuse the law of contract with constitutional values, including values of Ubuntu, which inspire much of our constitutional compact. On a number of occasions in the past this court has had regard to the meaning and content of the concept of Ubuntu. It emphasises the communal nature of society and 'carries in it the ideas of humaneness, social justice and fairness' and envelops the key values of group solidarity, compassion, respect, human dignity, conformity to basic norms and collective unity.[51]

Although the Constitutional Court recognizes the need to develop the law of contract in line with the spirit of the Constitution, the values of humanness, social justice, and fairness have not become self-standing requirements for the enforceability of contractual terms: in other words, these terms do not become unenforceable merely because a judge might deem them unfair, unreasonable, or unduly harsh. These values do, however, inform public policy, as a result of which they could render terms of contract unenforceable.[52] The court's protection of the principle of *pacta sunt servanda* against the backdrop of general equity jurisprudence has been based very much on the principle's direct link to the economy:

> [C]ontractual relations are the bedrock of economic activity and our economic development is dependent, to a large extent, on the willingness of parties to enter into contractual relationships. If parties are confident that contracts that they enter into will be upheld, then they will be incentivised to contract with other parties for their mutual gain. Without this confidence, the very motivation for social coordination is diminished. It is indeed crucial to economic development that individuals should be able to trust that all contracting parties will be bound by obligations willingly assumed.[53]

Having secured the basic ingredients of a market economy, the Bill of Rights focuses as well as measures for correcting a rampant free market. In the case of labour relations, section 23(1) secures the right of 'everyone' to 'fair labour practices'. This includes the right of workers to form or join a trade union and of employers to do the same by way of employers' organizations.[54] Labour protection is thus not subject to a purely market-led approach in which wages, hours of work, and other conditions of employment are determined by the

---

[49]   *Barkhuizen v Napier* [2007] ZACC 5 para 57.
[50]   *Beadica 231 CC and Others v Trustees for the time being of the Oregon Trust and Others* [2020] ZACC 13 (*Beadica 231* CC) para 81.
[51]   *Everfresh Market Virginia (Pty) Ltd v Shoprite Checkers (Pty) Ltd* 2012 (1) SA 256 (CC) para 71.
[52]   *Beadica 231* CC para 80.
[53]   ibid para 84.
[54]   ibid s 23(3).

employer and left to be regulated by the market. Instead, section 23 affords specific protections to both employees and employers; accordingly, the conduct of labour relations is subject to state regulation. Key provisions relate to fair labour practices as well as to the rights of employees and employers to unionize and take part in collective bargaining.

Section 23 also endows employees with the right to strike, a right which is no longer linked to collective bargaining as it had been under the interim Constitution. Indeed, this section was challenged in the constitutional certification process[55] for its failure to recognize employer's rights to lockout, rights which had been provided for in that earlier constitution; however, section 23 was found to be congruent with constitutional principles. A second area of contestation was that the Bill of Rights did not provide for the right of employers to bargain collectively with employees—a gap remedied in section 23(5) of the final text of the Constitution.

The significant innovation in the Bill of Rights was its inclusion of socio-economic rights that resonated with the Freedom Charter. Among the positive obligations imposed on the state is that it has to realize the unqualified right to 'a basic education, including basic adult education';[56] among the qualified socio-economic rights are the rights of access to 'adequate housing'[57] and 'health care services, including reproductive health care, sufficient food and water, and social security, including, if people are not able to support themselves and their dependents, appropriate social assistance'.[58] The state's duty to fulfil these rights is qualified in that it has only to take 'reasonable legislative and other measures, within available resources, to achieve [their] progressive realisation'.[59] Through these justiciable socio-economic rights, the framework for a 'social state' was established.

4. Land and Natural Resources

In view of South Africa's historical legacy of land dispossession and inequality, land reform was an important constitutional matter. The Constitution is mute on the subject of the control and ownership of other natural resources, but as 'land' is included in the term 'property',[60] it is as such protected from expropriation without some form of compensation. Given the skewed distribution of landownership along racial lines, the Constitution also makes provision for both land restitution and the reform of landownership.

In section 25, provision is hence made for the restitution of land to a person or community that was dispossessed after 19 July 1913 by racially discriminatory legislation or practice—this is the date on which the Land Act of 1913 came into effect and allocated 13 per cent of the country's land to the African population and the rest to whites. An Act of Parliament was thus foreseen that would provide for either restitution of the property or 'equitable redress'.[61] A second form of restitution is the conversion of insecure tenure of land to legal security or to 'comparable redress': a person or a community whose tenure of land

---

[55] *Ex Parte Chairperson of the Constitutional Assembly: In Re Certification of the Constitution of the Republic of South Africa, 1996* (1996) (10) BCLR 1253 (CC).
[56] 1996 Constitution, s 29(1).
[57] ibid s 26(1).
[58] ibid s 27(1).
[59] ibid ss 26(2), 27(2).
[60] ibid s 25(4)(b).
[61] ibid s 25(7).

was legally insecure owing to 'racially discriminatory laws or practices' was entitled to such redress as provided by an Act of Parliament. The Land Reform (Labour Tenants) Act,[62] the Extension of Security of Tenure Act (ESTA),[63] and Interim Protection of Informal Land Rights[64] were enacted to give effect to these provisions.

A more formidable constitutional project was deracializing landownership. Section 25(5) instructs the state to take 'reasonable legislative and other measures, within its available resources to foster conditions which enable citizens to gain access to land on an equitable basis'. This provision is bolstered by an interpretative clause indicating that no provision of section 25 '[may] impede the state from taking legislative and other measures to achieve land, water and related reform'; such measures, where they depart from the section, must comply with the general limitation clause.[65]

The 1996 Constitution has one direct reference to 'natural resources': given that property may be expropriated 'only for a public purpose or in the public interest', section 24(4)(a) states that 'the public interest includes the nation's commitment to land reform, and to reforms to bring about equitable access to all South Africa's *natural resources*'.[66] A further, indirect, reference is found in the envisaged action the state must take to 'achieve land, water or related reform'—'related reform' is conceivably concerned with mineral and petroleum rights. The import of section 25 was summed up by Chief Justice Mogoeng:

> We must therefore interpret section 25 with due regard to the gross inequality in relation to wealth and land distribution in this country. And by design, the MPRDA [Mineral and Petroleum Resources Development Act 28 of 2002] is meant to broaden access to business opportunities in the mining industry for all, especially previously disadvantaged people. It is not only about the promotion of equitable access, but also about job creation, the advancement of the social and economic welfare of all our people, the promotion of economic growth and the development of our mineral and petroleum resources for the common good of all South Africans.
>
> This brings to the fore the obligation imposed by section 25 not to over-emphasise private property rights at the expense of the state's social responsibilities. It must always be remembered that our history does not permit a near-absolute status to be given to individual property rights to the detriment of the equally important duty of the state to ensure that all South Africans partake of the benefits flowing from our mineral and petroleum resources.[67]

Such a measure was the enactment of the MPRDA to facilitate equitable redistribution and sustainable use of mineral and petroleum resources. The Act also transformed the common law position of landownership, which entailed ownership of what is above as well as below the land, and instead vested all mineral rights in the state.[68] This included changing pre-democracy mining licences to new-order prospecting and mining licences.

---

[62] Act 3 of 1996.
[63] Act 62 of 1997.
[64] Act 31 of 1996.
[65] 1996 Constitution, s 25(8) with reference to s 36.
[66] Emphasis added.
[67] *Agri South Africa v Minister for Minerals and Energy* 2013 (7) BCLR 727 (CC) para 62.
[68] MPRDA, s 3(1).

5. The Role of the State in the Market

While the Bill of Rights shields the market from the state to a certain extent (to an extent only, given that all rights are subject to reasonable limitations), the Constitution does not prevent a regulatory role for the state. Indeed, a broad framework is provided for national and subnational governmental engagement in the economy.

First, '[n]ational, provincial and municipal budgets and budgetary processes must promote transparency, accountability and *the effective financial management of the economy*, debt and the public sector'.[69] The concern is with how public money is managed effectively when the state engages with the private sector (the economy), borrows money, and manages state-owned enterprises (the public sector). These three elements are interconnected: poor management of a state-owned enterprise (eg Eskom, the electricity generator) results in desperate borrowing (to bail out a bankrupt Eskom), all of which impacts adversely on the economy (unreliable electricity supply hobbles domestic productivity and, combined with the ensuing unsustainable borrowing, leads to a lack of investment and poor credit ratings).

Secondly, as the state is a major buyer of goods and services from the private sector, public procurement has a significant bearing on how the market functions. The Constitution thus prescribes a system of procurement which is 'fair, equitable, transparent, competitive and cost effective'.[70] These elements affirm, first, an open market (competitive and cost-effective), secondly, equal treatment among the competitors (fairness and transparency), and thirdly, the need to transform the historical structure of the economy (equity). The Constitution thus makes specific allowance for a procurement policy that would provide for 'the protection or advancement of persons, or categories of persons, disadvantaged by unfair discrimination'.[71]

5.1 National Regulation

The national government has broad plenary powers which include regulation of the economy. More specifically, a number of functional areas dealing with the economy fall within the concurrent competences of both national and provincial governments.[72] The nature of these competences is discussed below.

The national executive's regulatory powers are limited in one crucial aspect—protecting the stability of the currency. In line with an international trend, the Constitution provides for an independent central bank called the South African Reserve Bank. Its primary mandate is 'to protect the value of the currency in the interest of balanced and sustainable economic growth in the Republic'.[73] Economic growth is thus not the only objective, albeit that this is a notion economists have derided—some have described 'balanced growth' as 'a curious and largely meaningless turn of phrase that has little or no traction in monetary

---

[69] 1996 Constitution, s 215(1), emphasis added.
[70] ibid s 217(1). In general, see Phoebe Bolton, *The Law of Public Procurement in South Africa* (LexisNexis 2012).
[71] 1996 Constitution, s 217(2)(b).
[72] ibid sch 4.
[73] ibid s 224(1).

or economic theory'.[74] In exercising this function, the Bank must do so 'independently and without fear, favour or prejudice, but there must be regulator consultation between the Bank and [the Minister of Finance]'.[75]

5.2 Subnational Regulation of the Economy

While the ANC's embrace of the market economy was almost complete, the same cannot be said of its enthusiasm for multilevel government. The powers of provinces were less than in the interim Constitution, but not substantively so after the amendment of the first draft of the 1996 Constitution.[76] The main beneficiary of this was local government, which gained an elevated status as one of the spheres of government.[77]

The list of exclusive provincial powers is meagre when it comes to the economy. They include abattoirs, liquor licences, and provincial planning, which could provide for a broad economic development policy.[78] Even then, the national parliament may intervene in this domain 'when it is necessary [inter alia] … to maintain economic unity'.[79] The powers enjoyed concurrently with the national government are much more extensive, however.[80] They may be categorized as those providing the necessary infrastructure for economic activity, those regulating the economy, those promoting economic activity, and those dealing with the state's participation in the economy. Provinces may provide economic infrastructure such as provincial airports and public transport. Their regulatory function covers agriculture, gambling, consumer protection, pollution control, and trade, while their promotional or facilitatory role includes agriculture, industrial promotion, regional planning and development, tourism, and trade. Provinces may also participate in the economy through public enterprises in the areas of their exclusive and concurrent competences.

As these powers are concurrent with the national government, a qualified override clause strongly in favour of the national government is provided in which economic concerns are important factors. First, economic unity is emphasized, and secondly, national economic policies are given paramountcy. Section 146(2)(c) of the Constitution provides that, in the case of a conflict, national legislation prevails over provincial legislation if the former is 'necessary for … (ii) the maintenance of economic unity; (iii) the protection of the common market in respect of the mobility of goods, services, capital and labour; [and] (iv) the promotion of economic activities across provincial boundaries'.[81]

Although the Constitution confers no direct taxing powers on provinces, those that are authorized by national legislation 'may not be exercised in a way that materially and

---

[74] Vishnu Padayachee, Imraan Valodia, and Robert van Niekerk, 'Evolution of ANC Economic Policy Sheds Light on Squabble over the Central Bank' *The Conversation* (3 July 2019) <https://theconversation.com/evolution-of-anc-economic-policy-sheds-light-on-squabble-over-the-central-bank-119401> accessed 25 August 2019.

[75] 1996 Constitution, s 224(2).

[76] Certification of the Amended Text of the Constitution of the Republic of South Africa, 1996 [1996] ZACC 24.

[77] Nico Steytler and Jaap de Visser, *Local Government Law of South Africa* (LexisNexis 2007) ch 1.

[78] 1996 Constitution, sch 5.

[79] ibid s 44(2)(b).

[80] ibid sch 4.

[81] Furthermore, s 146(3) provides that '[n]ational legislation prevails over provincial legislation if the national legislation is aimed at preventing unreasonable action by a province that—(a) is prejudicial to the economic, health or security interests of another province or the country as a whole; or (b) impedes the implementation of national economic policy'.

unreasonably prejudices national economic policies, economic activities across provincial boundaries, or the national mobility of goods, services, capital or labour'.[82] Furthermore, to cap the protection of a single economy, the national executive may intervene in a province which has failed to fulfil an executive obligation, doing so through the assumption of responsibilities 'to the extent necessary to ... maintain economic unity'.[83]

Local government, unlike the other two spheres of government, is given a particular mandate to promote economic development: one of the objects of local government is precisely 'to promote social and economic development'.[84] Accordingly, every municipality 'must structure and manage its administration and budgeting and planning processes to give priority to the basic needs of the community, and to promote the social and economic development of the community'.[85] Municipalities are thus given significant powers to: provide the necessary infrastructure for economic activity (electricity, water, roads, and public transport); regulate certain minor aspects of economic activities (air pollution, building regulations); and promote economic activity in general (through municipal planning and local tourism).

In the same manner as the national executive performs an oversight function over provinces, so do provinces over municipalities. The provincial government may intervene in a municipality through the assumption of responsibilities 'to the extent necessary to ... maintain economic unity'.[86]

Within this broad framework protecting a market economy, the division of powers between three levels of government could also impact on how the economy is regulated. As with various other federations, the overriding concept is the 'unity of the economy'. While all three spheres are endowed with forms of regulatory power, these powers have to be exercised in a way that observes the unified concept of the economy; furthermore, in view of the 'unity of the economy', the national government is posited as its chief regulator.

6. The Developmental State, Economic Growth, and Constitutionalism

While the grand compact of the 1993 and 1996 constitutions institutionalized a market economy, the goals it set included the transformation of landholding and, to a lesser extent, the deracialization of property relationships; the 1996 Constitution also established the basis for a 'social' state through its provisions for access to housing, education, health care, social security, food, and water. The bedrock of this framework is the main elements of constitutionalism—the separation of powers, the limitation of state power, and the rule of law—which, by and large, were subsequently given expression in practice.[87]

The compact delivered initial dividends in terms of political and societal peace, with the new 'developmental' state—in effect, a welfare state—dramatically extending services to all.

---

[82] 1996 Constitution, s 228(2)(a).
[83] ibid s 100(1)(b)(ii).
[84] ibid s 152(1)(c).
[85] ibid s 153(a).
[86] ibid s 139(1)(b)(iii).
[87] See Nico Steytler, 'The Dynamic Relationship between Devolution and Constitutionalism in South Africa' in Charles M Fombad and Nico Steytler (eds), *Constitutionalism and Decentralisation in Africa* (OUP 2019).

However, the four pillars of the compact (white elite, black elite, labour, and the poor) have for long been crumbling. At the core of the problem lies a faltering economy: as President Cyril Ramaphosa observed in 2019, the 1994 agreement has been unravelling because no changes have occurred in poverty, inequality, and the distribution of wealth.[88] This section takes up these questions by sketching out the political economy of the past twenty-five years and considering what role constitutionalism, or its absence, has played in South Africa's current malaise.

6.1 A Political-Economy Overview: From Mandela to Zuma

The ANC's election campaign in 1994 was based on the Reconstruction and Development Programme (RDP), which envisaged state intervention in an economy that had been in serious decline in the last two decades of apartheid rule. The Government of National Unity adopted this programme, the priorities of which were the creation of employment through economic growth and the alleviation of poverty and extreme inequality.[89] Two years later the RDP was replaced by the Growth, Employment, and Redistribution (GEAR) strategy, which focused on macroeconomic measures for ensuring growth: budget-deficit reduction, low inflation, trade liberalization, tax cuts, and deregulation.

The policy was criticized within the tripartite alliance—consisting of the ANC, the Congress of South African Trade Unions (Cosatu), and the South African Communist Party (SACP)—for being driven largely by neoliberal economic principles.[90] Indeed, while GEAR's immediate goals were achieved (low inflation, economic growth rising to 5 per cent), it came at the cost of job losses and increased inequality.[91] By the same token, immense strides were made in this period in the provision of housing, education, social security, health services, and—via municipalities—free electricity and water for indigent residents.

In 2006, at the peak of the country's economic growth, the Mbeki government introduced the Accelerated and Shared Growth Initiative—South Africa (ASGISA), which had the ambitious goal of reaching the Millennial Development Goals of cutting poverty and unemployment by half by 2014.[92] This was to occur through the trickle-down effect of a growing economy and investment in infrastructure, but no sooner was the policy in place than Mbeki lost the ANC presidency in 2007 and was removed from state office in the following year.

The new Zuma government faced increasing challenges after the global financial crisis of 2008. Although South African banks weathered the financial storm, the economy went into recession and more than a million jobs were shed.[93] The New Growth Path (NGP)

---

[88] Cyril Ramaphosa, 'Foreword' in Jonas (n 3) viii.

[89] White Paper on Reconstruction and Development Programme (Ministry in the Office of the President 1994).

[90] Geoffrey E Schneider, 'Neoliberalism and Economic Justice in South Africa: Revisiting the Debate on Economic Apartheid' (2003) 61(1) Review of Social Economy 23; SJ Mosala, JCM Venter, and EG Bain, 'South Africa's Economic Transformation Since 1994: What Influence has the National Democratic Revolution (NDR) Had?' (2017) 44 Review of Black Political Economy 327.

[91] Mosala, Venter, and Bain (n 90) 333.

[92] ibid 334.

[93] Nico Steytler and Derek Powell, 'The Impact of the Global Financial Crisis on Decentralised Government in South Africa' (2010) 358 L'Europe en Formation 149.

strategy thus focused intently on joblessness, poverty, and inequality, seeking to stimulate job creation through infrastructural investment and aiming to create 5 million new jobs by 2020 by supporting economic growth and a labour-absorbing economy. In 2011, the National Planning Commission, appointed by Zuma and chaired by Trevor Manuel, the former Minister of Finance under the Mandela and Mbeki administrations, produced its *National Development Plan: Vision for 2030* (NDP),[94] which sought to provide a blueprint for addressing the country's most intractable problems. Its three priorities were '[r]aising employment through faster economic growth; improving the quality of education, skills development and innovation; [and] building the capability of the state to play a developmental, transformative role'.[95]

With the NDP's objective being to create 11 million jobs by 2030, the tension this entailed was between economic growth and job growth. The best-case scenario was that they would be mutually supportive, with economic growth driving job growth and vice versa; the worst-case scenario was neither economic nor job growth but a rising public-service wage bill, low levels of investment, and falling educational standards.[96] Moreover, the thinking was that economic growth should not only generate jobs but transform ownership of the economy in order to ensure social cohesion. As the Commission noted,

> Social cohesion needs to anchor the strategy. If South Africa registers progress in deracialising ownership and control of the economy without reducing poverty and inequality, transformation will be superficial. Similarly, if poverty and inequality are reduced without demonstrably changed ownership patterns, the country's progress will be turbulent and tenuous.[97]

This transformation, the Commission admitted, would not be easy. It would have to take place without destroying the capabilities of the economy; in addition, for the economy to grow and become more inclusive, the education system would have to produce a skilled labour pool that could compete on the international market with export-driven economic growth. What is more, for the developmental state to lead economic development, this would require an ethical, non-corrupt state staffed by skilled persons appointed on the basis not of party loyalty but of merit. The Commission was clear that high levels of corruption would frustrate the state's ability to deliver on its developmental mandate and that the 'political will' to root it out was essential.[98]

Even in 2011, the Planning Commission, aware of Zuma's presidential ethos, may have had its misgivings about the ready availability of such political will, remarking that '[a] plan is only as credible as its delivery mechanism is viable'.[99] Since the existence of a capable state was a prerequisite for carrying out the NDP, '[t]here is a real risk that South Africa's national plan could fail because the state was incapable of implementation'.[100] Indeed, under Zuma's

---

[94] National Planning Commission, *National Development Plan: Vision for 2030*, RP270/2011 (National Planning Commission 2011). Trevor Manuel was then a minister in the presidency, having been Minister of Finance in both the Mandela and Mbeki cabinets.

[95] ibid 10.

[96] ibid.

[97] ibid.

[98] ibid 24.

[99] ibid 22.

[100] ibid.

rule the NDP was largely ignored:[101] the state was not only incapable of implementing it, but in many respects deliberately and systematically negated the goals it had ostensibly set for itself—which in a sense amounted to an attack on constitutionalism.

First, and most obviously, the rule of law was undermined. Corruption and mismanagement flourished, which meant that the state was increasingly less capable of giving leadership and providing essential economic infrastructure. While corruption was already a problem in 2010,[102] it reached unprecedented levels and culminated in 'state capture' by the Guptas and other business interests, with state-owned enterprises becoming principal sources for enrichment thanks to the appointment both of looters and of incompetent ANC cadres.[103] It is estimated that corrupt activities cost South Africa ZAR 1.6 trillion in lost revenue. The commentator Mcebisi Jonas was led to conclude that the ruling party, 'riven by patronage and corruption … has demonstrated contempt for the rule of law and constitutionalism'.[104]

The causes are manifold, but at their root lies the patrimonial state. Such a state is no longer aimed at developing society economically and socially but at serving the interests of the ruling elite and its minions. As if parodying the trickle-down effects of economic growth, the ethos of a self-serving state permeates the rank and file and seeps downwards from national government to provinces and municipalities. Although state employment was the primary source of new jobs, productivity was not the objective.

It is this ethos which Oscar Mabuyane, elected in 2019 as premier of the Eastern Cape, set out to change in a 120,000-person-strong provincial civil service responsible for providing some of the poorest people in the country with services in education and health. His goal, he said, was '[to inculcate a] new culture that says you are employed to work and earn a salary, not employed to earn a salary and then work'.[105] The prevailing ethos, by contrast, is that state employment is about salaries, not service delivery.

A corrupt and/or incapable state has proven to be devastating for the economy. Two examples suffice. First, due to large-scale theft, corruption, and maladministration, the state-owned electricity generator, Eskom, is bankrupt, burdened with a debt of ZAR 440 billion that places a huge drain on the state's revenue and credit rating; it is also, not coincidentally, unable to deliver electricity adequately and reliably enough to maintain, let alone expand, the economy, which in turn damages growth prospects and investment attractiveness.[106]

The second example is more mundane but equally devastating. Municipalities have the constitutional mandate to distribute electricity and water to consumers, including businesses. Thanks to poor financial management and corruption, some municipalities are unable to pay Eskom for the electricity they buy, compelling it to try to induce payment by interrupting electricity supply to that municipality. The impact is not only felt by paying consumers, but also adversely affects business activities.

---

[101] Jonas (n 3) 7.
[102] Recognized by the National Planning Commission in its *Diagnostic Report* (The Presidency 2011) 26.
[103] See Jacques Pauw, *The President's Keepers: Those Keeping Zuma in Power and out of Prison* (Tafelberg 2017); Adriaan Basson and Pieter du Toit, *Enemy of the People: How Jacob Zuma Stole South Africa and How the People Fought Back* (Jonathan Ball 2017); Robin Renwick, *How to Steal a Country: State Capture and Hopes for the Future of South Africa* (Jacana 2018); Pieter-Louis Myburgh, *Gangster State: Unravelling Ace Magashule's Web of Capture* (Tafelberg 2019).
[104] Jonas (n 3) 116.
[105] Luyolo Mkentane, 'No More Crybabies, Says Eastern Cape Premier' *Business Day* (8 August 2019) 3.
[106] Jonas (n 3) 30.

The same consequences are entrained by poor water distribution. In a 2019 case emblematic of the malaise of dysfunctional municipalities, the country's largest poultry producer had to halve its production at one of its plants, causing financial losses to the company (and perforce to the local community), because the municipality had not maintained its water delivery infrastructure.[107] As one news editorial noted, the government pursues a policy of distributing economic growth across the country, but 'it is a tough sell to investors if local government authorities in towns where factories will be located cannot guarantee water or electricity supplies'.[108]

A second subversion of constitutionalism is that a cardinal right, that of access to education, is proving to be an empty promise. As early in the Zuma years as 2011, the National Planning Commission lamented the education system's weak performance in regard to poor black learners.[109] Considerable progress has been made in providing near-universal coverage from Grades 1–12, mostly through no-fee schools; for example, pre-school learning among 5-year-olds increased from 22 per cent in 1996 to more than 80 per cent in 2007. But these figures do not speak to the quality of the education provided. Although South Africa spends more per capita on education than any other African country, and its teachers are among the highest paid in the world, the quality of education remains below African and global standards.[110] The Commission found that the main problems lie in teacher performance and the quality of school leadership.[111]

During the Zuma presidency, no improvements were seen in education outcomes. Education received the largest slice of the national budget, of which 93 per cent went to teachers' salaries, but school results remained dismal. In a 2018 study, 78 per cent of Grade 4 learners could not read for meaning, which is far below the standard in other comparable countries. Similar poor results were recorded in mathematics.[112] With a low throughput rate, only four out of 100 students proceed to post-matric education. Again, blame is placed on human agency: 'Corruption in national and provincial education departments, along with the over-extension of power of teachers' unions and school governing bodies, has played no small part in the collapse of our schooling system.'[113]

Thirdly, during the Zuma years the separation of powers between the executive and Parliament was weakened. Parliament hardly played an effective role in calling the executive to account—it required the intervention of the Constitutional Court[114] to instruct Parliament to enforce remedial measures the Public Protector imposed after finding that the President had been personally enriched by state-paid renovations to his private homestead, Nkandla.[115] What is more, figures in the ruling party spoke out against the notion of constitutional

[107] Siseko Njobeni, 'Deliver Basic Services, Astral Urges Government' *Business Day* (26 June 2019) 1.

[108] Business Day, 'Astral Shines Light on Service' *Business Day* (25 June 2019) 6.

[109] National Planning Commission, *Diagnostic Report* (n 102) 12.

[110] ibid 13–14.

[111] ibid 16.

[112] Jonas (n 3) 87.

[113] ibid 84.

[114] *Economic Freedom Fighters v Speaker of the National Assembly and Others; Democratic Alliance v Speaker of the National Assembly and Others* [2016] ZACC 11.

[115] Public Protector of South Africa, *Secure in Comfort: Report on an Investigation into Allegations of Impropriety and Unethical Conduct Relating to the Installation and Implementation of Security Measures by the Department of Public Works at and in Respect of the Private Residence of President Jacob Zuma at Nkandla in the Kwazulu-Natal Province* (2014) Report 25 of 2013/14.

supremacy.[116]

Fourth, the institutional independence of the South African Reserve Bank also came under attack. In responding to a complaint that the Reserve Bank gave a bank a bailout during the apartheid era that had not been repaid, the Public Protector, Busisiwe Mkhwebane, who succeeded Thuli Madonsela in September 2016,[117] used the opportunity to attack the Reserve Bank's independence. She proceeded, in an action unrelated to the complaint at hand, to instruct Parliament to amend the Constitution by removing, first, the object of protecting the value of the currency, and secondly, the independence of the institution.[118] When the Reserve Bank took the findings on review, the court set these instructions aside because they were 'unconstitutional', 'irrational', 'unlawful', and 'procedurally unfair'.[119]

This was not a case of mere incompetence: it was, as a commentator put it, 'calculated to undermine the authority of the Bank'.[120] It came to light that, shortly before releasing her report, the Public Protector had met with both the presidency and State Security Agency to discuss the 'vulnerabilities' of the Reserve Bank.[121] As a measure of its disapproval of her conduct, the trial court ordered her to pay 15 per cent of the litigation costs from her own pocket,[122] a decision the Constitutional Court confirmed.[123]

Fifth, there was a systematic attack on the judiciary. Whenever the courts, including the Constitutional Court, gave judgment against the state, senior ANC officials would claim that the judges were counter-revolutionaries betraying the cause of liberation.[124] The vehemence of the attacks increased as the courts became the last bastion between a constitutional state and a predatory state under Zuma. Ronald Lamola, the Minister of Justice and Correctional Services in Ramaphosa's cabinet, reportedly said that were it not for an independent judiciary, 'our fiscus would have been looted and depleted to a total collapse'.[125] He warned that continued unwarranted attacks on judges would damage the reputation of the judiciary.[126]

---

[116] See Nico Steytler, 'The "Financial Constitution" and the Prevention and Combating of Corruption: A Comparative Study of Nigeria, South Africa and Kenya' in Charles M Fombad and Nico Steytler (eds), *Corruption and Constitutionalism in Africa* (OUP 2020).

[117] After the departure of the highly independent and effective Madonsela, Parliament's choice of successor, Mkhwebane, was a safe bet for the majority party, as she had a background in the National Intelligence Agency. See 'Profile: Advocate Busisiwe Mkhwebane', SABC (Johannesburg, 24 August 2016) <https://bit.ly/2FfB18T> accessed 17 April 2017.

[118] Public Protector of South Africa, *Alleged Failure to Recover Misappropriated Funds: Report on an Investigation into Allegations of Maladministration, Corruption, Misappropriation of Public Funds and Failure by the South African Government to Implement the Ciex Report and to Recover Public Funds from Absa Bank* (2018) Report 8 of 2017/2018, para 5.3.25.

[119] *Reserve Bank of South Africa and Others v Public Protector and Others* [2017] ZAGPPHC 443 para 43. The entire report was also set aside in a subsequent case brought by Absa Bank, the Reserve Bank, the Minister of Finance, and the National Treasury (*Absa Bank Limited and Others v Public Protector and Others* [2018] ZAGPPHC 2).

[120] Stuart Theobald, 'Reserve Bank's Powers Trouble the Guptas' *Business Day* (3 July 2017) 7.

[121] *Public Protector v South African Reserve Bank* [2019] ZACC 29.

[122] *Absa Bank Limited and Others v Public Protector and Others* [2018] ZAGPPHC 2.

[123] *Public Protector v South African Reserve Bank* [2019] ZACC 29.

[124] See Steytler (n 87) 151.

[125] Legal Brief, 'Minister Condemns Unwarranted Attacks on Judges' *Legal Brief* (21 August 2019).

[126] ibid.

6.2 Ramaphosa: The Promise of the 'New Dawn'

The election of Cyril Ramaphosa as ANC president in December 2017, his selection as the country's president in February 2018, and his receipt of a new mandate after the 2019 national elections all seemed to portend that he would deal with the dire state the country found itself in after the Zuma years. Ramaphosa promised a 'new dawn': corruption would be rooted out, the economy revived, poverty and inequality addressed, and wealth ownership transformed. These are formidable goals, and some government action has already taken place. Certain of the challenges and initiatives intersect directly with constitutionalism.

First, a process is under way for restoring the rule of law. With 'state capture' having been the hallmark of the Zuma regime, President Ramaphosa appointed the Zondo Commission in 2018 to enquire into its extent and causes. The Commission, which has to complete its report by April 2021, dredged up corruption of flabbergasting scope and scale. Likewise, following the 'capture' by Zuma-ites of the National Prosecuting Authority (NPA), the National Director of Public Prosecutions, Shaun Abrahams, was dismissed and a new incumbent, Shamila Batohi, appointed after a public selection process. A new directorate in the NPA was established to pursue the findings of the Zondo Commission.

A number of other commissions of inquiry were also instituted to scrutinize corruption, in these cases in regard to the South African Revenue Service, the Public Investment Fund, and the fitness of two deputy National Directors of Public Prosecutions. The real test of whether the Secretary-General of the ANC, Ace Magashule, would be prosecuted for the alleged financial abuse of his office as premier of the Free State[127] was passed with his arrest in November 2020. Of concern here is that a fake-news campaign making accusations of bribery has begun against judges who found against Zuma.[128] The flip-side of ridding the state of corruption is building a capable state. This would include steering clear of ruling-party deployment and patronage and embracing meritocracy, a goal espoused in the NDP, but it may prove a bridge too far for the ANC, which is still a home to the corrupt.

Secondly, the revision of the right to property is in progress to allow the expropriation of land without compensation under certain circumstances. The initiative started with a breakaway group from the ANC, the Economic Freedom Fighters (EFF). Under the leadership of Julius Malema and in the context of a stagnant economy and little progress in land reform, the party has called for radical economic transformation and the nationalization of land.[129] The ANC, afraid of being outflanked on the left, approved the principle of expropriation without compensation at its national conference in 2017. In 2018, the National Assembly mandated the Constitutional Review Committee to review section 25 with the aim of making it more transformative.[130] At the request of this Committee, a Presidential Advisory Panel on Land Reform and Agriculture was established under the chairmanship of Dr Vuyokhazi Mahlati, its mandate being to consider expropriation without compensation.[131]

---

[127] See Myburgh (n 103).
[128] Legal Brief, 'Fake News Attack Launched against Judges, NDPP' *Legal Brief* (11 September 2019).
[129] Mosala, Venter, and Bain (n 90) 328.
[130] Parliamentary Monitoring Group (PMG), 'Call for Comment: Review of Section 25 of the Constitution (Property Clause)' <https://pmg.org.za/call-for-comment/654/> accessed 8 September 2019.
[131] Advisory Panel on Land Reform and Agriculture, *Final Report of the Presidential Advisory Panel on Land Reform and Agriculture* (Republic of South Africa 4 May 2019) <http://www.gov.za/sites/default/files/gcis_docum ent/201907/panelreportlandreform_1.pdf> accessed 30 November 2020.

The Panel's main recommendations were, first, that given that section 25 considers market value as only one of a number of factors in determining 'just and equitable' compensation, circumstances in which expropriation without compensation is appropriate should be specified in an amendment to section 25; and, secondly, that the registration system should be reformed to allow for security of tenure in communal lands (and hence for the repeal of the Ingonyama Trust Act of 1993, which placed 2.8 million hectares of communal land under the sole trusteeship of the ruler of the Zulu nation, King Zwelithini). A constitutional amendment bill was drafted, specifying that the limited circumstances in which no compensation is forthcoming would be determined by ordinary legislation. Although the bill did not receive the necessary support in Parliament in December 2021, the issue is politically still alive and the prospect that this principle will yet be constitutionalized has not encouraged the business community or improved the prospects of foreign investment.

Thirdly, linked to the land question is the transformation of the ownership of real wealth, which lies no longer in land and agriculture but in the service sector, industry, manufacturing, and mining.[132] The argument is that there has to be a shift in ownership from white dominance to a more inclusive economy, since this is necessary for political stability and political stability is in turn necessary for economic growth. How is this shift to be accomplished? Two pathways are mapped out, the one gradual, the other, radical.

In August 2019 the National Treasury released a draft policy entitled 'Economic Transformation, Inclusive Growth, and Competitiveness: Towards an Economic Strategy for South Africa'. Explicitly embedded in the NDP of 2011, its objectives are economic growth 'accompanied by interventions that change how the benefits of growth are distributed and fundamentally transform the systems and patterns of ownership and control that govern our economy'.[133] This change should not, however, compromise the long-term ability of the economy to compete internationally.

The many concrete proposals thus manoeuvre between a rock and a hard place: while preserving and expanding the role of the market and increasing investment attractiveness, they must ensure transformation of ownership.[134] The option taken is to prise open the market for newcomers (that is, black entrepreneurs) by, among other measures, easing the bureaucratic and other obstacles for entry into the market. Although much is said about the need for transformation, no mention is made of nationalization or expropriation.

A year later at the time of this writing, little or no progress has been made with the proposals,[135] which is not surprising given the reaction of the ANC's alliance partners, Cosatu and the SACP. It is exactly the same as their response to the GEAR policy of 1995—that it is neoliberal hogwash. They appear inclined to endorse the populist alternative punted by the EFF, namely nationalizing the land and putting a developmental state in control of the

---

[132] Even mining's share of GDP has declined, dropping to 7.3 per cent in 2018 from 10 per cent in 1994—which was already half of its peak of 22 per cent in 1980. Department of Planning, Monitoring and Evaluation, '4 Economic Transformation' in *Twenty Year Review: South Africa 1994–2014* (The Presidency 2014) <https://bit.ly/2JpjSgF> accessed 30 November 2020.

[133] National Treasury, 'Economic Transformation, Inclusive Growth, and Competitiveness: Towards an Economic Strategy for South Africa' (26 August 2019) <https://bit.ly/3fY2s6U> accessed 30 November 2020.

[134] Jonas is of a similar view: there is a need for a radical change in ownership, but he does not support nationalization or state-led development. See Jonas (n 3).

[135] Linda Ensor, 'David Masondo Tells MPs How Reforms Will Get Rolling' *Business Day* (24 July 2020) 4. The report of the ANC's Committee on Economic Transformation, *Reconstruction, Growth and Transformation: Building A New, Inclusive Economy* (10 July 2020), is said to be aligned to the Treasury's report. See Enoch Godongwana, 'ANC's Economy Policy Document Does Reference Mboweni's Paper' *Business Day* (27 July 2020) 6.

levers of power to end 'white monopoly capital'—a policy position seemingly oblivious to Zimbabwe's economic implosion or the disastrous Zuma years.

Fourth, the realization of the socio-economic rights of education and health is squarely on the agenda. The National Treasury draft policy emphasizes the importance of reforming the educational system, including early childhood development,[136] but what is more ambitious is the policy objective to introduce universal medical care through the National Health Insurance (NHI) system and thereby eliminate the vast disparities in services between the private and public health sectors. The aim is to equalize access by making private health practitioners available to non-paying patients as well through a system of health insurance. Although economists warn that South Africa cannot afford such a system at this stage, the government is proceeding apace with the National Health Insurance Bill, tabled in Parliament in August 2019. Economists argue that, as matters stand, the economy is unable to support even the government's current levels of spending and that a further burden of taxes may hasten the state's bankruptcy.

South Africa's dire finances and economic stagnation have been exacerbated by the COVID-19 pandemic of 2020. The measures taken to combat the pandemic, including the imposition of a national lockdown, involved draconian state interference in the market. Businesses big and small were either not permitted to operate at all or could operate only under very restrictive conditions; almost uniquely in the world, certain economic activities were banned entirely, notably the sale of alcohol and tobacco.

These measures resulted in a negative growth rate (a predicted contraction of the economy of between 8 and 10 per cent), the decimation of tax revenue (a projected shortfall of more than ZAR 300 billion for 2020/21), and a huge increase in spending on social grants.[137] On the latter score, expenditure on health services increased dramatically, as did that on social grants in ameliorating the economic consequences of the lockdown. It is estimated that by the end of 2020, 1.5 million persons would have lost their jobs and millions, their income. By June, 3.1 out of 6.5 million applications qualified for a basic support grant of ZAR 350 per month for a period of six months.

In the Supplementary Budget of 25 June 2020, the Minister of Finance disclosed that the budget deficit was 15.7 per cent and that the government's debt level rose from 65 per cent of GDP in the February 2020 budget to 81.1 per cent.[138] Loans were to be made by the IMF, World Bank, and African Development Bank. Although the government's position is that the IMF loan is only for health services, the spectre of general IMF bailouts has become real. Such bailouts are accompanied by structural adjustment programmes that come at the cost of democratic sovereignty: loan conditions oust democratic decision-making. The alternative is, of course, being bailed out by China; but that, as experience in Zambia and elsewhere suggests, comes at the high cost of losing the family silver.

The pandemic has exposed all the fault lines of South African society and its economy. How the latter will emerge from the current meltdown is not clear. The inevitable rise of populism in situations of dire economic distress, the continuation and expansion of the patrimonial state, a radical deracializing of the economy, and becoming one of Africa's

---

[136] National Treasury (n 133). See also the economic emphasis that Jonas places on the need for improving the quality of education (Jonas (n 3) 197–204).

[137] See Director-General of Finance, Lungisa Fuzile, 'With Hard Work and Heavy Lifting, R100bn in Spending Cuts Will Suffice' *Business Day* (17 July 2020) 7.

[138] Lynell Donnelly, 'Minister Says SA Needs to Reclaim Its "Fiscal Credibility"' *Business Day* (25 June 2020) 1.

highly indebted countries are all eventualities that would put enormous strain on constitutionalism in general and on the current constitutional framework in regard to the economy in particular.

7. The Connection between Constitutionalism and the Economy

What does the South African experience tell us thus far about the connection between the constitution, constitutionalism, and the economy? Is there a positive link between constitutionalism and economic growth, or has the relationship been negative or neutral? Whilst elsewhere in the world it is not a given that any positive link exists between the rule of law (broadly defined) and economic growth,[139] South Africa supports a converse case: the absence or weakening of constitutionalism has deleterious effects on the economy. One implication is that, in the various arguments doing the rounds about why the economy is ailing, blaming the Constitution is misplaced.

7.1 Constitutionalism as a Boon to Economic Growth

As the preceding discussion of the Zuma years and their erosion of constitutionalism shows, the weakening of the rule of law (narrowly defined) through corruption—with the capture of the state by private sector actors representing the most egregious instance of this—cost the state trillions in wasted or lost revenue, caused a loss of business confidence, and vitiated the hope that the 'developmental state' could lead to economic transformation. Corruption and state capture were made possible by a direct attack on constitutional institutions such as the NPA, the Public Protector, the police, the National Treasury, and the Reserve Bank.[140]

Conversely, it was only the courts that could prevent the then seemingly inevitable slide into a wholly patrimonial state and the collapse of the economy. They came to the rescue when all other political means failed. But the courts cannot bring an economy back to life: they are a brake on, not a lever for, state action. Some commentators nevertheless assert to the contrary that there is a positive link between the rule of law and economic growth. Madonsela, the former Public Protector whose findings brought Zuma to his knees, argues that the end of impunity would boost investor confidence;[141] for Mcebisi Jonas, a capable state is possible only without corruption.[142]

South Africa's poor implementation of the 'social' state illustrates another 'negative' or inverse connection between constitutionalism and economic growth (ie it shows that the absence of constitutionalism impairs economic growth). To provide 'schools but no learning'[143] has voided the right of access to education, and a poorly educated workforce cannot sustain a growing economy. With the Fourth Industrial Revolution busy unfolding worldwide, a workforce unskilled in IT further retards South Africa's competitiveness in the global market.

---

[139] See Nico Steytler, 'Constitutionalism and the Economy: Concepts and Questions' (Chapter 1 of this volume).
[140] See Steytler (n 116).
[141] Quoted in Londiwe Buthelezi, 'End to Impunity Good for Investment' *Business Day* (14 June 2019) 4.
[142] Jonas (n 3) 7.
[143] Jonas (n 3) ch 4.

7.2 Constitutionalism as an Impediment to Economic Growth

Given South Africa's population growth and the estimated 8–10 per cent contraction of its economy in 2020, the government anticipates a return to 2019 GDP levels (which showed no or insignificant growth) only by 2024—a scenario in which 'joblessness and inequality would reach dire levels'.[144] Even before the COVID-19 crisis, though, South Africa found itself in a deep malaise, with critics from the right and left alike in blaming the Constitution for it.

For their part, free marketeers point to five matters that hinder economic growth: governmental intrusiveness in the market; the possibility of expropriation without compensation; BEE; labour rights; and poor education.[145] Apart from poor education, these 'impediments', they claim, have their basis in the Constitution. From the left and populist perspectives, the Constitution is impeding development and social justice precisely because it prevents the government from being more 'intrusive', while land cannot be nationalized and BEE cannot be delivered quickly enough. The result is thus the popular strategy: if all else fails, blame the Constitution. In the era of COVID-19, such arguments increased in vehemence.

What is argued here is that, on the one hand, expecting the Constitution to deliver us from the evil of a collapsing economy, or, on the other, seeking to remove its 'harmful' elements, are both misconceived notions. In the first place, the constitutional scope for a 'developmental state' is wide. Few constraints inhibit the government from taking any initiative to advance economic policy or engage in the economy through state-owned enterprises. The only question is whether the state has the capacity to do so effectively and efficiently and is held accountable if it does not. The short answer that all the evidence points to is 'No'.

What else can be done, then? For one, in the absence of a parliament vigorously holding ministers and officials to account for maladministration, the courts have stepped into the breach by developing a new tool to vindicate the Constitution, namely sanctioning egregious conduct by state officials by imposing costs orders on them in their personal capacity.[146] Two examples suffice. The Constitutional Court saddled the Minister of Social Development, Bathabile Dlamini, with a personal cost order after her bungling of the distribution of social welfare grants put millions of grantees at risk.[147] As noted above, the same court affirmed a cost order against the Public Protector in her personal capacity as a measure of disapproval for her having acted 'in bad faith and in a grossly unreasonable manner'.[148]

Secondly, the protection of property stands centrally in the firing line of constitutional contestation. On the one hand, fiddling with the right to property by explicitly allowing expropriation without compensation is highly likely to scare off prospective investors; on the other, sticking to an unadulterated right may cause social instability, which is worse for the economy. Thomas Piketty has argued that obsessive protection of property does not provide the necessary stability but could lead to revolution and hence is inimical to the stability

---

[144] Fuzile (n 137).

[145] Institute of Race Relations, quoted in Hanlie Stadler, 'Die 5 Dinge Knou die Ekonomie' *Die Burger* (Cape Town, 6 June 2019).

[146] *Public Protector v South African Reserve Bank* [2019] ZACC 29 para 154.

[147] *Black Sash Trust (Freedom Under Law Intervening) v Minister of Social Development and Others* [2018] ZACC 36.

[148] *Public Protector v South African Reserve Bank* [2019] ZACC 29 para 205.

necessary for economic prosperity.[149] Although many commentators have pointed out that expropriation without compensation is possible under the current formulation of section 25,[150] the symbolic value of making a precise determination of the circumstances in which it may take place could be significant for social stability and at the same time not undermine investor confidence.

Central to any transformation measures of deracializing capital, whether or not supported by constitutional changes, stands the Constitutional Court. Previously, the court had to navigate the no less difficult task of transforming the inherited civil services and balancing affirmative action measures with equality. No blanket exclusion of whites was permitted, although measures benefiting persons from communities disadvantaged by apartheid were sanctioned. The court could play a similar role in mediating the different economic interests at stake during the process of ownership transformation.

Thirdly, the private sector as well as international financial institutions have argued that labour markets should become less rigid and allow for greater flexibility; a different but related argument is that the public sector wage bill should be trimmed. The problem does not lie in the protection of labour rights in the Bill of Rights, but in labour legislation that has fixated on job security and, moreover, in trade unions in state sectors that have achieved high salaries without commensurate increases in productivity. In both cases the problem lies, then, with the politics within the tripartite alliance, by dint of which Cosatu—increasingly dominated by unions representing state employees—plays a key role in labour economics.[151]

Fourth, those on the left claim that the Reserve Bank's independence allows it to construe its mandate narrowly as chasing inflation goals at the price of reducing the interest rate to spur economic growth; as a point of principle, the ANC has also demanded the nationalization of all private shareholding in the Bank. Again, the counter-argument is that the constitutional provisions are broad enough to accommodate different approaches to inflation targeting: it is a matter of policy rather than law. Furthermore, the Bank's private shareholders have no influence over policy, so paying compensation for their shares would add little (other than symbolic) value while nevertheless coming at a huge cost.

In summary, the quest for constitutionalism is not negatively linked to economic growth: the Constitution itself and its implementation have not impeded economic growth. While constitutionalism by itself does not promote growth (for that productive economic policies and actions are needed); however, by taking constitutionalism away, the economy will tank. The implication seems to be that constitutionalism is a necessary but not sufficient condition for economic growth. It is thus misconceived that when things go economically wrong, the Constitution becomes the easy object of blame as the font of all misery. This is no more than a searching for handy symbols to target for change: it is unlikely to have any positive effective on the health of the economy, but certainly could make matters worse.

---

[149] Thomas Piketty, *Capital in the Twenty-First Century* (Belknap Press of Harvard University Press 2014).
[150] This is also the view of the one of the drafters of the Bill of Rights, Enver Surty (see Surty (n 46) 181).
[151] Genevieve Quintal, 'State's Hands Tied as Unions Call the Shots' *Business Day* (2 August 2019) 6.

8. Conclusion

It is not audacious to state that the South African constitutions of 1993 and 1996 and the constitutionalism to which they gave rise have played a significant, if not central, role in the shaping of the economy. First, they were the battleground for different ideological perspectives on the economy and the vested interests they represented. In the socialist versus free market ideological debate between the ANC and the NP, the latter won handsomely: a market economy was given constitutional form. This result was inevitable. Inasmuch as whites had no option but to accept majority rule, the ANC in the post-Cold War era had little choice but to accept the dominance of the market and take consolation in the idea of a developmental state that would lead the way in transforming apartheid South Africa.

Secondly, the 1993 and 1996 constitutions cemented this result in the usual fashion. The right to property was protected in the Bills of Rights, but with the proviso that land restitution and reform were mandated. The freedom and sanctity of contract were indirectly protected. A competitive market was weakly catered for, and the freedom of contract secured. As corrective measures, the rights of workers and employees were safeguarded. The 1996 Constitution innovatively established a 'social' state through the entrenchment of socio-economic rights to guard against the market's failure to distribute resources equitably throughout society. Ample constitutional scope was given for the emergence of a developmental state, although, in line with best practice, decisions regarding currency stability were allocated to an independent central bank.

Thirdly, within this constitutional paradigm, considerable progress was made in the first three presidential terms in rolling out the 'social' state through the provision of housing, education, health care, social security, and the basic amenities of water and electricity. After twenty-seven years, however, the 1993 and 1996 economic compact is unravelling, with stagnant growth for the past decade (and, after 2020, negative growth) and lack of transformation of the economy's racial profile stirring up calls for action. Was the Constitution at fault? Has constitutionalism stifled economic growth?

It has been argued that it is the *lack* of constitutionalism that is responsible in good part for the deteriorating economy: instead of there being a developmental state driving development, a patrimonial state arose and operated outside the Constitution, in so doing proving detrimental to the economy. Moreover, the complaints that certain constitutional elements are hindrances to economic growth—for example, the property clause, workers' rights, or the independence of the Reserve Bank—are grasping at straws, as the problem lies in the realm of politics, policy, and an incapable state.

Both in the short and long term, South Africa's economic future looks bleak, even dire, after the COVID-19 crisis. However the government may intend to foster a growing economy, it is hamstrung by a deeply divided party, a tripartite alliance at odds with itself, and an incapable state. Thus immobilized, it will seek new policies, but these may well remain just that: mere policies. In the meantime populism is growing apace with the decline in the economy. Stark choices are being presented: a quick transfer of ownership which may accelerate an imploding economy, or a more gradualist sharing in a growing economy which may deepen political divisions? Populism, which by its nature promises the impossible, advocates the first choice, notwithstanding the clear warning of neighbouring Zimbabwe's economic implosion.

Neither the Constitution nor constitutionalism will solve South Africa's potential economic crises in the future: even the free marketeers are sanguine enough to admit that the rule of law is not enough.[152] The answer lies in political and economic policy choices, compacts, and transitions. But such policies and transitions should be grounded on the firm bedrock of constitutionalism. To the extent that constitutionalism brings stability, it is supportive and enabling of economic growth and the fair distribution of resources. As long as South Africa remains a constitutional democracy, the courts will be called upon ever increasingly to play the invaluable role of mediating diverse economic interests towards the attainment of social justice. To that extent, constitutionalism lies close to a prosperous and inclusive economy, and, in the end, a peaceful South Africa.

Bibliography

Advisory Panel on Land Reform and Agriculture, *Final Report of the Presidential Advisory Panel on Land Reform and Agriculture* (Republic of South Africa 4 May 2019) <http://www.gov.za/sites/defa ult/files/gcis_document/201907/panelreportlandreform_1. Pdf> accessed 30 November 2020

ANC (Committee on Economic Transformation), *Reconstruction, Growth and Transformation: Building A New, Inclusive Economy* (10 July 2020), <https://cisp. cachefly. net/assets/articles/attach-ments/82688_etc_document_final_8_july_2020. pdf> accessed 29 July 2020

ANC, Constitutional Guidelines for a Democratic South Africa: African National Congress Proposals—1955 & 1988 (1988)

ANC, ANC's Bill of Rights for a Democratic South Africa (1990)

ANC, *Bill of Rights: Policy Guide* (ANC Department of Information and Publicity, March 1993)

ANC, Draft Resolution on ANC Economic Policy for National Conference (Centre for Development Studies, UWC 1991)

Basson A and Du Toit P, *Enemy of the People: How Jacob Zuma Stole South Africa and How the People Fought Back* (Jonathan Ball 2017)

Bernstein A, 'Cleaning up is Not Enough—We Will Have to Slaughter Some Holy Cows' *Business Day* (26 March 2019)

Bolton P, *The Law of Public Procurement in South Africa* (LexisNexis 2012)

Business Day, 'Astral Shines Light on Service' *Business Day* (25 June 2019) 6

Buthelezi L, 'End to Impunity Good for Investment' *Business Day* (14 June 2019) 4

Davis D, 'The Freedom Charter: A Challenge and Bequest' in Steytler N (ed), *The Freedom Charter and Beyond: Founding Principles for a Democratic South African Legal Order* (Wyvern 1992)

Davis D, 'Freedom of Trade, Occupation and Profession' in Woolman S and others (eds), *Constitutional Law of South Africa* vol 4 (Juta 2014)

Donnelly L, 'Minister Says SA Needs to Reclaim Its "Fiscal Credibility"' *Business Day* (25 June 2020) 1

Dugard J, 'Unpacking Section 25: Is South Africa's Property Clause an Obstacle or Engine for Socio-Economic Transformation?' (2018) 4 <https://bit.ly/37ouvZh> accessed 30 November 2020

Ensor L, 'David Masondo Tells MPs How Reforms Will Get Rolling' *Business Day* (24 July 2020) 4

Friedman S, *Race, Class and Power: Harold Wolpe and the Radical Critique of Apartheid* (UKZN Press 2015)

Fuzile L, 'With Hard Word and Heavy Lifting, R100bn in Spending Cuts Will Suffice' *Business Day* (17 July 2020) 7

Godongwana E, 'ANC's Economy Policy Document Does Reference Mboweni's Paper' *Business Day* (27 July 2020) 6

---

[152] Ann Bernstein, 'Cleaning up is Not Enough—We Will Have to Slaughter Some Holy Cows' *Business Day* (26 March 2019) 7.

Hentz JJ, 'The Two Faces of Privatisation: Political and Economic Logics in Transitional South Africa' (2000) 38(2) Journal of Modern African Studies 203

Jonas M, *After Dawn: Hope after State Capture* (Picador Africa 2019)

Lazar D, 'Competing Economic Ideologies in South Africa's Economic Debate' (1996) 47(4) British Journal of Sociology 599

Legal Brief, 'Minister Condemns Unwarranted Attacks on Judges' *Legal Brief* (Cape Town, 21 August 2019)

Legal Brief, 'Fake News Attack Launched against Judges, NDPP' *Legal Brief* (11 September 2019)

Le Roux P, 'The Social Democratic Nature of the Charterist Economic Vision' in Steytler N (ed), *The Freedom Charter and Beyond: Founding Principles for a Democratic South African Legal Order* (Wyvern 1992) 120–35

Mkentane L, 'No More Crybabies, Says Eastern Cape Premier' *Business Day* (8 August 2019) 3

Mosala SJ, Venter JCM, and Bain EG, 'South Africa's Economic Transformation Since 1994: What Influence Has the National Democratic Revolution (NDR) Had?' (2017) 44 Review of Black Political Economy 327

Myburgh P, *Gangster State: Unravelling Ace Magashule's Web of Capture* (Tafelberg 2019)

Naidoo K and Pillay D, 'The Freedom Charter in the 1956 Treason Trial' in Steytler N (ed), *The Freedom Charter and Beyond: Founding Principles for a Democratic South African Legal Order* (Wyvern 1992)

National Planning Commission, *Diagnostic Report* (The Presidency 2011)

National Planning Commission, *National Development Plan: Vision for 2030*, RP270/2011 (National Planning Commission 2011)

National Treasury, 'Economic Transformation, Inclusive Growth, and Competitiveness: Towards an Economic Strategy for South Africa' (26 August 2019) <https://bit. ly/3fY2s6U> accessed 30 November 2020

Njobeni S, 'Deliver Basic Services, Astral Urges Government' *Business Day* (26 June 2019) 1

Padayachee V, Valodia I, and Van Niekerk R, 'Evolution of ANC Economic Policy Sheds Light on Squabble over the Central Bank' *The Conversation* (3 July 2019) <https://theconversation. com/evolution-of-anc-economic-policy-sheds-light-on-squabble-over-the-central-bank-119401> accessed 25 August 2019

Parliamentary Monitoring Group (PMG), 'Call for Comment: Review of Section 25 of the Constitution (Property Clause)' (15 June 2018) <https://pmg. org. za/call-for-comment/654/> accessed 8 September 2019

Pauw J, *The President's Keepers: Those Keeping Zuma in Power and out of Prison* (Tafelberg 2017)

Presidency, *White Paper on Reconstruction and Development Programme* (Ministry in the Office of the President 1994)

Public Protector of South Africa, *Secure in Comfort: Report on an Investigation into Allegations of Impropriety and Unethical Conduct Relating to the Installation and Implementation of Security Measures by the Department of Public Works at and in Respect of the Private Residence of President Jacob Zuma at Nkandla in the Kwazulu-Natal Province* (2014) Report 25 of 2013/14

Public Protector of South Africa, *Alleged Failure to Recover Misappropriated Funds: Report on an Investigation into Allegations of Maladministration, Corruption, Misappropriation of Public Funds and Failure by the South African Government to Implement the Ciex Report and to Recover Public Funds from Absa Bank* (2018) Report 8 of 2017/2018

Quintal G, 'State's Hands Tied as Unions Call the Shots' *Business Day* (2 August 2019) 6

Renwick R, *How to Steal a Country: State Capture and Hopes for the Future of South Africa* (Jacana 2018)

Schneider G, 'Neoliberalism and Economic Justice in South Africa: Revisiting the Debate on Economic Apartheid' (2003) 61(1) Review of Social Economy 23

Southall R, 'The ANC, Black Economic Empowerment and State-Owned Enterprises: A Recycling of History' in Sakhela Buhlungu and others (eds), *State of the Nation: South Africa 2007* (HSRC Press 2007)

Stadler H, 'Die 5 Dinge Knou die Ekonomie' *Die Burger* (6 June 2019)

Steytler N, 'The Dynamic Relationship between Devolution and Constitutionalism in South Africa' in Fombad CM and Steytler N (eds), *Constitutionalism and Decentralisation in Africa* (OUP 2019)

Steytler N, 'The Withering Away of Politically Salient Territorial Cleavages in South Africa and the Emergence of Watermark Ethnic Federalism' in Anderson G and Chowdry S (eds), *Territory and Power in Constitutional Transitions* (OUP 2019)

Steytler N, 'The "Financial Constitution" and the Prevention and Combating of Corruption: A Comparative Study of Nigeria, South Africa and Kenya' in Fombad CM and Steytler N (eds), *Corruption and Constitutionalism in Africa* (OUP 2020)

Steytler N and de Visser J, *Local Government Law of South Africa* (LexisNexis 2007)

Steytler N and Powell D, 'The Impact of the Global Financial Crisis on Decentralised Government in South Africa' (2010) 358 L'Europe en Formation 149

Surty ME, *In Pursuit of Dignity* (Awqaf South Africa 2019)

Theobald S, 'Reserve Bank's Powers Trouble the Guptas' *Business Day* (3 July 2017) 7

PART III
THE CONSTITUTIONAL FRAMEWORK FOR LAND AND NATURAL RESOURCES

6

Protecting the Land, Protecting the Resources

A Comparative Assessment of Constitutional Protections in Kenya, Sudan, and South Sudan

John Hursh

1. Introduction

> As in the rest of sub-Saharan Africa, the process of state creation itself involved an at best only very partially successful attempt to impose the imperatives of statehood on ecological zones and indigenous societies that in large measure failed to correspond to the political units into which they were squeezed by the assumption that statehood was a necessary constituent of global order—Christopher Clapham[1]

Few regions in Africa are as resource rich and as conflict prone as East Africa. Within this region, several states face alarming rates of corruption, as well as correspondingly low levels of transparency and checks on executive power. Historically, East African states have seen repressive governance, an over-concentration of executive authority, and the rampant misuse of natural resource wealth. This unfortunate combination has led to great personal enrichment for a subset of political leaders—typically those of an authoritarian or semi-authoritarian stripe—as well as a small circle of supportive and enabling elites, but widespread poverty and a lack of economic opportunity for the majority of citizens within these states.[2]

Throughout the region, jurists, scholars, activists, and civil society leaders have sought to challenge this unjust status quo by securing constitutional provisions that safeguard land and natural resources from state misuse. These reformist efforts are of great importance to the economic well-being and political economy of the state, since political power and personal enrichment frequently come from the control of natural resources and their misuse has left communities marginalized and underdeveloped. Here, the most obvious examples are extractive resources, such as oil, gold, and other valuable gems and minerals.

---

[1] Christopher Clapham, *The Horn of Africa: State Formation and Decay* (Oxford University Press 2017) 177.

[2] See especially Alex de Waal, *The Real Politics of the Horn of Africa: Money, War and the Business of Power* (Polity 2015); see also Joshua B Rubongoya, 'Political Leadership' in Paul J Kaiser and F Wafula Okumu (eds), *Democratic Transitions in East Africa* (Ashgate Publishing 2004) 76.

John Hursh, *Protecting the Land, Protecting the Resources* In: *Constitutionalism and the Economy in Africa*. Edited by: Charles M Fombad and Nico Steytler, Oxford University Press. © John Hursh 2022. DOI: 10.1093/oso/9780192886439.003.0008

Less obvious, but equally important examples include land and water rights, particularly as foreign entities seek to secure the legal rights to these resources, often at the expense of local communities.

The actors challenging the status quo have often sought legal reform following armed conflict and civil unrest, as these post-conflict moments allow for a potential reshaping of social values and constitutional relationships between state and citizen. This was the case in Kenya, Sudan, and South Sudan, where broad national peace efforts included constitutional reform projects. Thus, Sudan's 2005 Interim National Constitution, a product of the 2005 Comprehensive Peace Agreement that ended the Second Sudanese Civil War (1983–2005), included guiding principles for the equitable sharing of the country's resources. Likewise, the 2010 Constitution of Kenya, which followed the 2007–08 electoral violence that led to an investigation by the International Criminal Court, included a land policy that would ensure the 'equitable, efficient, productive and sustainable' use of land as well as 'equitable sharing' of the accruing benefits of the country's natural resources.[3]

The intent of these constitutional principles and policies is hugely significant and could reverse decades of economic development that allowed elite capture of key economic sectors and natural resource wealth flowing to the politically connected few in non-transparent and unsustainable ways. Indeed, these constitutional values would revise the relationship between state and citizen, recognizing the exclusion of most citizens from wealth generated by the state's natural resources and promising a shared inclusion in this wealth moving forward. However, despite these strong affirmations of equitable land and natural resource use, the implementation of these rights has been uneven at best.

Building on these points, this chapter examines the constitutional protection of land and natural resources, particularly as these protections relate to economic development and the political economies of the three states. It does so by offering a comparative assessment of how the constitutions of Kenya, Sudan, and South Sudan safeguard land and natural resources for the citizens of these states. The effectiveness (or lack thereof) of the safeguards carries heavy consequences for the citizens in terms of both environmental rights and economic opportunity. Kenya, Sudan, and South Sudan allow for a useful comparison of three distinct legal traditions within an important region of Africa. Moreover, these three constitutions emerged from violence and armed conflict and contribute to the growing study of constitutional reform in post-conflict settings. In this regard, the protracted violence and vast inequality in Sudan and South Sudan point to limitations in bringing about meaningful change by means of constitutional reform during externally imposed peace processes. All three examples demonstrate that constitutional protections are necessary but not sufficient to enact lasting reform, reshape economic relationships between the state and its citizens, and expand economic possibilities to include all citizens.

---

[3] See arts 60 and 69 of the 2010 Kenya Constitution and the discussion of them below.

2. Kenya: Constitutionalism, Natural Resources, and Economic Development

> The history of Kenya's electoral (and ethnic) violence is complex; it is, however, rooted in control of resources: land, government, and the economy—Stephen M Magu[4]

The British colonial economy centred on exploiting Kenya's wealth of natural resources, particularly its fertile land. Land and other natural resources have remained an important driver of economic growth in independent Kenya, especially for agrarian development. Many of the same legal, environmental, and economic issues debated decades ago consequently still resonate today. For example, writing in 1964, Clayton argued that land consolidation and better agricultural planning would help spur an agrarian revolution in Kenya.[5] He also noted that increased agricultural production and a growing population during the colonial era, among other factors, had resulted in high levels of soil erosion.[6] Although discussed in terms of agricultural development and economic growth, the unsustainable overuse of agricultural land is of course just as much an environmental issue. Clayton also identified several other issues pertaining to natural resource use, such as land tenure and landownership, rural unemployment and rural indebtedness, land speculation and a land tax, that are just as relevant in contemporary Kenya as they were in the country's first year of independence.[7]

Now, more than fifty years after independence, the sustainable and equitable use of natural resources endures as a paramount concern and an unmet goal. Many of the specific issues flowing from this broader problem stem from the imposition of a colonial legal system on Kenya's indigenous populations, as well as the continued struggle to reconcile European modes of ownership and resource use with indigenous ones. As Magu concludes,

> The adoption of European approaches to property ownership, and the notion that Kenya was for all Kenyans, which appeared to ignore traditional notions of community ownership, thus saw the stage set for grievances that have dominated the country since its independence, including the question of land ownership.[8]

In this sense, Kenya's natural resource use problem is perhaps foremost a land use and landownership problem. Moreover, the tension between these legal systems remains unreconciled, as illustrated by the contrasting priorities set by land and natural resource use supported by government centralization and backed by a strong executive branch and those supported by a decentralized and less formal approach allowing for greater decision-making by local communities.

---

[4] Stephen M Magu, *The Socio-Cultural, Ethnic and Historic Foundations of Kenya's Electoral Violence* (Routledge 2018) vii.

[5] Eric Clayton, *Agrarian Development in Peasant Economies: Some Lessons from Kenya* (Pergamon Press 1964) 32–40.

[6] ibid 10–14.

[7] ibid 147.

[8] Magu (n 4) 22.

2.1 British Colonialism

Kenya's colonial encounter with Britain lasted from 1895 until 1963. The dispossession of land and natural resources from indigenous communities followed the British colonial governance model applied throughout much of the African continent. The legal system, and particularly the constitution, served a key enabling function in this model. Invoking a version of the 'gentle civilizer' argument,[9] colonial officials created a legal framework to support the forcible displacement and dispossession of indigenous communities. For example, Oyaya and Poku note how the entrenchment of massive social and economic inequalities, including the alienation of land for white settlement, was a defining characteristic of colonial constitutionalism in Kenya.[10]

Under the colonial constitutional framework, Africans received occupation rights but no title to their lands.[11] This legal framework also contributed to the creation of native reserves.[12] Here, the most important legislation was the 1915 Crown Land Ordinance, which in many ways mirrored the 1913 Natives Land Act in South Africa that laid the groundwork for apartheid in the decades that followed.[13] Like the Natives Land Act, the Crown Land Ordinance was deeply unfair and racist, justifying the legal dispossession of indigenous communities while granting white European settlers 999-year leases.[14]

Government efforts of varying degrees of sincerity tried to address these issues. For example, a 1932 Land Commission formed to consider land grievances did little to improve land rights for Kenya's indigenous peoples.[15] As Rutten and Owuor note, the results of the commission 'were bitterly disappointing for the African population as they endorsed the segregated system of land holding'.[16]

Of course, different communities and different ethnic groups experienced land dispossession in different ways and with different effect. The Maasai was one of the most affected groups and refused to sign the 1962 Lancaster House Agreement, as the British government would not recognize its land claims stemming from agreements made between the Maasai and the colonial government in 1904 and 1911.[17] And while colonial era dispossession created many of Kenya's land issues, it is a mistake to characterize pre-colonial land use and landownership as without fault. Women and minorities in particular faced nearly insurmountable challenges to securing their own land rights. Likewise, it is also important to recall that following independence, Kenyan political elites acquired large tracts of land from departing Europeans, as class replaced race as the defining feature of unequal land distribution.[18]

---

[9] See Martti Koskenniemi, *The Gentle Civilizer of Nations: The Rise and Fall of International Law 1870–1960* (Cambridge University Press 2001).

[10] Charles O Oyaya and Nana K Poku, *The Making of the Constitution of Kenya: A Century of Struggle and the Future of Constitutionalism* (Routledge 2018) 38.

[11] Tom Ojienda and Matthews Okoth, 'Chapter Five: Land the Environment' in Plo Lumumna, MK Mbondenyi, and SO Odero (eds), *The Constitution of Kenya: Contemporary Readings* (LawAfrica Publication 2011) 159.

[12] ibid.

[13] Crown Land Ordinance of 1915; Natives Land Act of 1913.

[14] Crown Land Ordinance of 1915; see also Ojienda and Okoth (n 11) 160.

[15] Marcel Rutten and Sam Owuor, 'Weapons of Mass Destruction: Land, Ethnicity and the 2007 Elections in Kenya' in Peter Kagwanja and Roger Southall (eds), *Kenya's Uncertain Democracy: The Electoral Crisis of 2008* (Routledge 2010) 49.

[16] ibid 50.

[17] ibid 52.

[18] ibid 53.

2.2 From Independence until the 1992 Elections

Kenya gained independence on 12 December 1963, but the inability of Kenyan political leaders to reach a compromise on a number of key issues resulted in an independence constitution that the British government imposed on Kenya.[19] Perhaps the most contentious of these unresolved issues was the tension between centralized government power and regional autonomy, particularly in relation to natural resource use and landownership. This unresolved tension has had a lasting effect on Kenya's development as well as its legal system. As the historian Robert Maxon notes, the tension between these two governance models has vexed Kenya's constitutional order throughout the country's history.[20] At independence, the strong centralized model won out due to a combination of changes to the draft constitution and the political ascendency of Jomo Kenyatta, leader of the Kenya African National Union (KANU) political party.[21] For Maxon, this combination marked 'the beginning of the end for regionalism in independent Kenya' even before independence and the enactment of the independence constitution.[22]

With this critique in mind, it is perhaps unsurprising that the legal framework did not improve land rights for most Kenyans following independence. Most distressingly, Kenya's independent government often applied exclusionary and unjust land laws that closely resembled colonial legislation. For example, all government land vested exclusively with the president,[23] an arrangement that would prove crucial to the patronage networks that came to define Kenyan politics in the decades that followed.[24]

Several legislative acts further dispossessed local communities, while also confusing land tenure. The Registered Land Act of 1963 emphasized individual tenure, but the Land Adjudication Act of 1968 provided for the adjudication of group rights.[25] In turn, groups needed to register group rights under the Land (Group Representatives) Act of 1968.[26] Finally, while the independence constitution recognized three types of land tenure (public, customary, and private), colonial native reserves became trust lands administered by county councils that could then divide land within their jurisdiction into divisions that divisional land boards would administer.[27] As Ojienda and Okoth note, under this constitutional system, trust lands became 'one of the hubs for land grabbing'.[28]

While these acts created legal uncertainty and frustrated community development, the most damaging constitutional trend was the over-concentration of power in the executive branch, especially within the office of the president. It is not an overstatement to conclude that the amassment of political power in the executive threatened the viability of the Kenyan state. Most often accomplished through constitutional amendment, the continued

---

[19] Robert M Maxon, *Kenya's Independence Constitution: Constitution-Making and End of Empire* (Farleigh Dickinson University Press 2011) 245, 272.

[20] ibid 201, 220, 227, 239.

[21] ibid 267.

[22] ibid.

[23] Ojienda and Okoth (n 11) 165. Art 118 of the independence constitution granted the president broad powers to set apart land, although the landowners were entitled to receive 'prompt payment of full compensation'; ibid 168.

[24] Nic Cheeseman, *Democracy in Africa: Successes, Failures, and the Struggle for Political Reform* (Cambridge University Press 2015) 62, 65.

[25] Ojienda and Okoth (n 11) 163–64.

[26] ibid 164.

[27] ibid 164–66.

[28] ibid 169.

accumulation of executive power undermined all other facets of government and made national elections a winner-takes-all contest. Accordingly, as Murunga, Okello, and Sjogren argue, this proliferation of amendments created a one-party state and a judiciary 'emasculated by the executive'.[29] Likewise, after noting the twenty-four constitutional amendments passed between 1964 and 1989, Oyaya and Poku conclude that the concentration of power that these amendments afforded the president 'effectively put Kenya on the trajectory of constitutional dictatorship'.[30]

Government efforts to address land grievances following independence were only marginally more successful than those undertaken by the colonial government. The One Million Acre Scheme, a government plan to 're-Africanize' the White Highlands, is perhaps the best example, as the enactment of this policy created 'ethnic animosity' and 'laid a base for future conflicts'.[31] The scheme, a land purchase programme beginning in 1965 and running through the 1970s, resulted in ethnic rivalry between the Kikuyu and Kalenjin, while class division, usually between the landless and the landed elite, such as the Kikuyu in the Rift Valley, became much more evident.[32]

2.3 Towards a More Democratic Constitutional Order

In the eighteen years between the 1992 elections and the adoption of the 2010 Constitution, Kenya's constitutional order underwent a series of uneven developments. Following the 1992 and 1997 elections in which the incumbent president Daniel Arap Moi retained power, the 2002 election saw the defeat of the ruling party's candidate, a surprising political result demonstrating the possibility of meaningful reform. However, the betrayal of this possibility, and the rejected constitutional referendum of 2005, put the country on the path towards the 2007 election and the electoral violence that ensued.[33] In turn, international pressure and the national recognition that political change was necessary allowed for the progressive 2010 Constitution.[34] Though the promise of this constitution remains at best partially met, there is little doubt that Kenya's political process and legal system have improved considerably since the decades following independence.

In the 1990s, Kenyan politics began to improve, albeit slightly, as a reintroduction of multiparty politics spread throughout Africa, including Kenya's 1992 and 1997 elections.[35] Multiparty elections began to occur more frequently, as international donors came to require these elections as a condition for continued financial aid and foreign

[29] Godwin R Murunga, Duncan Okello, and Anders Sjogren, *Kenya: The Struggle for a New Constitutional Order* (Zed Books 2014) 4–5. Other scholars conclude that Kenya became a de facto one-party state much earlier. For example, Magu argues that Kenya had reached this outcome by 1982. See Magu (n 4) 27.
[30] Oyaya and Poku (n 10) 79.
[31] Karuti Kanyinga, 'The Legacy of the White Highlands: Land Rights, Ethnicity, and the Post-2007 Election Violence in Kenya' in Peter Kagwanja and Roger Southall (eds), *Kenya's Uncertain Democracy: The Electoral Crisis of 2008* (Routledge 2010) 71.
[32] ibid 73–76.
[33] Although the violence surrounding the 2007 election was on a different scale, it is important to recall that this was not the first instance of electoral violence. As Magu notes, electoral violence, largely along ethnic lines, occurred between 1991 and 1995. See Magu (n 4) 56.
[34] 'After almost twenty years of struggle for constitutional reforms in Kenya, it needed the short but intense period of civil unrest and violence to make the political elite agree to a rapid process of completing the review process'. Oyaya and Poku (n 10) 214.
[35] Cheeseman (n 24) 82.

investment. Moreover, by 1992, Kenyan governance approached its lowest point, as 'all key institutions—the judiciary, public services, security forces, provincial administration and parliament—had been reduced to instruments of authoritarian dominion'.[36] Thus, although hardly a radical break from Kenya's 'imperial presidency', 1992 marked the beginning of the struggle for a democratic constitutional order that would culminate with the passage of the 2010 Constitution.[37]

Between 1992 and 2010, the most significant constitutional moment was the 2005 constitutional referendum, as the political manipulation of this process not only ensured that the referendum failed, but also set the divisive and bitter political tone for the 2007 election.[38] The 2005 referendum featured two draft constitutions, a people-driven 'Bomas' draft, and a heavy-handed revision put forth by Attorney-General Amos Wako dubbed the 'Wako' draft.[39] Wako was a strong supporter of President Kibaki, and few Kenyans regarded his draft constitution as credible.[40] Opposition politicians dismissed it outright, derisively calling it a 'Kikuyu Constitution', a less-than-subtle insinuation that the constitution furthered only the interests of Kibaki's ethnic group.[41] The Wako draft undid many of the political changes that the Kenyan people most wanted and had clearly articulated in the Bomas draft, including the decentralization of authority and a less powerful executive.[42] The Bomas draft also provided for the creation of a prime minister, which would help check the power of the presidency.[43]

The Kenyan people did not have the opportunity to decide between the two drafts, as Kibaki replaced the Bomas draft with the Wako draft, a deeply unpopular decision.[44] The Wako draft undercut the most important changes in the Bomas draft by limiting decentralization, increasing presidential power, and subordinating the prime minister to the president.[45] In essence, it removed the political reforms that the majority of Kenyans most desired. Politically, it crippled the coalition between Kibaki and Raila Odinga, with the latter forming the Orange Democratic Movement as a result. Odinga and the Orange Democratic Movement then campaigned against the constitutional referendum and Kibaki, which led to the referendum's defeat in November 2005.[46]

The defeat of the 2005 draft constitution was due at least in part to a flawed land administration framework and uncertainty regarding changes to accessing and controlling land. Land remained central to Kenyan politics as ethnic-based land evictions followed the 2007

---

[36] Murunga, Okello, and Sjogren (n 29) 6.
[37] Oyaya and Poku conclude that the period of reform was even longer, beginning in 1989 and concluding in 2010, stating, 'The struggle for democratic constitutional reform in post-independence Kenya was difficult, complex, brutal and protracted, lasting almost two decades from 1989 to 2010'. Oyaya and Poku (n 10) 106.
[38] Rutten and Owuor (n 15) 57.
[39] ibid 56–57.
[40] ibid.
[41] ibid.
[42] Jill Cottrell and Yash Ghai, 'Constitution Making and Democratization in Kenya (2000–2005)' (2007) 14 Democratization 1, 16–17.
[43] Jérôme Y Bachelard, 'The Anglo-Leasing Corruption Scandal in Kenya: The Politics of International and Domestic Pressures and Counter-Pressures' (2010) 37 Review of African Political Economy 187, 190.
[44] Magu characterizes the Wako draft as a 'betrayal of the citizen-driven process and an attempt to continue the presidential system with its unchecked powers'. Magu (n 4) 74. In contrast, the Bomas draft enjoyed broad and popular consensus. Cottrell and Ghai (n 42) 11–17.
[45] Gabrielle Lynch, 'The Fruits of Perception: "Ethnic Politics" and the Case of Kenya's Constitutional Referendum' (2006) 65 Africa Studies 233, 240.
[46] Bachelard (n 43) 190.

election, particularly in the Rift Valley.[47] The inability of legal reforms to transcend political bias marks all of these unsuccessful land reform initiatives. As Kanyinga concludes:

> The land redistribution policy of the 1960s and its outcome clearly shaped the outcome of the December 2007 presidential election dispute. Both the procedure by which land settlement schemes were established and the skewed bias in favor of certain groups are responsible for the recurrence of violence.[48]

After the 2005 constitutional referendum failed, Kibaki dissolved the government and removed Odinga, his main political challenger, and Odinga's supporters from office.[49] This decision entrenched political division before the 2007 elections and heightened the possibility of violence, particularly given the likelihood of a closely contested election. Following the 2007 election and the 2007–08 electoral violence, the Kenyan government undertook several initiatives to ensure that such violence would not happen again. Here, it is important to note the role that Kenyan leaders ascribed to the inequitable sharing of resources and the misuse of authority when identifying the root causes of political violence. As Pheroze Nowrojee, a prominent Kenyan human rights lawyer, stated, 'The Kenyan problem is a product of dominant unresolved issues—these issues are political not legal. They touch on power sharing and resource allocation … They cannot be solved legally but politically.'[50]

2.4 A New Constitutional Order

In 2010, Kenya entered a new constitutional era with the passage of a progressive constitution. The struggle to decentralize executive power and share resources equitably among all Kenyans remained at the forefront of constitutional reform.

2.4.1 The devolution of authority and natural resource use
Although the path from the calamitous 2007 election to the 2010 Constitution was not direct,[51] the latter's drafting and strong public support—68.6 per cent of Kenyans voted to adopt it—demonstrates that a majority of Kenyans wished to see a less powerful executive branch and a more decentralized form of governance. As Magu notes, a key feature of the new constitution was that it distributed government authority more evenly and moved away from an overly powerful executive.[52] Accordingly, the new constitution contained numerous requirements to devolve authority from the national to the regional (county) level.[53]

The devolution of government authority is especially important for natural resource use and concomitant environmental concerns. After the 2007–08 electoral violence, Kenya's land policy—the most pressing natural resource issue in the country—was identified as one

---

[47] Kanyinga (n 31) 80–81.
[48] ibid 82.
[49] Bachelard (n 43) 190.
[50] Rutten and Owuor (n 15) 60. Nowrojee made this statement on 10 June 2008.
[51] Murunga, Okello, and Sjogren (n 29) 1. 'The decision by the Kenyan electorate in the 2010 referendum to support the proposed new constitution was the culmination of political work carried out over a generation'; ibid.
[52] Magu (n 4) 108. Many scholars note the progressive character of the 2010 Constitution, particularly the Bill of Rights, and the numerous checks on executive power. See Murunga, Okello, and Sjogren (n 29) 6.
[53] Magu (n 4) 109.

of the key areas that the government needed to reform.[54] As such, the 2010 Constitution, as well as a subsequent National Land Policy and various supporting pieces of legislation, sought to resolve the long-standing land question. The influence of human rights practice and human rights discourse is also evident throughout the 2010 Constitution.[55] In particular, the express justiciability of socio-economic rights is held as key to enforcing natural resource and environmental protections.[56]

Overall, the 2010 Constitution provides strong environmental protections and detailed provisions for the sustainable use of natural resources, particularly land. The inclusion of environmental protections in the Constitution's preamble speaks to the importance that the drafters gave this issue. The preamble contains only eight clauses, including the environmental clause, which declares that 'We, the people of Kenya' are 'RESPECTFUL of the environment, which is our heritage, and determined to sustain it for the benefit of future generations'.[57] The Constitution's progressive Bill of Rights[58] also addresses environmental protections, as article 42 provides '[e]very person has the right to a clean and healthy environment'. Specified within this right is environmental protection for the 'benefit of present and future generations'.[59] Article 42 requires the government to ensure this right through 'legislation and other measures', specifically referencing article 69, which details the government's environmental obligations, and article 70, which provides for the enforcement of environmental rights.[60] Both the preamble and article 42 establish the government's obligation to protect Kenya's environment. Moreover, both passages recognize the importance of intergenerational environmental rights, a recognition that remains rare in constitutional articles and constitutional jurisprudence.

While the preamble and article 42 establish the constitutional right to a clean and healthy environment, articles 69 to 72 detail the government's obligations for achieving this right. Article 69 sets out the government's environmental obligations by specifying eight duties the state has to fulfil. These duties range from the broad—such as the duty to 'ensure sustainable exploitation, utilization, management and conservation of the environment and natural resources, and ensure the equitable sharing of the accruing benefits'—to the specific, such as maintaining 'a tree cover of at least ten per cent of the land area of Kenya'.[61] The state must encourage public participation in the management, protection, and conservation of the environment,[62] while protecting genetic resources and biological diversity[63] and utilizing the environment and natural resources 'for the benefit of the people of Kenya'.[64] Technical requirements include protecting and enhancing the intellectual property and indigenous knowledge of biodiversity and the genetic resources of communities,[65] as well

---

[54] Murunga, Okello, and Sjogren (n 29) 7.

[55] Brian YK Sang, 'Horizontal Application of Constitutional Rights in Kenya: A Comparative Critique of the Emerging Jurisprudence' (2018) 26 African J International and Comparative Law 1, 5.

[56] Nlerum S Okogbule, *Globalization and Human Rights in Africa* (Sibon Books Limited 2012) 255–56.

[57] 2010 Kenya Constitution, preamble.

[58] Several scholars have noted the strong influence that the South African Constitution had on the drafters of the Kenyan Constitution. For example, Okogbule notes that the South African Constitution and its Bill of Rights clearly influenced the drafting of the 2010 Kenyan Constitution, resulting in a highly progressive constitution and strong bill of rights. Okogbule (n 56) 252–54.

[59] 2010 Kenya Constitution, art 42(a).

[60] ibid art 42(b).

[61] ibid arts 69(a)–(b).

[62] ibid art 69(d).

[63] ibid art 69(e).

[64] ibid art 69(h).

[65] ibid art 69(c).

as establishing systems for environmental impact assessments, environmental audits, and environmental monitoring.[66] Finally, the Constitution imposes a forward-looking, do no harm provision, as the state must 'eliminate processes and activities that are likely to endanger the environment'.[67] In turn, article 69(2) places a duty on all people to cooperate with the state and each other to protect and conserve the environment and to ensure the 'ecologically sustainable development and use of natural resources'.[68]

Article 70 provides for the enforcement of environmental rights and gives Kenyan courts considerable latitude in addressing acts and omissions that infringe upon article 42. Under article 70(1), once a person alleges the denial, violation, infringement, or threat to a clean and healthy environment, he or she may apply to a court for redress in addition to pursuing any other available legal remedies. Moreover, this procedure is available even when the denial, violation, infringement, or threat is likely, in addition to when it is happening or has happened. Once the application is received, the court may 'make any order, or give any directions, it considers appropriate' to 'prevent, stop or discontinue any act or omission that is harmful to the environment', 'to compel any public officer to take measures to prevent or discontinue any act or omission that is harmful to the environment', or 'to provide compensation for any victim of a violation of the right to a clean and healthy environment'.[69] In a further expansion of the court's authority, an applicant does not carry a burden to demonstrate that any person incurred a loss or suffered an injury from the alleged act or omission claimed under article 70(1).[70]

Lastly, article 71 addresses agreements relating to natural resources, making transactions that involve the grant or right of concession for the exploitation of any natural resource in Kenya subject to ratification by Parliament. These transactions include private transactions between individuals and transactions involving the government. Article 71(2) requires Parliament to enact legislation for such transactions, while article 72 provides a broader directive, requiring Parliament to 'enact legislation to give full effect to the provisions of this Part'.[71]

2.4.2 Strengthening land rights

The 2010 Constitution contains several provisions to strengthen land rights for Kenyan citizens. Article 60 sets forth the principles of Kenya's land policy, with article 60(1)(a) stating that land 'shall be held, used and managed in a manner that is equitable, efficient, productive and sustainable'. Notably, the Constitution makes a strong statement for gender equality in land and property rights, as article 60(1)(f) requires the 'elimination of gender discrimination in law, customs and practices related to land and property in land'.[72] It also encourages community resolution of land disputes at the local level through local practices.[73]

---

[66] ibid art 69(f).
[67] ibid art 69(g).
[68] ibid art 69(2). Moreover, all Kenyans have the duty to protect and conserve the environment. See Ojienda and Okoth (n 11) 175.
[69] 2010 Kenya Constitution, arts 70(2)(a)–(c).
[70] ibid art 70(3).
[71] The Part refers to arts 69 to 72.
[72] See also Ojienda and Okoth (n 11) 178.
[73] 2010 Kenya Constitution, art 60(1)(g). Art 60(1)(g) encourages communities to settle land disputes 'through recognized local community initiatives consistent with this Constitution'.

In addition to stating the importance of principles such as equity and sustainability, the 2010 Constitution sets out steps for implementing these principles. Article 60(1)(2) calls for a National Land Policy, and article 67 calls for the establishment of a National Land Commission to 'manage public land on behalf of the national and county governments'. The Constitution gives the Commission broad authority, which includes a mandate to conduct research into and make recommendations for land and natural resource use and to initiate investigations into 'present and historical land injustices' and 'recommend appropriate redress'.[74] It also encourages the Commission to apply traditional dispute resolution mechanisms in land conflicts and to monitor and provide oversight on land use planning throughout the country.[75]

The 2010 Constitution classifies land as public, community, or private,[76] and includes important restrictions on the unlawful allocation of land. This is important, as the unlawful allocation of land has played a prominent role in corruption and political patronage in Kenya.[77] Most importantly, article 62(4) requires that public land 'shall not be disposed of or otherwise used except in terms of an Act of Parliament specifying the nature and terms of that disposal or use'.[78] As Ojienda and Okoth note, this restriction serves '[a]s a bulwark against abuse of presidential discretion in the allocation of public land'.[79] Public land is a broad category that includes all minerals and oil, government forests falling outside community land as defined by article 63(2), as well as all rivers, lakes, and bodies of water. In many instances, public land now vests with the county government, which holds the land in trust for the people in the county. In the remaining instances, land vests with the national government, which holds the land in trust for the Kenyan people. In both situations, the National Land Administration administers the land on behalf of the Kenyan people.[80]

Community land vests in communities based on 'ethnicity, culture, or similar community of interest' and must be lawfully registered in the name of group representatives.[81] Private land consists of land held under freehold and leasehold tenure, as well as land declared private by an Act of Parliament.[82] Individuals that are not Kenyan citizens may hold land only through leasehold tenure and for a maximum of ninety-nine years.[83]

Finally, while the state retains strong rights to regulate the use of land,[84] the Constitution requires Parliament to enact legislation which ensures that property investments benefit local communities and local economies.[85] This provision follows article 65(3), which requires greater transparency and disclosure in relation to corporate ownership of land and property.[86] Here, it is hoped that greater transparency will allow for more effective devolution of authority and more effective land use by communities and local citizens.

---

[74] ibid arts 67(2)(d)–(e).
[75] ibid arts 67(2)(f)–(h).
[76] ibid art 61.
[77] Gabrielle Lynch, 'Histories of Association and Difference: The Construction and Negotiation of Ethnicity' in Daniel Branch, Nic Cheeseman, and Leigh Gardner (eds), *Our Turn to Eat: Politics in Kenya Since 1950* (Lit Verlag 2010).
[78] 2010 Kenya Constitution, art 62(4).
[79] Ojienda and Okoth (n 11) 175.
[80] 2010 Kenya Constitution, arts 62(2)–(3).
[81] ibid arts 63(1)–(2). See also Ojienda and Okoth (n 11) 176.
[82] 2010 Kenya Constitution, art 64.
[83] ibid art 65(1). See also Ojienda and Okoth (n 11) 174.
[84] 2010 Kenya Constitution, art 66(1).
[85] ibid art 66(2).
[86] ibid art 65(3). See also Ojienda and Okoth (n 11) 180.

2.4.3 Water rights

Water use is another example of the tension between the Kenyan government's central-ization of natural resource management and the need for flexible and informal resource management institutions at the local level. Carpenter, Baldwin, and Cole demonstrate this tension through an examination of water governance in Kenya by focusing on the extrac-tion of surface water for agricultural use.[87] First taking note of Kenya's productive agricul-ture sector, they observe how the government has increasingly centralized control over water resources in response to seasonal water scarcity, inefficient water use, and water use conflicts.[88]

Centralization was the dominant resource management approach employed throughout twentieth-century Kenya, but despite the dominance of this approach, less formal Water User Associations (WUAs) showed greater capacity and flexibility than centralized water use schemes.[89] The passage of the 2002 Water Act institutionalized this informal approach. Observing the success of WUAs, Carpenter, Baldwin, and Cole argue for a 'polycentric gov-ernance approach' that integrates informal institutions into a broader governance frame-work.[90] While questions of authority and hierarchal decision-making would remain, they contend that the integration of informal institutions into the governance system could create a 'network of overlapping decision centers', which could improve the efficiency and effectiveness of resource management.[91]

It is important to note that while WUAs often rely on the recognition or incorporation of informal or customary law, article 2(4) of the 2010 Constitution invalidates any law, in-cluding customary law, which is inconsistent with the Constitution.[92] Separate legislation supports WUAs, which helps to avoid constitutional objections, and could serve as an ex-ample for further efforts to recognize informal resource management without risking con-stitutional invalidation. Here, the controlling legislation is the 2016 Water Act.[93] This Act largely puts this issue to rest by expressly providing for the establishment of WUAs.[94] The Act refers to the 2010 constitutional acknowledgement of the access of clean and safe water as a basic human right, and seeks to realize this right by devolving water management to the county level.[95]

---

[87] Stefan Carpenter, Elizabeth Baldwin, and Daniel H Cole, 'The Polycentric Turn: A Case Study of Kenya's Evolving Legal Regime for Irrigation Waters' (2017) 57 Natural Resources J 101, 101.

[88] ibid 103.

[89] ibid 135. As the authors note, 'In practice, the early WUAs demonstrated the capacity to adopt, monitor, en-force, and mediate a much more flexible set of rules than those set out in existing legislation'; ibid.

[90] ibid 137.

[91] ibid. While the inclusion of informal institutions and overlapping decision centres implies a possible decrease in efficiency, these recommendations are more likely to increase efficiency and efficacy because of their legitimacy at the local level and recognition of local resource conditions. In contrast, centralized approaches that suggest im-proved efficiency and streamlined decision-making, but which lack local support and do not reflect local resource realities, will not prove successful.

[92] See also J Osogo Ambani and Ochieng Ahaya, 'The Wretched African Traditionalists in Kenya: The Challenges and Prospect of Customary Law in the New Constitutional Era' (2015) 1 Strathmore LJ 41, 49. The authors make this point clearly, concluding that 'African customary law has, therefore, to conform to the Constitution if it has to be considered legally sound and valid'; ibid.

[93] Water Act of 2016.

[94] ibid art 29.

[95] ibid art 63.

2.4.4 Natural resources and adjudication

The tension between centralized government institutions and less formal local institutions is evident in dispute settlement processes—especially adjudication—as well as legislation. One way to conceptualize the adjudication of natural resource disputes is to contrast the finality of judicial proceedings, particularly constitutional rulings, with the indefinite and contested nature of accessing land, water, and other natural resources at the local level. This dichotomy is present throughout Kenya, and indeed numerous African states. It is most evident in rural settings where cleavages between accessing and using natural resources—especially land—and ethnic groups can emerge.

Despite the ongoing negotiation for accessing natural resources at the local level, Kenyan citizens often prefer this approach. As Askew, Maganga, and Odgaard note, there are several reasons why local citizens prefer informal local institutions to courts: judicial proceedings require more time and money; local citizens fear that outsiders might not identify solutions that the community considers legitimate; and state officials may be biased or corrupt.[96] These authors base their conclusions on a lengthy review of attempts by pastoralists in East Africa, including the Maasai in Kenya and the Barabaig in Tanzania, to secure access to or ownership of their lands. In both cases, pastoralist communities lost on narrow technicalities despite having stronger legal claims than the defendants.[97]

Based on these and other examples, Askew, Maganga, and Odgaard argue that outside actors misuse courts 'to acquire institutional legitimacy for what amounts to theft of others' land', and aptly characterize this practice as 'property laundering'.[98] In several examples, a wealthier actor completes a land grab simply by outlasting and outspending the defendant, leaving courts 'no choice but to find in favor of the plaintiff, thus granting legally recognized claim to a land grabber'.[99] Okogbule reaches a similar conclusion when examining the African Commission's decision concerning the Endorois people.[100] Noting that African governments have consistently marginalized indigenous peoples 'under the guise of development', Okogbule concludes that 'the exploitation of natural resources found in lands belonging to indigenous peoples yields profits for transnational corporations and local elites, mostly from majority groups, but rarely "trickles down" to the indigenous people'.[101] There are notable similarities between the Endorois and their struggle to reclaim their land, the Maasai, displaced from their land by British colonial forces, and the Ogiek, fighting to maintain their land within the Mau Forest before and now well after independence. Although indigenous people and communities have nearly always lost such legal disputes, there is some evidence that the positive involvement of local and international non-governmental organizations, better education within indigenous communities, and strengthened constitutional claims to land and livelihood rights have stemmed these types of land grabs at least to some extent.[102]

---

[96] Kelly Askew, Faustin Maganga, and Rie Odgaard, 'Of Land and Legitimacy: A Tale of Two Lawsuits' (2013) 83 Africa 120, 135.

[97] ibid 122.

[98] ibid 136.

[99] ibid.

[100] Okogbule (n 56) 261. Okogbule notes the importance of this decision, stating, 'The decision of the African Commission has been hailed as a powerful statement on the need for states to respect and protect the rights of indigenous peoples as they strive to promote economic development in their countries'; ibid.

[101] ibid 263.

[102] Askew, Maganga, and Odgaard (n 96) 137.

In Kenya, a key question is to what extent the 2010 Constitution allows for the application of fundamental rights between private parties (horizontal application), as well as from individuals seeking redress from the state (vertical application). While the vertical application of constitutional rights is relatively straightforward, the horizontal application is not. However, as Sang notes, article 20 of the Constitution clearly envisions the horizontal application of fundamental rights, even though the extent to which Kenyan courts would allow for the indirect application of a fundamental right to create a remedy remains uncertain.[103] At present, Kenyan case-law suggests that parties must exhaust private-law remedies before they may seek a constitutional remedy.[104] Furthermore, Kenyan courts seem reluctant to apply horizontal constitutional rights directly when specific legislation exists to regulate the legal issue in question.[105]

In sum, Kenya's 2010 Constitution offers much promise for improved natural resource use and natural resource management that would benefit all Kenyans. The Constitution provides significant environmental protections and bottom-up economic development. Whether there is the political will to achieve such lofty aspirations is of course another question.

3. Sudan: Land Rights, Resource Management, and Centre–Periphery Economics

> Sudan's conflicts have many causes, but at the root of each conflict are questions over the control and distribution of resources. The most important resource is land: whether exploited for agriculture, cattle-herding or subterranean resources such as oil or water, land ownership is the key to wealth and power—
> Mona Ayoub[106]

Sudan fell under control of British colonial forces from 1899 until gaining independence in 1956. While formally governed by Egypt, Britain effectively ruled Sudan as a crown colony.[107] During this time, British colonialists and co-opted Sudanese elites used Sudanese land and natural resources to support Britain's colonial empire. Like other crown colonies, Sudan became a peripheral territory dedicated to maintaining the economic health of the colonial centre. This centre–periphery economic model replicated itself within Sudan after independence, as wealth derived from land and natural resources in Sudan's rural areas supported political and business elites in Khartoum.[108]

The centre–periphery economic model only became more entrenched after independence. And although Sudan has enjoyed a few brief periods of democratic governance, military-backed autocrats have ruled the country for much of its post-colonial history.[109] For Sudan's autocrats, political patronage is the key to remaining in power, and land and

---

[103] Sang (n 55) 6.
[104] ibid 13.
[105] ibid 14–15.
[106] Mona Ayoub, 'Land and Conflict in Sudan' (2006) 18 Accord 14, 14.
[107] Robert O Collins, *A History of Modern Sudan* (Cambridge University Press 2008).
[108] ibid 238, 300.
[109] See especially WJ Berridge, *Civil Uprisings in Modern Sudan: The 'Khartoum Springs' of 1964 and 1985* (Bloomsbury Academic 2015) 215–20.

natural resources provide the surest way to meet this objective. Accordingly, Sudan's polit-ical leaders have consistently looted much of the country's natural resource wealth for self-enrichment and to maintain political power.[110]

3.1 Dispossession by Legislation

After Sudan gained independence, General Ibrahim Abboud led the country as the mili-tary remained in power. Abboud resigned in 1964 when popular protests and demands for democratic rule led to a brief period of democratic governance. Only five years later, Gaafar Nimeiry seized power and returned Sudan to a military-led authoritarian state. Nimeiry named himself Prime Minister before abolishing Parliament and banning all political par-ties. Under his rule, Sudan enacted legislation and government policies that entrenched and expanded land dispossession, leading to poor environmental, social, and economic out-comes. Legislative and policy decisions affecting land rights were especially detrimental, making conflict over land and natural resources nearly inevitable.

The Nimeiry regime's two most damaging actions were the passage of the Unregistered Land Act in 1970 and the People's Local Government Act in 1971. The Unregistered Land Act (ULA) transferred all unregistered land to the Sudanese state, giving the government 'full ownership of unregistered lands, whether waste, forest, occupied or unoccupied, which had not been registered before the commencement of the Act on 6 April 1970'.[111] The Act also abolished the right of local authorities to allocate land.[112]

In effect, the Act was a massive land grab in which the government reclaimed much of Sudan's land from local communities. The Nimeiry regime used the colonial-era Land Settlement and Registration Act of 1925 to complete this land grab, as all land unregis-tered by the process set forth in that Act would then transfer to the government. The over-whelming majority of Sudanese communities relied on customary law to allocate land and determine land rights, and largely ignored the 1925 Act, which had little impact on their daily activities. As a result, the ULA caused an enormous shift in landownership, as the gov-ernment gained ownership of perhaps 90 per cent of all Sudanese land.[113]

Under the ULA, individuals can acquire usufruct rights, not proprietary rights, over now state-owned land. Moreover, the decision to abolish the rights of local authorities to allocate land moved key land use and natural resource management decisions away from local communities upwards to the centralized state bureaucracy. As such, the ULA alien-ated both agrarian and pastoral communities by denying legitimacy to traditional prop-erty rights, thereby damaging not just land rights but so too carefully negotiated water and grazing rights.[114] The ULA enabled corrupt practices and self-enrichment to flourish, as

---

[110] See eg De Waal (n 2) 70–73 (discussing Hamdi's Triangle).

[111] Unregistered Land Act of 1970, s 4. See also Suleiman Rahhal and AH Abdel Salam, 'Land Rights, Natural Resources Tenure and Land Reform' (2006) (Committee of the Civil Project) 2; Liz Alden Wily, ' "The Law is to Blame": The Vulnerable Status of Common Property Rights in Sub-Saharan Africa' (2011) 42 Development and Change 733, 742.

[112] As Rahhal and Salam note, the Unregistered Lands Act abolished the authority of native administrators to allocate land. Rahhal and Salam (n 111) 4. See also Ayoub (n 106) 15.

[113] 'USAID Country Profile, Property Rights and Resource Governance: Sudan' *United States Agency for International Development* (13 May 2013) <http://www.land-links.org/wp-content/uploads/2016/09/USAID_La nd_Tenure_Sudan_Profile.pdf> accessed 3 April 2021.

[114] Ayoub (n 106) 14.

government officials allocated land to private investors.[115] While customary land and natural resource management at the local level was not without fault, prioritizing a centralized state bureaucracy of a newly independent state to manage land and natural resources resulted in predictable failures, including modernized agricultural schemes that did not meet expectations, environmental degradation, and entrenched economic inequality.

The Nimeiry regime formally abolished Native Administration in 1971 by enacting the People's Local Government Act (PLGA).[116] Building on the ULA, this Act ended local governance and local courts based on customary law, the latter defined as native administration by British colonialists.[117] Instead, the PLGA called for the establishment of local councils linked to the Sudanese Socialist Union Party, which Nimeiry led as the only legal political party in the country.[118] In many rural areas, the state could not enforce this Act or the local councils for which it provided, as local communities retained their allegiance to existing local authorities.[119] This was especially true in southern Sudan.[120] Nonetheless, as Unruh and Abdul-Jalil note, in both the north and south, this Act and its attendant policies created an 'institutional vacuum' by eliminating 'the primary institution that allowed the customary and statutory tenure systems to effectively interface in a way that facilitated adaptation'.[121]

Finally, in 1984, a year before a popular uprising would remove Nimeiry from power, the government enacted the Civil Transactions Act (CTA). This Act reaffirmed state ownership of unregistered land, but also recognized usufruct rights for local communities occupying these lands.[122] Perhaps most importantly, the CTA ended all litigation pertaining to land claims and the ULA by prohibiting courts or other legal authorities from hearing challenges to state landownership stemming from the ULA.[123] Furthermore, the CTA amended the ULA to dismiss all pending cases concerning state ownership of unregistered land.[124]

The CTA did provide some benefits. It amended the ULA to afford occupants cultivating state lands with protection from removal.[125] It also partially recognized the customary acquisition of land,[126] and provided land use rights to any Sudanese citizen using wasteland for agriculture or irrigation, even if the land was not properly registered.[127] Nonetheless, these benefits hardly outweighed the harm that this Act caused by reifying the government's unjust appropriation of massive amounts of land and negating the attendant natural resource rights.

---

[115] M Suliman, 'The Nuba Mountains of Sudan: Resource Access, Violent Conflict, and Identity' in D Buckles (ed), *Cultivating Peace: Conflict and Collaboration in Natural Resource Management* (International Development Research Centre/World Bank Institute 1999). The 1990 Investment Act followed this precedent and allowed for the allocation of vast tracts of land to private capital investors, resulting in displacement, landlessness, and a loss of livelihoods for rural communities. Ayoub (n 106) 14.

[116] Douglas H Johnson, *The Root Causes of Sudan's Civil Wars* (International African Institute 2007).

[117] People's Local Government Act of 1971; John Ryle, *The Sudan Handbook* (James Currey 2011) 112–14.

[118] Ryle (n 117) 112–14.

[119] Rahhal and Salam (n 111) 4.

[120] As Ryle notes, traditional chiefs continued to exercise political and judicial functions in southern Sudan despite the Act. Ryle (n 117) 112–14.

[121] Jon Unruh and Musa Adam Abdul-Jalil, 'Land Rights in Darfur: Institutional Flexibility, Policy and Adaptation to Environmental Change' (2012) 36 Natural Resources Forum 274, 279.

[122] Civil Transactions Act of 1984. See also Carey N Gordon, 'Recent Developments in the Land Law of the Sudan: A Legislative Analysis' (1986) 30 Journal of African Law 143, 148.

[123] Rahhal and Salam (n 111) 3.

[124] ibid 11.

[125] Wily (n 111) 751.

[126] Unruh and Abdul-Jalil (n 121) 282.

[127] Gordon (n 122) 153.

Together, these three legislative acts led to profoundly negative environmental and economic outcomes, including the creation of a dual land tenure system that all but eliminated effective land use and natural resource management. Following Nimeiry's removal from power in 1985, the new government attempted to address these issues. The most prominent example was the reinstatement of native administration through the 1986 Native Administration Act.[128] This Act and other efforts were at best partially successful, as they lacked credibility with local communities and featured significantly weakened authorities for local leaders.[129] Furthermore, the government often worked to undermine the very efforts it supposedly supported. Thus, as Rahhal and Salam note, after the reinstatement of native administration the government still attempted to control local decisions through bribery or by replacing independent administrators with more pliant ones who would prioritize state policy over local concerns.[130]

3.2 The Interim National Constitution: Towards a New Constitutional Framework?

Sudan's 2005 Interim National Constitution resulted from the Comprehensive Peace Agreement that ended the Second Sudanese Civil War (1983–2005). For now, the Interim National Constitution remains 'the supreme law of the land', even though its interim status has lasted longer than anticipated.[131] In April 2018, Sudan's President Omar al-Bashir announced that Parliament would approve a permanent constitution following national elections in 2020.[132] However, months of popular protests led to the Sudan Armed Forces ousting Bashir on 11 April 2019.[133] Civilian protest leaders and the Transitional Military Council continue to negotiate the terms of a transitional government, including the drafting of a new constitution and the role that Islamic law should have in this constitution.[134] With the transition set to take at least three years, the Interim National Constitution is likely to remain in force for at least the next few years.[135]

The 2005 Interim National Constitution features considerable environmental protections as well as several provisions addressing natural resource use and land rights. Article

---

[128] Native Administration Act of 1986; USAID Country Profile (n 113) 11.

[129] Ayoub (n 106) 15.

[130] Rahhal and Salam (n 111) 4.

[131] Sudan Interim National Constitution of 2005, art 3. Art 3 states, 'The Interim National Constitution shall be the supreme law of the land.'

[132] 'Sudan's New Constitution to Be Approved by Next Parliament: al-Bashir' *Sudan Tribune* (28 April 2018) <http://sudantribune.com/spip.php?article65283> accessed 3 April 2021.

[133] Jen Kirby, 'Sudan's Longtime Leader Was Ousted in a Military Coup. Protesters Still Want Democracy' *VOX* (11 April 2019) <http://www.vox.com/world/2019/4/11/18306002/sudan-news-bashir-coup-protests-khartoum-auf> accessed 3 April 2021; John Hursh, 'Ouster of Sudan's Bashir Is Only the Beginning' *Just Security* (12 April 2019) <http://www.justsecurity.org/63601/ouster-of-sudans-bashir-is-only-the-beginning> accessed 3 April 2021.

[134] See 'Sudan Military Rulers Want Islamic Law to Guide Legislation' *Al Jazeera* (8 May 2019) <http://www. aljazeera.com/news/2019/05/sudan-military-rulers-sharia-laws-guide-legislations-190508061915754.html> accessed 3 April 2021; Mohammed Amin and Kaamil Ahmed, 'Sudan Protest Leaders Reject Army's Call for Islamic Law in New Constitution' *Middle East Eye* (8 May 2019) <http://www.middleeasteye.net/news/sudan-protest-leaders-reject-army-demand-use-Islamic-law-new-constitution> accessed 3 April 2021.

[135] On 4 August 2019, the transitional government, composed of civilian and military leaders, signed an Interim Constitutional Declaration. Although declared the 'supreme law of the land', this document focuses primarily on the transitional government and its competencies before elections planned for 2022. Furthermore, it addresses land and natural resources only at a superficial level.

11(1) provides that the people of Sudan 'shall have the right to a clean and diverse environment', while also declaring that the state and its citizens 'have the duty to preserve and promote the country's biodiversity'.[136] Article 11(2) ensures that the state will not pursue policies or take actions that adversely affect animal or vegetable (plant) life or the natural habitats of these species, while article 11(3) ensures that the state will use legislation to promote the 'sustainable utilization of natural resources and best practices with respect to their management'.[137] Furthermore, article 82 lists seven duties of the government, including the 'formulation of a repatriation, relief, rehabilitation, resettlement, reconstruction and development plan to address the needs of the areas affected by the conflict and redress the imbalances in development and resource allocation'. Thus, in addition to sustainable natural resource use, the Interim National Constitution commits the government to address inequitable resource allocation and imbalanced development policies—root causes of Sudan's two civil wars and a source of long-standing grievances between the capital, Khartoum, and the peripheral states in the north, including Darfur to the west, Red Sea State to the east, and South Kordofan and Blue Nile State to the south.

Article 185 contributes to the constitutional framework for natural resource and environmental management by setting forth the Guiding Principles for the Equitable Sharing of Resources and Common Wealth. Of these eleven principles, at least four invoke natural resources or the environment. Article 185(8) addresses natural resource management directly, stating that '[t]he best known practices in the sustainable utilization and management of natural resources shall be adopted by the State'. This requirement reinforces article 11(3), which requires the state to promote the sustainable use of natural resources through legislation. Likewise, article 185(1) requires the equitable sharing of resources and common wealth, while article 185(2) requires the government to share and allocate resources and the common wealth based on the premise that 'all parts of the country are entitled to development'. Lastly, article 185(6) requires revenue sharing to 'reflect a commitment to devolution of powers and decentralization of decision making' for the sake of development, service delivery, and governance. These articles clearly require the government to manage the country's natural resources in a sustainable manner and to share its natural resource wealth equitably across regions in a non-discriminatory way.[138]

Articles 186–89 address land rights. Article 186 regulates land registration, with article 186(1) calling for 'the appropriate level of government' to regulate land tenure, land use, and land rights, and article 186(3) requiring all levels of government 'to progressively develop and amend the relevant laws to incorporate customary laws, practices, local heritage, and international trends and practices'.

To ensure that the government meets these requirements, the Interim National Constitution establishes a National Land Commission to complete numerous tasks supporting these overarching requirements. Detailed in article 187, the National Land Commission has seven broad functions, including arbitrating land claims between individuals and the government, enforcing local land laws, accepting references and making

---

[136] Similarly, art 23(2) lists nine duties for every Sudanese citizen, including the duty to 'preserve the natural environment'.

[137] Sudan Interim National Constitution, arts 11(2)–(3).

[138] Arts 190–92 address the petroleum industry and contain similar language stressing the sustainable use of this natural resource. For example, art 190(a) recognizes the need to use oil in a sustainable manner and that oil constitutes a non-renewable resource.

recommendations concerning land reform and customary land law, assessing appropriate land compensation, and advising the government when national projects affect land rights. Article 187(2) ensures the independence of the Commission, although article 187(3) requires the President, with the consent of the First Vice-President, to appoint the chair of the Commission and article 187(4) requires the President to approve the Commission's budget. Thus, despite the assurances of independence given in article 187(2), articles 187(3) and 187(4) clearly undermine the Commission's independence.

3.3 Implementation and Identity

During the rule of President Nimeiry and especially that of President Bashir, the government's inability to govern land and natural resources in an equitable and sustainable manner was due in part to its failure to implement existing legal obligations, but much more so to an unwillingness to support an inclusive Sudanese identity that embraces the country's pluralistic nature and diverse peoples.[139] Perhaps the most important example of non-implementation frustrating better land and natural resource use is the failure to establish the Land Commissions set forth in the Interim National Constitution.[140] Likewise, the constitutional requirement to incorporate customary law into state legislation and to consider restitution for economic losses suffered during the last several decades has not moved forward, leaving communal land as vulnerable now as it was after enactment of the ULA.

Of course, creating an inclusive Sudanese identity is a more difficult task than bringing about greater implementation of the law. The inability to construct such an identity resulted in the secession of South Sudan and continues to perpetuate the centre–periphery dynamic that has proven so harmful to Sudan. As Francis Deng observes, 'Sudan has been intermittently at war with itself since independence on June 1, 1956, with only ten years of precarious peace between 1972 and 1983. At the heart of the conflict is a crisis of national identity.'[141]

Within Sudan, economic marginalization and violent conflict often flow from contested land and natural resource rights.[142] Salman makes this point regarding border communities between Sudan and South Sudan and the use of traditional rights to regulate grazing and water rights, the latter of which he calls 'the critical and ultimate claim'.[143] Moreover, as

[139] Noha Ibrahim Abdelgabar, 'International Law and Constitution Making Process: The Right to Public Participation in the Constitution Making Process in Post Referendum Sudan' (2013) 46 Law and Politics in Africa, Asia and Latin America 131, 150. Abdelgabar concludes that the Interim National Constitution is an 'exemplary constitution with the inclusion of a comprehensive bill of rights', but that since its adoption, it 'has faced ongoing attempts by the parties to the CPA to undermine it'; ibid.

[140] Wily (n 111) 744. Wily characterizes the follow-through as 'slow and diluted'; ibid.

[141] Francis M Deng, 'Sudan: A Nation in Turbulent Search of Itself' (2006) 603 The Annals of the American Academy of Political and Social Science 155. Accordingly, Abdulbari argues for constitutional efforts to strengthen, promote, and protect pluralism and diversity in Sudan. See Nasredeen Abdulbari, 'Identities and Citizenship in Sudan: Governing Constitutional Principles' (2013) 13 African Human Rights LJ 383, 413.

[142] The Nuba people who live mainly in South Kordofan are but one of several examples. GK Komey, 'The Denied Land Rights of the Indigenous Peoples and their Endangered Livelihood and Survival: The Case of the Nuba of the Sudan' (2008) 31 Ethnic and Racial Studies 991; Judith Large and El-Lazim Suleiman El Basha, 'A Bitter Harvest and Grounds for Reform: The Nuba Mountains, Conflict Land and Transitional Sudan' (2010) Berghof Peace Support Working Paper July 2010, <http://www.berghof-foundation.org/fileadmin/redaktion/Publications/Other_Resources/SUD_Bitter_Harvest_and_Grounds_for_Reform.pdf> accessed 3 April 2021.

[143] Salman MA Salman, 'Water Resources in the Sudan North–South Peace Process: Past Experience and Future Trends' (2008) 16 African Yearbook International Law 299, 328.

Mohamed notes, empirical evidence demonstrates that peripheral regions, such as Darfur and Kordofan, still 'stand out as clearly disadvantaged'.[144] A further and highly visible example of inequitable land and natural resource use is the Meroe Dam.[145] The construction of this dam displaced 70,000 people, almost all of them from Nubian communities.[146] Before flooding the land to allow for the dam, project engineers did not consult local communities, nor did local communities consent to this project.[147] Instead, government authorities forcibly displaced these communities, who then received inadequate compensation for their land.[148] Clearly, neither environmental sustainability nor economic development is possible when the relationship between citizen and state is as damaged as these examples illustrate.

There is, however, reason to expect considerable improvements from the transitional government that came to power after the peaceful demonstrations that ousted President Bashir. There is also reason for concern, as civil uprisings have removed authoritarian governments from power twice previously before the country reverted to non-democratic rule. Still, provided that civilian rule holds, Sudanese citizens should expect to see a better realization of their environmental and natural resource rights.

4. South Sudan: Marginalization, Independence, and Executive Power

Though debates in Juba are still being worked out, it is clear that the nature and scope of the newly independent South Sudanese state will be determined in large part by the outcome of debates over land—Naseem Badiey[149]

4.1 Pre-independence and the Interim Period

Before South Sudan gained independence in 2011, social, economic, and political marginalization—often resulting in armed conflict—largely defined its relationship with Sudan. While the marginalization of the south took many forms, the common theme was the exploitation of the south for the benefit of the north, and, more specifically, for the benefit of a small class of political elites in and around Khartoum. This exploitation

---

[144] Adam Azzain Mohamed, 'The Problem of Uneven Regional Development in the Northern Sudan' (2006) 30 Fletcher Forum of World Affairs 41, 50.

[145] On the construction of the Meroe Dam and the historical relationship between water rights and state power in Sudan, see especially Harry Verhoeven, *Water, Civilisation and Power in Sudan: The Political Economy of Military-Islamist State Building* (Cambridge University Press 2015) 1–11, 36–82.

[146] 'Petition to Stop the Dams in Sudan: European Committee for Preserving the Middle Nile' (2012) 29 The African Archaeological Review 1, 3.

[147] ibid.

[148] ibid. See also Trevor L Gross, 'Improvement with Impunity: Development-Induced Displacement and the Guiding Principle 6(2)(C) Proportionality Test Applied to the Merowe Dam Project in Sudan' (2008) 24 American University International L Rev 377, 406.

[149] Naseem Badiey, 'The Strategic Instrumentalization of Land Tenure in "State Building": The Case of Juba, South Sudan' (2013) 83 Africa 57, 75.

centred on natural resources, including the south's rich agricultural land and later its oil deposits.[150]

In large part, the Sudanese government replicated the core-periphery model of extractive governance that colonial British officials imposed during the Anglo-Egyptian Condominium (1899–1955). An enabling legal system was a key feature of this governance model, which exploited the country's peripheries for the enrichment of political elites within the capital. And while this model extended throughout Sudan, its deleterious effects were felt most strongly in the south due to the overwhelming reliance of the South Sudanese on agricultural and pastoral livelihoods. As discussed above, the Unregistered Land Act was especially harmful. As Badiey notes, 'This [Act] in effect dispossessed most of southern Sudan's ethnic communities of legal rights to the land which was held under customary law, and made southerners guests on the land on which they lived, farmed, and grazed their livestock.'[151]

As a result of this dispossession and persistent marginalization, the South Sudanese people took up arms against the north, resulting in two protracted civil wars that lasted throughout much of post-colonial Sudanese history. The first Sudanese Civil War began in 1955, the year before Sudan gained independence from Britain, and lasted until 1972, while the Second Sudanese Civil War began in 1983 and lasted until 2005, when the Government of Sudan and the Sudan Peoples' Liberation Movement (SPLM) signed the Comprehensive Peace Accord (CPA).[152] In addition to ending the armed conflict, the CPA provided for the possibility of secession, giving the South Sudanese people until 9 January 2011 to decide whether to remain within Sudan or to secede and form a new state. In 2011, the South Sudanese people voted overwhelmingly for secession, with more than 98 per cent of voters opting to leave Sudan and form a new state.[153]

4.2 Independence

Although the advent of independence in June 2011 was accompanied by high hopes, South Sudan returned to armed conflict in 2013. As was the case with the protracted civil wars with the north, conflict centred on access to natural resource wealth, as political leaders used this wealth to enlist fighters and garner support. While there are numerous, often overlapping and mutually reinforcing explanations for the collapse of South Sudan only two years after it gained independence, nearly all of these explanations involve the inequitable misuse of natural resource wealth.[154]

[150] Mario Silva, 'After Partition: The Perils of South Sudan' (2015) 3 University of Baltimore J of International L 63, 69–70. As Silva states, 'When the second civil war commenced, the government in Khartoum clearly had every intention of exploiting the South's natural resources'.

[151] Badiey (n 149) 62.

[152] The Comprehensive Peace Agreement between the Government of the Republic of the Sudan and the Sudan People's Liberation Movement/Sudan People's Liberation Army, 2005. See also United Nations Security Council Resolution 1574, 1 (19 November 2004). This Resolution required the implementation of the Comprehensive Peace Agreement by 31 December 2004.

[153] Josh Kron and Jeffrey Gettleman, 'South Sudanese Vote Overwhelmingly for Secession' New York Times (21 January 2011) <http://www.nytimes.com/2011/01/22/world/africa/22sudan.html> accessed 3 April 2021.

[154] Andrew S Natsios and Michael Abramowitz, 'Sudan's Secession Crisis: Can the South Part from the North without War?' (2011) 90(1) Foreign Affairs 19, 22. As Natsios and Abramowitz note, 'The rural areas of the south know little of the prosperity now evident in Juba; whether a new state could spread these benefits more equitably will determine its viability over the long term.'

In retrospect, the causes of South Sudan's collapse seem all too clear, but immediately after independence, regional observers feared a return to conflict with the north much more than a civil war between different factions of the government in the south. Again, these concerns typically involved natural resource wealth.[155] The best examples are the still unresolved border disputes over Abyei and South Kordofan and Blue Nile State. In both instances, the presence of significant natural resource wealth—oil in Abyei and gold in South Kordofan and Blue Nile—fuelled tensions and pushed actors towards conflict rather than peaceful resolution. Moreover, painstakingly negotiated land rights and natural resource sharing between the Misseriya and Ngok Dinka ethnic groups further complicated the resolution of the Abyei issue.[156]

Perhaps above all, the six-year transition period between the end of armed conflict and the vote for secession was a missed opportunity to resolve tension over natural resources. During this time, political leaders did little to resolve the outstanding issues found within the CPA. In addition to border disputes, the crucial issue of sharing oil wealth was not addressed in a satisfactory manner. Nearly 80 per cent of Sudanese oil is in the south, but southern entities have to use the northern pipeline to export the oil.[157] Likewise, the formation of regional land commissions, stipulated by the CPA, either did not occur or had little effect on resolving ongoing disputes over land and natural resources.

4.3 The Transitional Constitutional Framework and Natural Resource Governance

Now a decade into independence, South Sudan remains governed by its 2011 Transitional Constitution. The Transitional Constitution follows a 2005 interim constitution that resulted from the CPA. In the 2011 Constitution, part 12 addresses finance and economic matters, with chapter I of that part outlining the guiding principles for development and equitable sharing of national wealth in South Sudan. These principles include decentralized, broad-based, balanced, and participatory economic development; the devolution of government authority; sustainable development through transparent and accountable governance; and public participation in policy development and programming.

Perhaps most importantly, article 168(5) requires the sharing of national wealth and the allocation of resources 'on the premise that all states, localities and communities are entitled to equitable development without discrimination as shall be regulated by law'. Thus, the government must allocate national wealth and resources to ensure the quality of life and the

---

[155] Natsios and Abramowitz make this point well, stating, 'If the south does secede, Khartoum will have to negotiate to get access to the region's natural wealth: not only its vast oil reserves but also mineral resources in the region—gold, diamonds, copper, and coltan—that have yet to be fully explored, the plentiful water from the Nile River watershed and the Sudd marshlands, the region's luxuriant soil, and its thousands of square miles of open range with the greatest concentration of cattle per capita in sub-Saharan Africa'. ibid 23.

[156] Lere Amusan, 'Germinating Seeds of Future Conflicts in South Sudan' (2014) 4(1) African Conflict and Peacebuilding Review 120, 124.

[157] Roger Middleton, 'South Sudan: Labour Pains' (2011) 67(8/9) The World Today 26, 27; see also Michael L Ross, *The Oil Curse: How Petroleum Wealth Shapes the Development of Nations* (Princeton University Press 2012) 169–70. Ross notes how President Nimeiry decided to build the country's oil refinery in the north, which the SPLA deemed to be theft of southern Sudan's natural resource wealth. After the SPLA attacked the pipeline, which halted production, the Sudanese government, then led by President Bashir, responded by committing a series of atrocities that included killings, rape, torture, and forced displacement; ibid 169.

promotion of the dignity of all persons without discrimination. Accordingly, the national government must apportion revenue equitably among states and local governments, and revenue sharing must reflect a commitment to the devolution of power and the decentralization of decision-making.

4.3.1 Land rights

Chapter II consists of three articles that address landownership, land tenure, and natural resources. Article 169 regulates landownership, stating, 'All land in South Sudan is owned by the people of South Sudan and its usage shall be regulated by the government in accordance with the provisions of this Constitution and the law'. Article 169(2) allows the government to expropriate land when doing so is 'in the public interest as shall be prescribed by law'. Article 170 addresses land tenure, with article 170(2) providing for three types of land: public, community, and private. Public land includes all land owned, held, or otherwise lawfully acquired by the government and any other land not classified as community or private land.[158] Community land includes 'all lands traditionally and historically held or used by local communities or their members',[159] while private land includes 'registered land held by any person under leasehold tenure in accordance with the law'.[160] Private land also includes 'investment land', which is land leased by the government or the community, to further development.[161]

Despite these classifications, under article 170(4), the government retains 'rights over all subterranean rights and other natural resources through South Sudan', with specific reference to 'petroleum and gas resources and solid minerals'.[162] At the same time, article 170(7) recognizes 'customary land rights under customary land law', while requiring the government to exercise land and resource management at the 'appropriate or designated level of government' when it acquires rights in land and resources. Article 170(8) requires the government to 'progressively develop and amend the relevant laws to incorporate customary rights and practices and local heritage', while article 170(9) requires communities and persons to be consulted in decisions that 'may affect their rights in lands and resources'. Article 170(10) affords communities and persons 'prompt and equitable compensation on just terms' following the acquisition or development of their land to serve the public interest. Lastly, article 171 requires the establishment of 'an independent land commission', the composition of which must be 'persons of proven competence, experience, integrity and impartiality'.

4.3.2 Environmental protection

The Transitional Constitution provides several provisions to protect the environment and safeguard the country's natural resource wealth. Article 37(2)(b) requires the government to protect the country's natural resources, to manage these resources sustainably, and to ensure that all South Sudanese people benefit from the country's natural resource wealth.[163]

---

[158] Transitional Constitution of 2011, art 170(3).
[159] ibid art 170(5).
[160] ibid art 170(6)(a).
[161] ibid art 170(6)(b).
[162] ibid art 170(4).
[163] Art 37(2)(b) states, 'All levels of government shall protect and ensure the sustainable management and utilization of natural resources including land, water, petroleum, minerals, fauna and flora for the benefit of the people.'

Similarly, article 41(1) states that '[e]very person or community shall have the right to a clean and healthy environment'.

While the right to a clean and healthy environment extends to individuals or communities, the remainder of article 41 addresses individual rights and obligations. Thus, article 41(2) obligates 'every person … to protect the environment for the benefit of present and future generations'. Article 41(3) also emphasizes an intergenerational approach to environmental rights by restating the obligation of article 41(2) as a right to an environment 'protected for the benefit of present and future generations'. Article 41(3) continues by detailing how to achieve this right, namely through 'legislative action and other measures' that 'prevent pollution and ecological degradation', 'promote conversation', and 'secure ecologically sustainable development and use of natural resources', while also promoting 'economic and social development' and protecting 'genetic stability and biodiversity'. Finally, article 41(4) requires all levels of government to develop energy policies that ensure the basic needs of the South Sudanese people while also protecting and preserving the environment.

Article 46(g) repeats the obligation set out in article 41(2) by stating that South Sudanese citizens have a duty to 'protect the environment and conserve natural resources'. Finally, article 152(e) states that 'all members of armed forces shall not be involved in illicit activities that may affect the environment and natural resources'. That the Transitional Constitution contains a provision directly prohibiting all members of the armed forces from participating in illicit activities that may affect the environment and natural resources speaks volumes to the greatest threat to the environment in South Sudan. Likewise, the constitutional requirement to share the country's natural resource wealth equally among the South Sudanese people, along with the emphasis on intergenerational environmental concerns, reflects the country's history of inequitable resource management and short-term exploitation of natural resources.

While recognizing past failings and providing constitutional mandates to ensure future prevention is welcome, the country's post-independence political leaders and lawmakers have failed to meet these lofty standards. Indeed, instead of equitable resource sharing and policies designed to meet the needs of the South Sudanese people and protect the country's environment, the unsustainable exploitation of natural resources, particularly oil, has only contributed to war and the country's devastation.

4.3.3 The concentration of executive power and oil dependence

The strongest criticism of the 2011 Transitional Constitution is the concentration of power placed within the executive. For example, Amusan found that the concentration of executive power, including the president's ability to dismiss governors and dissolve Parliament, posed an obstacle to 'a true democracy' and could result in armed conflict in 'a weak rentier state'.[164] This very scenario came to pass in December 2013 when President Kiir dismissed his cabinet, including Vice-President Riek Machar, in response to a rumoured coup. South Sudan quickly descended into protracted armed conflict between Kiir's government and Machar's armed opposition. Although fighting largely followed ethnic lines, it is important to note that the collapse of the government was less the result of ethnic division than of irresponsible political leaders using ethnic identity and fear to mobilize their supporters.[165]

---

[164] Amusan (n 156) 129.
[165] Cheeseman (n 24) 204. Cheeseman notes, 'The problem was thus not so much one of ethnicity, but a lack of political inclusion'; ibid.

Similarly, Radon and Logan identify the 'concentration of power in the presidency' as one of three factors that led to South Sudan's civil war.[166] However, they note that these factors 'must be examined within the context of the country's excessively heavy independence on oil revenues'.[167] This is an important point. The over-concentration of authority in the executive is problematic in any democracy, but is especially damaging in institutionally weak states dependent on natural resource wealth[168]—and it is hard to imagine a state with less developed institutions or greater reliance on such wealth than South Sudan.[169] Exacerbating this situation is the fact that political actors use strong ethnic identities to mobilize supporters and make claims on valuable natural resources, including land.[170]

The excessively strong presidency and the overwhelming reliance on oil wealth significantly heightened the possibility that South Sudan would return to conflict following independence.

4.4 Constitutional Challenges

The most pressing issues for maintaining South Sudan's fragile peace directly relate to fundamental constitutional questions. Most of these questions also invoke natural resource use and the protection and management of the environment. In this sense, it is hard to understate the importance of land in terms of maintaining peace, fostering economic development, and, above all, establishing a constitutional order inclusive of all South Sudanese people. Indeed, as one recent study concluded:

> The intractability of conflicts in South Sudan derives from their complex local dynamics and the frequently changing linkages with national politics and developments in the larger region. Land issues have played a particularly important role both in generating poverty and in driving and sustaining protracted conflict.[171]

As one example, in her case study of urban land in Juba, Badiey illustrates how overlapping statutory and customary land tenure laws, particularly concerning less-regulated land such as peri-urban areas outside the capital, create tension among various claimants.[172]

---

[166] Jenik Radon and Sarah Logan, 'South Sudan: Governance Arrangements, War, and Peace' (2014) 68(1) Journal of International Affairs 149, 151. Radon and Logan also observe that the consolidation of presidential authority was at odds with the decentralized model of governance the Sudan Peoples' Liberation Movement applied during the interim period; ibid 154.

[167] ibid 151.

[168] For example, the South Sudanese anthropologist Jok Madut Jok argues that South Sudan's military will resist peace efforts that curtail the vast economic gains it receives from oil production, stating that '[a]bove all, the military is wracked by the enormous amount of money it has received in oil proceeds'. Jok Madut Jok, 'State, Law, and Insecurity in South Sudan' (2013) 37(2) Fletcher Forum of World Affairs 69, 74.

[169] The World Bank characterizes South Sudan as 'one of the most oil-dependent countries in the world', as oil accounts for nearly all of the country's exports and about 40 per cent of its GDP. See 'The World Bank in South Sudan: Overview' The World Bank (16 October 2019) <http://www.worldbank.org/en/country/southsudan/overv iew> accessed 3 April 2021; see also Tom Burgis, The Looting Machine: Warlords, Oligarchs, Smugglers, and the Theft of Africa's Wealth (PublicAffairs 2015) 73 (noting that crude oil and natural gas account for 98 per cent of government revenue in South Sudan).

[170] Amusan (n 156) 128.

[171] Mareike Schomerus and Lovise Aalen (eds), Considering the State: Perspectives on South Sudan's Subdivision and Federalism Debate (Overseas Development Institute 2016) 12. See also Badiey (n 149) 58.

[172] Badiey (n 149) 65.

Badiey demonstrates how multiple actors, including the local Bari ethnic group, the Central Equatoria state government, local elites, ex-combatants, and returning internally displaced persons and refugees, all made claims on this land by appealing to particular social and historical narratives in addition to or in lieu of legal claims supported by property titles or deeds.[173] Badiey's study is instructive because it shows the difficulty of resolving land disputes across multiple legal frameworks and the further challenge that extra-legal claims to land can create, two characteristics common to many land disputes throughout South Sudan.

One fundamental land and governance issue is the question of internal states within South Sudan. At independence, South Sudan consisted of ten states. However, after signing the 2015 Agreement on the Resolution of Conflict in South Sudan, Kiir issued a Presidential Decree that increased the number of states to twenty-eight.[174] Questions about the constitutionality of this action remain unresolved. Constitutionality aside, many observers criticized this decision as a gerrymandering effort to ensure political support and further entrench an already deep-seated patronage network.[175] Moreover, state boundaries have created substantial governing issues within South Sudan, particularly for land and natural resource use. The creation of numerous new boundaries raises the likelihood of more disputes at local and regional levels, even though the government could not adequately staff the many new state governments that it created through this decree.[176]

Another key issue is the relationship between constitutional and customary law. Throughout much of rural sub-Saharan Africa, customary law governs at the local level. This is especially so in South Sudan, where perhaps 90 per cent of all disputes are resolved through customary law.[177] The recognition of customary law in the Transitional Constitution follows from the 2005 Interim Constitution of South Sudan, which also recognized the customs and traditions of the South Sudanese people as a source of law and traditional authority as a valid institution of local governance.[178] Although the Transitional Constitution clearly allows for the application of customary law, the exact contours of this relationship remain unsettled.

Several provisions in the Transitional Constitution address customary law. In addition to articles 171(7) and 171(8), discussed above, articles 166, 167, and 168 recognize the role of traditional authority and customary law. Further, article 167(3) makes it clear that South Sudanese courts will apply customary law subject to the Constitution. Additional legislation, most notably the Local Governance Act and the Land Act, attempted to demarcate this relationship, and did so to a degree by clarifying that chiefs would serve as the focal point for conflict mitigation, especially for land-related conflicts.[179] Still, neither the Transitional Constitution, nor these legislative acts entirely succeeded, as questions remain about the

---

[173] ibid 61–72.

[174] 'South Sudan President Creates 28 New States' *Al Jazeera* (25 December 2015) <http://www.aljazeera.com/news/2015/12/south-sudan-president-creates-28-states-151225101750723.html> accessed 3 April 2021.

[175] Radon and Logan (n 166) 150. As the authors note, patronage networks, which often developed along ethnic lines, account for much of the conflict, and these networks require access to resources.

[176] Jok (n 168) 72 (noting that rural violence often involves contestations over land rights or natural resources, with disputes over grazing lands and cattle raids serving as two prominent examples).

[177] Jan Arno Hessbruegge, 'Customary Law and Authority in a State under Construction: The Case of South Sudan' (2012) 5 African Journal of Legal Studies 295, 296.

[178] ibid 304.

[179] Schomerus and Aalen (n 171) 14.

level of authority afforded to different types of chiefs, as do broader questions of legitimacy to administer land based on when and which government appointed the chief.[180]

Even without a clear understanding of how South Sudanese courts will resolve conflicting applications of constitutional and customary law, the recognition of customary law raises concern about the protection of human rights, most notably the rights of women, children, and ethnic minorities. Despite these concerns, customary courts retain a greater sense of legitimacy than many state institutions. As Hessbruegge observes, it is important to consider customary courts not against an idealized version of a statutory court, but against the reality of courts within South Sudan.[181] Thus, Hessbruegge concludes,

> the benchmark of comparison [has] to be existing central state institutions in post-conflict countries, where external assistance partners also face the dilemma of either refusing to work with state institutions that remain *de facto* patriarchal, unaccountable and prone to endorse inhumane practices or work towards their reform with the risk of inadvertently lending legitimacy to an unacceptable status quo.[182]

Moreover, customary courts may provide greater accountability through their familiarity and application of social norms prevalent within a given community.[183] Still, this is not a viable long-term strategy, and at some point, the government will have to clearly articulate the relationship between these two bodies of law.

In addition to the pressing questions of national identity and belonging, there are much more mundane, but nearly as problematic issues that challenge South Sudan's fledgling constitutional order. Professional capacity is but one example, as there is a substantial need for qualified judges and legal professionals.[184] This need is most pronounced in rural areas, as one study found that 85 per cent of South Sudan's lawyers live in Juba, whereas 80 per cent of the population lives in rural areas.[185]

The situation in South Sudan poses many more problems than solutions. But on a more optimistic note, the government and opposition finally formed a Transitional Government of National Unity on 22 February 2020, as required by the revitalized peace agreement.[186] While long overdue, this agreement at least makes a lasting peace and durable constitutional order possible. Nonetheless, the resolution of many constitutional questions remains unmet. Moreover, any legal or policy mechanism that would threaten the patronage networks benefiting South Sudan's political elites will encounter significant resistance. Thus, legal and policy recommendations that would undoubtedly benefit the country, such as Radon and Logan's proposal to create a natural resource fund that would 'collect oil revenues

---

[180] ibid.
[181] As Hessbruegge correctly concludes, '[I]t would be unfair to measure the customary systems against the benchmark of an idealized, fully human rights-compliant central state, because this ideal is removed from post-conflict realities'. Hessbruegge (n 177) 300.
[182] ibid 300–01.
[183] ibid 305.
[184] Stephanie L Schmidt, 'Emerging Rule of Law Priorities for Post-Conflict South Sudan' (2016) 11 Yale Journal of International Affairs 37, 42.
[185] ibid 47.
[186] See US Department of State, 'Troika Statement: Formation of South Sudan's Revitalized Transitional Government of National Unity' (23 February 2020) <https://2017-2021.state.gov/troika-statement-formation-of-south-sudans-revitalized-transitional-government-of-national-unity/index.html> accessed 3 April 2021.

and manage and spend funds in a transparent and accountable manner', are eminently sensible but also likely to be non-starters until political conditions improve.[187]

5. Conclusion

Having examined Kenya, Sudan, and South Sudan's constitutional provisions for protecting land and natural resources, as well as the historical contexts in which the provisions developed, we can now assess how this legal architecture relates to the broader political economy of these three states. Here, several common governing features and social dynamics are present within each state. The most obvious (and disheartening) is the misuse of natural resource wealth—particularly from the extractive resource sector and from the misappropriation of land—to secure and maintain political power. Corrupt financial practices and illicit patronage networks entrench these unjust governance structures and replicate the centre–periphery model of economic exploitation of the colonial era. Politicized ethnic identity also features heavily in all three states, giving rise to civil unrest, political violence, and even protracted civil wars. As noted above, the net result is the enrichment of a few at the expense of the majority, persistent underdevelopment, and underperforming economies.

The most salient constitutional feature of the political economies of Kenya, Sudan, and South Sudan is the struggle to establish a constitutional order that constrains executive power and ensures the implementation of legal reforms that devolve decision-making. Indeed, even when significant legal reforms are achieved, implementation has proven difficult, in large part because such reforms would not only check executive authority but also disrupt patronage networks and opportunities for personal enrichment. Recent constitutional amendments strengthening executive power in Sudan and South Sudan serve as an example, as does the non-implementation of key reforms in Kenya following the establishment of the 2010 Constitution. These outcomes demonstrate that political power still overwhelms the rule of law and that the constitutional orders of all three states remain less robust than hoped.

However, even authoritarian rulers can overplay their hand, and the 2018 constitutional amendment in Sudan that would have allowed President Bashir to run for yet another term (at the time Bashir had been in power for twenty-nine years) did little to assure the Sudanese people that economic conditions would improve. The converse is more likely, given that the sustained protests that would sweep Bashir from power only a few months later came from financial desperation and a sense that as long as Bashir and his National Congress Party remained in power, the economic situation would scarcely improve.

This outcome nonetheless raises uncomfortable questions about the possibility of meaningful political change in these three states without civil unrest or revolutionary tactics. Bashir's removal was an inspiring moment of social and political change, where a determined people refused to bow to an authoritarian leader that squandered the country's wealth through economic malfeasance, endless armed conflict, and gross misallocation of resources. But it was not a change accomplished through strictly democratic means

---

[187] Radon and Logan (n 166) 163.

or incremental reform. Nor is Sudan's political revolution or democratic transformation complete. Elements of Sudan's military and security apparatus killed hundreds of peaceful protesters only a few weeks after Bashir's ouster, leading to a protracted struggle between civilian leaders and the military over the future of the country. The civilians eventually prevailed, at least momentarily, but not without first forming a power-sharing arrangement with the military that many observers worry will at some point revert to authoritarian rule.

The removal of Bashir through (democratic) revolution and not reform also raises questions as to the broader relationship between constitutional provisions and political agency. In other words, do the well-drafted constitutions of Kenya, Sudan, and South Sudan lead to a greater realization of basic constitutional rights and fundamental freedoms in these countries?

Measuring the effects of a constitution is a notoriously difficult task and measuring the economic effects of a constitution perhaps even more so.[188] What is beyond dispute is that the post-colonial constitutional orders of Kenya, Sudan, and South Sudan featured a subversion of the rule of law that resulted in the formation of governance structures that distributed resources unjustly and inequitably, typically along politicized ethnic group status. Constitutional provisions and subsequent legislation allowed for the over-concentration of executive power and the centralization of decision-making, which in turn undermined economic opportunity and denied citizens their basic rights and freedoms.

Here, it is crucial to recall the connection between environmental and land rights and economic security in these three states, where the majority of livelihoods involve agricultural and pastoral activities. The manipulation or non-implementation of constitutional provisions intended to protect these rights betrayed the citizens of these states and led to economic arrangements where the unjust distribution of resources matched the unjust distribution of power. Beginning with indigenous dispossession and moving through the re-creation of centre–periphery exploitation, the relationship between the inequitable use of natural resources and inequality is clear. This inequality, fuelled by corruption and repression, leads to further grievances and a greater risk of civil unrest or armed conflict. And few, if any, phenomena are more detrimental to economic growth and development than civil war.[189]

Neither environmental sustainability, nor lasting economic development is possible until these conditions change. In Kenya, the struggle to decentralize government authority and move the country away from a winner-takes-all political model has proved challenging, even with the 2010 Constitution and subsequent electoral reforms. The persistence of the centralized state has undercut county decision-making that more accurately reflects local needs both from an environmental and economic perspective. Similarly, within Sudan, centre–periphery economics outlasted the colonial era and became a defining trait of authoritarian rule under President Bashir. The 2019 ouster of Bashir and the early successes of the transitional government to re-establish a democratic and inclusive Sudanese constitutional order provide hope. While the 2005 Interim Constitution provided strong environmental safeguards, the non-implementation of these provisions, as well as the non-inclusive

---

[188] Torsten Persson and Guido Tabellini, *The Economic Effects of Constitutions* (MIT Press 2005); see also Daron Acemoglu, 'Constitutions, Politics, and Economics: A Review Essay on Persson and Tabellini's *The Economic Effects of Constitutions*' (2005) 43 Journal of Economic Literature 1025.

[189] As Collier notably observed, civil war is 'development in reverse'. Paul Collier, *The Bottom Billion: Why the Poorest Countries are Failing and What Can Be Done about It* (Oxford University Press 2007) 27.

order that the Bashir regime employed to remain in power, dulled these protections. The new government must improve implementation and inclusiveness when it begins work on a new constitution.

South Sudan also suffers from entrenched centre–periphery economics, but it feels the negative effects even more than Sudan due to its nascent institutions, underdevelopment, and of course, the civil war that devastated the country almost immediately after independence. South Sudan's political leaders showed little ability or willingness to end this conflict, and the dire situation of this already fragile state raises foreboding parallels to the breakdown of government authority in Somalia or at least the darkest days of repression in Kenya in the late 1980s and early 1990s. The formation of the Transitional Government of National Unity provides at least some hope that brighter days are ahead and that South Sudanese political leaders finally will prioritize peace and allow a more robust constitutional order to take hold.

Thus, despite obvious shortcomings and historical injustices, there is still room for some degree of optimism. The constitutional provisions discussed above are quite strong and even a modest improvement in implementation could yield significant gains. Likewise, and again despite some very dark moments for all three states, Kenya, Sudan, and even South Sudan retain a strong culture of constitutionalism, particularly among civil society, where leaders have fought for years and even decades to achieve constitutional reforms. Here, the most obvious example is the eighteen-year odyssey from Kenya's multiparty elections in 1992 to the passage of the new constitution in 2010. Likewise, the ouster of President Bashir after thirty years of authoritarian rule and the promise of a new constitutional order raise hope for improved rule of law and better governance in Sudan.

Whether the environmental safeguards in these three constitutions will directly result in the more effective management of natural resources, better environmental outcomes, or more equitable sharing of natural resource wealth and economic opportunity is difficult to know. However, the drafters of the constitutions incorporated these provisions to address specific problems based on historical experience. Such a direct reckoning with past injustices is itself noteworthy and shows that the constitutional drafters sought to address the legal inequalities that resulted in unjust economic outcomes and environmental degradation. Whether the constitutional drafters will see the realization of their vision will depend on implementation and political will, as in all three states, constitutional reform is a necessary, but not sufficient step towards a stronger constitutional order that allows all citizens to enjoy economic opportunity and a clean and healthy environment. While the constitutional drafters recognized this point, it remains to be seen if the political leaders will.

Bibliography

'Petition to Stop the Dams in Sudan: European Committee for Preserving the Middle Nile' (2012) 29 The African Archaeological Review 1

'South Sudan President Creates 28 New States' *Al Jazeera* (25 December 2015) <http://www.aljazeera.com/news/2015/12/south-sudan-president-creates-28-states-151225101750723.html> accessed 3 April 2021

'Sudan Military Rulers Want Islamic Law to Guide Legislation' *Al Jazeera* (8 May 2019) <http://www.aljazeera.com/news/2019/05/sudan-military-rulers-sharia-laws-guide-legislations-190508061915754.html> accessed 3 April 2021

'Sudan's New Constitution to Be Approved by Next Parliament: al-Bashir' *Sudan Tribune* (28 April 2018) <http://sudantribune.com/spip.php?article65283> accessed 3 April 2021

Abdelgabar NI, 'International Law and Constitution Making Process: The Right to Public Participation in the Constitution Making Process in Post Referendum Sudan' (2013) 46 Law and Politics in Africa, Asia and Latin America 131

Abdulbari N, 'Identities and Citizenship in Sudan: Governing Constitutional Principles' (2013) 13 African Human Rights Law Journal 383

Acemoglu D, 'Constitutions, Politics, and Economics: A Review Essay on Persson and Tabellini's *The Economic Effects of Constitutions*' (2005) 43 Journal of Economic Literature 1025

Ambani JO and Ochieng A, 'The Wretched African Traditionalists in Kenya: The Challenges and Prospect of Customary Law in the New Constitutional Era' (2015) 1 Strathmore Law Journal 41

Amin M and Ahmed K, 'Sudan Protest Leaders Reject Army's Call for Islamic Law in New Constitution' *Middle East Eye* (8 May 2019) <http://www.middleeasteye.net/news/sudan-protest-leaders-reject-army-demand-use-Islamic-law-new-constitution> accessed 3 April 2021

Amusan L, 'Germinating Seeds of Future Conflicts in South Sudan' (2014) 4 African Conflict and Peacebuilding Review 120

Askew K, Maganga F, and Odgaard R, 'Of Land and Legitimacy: A Tale of Two Lawsuits' (2013) 83 Africa 120

Ayoub M, 'Land and Conflict in Sudan' (2006) 18 Accord 14

Bachelard JY, 'The Anglo-Leasing Corruption Scandal in Kenya: The Politics of International and Domestic Pressures and Counter-Pressures' (2010) 37 Review of African Political Economy 187

Badiey N, 'The Strategic Instrumentalization of Land Tenure in "State Building": The Case of Juba, South Sudan' (2013) 83 Africa 57

Berridge WJ, *Civil Uprisings in Modern Sudan: The 'Khartoum Springs' of 1964 and 1985* (Bloomsbury Academic 2015)

Burgis T, *The Looting Machine: Warlords, Oligarchs, Smugglers, and the Theft of Africa's Wealth* (PublicAffairs 2015)

Carpenter S, Baldwin E, and Cole DH, 'The Polycentric Turn: A Case Study of Kenya's Evolving Legal Regime for Irrigation Waters' (2017) 57 Natural Resources Journal 101

Cheeseman N, *Democracy in Africa: Successes, Failures, and the Struggle for Political Reform* (Cambridge University Press 2015)

Clapham C, *The Horn of Africa: State Formation and Decay* (Oxford University Press 2017)

Clayton E, *Agrarian Development in Peasant Economies: Some Lessons from Kenya* (Pergamon Press 1964)

Collier P, *The Bottom Billion: Why the Poorest Countries are Failing and What Can Be Done about It* (Oxford University Press 2007)

Collins RO, *A History of Modern Sudan* (Cambridge University Press 2008)

Cottrell J and Ghai Y, 'Constitution Making and Democratization in Kenya (2000–2005)' (2007) 14 Democratization 1

Deng FM, 'Sudan: A Nation in Turbulent Search of Itself' (2006) 603 The Annals of the American Academy of Political and Social Science 155

De Waal A, *The Real Politics of the Horn of Africa: Money, War and the Business of Power* (Polity 2015)

Gordon CN, 'Recent Developments in the Land Law of the Sudan: A Legislative Analysis' (1986) 30 Journal of African Law 143

Gross TL, 'Improvement with Impunity: Development-Induced Displacement and the Guiding Principle 6(2)(C) Proportionality Test Applied to the Merowe Dam Project in Sudan' (2008) 24 American University International Law Review 377

Hessbruegge JA, 'Customary Law and Authority in a State under Construction: The Case of South Sudan' (2012) 5 African Journal of Legal Studies 295

Hursh J, 'Ouster of Sudan's Bashir Is Only the Beginning' *Just Security* (12 April 2019) <http://www.justsecurity.org/63601/ouster-of-sudans-bashir-is-only-the-beginning> accessed 3 April 2021

Johnson DH, *The Root Causes of Sudan's Civil Wars* (International African Institute 2007)

Jok JM, 'State, Law, and Insecurity in South Sudan' (2013) 37 Fletcher Forum of World Affairs 69

Kanyinga K, 'The Legacy of the White Highlands: Land Rights, Ethnicity, and the Post-2007 Election Violence in Kenya' in Kagwanja P and Southall R (eds), *Kenya's Uncertain Democracy: The Electoral Crisis of 2008* (Routledge 2010)

Kirby J, 'Sudan's Longtime Leader Was Ousted in a Military Coup: Protesters Still Want Democracy' *VOX* (11 April 2019) <http://www.vox.com/world/2019/4/11/18306002/sudan-news-bashir-coup-protests-khartoum-auf> accessed 3 April 2021

Komey GK, 'The Denied Land Rights of the Indigenous Peoples and their Endangered Livelihood and Survival: The Case of the Nuba of the Sudan' (2008) 31 Ethnic and Racial Studies 991

Koskenniemi M, *The Gentle Civilizer of Nations: The Rise and Fall of International Law 1870–1960* (Cambridge University Press 2001)

Kron J and Gettleman J, 'South Sudanese Vote Overwhelmingly for Secession' *New York Times* (21 January 2011) <http://www.nytimes.com/2011/01/22/world/africa/22sudan.html> accessed 3 April 2021

Large J and El Basha ELS, 'A Bitter Harvest and Grounds for Reform: The Nuba Mountains, Conflict Land and Transitional Sudan' (2010) (Berghof Peace Support, Working Paper)

Lynch G, 'The Fruits of Perception: "Ethnic Politics" and the Case of Kenya's Constitutional Referendum' (2006) 65 Africa Studies 233

Lynch G, 'Histories of Association and Difference: The Construction and Negotiation of Ethnicity' in Branch D, Cheeseman N, and Gardner L (eds), *Our Turn to Eat: Politics in Kenya Since 1950* (Lit Verlag 2010)

Magu SM, *The Socio-Cultural, Ethnic and Historic Foundations of Kenya's Electoral Violence* (Routledge 2018)

Maxon RM, *Kenya's Independence Constitution: Constitution-Making and End of Empire* (Farleigh Dickinson University Press 2011)

Middleton R, 'South Sudan: Labour Pains' (2011) 67(8/9) The World Today 26

Mohamed AA, 'The Problem of Uneven Regional Development in the Northern Sudan' (2006) 30 Fletcher Forum of World Affairs 41

Murunga GR, Okello D, and Sjogren A, *Kenya: The Struggle for a New Constitutional Order* (Zed Books 2014)

Natsios AS and Abramowitz M, 'Sudan's Secession Crisis: Can the South Part from the North without War?' (2011) 90(1) Foreign Affairs 19

Ojienda T and Okoth M, 'Chapter Five: Land the Environment' in Lumumna P, Mbondenyi MK, and Odero SO (eds), *The Constitution of Kenya: Contemporary Readings* (LawAfrica Publication 2011)

Okogbule NS, *Globalization and Human Rights in Africa* (Sibon Books Limited 2012)

Oyaya CO and Poku NK, *The Making of the Constitution of Kenya: A Century of Struggle and the Future of Constitutionalism* (Routledge 2018)

Persson T and Tabellini G, *The Economic Effects of Constitutions* (MIT Press 2005)

Radon J and Logan S, 'South Sudan: Governance Arrangements, War, and Peace' (2014) 68 Journal of International Affairs 149

Rahhal S and Abdel Salam AH, 'Land Rights, Natural Resources Tenure and Land Reform' (2006) (Committee of the Civil Project)

Ross ML, *The Oil Curse: How Petroleum Wealth Shapes the Development of Nations* (Princeton University Press 2012)

Rubongoya JB, 'Political Leadership' in Kaiser PJ and Wafula Okumu F (eds), *Democratic Transitions in East Africa* (Ashgate Publishing 2004)

Rutten M and Owuor S, 'Weapons of Mass Destruction: Land, Ethnicity and the 2007 Elections in Kenya' in Kagwanja P and Southall R (eds), *Kenya's Uncertain Democracy: The Electoral Crisis of 2008* (Routledge 2010)

Ryle J, *The Sudan Handbook* (James Currey 2011)

Salman SMA, 'Water Resources in the Sudan North-South Peace Process: Past Experience and Future Trends' (2008) 16 African Yearbook International Law 299

Sang BYK, 'Horizontal Application of Constitutional Rights in Kenya: A Comparative Critique of the Emerging Jurisprudence' (2018) 26 African Journal of International and Comparative Law 1

Schmidt SL, 'Emerging Rule of Law Priorities for Post-Conflict South Sudan' (2016) 11 Yale Journal of International Affairs 37

Schomerus M and Aalen L (eds), *Considering the State: Perspectives on South Sudan's Subdivision and Federalism Debate* (Overseas Development Institute 2016)

Silva M, 'After Partition: The Perils of South Sudan' (2015) 3 University of Baltimore Journal of International Law 63

Suliman M, 'The Nuba Mountains of Sudan: Resource Access, Violent Conflict, and Identity' in Buckles D (ed), *Cultivating Peace: Conflict and Collaboration in Natural Resource Management* (International Development Research Centre/World Bank Institute 1999)

United States Agency for International Development, 'USAID Country Profile, Property Rights and Resource Governance: Sudan' *United States Agency for International Development* (13 May 2013) <http://www.land-links.org/wp-content/uploads/2016/09/USAID_Land_Tenure_Sudan_Profile.pdf> accessed 3 April 2021

Unruh J and Abdul-Jalil MA, 'Land Rights in Darfur: Institutional Flexibility, Policy and Adaptation to Environmental Change' (2012) 36 Natural Resources Forum 274

US Department of the State, 'Troika Statement: Formation of South Sudan's Revitalized Transitional Government of National Unity' (23 February 2020) <https://2017-2021.state.gov/troika-statem ent-formation-of-south-sudans-revitalized-transitional-government-of-national-unity/index.html> accessed 3 April 2021

Verhoeven H, *Water, Civilisation and Power in Sudan: The Political Economy of Military-Islamist State Building* (Cambridge University Press 2015)

Wily LA, ' "The Law is to Blame": The Vulnerable Status of Common Property Rights in Sub-Saharan Africa' (2011) 42 Development and Change 733

7

The Political Economy of Post-colonial Constitutionalism in Southern Africa

Heinz Klug

1. Introduction

Post-colonial constitutions across southern Africa contain a range of provisions that either address economic rights and regulation directly or impact indirectly on the economic potential of their societies. The varying histories of southern African polities, including differences in the colonial origins of their legal orders, have affected the form and development of constitutionalism in each of them, yet viewed from the perspective of the political economy of constitutions, it is possible to identify salient constitutional features that can be compared across the region. This chapter explores the political economy of these constitutions by seeking to understand the articulation of salient features that together establish the conditions for achieving the goals of democracy and economic development set out in the constitutions. In contrast to undertaking a simple economic analysis, a political-economy approach asks the question: what is required to fulfil the promise of post-colonial constitutionalism in southern Africa?

The political economy of southern African rests on a variety of economic pillars, including extractive industries, tourism, and manufacturing, yet control over land remains a core and contested feature of the post-colony throughout the region. Tenure relations have been a central issue of conflict since the earliest days of colonization. While there have been significant shifts in tenure systems since the end of colonization, these have been contested and remain politically salient features of law and governance today.

Accordingly, while conducting a general comparative analysis of the relationship between the economic constitution and governance in southern Africa, this chapter places specific emphasis on the significance of property rights and tenure relations to constitutionalism in the region. The complex history of tenure relations in each of these countries cannot be addressed adequately in a single chapter; thus the task here, is to highlight some of the most significant features of each country's history in order to compare the relationship between land tenure and constitutionalism at a relatively high level of abstraction. Although this approach entails eliding some key details, it is hoped that it enables important trends to be identified and raises questions for further research.

Given the different economic conditions in four of these post-colonial societies—Botswana, Mozambique, South Africa, and Zimbabwe—a comparative analysis of their post-colonial constitutional development may shed light on the potential impact of various constitutional provisions that address economic governance in these countries. Although there is substantial literature to suggest that constitutional choices and provisions have real

Heinz Klug, *The Political Economy of Post-colonial Constitutionalism in Southern Africa* In: *Constitutionalism and the Economy in Africa*. Edited by: Charles M Fombad and Nico Steytler, Oxford University Press. © Heinz Klug 2022. DOI: 10.1093/oso/9780192886439.003.0009

impacts on economic development, the existence of often conflicting provisions within constitutions, as well as the convergence among constitutions, raises caveats for claims that any specific constitutional provision or structure will produce positive or negative economic outcomes. Nevertheless, the relationship of constitutionalism to economic development remains an important question. The chapter argues that, to understand this relationship, it is necessary to identify the political economy of a constitution—a task which is to be distinguished from an economic analysis of the constitution. As William Forbach maintains, while '[e]conomics sidelines the distribution of wealth and power[,] political economy puts it at the center. Economics claims to be value-free; political economy asks: "What is the good economy?"'[1]

Methodologically, this chapter takes a New Legal Realist approach by first drawing on social science literature to identify the relevant constitutional elements to consider in comparing these four orders across southern Africa. While the analysis identifies the institution of property rights in land as the most significant constitutional element shaping the political economy for purposes of comparison, it remains essential that the comparison include those aspects of the constitutions that underpin the guarantee of democracy as a means of sustaining the popular will these constitutions claim to represent. As compared to a purely economic approach, political economy 'blends the normative with the analytical and the economic with the political'[2] in order to define what the constitution requires. Finally, the chapter evaluates the different theoretical approaches to constitutional political economy as applied to the four countries under study.

2. Theories of Economic Constitutionalism

The Norwegian social and political theorist Jon Elster argues that 'constitutions matter for economic performance to the extent that they promote the values of stability, accountability, and credibility'.[3] This broad statement on the economic impact of constitutions does not clarify the relationship, if any, between specific characteristics or clauses of any constitution and economic outcomes. Furthermore, unlike political economy, it does not put the distribution of wealth and power at the centre of the analysis. Instead, it assumes that the constitution merely establishes the rules of the game and that these rules impact on economic performance to the degree that they incorporate specific values. This understanding of the relationship between constitutional provisions and economic development underpins much of the economic literature, albeit that the literature varies dramatically according to the strains of economic thought that underlie the different approaches to economic constitutionalism or constitutional political economy.

An early contribution in economics came from the 'ordoliberal or "Freiburg" school of thought' in early twentieth-century Germany which, responding to the historical conditions of Weimar and national socialism, 'believed the economy needed to be embedded in a constitutional legal framework that would both protect it [the economy] and help integrate

---

[1]   William Forbach, 'A Political Economy the Constitution Requires' *LPE Project* <https://lpeblog.org/2019/10/23/title-tk/> accessed 12 August 2020.

[2]   ibid.

[3]   Jon Elster, 'The Impact of Constitutions on Economic Performance' (1995) Proceedings of the World Bank Annual Conference on Development Economics 1994, 209–26, 210.

society around it'.[4] The basic idea of this approach was that the 'community chooses its economic constitution, and from that point, governmental decisions must be justified by reference to it'.[5]

In contrast to this view, Justice Holmes of the United States Supreme Court stated in his 1905 dissent in *Lochner* that 'a constitution is not intended to embody a particular economic theory, whether of paternalism and the organic relation of the citizen to the State or of *laissez faire*'.[6] While Holmes was arguing against the Supreme Court's use of its theory of substantive due process to strike down legislation that constrained the economic decisions of proprietors, a claim of economic neutrality also precludes a more robust discussion of the political economy of a constitution, one which asks what form of economic order best protects the democratic and social interests of citizens and the society more generally.

A long-standing branch of economic literature that addresses the consequences of constitutions for economic change is the institutionalist school, which originated with the work of Thorsten Veblen, Wesley Mitchell, and, most importantly, John R Commons.[7] Working in this tradition, Douglass North, a prominent new institutionalist, notes at the beginning of his classic work *Structure and Change in Economic History* that the 'basic services that the state provides are the underlying rules of the game'.[8] Criticizing '[neo-classical] economists who talk about their discipline as a theory of choice and the menu of choices being determined by opportunities and preferences',[9] North argues that they have 'simply left out that it is the institutional framework which constrains people's choice sets'.[10] Institutions, in his view, are 'a set of rules, compliance procedures and moral and ethical behavioural norms',[11] and he concludes that '[c]onstitutional rules are the fundamental underlying rules designed to specify the basic structure of property rights and control of the state'.[12]

Significantly, when it comes to economic development, North emphasizes the institution of property rights, arguing that it was 'better-specified property rights over inventions' that raised the rate of the return on innovation that fostered the first industrial revolution.[13] Likewise stressing the importance of an institutional approach to understanding economic development in developing and transitional economies, Biman Prasad argues that 'the theory of property rights and the institutions that support the maintenance of particular types of property rights invariably imply that it is an important factor in explaining the difference in economic growth'.[14]

Another perspective that supports an emphasis on the specification and institutional role of property rights is found in recent work by Katerina Pistor. She argues that it is the continuing reconfiguration or 'coding of capital' through a toolkit of traditional legal

---

[4] David J Gerber, 'Economic Constitutionalism and the Challenge of Globalization: The Enemy is Gone? Long Live the Enemy' (2001) 157 Journal of International and Theoretical Economics 14, 15.

[5] ibid 17.

[6] *Lochner v New York* 198 US 45 (1905) 75.

[7] John R Commons, *The Legal Foundations of Capitalism* (MacMillan 1924).

[8] Douglas C North, *Structure and Change in Economic History* (Norton 1981) 24.

[9] ibid 201.

[10] ibid.

[11] ibid.

[12] ibid 203.

[13] ibid 159.

[14] Biman C Prasad, 'Institutional Economics and Economic Development: The Theory of Property Rights, Economic Development, Good Governance and the Environment' (2003) 30(6) International Journal of Social Economics 741, 749.

modules—including 'the rules of property and collateral law; the principles of trust, corporate and bankruptcy law; and contract law'—that 'are ready to be moulded and grafted onto an ever-changing roster of assets' which explains both the creation of wealth and inequality.[15] Although Pistor does not focus on constitutions, it is clear that, for the process of legal creativity and capture of assets she describes to occur, what has to exist is a degree of legal certainty engendered by a stable legal system and the recognition of property rights, among other legal rules. Furthermore, the ability of lawyers to refashion the modules of law that Pistor identifies as key to the 'coding of capital' requires a guarantee of the rule of law to ensure that the refashioned modules which incorporate each new asset class as capital remain secure. From this perspective, economic development depends on the stability provided by a constitutional order's recognition of property rights as well as by a functioning set of institutions that uphold the rule of law.

The one branch of economics that does lay claim to the idea that constitutional provisions can determine the direction of economic development is the work on constitutional political economy that emerged from public choice theory. This approach, 'best ... described as the economics of rules',[16] was 'initiated by the work of James M Buchanan', although as Vanberg notes, it also draws on other sources including Hayek and the Freiburg school.[17] Proceeding from the idea that 'economists should look to the structure within which political decisions are made',[18] Buchanan and Tullock argued in their 1962 work *The Calculus of Consent: Logical Foundations of Constitutional Democracy* that '[the] individual will find it advantageous to agree in advance to certain rules (which he knows may work occasionally to his own disadvantage) when the benefits are expected to exceed the costs'.[19] Emphasizing individual self-interest and the notion of rent-seeking, Buchanan argued that

> [a]lthough we do not believe that narrow self-interest is the sole motive of political agents ... [t]his differentiates our approach from the alternative model, implicit in conventional welfare economics and ... political science, that political agents can be satisfactorily modeled as motivated solely to promote the 'public interest,' somehow conceived.[20]

While Neil Komesar argues that the 'mistaken focus on motive is unfortunate'[21] and proceeds to supplement the 'so-called interest group theory of politics'[22] with a twofold model that recognizes both minoritarian and majoritarian bias in the political process, his comparative institutional analysis highlights the structural elements in a constitution that create 'the complex but essential trade-off between majoritarian and minoritarian bias',[23] rather than the individual economic clauses within a constitution.

---

[15] Katharina Pistor, *The Code of Capital: How the Law Creates Wealth and Inequality* (Princeton 2019) 160.

[16] Viktor J Vanberg, 'Market and State: The Perspective of Constitutional Political Economy' (2004) Freiburg Discussion Papers on Constitutional Economics 04/10, 2.

[17] ibid.

[18] James M Buchanan, 'The Constitution of Economic Policy' (1987) 77(3) The American Economic Review 243, 243.

[19] James Buchanan and Gordon Tullock, *The Calculus of Consent: Logical Foundations of Constitutional Democracy* (1962) Collected Works of James M Buchanan Vol 3 (Liberty Fund 1999) 7.

[20] Geoffrey Brennan and James M Buchanan, 'Is Public Choice Immoral? The Case for the "Nobel" Lie' (1988) 74 Virginia Law Review 179, 181.

[21] Neil K Komesar, *Imperfect Alternatives: Choosing Institutions in Law, Economics and Public Policy* (Chicago 1994) 60.

[22] ibid 53.

[23] ibid 230.

Despite these and other criticisms[24] of the notion that 'political constitutions "emerge" from a process of discussion where individual deliberation and individual choice are assumed to play a key role in the development of the constitutional framework',[25] Buchanan's idea has remained a core component of the neoliberal approach to economic constitutionalism. As Nancy MacLean observes in *Democracy in Chains*, Buchanan and Tullock's premise in *The Calculus of Consent* was that majority-based voting tends to create 'powerful coalitions of voters, politicians, and bureaucrats' who would overinvest in the public sector and 'foist most of the costs onto a minority whom they ... [would subject] to "discriminatory taxation" or create deficits that would be imposed on future generations'.[26] According to MacLean, the authors felt that this not only 'wronged minority interests ... but also held down private capital accumulation and investment and therefore overall economic growth'.[27]

In this sense, then, simple majority rule was not only bad for economic development but also normatively questionable, since it 'tended to violate the liberty of the minority, because it yoked some citizens unwillingly to others' goals'.[28] From such a perspective, the 'only truly fair decision-making model ... was unanimity', one giving 'each individual the capacity to veto the schemes of others so that the many could not impose on the few'.[29]

For Buchanan, the opportunity to see his ideas applied to the creation of a new constitutional order came in the context of General Pinochet's efforts to create a constitution that would provide a legal structure for the social and economic changes imposed by the post-1973 military junta in Chile. Invited on a week-long lecture tour in May 1980, Buchanan delivered 'five formal lectures to top representatives of a governing elite that melded the military and the corporate world',[30] arguing for constitutional provisions on 'matters ranging from "the power of a constitution over fiscal policy" to "what the optimum number of lawmakers in a legislative body should be" '.[31] Describing public choice theory as a science, he argued that economic constitutionalism as applied by 'members of his school of thought ... [was] "formulating constitutional ways in which we can limit government intervention in the economy and make sure it keeps its hand out of the pockets of productive contributors" '.[32]

Such was Buchanan's commitment to economic liberty that when it was applied in practice, 'he simply did not care about the invitation to abuse inherent in giving nearly unchecked power to an alliance of capital and the armed forces'.[33] As a result, with Chile's 1980 Constitution '[bearing] the same name as Hayek's classic *The Constitution of Liberty*',[34] its idea of freedom was best described by Rolf Luders, a Chilean who, in a presentation to the

---

[24] See Andre Azevedo Alves, 'No Salvation through Constitutions: Jasay versus Buchanan and Rawls' (2015) 20(1) The Independent Review 33. For a libertarian perspective, see Walter Block and Thomas J DiLorenzo, 'Constitutional Economics and *The Calculus of Consent*' (2001) 15(3) Journal of Libertarian Studies 37.

[25] Alves (n 24) 34.

[26] Nancy MacLean, *Democracy in Chains: The Deep History of the Radical Right's Stealth Plan for America* (Viking 2017) 79.

[27] ibid.

[28] ibid.

[29] ibid.

[30] ibid 157.

[31] ibid 158.

[32] ibid.

[33] ibid 163.

[34] ibid 159.

1980 meeting of the Mont Pelerin Society, said approvingly that the new constitution had restored 'individual freedom to consume, produce, save and invest'.[35]

Chile's 1980 Constitution and economic growth are still represented as an example of neoliberal success, yet a close look at both its structure and the country's subsequent history of growing economic inequality should give pause for thought. As Steve Stern, the eminent historian of the Pinochet era, notes, the 'Constitution of Liberty'

> enshrined the concept of a restrictive or 'protected' democracy through strong presidentialism; a National Security Council with powers to appoint military officers to policy and advisory positions; division of the Senate into designated and elected seats, with former military commanders among the designated senators; military representatives on powerful regional councils; and prohibition of political parties, social movements, and rights of association that promoted doctrines of violence, totalitarianism, or class conflict.[36]

Although Pinochet fell from power after losing a referendum in 1988 and was disgraced when it was discovered that he had stashed at least USD 15 million in foreign bank accounts under false names during his rule, the effects of the Constitution in limiting democratic decision-making, especially on economic issues, continued to be felt. The most blatantly anti-democratic features of the Constitution were removed by a series of amendments between 1989 and 2005, but a significant gap remains between the traditional political parties and citizens, who feel they have no influence in policy decisions since 'the document baked in the fundamental rules of Pinochet's economic model' and led to increasing inequality and economic insecurity.[37] What is more,

> [the] constitution itself makes any significant attempt at reform impossible, with super-majority requirements over a bicameral system ... [meaning] any attempt to change the system—in terms of the distribution of political power, the economic model, or the role of the state—requires the support of right-wing parties that supported the military regime.[38]

Echoing the complaint in 2014 of Chile's former Socialist Party president, Michelle Bachelet, that '[w]e want a constitution without locks and bolts',[39] millions of Chileans demonstrated in October 2019 'to transform an institutional model that has increased inequality for decades and excluded the population in decision-making'.[40]

Despite the Chilean experience, public choice theory continues to claim that its tools of analysis can explain the effects of different constitutional forms. The empirical work of Persson and Tabellini provides an excellent example of how this branch of economic constitutionalism understands the impact of different constitutional provisions. Their book, *The Economic Effects of Constitutions*, investigates the policy and economic implications of

---

[35] ibid 161.
[36] Steve J Stern, *Battling for Hearts and Minds: Memory Struggles in Pinochet's Chile, 1973–1988* (Duke 2006) 171.
[37] MacLean (n 26) 165.
[38] Rodrigo Espinoza Troncoso and Michael Wilson Becerril, 'Chile Will Never Make Progress under Pinochet's Constitution' *Washington Post* (29 October 2019).
[39] MacLean (n 26) 168.
[40] Troncoso and Becerril (n 38).

alternative forms of government and electoral rules. Stating that their goal 'is to draw conclusions about the causal effects of constitutions on specific policy outcomes',[41] Persson and Tabellini use sophisticated econometric analyses to show that presidential and majoritarian or first-past-the-post electoral systems have smaller governments than parliamentary and proportional representation systems. They also find that countries with parliamentary systems have more persistent fiscal outcomes than countries with a presidential system. While these general correlations are important and fascinating, they are at a level of comparative generality that does not necessarily provide the kind of guidance, or even arguments, that might be used in any process of constitutional reform.[42]

In sum, while these economic theories and their application confirm Elster's claim that 'constitutions matter', they provide only a very general conception of what constitutional forms or clauses might be of greatest significance. If a functioning constitutional order guarantees 'stability, accountability and credibility', the project of this volume seems to be to identify what specific aspects of it or clauses within it are most salient. This task is particularly difficult from a socio-legal or New Legal Realist perspective in which any constitution contains a variety of clauses and institutions that, under different circumstances, can be in tension with one another.

However, a comparison of constitutions in southern Africa provides one means of exploring the effects that different constitutional forms and formulations may or may not have on economic development in the region. To this end, the chapter proceeds to explore whether the correlations suggested by Persson and Tabellini's analysis have any explanatory power in this context. Finally, it examines land reform with a view to comparing the allocation of land in the various constitutions and considering its implications for the political economy.

3. Economic Dimensions of Southern African Constitutions

Comparing the economic dimensions of southern African constitutions raises several questions. First, what specific elements are most pivotal in shaping the political economy of each of these constitutional orders? Secondly, if we agree to focus on aspects of the constitution that seem to address the political economy most directly—property rights, democratic participation (electoral systems), fiscal policy, corruption, and the rule of law (judicial autonomy)—what factors shape them? It has to be recognized that these elements are shaped both by the histories of each country and the global context and, moreover, that this amalgam of factors will vary according to the era in which the constitution was produced and in which subsequent amendments or reforms occurred.[43] A third issue is that, in evaluating the impact any of the elements may have had on economic outcomes, it is important to note that the different rights and institutions contained in any single constitution may pull in different directions. With these questions in mind, it is useful to begin by describing the

---

[41] Torsten Persson and Guido Tabellini, *The Economic Effects of Constitutions: What Do the Data Say?* (MIT 2003) 7.

[42] Torsten Persson, 'Presidential Address: Consequences of Constitutions' (2004) 2(2–3) Journal of the European Economic Association 139.

[43] Heinz Klug, *Constituting Democracy: Law, Globalism and South Africa's Political Reconstruction* (Cambridge University Press 2000) 2–5.

similarities and differences between the economic elements in the four constitutional orders that are the subject of this comparison.

The simplest formal distinction among them relates to how each most explicitly addresses economic rights and duties. All four of them address property rights, but that apart, it is the Mozambican Constitution that gives economic rights and duties the most extensive coverage, with a separate section containing economic, social, financial and fiscal provisions. Title IV of the Constitution has thirty-seven articles addressing the country's economic, social, financial, and fiscal organization. The article on economic policy declares that

> [s]tate economic policy shall be directed towards laying the fundamental bases for development, improving the living conditions of the people, strengthening the sovereignty of the State, and consolidating national unity, through the participation of citizens and the efficient use of human and material resources.[44]

This is followed by a host of more specific clauses constitutionalizing a detailed conception of economic development ranging from the distribution of national wealth to the ownership of the means of production, as well as dealing with taxes, the coordination of economic activity, foreign investment, and the drafting and executing of a five-year economic and social plan.[45]

In contrast to Mozambique, the Constitution of Botswana has no explicit economic provisions aside from the protection of property. The constitutions of South Africa and Zimbabwe fit between these two extremes, including both property and specific social and economic rights. Neither of them has provisions defining the process of setting, forming, or directing economic policy; nevertheless, both of them include further specificity on the question of land and, in the case of Zimbabwe, agricultural land in particular.

The exploration and comparison of the political economy of these four constitutional orders require us to identify elements of their constitutions that are likely to impact their respective economic environments. Here, the political-economy approach recognizes the significance of both constitutional rights and institutions in affecting the allocation of resources. It is hence important to identify all those constitutional elements that determine economic decision-making and sustain the democratic order within which that decision-making occurs. The elements identified for comparison are those relating to economic rights, democratic participation, fiscal policy, corruption, and the rule of law or judicial authority. The specific constitutional clauses which are relevant concern, inter alia: rights to property; electoral systems; the status of central banks; anti-corruption or integrity institutions; and the status and role of the judiciary, including the nature of constitutional review established in the constitution.

While some of these clauses are long-standing elements of modern constitutionalism, such as constitutional rights and judicial or constitutional review, the recent inclusion of fiscal institutions such as central banks and the constitutionalization of anti-corruption and other independent institutions reflects a post-Cold War or neoliberal form of constitutionalism.

---

[44] Constitution of Mozambique, art 96.
[45] ibid arts 96–132.

3.1 The Right to Property

The right not to be deprived of property without compensation is explicitly protected in all four constitutions, with notable variations in the case of land rights. The Constitution of Botswana provides the most explicit and all-encompassing protection of property, doing so in a manner that reflects its origins as one of the independence constitutions drafted by Britain's Colonial Office and negotiated in the 1960s at Lancaster House as decolonization swept across Africa.

Not only is the right to protection from 'deprivation of property without compensation'[46] recognized among the 'fundamental rights and freedoms of the individual',[47] but section 8 provides that '[n]o property of any description shall be compulsorily taken possession of, and no interest in or right over property of any description may be compulsorily acquired', except where the extensive conditions in subsections 8(1)–(6) are satisfied. Significantly, some of these conditions, such as the stipulation that '[n]o person ... entitled to compensation under this section shall be prevented from remitting, within a reasonable time ... the whole of [the compensation received] ... to any country of his or her choice outside of Botswana', are similar to those imposed on Zimbabwe in the Lancaster House Constitution of 1980.

While the Botswana Constitution does not guarantee a positive right to ownership, the Mozambican Constitution of 2004 includes both the positive and negative dimensions of the right, stipulating that '[t]he State shall recognise and guarantee the right of ownership of property'[48] and providing that '[e]xpropriation may take place only for reasons of public necessity, utility, or interest, as defined in the terms of the law, and subject to payment of fair compensation'.[49] Despite the generality of the language in which it protects property, the Constitution explicitly distinguishes land from property: article 109 provides that '[a]ll ownership of land shall vest in the State' and that '[l]and may not be sold or otherwise disposed of, nor may it be mortgaged or subject to attachment'.[50]

Unlike the statute-like detail of Botswana's property clauses or the positive guarantee of property rights in the Mozambican Constitution, the South African Constitution does not have a positive right to property or guarantee the right of ownership, but rather states in section 25(1) that '[n]o one may be deprived of property except in terms of law of general application, and no law may permit arbitrary deprivation of property'.[51] As in the Mozambican Constitution, there are provisions relating specifically to land; however, in the case of South Africa, land is not nationalized—instead, in recognition of a history of land dispossession and forced removals, the Constitution contains specific provisions including a right to restitution,[52] a duty on the state to 'enable citizens to gain access to land on an equitable basis',[53] and an exception to the entire clause which ensures the state is unimpeded in taking 'legislative and other measures ... to achieve land, water and related reform, in order to redress the results of past racial discrimination'.[54] The Constitution also requires

---

[46] Constitution of Botswana, s 3(c).
[47] ibid s 3.
[48] Constitution of Mozambique, art 82(1).
[49] ibid art 82(2).
[50] ibid art 109(1) and (2).
[51] Constitution of South Africa, s 25(1).
[52] ibid art 25(7).
[53] ibid art 25(5).
[54] ibid art 25(8).

the legislature to enact legislation to address circumstances in which individuals or communities lack secure tenure as a result of past racially discriminatory laws.[55]

In the case of Zimbabwe, land is again distinguished from other forms of property but, in this respect more akin to Mozambique than South Africa, the general clause granting property rights both guarantees a positive right to property and explicitly exempts agricultural land from the extensive protections guaranteed.[56] These protections include the right of every person 'in any part of Zimbabwe, to acquire, hold, occupy, use, transfer, hypothecate, lease or dispose of all forms of property, either individually or in association with others'.[57] However, the exclusion provides that

> [w]here agricultural land, or any right or interest in such land, is required for a public purpose, including—(a) settlement for agricultural or other purposes; (b) land reorganisation, forestry, environmental conservation or the utilisation of wild life or other natural resources; or (c) the relocation of persons dispossessed as a result of the utilisation of land for a purpose referred to in paragraph (a) or (b); the land, right or interest may be compulsorily acquired by the State by notice published in the Gazette identifying the land, right or interest, whereupon the land, right or interest vests in the State with full title with effect from the date of publication of the notice.[58]

Compulsory acquisition of agricultural land under these conditions does not include a right to compensation, 'except for improvements effected on it before its acquisition'.[59] Furthermore, section 72(7) provides that

> [in the case of] compulsory acquisition of agricultural land for the resettlement of people in accordance with a program of land reform ... the former colonial power has an obligation to pay compensation [and if it] ... fails to pay compensation ... the Government of Zimbabwe has no obligation to pay compensation for agricultural land compulsorily acquired for resettlement.[60]

3.2 Electoral Systems

Significantly, given the theoretical importance which the literature on constitutional political economy gives to the distinction between first-past-the-post majoritarian electoral systems and proportional representation,[61] the four constitutional orders under comparison here are, on the whole, divided evenly between these systems.

First, Mozambique and South Africa are primarily proportional systems at the national level, while Botswana and Zimbabwe are primarily constituency-based electoral systems. Secondly, the upper houses in each of these bicameral legislatures have different forms of

---

[55] ibid art 25(6) read with art 25(9).
[56] Constitution of Zimbabwe, s 72.
[57] ibid s 71(2).
[58] ibid s 72(2).
[59] ibid s 72(3)(a).
[60] ibid s 72(7)(i) and (ii).
[61] See Persson and Tabellini (n 41).

representation—chiefs in Botswana, provinces in South Africa, and, in Zimbabwe, a combination of provinces, chiefs, and two representatives of persons with disabilities.

Finally, when it comes to the election of the executive authority, the electoral processes range from a direct 50-plus-one per cent majoritarian system in Mozambique to purely indirect election by the National Assembly in South Africa. In Botswana and Zimbabwe, the executives are directly elected as part of the general parliamentary elections.

In the case of Botswana, the nomination of the president is explicitly tied to the election of Members of Parliament. Before a general election, nominations for president may be made with the support of at least 1,000 eligible voters. Candidates for Parliament in the election may then declare their support of a nominee as part of their election and, if a majority of elected Members of Parliament have declared support for a particular presidential candidate, that candidate is automatically declared president. Alternatively, in the case of a vacancy during a parliamentary term, Parliament must elect a president.

In Zimbabwe, the election of the President and two vice-presidents will, once that section of the Constitution is implemented in 2023, be by direct ballot, which must take place simultaneously with a general election in which voters select members of the legislature on a first-past-the-post constituency-based system. However, recently the ruling Zimbabwe African National Union—Patriotic Front (ZANU-PF) proposed a constitutional amendment to preclude the direct election of vice-presidents, though this amendment is yet to be adopted.

3.3 The Status of Central Banks

While the inclusion of fiscal policy institutions in national constitutions was not unknown before the post-Cold War era, with the rise of neoliberalism the explicit inclusion of central banks as independent constitutional institutions has become ubiquitous. In southern Africa, the revision or emergence of new constitutions post-1990 reflected this global trend, with only Botswana, of the cases being compared, not following suit. Even so, despite their inclusion of central banks, the constitutions of Zimbabwe, South Africa, and Mozambique vary in the degree of independence which they grant them.

Zimbabwe's Constitution of 2013 declares that the Reserve Bank of Zimbabwe is the country's central bank and that its object is to regulate the monetary system to 'protect the currency of Zimbabwe in the interest of balanced and sustainable economic growth' but grants it no guarantee of independence from government. In contrast, the South African Constitution both provides for a central bank,[62] the 'primary object' of which 'is to protect the value of the currency in the interest of balanced and sustainable economic growth in the Republic',[63] and states that '[t]he South African Reserve Bank, in pursuit of its primary object, must perform its functions independently and without fear, favour or prejudice'.[64] However, it also requires that 'there must be regular consultation between the Bank and the Cabinet member responsible for national financial matters'.[65]

---

[62] Constitution of South Africa, s 223.
[63] ibid s 224(1).
[64] ibid s 224(2).
[65] ibid.

Significantly, while the Mozambican Constitution is in one respect more like the Zimbabwean model than the South African inasmuch it sets up a central bank but does not explicitly guarantee its independence, it does include a provision that ties the Bank of Mozambique's constitutional authority to international norms, stating that '[t]he operation of the Bank of Mozambique shall be governed by specific legislation and by international norms that bind the Republic of Mozambique and apply to it.'[66]

3.4 Independent Integrity Institutions

The constitutionalization of independent integrity institutions is another feature of post-Cold War constitutionalism with implications for the political economy. While some constitutions have long included independent institutions such as electoral commissions and ombuds, they have been an increasingly important feature of the many new and revised constitutions of the post-Cold War era. These integrity institutions often address competing aspects of post-Cold War constitutionalism—on the one hand, the guarantee of democracy and, on the other, neoliberal constraints on fiscal policy. Anti-corruption and human rights institutions—ranging from auditors-general and ombudspersons to public protectors and human rights commissions—serve to advance democratic ends as well as build confidence among external audiences such as foreign investors. As such, they reflect both the democratic and neoliberal visions of the post-Cold War constitutional era.

In southern Africa, it is not surprising to see these institutions in three of the case studies. The South African Constitution contains the most extensive set of them, most of which are gathered together in chapter 9 under the rubric of 'State Institutions Supporting Constitutional Democracy'. Of the six institutions created to 'strengthen constitutional democracy in the Republic', at least three—the Public Protector, Auditor-General, and Electoral Commission—may be considered 'integrity institutions', while the Human Rights Commission has the dual function of monitoring the observance of human rights and promoting '[the protection of and] respect for human rights and a culture of human rights'.[67]

A marked feature of these institutions is that their constitutional status includes extensive guarantees of their independence as well as interrelatedness with fellow state institutions. Among other things, first, '[t]hese institutions are independent, and subject only to the Constitution and the law, and they must be impartial and must exercise their powers and perform their functions without fear, favour or prejudice';[68] secondly, '[o]ther organs of state, through legislative and other measures, must assist and protect these institutions to ensure the independence, impartiality, dignity and effectiveness of these institutions';[69] and, thirdly, '[n]o person or organ of state may interfere with the functioning of these institutions'.[70]

The Mozambican Constitution, by comparison, designates only two integrity institutions with explicit guarantees of independence, the Ombudsman and the Superior Council for the Media. Set out in the Constitution's chapter on Rights, Duties and Freedoms, the

---

[66] Constitution of Mozambique, art 132(2).
[67] Constitution of South Africa, s 184(1)(a).
[68] ibid s 181(2).
[69] ibid s 181(3).
[70] ibid s 181(4).

Superior Council for the Media is an independent body that 'shall guarantee the right to information, to freedom of the press and the independence of the media, as well as the exercise of broadcasting rights and the right of reply'.[71] As for the Ombudsman, it 'is an office established to guarantee the rights of citizens and to uphold legality and justice in the actions of the Public Administration',[72] and 'shall be independent and impartial in the exercise of his functions and he shall owe obedience only to the Constitution and the laws'.[73]

Nevertheless, this office does not have the power to make decisions in the cases it investigates. As is common among other ombuds the world over, its powers are instead limited to submitting 'recommendations to the appropriate offices to correct or prevent illegalities or injustices'[74] and reporting any 'serious mistakes, irregularities or violations ... [committed by the Public Administration to] the Assembly of the Republic, the Attorney General of the Republic and the central or local authority, with recommendations for pertinent measures'.[75]

In the case of Zimbabwe, the Electoral Commission and Media Commission are appointed by the President, who, in addition to selecting the chair of the commissions in consultation with the Judicial Service Commission and the Committee on Standing Rules and Orders, must choose the remaining eight members of these commissions from a list of at least twelve candidates submitted by the Judicial Service Commission.[76] Despite their constitutional enshrinement, provisions explicitly guaranteeing the independence of the commissions, including the protection of their members against removal—which is the same as for judges[77]—have been undermined by the appointment process. Furthermore, these protections did not prevent Mugabe's government from forcing out judges it deemed unsupportive; as for the Electoral Commission, the members of which may serve only two six-year terms, the guarantee of independence has been meaningless.

Botswana's Constitution contains far fewer integrity institutions by comparison. Aside from an independent electoral commission,[78] which was introduced by a constitutional amendment in 1999, the only other integrity institution is the Auditor-General, who 'shall not be subject to the direction or control of any other person or authority'.[79] The country's Constitution instead relies primarily on the separation of powers rooted in the traditional governmental structure of the *tres politica*—legislature, executive, and judiciary.

3.5 Judicial Authority and Constitutional Review

Another worldwide feature of post-Cold War constitutionalism is the expansion of judicial authority in the form of constitutional review,[80] albeit that it differs in nature and

---

[71] Constitution of Mozambique, art 50(1).
[72] ibid art 256.
[73] ibid art 258(1).
[74] ibid art 259(1).
[75] ibid art 259(2).
[76] Constitution of Zimbabwe (2013), s 238.
[77] ibid ss 235–37.
[78] Constitution of Botswana, s 65A.
[79] ibid s 124(5).
[80] See C Neal Tate and Torbjorn Vallinder (eds), *The Global Expansion of Judicial Power* (New York University Press 1995).

consequence from one country to the next.[81] In the southern African case studies, there are two distinct forms of constitutional review, each with implications for judicial authority as well as the constitutional order at large.

The first form, represented by Botswana, is the traditional post-colonial model of judicial review in which courts have the authority to interpret the constitution and protect individuals from violations of their rights under it.[82] In the second, constitutional review is given explicit recognition, with the constitution designated as the supreme law and a specialized constitutional court established with the ultimate authority to uphold it. Although the three other countries follow this model, the structure of their courts and the specific forms of access to constitutional review lead to significantly different outcomes in each case.

In South Africa, all high courts may exercise constitutional review in all cases before them; however, the Constitutional Court, which retains original jurisdiction over constitutional matters, must confirm any order of unconstitutionality in regard to parliamentary and provincial statutes or presidential conduct.[83] Zimbabwe's Constitution follows a similar pattern of diffuse constitutional review,[84] but in Mozambique the Constitution limits it to a constitutional council with the sole authority to 'evaluate and pronounce upon the unconstitutionality of laws and the illegality of other normative acts of State offices'.[85] For the Constitutional Council to 'pronounce on the unconstitutionality of laws, or on the illegality of normative acts of State offices',[86] one of a number of designated actors, including the President, Prime Minister, Attorney-General, Ombudsman, President of the Assembly (that is, the legislature) or 2,000 citizens, must make a request to it.[87]

In Botswana, the High Court and Court of Appeal have jurisdiction both to interpret the Constitution[88] and provide redress 'if any person alleges that any of the provisions of [the chapter on fundamental rights and freedoms of the individual] ... has been, is being or is likely to be contravened in relation to him or her'.[89] In the event that an act of government or legislation is considered *ultra vires* the Constitution, the High Court, subject to appeal to the Court of Appeals, shall 'dispose of the case in accordance with the decision'.[90]

While the discussion above has noted the similarities and differences between constitutional elements that could impact on the economic constitution of each of the countries, the difficult task is to ascertain the salience of these elements in shaping their respective political economies. Allocations of political authority and accountability clearly affect whether and how constitutional or other legal protections are upheld in practice, but democratic participation and fealty to the rule of law do not alone account for the failure to achieve the political economy of economic prosperity and equality promised in the texts of these constitutions.

Another means of exploring our question about the political economy of constitutions is thus to focus on a specific issue within the political economy of southern Africa that might

---

[81] See Stephen Gardbaum, *The New Commonwealth Model of Constitutionalism: Theory and Practice* (Cambridge University Press 2013); Robery Leckey, *Bills of Rights in the Common Law* (Cambridge University Press 2015).
[82] Constitution of Botswana, s 105.
[83] Constitution of South Africa, ss 167 and 172.
[84] Constitution of Zimbabwe, s 175.
[85] Constitution of Mozambique, art 245(1).
[86] ibid art 245(2).
[87] ibid.
[88] Constitution of Botswana, ss 105–106.
[89] ibid s 18(1).
[90] ibid s 105(2).

shed light on the effect of these different elements. With this as a goal, this chapter now focuses on the problem of land rights, which remains a burning issue throughout the region.

4. Property Rights, Land Tenure, and Land Reform

The relationship between land and constitutional structure is embedded in the history of southern Africa. At the dawn of the colonial era, a process of violent dispossession began that would span more than 250 years and culminate, in South Africa, in the adoption of the 1913 Land Act—which created a legal structure that sought both to legitimize the history of dispossession and prevent future access to the land by the African majority.

The pattern of colonial settlement combined with the creation of African reservations (later called 'bantustans' or 'homelands' in apartheid South Africa) was repeated in Zimbabwe (Southern Rhodesia), though the relationship between land and people in the protectorates of Basutoland (Lesotho), Bechuanaland (Botswana), and Swaziland (Eswatini) was slightly different. In Botswana, for example, most of the arable rural land remained under the control of traditional authorities until after independence in 1966, at which point the new government introduced tenure reforms that altered the relationship between traditional authorities and land as well as expanded the area of land available for private ownership. As for the former Portuguese colonies of Angola and Mozambique, there again the pattern of tenure relations, especially in the post-colonial period, was significantly different. While there are clear differences in these cases, the fundamental distinction nevertheless lies in the level of dispossession that distinguishes the settler colonies of South Africa, Rhodesia, and Mozambique, on the one hand, from the Protectorates, including Botswana, on the other.

While property extends far beyond the idea of landownership and wealth in the contemporary era is no longer based primarily on landholdings, the focus of this comparison is on property rights in land. It has to be recognized as such that, in southern Africa at least, the form of tenure under which property in land is held varies greatly from fee simple (the notion of full private ownership) and extends to a diversity of other arrangements, such as common ownership, leasehold, public ownership, and various indigenous forms of landholding and control. When considering rights to land, we are, in short, looking at a range of land tenure arrangements and not simply private ownership of property.

In addition, it is necessary to recognize that, among these different forms, tenure may be held by quite different social and legal entities, including the state, private individuals, legal entities such as corporations or trusts, or even communities. While these different forms of tenure are often determined by the history, location, and use of the relevant parcels of land, another broad and significant distinction is between rural and urban land. Although this is an artificial distinction, it maps onto geographical and use distinctions that fundamentally impact on the nature of tenure at various points in time and location. Furthermore, the distinction between rural or agricultural land and urban or housing property is a distinction of vital importance in understanding the relationship between the state and property in southern Africa.[91]

---

[91] Heinz Klug, 'Property's Role in the Fundamental Political Structure of Nations: The Southern African Experience' (2017) 6 The Brigham Kanner Property Conference Journal 145.

The histories of the different countries in the region and the evolution of property relations within each had significant consequences for the nature of the state during the colonial period. In the post-colonial era, it is the legacy of these relationships and how they shape relations between public authorities and the governed that are of central concern to the future of democracy and constitutionalism in the region.[92] Democratic legitimacy is tied to the processes of land reform and restitution that have been undertaken in the post-colonial era. Where these processes have stalled or failed, there remains a sense of betrayal and a belief that the country has still to be fully decolonized or returned to the people,[93] while in other contexts land reforms or transfers of property through illegitimate means have led to political instability and international isolation.[94]

It is in this sense that it may be argued that the constitutional orders of the post-colonial states of southern Africa have been fundamentally shaped by the nature of property relations. This is especially so in the cases of Mozambique, Zimbabwe, and South Africa, where the dispossession of land was a central grievance in the liberation struggles; it is also significant to the structure of post-colonial Botswana, where the relationship between communal land and public authority remained a key area of contestation in the shaping of local government, particularly in the rural villages of the country.

Dispossession and forced removals were central to the colonial and apartheid projects. They were not only the basic means of colonization but continued late into the twentieth century as the darkest face of apartheid policy,[95] justifying the international community's condemnation of apartheid as a crime against humanity.[96] It is this legacy—in which millions were forced from their homes and declared pariahs in the land of their birth;[97] in which communities were dismantled brick by brick and their members scattered across the most barren wastelands of the country,[98] in which people clung to the land and refused to give up their claims[99]—that set the stage for the recognition and shaping of property rights in post-apartheid South Africa.

Similarly, in Zimbabwe the liberation struggle was premised on the demand for land, with the country's post-independence history in turn having been shaped by conflict between the government and white farmers, culminating at the turn of the century in the fast-track land reform programme and subsequent collapse of the economy.[100] In Mozambique,

---

[92] See Maria Paula Meneses and Boaventura de Sousa Santos, 'Mozambique: The Rise of a Micro Dual State' (2009) 34(3–4) Africa Development 129.

[93] See Joel M Modiri, 'Conquest and Constitutionalism: First Thoughts on an Alternative Jurisprudence' (2018) 34(3) South African Journal on Human Rights 300.

[94] International Crisis Group, 'Zimbabwe: Stranded in Stasis' (29 February 2016) 118 Crisis Group Africa Briefing. See also Munoda Mararike, *Zimbabwe Will Never Be a Colony Again! Sanctions and Anti-Imperialist Struggles in Zimbabwe* (Langaa RPCIG 2019).

[95] Cosmos Desmond, *The Discarded People: An Account of African Resettlement in South Africa* (Penguin African Library 1972).

[96] United Nations General Assembly Resolution: The Policies of Apartheid of the Government of the Republic of South Africa, GA Res 2202, UN GAOR, 21st Sess, UN Doc A/RES/2202 A (1966); United Nations General Assembly Resolution: The Policies of Apartheid of the Government of South Africa, GA Res 2396, UN GAOR, 23rd Sess, UN Doc A/RES/2396 (1968); United Nations General Assembly Resolution: International Convention on the Suppression and Punishment of the Crime of Apartheid, GA Res 3068, UN GAOR 28th Sess, UN Doc A/RES/3068 (1973) reprinted in United Nations, *The United Nations and Apartheid 1948–1994* (UN 1994).

[97] Sol T Plaatjie, *Native Life in South Africa* (1916, Longman 1987) 6.

[98] Surplus People Project, *Forced Removals in South Africa: The Surplus People Project Reports*, vols 1–5 (Surplus People Project 1983).

[99] Transvaal Rural Action Committee, *A Toehold on the Land: Labour Tenancy in the South Eastern Transvaal* (TRAC 1988).

[100] Joseph Hanlon, Jeanette Manjengwa, and Teresa Smart, *Zimbabwe Takes Back Its Land* (Jacana 2013).

the history of post-colonial socialist ideology that saw the nationalization of all land at independence is still reflected in the Constitution, yet access to and use of land is no longer based on socialist principles but on both a system of long-term leasehold and indigenous forms of landholding. Although dispossession of land was not a direct driver of the relationship between the colonial state and communities in the Bechuanaland Protectorate, the Tswana chiefdoms that made up the Protectorate had all experienced conflict over land as a result of state formation and colonial expansion in the nineteenth and early twentieth centuries.[101]

In South Africa, the history of land dispossession, primarily of rural land, now defines the relationship between the state and property. The framework of land law inherited by post-apartheid South Africa is characterized by historical legacies that undermine its legitimacy and have profound consequences for the establishment of a functional system of land law. These elements include a hierarchy of land tenure in which freehold title is privileged; the fragmentation of land law in different parts of the country; the lack of an adequate system for recording all land rights; the prevalence of bureaucratic discretion over the land rights of many landholders (particularly in the former bantustans); and the need to establish new laws and forms of regulation to address this history.

Since 1994, major efforts have been made to address this legacy. Although the degradation and pain of communities and individuals who had policies of dispossession and forced removal thrust upon them can never be adequately documented,[102] there is an intimate link between these struggles and the shaping of property rights in South Africa today. As a result, the legacy of dispossession and forced removals has become as central to the project of achieving justice in post-apartheid South Africa as these processes were in perpetuating apartheid.

Market-led reform was the mantra of the World Bank in the 1990s as it attempted to mediate between claims for restitution and redistribution and the need to resuscitate and stabilize markets in countries emerging from state socialism, authoritarian dictatorships, apartheid, and civil conflict.[103] These policies have faltered in southern Africa, however. In Zimbabwe, where the post-colonial settlement dictated a 'willing-buyer, willing-seller' process, the failure to provide the resources required to address vast colonially derived inequalities in landownership undermined all property rights. By comparison, in South Africa there has been less economic and political disruption thus far, with the process of restitution providing some relief and promise of change. Yet the process remains extremely slow, and the overall disparities continue to raise agrarian and political tension, leading at times to violent disruption. In other contexts, processes of privatization and individual titling have continued apace, but there is little evidence that this has significantly stimulated agrarian economies and livelihoods.

---

[101] Neil Parsons, *A New History of Southern Africa* (MacMillan 1982) 130–38; Andrew Manson and Bernard K Mbenga, *Land Chiefs Mining* (Wits Press 2014).

[102] Desmond (n 95); Laurine Platzky and Cherryl Walker, *The Surplus People: Forced Removals in South Africa* (Ravan 1985).

[103] Klaus Deininger, *Land Policies for Growth and Poverty Reduction: A World Bank Policy Research Report* (OUP 2003).

4.1 Land Reform in Southern Africa

If land reform in southern Africa today is immediately associated with the economic trav- ails of Zimbabwe, a more nuanced history will recognize that the region's first experience of post-colonial land reform occurred in Botswana after it gained independence in 1966.

With nearly half of the country's land formally designated as tribal reserves and about 80 per cent of the population living in them, the government adopted the Tribal Land Act in 1968 with the aim of transforming existing tenure relations. At independence, Botswana's land mass was divided in terms of three forms of tenure: state land (formerly crown lands), freehold land, and tribal land. While freehold tenure was limited to a few areas of former white settlement, comprising about 6 per cent of the land, the colonial division between crown land and native reserves was never as clear, with some estimating that up to 70 per cent of the land area was under tribal authority, rather than the 48 per cent formally des- ignated as native reserves. It was in this context that land reform took place, first with the adoption of the Tribal Land Act in 1968, then with the State Land Act of 1970, and finally with the Tribal Grazing Land Policy,[104] introduced by President Sir Seretse Khama in 1975, and its counterpart, the Arable Lands Development Programme of 1980.

Land reform in Botswana had a profound impact on access to land and the country's political structure. Instead of traditional authorities having the power to allocate land, the Tribal Land Act placed all tribal land under the jurisdiction of twelve land boards that began operations in 1970.[105] Initially the land boards continued to be dominated by local traditional authorities, but amendments to the Tribal Land Act in 1989 removed both chiefs and councillors from membership,[106] ensuring that broader interests gained greater influ- ence on the boards, particularly those of the national government by virtue of appointments made by the Minister of Local Government, Lands and Housing as well as the appointment of two *ex officio* members by the Minister of Commerce and Industry and the Minister of Agriculture. Five of the twelve members of the main land boards are still elected in the local *kgotla*—the traditional court of the chief—while the remaining seven are appointed.

The main role of the boards continues to be land allocation, land use planning, and ad- judication of land disputes.[107] In larger districts, subordinate land boards were created to address applications for land use and hear local disputes, although their decisions remained subject to appeal to the main land board under which they were created.

The operational difficulties of the land boards have been well documented, including the persistent influence of local traditional authorities as well as the problem of self-allocation and pre-allocation, in which applicants would justify their requests by claiming that they had been granted the land before the creation of the land boards,[108] yet the system has con- tinued to evolve and represents a unique feature of governance in Botswana.

---

[104] National Policy on Tribal Grazing Land, Government Paper No 1 of 1975.

[105] B Machacha, 'Botswana's Land Tenure: Institutional Reform and Policy Formulation' in JW Arntzen, LD Ngcongco, and SD Turner (eds), *Land Policy and Agriculture in Eastern and Southern* (UN University 1986) <http://www.unu.edu/unupress/unupbooks/80604e/80604E00.htm> accessed 9 April 2017.

[106] BM Mathuba, 'Land Boards and Customary Land Administration in Botswana' (1999). Paper presented at the DFID Workshop on Land Rights and Sustainable Development in Sub-Saharan Africa: Lessons and Way Forward in Land Tenure Policy, Sunningdale, UK, 16–19 February 1999, cited in B Nkwae, 'Botswana's Experience on Recognizing Traditional Land Rights on a Large Scale' <https://bit.ly/3qk6TxI> accessed 30 November 2020.

[107] ibid.

[108] John Comaroff, *The Structure of Agricultural Transformation in Barolong: Towards an Integrated Development Plan* (Good Hope 1977).

While resisting the formal expansion of freehold tenure, Botswana's land reform has fundamentally transformed the traditional land tenure system. Through the implementation of the Tribal Grazing Land Policy since 1975 and the Arable Lands Development Programme since 1980, the land boards have granted individualized rights based on the demarcation and fencing-off of land. Introduced in response to the problem of overgrazing, on the one hand, and recognition of the fact, on the other, that 45 per cent of Batswana owned no livestock at all,[109] these policies have engendered a diversity of tenure forms within the former tribal lands.

Although critics describe the grazing policies' creation of individual ranches as synonymous with the historic highlands enclosure and maintain that inequality in access to land has continued to grow, politically the outcome has been profound. Before the Tribal Land Act, a 'strong chief enjoyed … sole control over the distribution of fields, pasturage, and residential plots … and a monopoly over the creation of new political constituencies',[110] but the introduction of land boards has diffused local power and given more authority to national post-colonial state institutions. At the same time, the retention of tribal lands and the role of the *kgotla* and traditional authorities within the political system has provided what Jean and John Comaroff describe as a 'civic culture that specified the means of producing a certain kind of participatory politics, a politics grounded in an articulate popular ideology of good government'.[111]

In the case of Botswana, the retention of forms of land tenure that are rooted in historic forms of governance (despite their transformation through land reform) has had a fundamental impact on the nature of the post-colonial state and what the Camoroffs identify as a form of 'popular sovereignty and direct state accountability'[112] in post-independence Botswana. As Griffiths demonstrates in *Transformations on the Ground*, Botswana's land boards have provided a space in which 'competing normative orders' embedded in legal pluralism are applied to decisions about land and 'have a mutually constitutive bearing on how land is distributed'.[113] Basing her analysis on networks of families and households and 'taking account of gender and the lifecycle', Griffiths examines how globalized notions of the 'entrepreneurial vision of land development' promoted by international and transnational agencies impact on 'structures of inequality concerning class relations and empowerment (or disempowerment)' and how positioning within social networks affects 'access to resources, including land'.[114]

These distinctions are exacerbated by the government's adoption in 2015 of a new land policy which provides that, while allocations of free residential plots on tribal land are restricted to one plot per applicant, 'there should be no restrictions where parties are prepared to pay for tribal land that has already been allocated to be transferred to them'.[115] Thus, although the land boards are 'configured to administer and allocate land that was previously vested in dikgosi [chiefs]' and reflect an incremental approach to change, they must

---

[109] Machacha (n 105).
[110] Jean Comaroff and John Comaroff, *Theory from the South: How Euro-America is Evolving toward Africa* (Sun MeDia 2014) 104.
[111] ibid 111.
[112] ibid 113.
[113] Anne MO Griffiths, *Transformations on the Ground: Space and the Power of Land in Botswana* (Indiana University Press 2019) 14.
[114] ibid 11–12.
[115] ibid 51.

now 'meld past tradition and the implementation of present realities with the attainment of future goals that are aligned with broad global capitalist and sustainable visions of land tenure'.[116]

In contrast to Botswana's incremental land reform, the history of post-independence Mozambique shows a dramatic initial intervention followed by a series of measures reflecting a shift post-civil war to neoliberal policies. Mozambique at independence inherited an agrarian land economy in which a commercial sector controlled by colonial settlers was interdependent with a peasant sector where landholding was controlled by 'regulos (traditional chiefs) through which both labour recruitment and peasant access to land were regulated'.[117] With settlers having taken flight, the Mozambique Liberation Front (Frelimo) government nationalized the land, but then proceeded to reinscribe the basic structure of the agrarian system by turning former commercial farms into state farms and defining peasant holdings as family farms.[118]

The civil war was in part fuelled by and undermined these initial efforts at land reform; consequently, the failure of state farms and the marginalization of the peasantry forced land reform back on the agenda in the mid-1990s after a political settlement brought the war to a close.[119] The return of war refugees, both as returnees from neighbouring countries and as internally displaced persons, the return of some former settlers, and the arrival of new investors led to multiple claims on the land.[120] While the constitutional status of land remained unchanged, the government introduced a new land law in 1997 'as a compromise between elite interests in privatizing land and more populist interests in protecting the rural poor and creating development opportunities that would help alleviate rural poverty'.[121]

This reform introduced three forms of tenure: customary; good faith occupation; and fifty-year lease holds for commercial land 'by the State to a private investor, after consultation with the affected local community'.[122] The effect of the reform has been to decentralize control over land and natural resources to the local level. Although it was undertaken on the basis that there would be security for community land rights, it has created tensions between local communities and raised concerns that powerful interests seeking access to natural resources, including oil, gas, and other minerals, are able to exert influence over local authorities to the detriment of community interests.[123]

If Mozambique's land reform is proceeding without constitutional change, in Zimbabwe the Constitution has been central to claims that conflict over land and land reform is key to the country's economic travails and erosion of democratic governance. At independence,

---

[116] ibid 58.

[117] Bridget O'Laughlin, 'Past and Present Options: Land Reform in Mozambique' (1995) 63 Review of African Political Economy 99.

[118] ibid 102.

[119] M Anne Pitcher, 'Disruption without Transformation: Agrarian Relations and Livelihoods in Nampula Province, Mozambique 1975–1995' (1998) 24(1) Journal of Southern African Studies 115.

[120] M Anne Pitcher, 'Recreating Colonialism or Reconstructing the State? Privatisation and Politics in Mozambique' (1996) 22(1) Journal of Southern African Studies 49.

[121] Elizabeth Lunstrum, 'Mozambique, Neoliberal Land Reform, and the Limpopo National Park' (2008) 98(3) The Geographical Review 339, 342.

[122] Simon Hull and Jennifer Whittal, 'Filling the Gap: Customary Land Tenure Reform in Mozambique and South Africa' (2018) 7(2) South African Journal of Geomatics 102, 104.

[123] See Nilza Matavel, Sílvia Dolores, and Vanessa Cabanelas, 'Lords of the Land: Preliminary Analysis of the Phenomenon of Land Grabbing in Mozambique' (Justiça Ambiental & UNAC 2011); Josipa Bicanic, Rasmus Fejer Nielsen, and Flemming Sehested, 'Securing Community Land Rights in Northern Mozambique' (Danish Forestry Extension 2014).

Zimbabwe was a settler colony in which 6,000 white farmers owned 42 per cent of the arable land while 4.5 million black Zimbabweans lived in overcrowded communal areas, the former 'native reserves'.[124] It was in this context that the 1979 Lancaster House Agreement[125]—which ended the war and led to democratic elections in Zimbabwe in 1980—included the text of Zimbabwe's independence constitution in summary form.

This summary contained, among other things, a guarantee of a specific number of seats for white settlers in the new parliament until 1987,[126] as well as a clause in the Declaration of Rights that protected existing property rights and specified that the new government could expropriate land only for specific purposes and under stringent conditions.[127] It also provided that, except by unanimous agreement, there could be no amendment of the Declaration of Rights, and hence the property clause, for the first ten years of independence.[128]

As a result, the Zimbabwe Constitution Act of 1979, which came into force as the Constitution of Zimbabwe at independence in April 1980, prevented the government from obtaining land for land reform except under circumstances in which the land was obtained in conformity with the 'willing-seller, willing-buyer' principle.[129] While the principle refers in the common law to the idea of market value, in this context, rather than merely defining the measure of compensation that would be due in the aftermath of expropriation, it entailed a limitation on the ability of the new government to exercise its inherent power of eminent domain. Under the independence Constitution, this settlement was in effect restricted to ten years,[130] after which Parliament, which remained sovereign in the tradition of parliamentary sovereignty inherited from Britain, would be free to amend the Constitution.

Although the Zimbabwean legislature moved quickly in 1990 to remove the 'willing-buyer, willing-seller' limitations in the Constitution,[131] in practice the government continued, in the interests of economic stability and foreign investment, to follow 'willing-buyer, willing-seller' principles when it purchased land from white farmers for its resettlement and related land reform efforts. It was only when the ruling ZANU-PF party and President Robert Mugabe began to face serious electoral challenges in the late 1990s that the slow pace of land redistribution became a refrain in government rhetoric.[132] Against this backdrop, Zimbabwe adopted ever more aggressive policies of land acquisition, policies which after 2000 led to farm invasions, political turmoil, and the collapse of the economy.

While the conditions that led to economic collapse are multiple and complex, what has been the focus of attention was the adoption of constitutional changes that revoked the duty to pay compensation altogether by tying it to the willingness of the former colonial power to offer financial aid to cover the costs of compensation.[133] Significantly, these provisions of the Constitution remained a core element of contestation in the process of constitutional

[124] R Palmer, 'Land Reform in Zimbabwe, 1980–1990' (1990) 89 African Affairs 163.
[125] 'Southern Rhodesia Constitutional Conference Held at Lancaster House, London, September—December 1979: Report' <https://peacemaker.un.org/sites/peacemaker.un.org/files/ZW_791221_LancasterHouseAgreement.pdf> accessed 30 November 2020.
[126] ibid annex C, s E, para 29.
[127] ibid annex C, s C, para V(1)–(3).
[128] ibid annex C, s E, para 30.
[129] Zimbabwe Act of 1979, ch 60.
[130] Constitution of Zimbabwe of 1980, art 52(4).
[131] Amendment No 16, Constitution of Zimbabwe of 1980, s 16A, inserted by s 3 of Act 5 of 2000.
[132] Hanlon, Manjengwa, and Smart (n 100).
[133] Constitution of Zimbabwe of 1980 (as amended by Act 5 of 2000), s 16A (1)(i) and (ii).

amendment or constitution-making that produced a new constitution in 2013 but which failed to resolve the political crisis in Zimbabwe. As Muna Ndulo has argued, '[t]he Lancaster House Constitution itself failed to serve as a framework for local political and economic actors to negotiate the transformation from a colonial state with great economic disparities to a more equitable Zimbabwe'; as a result, '[it] failed to gain legitimacy or provide a framework for the democratic governance of Zimbabwe'.[134]

Not unlike Zimbabwe's, South Africa's system of landownership historically benefited only a small percentage of the population. This was primarily the result of the racial division of land that predated formal apartheid and found legal enshrinement in the 1913 and 1936 Land Acts. As mentioned, the 1913 Land Act denied the land rights of black South Africans and established the spatial distribution of land use that became the basis of apartheid. It has been 'estimated that some 3.5 million black South Africans had been uprooted from their homes and relocated in furtherance ... of the apartheid agenda between 1960 and 1982' alone.[135] The combined effects of this often-violent dispossession were twofold: first, it created a land market from which nearly 80 per cent of the population were excluded, and secondly, it privileged freehold tenure—denied to all but white South Africans—over other forms of tenure which were recognized. In time this distinction would determine not only the racialized socio-economic conditions of wealth and poverty but also the distribution of political rights, leading to a system of racial oppression under apartheid.

Unsurprisingly, the issue of property was and remains a significant point of contention in South Africa. While the internationally endorsed process for the democratic transition from apartheid included a commitment to the rule of law and the inclusion of a justiciable bill of rights, there was no clarity on the contents of these commitments. Prior to the start of substantive constitutional negotiations in early 1993, the two main parties, the African National Congress (ANC) and the apartheid government, presented dramatically different proposals for how they wished to see property addressed in a post-apartheid constitution. On the one hand, the ANC was willing to protect the undisturbed enjoyment of personal possessions; however, property entitlements were to be determined by legislation and provision was to be made for the restoration of land to people dispossessed under apartheid. On the other hand, the apartheid government's proposals were aimed at protecting all existing property rights and would allow expropriation only for public purposes and subject to cash compensation determined by a court of law according to the market value of the property. In response, the ANC suggested that no property clause was necessary at all.

As the negotiations progressed, the conflict over the property clause continued, with the apartheid government insisting that property rights be included in the constitution and that the measure of compensation include specific reference to the market value of the property. In contrast, the ANC insisted that the property clause should not frustrate efforts to address land claims and that the state ought to have the power to regulate property without the obligation to pay compensation unless there was a clear expropriation of the property. The interim 1993 Constitution resolved these conflicts by providing a separate institutional basis for land restitution, which was guaranteed in the corrective action provisions of the

---

[134] Muna Ndula, 'Zimbabwe's Unfulfilled Struggle for a Legitimate Constitutional Order' in LE Miller (ed), *Framing the State in Times of Transition: Case Studies in Constitution Making* (United States Institute of Peace 2010) 182.

[135] Cherryl Walker, *Land-Marked: Land Claims & Land Restitution in South Africa* (Jacana 2008) 2.

equality clause, and by compromising on the question of compensation by including a range of factors which the courts would have to consider in determining just and equitable compensation.

Despite predictions that there would be very little change in the Constitution during the second phase of constitution-making, particularly regarding such sensitive matters as the property clause and the Bill of Rights, property again became a lightning-rod issue. Political agreement on the property clause was finally reached only at midnight on 18 April 1996, when section 28(8), the clause insulating land and water reform from the property clause, was modified to make it subject to the general limitations clause of the Constitution.[136]

As a result, the final property clause guarantees the restitution of land dispossessed after the 1913 Land Act was adopted[137] and a right to legally secure tenure for those whose tenure is insecure as a result of racially discriminatory laws or practices.[138] It also includes an obligation on the state to enable citizens to gain access to land on an equitable basis.[139] Furthermore, the state is granted a limited exemption from the protective provisions of the property clause to empower it to take 'legislative and other measures to achieve land, water and related reform, in order to redress the results of past racial discrimination'.[140] At the same time, it protects the rights of property-holders, stipulating in section 25(1) that '[n]o one may be deprived of property except in terms of law of general application, and no law may permit arbitrary deprivation of property'.

While the clause does indeed recognize the state's power to expropriate property for 'a public purpose or in the public interest'[141] and 'subject to compensation',[142] there is a clear attempt both to protect land reform from constitutional challenge and to ensure that the payment of compensation is tied to recognition of the history and use of the relevant property.[143] In the last quarter-century, this led to the establishment of a land claims process that in its first iteration saw 64,000 claims based on the constitutional right of 'a person or community dispossessed of property after 19 June 1913 as a result of past racially discriminatory laws or practices' to claim either 'restitution of that property or to [obtain] equitable redress'. By the end of the first land restitution process, nearly 80,000 claims (mostly to urban land) were received by regional land claims commissions and in some cases adjudicated by a land claims court.

Combined with the additional processes of land redistribution and land tenure reform introduced by statute, the result is that more than 3.4 million hectares have been redistributed, albeit that this remains far short of the 30 per cent target—of 82 million hectares of white-owned farmland—initially set by the new government in 1994.[144]

---

[136] P Bell (ed), *The Making of the Constitution: The Story of South Africa's Constitutional Assembly, May 1994 to December 1996* (Churchill Murray Publications 1997).

[137] Constitution of South Africa of 1996, s 25(7).

[138] ibid s 25(6).

[139] ibid s 25(5).

[140] ibid s 25(8).

[141] ibid s 25(2)(a).

[142] ibid s 25(2)(b).

[143] ibid s 25(3). This section states: 'The amount of the compensation and the time and manner of payment must be just and equitable reflecting an equitable balance between the public interest and the interests of those affected, having regard to the relevant circumstances, including: (a) the current use of the property; (b) the history of the acquisition and use of the property; (c) the market value of the property; (d) the extent of direct state investment and subsidy in the acquisition and beneficial capital improvement of the property; and, (e) the purpose of the expropriation.'

[144] Lungisile Ntsebeza and Ruth Hall (eds), *The Land Question in South Africa* (HSRC 2007); Ben Cousins and Cherryl Walker (eds), *Land Divided, Land Restored* (Jacana 2015).

Another major challenge facing the post-apartheid land system is the effective incorporation of existing non-freehold rights into the legal system.[145] Despite the adoption of laws to address this legacy and reduce insecurity of tenure, the task of providing security of tenure through formal processes of survey, titling, and registration remains daunting. Even the reduction of the levels of accuracy required for traditional modes of land survey is unlikely to bring about reduced costs, given that although the technology is readily available to surveyors, professional control of the process and reluctance to abandon past practices have prevented significant reductions in cost.

The new legal regime designed to increase security of tenure includes the provision of tenure rights to persons occupying land with the owner's permission in rural and peri-urban areas;[146] legislation protecting and allowing labour tenants to gain permanent rights to the use of land held as tenants;[147] law providing temporary protection to those who might gain rights to land as a result of land and tenure reform;[148] and new legislation prohibiting unlawful evictions, which has fundamentally changed the legal and practical relationship between occupiers and titleholders.[149] In spite of these attempts to protect existing occupiers, the future legitimation of all landholdings was understood to rest on the recognition of historical land claims and the creation of a process of restitution for those who had already been denied possession of their lands.

Despite the constitutional focus on rural land, urban land and housing are today the most significant form of property for the majority of individual South Africans, who live in a country that has seen massive urbanization since the collapse of apartheid's internal pass system in the mid-1980s. A separate constitutional provision states that 'everyone has a right to have access to adequate housing'[150] and imposes the same duty on the state to provide for this right within its available resources.[151] This provision also guarantees that 'no one may be evicted from their home, or have their home demolished, without an order of court ...'.[152] Constitutional Court jurisprudence has subsequently interpreted the right to housing to include a right not to be evicted unless provided with alternative accommodation and only after 'meaningful engagement' by the relevant governmental authority.

Moreover, in its attempts to address the vast urban housing shortage created by apartheid as well as post-apartheid urbanization and immigration, the government first adopted a housing policy under its Reconstruction and Development Programme (RDP) of 1994 that produced more than 3.3 million low-cost housing units in the first twenty years of democracy.[153] Over the same period, the population grew by approximately 13 million (to over 53 million), with only about 15 per cent of the country's approximately 14.5 million households earning enough income to secure financing in the formal banking system.

---

[145] In particular, the rights in sch 2 to the Upgrading of Land Tenure Rights Act 113 of 1991, as well as the occupation and site permits referred to in the Conversion of Certain Rights into Leasehold or Ownership Act 81 of 1988.

[146] Extension of Security of Tenure Act 62 of 1997.

[147] Labour Reform (Labour Tenants) Act 3 of 1996.

[148] Interim Protection of Informal Land Rights Act 31 of 1996.

[149] Prevention of Illegal Eviction from and Unlawful Occupation of Land Act 19 of 1998.

[150] Constitution of South Africa of 1996, s 26(1).

[151] ibid s 26(2).

[152] ibid s 26(3).

[153] National Department of Housing, *White Paper: A New Housing Policy and Strategy for South Africa* (1994); Financial and Fiscal Commission, Exploring Alternative Finance and Policy Option for Effective and Sustainable Delivery of Housing in South Africa, RP303/2013 (FFC 2013).

In keeping with changes in economic policy, the government's housing policy shifted in the first decade of this century towards a bifurcated policy which, on the one hand, promoted a rental housing sector under a social housing policy and law[154] and, on the other, sought to promote a more market-based housing policy in which the granting of title would facilitate private investment and improvement in housing.[155]

4.2 Tensions and Trajectories

Different patterns of land tenure and reform efforts have produced very different impacts on access to land and economic opportunity across the four southern African countries of Botswana, Mozambique, South Africa, and Zimbabwe. To what extent have the different constitutional provisions affected these trajectories? The outcome of a continuous process of land conflict is a product of both the inherited pattern of colonial land relations and the choices made by the post-colonial state in these different circumstances.

In Mozambique, the constitutional solution to the question of tenure relations has been to maintain the post-independence nationalization of land even as the Constitution guarantees the protection of all other forms of property. As a result, the new land law of 1997 made leasehold, occupation, and indigenous forms of tenure the means through which individuals, communities, and corporations access land. However, the country's economic trajectory seems less impacted on by the institution of property and its constitutional status than by concerns about corruption and failures of democratic accountability.

If in Botswana the limited amount of freehold tenure and the political strength of traditional authorities at the time of independence saw land policies focus on the 'tribal areas', it was the slowly evolving process of national intervention and the continued vitality of the political culture of the *kgotla* that produced a gradual transformation in land rights as well as a relatively stable political regime. The dominant political party—the Botswana Democratic Party—has relied on rural support to continue to win national elections, even as the major urban areas have seen local governments controlled by the political opposition. The net result has been the emergence of a democratic state where national and local politics are quite distinct. Even if there are questions about the exact form of local democracy, there is recognition that national elections are free and fair.

While it may be argued that the variation in tenure relations across Botswana affects the political choices of citizens, there is little evidence that any specific constitutional provisions were of salience. Instead, it is more likely that if the constitutional order has had any impact on economic development, it is to the degree that its unchanging character is part of the overall stability the country has enjoyed since independence notwithstanding that it was geographically at the centre of the wars of liberation in Zimbabwe, Namibia, and South Africa that shaped the region as a whole.

This is in stark contrast to developments in Zimbabwe, where the failure to engage in effective land reform in the immediate post-independence era saw a perpetuation of inequality and land hunger reminiscent of the colonial era. The continuing inequality

---

[154] Social Housing Act 16 of 2008.
[155] Department of Human Settlements, 'Breaking New Ground': A Comprehensive Plan for the Development of Integrated Sustainable Human Settlements (Republic of South Africa 2004).

produced, first, a political crisis and then—when Robert Mugabe's government responded by adopting 'fast-track land resettlement', including land invasions from 2000 to 2003— economic disruption. Despite the overall economic situation, however, there is increasing evidence that the process has seen black Zimbabweans gain more access to land and 'has unleashed a process of radical agrarian change'.[156]

As Scoones and others note in this regard, their 'data identifies an emerging process of "accumulation from below", rooted in petty commodity production and small-scale capitalist farming ... [I]f the new resettlements are to contribute not only to local livelihoods, but also national food security and economic development, they require investment and support', including in infrastructure, financing, input supply, technology, and 'coordination mechanisms (institutions and policy) that allow agriculture to grow and be sustained'.[157] However, a lack of incentives and a 'vacuum in policy thinking'[158] on agrarian reform, as well as a more general failure to uphold the rule of law, including an undermining of the courts by the government, have had a longer-term impact on the constitutional order. After flawed elections and increasing authoritarianism, there has been an attempt to reconstitute the state through a process of constitutional renewal. But the failure of the democratic process as well as the constitutional reforms has produced 'a government which lacks both national and international legitimacy'.[159]

It is in this context that we might consider developments in South Africa and ask what effect land reform might have on the future structure of the new constitutional state that emerged from apartheid in the mid-1990s. The debate about South Africa's land reform programme has become an argument over whether the glass is half-full or half-empty. Although the promise of the ANC's 1994 election manifesto—a transfer of 30 per cent of the land—has not been met, thousands of families and individuals from the most marginalized sections of society have been beneficiaries of the government's threefold land reform strategy: land restitution; land redistribution and land tenure reform; and a massive, subsidized housing programme. These slow gains notwithstanding, it remains the fact that the clearest indicator of poverty in South Africa, even after twenty-five years of democracy, is being black, female, and living in a rural area.

Unfortunately, after a change in land reform policy in the early 2000s, when the government re-evaluated its focus and decided to target black commercial farmers instead of marginalized rural communities as beneficiaries of land reform, this set of indicators seems little likely to change. Whether it be in terms of access to land, housing, or simply the continuing unequal distribution of wealth, the failure to effect significant economic change has led to increasing challenges to the legitimacy of the government's land reform policies and to the constitutional order more generally.

This comparison of the institution of property and land reform in four post-colonial states in southern Africa has explored the relationship between the history and nature of property rights and the constitutional status of land in each of them. In each case, the economic structure of the post-colonial state has been or is still being formed around the history and nature of tenure relations—whether based on indigenous and colonial relations to

---

[156] Ian Scoones and others, *Zimbabwe's Land Reform: Myths & Realities* (James Currey 2010) 233.
[157] ibid 233–34.
[158] ibid 235.
[159] Ndula (n 134) 177.

the land or being forged through claims of historical dispossession and restitution. In each of these cases, the history of land reform post-independence has had a profound impact on the structure of democratic politics and legal institutions—whether at the local level, in Botswana, or at multiple levels, in Zimbabwe, South Africa, and Mozambique.

Where land reform has failed or been inadequate to the legacy of colonialism, there have been profound political consequences. In Zimbabwe, these early failings put the very structure of the state in jeopardy, while in South Africa the inability to address economic inequality has led politicians to point to the question of land and reassert the claim that the land must be returned to the people.[160] While often serving as a proxy for a more general claim for the redistribution of wealth, it is the continuing inequality in access to land, both urban and rural, that enables these claimants to question the legitimacy of the post-apartheid constitutional order.

5. Conclusion

Considering the different theories of economic constitutionalism, the relationship between specific constitutional provisions and their economic impact remains unclear. First, there is the difficulty of deciding which elements of a constitution matter, especially when different provisions of the constitution might be expected to pull in different directions. While an institutional approach seems to provide the most useful means of explicating the potential effects of the constitution, the different forms and range of institutions in the four constitutions compared make it clear that the simple incorporation of any specific clause or institution in the constitution does not produce any standard effect on economic development. Even the protection of property, an institution that might be considered central to economic development, depends more on the history of tenure relations within each polity than on the form of the constitutional provisions.

Secondly, differences in the constitutional form of government and electoral system, so central to neoliberal analyses of constitutional political economy, produce rather counter-intuitive results. On the one hand, South Africa and Mozambique have electoral systems based on proportional representation, while, on the other, Botswana and Zimbabwe have constituency-based first-past-the-post systems. All four cases have presidential forms of executive government; however, aside from Mozambique, they are essentially parliamentary systems. While these distinctions are considered theoretically significant, especially when it comes to the role of proportional representation, the nature of post-liberation politics and dominant-party democracy in all four cases seems to negate these theoretically expected effects.

Thirdly, Elster's statement that 'constitutions matter for economic performance to the extent that they promote the values of stability, accountability and credibility'[161] seems to be vindicated at the highest level of abstraction, yet it does not provide much guidance on the import of particular constitutional provisions. This chapter suggests that a political-economy approach might provide a more useful means of addressing the relationship

---

[160] Heinz Klug, 'Decolonization, Compensation and Constitutionalism: Land, Wealth and the Sustainability of Constitutionalism in Post-apartheid South Africa' (2018) 34(3) South African Journal on Human Rights 469.
[161] Elster (n 3) 210.

between constitutions and economic development. It is an approach that places the distribution of wealth and power at the centre of its analysis and explores how different features of constitutions either promote or frustrate the promises of democracy and economic well-being that constitutionalism offers. Even as constitutions, including all the post-colonial constitutions in southern Africa, have incorporated justiciable bills of rights, independent mechanisms to protect democracy, and independent courts with powers of constitutional review, civil conflict and economic inequality have continued to undermine the promise of constitutionalism.

Central to these problems is the issue of land: in spite of their similarities in the constitutional protection of property rights in general, in the countries under study it is the history of tenure relations, and level of confidence in the stability and application of the rules of the game as defined in the constitution, that seem to have had the most important consequences for economic development. While Botswana has constitutional provisions closely associated with the negotiated post-colonial constitutions that dominated the first wave of African independence, including a first-past-the-post parliamentary democracy and limited constitutional review of fundamental rights, its history of stability—based on socially redistributive economic policies as well as its fortunate post-colonial mineral discoveries—appears to be a more significant factor in its economic development than its constitutional provisions. In comparison, the economic collapse of Zimbabwe and problems of accountability in South Africa and Mozambique seem more related to political failures than to the presence or absence of specific provisions in each country's constitution.

Finally, if we adopt a political-economy lens, one in which constitutional analysis brings together the economic and the political while taking a normative stance in favour of democratic participation and economic equality, we might see beyond the formal terms of each constitution and consider which elements could promote constitutionalism in southern Africa. From this perspective, we would recognize the significance of the constitutionalization of electoral commissions and integrity institutions but emphasize that unless the latter are supported and their independence guaranteed, the democratic underpinnings of economic change will be undermined.

It is here that the relationship between the constitutional status of land and property and democratic accountability for economic policies and behaviours, including patronage and corruption, comes into focus. The legacies of colonial dispossession and the limits of post-colonial land reform in the region require us to reconsider the forms of democratic representation in our constitutions. This means exploring the relationship between the constitutionally enshrined electoral systems and the nature of democratic accountability within dominant political parties, the lack of which inhibits the adoption and implementation of policies that might further the political-economic vision of each of these constitutions.

Bibliography

Alves AA, 'No Salvation through Constitutions: Jasay versus Buchanan and Rawls' (2015) 20(1) The Independent Review 33

Bell P (ed), *The Making of the Constitution: The Story of South Africa's Constitutional Assembly, May 1994 to December 1996* (Churchill Murray Publications 1997)

Bicanic J, Nielsen RF, and Sehested F, 'Securing Community Land Rights in Northern Mozambique' (Danish Forestry Extension 2014)

Block W and DiLorenzo T, 'Constitutional Economics and the Calculus of Consent' (2001) 15(3) Journal of Libertarian Studies 37

Brennan G and Buchanan JM, 'Is Public Choice Immoral? The Case for the "Nobel" Lie' (1988) 74 Virginia Law Review 179

Buchanan, JM and Tullock G, *The Calculus of Consent: Logical Foundations of Constitutional Democracy* (1962) Collected Works of James M Buchanan Vol 3 (Liberty Fund 1999)

Buchanan, JM, 'The Constitution of Economic Policy' (1987) 77(3) The American Economic Review 243

Comaroff J, *The Structure of Agricultural Transformation in Barolong: Towards an Integrated Development Plan* (Good Hope 1977)

Comaroff J and Comaroff J, *Theory from the South: How Euro-America is Evolving toward Africa* (Sun MeDia 2014)

Commons JR, *The Legal Foundations of Capitalism* (MacMillan 1924)

Cousins B and Walker C (eds), *Land Divided, Land Restored* (Jacana 2015)

Deininger K, *Land Policies for Growth and Poverty Reduction: A World Bank Policy Research Report* (OUP 2003)

Department of Human Settlements, 'Breaking New Ground': A Comprehensive Plan for the Development of Integrated Sustainable Human Settlements (Republic of South Africa 2004)

Desmond, Cosmos, *The Discarded People: An Account of African Resettlement in South Africa* (Penguin African Library 1972)

Elster J, 'The Impact of Constitutions on Economic Performance' (1995) Proceedings of the World Bank Annual Conference on Development Economics 1994

Financial and Fiscal Commission, *Exploring Alternative Finance and Policy Option for Effective and Sustainable Delivery of Housing in South Africa*, RP303/2013 (FFC 2013)

Forbach W, 'A Political Economy the Constitution Requires' *LPE Project* <https://lpeblog. <org/2019/10/23/title-tk/> accessed 12 August 2020

Gardbaum S, *The New Commonwealth Model of Constitutionalism: Theory and Practice* (Cambridge University Press 2013)

Gerber DJ and David J, 'Economic Constitutionalism and the Challenge of Globalization: The Enemy is Gone? Long Live the Enemy' (2001) 157 Journal of International and Theoretical Economics 14

Griffiths AMO, *Transformations on the Ground: Space and the Power of Land in Botswana* (Indiana University Press 2019)

Hanlon J, Manjengwa J, and Smart T, *Zimbabwe Takes Back Its Land* (Jacana 2013)

Hull S and Whittal J, 'Filling the Gap: Customary Land Tenure Reform in Mozambique and South Africa' (2018) 7(2) South African Journal of Geomatics 102

International Crisis Group, 'Zimbabwe: Stranded in Stasis' (29 February 2016) 118 Crisis Group Africa Briefing

Klug H, *Constituting Democracy: Law Globalism and South Africa's Political Reconstruction* (Cambridge University Press 2000)

Klug H, 'Property's Role in the Fundamental Political Structure of Nations: The Southern African Experience' (2017) 6 The Brigham Kanner Property Conference Journal 145

Klug H, 'Decolonization, Compensation and Constitutionalism: Land, Wealth and the Sustainability of Constitutionalism in Post-apartheid South Africa' (2018) 34(3) South African Journal on Human Rights 469

Komesar NK, *Imperfect Alternatives: Choosing Institutions in Law, Economics and Public Policy* (University of Chicago 1994)

Leckey R, *Bills of Rights in the Common Law* (Cambridge University Press 2015)

Lunstrum E, 'Mozambique, Neoliberal Land Reform, and the Limpopo National Park' (2008) 98(3) The Geographical Review 339

Machacha B, 'Botswana's Land Tenure: Institutional Reform and Policy Formulation' in Arntzen JW, Ngcongco L, and Turner SD (eds), *Land Policy and Agriculture in Eastern and Southern* (UN University 1986)

MacLean N, *Democracy in Chains: The Deep History of the Radical Right's Stealth Plan for America* (Viking 2017)

Manson A and Mbenga BK, *Land Chiefs Mining* (Wits Press 2014)

Mararike M, *Zimbabwe Will Never Be a Colony Again! Sanctions and Anti-Imperialist Struggles in Zimbabwe* (Langaa RPCIG 2019)

Matavel N, Dolores S, and Cabanelas V, 'Lords of the Land: Preliminary Analysis of the Phenomenon of Land Grabbing in Mozambique' (Justiça Ambiental & UNAC 2011)

Meneses MP and de Sousa Santos B, 'Mozambique: The Rise of a Micro Dual State' (2009) 34(3–4) Africa Development 129

Modiri JM, 'Conquest and Constitutionalism: First Thoughts on an Alternative Jurisprudence' (2018) 34(3) South African Journal on Human Rights 300

Ndula M, 'Zimbabwe's Unfulfilled Struggle for a Legitimate Constitutional Order' in Miller LE (ed), *Framing the State in Times of Transition: Case Studies in Constitution Making* (United States Institute of Peace 2010)

Nkwae B, 'Botswana's Experience on Recognizing Traditional Land Rights on a Large Scale' (2015) <https://bit. ly/3qk6TxI> accessed 30 November 2020

North DC, *Structure and Change in Economic History* (Norton 1981)

Ntsebeza L and Hall R (eds), *The Land Question in South Africa* (HSRC 2007)

O'Laughlin B, 'Past and Present Options: Land Reform in Mozambique' (1995) 63 Review of African Political Economy 99

Palmer R, 'Land Reform in Zimbabwe, 1980–1990' (1990) 89 African Affairs 163

Parsons N, *A New History of Southern Africa* (MacMillan 1982)

Persson T, 'Presidential Address: Consequences of Constitutions' (2004) 2(2–3) Journal of the European Economic Association 139

Persson T and Tabellini G, *The Economic Effects of Constitutions: What do the Data Say?* (MIT 2003)

Pistor K, *The Code of Capital: How the Law Creates Wealth and Inequality* (Princeton 2019)

Pitcher MA, 'Recreating Colonialism or Reconstructing the State? Privatisation and Politics in Mozambique' (1996) 22(1) Journal of Southern African Studies 49

Pitcher MA, 'Disruption without Transformation: Agrarian Relations and Livelihoods in Nampula Province, Mozambique 1975–1995' (1998) 24(1) Journal of Southern African Studies 115

Plaatjie ST, *Native Life in South Africa* [1916] (Longman 1987)

Platzky L and Walker C, *The Surplus People: Forced Removals in South Africa* (Ravan 1985)

Prasad BC, 'Institutional Economics and Economic Development: The Theory of Property Rights, Economic Development, Good Governance and the Environment' (2003) 30(6) International Journal of Social Economics 741

Scoones I and others, *Zimbabwe's Land Reform: Myths & Realities* (James Currey 2010)

Stern SJ, *Battling for Hearts and Minds: Memory Struggles in Pinochet's Chile, 1973–1988* (Duke 2006)

Surplus People Project, *Forced Removals in South Africa: The Surplus People Project Reports*, vols 1–5 (Surplus People Project 1983)

Tate NC and Vallinder T (eds), *The Global Expansion of Judicial Power* (New York University Press 1995)

Transvaal Rural Action Committee, *A Toehold on the Land: Labour Tenancy in the South Eastern Transvaal* (TRAC 1988)

Troncoso RE and Becerril MW, 'Chile Will Never Make Progress under Pinochet's Constitution' *Washington Post* (29 October 2019)

Vanberg VJ, 'Market and State: The Perspective of Constitutional Political Economy' (2004) Freiburg Discussion Papers on Constitutional Economics 04/10

Walker C, *Land-Marked: Land Claims & Land Restitution in South Africa* (Jacana 2008)

8

Land, Conflict, and the Economy

The Role of the Constitution in Addressing the Land Issue in Post-independence Zimbabwe

Makanatsa Makonese

1. Introduction

This chapter seeks to analyse the implementation of the constitutional and legal framework for Zimbabwe's post-independence land reform, acquisition, and redistribution programmes and the impact of such implementation on the country's economy. It examines how the Zimbabwean government applied, or failed to apply, the law and the constitution in implementing these programmes and how this affected the country's economy. Following independence in 1980, the government touted the need to reverse the impact of colonialism on the ownership and control of land and the attendant economic exclusion of the previously disadvantaged population. The post-independence government was envisaged as addressing the land question, given that '[l]and was at the heart of the first ... liberation struggle [and] the second liberation struggle which gave birth to an independent Zimbabwe in 1980'.[1] The land question was hence a key issue in the Lancaster House negotiations of 1979 which led to the adoption of the independence constitution and to the independence of Zimbabwe.

This chapter discusses Zimbabwe's constitutional and legislative framework for land and its implementation since independence until the present, with a focus on three issues. The first is the 1980 independence constitution and how it addressed the land rights of white landowners and the landless black majority. The chapter looks at the period between 1980 and 1998 and examines how the government tackled land reform and redistribution with a view to addressing historical land imbalances whilst adhering to constitutional provisions on the protection of property rights.

The second set of issues are the land provisions in constitutional amendments numbers 16 of 2000 and 17 of 2005; the land contestations that triggered the amendments; and the economic fallout from these developments. These issues can be seen as a natural progression from the government efforts that were made between 1980 and 1998 to acquire and redistribute land but which were unable to make progress in achieving racial equity in land-ownership in the country—developments which, it is argued, partly triggered the land invasions of 2000. This section of the chapter also discusses subsequent government attempts to legalize land invasions retroactively through constitutional and legislative amendments.

---

[1] Klaus Deininger, Hans Hoogeveen, and Bill H Kinsey, 'Economic Benefits and Costs of Land Redistribution in Zimbabwe in the Early 1980s' (2004) 32(10) World Development 1697.

Makanatsa Makonese, *Land, Conflict, and the Economy* In: *Constitutionalism and the Economy in Africa*. Edited by: Charles M Fombad and Nico Steytler, Oxford University Press. © Makanatsa Makonese 2022. DOI: 10.1093/oso/9780192886439.003.0010

The third issue concerns the 2013 Constitution and how it addresses the land question; the government's implementation of the Constitution; and the economic impact of these developments. In this respect, the chapter looks at government efforts to implement the constitutional provisions for compensating former white farmers for improvements on the acquired farms and for returning land to, or paying compensation for land lost by, black Zimbabwean farmers and farmers whose land was protected under the bilateral investment protection and promotion agreements (BIPPAs) and the bilateral investment treaties (BITs).[2] The government, in undertaking this initiative, emphasized the importance of the gesture in its attempts at international re-engagement and resuscitation of the economy. It maintained that this was an indication of its willingness to respect the Constitution and property rights and was therefore a rallying point for the international community and investors to invest in the country.

Using the framework above as the basis for analysis, I make the argument that the rule of law and constitutionalism are key prerequisites for economic development, albeit not the only ones. I also argue that constitutionalism and the rule of law must be in line with principles of fairness, equity, and social justice, particularly when redress is sought against the historical injustices of colonialism in Africa. Constitutionalism and the rule of law provide for the protection of the fundamental rights and freedoms that encourage business development and investment, protect workers and investors, and allow the courts to adjudicate without fear or favour on business, labour, and property disputes. The absence of the rule of law and constitutionalism, as the case of Zimbabwe's twenty-first-century land reform programme (also known as the fast-track land reform programme, FTLRP) will show, is often a recipe for economic collapse, as it leads to disinvestment, non-investment, and the collapse and failure of existing businesses and enterprises.

It is argued, furthermore, that the rule of law and constitutionalism are better protected and observed by the citizenry when they have a sense that the law is fair, just, and protects everyone equally. The chapter shows that land reform and redistribution after independence were essential for correcting Zimbabwe's historical land injustices. However, the intransigence of former white commercial farmers and the government's use of the land issue to cling to power led to an implosion that undermined constitutionalism and the rule of law and brought about the subsequent collapse of the Zimbabwean economy.

2. The Role of Land and Agriculture in the Economy

The agricultural sector is critical for the Zimbabwean economy, as it is responsible for producing the bulk of the raw materials needed in the country's industrial sector. Zimbabwe's second-largest export product after gold is tobacco, which in 2019 earned the country USD 818.1 million and contributed 19.2 per cent to its total export earnings.[3] Other important

---

[2] Section 295(1) and (2) of the Constitution provides that '[a]ny indigenous Zimbabwean whose agricultural land was acquired by the State before the effective date is entitled to compensation from the State for the land and any improvements that were on the land when it was acquired'; it also provides: 'Any person whose agricultural land was acquired by the State before the date and whose property rights at that time were guaranteed or protected by an agreement concluded by the Government of Zimbabwe with the government of another country, is entitled to compensation from the State for the land and any improvements in accordance with that agreement.'

[3] Daniel Workman, 'Zimbabwe's Top 10 Exports' *Worlds Top Exports* (nd) <http://www.worldstopexports.com/zimbabwes-top-10-exports> accessed 31 July 2020.

agricultural exports in 2019 were sugar and sugar confectionery, cotton, fruits, and nuts,[4] all of which helped prop up an ailing economy reeling from foreign exchange shortages.[5]

Land is also important for the majority of citizens, especially the poor and marginalized, who depend on land and agriculture for their subsistence. The Food and Agricultural Organization (FAO) of the United Nations finds that about 86 per cent of women in Zimbabwe depend on land for their livelihoods and food production for their families.[6] Even as the country's economy teeters on the brink of collapse as a result of political turmoil, a governance crisis, and the impact of COVID-19, the agricultural sector still employs the majority of the formally employed—the World Bank estimates that, in 2019, the figure was as high as 66.54 per cent.[7]

This is a significant proportion, given that the majority of the population are employed in the informal sector following the decimation of the formal sector due to years of economic mismanagement, poor governance, and the collapse of constitutionalism and the rule of law. These factors are attributable partly to the land reform programme, the consequences of which have led since 2000 to about 90 per cent of the population being employed in the informal sector in fields such as vending, small-scale trading, and artisanal mining.[8] Nevertheless, in spite of the informal sector's increasing importance as a source of subsistence livelihoods for the majority of the country's people, government responses to it have been at best ambivalent and ad hoc.[9]

Farmers and the informal sector have borne the brunt of prohibitions on trade and movement imposed due to the COVID-19 outbreak. For example, at the beginning of the national lockdown, police in the town of Mutare confiscated and burnt agricultural produce which had been brought to its main fresh-produce market,[10] citing lockdown regulations as the reason for their actions. In the town of Masvingo, farmers reported that 35 tonnes of bananas, 21 tonnes of avocados, and other quantities of fruits and vegetables went to waste when authorities abruptly closed the town's largest market under the COVID-19 regulations.[11] The local Fruit and Vegetables Vendors Association reported that the closure was announced at a point when the produce had been ordered and delivery trucks were en route to the town. Farmers arrived at a closed market and had to remove their tomatoes while bananas and avocados rotted.[12]

---

[4] ibid.

[5] The International Monetary Fund predicted the economy would shrink by 7.2 per cent in 2019 and by a further 7.4 per cent in 2020, with COVID-19 exacerbating economic challenges. See Elen Mabunda, 'Zim Economy to Shrink 7.4% in 2020—IMF' (EquityAxis, 15 April 2020) <https://equityaxis.net/2020/04/15/zim-economy-to-shrink-7-4-in-2020-imf/> accessed 20 November 2020.

[6] Food and Agricultural Organization of the United Nations, 'National Gender Profile of Agriculture and Rural Livelihoods' (FAO 2017).

[7] Trading Economics, 'Zimbabwe: Employment in Agriculture (% of Total Employment)' Trading Economics (nd) |<https://tradingeconomics.com/zimbabwe/employment-in-agriculture-percent-of-total-employment-wb-data.html> accessed 31 July 2020.

[8] International Labour Organization, 'Enabling Environment for Sustainable Enterprises in Zimbabwe' (ILO 2018).

[9] Government focus on the informal sector has been on tax collection and not on helping the sector to develop despite its importance to the economy. A 2 per cent electronic money tax imposed in October 2018 sought to capture tax from the informal economy, especially from mobile money transfers, which the majority of informal sector actors who are unbanked use in their financial transactions.

[10] Rumbidzai Zinyuke, 'Lockdown: Police Confiscate Vegetables' Herald (Harare, 3 April 2020).

[11] Morris Bishi, '35 Tonnes of Tomatoes and 21 Tonnes of Avocados Rot in Shut Down Masvingo Fruit and Vegetables Market' Masvingo Mirror (21 April 2020).

[12] ibid.

Incidents like these have brought hardship to a populace dependent for their livelihoods on agriculture and the informal trade in agricultural produce. The central fresh-produce markets in the urban areas were, however, amongst the first to be reopened following protests from farmers who had struggled to sell their produce under the restrictive lockdown regulations,[13] a fact that again highlights the importance of agriculture to the country's economy and national food security.

COVID-19 also impacted on the sale of tobacco on the auction floors in the capital, Harare, where the bulk of tobacco is usually sold. Farmers travel to Harare and spend days sleeping at the auction floors as they await the auctioning of their tobacco and processing of their payments. With the outbreak of COVID-19, this was no longer possible. As a result, tobacco auctioning was decentralized, with floors being opened in major tobacco-growing regions such as Karoi in Mashonaland West Province. This was costly to the auction floors but beneficial to farmers, who spent less on transport and other costs associated with travel to Harare.

On the strength of these measures, the Tobacco Industry Marketing Board could report that, by the end of July 2020, tobacco sales had reached USD 383.1 million, representing growth of 8 per cent on sales in the same period in 2019.[14] The authorities had realized the importance of tobacco to the economy and put measures in place to ensure minimum disruption to sales in the face of the pandemic. Indeed, the bulk of the country's tobacco grown these days is by small-scale farmers who benefited from the land reform programme. They constitute 80 per cent of Zimbabwe's tobacco growers and produce two-thirds of the annual tobacco output,[15] which shows that to some extent the black people who benefited from the land reform programme are beginning to make a meaningful, albeit small, contribution to the economy. This contribution pales into insignificance, however, in view of the economic collapse brought about by the chaotic, unplanned implementation of the fast-track land reform programme.

3. Colonial Land Acquisition and the Social Justice Argument

To understand the place of the rule of law and constitutionalism in Zimbabwe's current debates on land and the economy, one has to go back to the country's colonial history. It is also important to recognize that, other than being an economic asset, land also played and continues to play many other roles in the lives of Zimbabweans. These include a spiritual role, with many Zimbabweans closely tied to their villages of origin or ancestral homes regardless of their location in the world.

In recognition of this reality, the Traditional Leaders Act, 1998 in dealing with access and occupation of customary land in the country, provides that '[e]very person who, in terms of local customs and traditions, is entitled to reside in communal land and has maintained a homestead there may continue to do so ... notwithstanding that he/she may reside elsewhere'.[16] This is in recognition of the spiritual link many Zimbabweans have with their

---

[13] Reuters, 'Zimbabwe Reopens Produce Markets after Protests by Drought-Hit Farmers' *Daily Maverick* (9 April 2020).

[14] NewsDay, 'Tobacco Sales Reach US$383,1m' *NewsDay* (31 July 2020) <http://www.newsday.co.zw/2020/07/tobacco-sales-reach-us3831m/> accessed 1 August 2020.

[15] Ian Nkala, 'Tobacco Farming in Zimbabwe: Profit, Problems and Solutions' *FarmBiz* (31 December 2019).

[16] Traditional Leaders Act, s 27(1).

ancestral lands. This spiritual dimension was also reflected in the country's liberation struggle, when nationalists and freedom fighters emphasized the notion that the fight was over land and the restoration of the identity and dignity of the people of Zimbabwe. Phrases such as 'mwana wevhu' (son of the soil) were used to describe all black people in the then Rhodesia without regard to ethnicity.[17] Land was thus a large political question that went beyond its role in the economy and the daily subsistence of the population.

In the colonial-era contestation around land, laws, often unjust, played an important role in determining access, control, and ownership of it. The law was used by the colonial government in compulsory land and livestock acquisition and in livestock population control, thereby shaping the colonial economic and political system. Laws such as the Native Land Husbandry Act of 1951, the Land Apportionment Act of 1930, the Maize Control Act of 1930, the Cattle Levy Act of 1931, the Land Tenure Act of 1969, and the Tribal Trust Land Act of 1965 were used to regulate and justify land acquisition, to support white agriculture, and to limit the black population's involvement in the country's agricultural economy. The same laws were used to segregate land occupation and ownership along racial lines whilst giving the white population a stronghold in the country's economy.

The same laws were used to limit the amount of livestock that blacks could keep on their decreasing landholdings as they were pushed into native reserves[18] following the compulsory acquisition of their land. The limit on livestock numbers led to massive destocking, with much of the destocked cattle taken over by white settlers or forcibly sold to the white population. In addition to drastically reducing the number of cattle that blacks could keep, the veterinary disease control regulations imposed by the settler government further disrupted the social and economic lives of the majority black population in that livestock was often killed on the pretext that it was diseased.

Blacks clearly and justifiably saw the white settler economy as a threat to their social, political, and economic structure. The fact that laws and rules were enforced with brute force intensified resentment towards the laws of the white settler system, leading to the country's first and second *chimurenga* or *umvukela*[19] wars (wars of liberation). As successive white settler governments put in place race-based land occupation and segregation laws, better legal protections were provided for land that was owned and occupied by the white population through strong tenure systems, whilst minimal protections were given for land occupied by black people in the native reserves, later named communal land after independence. To the present day, the lack of security of tenure in communal areas is cited as one of the reasons for poor investment and agricultural productivity in these areas; conversely, it has been argued that improved security of tenure there would increase investment and improve productivity.[20]

The two Zimbabwean Liberation Wars (1896–97 and 1966–79) were therefore primarily fought over land. However, the wars also sought to dismantle colonial ideologies, including

---

[17] I Muwati, DE Mutasa, and ML Bopape, 'The Zimbabwean Liberation War: Contesting Representations of Nation and Nationalism in Historical Fiction' (2010) 31(1) Literator 147.

[18] Native reserves were created by Native Reserves Order in Council in 1898 to set aside land where black people could be concentrated, whereas white people took the bulk of the best land in the country. Native reserves were established in the marginal and arid areas characterized by poor soils and rainfall.

[19] *Chimurenga* and *umvukela* are Shona and Ndebele words, respectively, meaning 'uprising' or 'liberation war'.

[20] Toby Penrhys, 'Land and Tenure in Zimbabwe's Communal Areas: Why Land Reform Was Needed' *Future Agricultures* (14 October 2019) <http://www.future-agricultures.org/blog/land-and-tenure-in-zimbabwes-communal-areas-why-land-reform-was-needed/> accessed 2 August 2020.

in relation to racial segregation and discrimination. Further areas of contention were the exclusion of blacks from mainstream economic activities and other opportunities such as access to education. Land was central, then, and it continues to define politics in the country today, where it is regarded as key to the black majority's economic emancipation. As such, although other economic sectors, such as manufacturing and mining, also excluded the majority black population, it was the agricultural economy that captured the minds of all— the unfairness of compulsory land acquisition and mass evictions from ancestral land was unquestionable and glaringly visible to everyone.

Accordingly, when the war of liberation ended in 1979, leading to the country's independence in 1980, the country's constitution and laws were expected to address the inequalities in the country's race-based landownership structures. At independence, 'about 15 million hectares of predominantly good quality land [were] owned by about 6,100 families of European descent, and 16.4 million hectares of less fertile land [were] occupied by a little less than 800,000 indigenous families'.[21] This situation had to be addressed through a new constitutional and legal order, taking into consideration that most of this land had been forcibly taken away from the black people. The section below provides insight into how the independence constitution engaged with the land issue and how the independence government implemented its provisions in regard to acquisition and redistribution of land.

4. Land Reform between 1980 and 1990

Despite the centrality of the land question in the independence negotiations, Britain has argued that there was never an agreement regarding its role in paying for the costs of land reform in independent Zimbabwe.[22] The Zimbabwean government, on the other hand, has insisted that Britain and the United States of America made commitments to support it financially in paying for land acquisition for redistribution to the black majority but later reneged on this agreement.[23] This lack of clarity about the nature of the agreement reached in the Lancaster House negotiations would partly trigger chaotic farm invasions almost two decades later, when the British government openly told Zimbabwe that it was not responsible for funding the country's land reform programme.[24]

The independence constitutional arrangements were a compromise, though one which the leaders of the liberation movement viewed as anything but ideal. Indeed, some authors have argued that far from entering into a compromise, the liberation leaders were essentially ignored and emasculated during the negotiations, with many of their proposals regarding the land question having been disregarded. Madhuku argues that

> they lacked the political muscle to ensure a different framework. Real political power at the Lancaster House Conference lay with the British government whose avowed aim was to preserve white settler privileges. The framework which eventually appeared in the

---

[21] Deininger, Hoogeveen, and Kinsey (n 1).
[22] Africa All Parliamentary Group, 'Land in Zimbabwe: Past Mistakes, Future Prospects' (2009).
[23] Martin Plaut, 'US Backed Zimbabwe Land Reform' BBC News (22 August 2007).
[24] In a letter dated 5 November 1997, the then British Secretary of State for International Development, Claire Short, wrote a letter to the Zimbabwean Minister of Agriculture in which she stated, 'I should make it clear that we do not accept that Britain has a special responsibility to meet the costs of land purchase in Zimbabwe.'

constitution was derived, almost *verbatim*, from the proposals put forward by the British government.[25]

The independence constitution hence maintained the status quo under the pretext of protecting property rights. The relevant provision stated:

> Every person shall be protected from having his property compulsorily acquired except when the acquisition is in the interests of defence, public safety, public order, public morality, public health, town and country planning, the development or utilisation of that property in such a manner as to promote public benefit or, in the case of *under-utilised land*, settlement of land for agricultural purposes. Once property is wanted for one of these purposes, its acquisition will be lawful only on condition that the law provides for the prompt payment of adequate compensation and, where the acquisition is contested, that a court order is obtained. A person whose property is so acquired will be guaranteed the right of access to the High Court to determine the amount of compensation.[26]

With this provision, the Lancaster House Independence Constitution ensured the protection of the white minority's economic interests by stipulating that the state had to buy land on a willing-seller-willing-buyer basis and that only 'under-utilised land' could be acquired compulsorily—in the event that such land was compulsorily acquired, compensation still had to be paid promptly and could be sent to any country in the world as chosen by the owner of the acquired land.[27] Those who received compensation also sent their money outside the country, thus depriving the local economy of an opportunity for it to be reinvested there.

Moreover, the provision was entrenched in the Bill of Rights and could not be amended for ten years after independence except with the agreement of all members of the House of Assembly.[28] Given that the same constitution reserved twenty seats in the Assembly for the white minority for the same ten-year period by stating that '20 members [of Parliament] will be elected by voters on the White Voters Roll',[29] it meant in effect that the clause could not be changed during the period. This ensured minimal disruption to landownership patterns, with the result that the independence constitution did little to aid land redistribution and correct the injustices of colonialism. Although the new government was determined to address the land issue, it was legally and constitutionally hamstrung.

The first piece of legislation used to implement the constitutional provisions on land acquisition was the 1985 Land Acquisition Act. To increase the amount of land available for acquisition and redistribution, the Act gave the government a right of first refusal in all agricultural land sales. However, even with this provision, the government argued that, given the protections that white farm owners enjoyed, very little land was made available for

---

[25] Lovemore Madhuku, 'Law, Politics and the Land Reform Process in Zimbabwe' in Medicine Masiiwa (ed), *Post-independence Land Reform in Zimbabwe* (FES and IDS 2004).

[26] Zimbabwe Lancaster House (Independence) Constitution, 1979; emphasis added.

[27] The Lancaster House Agreement in art V(3) provided that 'Compensation paid in respect of loss of land to anyone who is a citizen of or ordinarily resident in Zimbabwe (or to a company the majority of whose shareholders are such persons) will, within a reasonable time, be remittable to any country outside Zimbabwe, free from any deduction, tax or charge in respect of its remission.'

[28] ibid art 30.

[29] ibid art 10(b).

purchase; that the prices charged for it were exorbitant; and that there were not enough con-tiguous farms to make large-scale resettlement viable;[30] the farms that were made available were also mainly in the arid Natural/Agricultural Regions IV and V. Some researchers have argued that the government was in fact offered land in high-value areas but rejected it as ei-ther too expensive or too small for resettlement purposes.[31]

Although there were varying reasons for the unavailability of land, the result was that the pace of land reform was slow. Section 3 of the Land Acquisition Act, in line with the constitution, allowed for compulsory acquisition only if the land was considered derelict or underutilized; in this regard, white farmers resisted the new Act, charging exorbitant prices for derelict or abandoned land or simply holding on to it.[32] Furthermore, the requirement for prompt payment of adequate compensation meant that the government needed money even for land that was not considered ideal. Consequently, it was difficult for the new gov-ernment or any beneficiaries of the available land to establish a successful agricultural eco-nomic sector,[33] with the result that 'between 1980 and 1990 only 71,000 out of a target of 162,000 were resettled'[34]—a level of resettlement that was below the targets the government considered ideal for meeting the land needs of the black population.

Given that the resettlement was on derelict, abandoned, or low-rainfall land, the majority of people who obtained land did not necessarily get allocations that made it possible to use agriculture to engage competitively in the country's economy. Named 'minda mirefu', or 'the long fields', the land allocated in this first phase of the resettlement programme came to mirror the communal lands from which many of the beneficiaries originated. Over time, it became fragmented as families allocated pieces of land to children who had grown up and wanted to build homes for their new families. Marongwe notes that 'the continued frag-mentation of farming plots (largely due to population increases), 60% of which ranged from 1.6–3.2 ha, [has contributed] to reduced productivity'.[35]

The initial selection criteria for resettlement were social and political, with priority given to refugees from the recently ended liberation war, landless people, those displaced by the war, former freedom fighters, and former farmworkers and other persons in need.[36] The al-location was made 'irrespective of age, literacy levels, farming experience and management capacity'.[37] Although this approach was necessary from a social and political perspective, it was not geared towards people who would be serious participants in the country's agricul-tural economy, given that beneficiaries mostly lacked the capacity and resources to use the land for anything beyond meeting subsistence needs.

---

[30] Michael R Roth and John W Bruce, 'Land Tenure, Agrarian Structure, and Comparative Land Use Efficiency in Zimbabwe: Options for Land Tenure Reform and Land Redistribution' (University of Wisconsin-Madison, 1994).

[31] ibid.

[32] Sobona Mtisi, 'Water Reforms during the Crisis and Beyond: Understanding Policy and Political Challenges of Reforming the Water Sector in Zimbabwe' (Overseas Development Institute, 2011).

[33] Emmanuel R Marabuka, 'Critical Analysis of Willing Buyer Willing Seller Framework in Relation Reform in Zimbabwe' (Lupane State University 2013).

[34] Prince Mario, *Zimbabwe, Land and the Dictator* <https://books.google.co.za/books?id=zi-tWekXb D8C&printsec=frontcover&source=gbs_vpt_buy#v=onepage&q&f=false> accessed 23 May 2019.

[35] Nelson Marongwe, 'Redistributive Land Reform and Poverty Reduction in Zimbabwe: A working paper for the research project on "Livelihoods after Land Reform"'.

[36] Zimbabwe Land Reform and Resettlement Programme, Phase I.

[37] Francis T Gonese and others, 'Land Reform and Resettlement Implementation in Zimbabwe: An Overview of the Programme against Selected International Experiences' <https://minds.wisconsin.edu/bitstream/handle/1793/23060/LRRPOverview.pdf?sequence=1> accessed 2 August 2020.

The agricultural economy therefore remained in the hands of the large-scale commercial farmers, the majority of whom were still white. It is pertinent to note, however, that given the 'willing-buyer-willing-seller' principle, during this period some black people managed to buy high-value farms from white farmers outside the government's land reform programme. They were, nevertheless, a small political and economic elite, and their access to land could not be equated with meeting the needs of the majority of the population, who remained without land and were growing increasingly disillusioned by the government's failure to avail this resource.

As a result of this disillusionment, there were many incidents soon after independence when people invaded land[38] to express their need for land and call on the government to provide it. As will be shown, such disillusionment fuelled the major land invasions of the late 1990s and early 2000s and led to the economic disruption that haunts Zimbabwe to this day.

5. Land Reform between 1990 and 1998

Realizing the shortcomings of the independence land-acquisition framework, the government moved to amend the Constitution after the expiry of the ten-year entrenchment period in order to speed up land acquisition. Constitutional Amendment No 11 of 1990 provided for the compulsory acquisition of land and also ousted the courts' jurisdiction over deciding whether compensation paid for such land was fair or not. This gave the government greater latitude to acquire land and pay what it considered fair without having to worry about the payments being contested in the courts of law.

Following the 1990 constitutional amendments, the Land Acquisition Act: Chapter 20:10 was promulgated in 1992, repealing the similarly named 1985 Act. As with previous laws (such as the 1985 Land Acquisition Act), white commercial farmers opposed both the constitutional amendments and the 1992 Land Acquisition Act. Litigation was often used as a strategy to fight the laws and the government's implementation efforts. Slow and ineffectual as the programme might have been, the landowners could not take any chances by appearing to acquiesce in the government's compulsory acquisition efforts.

In instances where litigation was used, the courts gave judgments that seemed to support the land reform programme. Madhuku argues that the dismissal of the case of *Davies and Ors v Minister of Lands, Agriculture and Water Development*[39] by both the High Court and the Supreme Court 'demonstrated the readiness of the courts to support the thrust of the land reform process'.[40] This was the first case to be brought to court by white commercial farmers after the 1990 constitutional amendments, the aim being to challenge government processes in designating land for compulsory acquisition for resettlement purposes.

Despite the dismissal of the case by the courts, such challenges to the country's land reforms raised tensions between white commercial farmers and the government, with questions being raised about the sincerity of the farmers' commitment to land reform. In effect,

---

[38] Thomas W Mitchell, 'The Land Crisis in Zimbabwe: Getting Beyond the Myopic Focus upon Black and White' (2001) 11(3) Indiana International and Comparative Law Review 587–603.

[39] 1996 (1) ZLR 681 (S).

[40] Madhuku, (n 25).

then, due to resistance by the farmers and the government's desire to proceed with caution so as not to wreck the economy, the passing of Constitutional Amendment No 11 and the new Land Acquisition Act did not substantially increase the pace of land reform. These delays, however, only served to increase frustration amongst people eager to receive land from the government.

As resistance by white commercial farmers and legal challenges to the land reform programme dragged on, questions were raised about whether land reform in Zimbabwe could be achieved by the legal and constitutional route or by adopting a more radical approach. The latter approach, as will be shown below, was adopted by some of the country's citizens and acquiesced to by the ZANU-PF government at a critical moment as it fought for its political survival, triggering a crisis in the rule of law and constitutionalism that brought about the country's economic downfall.

6. Mass Land Invasions and the Crisis of Constitutionalism

In 1998, frustrations over the slow pace of land reform and redistribution boiled over and resulted in widespread farm invasions. The Svosve people of Mashonaland East Province, led by their chief, invaded farms in the highly productive Marondera area. In previous land invasions, invariably of land that was unproductive or appeared abandoned, the government had evicted the invaders in line with the need to protect the land rights of the affected owners. Similarly, in the Svosve incident, the government, through then Vice-President Simon Muzenda, again ordered people to leave the occupied farms and await proper allocation of land in terms of the country's laws.[41] Although the Svosve people left the farms, this was the most highly visible farm invasion to date, given that, for the first time, invaders had targeted highly productive farms. The seeds of protest over land inequalities had been sown.

Numerous sporadic invasions were witnessed in the following years, mainly as protest action taken by communal land dwellers seeking to highlight their land needs. Eventually, these protests found favour with the ZANU-PF ruling party when it lost the 2000 national referendum on the draft constitution, with the result that ZANU-PF-aligned war veterans of the liberation struggle led mass land occupations. The refusal by the police to enforce High Court eviction orders following these invasions—on the argument that the land issue was political and not the responsibility of the police[42]—was the first sign of the erosion of the rule of law and constitutionalism in the country. The government supported this stance, which emboldened the farm invaders.

In *Commissioner of Police v Commercial Farmers' Union*,[43] the mainly white commercial farmers initially sought and obtained an order by consent for the police to evict farm invaders from the farms they had occupied across the country. However, the police eventually refused to comply with the order, citing lack of personnel to enforce the court order even though the real reason was clearly that the executive branch of government, including its ministers and the President, had in effect ordered them not to abide by the court order.[44]

---

[41] Fortious Nhambura, 'Celebrating Pioneers of Land Reform' *Herald* (Harare, 30 July 2015).

[42] 'How We Were Dispossessed' *PoliticsWeb* (28 August 2018) <http://www.politicsweb.co.za/opinion/how-we-were-dispossessed> accessed 24 August 2018.

[43] 2000 (1) ZLR 503 (HC).

[44] In its ruling, the court noted that 'from the consent paper, there is enough indication on the papers filed of record in this matter that the Executive has been unwilling to assist him [Commissioner General of Police] in the

In an unusual turn of events, the police approached the High Court for them to be absolved from the implementation of the court order. The High Court dismissed the Commissioner of Police's plea not to implement the court order, declaring the invasions illegal and ordering the Commissioner to assist the Sherriff of the High Court in effecting the eviction of the farm invaders. Still the Commissioner of Police did not implement the court order.

In an earlier case in 2000, *Commercial Farmers' Union v Minister of Land, Agriculture and Resettlement*,[45] the Supreme Court of Zimbabwe had an opportunity not only to deal with the land invasions but to determine the legality of the country's FTLRP. In this case, the full bench of the Supreme Court sitting as the Constitutional Court ruled that the programme was unplanned, unlawful, and unconstitutional. This, the court ruled, was because it infringed on the white farmers' property rights and failed to accord the farmers and farmworkers the full protection of the law, as guaranteed in the Constitution.

At the time of this ruling, there was open hostility between the courts and the government, with war veterans disrupting Supreme Court sessions[46] and the executive castigating judges and pressuring them to resign. The Minister of Justice visited some of the judges, telling them the government had 'lost confidence in them'[47] and they should step down. Although they initially resisted, the targeted judges, including the Chief Justice,[48] who was white, all eventually resigned—the then Minister of Justice, Patrick Chinamasa, had accused the Chief Justice of racism for not supporting the land reform programme.[49] Justice Godfrey Chidyausiku, who was viewed as supportive of the government's land reform, was appointed as Chief Justice. In supporting the appointment, the then Minister of Information and Publicity, Jonathan Moyo, said that '[n]o sane Zimbabwean should expect the judiciary to be headed by a foreigner—especially a British—20 years after our independence, just like it would be insane to have a foreign or British President or Speaker of Parliament'.[50]

Instead of following due process in dealing with court judgments with which they disagreed, the government vilified judges as racists if they were in support of white farmers and thus unlikely to rule in favour of the land reform programme. On this basis, the government could purport to justify failure to abide by court judgments and the rule of law.

Over time, the government's failure to obey court judgments and respect the rule of law exacerbated the economic challenges caused by the farm invasions as it clearly showed that the government would not protect the property rights of investors and obey court orders if courts ruled in their favour. Investors consequently shunned Zimbabwe as an investment destination, whilst some of those already in the country disinvested and took their capital

---

task before him. I would like to urge to the Executive to recognise that the permanent interest of Zimbabwe and the rule of law are served by ensuring that the land invasions are brought to an immediate end … On one side, the courts have issued an order which he should enforce and, on the other, the Executive is giving conflicting signals as to what he must do, if it is not showing outrightly that it condones the farm invasions.'

[45]   Constitutional Application No 262/2000.

[46]   Reuters reported on 25 November 2000 that 'about 300 self-styled independence war veterans disrupted the hearing when they broke into the court building and chased away lawyers representing the mainly white Commercial Farmers' Union. Order was restored, and the court reconvened later.' See Reuters, 'Ruling Favoring Black Squatters Nullified' *Los Angeles Times* (California, 25 November 2000).

[47]   SAPA-AFP, 'Zim to Start Firing Judges' *News24* (23 February 2001).

[48]   Anthony Gubbay.

[49]   Lewis Machipisa, 'Politics-Zimbabwe: A Top Judge Appointed Chief Justice' *Inter Press Service News Agency* (Harare, 9 March 2001).

[50]   ibid.

elsewhere. As will be seen, the government used the constitutional amendment route to ensure that, in future, judges would have no role to play in determining land-related matters.

With the courts having been emasculated, the rule of law disregarded, and constitutionalism ignored, white landowners were forcibly evicted from their farms on scale, an episode that has been described as 'arguably one of the primary drivers of Zimbabwe's sudden economic downfall'.[51] The question that needs to be asked is: why did the government support the farm invasions at this point in time? The political and economic consequences were clearly adverse, and in the past, acutely aware of them, the government had discouraged land invasions. There has been debate as to whether it was in control of the farm invasions when war veterans and others went on the rampage, or instead was caught off-guard and, aware that it had lost control, tried to save face by condoning them. It could also be argued that the ZANU-PF government realized that its power was waning, especially after losing the vote—the first time since independence—in the 2000 constitutional referendum, and thus encouraged the invasions as a populist move to gain political support from the landless majority.

In supporting the land invasions, the government and ZANU-PF party argued that white farmers and the international community had campaigned against the draft constitution because of its provisions for compulsory land acquisition. This was true, as white commercial farmers and the international community were indeed against these proposed constitutional provisions. However, in addition, at this stage the country's economy was already on a downward trend, with the state of the economy having been cited as one of the reasons for the disillusionment that led to the rejection of the draft constitution in the referendum.[52] Moreover, civil society organizations, the opposition, and some members of the Constitutional Commission campaigned for people to vote 'No' on the draft constitution because clauses had been changed by President Mugabe outside the constitution-making process.

In particular, the draft constitution proposed that Mugabe step down as executive president to assume the position of a ceremonial presidential position while an elected prime minister took up executive functions. This was replaced by a clause allowing for an executive president with a two-term limit.[53] It therefore enabled Mugabe, who by then had been in power for more than twenty years, to stand for two future terms notwithstanding the new two-term limit in the draft constitution, which, it was argued, was not retroactive.[54]

The campaigns for and against the draft constitution were vigorous and often turned violent. The blame for the violence was placed on ZANU-PF, which was accused of waging a campaign of terror to force people to vote in favour of the draft constitution. In the run-up to the referendum, one newspaper reported:

> President Robert Mugabe's ruling ZANU-PF party has been accused of unleashing a campaign of violent intimidation against people campaigning for a no vote in Zimbabwe's

---

[51] Zimbabwe Human Rights NGO Forum, 'Land and Property Rights in Zimbabwe Reform' (2010).

[52] Henri E Cauvin, 'Zimbabwe Signals It Still Plans to Seize White-Owned Farms' *New York Times* (New York, 3 March 2000).

[53] Draft Constitution of Zimbabwe of 2000, s 3(2)(6).

[54] Barbara Slaughter and Stuart Nolan, 'Zimbabwe: Referendum Defeat for Mugabe Shakes Zanu-PF Government' *World Socialist Web Site* (22 February 2000) <http://www.wsws.org/en/articles/2000/02/zimb-f22.html> accessed 28 May 2019.

constitutional referendum, to be held this weekend. Several recent incidents indicate that Mr Mugabe's supporters have been beating up and threatening those working to reject the draft constitution in the referendum. Police are accused of failing to take action against those responsible for the attacks.[55]

As farm invasions spread across the country, they even extended to farms and estates protected internationally through BIPPAs and BITs. These were two-way agreements or treaties signed between the government and other countries to promote, protect, and encourage investment between Zimbabwe and the signatory country; in particular, they ensured the protection of the investors' property rights in either country. Land that was bought or leased through BIPPAs and BITs was thus immune from compulsory acquisition under the land reform programme.

BIPPAs and BITs were vital to Zimbabwe's investment promotion architecture and had 'a significant bearing on the ability of the country to mobilise financial and material resources from other countries for the much-needed foreign direct investment'.[56] However, by allowing the invasions of BIPPA- and BIT-protected farms and estates, the government showed that it was unconcerned not only about protecting the property rights of investing farmers but about the implications of the farm invasions for international trade and investment. This pushed existing and potential investors away and, with investor confidence waning, further weakened the country's economy and its prospects of growth.

The invasion of BIPPA- and BIT-protected farms was also an indication of how chaotic the land reform programme was, given that these farms were divorced from the country's history of colonialism. The farmers who owned such land had bought it after independence and could not be regarded as being among the beneficiaries of colonialism whose land could be targeted for acquisition and redistribution. Indeed, the chaos extended to farms owned by black Zimbabwean farmers, who likewise lost their land in the turmoil and failure to make the necessary assessments and distinctions. In its haste to turn the land issue into a political and electoral campaign issue, the ZANU-PF government encouraged lawlessness and created a haphazard land occupation scenario that brought social, economic, and political upheaval.

7. Constitutional Amendments Numbers 16 of 2000 and 17 of 2005

Soon after losing the draft constitution referendum in 2000, the government moved to pass the contentious provisions on compulsory land acquisition in the rejected draft constitution through a constitutional amendment. This expedited process was strategic, as the ruling ZANU PF party wanted to use its overwhelming parliamentary majority to pass the constitutional amendments ahead of the parliamentary elections scheduled for June of the same year (2000). The amendment was hence enacted into law on 6 April 2000. With regard to the land issue, it provided that the colonial power, Britain, was responsible for paying compensation for land acquired for resettlement purposes, and that if the latter failed to pay

---

[55] Andrew Meldrum, 'Violence before the Vote' *The Guardian* (Harare, 9 February 2000).
[56] Former Minister of Finance Herbert Murerwa during the presentation of the 2006 National Budget. See A Mukaro, 'Govt in Climbdown on Bilateral Agreements' *Zimbabwe Independent* (Harare, 28 October 2005).

for such compensation, the government had no obligation to do so. The amendment stated further that this provision was made in consideration of the following:

- that under colonial domination, the people of Zimbabwe were unjustifiably dispossessed of their land and other resources without compensation;
- that the people consequently took up arms in order to regain their land and political sovereignty, and this ultimately resulted in the independence of Zimbabwe in 1980; and
- that the people of Zimbabwe must be enabled to reassert their rights and regain ownership of their land.[57]

In plain terms, the government's claim was that colonialists had stolen land from the black majority and that it would not pay to get that land back. The provisions opened the way for the government to gazette more land for acquisition and protect people who had invaded farms by the time of the constitutional amendment. To reinforce these provisions, the government in 2001 promulgated the Rural Land Occupiers (Protection from Eviction) Act, Chapter 20:26. The Act sought to protect from eviction people who had illegally invaded farms; moreover, it barred the courts from issuing orders for eviction against occupiers or for compensation for damages to white farmers whose land would have been occupied. The Act stated in part that

> no court shall issue any order for the recovery of possession from a protected occupier of any rural land, or the ejectment therefrom of a protected occupier, or the payment of damages by such protected occupier in respect of the occupation or trespass of such land during any period referred to in section four.[58]

Given the tension between the courts and the executive on the land issue, the government sought to clip the courts' wings even further. To this end, Constitutional Amendment No 17 was passed in 2005, barring landowners from approaching the courts to challenge the acquisition of their land or the compensation paid for improvements on the farms. The provision stated that no person shall

> apply to a court to challenge the acquisition of the land by the State, and no court shall entertain any such challenge [and] ... challenge the amount of compensation payable for any improvements effected on the land before it was acquired.[59]

With these provisions, it effectively became impossible for any person to approach the courts for relief in relation to the agricultural land acquisition programme, be it with regard to the acquisition of the land or the amount of compensation to be paid for the improvements upon such acquisition. This further undermined the role and authority of the courts in dealing with the land issue, and denied citizens their rights to property, access to justice, and equal protection of the law. All these tenets were protected in the Bill of Rights but were

---

[57] Section 16A(1).
[58] Rural Land Occupiers (Protection from Eviction) Act: Chapter 20:26, s 3(2).
[59] Section 16B(3)(a) and (b).

excepted when it came to their application in relation to the land reform programme. The constitutional provisions in turn required amendment of the Land Acquisition Act to facilitate its implementation.

The challenge with these constitutional and legal amendments was that they were promulgated to legalize land invasions that had occurred outside of the provisions of the Constitution and the law at the time of the invasions. This undermined the legitimacy of subsequent land reform processes that were implemented in terms of the new constitutional and legal order, despite their being clothed with legality and constitutionalism. It was in essence a continuation of the colonial system which had used laws to clothe illegitimate and unfair land and property grabs from black people and give land and property to the white minority. The difference was that the land invasions and the constitutionally clothed land grabs in post-independence Zimbabwe happened at a time when the new world order and the international community was more averse to human rights violations and attentative to promoting constitutionalism and the rule of law. A departure from such tenets therefore would inevitably have economic and political consequences.

Before the advent of the land invasions and that of the subsequent constitutional and legal provisions legalizing them and the state take-over of farms, Zimbabwe was considered the bread basket of southern Africa, with agriculture as the mainstay of its economy. As Sachikonye notes, 'prior to land reform, an estimated 320,000 to 350,000 farm workers were employed on commercial farms owned by about 4,500 white farmers'.[60] The farm invasions and eviction of white farmers led to the decimation of the agriculture sector and to attendant job losses. Perhaps more significantly, the collapse of this sector led in turn to the collapse of the industrial sector, given that the latter was largely dependent on inputs from agriculture. This led to job losses not only in agriculture but industry as well. Tax revenues from both employee and company taxes were wiped out, leaving the government unable to meet its obligations, including to multilateral lending institutions such as the International Monetary Fund (IMF) and the World Bank, and resulting in the suspension of further lending from these institutions.

The government insisted that the suspension of lending by the IMF and the World Bank was due the sanctions imposed by the European Union (EU) and US in reaction to the land reform programme and had nothing to do with its failure to service its debts. My argument, however, is that the country's disregard of the rule of law, human rights, and constitutionalism through the manner in which the land reform programme was implemented triggered a response from the international community (individual countries, economic communities, and multilateral financial and lending institutions) at both a political and economic level that contributed to the deterioration of the economy. The fact that the ZANU-PF government leapt on to an otherwise legitimate rally by Zimbabweans for racial equity in landownership for its own political survival also undermined the social-justice argument for land reform in the country.

---

[60] Llyod Sachikonye, 'The Situation of Commercial Farm Workers after Land Reform in Zimbabwe' (Farm Community Trust 2003).

8. White Farmers' Efforts to Seek Justice outside Zimbabwe

The provisions ousting the jurisdiction of the courts and denying citizens access to the courts became the subject of a long-running international battle between the government and white commercial farmers after they took the matter to the Southern African Development Community (SADC) Tribunal[61] for determination.

Before doing so, the farmers had attempted without success to approach the Supreme Court of Zimbabwe for adjudication of their grievances.[62] In that case, the Supreme Court ruled that the Constitution was clear and unambiguous that the courts had no jurisdiction over land matters and dismissed the case in its entirety. The litigants decided to approach the SADC Tribunal, a regional court established in terms of the SADC Treaty of 1992 and operationalized in 2005, in the case of *Mike Campbell (Pvt) Ltd and Others v Republic of Zimbabwe*.[63] The *Campbell* case was the most high-profile case the Tribunal had been seized with since its establishment and, ironically, also led to its demise.

The applicants argued that the land reform programme in Zimbabwe was unconstitutional and its implementation constituted discrimination on the grounds of race; in addition, they argued that they had approached the SADC Tribunal for relief because they had been barred in effect from approaching any court in Zimbabwe to present their cases. The SADC Tribunal agreed with the applicants, declaring that they had been denied access to the courts in Zimbabwe; had been discriminated against on the ground of race; and that fair compensation was payable to them for their lands compulsorily acquired by the respondent. In view of these conclusions, the Tribunal ordered the government to take all 'necessary measures, through its agents, to protect the possession, occupation and ownership of the lands of the Applicants, except those that had already been evicted', and to pay the applicants fair compensation.

The ruling emphasized Zimbabwe's obligations under international law regardless of the laws it passed at the national level, including constitutional provisions that had the effect of unfairly limiting the rights of the applicants. Moyo rightly argues that 'the implication [was] that national legislation and policy should be consistent with the [SADC] Treaty and other international instruments'.[64] However, when the applicants applied to register the judgment with the courts in Zimbabwe for enforcement, the application was dismissed, with the High Court ruling as follows:

> In the result, having regard to the foregoing considerations and the overwhelmingly negative impact of the Tribunal's decision on domestic law and agrarian reform in Zimbabwe, and notwithstanding the international obligations of the Government, I am amply satisfied that the registration and consequent enforcement of that judgment would be fundamentally contrary to the public policy of this country.[65]

---

[61] The SADC Tribunal was established by the SADC Treaty, and before its abolishment was the judicial arm of the fifteen-member SADC.

[62] *Mike Campbell (Pty) Ltd v Minister of National Security Responsible for Land, Land Reform and Resettlement* (SC 49/07).

[63] (2/2007) [2008] SADCT 2.

[64] Admark Moyo, 'Defending Human Rights and the Rule of Law by the SADC Tribunal: Campbell and Beyond' (2009) 9(2) African Human Rights Law Journal 590.

[65] *Gramara (Private) Limited and Another v Government of the Republic of Zimbabwe and Ors* HH 5483/09.

With this ruling providing no platform to enforce their judgment, the white commercial farmers were left with an empty victory. The government was not satisfied with this, though, and sought to dismantle any opposition to its land reform programme. It embarked on a campaign to have the SADC Tribunal disbanded, successfully achieving this when the Tribunal was reconstituted through a new protocol in 2014 that reduced it to an inter-state court in which individuals, both natural and juristic, were barred from suing their governments.

Farmers who held their land in terms of BIPPAs and BITs with the government also sought international justice through international arbitration procedures, given that the agreements provided for such remedies. In the cases of *Border Timbers Limited, Timber Products International (Private) Limited, and Hangani Developments Co (Private) Limited v Zimbabwe*[66] and *Bernhard von Pezold and others v Zimbabwe*,[67] the International Centre for Settlement of Investment Disputes (ICSID) ordered the government to return applicants' farms that had been seized without compensation. In addition, the ICSID ordered it to pay one of the applicants USD 65 million as compensation for lost value.

Predictably, the government did not comply with these orders. This further exposed Zimbabwe as a country that does not respect the rule of law and constitutionalism with regard to the protection of property rights. This again discouraged investment in the country, serving to underline that the protection of property rights and the ability of the courts to mediate in commercial and other business-related disputes is critical to attracting both foreign direct and local investment: without such protections, investments will be limited or dry up, leading to economic collapse or stagnation. As will be shown later, in 2020 the government initiated legal processes to compensate farmers from whom land protected under BIPPAs and BITs had been acquired, as provided for in the 2013 Constitution.

9. The 2013 Constitution

The 2013 Constitution preserved most of the land-related provisions in Constitutional Amendments Nos 16 and 17. It retained provisions in regard to compulsory acquisition and Britain's responsibility for paying compensation for acquired land. It also retained the provisions relating to the government's responsibility for compensating for improvements on the land. The retention of these provisions in the 2013 Constitution in effect seals the fate of the former white landowners with regard to the acquisition of their land and the non-payment of compensation. In the absence of another constitutional amendment, the position is that compensation will be paid only for improvements on the land and not for the land itself, except for BIT and BIPPA farms and those owned by black Zimbabweans.

President Mnangagwa's government, which took over from Mugabe after a coup in November 2017,[68] has made the issue of compensation (for improvements and protected acquired land) one of its focus areas in implementing the Constitution, taking its first

---

[66] ICSID Case No ARB/10/25.

[67] ICSID Case No ARB/10/15.

[68] There has been controversy about what to call this event in the history of Zimbabwe. While some term it a coup, the High Court of Zimbabwe, in *Sibanda and Another v The President of the Republic of Zimbabwe and Others*, concluded that the actions of the Zimbabwe Defence Forces were constitutional and therefore did not amount to a coup. African intergovernmental bodies such as the African Union and SADC have also taken this view.

serious steps in this regard in 2019. In April of that year, it announced that an ad hoc committee would complete its valuations of farm improvements by the end of May, after which compensation would be paid to various of the affected farmers.[69] On 30 May, the government announced further that it had completed the registration of 737 farmers who were due to receive compensation immediately, with initial amounts set at ZWL 55,000 (then USD 10,000). Media coverage noted that 'President Emmerson Mnangagwa's government [was] eager to bring closure to the controversial land reform that had disastrous consequences on the economy, which is still in the doldrums two decades later'.[70] In a significant development, on 29 July 2020 the government and former commercial farmers signed a Global Compensation Deed awarding USD 3.5 billion for improvements to agricultural land.

While the government insisted the agreement was in line with constitutional provisions that required it to pay such compensation, its decision met with criticism from various quarters. Julius Malema, the leader of the Economic Freedom Fighters (EFF), the third biggest opposition political party in South Africa, claimed that Mnangagwa's government had sold out the black economic empowerment struggle by offering to pay former white farmers for land originally stolen from black people. Malema said '[a]nyone who compensates them for stolen land is a sell-out', maintaining they did not deserve it.[71] Added to this was an EFF press statement that excoriated Mnangagwa's actions as treasonous capitulation to pressure; paying compensation, the party said, amounted to 'pissing on the graves of the many heroic men and women who laid down their lives for the return of Zimbabwean land, ... [and in so doing] desecrating the legacy of Robert Mugabe'.[72]

This strongly worded response illustrates the intensity of feeling that the land issue elicits not only in Zimbabwe but other countries in the region as well. In Zimbabwe, citizens maintained that the bill for the compensation should be footed not by the government or taxpayers but by those who have benefited from the land. It was argued that although land recipients, the political elite in particular, had gained land and been supported by initiatives such as the Reserve Bank's Farm Mechanization Programme[73] and Command Agriculture Programme,[74] they had done little to improve the economy and food security.[75] Along with politicians in the ruling party and opposition, senior government officials and their relatives had been given free farm equipment worth more than US 200 million under the Farm Mechanization Programme, but very few have produced a notable harvest.[76] The war veterans of the 1970s liberation struggle argued, as did others, that irrespective of what the

---

[69] Godfrey Marawanyika, 'Zimbabwe to Complete Land Valuations in May to Pay Compensation' *Bloomberg* (7 April 2019).

[70] Kevin Samaita, 'Zimbabwe to Compensate More than 700 White Farmers' *Business Day* (Harare, 30 May 2019).

[71] Loyiso Sidimba, 'Julius Malema calls Mnangagwa a Sellout for Plans to Compensate White Farmers' *IOL* (11 April 2019).

[72] EFF statement issued on 31 July 2020.

[73] This programme was implemented by the Reserve Bank of Zimbabwe between 2007 and 2008 to give land recipients farm equipment such as tractors, combine harvesters, disc harrows, and ploughs.

[74] The programme was initiated by government in 2016 to give farmers support through irrigation equipment, inputs and chemicals, mechanized equipment, electricity, and water charges. An investigation by the Parliamentary Portfolio Committee on Public Accounts in 2019 concluded that, under the scheme, more than USD 3.2 billion had been syphoned out of Treasury coffers through corruption.

[75] The late Dr Alex Magaisa, a Zimbabwean lawyer and academic, argued this was just another way of saddling taxpayers with debts for resources that were benefiting a few politically connected individuals.

[76] Crecey Kuyedzwa, 'Can It Work? Zimbabwe's US$3.5bn Land Reform Compensation Plan Explained' *News24* (1 August 2020).

constitutional provisions are, the former white farmers did not deserve compensation at all because the land in question was never theirs to begin with and had been stolen from black Zimbabweans; the war veterans threatened they would sue the government to prevent the compensation from being paid.[77]

The government had but one response to all the criticism: it was a constitutional requirement to pay the compensation.[78] It has been argued that this stance was borne of a realization that a continued stand-off with the former white farmers over the land and compensation issue would persist in harming the economy[79] and fuelling perceptions of Zimbabwe as a pariah state; on the other hand, paying the farmers would suggest that a modicum of constitutionalism and resolve to protect property rights and observe the rule of law was being restored in the aftermath of the farm invasions and FTLRP during which these principles had been infringed.

The argument, in other words, was that in now demonstrably adhering to these principles in the case of the compensation issue, the government was mobilizing to attract foreign direct investment and the support of international lenders. For example, when the Minister of Finance approached the IMF in April 2020 in search of relief and arrears clearance to support the government's response to the COVID-19 pandemic, he pointed out that by June of the year the government would complete its valuation exercise for determining the compensation amount and laying the basis for a settlement agreement. This was meant to elicit the good favour of the IMF on the understanding that the government was working towards resolving the issue of compensation as required of it by its constitutional obligations.

The IMF's response, however, was still negative, as it urged the government to address the country's human rights and rule of law challenges before such a request could be considered. The argument was that, the land issue aside, Zimbabwe had continued to violate the Constitution and citizens' human rights in many other aspects. This was at a time when citizens' rights to freedom of association, political opinion and dissent, and freedom of expression were being violated under the pretext of enforcing COVID-19 regulations.[80]

In March 2020, the government indicated that it would return acquired farms that were held under the BIPPAs and BITs. It duly gazetted Statutory Instrument 62 of 2020—entitled Land Commission (Gazetted Land) (Disposal in Lieu of Compensation) Regulations, 2020—with the object 'to provide for the disposal of land to persons ... who are, in terms of section 295 of the Constitution, entitled to compensation for acquisition of previously compulsorily acquired agricultural land'.[81] The persons referred to in section 295 are indigenous Zimbabweans and individuals or partnerships and companies whose partners or shareholders were citizens of BIPPA or BIT countries. By way of this Statutory Instrument, the government is seeking to give these entities and individuals their land back (or alternative land, if it is impractical in view of a farm's current occupation status) in lieu of compensation.

[77] Wilf Mbanga, 'Is Zimbabwe Extending an Olive Branch to Its White Farmers?' *BBC News* (4 September 2020).

[78] Fin24, 'Land Compensation: I am Simply Following the Constitution, Says Zim President' *Fin24* (14 April 2019).

[79] 'Zim to Pay Partial Compensation to White Ex-Farmers' *Mail & Guardian* (8 April 2019).

[80] UN News, 'Zimbabwe: COVID-19 Must Not be Used to Stifle Freedoms, Says UN Rights Office' *UN News* (24 July 2020).

[81] Section 3 Land Commission (Gazetted Land) (Disposal in Lieu of Compensation) Regulations, Statutory Instrument 62/2020.

This is a further attempt by Zimbabwe's new government to provide compensation for acquired land, as required by the 2013 Constitution and, more widely, demonstrate its commitment to constitutionalism and the rule of law—commitment which includes granting recognition to the outstanding judgments made against the country by ICSID.

10. Conclusion

Constitutionalism and the rule of law have been tested in Zimbabwe's land reform programme. Given that land has been an enduring issue in the country's history and vital to its economy, it was inevitable that, if not addressed properly, the issue would lead to upheaval and impact negatively on the economy.

To pre-empt such challenges, the post-independence government put in place legal and constitutional provisions to ensure racial equity in landownership, but for the first twenty years of independence, effective land reform remained a pipe-dream. The government lacked the funds to buy land for resettlement, while white farmers resisted the land reform agenda; it was also the case that, until the situation imploded, the government did not appreciate the magnitude of the need for land or the frustration among black citizens at failure to implement land reform. It was only when its stay in power was threatened that it appeared to become serious about land.

This, however, did not resolve the issue because, as the situation became riotous and disorderly due to land invasions, the government implemented its programme outside the provisions of the law and the principles of constitutionalism, using the land question as a political tool to maintain its hold on power. The impact on the economy was immediate and continues to be felt today, which underlines the importance of constitutionalism and the rule of law in maintaining and growing a prosperous economy.

It is equally important, though, to acknowledge that laws and constitutions should be used to ensure fairness, equity, and the equal protection of the rights of all citizens. As such, post-independence laws and constitutional frameworks that failed to recognize and correct the history of colonialism and its impact on landownership in Zimbabwe were destined to face resistance from the majority of the citizens. The immediate post-independence legal framework protected white farmers and landowners and perpetuated the injustices of the colonial period. The independence government should have done more to address these injustices timeously and before citizens resorted to self-help measures. The government's initial failure to implement a timely post-independence land reform programme, along with its later efforts to promulgate laws to rectify the injustices only when its political power was under threat, showed that it was concerned more about its hold on power than in implementing a genuine land reform programme.

The failure of the government to deal properly with the land question does not diminish the fact that land reform and redistribution were and remain necessary. To date, fairness and equity in land access and ownership are unresolved in many respects. Land reform still needs to ensure racial, gender, and intergenerational equality, as well as ensure access to this resource without discrimination on any of the grounds stated in the Constitution.[82] Only

---

[82] Section 56(3) of the Constitution is the non-discrimination clause, and states: 'Every person has the right not to be treated in an unfairly discriminatory manner on such grounds as their nationality, race, colour, tribe, place of birth, or social origin, language, class, religious belief, political affiliation, opinion, custom, culture, sex,

then would true constitutionalism be achieved with regard to the land question, the true economic value of land unlocked, and the economic prosperity of the country facilitated. In promoting constitutionalism and the rule of law with regard to land rights in Zimbabwe, the international community must not lose sight of the colonial history of the country and its impact in creating racially unjust landownership patterns.

Whilst this contestation continues to play out, the role of land beneficiaries in the country's economy is beginning to emerge. The small-scale farmers who obtained A1[83] land allocations are using their land effectively and playing an important role in the country's tobacco production. This is an indication that these farmers were in need of the land and have proceeded to utilize it fully. Their success, however, has done little so far to address the economic challenges that the country is facing after years of battering.

Most of the political elites and senior government officials who received large tracts of land under the A2[84] land allocations have used it to syphon money from the fiscus through controversial agricultural support programmes, with little production coming out of their farms. Instead of helping to build the economy, these land beneficiaries have further drained the economy through corruption and other malfeasance. They are the clearest sign of how the implementation of the land reform programme outside constitutionally protected tenets led to corruption, cronyism, and the allocation of resources to the undeserving, thereby contributing to the collapse of the country's economy.

Bibliography

'How We Were Dispossessed' *Politics Web* (28 August 2018) <http://www.politicsweb.co.za/opinion/how-we-were-dispossessed> accessed 24 August 2018

'Zim to Pay Partial Compensation to White Ex-Farmers' *Mail & Guardian* (8 April 2019)

Africa All Parliamentary Group, 'Land in Zimbabwe: Past Mistakes, Future Prospects' (2009)

Bishi M, '35 Tonnes of Tomatoes and 21 Tonnes of Avocados Rot in Shut Down Masvingo Fruit and Vegetables Market' *Masvingo Mirror* (21 April 2020)

Cauvin HE, 'Zimbabwe Signals It Still Plans to Seize White-Owned Farms' *New York Times* (New York, 3 March 2000)

Deininger K, Hoogeveen H, and Kinsey BH, 'Economic Benefits and Costs of Land Redistribution in Zimbabwe in the Early 1980s' (2004) 32(10) World Development 1697

EISA, 'Zimbabwe: 2000 Constitutional Referendum Results' *African Democracy Encyclopaedia Project* (June 2007) <https://www.eisa.org.za/wep/zimresults2000r.htm> accessed 29 May 2019

Fin24, 'Land compensation: I am Simply Following the Constitution, Says Zim President' *Fin24* (14 April 2019)

Food and Agricultural Organization of the United Nations, 'National Gender Profile of Agriculture and Rural Livelihoods' (FAO 2017)

gender, marital status, age, pregnancy, disability, or economic or social status, or whether they were born in or out of wedlock.'

[83] A1 land under the FTLRP was allocated for smallholder production through either villagized settlements or small self-contained farms (see Ian Scoones and others, *Zimbabwe's Land Reform: Myths and Realities* (James Currey 2010). The allocations ranged from 6 to 37 hectares.

[84] A2 land under the FTLRP was allocated for large-scale commercial production and allocated individually. The farm sizes under this land resettlement model were determined by the agricultural region in which the land was allocated, with maximum farm sizes currently regulated in terms of the Rural Land (Farm Sizes) (Amendment) Regulations, Statutory Instrument 41 of 2020.

Gonese FT and others, 'Land Reform and Resettlement Implementation in Zimbabwe: An Overview of the Programme against Selected International Experiences' (n.d.) <https://minds.wisconsin.edu/bitstream/handle/1793/23060/LRRPOverview.pdf?sequence=1> accessed 2 August 2020

Government of Zimbabwe, 'Report of the Presidential Land Review Committee on the Implementation of the Fast Track Land Reform Programme, 2000–2002' ('The Utete Commission Report') (2008)

Grundy T, 'Carrington and Mugabe' *PoliticsWeb* (16 July 2018) <http://www.politicsweb.co.za/opinion/carrington-and-mugabe> accessed 23 May 2019

International Labour Organization, 'Enabling Environment for Sustainable Enterprises in Zimbabwe' (ILO 2018)

KPMG, 'Zimbabwe Economic Snapshot' (H2, 2017)

Kuyedzwa C, 'Can It Work? Zimbabwe's US$3.5bn Land Reform Compensation Plan Explained' *News24* (1 August 2020)

Mabunda E, 'Zim Economy to Shrink 7.4% in 2020—IMF' *EquityAxis* (15 April 2020) <https://equityaxis.net/2020/04/15/zim-economy-to-shrink-7-4-in-2020-imf/> accessed 20 November 2020

Machipisa L, 'Politics-Zimbabwe: A Top Judge Appointed Chief Justice' *Inter Press Service News Agency* (Harare, 9 March 2001)

Madhuku L, 'A Survey of Constitutional Amendments in Post-Independence Zimbabwe (1980–1999)' (1999) 16 Zimbabwe Law Review 82

Madhuku L, 'Law, Politics and the Land Reform Process in Zimbabwe' in Masiiwa M (ed), *Post-independence Land Reform in Zimbabwe* (FES and IDS 2004)

Marabuka ER, 'Critical Analysis of Willing Buyer Willing Seller Framework in Relation Reform in Zimbabwe' (Lupane State University 2013)

Marawanyika G, 'Zimbabwe to Complete Land Valuations in May to Pay Compensation' *Bloomberg* (7 April 2019)

Mario P, *Zimbabwe, Land and the Dictator* (Godfrey 2009)

Marongwe N, 'Redistributive Land Reform and Poverty Reduction in Zimbabwe: A Working Paper for the Research Project on "Livelihoods after Land Reform"' (nd)

Mbanga W, 'Is Zimbabwe Extending an Olive Branch to Its White Farmers?' *BBC News* (4 September 2020)

Meldrum A, 'Violence before the Vote' *The Guardian* (Harare, 9 February 2000)

Mitchell TW, 'The Land Crisis in Zimbabwe: Getting Beyond the Myopic Focus upon Black and White' (2001) 11(3) Indiana International and Comparative Law Review 587

Moyo A, 'Defending Human Rights and the Rule of Law by the SADC Tribunal: Campbell and Beyond' (2009) 9(2) African Human Rights Law Journal 590

Mtsi S, 'Water Reforms during the Crisis and Beyond: Understanding Policy and Political Challenges of Reforming the Water Sector in Zimbabwe' (2011) Working Paper 333, Overseas Development Institute

Mukaro A, 'Govt in Climbdown on Bilateral Agreements' *Zimbabwe Independent* (Harare, 28 October 2005)

Muwati I, Mutasa DE, and Bopape ML, 'The Zimbabwean Liberation War: Contesting Representations of Nation and Nationalism in Historical Fiction' (2010) 31(1) Literator 147

NewsDay, 'Tobacco Sales Reach US$383,1m' *NewsDay* (31 July 2020) <http://www.newsday.co.zw/2020/07/tobacco-sales-reach-us3831m/> accessed 1 August 2020

Nhambura F, 'Celebrating Pioneers of Land Reform' *Herald* (Harare, 30 July 2015)

Njowa G, 'Leveraging on the Mining Sector for Economic Stimulation in Zimbabwe' *Deloitte* (May 2014) <https://www.icaz.org.zw/imisdocs/mining.pdf> accessed 14 May 2019

Nkala I, 'Tobacco Farming in Zimbabwe: Profit, Problems and Solutions' *FarmBiz* (31 December 2019)

Penrhys T, 'Land and Tenure in Zimbabwe's Communal Areas: Why Land Reform Was Needed' *Future Agricultures* (14 October 2019) <http://www.future-agricultures.org/blog/land-and-tenure-in-zimbabwes-communal-areas-why-land-reform-was-needed/> accessed 2 August 2020

Plaut M, 'US Backed Zimbabwe Land Reform' *BBC News* (22 August 2007)

Pottie D, 'Parliamentary Elections in Zimbabwe, 2000' (2001) 1(1) Journal of African Elections <https://www.eisa.org.za/pdf/JAE1.1Pottie.pdf> accessed 31 May 2019

Reuters, Aaron Ufumeli, 'Ruling Favoring Black Squatters Nullified' *Los Angeles Times* (California, 25 November 2000)

Reuters, Aaron Ufumeli, 'Zimbabwe reopens Produce Markets after Protests by Drought-Hit Farmers' *Daily Maverick* (9 April 2020)

Roth MR and Bruce JW, 'Land Tenure, Agrarian Structure, and Comparative Land Use Efficiency in Zimbabwe: Options for Land Tenure Reform and Land Redistribution' (1994) Research Papers 12750, University of Wisconsin-Madison, Land Tenure Center

Sachikonye L, 'The Situation of Commercial Farm Workers after Land Reform in Zimbabwe' (Farm Community Trust 2003)

Samaita K, 'Zimbabwe to Compensate More than 700 White Farmers' *Business Day* (Harare, 30 May 2019)

SAPA-AFP, 'Zim to Start Firing Judges' *News24* (23 February 2001)

Scoones I and others, *Zimbabwe's Land Reform: Myths and Realities* (James Currey 2010)

Sibanda G, 'Zim Eyes US$2bn from G7 Nations' *Herald* (Harare, 19 August 2019)

Sidimba L, 'Julius Malema calls Mnangagwa a Sellout for Plans to Compensate White Farmers' *IOL* (11 April 2019)

Slaughter B and Nolan S, 'Zimbabwe: Referendum Defeat for Mugabe Shakes Zanu-PF Government' *World Socialist Web Site* (22 February 2000) <http://www.wsws.org/en/articles/2000/02/zimb-f22. html> accessed 28 May 2019

Trading Economics, 'Zimbabwe: Employment in Agriculture (% of Total Employment)' Trading Economics (nd) <https://tradingeconomics.com/zimbabwe/employment-in-agriculture-percent-of-total-employment-wb-data.html> accessed 31 July 2020

UN News, 'Zimbabwe: COVID-19 Must Not be Used to Stifle Freedoms, Says UN Rights Office' *UN News* (24 July 2020)

Workman D, 'Zimbabwe's Top 10 Exports' *Worlds Top Exports* (nd) http://www.worldstopexports. com/zimbabwes-top-10-exports accessed 31 July 2020

Zimbabwe and Related Topics, 'Zimbabwe's Pre-Colonial History' (n.d.) <https://zimbabweandrelate dtopics.weebly.com/zimbabwes-pre-colonial-history.html> accessed 21 May 2019

Zimbabwe Election Support Network, 'Report on the 2000 Parliamentary Elections Zimbabwe 24—25 June 2000' (2000)

Zimbabwe Human Rights NGO Forum, 'Land and Property Rights in Zimbabwe Reform' (2010)

Zinyuke R, 'Lockdown: Police Confiscate Vegetables' *Herald* (Harare, 3 April 2020)

9

Custodial Resource Holding as an Expression of Constitutional and Economic Intent in Africa

Hanri Mostert[*]

1. Introduction

In an ideal world, there would be coherence between a state's constitutional ideals, economic policy, and legal framework. These would be the foundations upon which that state's extractive sector[1] could serve its society by enabling prosperity and sustainability. The reality is often far more incoherent. The fault lines in the relationship between a state's legal-constitutional framework and its economic approach often show up clearly in the extractive sectors, especially in 'resource-dependent' states.[2]

These states' constitutional provisions may affirm sovereignty over their natural resources and/or acknowledge the importance of their natural resource wealth, for example through provisions on property and governance. Resource-dependent states also typically have laws, codes, or statutes affirming their particular understanding of resource sovereignty. The attributed powers of use, control, and ownership of mineral resources constitute a state's 'resource holding'. The state's preferred manner of exercising and/or managing such powers of use, control, and ownership over mineral resources represents its 'resource-holding model'.

[*] The chapter was written with the financial support of the DST/NRF South African Research Chairs Initiative. The author acknowledges the advice of colleagues Bethany Berger, Hanoch Dagan, Priya Gupta, Laura Underkuffler, Rashmi Dyal-Chand, Greg Alexander, Joe Singer, Nadav Shoked, Avihay Dorfman, and Cathy Powell; the research assistance of Fezeka Ntsanwisi and Chiyedza Mutendera and input from students from the Masters Programme on the Law of Extraction and Use of Mineral and Petroleum Resources (2020), inter alia Inga Dyan, Tasha Makowe, Keanan Wheeler, Terrence Mutambara, Ahmed Mussa, and Leezola Zongwe. Opinions and errors are my own and should not be attributed to any of the institutions or persons mentioned. The chapter was written with the financial support of the DST/NRF South African Research Chairs Initiative.

[1] Those parts of the economy that pertain to the extraction of minerals and hydrocarbons.

[2] That is, where the mineral or petroleum sectors play a dominant economic role. The report of the International Council on Mining & Metals (ICMM), 'Social Progress in Mining-Dependent Countries: Analysis through the Lens of the SDGs' (ICMM 2018) 12 uses two criteria to define resource-dependent states: (1) resources must represent more than 20 per cent of exports by value; and (2) resource rents must be more than 10 per cent of GDP. In sub-Saharan Africa—in respect of either hydrocarbons or hard minerals (or sometimes both), over the period between 1995 and 2015—these criteria applied to Angola, Botswana, Cameroon, Central African Republic, the Democratic Republic of the Congo, the Republic of Congo, Equatorial Guinea, Gabon, Ghana, Guinea, Libya, Mauritania, Namibia, Niger, Nigeria, South Africa, Togo, and Zambia. A separate study (Haroon Bhorat and others, 'Resource Dependence and Inequality in Africa: Impacts, Consequences and Potential Solutions' in Ayodele Odusola and others (eds), *Income Inequality Trends in Sub-Saharan Africa: Divergence, Determinants and Consequences* (UNDP 2019) considers a country resource dependent if, over five years, 25 per cent or more of export revenue is derived from natural resources. On this criterion, between 2008 and 2012, the following African countries qualified (listed from highest level of resource dependency to the lowest): Angola, Algeria, Libya, Equatorial Guinea, Nigeria, Chad, Democratic Republic of the Congo, the Republic of Congo, Guinea, Gabon, Botswana, Sudan, Zambia, Mauritania, Mozambique, Mali, Sierra Leone, Namibia, Cameroon, South Africa, Egypt, Niger, Central African Republic, Tanzania, Burkina Faso, Senegal, Benin, Zimbabwe, Rwanda, Ghana, Lesotho, Côte d'Ivoire, Togo, and Liberia.

Hanri Mostert, *Custodial Resource Holding as an Expression of Constitutional and Economic Intent in Africa* In: *Constitutionalism and the Economy in Africa*. Edited by: Charles M Fombad and Nico Steytler, Oxford University Press. © Hanri Mostert 2022.
DOI: 10.1093/oso/9780192886439.003.0011

The economic policies of resource-dependent states become evident in their extractive sectors. Compelled to deal with persistently challenging realities rooted in historically problematic positions, almost all African peoples entrust their states with the responsibility of managing, and even holding, their mineral resources. A state's preferences regarding resource holding will determine its choices in resource governance. Its resource-holding 'model', irrespective of how the constitution and economic policies express it, will find further expression in laws dealing with resource extraction. Consequently, the ideologies underlying a state's economic and political choices, whether command or market oriented, are given effect in the extractives context.

The introductory chapter to this volume notes the disastrous effects that command economies have wrought upon the African societies they were supposed to serve. It acknowledges the corruption and mismanagement to which market economies are vulnerable. This chapter contributes to the general theme by narrowing the focus to the resource context. The chapter seeks to identify broad trends in law-making and policy formulation.

In the face of the persistent failures of command and market economic approaches to establish thriving societies on the back of ample resource wealth, African states must find ways to avoid the pitfalls of extractive policies, irrespective of whether they lean towards privatization or nationalization. This chapter explores this reality and current responses to it in the mineral-resource context. It argues that historical policies, be they oriented to the market or command economy, have not served Africa's extractives sectors well enough. It presents a third option, state custodianship, in response to failures of transparency and state accountability under both market and command economies.

The chapter examines, first, how constitutions in sub-Saharan Africa translate the notion of permanent sovereignty of natural resources in country-specific contexts. Demonstrating that constitutions generally do little more than affirm resource sovereignty, the chapter then considers how selected country-specific economic orders in sub-Saharan Africa define resource holding. It observes that command- and market-economy approaches in Africa have been near universal in their failure to promote human flourishing. The chapter posits that recent legislative expressions of resource governance as state custodianship may provide a strategy to sidestep the binary of command- and market-economic approaches. The chapter then analyses the concept of custodial resource holding to determine how sub-Saharan African constitutional and legal frameworks envision and manage future state accountability for mineral-resource exploitation.

2. Resource Sovereignty and African Constitutions

Colonialism had devastating effects[3] on the self-determination of peoples. It also compromised the ability of the colonized parts of the world to manage resource wealth within their territories.[4] Colonial powers often concluded concession agreements[5] with investors

---

[3] See eg *Social and Economic Rights Action Centre (SERAC) v Nigeria* [2001] AHRLR 60 (ACHPR 2001) Communication 155/96, 15th Annual Report [56].

[4] Bonnie Campbell, 'Revisiting the Reform Process of African Mining Regimes' (2010) 30(1-2) Canadian Journal of Development Studies 197, 200; Kobena T Hanson, Cristina D'Alessandro, and Francis Owusu (eds), *Managing Africa's Natural Resources: Capacities for Development* (Palgrave Macmillan 2014) 16.

[5] Danièle Barberis, *Negotiating Mining Agreements: Past, Present and Future Trends: Past, Present and Future Trends* (1st edn, Kluwer Law International 1998) 1.

from abroad—for instance via transnational mining companies (TMCs)—for resource exploitation.[6] These concession agreements typically gave the investor the right to operate a specific business (eg extracting minerals) within a territory under the rule of the colonial power and subject to certain terms. These agreements were often one-sided,[7] favouring the interests of foreign, non-African investors to the detriment of local communities and colonies.[8]

In the post-war period, many colonies gained independence from oppressive and exploitative rule. This section considers how, during this time, the international community attempted to correct course by developing a recognition of permanent sovereignty of natural resources ('resource sovereignty' for short) in international law. It then discusses the resource-holding models founded on resource sovereignty. The section highlights the dilemma caused by the binary approach to resource holding that emerged under postcolonial independence.

2.1 Permanent Sovereignty over Natural Resources

After the Second World War, the international community engaged repeatedly[9] with the imbalances which colonialism had caused in relation to natural resources.[10] It began canvassing, successfully, for increased levels of state control and the concomitant parameters of state action.[11] A notable instrument adopted to address some of the consequences of the so-called 'scramble for Africa'[12] was the United Nations 1962 Resolution[13] on the Permanent

---

[6] Sangwani Patrick Ng'ambi, 'Permanent Sovereignty Over Natural Resources and the Sanctity of Contracts, from the Angle of Lucrum Cessans' (2015) 12(2) Loyola University Chicago International Law Review 153.

[7] Joseph E Stiglitz, 'What Is the Role of the State?' in Marcatan Humphreys and others (eds), *Escaping the Resource Curse* (Columbia University Press 2007) 24.

[8] Hugo Meyer van den Berg, 'Regulation of the Upstream Petroleum Industry: A Comparative Analysis and Evaluation of Regulatory Frameworks of South Africa and Namibia' (PhD thesis, University of Cape Town 2014) 3–4. Ricardo Pereira and Orla Gough, 'Permanent Sovereignty over Natural Resources in the 21st Century: Natural Resource Governance and the Right to Self-Determination of Indigenous Peoples under International Law' (2013) 14(2) Melbourne Journal of International Law 451, 455. Also Stephen Ocheni and Basil C Nwankwo, 'Analysis of Colonialism and Its Impact in Africa' (2012) 8(3) Cross-Cultural Communication 48.

[9] For example, UNGA Resolution 1515 (XV) of 15 December 1960, *Concerted Action for Economic Development of Economically Less Developed Countries* recommended that every state's sovereign right to dispose of its natural wealth and resources should be respected. UNGA Resolution 1803 (XVII) of 14 December 1962, *Permanent Sovereignty Over Natural Resources*, para 1 declared that the right of permanent sovereignty over natural wealth and resources should be exercised in the interest of the well-being of the people and development of the nation in question.

[10] Ng'ambi (n 6) 153.

[11] See n 9 above. Eg Clause 4, UNGA Resolution 1803, 1962 (n 9) suggested that nationalization and expropriation of these resources must be possible but based on grounds or reasons of public utility, security, or national interest that override purely individual or private interests, and that appropriate compensation must be paid. See the more detailed discussion in Van den Berg (n 8) 53.

[12] Walter Rodney, *How Europe Underdeveloped Africa* (Bogle-L'Ouverture Publications, London with the Tanzanian Publishing House, Dar-Es-Salaam 1972) 214 explains that the 'scramble for Africa' was a drive by European powers to 'grab ., . . whatever they thought spelt profits in Africa', along with even more acquisitions with 'an eye to the future'. Africa hence became the vessel for Europe's short-term and long-term economic interests, which resulted in European political domination of Africa.

[13] UNGA Resolution 1803, 1962 (n 9) reiterated a principle already formally endorsed a decade earlier in UNGA Resolution 626 (VII) of 21 December 1952, *Right to Exploit Freely Natural Wealth and Resources*. The 1962 Resolution states that '[t]he right of peoples and nations to permanent sovereignty over their wealth and resources must be exercised in the interest of their national development and the well-being of the people of the State concerned'.

Sovereignty of Natural Resources (PSNR).[14] Further acknowledgements followed,[15] until states' resource sovereignty became a recognized principle in customary international law[16] (hereafter 'the principle of resource sovereignty'). These developments endorsed the importance of protecting developing states from being exploited.[17] They contained increasingly assertive recognitions of states' rights, within their territories,[18] to exercise permanent sovereignty (ie exclusive ownership and control) over their natural resources, wealth, and economic activities,[19] for the ultimate benefit of their citizens.[20] In 1986, article 21 of the African Charter on Human and Peoples' Rights[21] also endorsed PSNR.[22] It emphasizes the need for the state to exercise its related powers in the interests and benefit of each nation's people[23] rather than monopolistic international entities.[24]

The Africa Mining Vision of 2009 (AMV)[25] proclaims itself to be an initiative to refine the varying expressions of resource sovereignty practised in the extractive sectors of many African states since independence.[26] It seeks to promote equitable and broad-based development through the prudent exploitation of the continent's natural wealth.[27] It represents

---

[14] See further also art 4(e) of UNGA Resolution 3201 (S-VI) of 1 May 1974 *Declaration on the Establishment of a New International Economic Order*, which states: 'The new international economic order should be founded on full respect for the following principles: "[f]ull permanent sovereignty of every State over its natural resources ... each State is entitled to exercise effective control over them and their exploitation" '; and art 2 of UNGA Resolution 3281 (XXIX) of 12 December 1974 *Charter of Economic Rights and Duties of States*, which states that '[e]very State has and shall freely exercise full permanent sovereignty, including possession, use and disposal, over all its wealth, natural resources and economic activities'.

[15] Notably in UNGA Resolution 3281, 1974 (n 14). David Harris, *Cases and Materials on International Law* (7th edn, Sweet & Maxwell 2010) 475–76. Also Fritz Visser, 'The Principle of Permanent Sovereignty over Natural Resources and the Nationalization of Foreign Interests' (1988) 21(1) The Comparative and International Law Journal of Southern Africa 76–91; and Onur Ulas Ince, 'Development' in Jean d'Aspremont and Sahib Singh (eds), *Concepts for International Law—Contributions to Disciplinary Thought* (Edward Elgar 2019), 193–94.

[16] Hillary Charlesworth, 'Democracy' in Jean d'Aspremont and Sahib Singh (eds), *Concepts for International Law—Contributions to Disciplinary Thought* (Edward Elgar 2019), 166; Fernando Loureiro Bastos, 'A Southern African Approach to the Permanent Sovereignty over Natural Resources and Common Resource Management' in Marc Bungenberg and Stephan Hobe (eds), *Permanent Sovereignty over Natural Resources* (Springer 2015) 66.

[17] See eg the Preamble to the 1962 Resolution, which emphasizes the economic development of developing countries through the observance of equality and fairness and respect of the right to self-determination when agreements are entered into between developed and developed countries. See also cl 6, which declares that dealings in developing countries must advance their independent national development and respect their sovereignty over their resources.

[18] That is, the fixed area of the state's jurisdiction.

[19] Ng'ambi (n 6) 154.

[20] Nico J Schrijver, 'Permanent Sovereignty over Natural Resources versus Common Heritage of Mankind: Complementary or Contradictory Principles of International Economic Law' (1987) 21 Series: Development & Security 1. Thomas Wälde, 'Permanent Sovereignty over Natural Resources Recent Developments in the Mineral Sector' (1993) 7(3) National Research Forum 240. Samantha Besson, 'Sovereignty' (Max Planck Encyclopaedias of International Law [MPIL], Max Planck Encyclopaedia of Public International Law [MPEPIL] (April 2011) <https://opil.ouplaw.com/view/10.1093/law:epil/9780199231690/law-9780199231690-e1472?prd=MPIL> accessed 14 February 2021.

[21] African (Banjul) Charter on Human and Peoples' Rights, 1981.

[22] ibid art 21.

[23] ibid art 21(1).

[24] See also *Social and Economic Rights Action Centre (SERAC) v Nigeria* [2001] AHRLR 60 (ACHPR 2001) Communication 155/96, 15th Annual Report [56].

[25] African Union, 'Africa Mining Vision' (February 2009) <https://docs.igihe.com/IMG/pdf/africa_mining_vision_english.pdf> accessed 14 February 2021.

[26] ibid 11–13. Also Gavin Hilson, 'The Africa Mining Vision: A Manifesto for More inclusive Extractive industry-Led Development?' (2020) 41 Canadian Journal of Development Studies/Revue canadienne d'études du développement, 417–31.

[27] Paul Bagabo and others, 'Contract Transparency in Uganda's Petroleum and Mining Sectors' (2019) Kampala: ACODE Policy Research Paper Series No 94, 9. Also Gavin Bridge, 'Global Production Networks and the Extractive Sector: Governing Resource-Based Development' (2008) 8 Journal of Economic Geography 389, 390.

an attempt to formulate a unified expression of the continent's endorsement of the principle of resource sovereignty, which has found its way into the legal frameworks of African states in many, varied ways. Some states (eg Zimbabwe[28]) acknowledge resource sovereignty explicitly in their constitutions; others (eg South Africa,[29] Tanzania,[30] and Botswana[31]) have woven the principles into their domestic laws with either explicit or implicit references in their constitutions (discussed in more detail below).

More recently, the principle of resource sovereignty has featured in indigenous peoples' self-determination claims in international law.[32] Such claims indicate the expectations this principle must fulfil in a post-colonial era characterized by endorsement of political independence and constitutionalization. The principle also raises questions about the role and responsibilities of the state in harnessing the economic wealth emanating from resource extraction.[33]

Bastos categorizes African responses to the principle of resource sovereignty into three types: those classically focused on the pursuit of *national interest*; those traditionally focused on *community interests*; and those focused on *sustainability and interdependence*.[34] This categorization is useful for understanding the reach of the principle in the regulation of

---

[28] Zimbabwe's supreme law, the Constitution of Zimbabwe Amendment (No 20) Act of 2013, affirms that the state 'is a unitary, sovereign and democratic republic'. The Preamble recognizes Zimbabwe's natural resource wealth and acknowledges 'the need to entrench democracy, good, transparent and accountable governance and the rule of law'. Simultaneously, s 3(c) of the Constitution states that Zimbabwe is founded on upholding 'fundamental human rights and freedoms'. Section 315(2) mandates that an Act of Parliament 'must provide for the negotiation and performance of State contracts'. The negotiation of concessions of mineral rights, among others, are brought under the constitutional ambit, under s 315(2)(c), in an attempt to achieve transparency, accountability, cost-effectiveness, and competitiveness. The Constitution commits the state to good governance of the minerals sector (among others) in s 270 (1)(c), dealing with the management of natural resources, and recognizes, under s 73(1)(iii), the right to 'secure ecologically sustainable development and use of natural resources while promoting economic and social development'.

[29] The Constitution of the Republic of South Africa of 1996 does not explicitly recognize the principle of sovereignty over natural resources, but the Preamble of the Mineral and Petroleum Resources Development Act 28 of 2002 recognizes 'that South Africa's mineral and petroleum resources belong to the nation and the State is the custodian thereof'. This is reiterated in s 3(1) which provides that 'mineral and petroleum resources are the common heritage of all the people of South Africa and the State is the custodian thereof for the benefit of all South Africans'. See also Johan D van der Vyver, 'Nationalisation of Mineral Rights in South Africa' (2012) 45(1) De Jure 125, 139.

[30] Tanzania—as a signatory to several pertinent international and regional instruments confirming permanent sovereignty over natural resources (notably, UNGA Resolution 1515, 1960; UNGA Resolution 1803, 1962 (both in n 9); and the African (Banjul) Charter on Human and Peoples Rights, 1981)—has adopted the Natural Wealth and Resources (Permanent Sovereignty) Act of 2017 as a domestic embodiment of these regional and international instruments. Section 4(1) of this Act asserts the country's permanent sovereignty over its natural resources. Section 4(2) provides that ownership and control over natural resources is 'exercised by, and through the Government on behalf of the People and the United Republic'. The Act is complemented by the Natural Wealth and Resources Contracts (Review and Renegotiation of Unconscionable Terms) Act of 2017 and the Written Laws (Miscellaneous Amendments) Act of 2017.

[31] Although Botswana's Constitution of 1996 is silent on permanent sovereignty of natural resources, referring only to the promotion of sustainable development or utilization of minerals in ss 8(1)(a)(ii) and 9(2)(a)), the principle is entrenched in ordinary legislation. To this effect, s 3 of the Mines and Minerals Act 17 of 1999 endows the state with ownership of mineral resources. This section should be read with s 2 of the Mineral Rights in Tribal Territories Act 31 of 1967, which vests ownership of tribal mineral deposits in the state.

[32] Pereira and Gough (n 8) 453.

[33] See in general Gary Flomenhoft, 'Historical and Empirical Basis for Communal Title in Minerals at the National Level: Does Ownership Matter for Human Development?' (2018) 10(6) Sustainability1958 https://www.mdpi.com/2071-1050/10/6/1958#cite; Pauline Jones Luong and Erika Weinthal, 'Rethinking the Resource Curse: Ownership Structure, Institutional Capacity and Domestic Constraints' (2006) 9 Annual Review of Political Science 241, 241–63; Nicolaas Schrijver, 'Self-determination of Peoples and Sovereignty over Natural Wealth and Resources' in United Nations, *Realizing the Right to Development* (United Nations Publication 2013) 95–102; Petra Gümplová, 'Sovereignty over Natural Resources—A Normative Reinterpretation' (2020) 9 Global Constitutionalism 7ff.

[34] Bastos (n 16) 66.

extractive activity within a given jurisdiction. The principle confers great breadth and depth of power on the state; it also imposes responsibilities for managing different interests within the extractive sector. In view of these powers and responsibilities, the impact of choices regarding resource holding is felt by the state, mining companies, landowners, and communities affected by mining. See further section 3 below.

2.2 Expressions of Resource Sovereignty in Constitutions: A Survey

The principle of resource sovereignty expresses the state's right to determine the property regime in which mineral and petroleum resources are to be owned and regulated.[35] It is widely understood to relate to, inter alia, the state's right to seek, possess, use, regulate, and dispose of such natural resources and to settle related disputes.[36] Economic and sociopolitical preferences further influence particular understandings of the state's role in extracting, managing, and drawing benefit from such resources.

Table 9.1 presents the results of a survey of expressions of resource sovereignty in sub-Saharan constitutions. Expressions differ: references to 'natural resources' are sometimes granulated into different types of resources—for example, specific mention is made of 'solid minerals', 'hydrocarbons', 'oil', 'gas' or 'petroleum'—or resources with differing locations (eg 'soil', 'subsoil', and 'territorial waters'). This survey has not made such granulated distinctions.

Figure 9.1 presents a summary of the findings. Five countries[37] recognize resource sovereignty in the preambles to their constitutions, while two[38] more make general references to 'sovereignty' or 'territorial integrity': references which are further defined in domestic legislation dealing with resource extraction. These 'indirect' types of acknowledgement of resource sovereignty are eclipsed by the number of countries (22)[39] that include some form of recognition of resource sovereignty in the substantive parts of their constitutions.

However, a surprisingly large number (16)[40] of the countries surveyed make *no* discernible reference to resource sovereignty in their constitutions, but instead rely only on domestic legislative frameworks to establish their control of natural resources. The sizeable number of jurisdictions containing no form of constitutional assertion of resource sovereignty is all the more interesting given the number of countries within this subcategory (11 out of 16, or 68 per cent), which have known resource dependency in their economies.

Further scrutiny reveals that those countries with neither direct nor indirect endorsement of the principle of resource sovereignty mostly have constitutions hailing from before the turn of the century. There are significant exceptions, however, in terms both of more recent constitutions and of recent amendments to older constitutions. Hence, no

---

[35] Anita Rønne, 'Public and Private Rights to Natural Resources and Differences in Their Protection?' in Aileen McHarg and others (eds), *Property and the Law in Energy and Natural Resources* (9th edn, Oxford University Press 2010) 60–79.

[36] Art 1, UNGA Resolution 3281, 1974 (n 14). See Elmarie van der Schyff, *Property in Minerals and Petroleum* (Juta 2016) 165. Ng'ambi (n 6) 154.

[37] Cameroon, Central African Republic, Congo (Brazzaville), South Africa, and Zimbabwe.

[38] Mali, Togo.

[39] See Table 9.1.

[40] ibid.

Table 9.1 Constitutional recognition of resource sovereignty in sub-Saharan Africa

Country	Date of latest constitution	Constitutional recognition of resource sovereignty		
		Direct	Indirect	None (domestic law affirmation only)
Angola*	2010	Art 16: 'property of the state'	-	-
Benin*	1990	-	-	X
Botswana*	1966/2006 Amendments	-	-	X
Burkina Faso*	1991/2012 Amendments	Art 14: 'resources belong to the people'	-	-
Burundi	2018	-	-	X
Cameroon*	1972/2008 Amendments	-	Preamble: 'we the people … *our* natural resources'	-
Cntrl Afrn Republic*	2016	-	Preamble: 'right to … sovereignty on its soil, its subsoil and its airspace'	-
Chad*	2018	Art 63: 'State exercises its sovereignty … natural riches and resources'	-	-
Comoros	2018	Art 7: Union … possesses sovereign rights in … living and non-living natural resources …'	-	-
Congo (Brazzaville)*	2015	-	Preamble: people … reaffirm its permanent … sovereignty over … resources	-
Côte d'Ivoire*	2016	-	-	X
Dem Rep of Congo*	2005/2011 Amendments	Art 9: 'State exercises a permanent sovereignty … over … soil, the subsoil, the waters and the forests …'	-	-

(continued)

Table 9.1 Continued

Country	Date of latest constitution	Constitutional recognition of resource sovereignty		
		Direct	Indirect	None (domestic law affirmation only)
Djibouti	1992/2010 Amendments	-	-	X
Equatorial Guinea*	1991/2012 Amendments	Art 3(2): 'State exercises its sovereignty … resources and mineral wealth and hydrocarbons'	-	-
Eswatini	2005	S 213: 'minerals … shall … continue to vest in iNgwenyama in trust for the Swazi Nation'	-	-
Gabon*	2011		-	X
Gambia	1996/2018 Amendments	-	-	X
Ghana*	1992/1996 Amendments	Art 257(1) & (6): 'property of the Republic of Ghana … vested in the President … in trust for the people'	-	-
Guinea*	2010	Art 10: 'State … holds exclusive competence to … natural resources'	-	X
Guinea-Bissau	1984/1996 Amendments		-	-
Kenya	2010	Art 62(3) read with art 62(1)(f): '[minerals] … vest in … national government in trust for the people'	-	-
Lesotho*	1993/1998 Amendments	-	-	X
Liberia*	1986	Art 22(b): 'all mineral resources … shall belong to the Republic'	-	-
Madagascar	2010		-	X
Malawi	1994/2017 Amendments		-	X
Mali*	1992		Art 50: 'national sovereignty or territorial integrity'	-

Country	Year/Amendments	Provision		
Mauritania*	1991/2012 Amendments		-	X
Mauritius	1968/2016 Amendments	S 8(5): 'state … ownership of … unextracted minerals'	-	-
Mozambique*	2004/2007 Amendments	Article 98: 'Natural resources in the soil and the subsoil … shall be the property of the State'	-	-
Namibia*	1990/2014 Amendments	Article 100: natural resources … shall belong to the State if … not otherwise lawfully owned'	-	-
Niger*	2010/2017 Amendments	Art 148: 'natural resources … are the property of the Nigerien people' read with Art 149: 'The State exercises its sovereignty over the natural resources and the subsoil'	-	-
Nigeria*	1999	S 44: 'minerals … vest in the Government'	-	-
Rwanda*	2003/2005 Amendments	-	-	X
Senegal*	2001/2016 Amendments	Art 25-2: 'natural resources belong to the people … exploitation and management of natural resources … to promote the wellbeing of the population in general'	-	-
Seychelles	1993/2017 Amendments	S 26(2)(i): 'vesting in the Republic … ownership of … unextracted … minerals'	-	-
Sierra Leone*	1991	—	-	X
Somalia	2012	Art 41: 'Natural resources … shall be state property'	-	-
South Africa*	1996	-	Preamble: 'mineral and petroleum resources belong to the nation and the State is the custodian thereof'	-
South Sudan	2011	S 2: 'sovereignty is vested in the people', read with	-	-

(continued)

Table 9.1 Continued

Country	Date of latest constitution	Constitutional recognition of resource sovereignty		
		Direct	Indirect	None (domestic law affirmation only)
Sudan*	2019	S 170(4): 'petroleum and gas resources and solid minerals, shall belong to the National Government', and S 172(1): 'Ownership of petroleum and gas shall be vested in the people ... and shall be developed and managed by the National Government on behalf of and for the benefit of the people'	-	X
United Rep of Tanzania*	1977/1995 Amendments	-	-	X
Togo*	2007	-	Art 4: 'Sovereignty belongs to the people ... exercised by their representatives'	-
Uganda	1995/2006 Amendments	National Objectives XIII: 'The State shall protect important natural resources, including land, water, wetlands, minerals, oil, fauna and flora on behalf of the people'	-	-
Zambia*	1991/2016 Amendments	Art 5(1): 'Sovereign authority vests in the people of Zambia ... exercised directly or through elected or appointed representatives or institutions' and Art 255(a): 'benefits accruing from ... natural resources shall be shared equitably amongst the people'	-	-
Zimbabwe*	2013	-	Preamble: 'we the people ... *our* natural resources'	-

An asterisk (*) next to the country's name indicates known resource-dependency levels (see n 2)

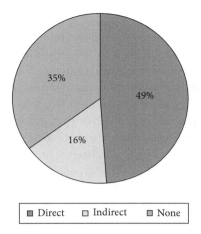

Figure 9.1 Summary of constitutional expressions of resource sovereignty in sub-Saharan jurisdictions

firm deductions can be made from this observation. Also, several countries with direct and strong endorsements of resource sovereignty have older constitutions.[41]

Where constitutions contain an acknowledgement—either direct or indirect—of resource sovereignty, the formulations vary, with some attributing property in natural resources to 'the state' and others, to 'the nation' or 'the people' of a particular country. (See further section 4.1 below.)

However, even in jurisdictions that have constitutions directly acknowledging, such assertions only affirm the extractive sectors' economic relevance. The details of resource management and governance are to be sought in other kinds of commitments, be they in the constitutions themselves, or in their accompanying legal frameworks. For instance, one may find a particular constitutional order's commitment to holding the state accountable for proper governance of mineral resources in its mechanisms to ensure transparency and accountability and uphold the rule of law. Article 132(4) and (5)(f) of Tanzania's Constitution contains provisions on the ethical conduct of public leaders, for example. It mandates the formulation of 'basic rules of ethics for public leaders' that, among other duties, must prescribe ways to promote honesty, transparency, impartiality, and integrity in public affairs, and to protect public funds and any other public property.

Provisions for protecting property and the environment, prevalent in several African constitutions,[42] may give insight into country-specific understandings of resource sovereignty.[43] An acknowledgement of constitutional property protection—even if it is a

---

[41] Guinea-Bisseau, Mauritius, Burkina Faso.

[42] For example, s 24 (Environment) and s 25 (Property) in South Africa's Constitution of 1996; arts 23 and 41 of the Constitution of the Democratic Republic of Congo, 2015; arts 13 and 15 of the Constitution of the Republic of Mali, 1992; and ss 13 and 28 of the Constitution of the Republic of Malawi, 1994.

[43] In some jurisdictions (eg ss 24, 27, and 30(2) of the Constitution of the United Republic of Tanzania of 1977) the expression of resource sovereignty is encompassed in the constitutional provisions dealing with the management and protection of property and/or land rights.

weak—would demonstrate the state's position on the protection of mineral tenure security and, by extension, mineral investment protection.[44] Sometimes, as with Botswana's Constitution,[45] the recognition of the right to and protection of property accompanies an affirmation of the state's right to utilize mineral resources.[46] Botswana's Constitution mentions this affirmation in conjunction with the right to secure development.

Constitutions may contain general assertions of, say, a democratic state model or constitutional supremacy, but the survey shows that such generalized confirmations of state organizational models do not usually provide enough detail to discern, with any certainty, the state's position on mineral governance. Rather, the broad survey reveals that most constitutions have few (if any) real features that give specific guidance on how mineral resources should be managed. The apparent trend instead is that constitutional provisions rarely go beyond asserting sovereignty over natural resources.[47] In some constitutions, such assertions accompany expressions of state ownership of such resources; in others, they do not.[48]

In all the jurisdictions in the survey, domestic legislation contained more detailed regulation, as Table 9.2 demonstrates. The applicable domestic law hence becomes important as a reflection of constitutional principles or values. The survey results in Table 9.2 are limited only to what can be taken from these countries' mining codes or laws. A consideration of environmental and property law principles would have far exceeded the scope of the current brief.

Figure 9.2 summarizes the survey undertaken in Table 9.2, as regards types of regulation found in domestic legal frameworks. The summary is based on a categorization of provisions according to the type of resource ownership foreseen. In most (28) of the jurisdictions included in the survey, domestic legislation affirms natural resources as state property. A smaller number (8) affirm natural resources as some form of public property or national heritage. Four jurisdictions contained references to natural resources as *both* state property *and* public property. Three further jurisdictions vest the mineral resources in a public office-bearer or institution (such as the president or government); one (Tanzania) contains references both to the latter type of vesting and the resources being public property. Only Mauritania's law vests mineral resources specifically in the landowner.

The ownership provisions in domestic legislation afford a clearer perspective on how the type of commitments states are prepared to make for the protection of proprietary positions can influence resource management. This is explored in the following section.

---

[44] See eg Robert Pritchard, 'Safeguards for Foreign Investment in Mining' in Elizabeth Bastida, Thomas Wälde, and Janeth Warden-Fernández (eds), *International and Comparative Mineral Law and Policy: Trends and Prospects* (Kluwer Law International 2005) 73 at 88ff and Heleen van Niekerk, 'Towards a New Understanding of Mineral Tenure Security: The Demise of the Property-Law Paradigm' (PhD thesis, University of Cape Town 2016) 71 and 92.

[45] 1966 (as amended 2006).

[46] Section 8(1)(a)(ii) and 8(1)(iii) read with s 9(2)(a), Constitution of the Republic of Botswana of 1966 (as amended).

[47] See Table 9.1.

[48] See Table 9.3. It was posited—but not tested—that assertions of direct state ownership of resources are more likely to appear in the constitutions of countries politically oriented to the left.

Table 9.2 Domestic legal affirmations of resource sovereignty in sub-Saharan Africa

Country	Domestic legislative affirmation of resource sovereignty			
	Mineral resources as state/government/republic/public property	Mineral resources as public good/public property/national heritage under state's custodianship	Mineral resources vested in office-bearer (president/government)	Mineral resources vested in private entity/landowner
Angola*	Art 42, Mining Code 2011	-	-	-
Benin*	Art 12, Mining Code 2006	-	-	-
Botswana*	-	S 3, Mines & Minerals Act 1999	-	-
Burkina Faso*	Art 6, Mining Code 2015	-	-	-
Burundi	Art 7, Mining Code 2013	-	-	-
Cameroon*	Art 5, Mining Code 2016	-	-	-
Cntrl Afrn Republic*	Art 6, Mining Code 2009	-	-	-
Chad*	Title 1, Mining Code 2018	-	-	-
Comoros	Art 5, Mining Code 1954	-	-	-
Congo (Brazzaville)*	-	Art 11, Revised Mining Code 2018	-	-
Côte d'Ivoire*	Art 3, Mining Code 2014	-	-	-
Dem Rep of Congo*	Art 3, Mining Code 2002	-	-	-
Djibouti	Art 3, Mining Code 2016	-	-	-
Equatorial Guinea*	S 2, Mining Law 2006	S 2, Mining Law 2006	-	-
Eswatini	S 41, Mines and Minerals Act 2011	-	-	-
Gabon*	Art 7, Mining Code of Gabon, 2019	Art 3, Art 7, Mining Code of Gabon, 2019	-	-

(continued)

Table 9.2 Continued

Country	Domestic legislative affirmation of resource sovereignty			
	Mineral resources as state/ government/republic property	Mineral resources as public good/public property/national heritage under state's custodianship	Mineral resources vested in office-bearer (president/government)	Mineral resources vested in private entity/landowner
Gambia	S 4, Mines and Quarries Act 2005	-	-	-
Ghana*	-	S 1, Minerals and Mining Act 2006	-	-
Guinea-Bissau	Art 3, Mining Code 2014	-	-	-
Guinea	Art 3, Mining Code of the Republic of Guinea, 2011	-	-	-
Kenya	-	S 6(1), Mining Act 2016	-	-
Lesotho*	-	S 3, Mines and Minerals Act 2005	-	-
Liberia*	Section 2.1, Minerals and Mining Law 2000	-	-	-
Madagascar	Art 3, Mining Code 2005	-	-	-
Malawi	S 4(1), Mines and Minerals Act 2018	-	-	-
Mali*	Art 3, Mining Code 2019	-	-	-
Mauritania*	-	-	-	Art 9, Mining Code 2008
Mauritius	-	-	S 4, Minerals Act 1966	-
Mozambique*	Art 4, Mining Code 2014	-	-	-
Namibia*	S 2, Namibian Minerals Act, 1992 (read with Minerals (Prospecting and Mining) Amendment Act 2008)	-	-	-

Country			
Niger*	Art 2, Mining Code 2006	Art 5, Mining Code 2006	-
Nigeria*	S 1, Minerals and Mining Act, 2007	-	-
Rwanda*	Art 4, Law on Mining and Quarry Operations 2018	-	-
Senegal*	Art 3, Mining Code 2016	-	-
Seychelles	S 3, Minerals Act 1962	-	-
Sierra Leone*	S 9(1), Mines and Minerals Act 2009	S 9(2), Mines and Minerals Act 2009	-
Somalia	S 2, Mining Law 1984	-	-
South Africa*	-	S 3(1), Mineral and Petroleum Resources Development Act 2002	-
South Sudan	S 6, Mining Act 2012	S 6, Mining Act 2012	-
Sudan*	S 8, Mineral Wealth and Mining (Development) Act 2015	-	-
United Rep of Tanzania*	-	Art 5, Mining Act 2010/2019	Art 5, Mining Act 2010/ 2019
Togo*	-	Art 3, Mining Code 1996	-
Uganda	S 3, Mining Act 2003	-	-
Zambia*	-	Art 3, Mines and Minerals Development Act 2015	Art 3, Mines and Minerals Development Act 2015
Zimbabwe*	-	-	S 2, Mines and Minerals Act 1961

An asterisk (*) next to the country's name indicates known resource-dependency levels (n 2)

3. Mineral Resource Holding as an Expression of Economic Policy

It is notable, when comparing the information in Tables 9.1 and 9.2, that direct constitutional expressions of resource sovereignty frequently overlap with further domestic-level legal assertions of resources as outright state property. Similarly, there is a significant correlation between jurisdictions with direct constitutional expressions of resource sovereignty and those with assertions of resources as public property. To be specific ten jurisdiction, of which three also assert state ownership, display the combination of direct constitutional expression of resource sovereignty, coupled with acknowledgements that these resources are public property.

However, these insights do not enable sufficient understanding of countries' specific choices around resource holding. Section 3.2 below links and problematizes states' economic policy choices with their preferred expressions of resource holding. The focus is on hard minerals only. A brief reference to the resource-curse phenomenon in section 3.1 provides context.

3.1 The Resource-Curse Syndrome

Paradoxically, states with vast natural resource wealth are often unable to translate it into enhanced quality of living for their peoples. Instead, they suffer from slower-than-expected economic growth, abject poverty, political instability, rampant corruption, and authoritarianism.[49] In economic and political theory, this phenomenon is referred to as the 'resource curse'.[50] Prevalent where states' economies rely too heavily on resource extraction,[51] the resource curse causes industries other than the extractive industries to wane,[52] obliterating the complex and diverse industrial context needed for any country to thrive. States afflicted by the resource curse tend to have governments more likely to be undemocratic and unaccountable.[53] Moreover, in

---

[49] Jeffrey D Sachs and Andrew M Warner, 'The Curse of Natural Resources' (2001) 45 European Economic Review 827, 827–31, demonstrate the missing link between resource wealth and economic growth. See also the general discussions by Africa Progress Panel in Africa Progress Report 2013, 'Equity in Extractives: Stewarding Africa's natural resources for all', 12–16 <https://reliefweb.int/sites/reliefweb.int/files/resources/relatorio-africa-progress-report-2013-pdf-20130511-125153.pdf> accessed 23 February 2021; Michael L Ross, *The Oil Curse: How Petroleum Wealth Shapes the Development of Nations* (Princeton University Press 2012) 1–3; Macartan Humphreys, Jeffrey D Sachs, and Joseph E Stiglitz, 'Introduction: What is the Problem with Natural Resource Wealth?' in Macartan Humphreys and others (eds), *Escaping the Resource Curse* (Columbia University Press 2007) 1–5; Michael L Ross, 'The Political Economy of the Resource Curse' (1999) World Politics 297, 297–98; M Dell, 'The Devil's Excrement: The Negative Effect of Natural Resources on Development (2004) Harvard International Review 38, 38. Afeikhena Jerome and others, 'Addressing Oil Related Corruption in Africa: Is the Push for Transparency Enough? (2005) 11(1) Review of Human Factor Studies Special Edition 7, 15.

[50] Phrase coined in Richard M Auty, *Sustaining Development in Mineral Economies: The Resource Curse Thesis* (Routledge 1993) 1.

[51] See Fabrizio Carmignani and Abdur Chowdhury, 'Why are Natural Resources a Curse in Africa, but not Elsewhere?' (2010), 3–4.

[52] Humphreys, Sachs, and Stiglitz (n 49) 5. Argentino Pessoa, 'Natural Resources and Institutions: The "Natural Resources Curse" Revisited' (2008) MPRA Paper No 8640, 4.

[53] Abdullah Al Faruque, 'Transparency in Extractive Revenues in Developing Countries and Economies in Transition: A Review of Emerging Best Practices' (2006) 24(1) Journal of Energy and Natural Resources 66, 66–67; Andrew Rosser, 'The Political Economy of the Resource Curse: A Literature Review' (2006) Institute of Development Studies Working Paper 268, 20. Also Andrew Williams, 'Shining a Light on the Resource Curse: An Empirical Analysis of the Relationship Between Natural Resources, Transparency, and Economic Growth' (2011) 39(4) World Development 490, 490.

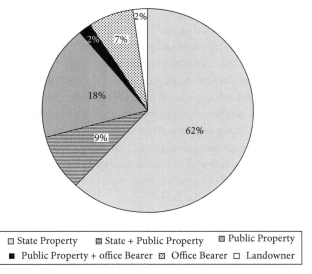

Figure 9.2 Types of resource-ownership expression in domestic legislation

such states revenue leakage is rife[54] and their societies are prone to conflict.[55] Such states often depend on extra-national and -continental entities for support.[56]

Attempts to explain the reasons for occurrences of the resource curse abound.[57] From the political science angle, such explanations focus on the prevalence of weak governance,[58] corruption,[59] and rent-seeking.[60] There is further focus on how such phenomena weaken democracy[61] and concentrate the proceeds of natural resource extraction in the hands of small elite groups of beneficiaries.[62] Rent-seeking also receives attention in economic

[54] Boniphace Luhende, 'Towards A Legal Framework for Preventing Tax Revenue Leakage in the Upstream Oil and Gas Industry in Tanzania: An Analysis of the Concepts, Methods and Options available in a Public Trusteeship Model of Natural Resource-holding' (PhD thesis, University of Cape Town 2017) 1–21.

[55] Nathan Jensen and Leonard Wantchekon, 'Resource Wealth and Political Regimes in Africa' (2004) 37(7) Comparative Political Studies 816, 821–22.

[56] Humphreys, Sachs, and Stiglitz (n 49) 8.

[57] Paul Stevens and Evelyn Dietsche, 'Resource Curse: An Analysis of Causes, Experiences and Possible Ways Forward' (2008) 36 Energy Policy 56–65. Emeka Duruigbo, 'The World Bank, Multinational Oil Corporations, and the Resource Curse in Africa' (2005) 26 U Pa J Int'l L 1, 12. Humphreys, Sachs, and Stiglitz (n 49) 4–14.

[58] Most notably the absence of transparency and accountability. See eg Ross (n 49) 59.

[59] Carlos Leite and Jens Weidmann, 'Does Mother Nature Corrupt? Natural Resources, Corruption, and Economic Growth' (1999) IMF Working Paper No 99/85, 3; Anthony J Venables, 'Using Natural Resources for Development: Why Has It Proven So Difficult' (2016) 30(1) Journal of Economic Perspective 161, 173; and Alberto Ades and Rafael Di Tella, 'Rents, Competition, and Corruption' (1999) 89(4) American Economic Review 982, 982–83.

[60] Term attributed to Anne O Krueger, 'The Political Economy of the Rent-Seeking Society' (1974) 64(3) American Economic Review 291, 291–303; rent-seeking refers to the actions of politically well-connected entrepreneurs who use their networks and relationships to profit from advantageous contracts concluded with the state. See eg Ragnar Torvik, 'Natural Resource, Rent Seeking and Welfare' (2002) 67(2) Journal of Development Economics 455.

[61] Dominik Kopiński and others, 'Resource Curse or Resource Disease? Oil in Ghana' (2013) 112 African Affairs 583, 584.

[62] Ramez Badeeb and others, 'The Evolution of the Natural Resource Curse Thesis: A Critical Literature Survey' (2017) Resources Policy 51, 123, 124. Kopiński and others (n 61) 584 citing Jeffrey D Sachs and Andrew M Warner, 'Natural Resource Abundance and Economic Growth' (1995) National Bureau of Economic Research Working Paper 5398. RM Auty, 'Introduction and Overview' in Richard Auty (ed), *Resource Abundance and Economic*

analyses, which consider, inter alia, price volatility[63] in natural resource markets, the repercussions of the so-called Dutch disease,[64] the lack of economic linkages[65] between the extractive industries and the local economies in which they operate, and the emphasis on natural resource extraction to the detriment of human resource development.[66]

Commentators agree that the resources themselves are not 'cursed'.[67] Human behaviour is what turns a national asset into a collective liability.[68] Some posit that the resource curse results ultimately from an institutional failure to enforce property rights.[69] Others opine that the failure at the heart of the resource curse is even broader: the root cause is the state's failure to discharge its duties in managing its mineral and petroleum resources.[70] They suggest that the quality of governance and the competence of a country's governmental institutions are crucial in determining the nexus between the prevalence of natural resources in a country and the society's living standards.[71]

Scholars who follow the effects of the resource curse in African states such as the Republic of the Congo, Gabon, Nigeria, and Sudan observe that sub-Saharan Africa has some of the world's poorest natural-resource-exporting states, and that this region hence is the one most affected by the resource curse.[72] Analysts[73] who are more cautious about assuming

---

Development (Oxford University Press 2001). Humphreys, Sachs, and Stiglitz (n 49) 12. Elissaios Papyrakis and Reyer Gerlagh, 'The Resource Curse Hypothesis and Its Transmission Channels' (2004) 32(1) Journal of Comparative Economics 181, 181–82 and 190.

[63] Raymond F Mikesell, 'Explaining the Resource Curse, with Special Reference to Mineral Exporting Countries' (1997) 23(4) Resources Policy 191, 193. Frederick van der Ploeg and Steven Poelhekke, 'Volatility and the Natural Resource Curse' (2009) 61(4) Oxford Economic Papers 727, 736.

[64] That is, the singular focus on the extractives sector to the neglect of the other sectors of the economy. See eg Zuzana Brinčiková, 'The Dutch Disease: An Overview' (2016) 12(10) European Scientific Journal, Special Edition 95, 95.

[65] William R Freudenburg and Robert Gramling, 'Linked to What? Economic Linkages in an Extractive Economy' (1998) 11(6) Society & Natural Resources 569, 569–70; Michael W Hansen, 'From Enclave to Linkage Economies? A Review of the Literature on Linkages between Extractive Multinational Corporations and Local Industry in Africa' (2014) DIIS Working Paper, 2, 5.

[66] Thorvaldur Gylfason, 'Natural Resources, Education and Economic Development' (2001) 45 European Economic Review 847, 850.

[67] Carmignani and Chowdhury (n 51); Mikesell (n 63) 191; Ragnar Torvik, 'Why do Some Resource-Abundant Countries Succeed while Others do not?' (2009) 25(2) Oxford Review of Economic Policy 241, 245–50.

[68] Leif Wenar, 'Property Rights and the Resource Curse' (2008) 36(1) Philosophy & Public Affairs 2, 9.

[69] ibid.

[70] John R Heilbrunn, *Oil, Democracy and Development in Africa* (Cambridge University Press, 2014) 2; Jorge E Viñuales 'The "Resource Curse"—A Legal Perspective' (2011) 17(2) Global Governance 197, 208; Erika Weinthal and Pauline Jones Luong, 'Combating the Resource Curse: An Alternative Solution to Managing Mineral Wealth' (2006) 4(1) Perspectives on Politics 35, 38–39; Wenar (n 68) 9–12; African Development Bank and the African Union, *Oil and Gas in Africa* (Oxford University Press 2009) 110; JR Mailey, *The Anatomy of the Resource Curse: Predatory Investment in Africa's Extractive Industries* ACSS Special Report No 3 (Africa Center for Strategic Studies 2015) 5.

[71] See eg William Hogan, Federico Sturzenegger, and Laurence Tai, 'Contracts and Investment in Natural Resources' in William Hogan and Federico Sturzenegger (eds), *The Natural Resources Trap: Private Investment without Public Commitment* (MIT Press, 2010) 2. UNCTAD, *World Investment Report 2007: Transnational Corporations, Extractive Industries and Development* (2007) 94.

[72] Petar Kurečić and Marija Seba, 'The Resource Curse in Sub-Saharan Africa: A Reality Corroborated by the Empirical Evidence' (conference paper for the 15th International Scientific Conference on Economic and Social Development—Human Resources Development, Varazdin. Vol 1, June 2016) <https://bib.irb.hr/datoteka/820620. The_Resource_Curse_in_Sub-Saharan_Africa.pdf> accessed 15 February 2021.

[73] Charlotte J Lundgren, Alun H Thomas, and Robert C York, 'Boom, Bust, or Prosperity? Managing Sub-Saharan Africa's Natural Resource Wealth', 4-15 (International Monetary Fund, Washington, DC, 2013).

the prevalence of the resource curse in resource-rich states in Africa cite compelling data to show that states classified as 'fiscally dependent on budget revenue derived from natural resource extraction' are vulnerable to the resource curse, or most of its symptoms.[74] Even Botswana, arguably the only African country to have avoided the resource curse,[75] faces challenges.[76]

3.2 Resource-Holding Models as Response to the Resource Curse

For law scholarship, one entry point into the problem of the resource curse and the context of PSNR is to ask how existing or yet-to-be-developed legal mechanisms can contribute to the design of models for generating better economic outcomes: models that can improve the material conditions of people living under the triple burdens of poverty,[77] inequality,[78] and unemployment[79] in Africa.

Famously dubbed the 'evil triplets',[80] these burdens relating to underdevelopment are part of the great moral challenges facing humanity.[81] A state's choices around how to manage and administer its mineral resources[82] respond to the challenge of the 'evil triplets'

---

[74] ibid.

[75] See Halvor Mehlum, Karl Moene, and Ragnar Torvik, 'Cursed by Resources or Institutions?' (2006) 29(8) The World Economy 1117, 1117–20. Also Carmignani and Chowdhury (n 51), Ross (n 49) 3–4, and UNCTAD (n 71) 93.

[76] Scholars have noted Botswana's struggles with eg the repercussions of the AIDS pandemic, a weak civil society, poor rural areas, high unemployment rates, and minority discrimination. See Ellen Hillbom, 'Diamonds or Development? A Structural Assessment of Botswana's Forty Years of Success' (2008) 46(2) Journal of Modern African Studies 191, 192–93. Also Robert L Curry, Jr, 'Poverty and Mass Unemployment in Mineral-Rich Botswana' (1987) 46(1) The American Journal of Economics and Sociology 71, 71–87; Ian Taylor, 'As Good as It Gets? Botswana's "Democratic Development"' (2003) 21(2) Journal of Contemporary African Studies 225, 215–16.

[77] South Africa recorded a poverty headcount ratio of 55.5 per cent in 2015. See The World Bank, 'Poverty Headcount Ratio at National Poverty Lines (% of Population)—South Africa' <https://data.worldbank.org/indicator/SI.POV.NAHC?locations=ZA> accessed 15 February 2021.

[78] In 2014, South Africa's Gini coefficient of 0.63 (where 0 represents perfect equality and 1, maximal inequality) made it one of the most unequal countries in the world. See The World Bank, 'Gini Index (World Bank Estimate)—South Africa' <https://data.worldbank.org/indicator/SI.POV.GINI?locations=ZA> accessed 15 February 2021. See also Anton van Dalsen and Charles Simkins, 'Does Gini Index really Show SA as Most Unequal Society in the World?' Politics Web (13 June 2019) <https://www.politicsweb.co.za/opinion/does-the-gini-index-show-that-sa-is-the-most-unequ> accessed 17 February 2021.

[79] South Africa's unemployment rate increased from 23.3 per cent in the second quarter of 2020 to 30.8 per cent in the third quarter. See Trading Economics, 'South Africa Unemployment Rate' <https://tradingeconomics.com/south-africa/unemployment-rate> accessed 15 February 2021. See also Statistics South Africa, 'SA economy sheds 2,2 million jobs in Q2 but unemployment levels drop' (29 September 2020) <http://www.statssa.gov.za/?p=13633> accessed 15 February 2021.

[80] The phrase is attributed to the former South African Mineral Resources Minister Susan Shabangu, who in a 2011 speech referred to the 'evil triplets' of the mining sector as poverty, inequality, and unemployment. See eg Sekai Chiwandamira and Tiyani Majoko, 'South Africa: The Evil Triplets and the Mining Industry' Modise (2 February 2012) <https://www.mondaq.com/southafrica/mining/163204/the-evil-triplets-and-the-mining-industry> accessed 17 December 2020. See also Sekai Chiwandamira and Tiyani Majoko, 'The Evil Triplets and the Mining Industry' (2011) 11 Without Prejudice 53–55.

[81] South Africa's National Development Plan seeks to address this 'triple challenge' of poverty, inequality, and violence by 2030. See Victor Sulla and Precious Zikhali, 'Overcoming Poverty and Inequality in South Africa: An Assessment of Drivers, Constraints and Opportunities' (2018) International Bank for Reconstruction and Development/The World Bank, 1. See also in general Pius N Langa, 'The Role of the Constitution in the Struggle against Poverty' (2011) 22(3) Stellenbosch Law Review 446–51 for the Constitution's aspiration for the achievement of equality and fighting poverty.

[82] Hanri Mostert and Cheri-Leigh Young, 'Natural Resources as "Regulated Property": The Challenges of Resource Stewardship in South Africa' in Christine Godt (ed), Regulatory Property Rights: The Transforming Notion of Property in Transnational Business Regulation (Brill Nijhoff 2016) 141.

in the mining sector and reveal its preferred resource-holding model. The resource-holding model usually indicates how and upon whom the powers of use, control, and ownership of mineral resources are conferred, and how they should be exercised legitimately within the legal framework.

A state's legal heritage, which underlies political and economic convictions and context, has a significant influence on the state's resource-holding model.[83] For instance, in historically 'regalian' systems of mineral ownership, surface ownership is distinguished from ownership of the subsoil.[84] Yet, even within such regalian systems, the character of the state's ownership differs from jurisdiction to jurisdiction.[85] In some, referred to as 'domanial' systems,[86] minerals fall under the absolute ownership of the state. In contrast, in 'true' regalian systems, control (but not necessarily absolute ownership) of all mines is vested in the state.[87]

These choices around management and administration of resources are not static. They tend to pendulate along with the policy shifts between nationalization and privatization that have characterized regulation of extractives sectors in post-colonial Africa. There are at least two holding models worth mentioning at the outset:

'Privatized holding' refers to models in which the state decentralizes ownership rights and control of the mineral resource and/or specific related industries by allowing private-sector regulation. An example is a system that enables private landowners, rather than the state, to control who can access a resource and how the resource is to be extracted. Admittedly, this type of control is not widespread in modern Africa,[88] but a close historical example is available. Around 1911 and 1912, the British South African Company (BSAC) of Cecil John Rhodes in effect usurped control of mineral resources in two regions now located in present-day Zambia.[89] It did so by negotiating British 'protection' treaties with local chieftains and gaining exclusive rights of extraction over the region.[90] Even the first statute regulating mining in the area, the Mining Ordinance of 1912, was designed to provide Rhodes's company with a mechanism to regulate the mining rights it could grant to anyone who could pay a minimal fee to obtain a prospecting right.[91] The benefit of more than a century's worth of hindsight[92] exposes this arrangement as untoward,[93] at the very least. It also cultivates understanding of the Zambian state's reaction in favour of an alternative resource-holding model.

---

[83] See in general Antony Butler, 'Resource Nationalism and the African National Congress' (2013) 113 The Journal of the Southern African Institute of Mining and Metallurgy 11, 11–19.

[84] Nicholas J Campbell, Jr, 'Principles of Mineral Ownership in the Civil Law and Common Law Systems' (1956) (31) Tulane Law Review 303, 306.

[85] Van den Berg (n 8).

[86] Campbell (n 84) 307.

[87] ibid.

[88] The closest current example is in the wording of the mining code of Mauritania: see art 9 of the Mining Code adopted by Law No 2008-011 dated 27 April 2008.

[89] North-East and North-West Rhodesia.

[90] Muna Ndulo, 'Mining Legislation and Mineral Development in Zambia' (1986) 19(1) Cornell International Law Journal 1, 6–7.

[91] ibid 7.

[92] There is no scope here to explore the insights gained from analyses in decolonialist literature, but see eg Rodney (n 12).

[93] Indeed, the legitimacy of the BSAC's title to minerals became an especially sore point in the run-up to Zambian independence in 1964. Ndulo (n 90) 1, 9–10.

The alternative model, the polar opposite of privatized holding, is assumed to be the most widespread.[94] It concentrates the vesting of rights of ownership and control over the mineral resource (or even specific related industries) in the state. The shorthand reference for this model here is 'nationalized' holding; however, the term 'resource nationalism'[95] is also used in the literature to signify a state's predisposition towards increased control of economic activities relating to natural resources within its borders.[96] 'Resource nationalism' may refer either to outright state ownership of such resources, or to a regulatory and fiscal regime adjustment to increase the benefit the state derives from economic activities in the sector.[97] As such, the term is less discerning than 'nationalized' holding, and for purposes of this chapter, less useful.

In keeping with the Zambian example, after the BSAC had been pressured to relinquish its claims to Zambia's newly formed independent state,[98] the Zambian government veered towards nationalizing the mining sector from 1969 onwards.[99] Nationalization involved the creation of a state mining company with stakes in each mine.[100] It was born of the belief that stronger state influence was needed if management policies were to benefit the Zambian people through skills building and if the out-flow of value from the mining sector was to be slowed down.[101] Nationalization responded, in other words, to the realization that poverty, unemployment, and inequality could not be eradicated by allowing the private sector, consisting mostly of foreign investors, to regulate Zambia's mineral resource wealth.[102]

The Zambian state held its mining sector in an iron grip for decades. This approach bore initial successes through the up-skilling of Zambia's local workforce and the enhancement of its educational system to benefit the local people.[103] However, declines in productivity, a sustained copper-price bust, and lack of reinvestment in the maintenance of the mines ultimately placed Zambia's nationalized mining sector under severe strain. This led to a reprivatization of the sector between 1990 and 2000.[104] The state mining company, Zambia

---

[94] Luong and Weinthal (n 33), 241–63; Flomenhoft (n 33).

[95] Resource nationalism is understood as the inclination of a state to increase (either outright or indirectly through regulatory or fiscal measures) its control over economic activities that are related to natural resources within its territorial boundaries. Siri Lange and Abel Kinyondo, 'Local Content in the Tanzanian Mining Sector' (2016) 15(3) CMI Brief, 2.

[96] Lange and Kinyondo (n 95).

[97] ibid.

[98] Ndulo (n 90) 9–10.

[99] J Sikamo, A Mwanza, and C Mweemba, 'Copper Mining in Zambia—History and Future' (2016) 116(6) The Journal of the Southern African Institute of Mining and Metallurgy 491, 492ff provides a succinct account of the Matero reforms that paved the way to state appropriation of majority shareholding in all mines. See also Ndulo (n 90) 11.

[100] The undeveloped concessions and special grants bestowed on (in particular) Anglo-American and Roan Select Trust during the pre-independence period were terminated, releasing areas in which these companies were not mining at full scale. Later, a dividend share buy-out arrangement with the mining companies resulted in a take-over of a 51 per cent equity share in existing mines. Sikamo, Mwanza, and Mweemba (n 99) 493.

[101] Ndulo (n 90) 1, 10–11; Sikamo, Mwanza, and Mweemba (n 99) 491. Also see Alastair Fraser and Miles Larmer (eds), *Zambia, Mining, and Neoliberalism: Boom and Bust on the Globalized Copperbelt* (Palgrave Macmillan 2010) 7.

[102] The Zambian example resonates with the findings of an earlier study of post-colonial economic 'policy oscillation' in Asia and Latin America. There, the established pattern was found to be a shift from a colonial free-trade economy to post-independence nationalization, and then back again to subsequent rounds of privatization. See Amy L Chua, 'The Privatization-Nationalization Cycle: The Link between Markets and Ethnicity in Developing Countries' (1995) 95(2) Columbia Law Review 223, 254.

[103] Sikamo, Mwanza, and Mweemba (n 99) 493–94.

[104] ibid 494.

Consolidated Copper Mines, was unbundled and sold off in smaller units.[105] Unlike the privatized model of pre-independence, however, private mining companies in Zambia now operate within the bounds of the law set by the Zambian state, rather than within the dictates of a private, foreign entity such as the BSAC. The law provides[106] for a model based on the notion of mineral resources as 'property of the public'.[107] This model entails a different role for the state, namely a custodial role (discussed further below).

The phenomenon of policy careening between market-economy privatization and command-economy nationalization models in post-colonial independent states[108] has especially profound effects in the extractives context. Earlier research drew attention to the ever-increasing cost of sustaining the pendulation between privatization and nationalization.[109] The latter insight is important for present purposes: constant political manipulation of ownership patterns is costly.[110] Moreover, it is not eradicating 'the evil triplets'. Instead, in the accompanying legal and bureaucratic reorganization, the costs rack up, while public trust in the legitimacy of the state or the governing party plummets, with an accompanying dive in investor confidence and losses in production.[111] Often, economically destructive political violence follows.[112] Economists have also been unable to conclude that a return to privatization necessarily improves production or growth trajectories.[113] In some instances, it can even be more destructive.[114] Further, the success of the state-owned resource sectors of some states (the Scandinavian countries generally and Norway in particular)[115] continue to garner support for models sporting some forms of resource nationalization.[116]

Basically, the swings in economic policy fail to address the paradox at the heart of attempts to regulate resource holding: one cannot nationalize what is internally fractured; yet, privatizing it simply widens the cracks in society by reintroducing dependence on foreign capital and skills.[117] Neither the privatized nor the nationalized model of resource holding has thus proven effective in addressing the main concerns in post-colonial states afflicted by the resource curse. Indeed, research suggests that, almost without fail, the rotation of such policies in post-colonial states causes further problems.[118] To avoid a downward spiral, large-scale institutional reform of the state is often necessary.[119] Such institutional reform should be conscious of the predatory tendencies[120] that accompany the struggle for political

---

[105] ibid.

[106] Art 16(1), Zambian Mines and Minerals and Minerals Development Act, 2015.

[107] Muna Ndulo, 'The Ownership of Base Minerals in Zambia' (1980) 13(1) The Comparative and International Journal of Southern Africa 78–85.

[108] Chua (n 102) 254.

[109] Butler (n 83) 12.

[110] CP Mayer and SA Meadowcroft, 'Selling Public Assets: Techniques and Financial Implications' (1985) 6(4) Fiscal Studies 42, 42, 44 and 47.

[111] Butler (n 83) 12.

[112] Chua (n 102) 223–303.

[113] Mayer and Meadowcroft (n 110) 48–52.

[114] Christoffer Guldbrandsen 'Why Poverty? Stealing Africa', Denmark: Guldbrandsen Film, 2012. HD, 58 min. Available at <https://www.youtube.com/watch?v=WNYemuiAOfU> accessed 25 September 2021. This exposes a global trade in which money and natural resources flow in only one direction, namely away from those who are regarded as deserving of benefit.

[115] See eg Juan Manuel Ramírez-Cendrero and Eszter Wirth, 'Is the Norwegian Model Exportable to Combat Dutch Disease' (2016) 48 Resource Policy 85, 85.

[116] Butler (n 83) 13.

[117] Butler (n 83) 12; Chua (n 102) 263ff, 283–84.

[118] Chua (n 102) 285–86.

[119] Chua (n 102) 298–99.

[120] ibid 299.

Table 9.3 Resource-holding provisions in the mining statutes of sub-Saharan African countries

Country	Date of legislation / code	Vesting clause					Benefit clause	
		In people / public property	In republic / state	In government	In president	In landowner	Acknowledgement of benefit of people	Trustee / fiduciary / custodial language
Angola*	2011	-	yes		-		-	-
Benin*	2006	-	yes		-		-	-
Botswana*	1999	-	yes		-		yes	-
Burkina Faso*	2015	-	yes				-	-
Burundi	2013	-	yes		-		-	-
Cameroon*	2016	-	yes				-	-
Cntrl Afrn Republic*	2009	-	yes		-		-	-
Chad*	2018	-	yes		-		-	-
Comoros	1954	-	yes		-		-	-
Congo (Brazzaville)*	2005	yes	-		-		yes	yes
Côte d'Ivoire*	2014	-	yes		-		-	-
Dem Rep of Congo*	2002	-	yes		-		-	-
Djibouti	2016	yes	-		-		yes	yes

(continued)

Table 9.3 Continued

Country	Date of legislation / code	Vesting clause					Benefit clause	
		In people / public property	In republic / state	In government	In president	In landowner	Acknowledgement of benefit of people	Trustee / fiduciary / custodial language
Equatorial Guinea*	2006	-	yes	-	-	-	-	-
Eswatini	2011	-	-	-	yes	-	-	-
Gabon*	2005	-	yes	-	-	-	yes	-
Gambia	2005	-	yes	-	-	-	-	-
Ghana*	2006	-	-	-	yes	-	yes	yes
Guinea*	2011	-	yes	-	-	-	-	-
Guinea-Bissau	2014	-	yes	-	-	-	-	-
Kenya	2016	-	yes	-	-	-	yes	yes
Lesotho*	2005	yes	-	-	-	-	yes	-
Liberia*	2000	-	yes	-	-	-	-	-
Madagascar	2005	-	yes	-	-	-	-	-
Malawi	2018	-	yes	-	-	-	yes	-
Mali*	2019	-	yes	-	-	-	-	-
Mauritania*	2008	-	-	-	-	yes	-	-
Mauritius	1966	-	-	yes	-	-	-	-

Country	Year						
Mozambique*	2014	yes	-	-	-	-	-
Namibia*	1992	yes	-	-	-	-	-
Niger*	2006	yes	-	-	-	-	-
Nigeria*	2007	-	yes	-	-	yes	yes
Rwanda*	2018	yes	-	-	-	-	-
Senegal*	2016	yes	-	-	-	-	-
Seychelles	1962	yes	-	-	-	-	-
Sierra Leone*	2009	yes	-	-	-	yes	yes
Somalia	1984	yes	-	-	-	-	-
South Africa*	2002	-	-	yes	-	yes	yes
South Sudan	2007	-	yes	-	-	yes	yes
Sudan*	2015	yes	-	-	-	-	-
United Rep of Tanzania*	2019	-	-	-	yes	yes	yes
Togo*	1996	-	-	yes	-	-	-
Uganda	2003	-	yes	-	-	-	-
Zambia*	2015	-	-	-	yes	-	yes
Zimbabwe*	1961	-	-	-	yes	-	-

An asterisk (*) next to the country's name indicates known resource-dependency levels (n 2)

and economic power in states attempting to overcome the resource curse.[121] With this insight in mind, the next section analyses the legal mechanisms, already available in many
African states, that allow new approaches to resource holding in Africa to emerge.

4. New Approaches to Resource Holding in Africa

A survey of 'holding model' clauses in the domestic laws of sub-Saharan African states reveals a trend towards vesting resources in the 'nation' or 'people' and, as such, stipulating
that the management of such resources is 'for the benefit of' the nation or people. Section 4.2
below explores what this might mean on a conceptual level; section 4.3 considers whether
such an approach might avoid the problems caused by repeated policy careening between
nationalization and privatization.

4.1 A Survey of 'Holding Model' Clauses

Table 9.3 shows the result of a survey[122] of 'holding model' clauses from mining codes in
forty-five sub-Saharan states. With the resource-holding options above in mind, the survey
categorizes states according to the way in which their mining statutes express the vesting of
control over such resources. The survey also identifies states whose legislative frameworks
expressly provide for sharing of the benefits of mining.

Most states in sub-Saharan Africa have revised their mineral resource laws in the past
twenty years.[123] International financial institutions, in particular the World Bank, were in-
strumental in effecting many of these reforms.[124] Such reforms focused on 'mining as a
driver of development.'[125] Mineral-rich jurisdictions received financial and technical support for mining-law and governance reforms. The preference was for reforms that enabled
increased foreign direct investment in the mining sector, for example through liberalization
of import and export promotion, liberalization of exchange controls, and fiscal reform. The
institutions also favoured reduced state involvement, for example through state-owned enterprise reform, privatization, reduction of public expenditure, and reform of public sector
management.[126] Worldwide, more than ninety states, many of them in Africa, responded to
these incentives.

Most of the clauses from African mining laws that came from twenty-first-century reform refer to the vesting of mineral resources in the state, with some of them endorsing a
stronger model of state control than others. There are also different ways to reference state
control. Thirty statutes vest mineral resources in the 'state' or 'republic', four vest them in

---

[121] Papyrakis and Gerlagh (n 62), 187–89.
[122] The author is grateful to Chiyedza Mutendera, LLM Researcher at the SARChI: MLiA Chair, for undertaking
this wide-ranging collection of data from the African Mining Legislation Atlas (<http://www.a-mla.org>).
[123] The only states with mining codes or laws older than two decades are Botswana, Comoros, Namibia,
Mauritius, Seychelles, Somalia, Togo, and Zimbabwe.
[124] Tracy-Lynn Field, *State Governance of Mining, Development and Sustainability* (Edward Elgar Publishing
Limited 2019) 17.
[125] ibid.
[126] ibid.

the 'government', and five vest them in the 'president'. Another five have phraseology either referring to mineral resources as 'public property' or vesting them in 'the people' or 'nation'.

Beneath these differences of terminology and ideology, the growing legislative trend is to position the state (or its functionaries) in a custodial or fiduciary role in respect of mineral resources. Even where the terminology is unusual (such as in the vesting clause in the mining law of Congo Brazzaville),[127] the choice of typifying the country's mineral resources as the 'national mining heritage' and entrusting the state to 'protect' and 'guarantee' its development suggests a fiduciary duty resting upon the state.

The trending provisions also regularize the idea that the state must administer resources 'for the benefit of' the 'people' or the 'nation'. Of the thirty legal frameworks that vest mineral resources in the republic or the state, five—Botswana,[128] Kenya,[129] Malawi,[130] Gabon,[131] and Sierra Leone[132]—have wording in their mining laws acknowledging that the state must act to benefit its people when managing mineral resources. Kenya, in addition, includes a reference to the state's role as trustee.[133]

Nine of the surveyed mining laws vest the respective states' mineral resources in the government or the president.[134] A further five[135] vest the mineral resources directly in the people or the nation of the particular state, with some using language rendering the resources 'public property'. All but one[136] couples such vesting with express statements that the state must manage the mineral resources to benefit the people of the relevant country. Except for the laws of Malawi and Botswana, which acknowledge popular benefit without referring to custodial holding, these clauses additionally refer to the states' duties in language suggesting a trust, fiduciary, or custodial responsibility. For the sake of simplification, the denominator for this type of holding here is 'custodial', irrespective of specific jurisdictions' terminology.

What can be gleaned from a side-by-side study of the resource-holding clauses in many sub-Saharan states is a growing trend towards overt acknowledgement of popular benefit through resource extraction, sometimes with an added directive about the state's fiduciary or custodial responsibilities. Twelve of the African states in the survey have revised their mining laws since 2015. Of these, five have coupled the vesting provisions with directives around popular benefit and fiduciary or custodial holding.[137]

The survey focused only on explicit vesting and benefit clauses in mining laws. Nonetheless, in some contexts, judicial interpretation of clauses that, on first glance, favour a strong model of state control without qualifications of popular benefit or fiduciary/custodial holding, could slant the categorization towards custodial holding. Analysing these nuances is beyond the scope of this chapter, so the discussion of Namibia below must suffice as an example.

---

[127] Art 11 of the Mining Code of Congo, Law No 4/2005.
[128] Section 3 Mines and Minerals Act No 17 of 1999.
[129] Section 6(1) of Mining Act No 12 of 2016.
[130] Section 4(1) of the Mines and Minerals Act of Malawi, 2018.
[131] Art 3 and 7, Mining Code of Gabon, 2019.
[132] Section 9 of the Mines and Minerals Act 12 of 2009.
[133] Section 6(1)(c) of the Mining Act 12 of 2016.
[134] Government: Mauritius, Nigeria, South Sudan, Uganda. President: Eswatini, Ghana, Tanzania, Zambia, Zimbabwe.
[135] Congo (Brazzaville), Djibouti, Lesotho, South Africa, and Togo.
[136] See s 3 of Uganda's Mining Act of 2003.
[137] Tanzania in 2019, Zambia in 2015, Malawi in 2018, Djibouti in 2016, and Kenya in 2016.

Also, as to vesting clauses mentioning the 'republic' or the 'state', what is omitted is a deeper analysis of related legislation circumscribing the powers of the holding entity, especially under a new wave of constitutionalism. Such analyses could change the picture even more. For example, Zimbabwe's mining law, one of the longest-standing in Africa, harks back to 1961 and vests the country's mineral resources in 'the President'.[138] However, the 2013 Constitution articulates the role of the President to include the duty to 'promote unity and peace in the nation for the benefit and well-being of all the people of Zimbabwe'.[139] Such wording lends credence to an interpretation of custodial holding even in a country whose mining code has (so far) evaded twenty-first-century reform. Further in-depth analyses are likely to reveal similar positions in other states where resources are vested in the state or republic.

A further note of caution: to stay on trend, a state could revise its laws to introduce the notions of state custodial holding and popular benefit, yet without changing its approach in practice to granting concessions or licences. For fuller understanding, more in-depth, jurisdiction-specific research is needed—this, too, is beyond the scope of the chapter.

For now, the focus remains on the possibility that recent attempts at articulating how African states should hold and administer mineral resources is a response to the realization that neither a nationalizing nor a privatizing approach to resource holding has served African jurisdictions particularly well. The notion of custodianship, resource stewardship/trusteeship, or fiduciary holding—often accompanied by an acknowledgement that the state must manage resources for popular or national benefit—may thus be the medium for acknowledging the various interests at play and creating an equilibrium of such interests. The next section considers the conceptualization of custodial resource holding in a sample of African jurisdictions.

4.2 Conceptualizing Custodial Resource Holding

Although custodial resource holding prevails in many of Africa's mining laws, state custodianship of mineral resources remains a fluid concept. Disagreement about its substance continues to arise in scholarship.[140] However, across various jurisdictions, it is a constant that custodial resource holding targets a specific interest group—'the people' or 'the citizens' of a particular country—as its beneficiaries. This characteristic is a key commonality across all jurisdictions grouped in the custodial-holding category. It has led several scholars to regard custodial holding as a manifestation of a fiduciary relationship[141]

---

[138] Section 2 of the Mines and Minerals Act of Zimbabwe [Chapter 21:05], 1961.

[139] Sections 13, 73, and 90 of the Constitution of Zimbabwe Amendment (No 20) Act, 2013.

[140] cf Elmarie van der Schyff, 'Who "Owns" the Country's Mineral Resources? The Possible Incorporation of the Public Trust Doctrine through the Mineral and Petroleum Resources Development Act' (2008) 4 TSAR 757, 758–59; PJ Badenhorst and H Mostert, *Mineral and Petroleum Law of South Africa* (Juta 2004) 13-4 to 13-11 (RS10, 2014); PJ Badenhorst and H Mostert, 'Artikel 3(1) en (2) van die Mineral and Petroleum Development Act 28 of 2002: 'n herbeskouing' (2007) TSAR 469, 476; HM van den Berg, 'Ownership of Minerals under the New Legislative Framework for Mineral Resources' (2009) 20 Stellenbosch Law Review 139, 145; MO Dale and others, *South African Mineral and Petroleum Law* (LexisNexis Butterworth 2005) 20–122 to 20-129 (s 91) (RS 29, 2020).

[141] A fiduciary relationship exists where the responsible party (fiduciary) acts responsibly and to the benefit of the beneficiary, often, but not always, with the latter's consent. See Evan Fox-Decent, 'The Fiduciary Nature of State Legal Authority' (2005) 31 Queen's Law Journal 259, 263, where the state exercises its fiduciary power in the

between the state and its people regarding the country's mineral (and other natural) resources.[142]

Under custodial resource-holding models, state control is generally constrained and the state's powers circumscribed in various ways.[143] Writing custodianship into a country's mining law is, in other words, a mechanism to hold the state *responsible and accountable* for administering mineral resources in a particular way such that all its people can benefit.[144] At the very least, therefore, custodial holding, endorsed in law, can inform decision-making and give direction to further policy-making. Hence this form of resource holding may seek to ensure that the state does not succumb to the resource curse.

In some African jurisdictions, it is hard to come by any systematic legislative engagement with the meaning and content of such holding. Gaps like these lead to scholarly conjecture, as has been the case, for instance, in South African law. The country's Constitution of 1996 is oblique about resource sovereignty.[145] Still, its Mineral and Petroleum Resources Development Act (MPRDA)[146] is clear: resource holding is based on the principle of state custodianship.[147] Few other statutory innovations have given rise to as much academic speculation as the legislative introduction of state custodianship of mineral and petroleum resources.[148]

Section 3(1) of the MPRDA is pivotal. It states that mineral and petroleum resources belong to the nation, with the state (as custodian) responsible for ensuring that the exploitation of these resources occurs for the nation's benefit. Scholarly opinion diverges on the meaning and consequences of this legislative construct. One vein of opinion is that section 3(1) renders the country's mineral resources a *res publica*.[149] Another is that the collective wealth of mineral and petroleum resources, comprising unextracted minerals and petroleum, is what vests in the nation; the minerals *in situ* on individual properties belong to individuals.[150] Yet another scholarly view is that individual landowners remain the owners of the minerals contained in and on their land, subject to the public trust doctrine.[151] A variation on this theme is that South Africa's mineral resources became statutory public property and vested in the state as custodian for the people of South Africa.[152]

---

interests of its people, the state-subject may withhold consent or reject the state's authority. However, see the application of this concept in the context of resource sovereignty in Emeka Duruigbo, 'Permanent Sovereignty and Peoples' Ownership of Natural Resources in International Law' (2006) 38(1) George Washington International Law Review 33, 67.

[142] Fox-Decent (n 141) 263.
[143] Van den Berg (n 140) 145.
[144] See eg in relation to South Africa, Van der Schyff (n 140).
[145] As indicated in Table 9.1, South Africa's Constitution contains a reference, in its preamble, to its sovereignty as a nation. In the constitutional property clause, s 25(4)(a) defines property as inclusive of natural resources, which means these resources qualify for protection under this clause. The property clause further mandates the state to undertake land and resource reform to bring about a more equitable dispensation.
[146] 28 of 2002.
[147] Sections 2 and 3 of the Mineral and Petroleum Resource Development Act 28 of 2002; Van der Schyff (n 36) 165.
[148] Badenhorst and Mostert 2004 (n 140) 13-4 to 13-11 (RS10, 2014); Badenhorst and Mostert 2007 (n 140) 476; Van der Schyff (n 36) 230ff; Van den Berg (n 140) 139ff; Dale and others (n 140) 20-122 to 20-129 (s 91) (RS 29, 2020); Van der Vyver (n 29) 125ff.
[149] Badenhorst and Mostert 2004 (n 140) 13-14.
[150] Dale and others (n 140) 20-123 to 20-125 (s 91) (RS 29, 2020).
[151] Jan Glazewski, *Environmental Law in South Africa* (2nd edn, LexisNexis 2005) para 17.5.22.
[152] Van der Schyff (n 36) 229-300.

The South African judiciary has now acknowledged that the custodianship provision of section 3(1) represents a fundamental departure from previous legal positions.[153] It has also indicated that, at its core, the provision commits to transforming the extractives sector and improving access to it for previously disadvantaged citizens.[154] *De Beers Consolidated Mines Ltd v Ataqua Mining (Pty) Ltd and Others*[155] dealt with whether tailings were subject to the provisions in the MPRDA. In an *obiter dictum*, the provincial High Court engaged with the meaning of custodianship, comparing South Africa's fishing resources with its mineral and petroleum resources.[156] Based on this analogy, the court's opinion was that—as with fishing resources—custodianship did not mean that the minerals belonged to the state but amounted to *res publicae* (public things). However, Van den Berg's analysis of the *dictum* draws a clear distinction between the resources and their products:

> When one applies the *res publica* argument to fishing resources, one might argue that the wealth of fishing resources is in fact 'a' *res publica* and that the state controls it as custodian for the benefit of the nation. This does not mean that the fish belong to the state in private ownership or that the fish are *res publicae*.

The MPRDA was challenged before the International Tribunal for the Settlement of Investment Disputes[157] and before the domestic courts,[158] in two separate matters alleging unlawful expropriation. The former challenge was settled before it was heard; the latter was pursued through all levels of the judiciary and eventually decided by the Constitutional Court in *Agri South Africa v Minister for Minerals and Energy* ('*AgriSA*').[159]

When given this opportunity to consider the meaning and implications of state custodianship of mineral and petroleum resources in *AgriSA*, the Constitutional Court upheld the MPRDA and rejected the appellant's argument about the Act's unconstitutionality.[160] The court did not regard the custodianship model, imposed by the MPRDA, as bringing about large-scale expropriation of mineral rights, nor as effecting a nationalization of the resource. Instead, it was prepared to hold only that whatever state custodianship might mean, it did not mean that the state became owner of all rights to minerals.[161] Instead, the Constitutional Court explained,

> [t]he state, as the custodian of these resources, is not seeking or supposed to be a co-contender with people or business entities for the right to prospect for or mine these minerals. *It is a facilitator or a conduit through which broader and equitable access to mineral and petroleum resources can be realised.*[162]

---

[153] *Xstrata South Africa (Pty) Ltd and Others v SFF Association* 2012 (5) SA 60 (SCA) at para 1.
[154] *Maledu and Others v Itereleng Bakgatla Mineral Resources (Pty) Ltd and Another* 2019 (2) SA 1 (CC) para 50.
[155] *De Beers Consolidated Mines Ltd v Ataqua Mining (Pty) Ltd and Others* (3215/06) [2007] ZAFSHC [74].
[156] ibid [38].
[157] *Piero Foresti, Laura de Carli and Others v the Republic of South Africa*, ICSID Case No ARB(AF) 07/01.
[158] *Agri South Africa v Minister of Minerals and Energy* 2012 (1) SA 171 (GNP); *Minister of Minerals and Energy v Agri South Africa* 2012 (5) SA 1 (SCA); *Agri South Africa v Minister for Minerals and Energy* 2013 (4) SA 1 (CC).
[159] 2013 (4) SA 1 (CC) [68].
[160] ibid [53], [66].
[161] ibid [68].
[162] ibid, emphasis added.

The clearest indication of the substance of custodial resource holding has come in the context of questions around black economic empowerment (BEE), a far-reaching legislative and policy intervention in South Africa which seeks to promote equality and redress past discrimination.[163] For the extractives sector, as for many others, industry-specific laws and generic laws combine to create a framework for empowerment through affirmative action, employment equity, ownership transfer, and skills development. For the South African extractive sectors, these provisions activate the government's attempts at ensuring local benefit through the legal framework. In such an important law and policy context, scrutiny of the custodial role of the state in respect of mineral resources was inevitable.

The 2018 provincial division judgment of *Chamber of Mines of South Africa v Minister of Mineral Resources and Others*[164] provided the opportunity for such scrutiny. The applicants and respondents jointly applied for a declaratory order clarifying the legal position relating to a provision that mining company should have 26 per cent of its ownership shares designated to historically disadvantaged South Africans (HDSAs). The question related to the perpetuity of such a requirement: would the ownership provision apply only until the 26 per cent mark had been reached, or would mining companies be obliged to have a 26 per cent share allocated to HDSAs forever? The matter—dubbed the 'once empowered, always empowered' question—was rather politicized.

In answering this question, the provincial court commented that custodianship confers on the state 'directional authority, governing power and oversight over mineral resources'.[165] It further indicated that the function of granting mining rights is an inherent, constituent component of the state's power to control the mineral resources.[166] The court indicated that the state's power reaches even further: 'State custodial rights … signpost … a composite of multi-facet functions and objectives the State should bear in mind when fulfilling the role set out in section 3(2)',[167] which mandates the state to 'control', 'administer', and 'manage' mining rights.

In the most recent episode of judicial engagement with the status and binding nature of the provisions on empowerment,[168] the Gauteng Provincial Division of the High Court reiterated the position as expressed by the Constitutional Court in *AgriSA*: '[T]he State as custodian of the resources is a facilitator or a conduit through which broader and equitable access to mineral and petroleum resources can be realised.'[169]

The South African judiciary's engagement with custodial resource holding provides a point of departure for an alternative relationship between the state and its people regarding resource sovereignty. A fiduciary relationship between the state and its people can provide the legal basis for the state to act *on behalf of* its subjects. It can also constrain the exercise of public powers.[170]

---

[163] Hanri Mostert and Meyer van den Berg, 'Expressing Local Content through Black Economic Empowerment in the South African Petroleum Industry' in Damilola S Oluwayi (ed) *Local Content, Sustainable Development and Treaty Implementation in Global Energy Markets* (Cambridge University Press 2021).

[164] (41661/2015) [2018] ZAGPPHC 8.

[165] ibid, para 154.

[166] ibid.

[167] ibid [154].

[168] *Minerals Council of South Africa v Minister of Mineral Resources and Energy* [2021] ZAGPPHC 623.

[169] *Agri SA* CC [68].

[170] Fox-Decent (n 141) 271.

Fox-Decent conceptualizes the fiduciary state as encapsulating a 'trust relationship' between citizens and the state. Nussbaum[171] articulates 'trust' as a surrender to the helplessness of exposing oneself to the possibility of deep harm. For the relationship between the state and the citizen, this would mean that citizens' interests are vulnerable but voluntarily relinquished to the fiduciary state, which assumes a benevolent discretionary power over them. Fox-Decent[172] points out that this relationship between the state and its people presumes that 'the law cannot authorise any kind of fiduciary power [for the state] that can be exercised arbitrarily'.

For a state to adhere to a fiduciary mandate (and thus be a 'fiduciary state'), it must have reasonable justification for compelling its citizens' compliance with its laws.[173] Such justification is needed for the state to fulfil its most basic function: securing and protecting the rights of all its citizens.[174] It also motivates adherence to the rule of law, and underlies the state's claim to govern and to expect allegiance from its subjects.[175] The obvious expectation is that a fiduciary duty on the state will preclude government officials from misusing their position of trust, and/or enriching themselves unjustly.[176] Hence the idea of the state as a fiduciary is a potent response to some of the consequences brought about by the resource curse.

Moreover, custodial resource holding can be a means to constrain the fiduciary state. By authorizing the state to control access to the mining industry for popular or national benefit, the law places a duty upon the state to do the same. The South African Minerals and Petroleum Resources Development Act 28 of 2002 provides a good example of the content of such a duty: after the pivotal confirmation, in section 3(1), of the state's custodial role, section 3(2) permits the state to 'grant, issue, refuse, control, administer and manage any reconnaissance permission, prospecting right, permission to remove, mining right, mining permit, retention permit, technical co-operation permit, reconnaissance permit, exploration right and production right'; and to prescribe relevant levies and fees. Section 3(3) then compels the relevant minister to 'ensure the sustainable development of South Africa's mineral and petroleum resources within a framework of national environmental policy, norms and standards while promoting economic and social development'. Section 6(1) also subjects the state's compelled or permitted actions to the principles of administrative justice, namely lawfulness, reasonableness, and procedural fairness.[177]

These provisions already guide interpretation of the state's custodial role. Read with the Act's preamble and its stated objectives in section 2(a)–(i), the emerging vision is that of a developmental state, one committed to redressing past injustice and ensuring equitable

---

[171] Martha C Nussbaum, *Anger and Forgiveness: Resentment, Generosity, Justice* (Oxford University Press 2016) 94.

[172] Fox-Decent (n 141) 265-67.

[173] ibid 271.

[174] ibid.

[175] ibid 272.

[176] Duruigbo in Ndiva Kofele-Kale 'Patrimonicide: The International Economic Crime of Indigenous Spoliation' (1995) 28(1) Vanderbilt Journal of Transnational Law 45, 116.

[177] See in general Lauren Kohn and Hugh Corder, 'Judicial Regulation of Administration Action' in C Murray and C Kirkby (eds), *South African Monograph on Constitutional Law* (Suppl. 108 International Encyclopaedia of Laws (IEL), 2014) regarding lawfulness, reasonableness, and procedural fairness; see also Cora Hoexter, *Administrative Law in South Africa* (2nd edn, Juta 2012) 252-459.

access to resources, while also promoting environmental sustainability, economic growth, and socio-economic welfare.[178] These are high expectations indeed.

Custodial resource-holding circumscribes a state's power to regulate mineral exploitation. It might include the duty to reform holding and licensing to achieve redress for past injustice. Beyond the South African example already mentioned, Namibia is a case in point. At first glance, its laws—dating from the early 1990s—correspond to a 'nationalized' model.[179] However, twenty-first-century policy developments[180] along with the Namibian judiciary's specific interpretation of the resource-holding provision in the Constitution,[181] have shifted Namibian resource holding towards a 'custodial' model. In particular, the widely accepted *obiter dictum* in *Rostock CC and Another v Van Biljon*[182] ('*Rostock*') interpreted Namibian resource holding as custodial, and presents a less literal interpretation of the constitutional reservation[183] of natural resources in favour of the state. The court based its opinion on article 1(2) in the Namibian Constitution, which vests all power in the people of Namibia and stipulates that the state's democratic institutions must exercise such power. This provision induced the court to endorse the idea of popular resource holding coupled with state administration of resources on behalf of the Namibian people.[184]

These examples suggest that custodial resource holding circumscribes the state's powers and heightens its responsibilities: it requires the state to demonstrate a particular kind of responsibility and duty of care in managing existing and new interests. In understanding a custodial holding to include the fiduciary role of the state, Duruigbo points out that when governments act as trustees of their states' natural resources, they must discharge their obligations *bona fide*.[185]

The meaning and content of the state's responsibility and duty of care intertwines with a state's political and economic ideology. This accounts for the differences between jurisdictions that subscribe to the custodial resource-holding model. The differences between Tanzania and Botswana may serve as an example. From the provisions quoted in the survey above, it would appear that these two jurisdictions both subscribe to the custodial resource-holding model in that they vest their 'republics' with fairly encompassing rights of control over minerals. However, the exercise of these rights looks different in the various jurisdictions.

---

[178] See eg Fabrice Tambe Endoh, 'Democratic Constitutionalism in Post-apartheid South Africa: The Interim Constitution Revisited' (2015) 7(1) Africa Review, 67–79; SJ Mosala, JCM Venter, and EG Bain, 'South Africa's Economic Transformation since 1994: What Influence has the National Democratic Revolution (NDR) Had? (2017) 44(3–4) The Review of Black Political Economy, 327–40.

[179] Eg art 100 of the Namibian Constitution provides that 'natural resources ... shall belong to the State if ... not otherwise lawfully owned'. See further s 2, Namibian Minerals Act, 1992 (read with Minerals (Prospecting and Mining) Amendment Act 2008).

[180] The Namibian Government's Minerals Policy of 2002, formulated in an attempt to reform the law, does not refer to the state as owner of mineral resources, but provides that the Ministry of Mines and Energy is a custodian of Namibia's mineral resources. See also the Mission and Vision of the Namibian Ministry of Mines and Energy, 'Mission and Vision' <http://www.mme.gov.na/about-us/mission/> accessed 19 February 2021, where the Ministry refers to itself as having been 'established to take custody of the ... mineral and energy resources'.

[181] *Rostock CC and Another v Van Biljon* [2011] NAHC 259 [8]–[10].

[182] ibid.

[183] Art 100 of the Constitution of the Republic of Namibia, 1990 (Act No 1 of 1990).

[184] The court further stated, without elaborating, that these resources are either *res publicae* or *res omnium communes*. However, Van den Berg (n 8) 93 argues that unsevered mineral resources in Namibia must be seen as *res publica*.

[185] Duruigbo (n 141) 67.

Tanzania's Constitution offers no overt affirmation of resource sovereignty.[186] Nevertheless, its complement of recently enacted domestic laws on resource extraction[187] aims to enable citizens to benefit better from the country's mineral resources.[188] First, the constitutionally mandated[189] Permanent Sovereignty Act[190] of 2017 states that natural resources are 'held in trust by the President on behalf of the people of the United Republic',[191] and provides expressly for benefit-sharing and state participation in mining activities.[192] The Natural Wealth and Resources Contracts (Review and Renegotiation of Unconscionable Terms) Act[193] of 2017 provides for renegotiation of all mining contracts containing unreasonable and excessive terms. It also contains clauses to increase the mining sector's benefit-sharing potential.[194] The features of the Tanzanian resource-holding model hence include a mandatory state ownership share of 16 per cent of future mining operations; the entitlement of state-owned enterprises to acquire a 50 per cent shareholding in mining companies; and parliamentary review and renegotiation of existing mining agreements.[195]

In Tanzania, therefore, custodial resource holding seems closely modelled on the country's socialist-inspired and state-centric economic approach.[196] But the Tanzanian government's position is that this model does not intend to nationalize the mining sector.[197] Rather, the stated purpose is to achieve local benefit from mining enterprises by ensuring sovereign ownership of natural resources as prescribed by international instruments.[198]

At first glance, Botswana's position on strong state control of mineral resources[199] seems similar to Tanzania's inasmuch as its Constitution contains no outright affirmation of resource sovereignty.[200] The wording in Botswana's Mines and Minerals Act,[201] however, curtails the right to privatized resource holding.[202] The provision reads that 'all rights of ownership in minerals are vested in the Republic', and compels the state, through the minister, to ensure, 'in the public interest', that Botswana's mineral resources 'are investigated

---

[186] See Table 9.1.
[187] See ss 4(1) and (2) of the Natural Wealth and Resources (Permanent Sovereignty) Act No 5 of 2017; ss 4(2), 6(2)(g) and (k) of the Natural Wealth and Resources Contracts (Review and Re-negotiation of Unconscionable Terms) Act No 6 of 2017.
[188] Burure Ngocho and Sadock Magai, 'Mining in Tanzania: Effects of the Mining Legal Framework Overhaul' DLA Piper (11 August 2020) <https://www.dlapiper.com/nl/global/insights/publications/2020/08/africa-connec ted-issue-4/6tanzania-mining-legal-framework-overhaul/> accessed 22 February 2021.
[189] Art 27 of the Constitution of the United Republic of Tanzania, 1977.
[190] The Natural Wealth and Resources (Permanent Sovereignty) Act No 5 of 2017.
[191] ibid s 5(2).
[192] ibid ss 7 and 8.
[193] Natural Wealth and Resources Contracts (Review and Re-negotiation of Unconscionable Terms) Act of 2017.
[194] ibid, ss 4 and 5.
[195] Thabit Jacob and Rasmus Hundsbæk Pedersen, 'New Resource Nationalism? Continuity and Change in Tanzania's Extractive Industry' (2018) 5(2) The Extractive Industries and Society 287, 288.
[196] Jacob and Pedersen (n 195) 288 even argue that these features smack of a contemporary resource nationalism.
[197] Jody Emel and others, 'Extracting Sovereignty: Capital, Territory and Gold Mining in Tanzania' (2011) 30(2) Political Geography 70, 72 and 75; Jacob and Pedersen (n 195) 289.
[198] See the discussion of the Tanzania Development Vision 2025 (United Republic of Tanzania, Planning Commission, 2000) and the Tanzania Five Year Development Plan 2011/12–2015/16: Tanzania's Latent Growth Potentials (United Republic of Tanzania, President's Office, Planning Commission) by Jacob and Pedersen (n 195) 289ff. Also Emel and others (n 197), 75-76.
[199] IB Matshediso, 'A Review of Mineral Development and Investment Policies of Botswana' (2005) 30(3) Resource Policy 203, 204.
[200] See Table 9.1.
[201] Mines and Minerals Act No 17 of 1999, s 3.
[202] Matshediso (n 199) 204. Keith Jefferies, 'The Role of TNCs in the Extractive Industry of Botswana' (2009) 18(1) Transnational Corporation 62.

and exploited in the most efficient, beneficial and timely manner'.[203] Botswana[204] manages its mineral resources through Debswana, a mining corporation representing a 50/50 joint venture partnership (described as a 'marriage of convenience')[205] between Botswana's government and leading diamond-mining multinational corporation, De Beers Consolidated Mines[206] (De Beers). Through this joint venture, Debswana operates four diamond mines and one coal mine. Botswana thus hopes to ensure benefit through equity stakes and profit-sharing beyond the 15 per cent profit share foreseen by the Mines and Minerals Act.[207] It boosts the economy with resource revenue through taxation and royalties, and through shareholder dividends from the mining company.[208]

Despite their significantly different interpretations of how custodial holding should work, Tanzania and Botswana both appear to support the custodial resource-holding model. This comparison should demonstrate that such a model may be as applicable in a market-oriented economic context as in a command economy. Hence economic and political preferences do not have to compel a legislative choice of either a nationalized or privatized mining sector. This is supported further by the Namibian example, in which the judiciary imposed a custodial holding model upon wording that seems to support nothing more than a nationalized holding model.

This leads to the point of this chapter: custodianship as written (or read) into the mining laws of various African states allows African legislatures (or judiciaries) to engage the tenets of constitutionalism in the extractive sectors where the relevant constitutions do not contain sufficiently clear expressions of resource sovereignty. These tenets include, inter alia, the applicability of the rule of law, protection of property and the environment, socio-economic development, transparent and accountable government, and participatory justice. Above all, these tenets explain the relationship between the state and its subjects in the resource context.

Seen in this light, custodial resource holding serves as a response to the inevitable problems ensuing from switching from one economic model to its opposite (especially since neither model has proven itself appropriate to serve the African political, economic, or indeed extractive contexts). The remaining question is whether custodial resource holding, as an expression of African constitutionalism, can indeed address the problems arising from resource dependency. This is the topic of the final subsection below.

4.3 Is Custodial Resource Holding a Panacea?

In modern, operative democracies it might be easy to trust that the state is fulfilling its functions and working towards its electorate's mandate. Where a democracy is

---

[203] Mines and Minerals Act No 17 of 1999, s 3.

[204] Jefferies (n 202).

[205] David van Wyk, 'Policy Gap 5 SADC Research: Corporate Social Responsibility in the Diamond Mining Industry in Botswana', 22 Bench Marks Foundation (2009).

[206] Angela Gapa, 'Strategic Partner or Shot Caller? The De Beers Factor in Botswana's Development' (2016) 33(1) Journal of Global South Studies 49, 60.

[207] Ian Taylor, 'Botswana's "Developmental State" and the Politics of Legitimacy' 3 (conference paper: 'Towards a New Political Economy of Development: Globalisation and Governance', University of Sheffield, United Kingdom, 4-6 July 2002). Section 40 of the Mines and Minerals Act provides the government a once-off option of acquiring 15 per cent working interests and shares in a mining company which has been granted mining rights.

[208] Gapa (n 206) 61.

functional, the custodial resource-holding model may well offer a means to escape the nationalization–privatization cycle as it applies to the mineral resource context. It can shift focus to the role of the sovereign state in the era of constitutionalism—an era of 'positive sovereignty', in the words of Emel and others, in which the state becomes responsible for creating and maintaining an enabling environment for revenue generation and local wealth accumulation.[209] In an ideal world, custodial resource holding might transcend the nationalization–privatization binary, avoiding resource nationalism's hostility towards foreign capital, while promoting responsible, ethical investment that results in local benefit.

One must ask whether the response would hold up in the African context. To link resource custodianship with constitutionalism in Africa means placing a range of expectations upon the concept and the model. Such a link could be forged by the way in which a given jurisdiction's constitution informs the practice of resource custodianship. As Table 9.1 indicates, however, there are many constitutions in which overt indications of this nature are absent. In such jurisdictions—of which Tanzania and Botswana were the examples discussed—the link is more difficult to make, albeit not impossible: domestic legislation, or even resource contracts, can put custodial holding into practice, even where a country's constitution does not fully envision custodianship. Moreover, Table 9.1 demonstrates that most sub-Saharan African jurisdictions in the survey already make a clear link between resource sovereignty and resource custodianship.

It is beyond the scope of this chapter to assess the likelihood of custodial resource holding being able to halt or reverse the negative effects of oscillation between the inappropriate models of nationalization and privatization. Even so, some observations are warranted:

For one, South Africa's recent experience of state capture[210] has exposed the fallacy of assuming the state is dependable. It showed the tragedy of how entrenched yet weak leadership can atrophy a state's ability to perform positively for its citizens. Now it serves as cautionary lesson that failure to adhere to the rule of law,[211] (or, put differently, tolerating outright gaps in the law or its implementation) may jeopardize a custodianship model, given that it depends heavily on how the law defines the state's fiduciary duties. By the same token, poor intra-governmental governance and corruption[212] would threaten the custodial model.

Secondly, South Africa may look like an extreme example, but it is not an outlier. Other commentators have already established the systemic nature of corruption in African countries.[213] For present purposes, it must be added that unimplemented and unenforced

---

[209] Emel and others (n 197) 76.

[210] See Public Protector South Africa, 'State of Capture Report No: 6 of 2016/17' <http://www.saflii.org/images/329756472-State-of-Capture.pdf> and commentaries, for example Francois Venter, 'State Capture, Corruption, and Constitutionalism in South Africa' in Charles M Fombad and Nico Steytler (eds), *Corruption and Constitutionalism in Africa* (Oxford University Press 2020) 69–89; Sanet Madonsela, 'Critical Reflections on State Capture in South Africa' (2019) 11(1) Insight on Africa, 113–30; Maurice O Dassah, 'Theoretical Analysis of State Capture and its Manifestation as a Governance Problem in South Africa' (2018) 14(1) The Journal for Transdisciplinary Research in Southern Africa, 1–10 <https://doi.org/10.4102/td.v14i1.473> accessed 27 February 2021; Loammi Wolf, 'The Remedial Action of the "State of Capture" Report in Perspective' (2017) 20 PER/PELJ 2017 (20), 2–46 <https://pdfs.semanticscholar.org/68ee/4497c18bc72d0b1328a6fbd96e61a5c1d20f.pdf?_ga=2.39197027.1330516977.1614440237-1564413288.1613335593> accessed 27 February 2021.

[211] Venter (n 210) 85–88.

[212] Dassah (n 210) 1–10. Detailed analyses of the challenges of corruption to African constitutions may be found in the earlier volume in this series: Charles M Fombad and Nico Steytler (eds), *Corruption and Constitutionalism in Africa* (Oxford University Press 2020).

[213] Charles M Fombad, 'Corruption and the Crisis of Constitutionalism in Africa' in Charles M Fombad and Nico Steytler (eds), *Corruption and Constitutionalism in Africa* (Oxford University Press 2020) 15–16.

constitutional and legal frameworks are worth little. They certainly would have no power to combat the resource curse.

Thirdly, the Natural Resource Governance Index (NRGI)[214] assesses the policies and practices that resource-producing states employ to govern their extractive industries.[215] The NRGI's latest questionnaire-based assessment of eighty-nine states (from 2017), supported by vast documentary evidence, is damning in its assessment of African states. Most of them are in the index's lower spectrum.[216] The NRGI's work makes it easy to see that many states face daunting governance challenges. Problems are compounded where states fail to honour their own legal and regulatory frameworks through proper implementation.[217] These insights suggest that many African states' ability to fulfil a custodial role is compromised from the start.

Custodial resource holding in Africa will be compromised, inter alia, by weaknesses in the institutions supporting, and the cultures determining, the management of resources for popular benefit in the relevant states. African states' experience with corruption and bribery in the natural resource context provides obvious and multiple examples.[218] To mention only two, Zambia's former Minister of Mines was convicted in 2015 for extorting bribes for awarding operating licences.[219] Scholarship also points out that corruption and lack of good governance have resulted in continued misappropriation of public funds in Nigeria.[220] The loss of the means to fund well-being in African states is particularly irksome where a combination of greed, incompetence, and lack of political will keeps communities in endless cycles of poverty and underdevelopment.

Furthermore, insufficient levels of transparency and accountability also contribute to challenges in African mineral resource sectors.[221] Commentators have pointed out, for instance, how shortcomings on this front in Zimbabwe contributed to the depletion of the fiscus,[222] reduction of the country's economic performance,[223] and an exponential increase

---

[214] Natural Resource Governance Institute, '2017 Resource Governance Index: Measuring the quality of governance in the oil, gas and mining sectors of 81 countries' <https://resourcegovernanceindex.org> accessed 22 February 2021. The NRGI Index measures the quality of resource governance in the countries worldwide that are responsible for producing the lion's share of the world's oil and gas resources, along with a 'significant proportion' of its minerals.

[215] The NRGI Index (n 214) does so by considering the extent to which, first, value realization is enabled through the governance of allocating extraction rights, exploration, production, environmental protection, revenue collection and state-owned enterprises. Secondly, it scrutinizes countries' revenue management by considering national budgeting, subnational resource revenue sharing, and sovereign wealth-funds practices. Thirdly, it assesses a country's enabling environment through legal and political markers, such as the presence of the rule of law, strong governing institutions, and regulatory frameworks and a culture of accountability and transparency. An enabling environment is also characterized by the control of corruption and the absence of political instability and violence.

[216] NRGI Index (n 214) 4–5.

[217] ibid 15.

[218] See in general Fombad (n 213).

[219] Reuters Staff, 'Zambian Ex-Mines Minister Found Guilty of Corruption' Reuters (2015) <https://www.reuters.com/article/us-zambia-mining-corruption/zambian-ex-mines-minister-found-guilty-of-corruption-idUSKBN0LT1X420150225> accessed 22 February 2021.

[220] Ifeanychukwu Michael Abada and Elias Chukwuemeka Ngwu, 'Corruption, Governance, and Nigeria's Uncivil Society, 1999-2019' (2019) 387, 387–88.

[221] Christopher Hood, 'Accountability and Transparency: Siamese Twins, Matching Parts, Awkward Couple?' (2010) 33(5) West European Politics, 989.

[222] James Mupfumi and Tyanai Masiya, 'An Analysis of Zimbabwe's Mines and Minerals Amendment Bill' (2016) 1 (1) Policy Analysis 1, 3.

[223] Brian Latham, 'Zimbabwe Eyes Taking Back Unused Mining Licences to Boost Output' Business Day (19 May 2017) <https://www.businesslive.co.za/bd/world/africa/2017-05-19-zimbabwe-eyes-taking-back-unused-mining-licences-to-boost-output/> accessed 22 February 2021.

in inflation.[224] They blame poor systems and institutions[225] for the plunder of Zimbabwe's resources in the Marange diamond fields.[226]

Many African governments attempt to respond to such types of challenges, notably by instituting more rigorous legal frameworks and establishing independent institutions with oversight functions. For instance, in the 1990s Botswana sought to curb corruption[227] by establishing the independent Directorate on Corruption and Economic Crime (DCEC)[228] to promote transparency in mining and all other industries and combat economic crimes.[229] This measure impacted positively across sectors in Botswana.[230] Another anti-corruption measure was the establishment of the Public Procurement and Asset Disposal Board (PPADB), a parastatal organization for curbing corruption in '[the] procurement of works, supplies and services, for the disposal of public assets and related matters'.[231]

Many states also rely on initiatives at the international level to support the implementation of better systems at home. Several have joined the Extractive Industries Transparency Initiative (EITI), a 'global standard to promote the open and accountable management of oil, gas, and mineral resources'.[232] Tanzania is one example.[233] As a result of concerns about disproportionate growth trends in the extractive industry, on the one hand, and economic and human development, on the other, Tanzania joined the EITI in 2009 to promote good governance of its natural resources.[234] It then enacted the Tanzania Extractive Industries (Transparency and Accountability) Act (TEITA Act),[235] which integrates the EITI requirements into national legislation. The Act established the TEITA Commission, an independent government body that must ensure that 'the benefits of the extractive industry are verified, duly accounted for and prudently utilised for the benefit of the citizens of Tanzania'.[236] It does so by monitoring the promotion of transparency and accountability.[237]

---

[224] JP Casey, 'Mining in Zimbabwe: Time to Use it or Lose it' *Mining Technology* (4 March 2020) <https://www.mining-technology.com/features/mining-in-zimbabwe-time-to-use-it-or-lose-it/> accessed 27 February 2021.

[225] Nelson Banya, 'About the Missing $15 Billion Diamond Revenue … ' *Zimfact* (16 March 2018) <https://zimfact.org/did-zimbabwe-lose-15-billion-in-diamond-revenue-zimbabwes-15-billion-diamond-question/> accessed 28 February 2021.

[226] An estimated $15 billion of potential revenue from Marange disappeared due to corruption involving public officials and private entities. Banya (n 225).

[227] David Sebudubudu, 'Corruption and its Control in Botswana' (2003) 35 Botswana Notes and Records 125, 125.

[228] See s 3(1) of the Corruption and Economic Crime Act 13 of 1994, which provides for the establishment of a Directorate on Corruption and Economic Crime; Sebudubudu (n 227) 125.

[229] Sebudubudu (n 227) 125.

[230] See ibid 125, 132–34, for distributional cost-effectiveness analysis (DCEA) cases across various sectors.

[231] Isaac Pinielo, 'PPADB Battles to Stamp out Tender Corruption' *MmegiOnline* (7 July 2017) <https://www.mmegi.bw/index.php?aid=70113&dir=2017/july/07> accessed 22 February 2021. See also Emmanuel Botlhale, 'Infusing Value for Money (VfM) into the Public Procurement System in Botswana' (2017) 17(3) Journal of Public Procurement 281, 287.

[232] The EITI is an international standard for transparency in extractive industry payments and receipts. Companies in the countries participating in the EITI are required to publish what they pay to the governments. Governments are also expected to release what they receive from the companies. These figures are reconciled by an independent administrator. See Extractive Industries Transparency Initiative, 'The Global Standard for Good Governance of Oil, Gas and Mineral Resources' *EITI* (October 2020) <https://eiti.org/files/documents/en_eiti _factsheet_2020.pdf> accessed 22 February 2021; see also Benjamin K Sovacool and Nathan Andrews, 'Does Transparency Matter? Evaluating the Governance Impacts of the Extractive Industries Transparency Initiative (EITI) in Azerbaijan and Liberia' (2015) 45 Resources Policy 183, 185.

[233] Natural Resource Governance Institute, 'Tanzania's 2015 Extractive Industry Legislation: Recommendations for Implementation' *NRGI Briefing* (November 2016) 2.

[234] Japhace Poncian and Henry Kigodi, 'Transparency Initiatives and Tanzania's Extractive Industry Governance' (2018) 5(1) Development Studies Research 106, 109.

[235] Tanzania Extractive Industries (Transparency and Accountability) Act No 23 of 2015.

[236] ibid s 10(1).

[237] ibid s 4(2).

Meanwhile, Tanzania has reached EITI-compliant status.[238] Along with other efforts to en-hance transparency,[239] these initiatives show a commitment by the Tanzanian government to fulfil its constitutional obligation to allow natural resource wealth to serve the common good of its people.

A range of other African states have taken similar initiatives.[240] Among them, Tanzania, Nigeria,[241] Zambia,[242] and the Democratic Republic of the Congo[243] have promulgated le-gislation to this effect.

5. Concluding Remarks

In Africa, poverty, inequality, underdevelopment, and lack of productivity are more than just the by-products of the systemic and ideological failures of command and market economies—they are tragic constraints on the continent's future prosperity. It is disturbing when one contrasts the wealth of Africa's natural resources with the scarcity Africa's peoples experience in almost every other respect.

Amid global trends toward multi-polarity, states need to assert sovereignty over their natural resources. In Africa they do so from a precarious position,[244] balancing hopeful ideals about the potential of the extractives sectors to contribute to development and pros-perity[245] against the debilitating realities of pervasive poverty, political instability, systemic

---

[238] Poncian and Kigodi (n 234) 109.

[239] See Tanzania EITI legal framework explained in Poncian and Kigodi (n 234) 110–11.

[240] See Extractive Industries Transparency Initiative, 'EITI in Africa' *EITI* (October 2018) <https://eiti.org/files/documents/eiti_africa_brief_en.pdf> accessed 11 February 2021.

[241] Section 2(a) of the Nigerian Extractive Industries Transparency Initiative (NEITI) Act of 2007. The NEITI Act condemns all acts of corruption when dealing with the revenue payable to the government by closely observing and checking the applicability and disbursement of resources realized from mining industries as revenue to the government (s 2(e)). It also operationalizes a working model to ensure achievement of the intended transparency and accountability by, for instance, evaluating the discharge of obligations and responsibilities of both the govern-ment and the mining companies (s 3).

[242] Extractive Industries Transparency Initiative, 'Zambia Declared EITI Compliant' <http://eiti.org/news-eve nts/zambia-declared-eiti-compliant> accessed 23 February 2021.

[243] Nicholas Garrett, 'The Extractive Industries Transparency Initiative (EITI) & Artisanal and Small-Scale Mining (ASM): Preliminary Observations from the Democratic Republic of the Congo (DRC)', 35; Felix Todd, 'DRC Mining Becoming more Transparent but Lacks Accountability, says EITI, 2019', Extractive Industries Transparency, para 9. See also Africa Progress Panel Report 2013 (n 49) 63.

[244] See Field (n 124) 2 who cites Anthony Bebbington and others, 'Contention and Ambiguity: Mining and the Possibilities of Development' (2008) 39(6) Development and Change 965, 966.

[245] Diamond-rich Botswana's extractive sector has been described as the 'lifeline of its economy'. Apollo Rwomire, 'Economic Growth, Poverty and Governance: The Case of Botswana' in Organization for Social Science Research in Eastern and Southern Africa (OSSREA), *Good Governance and Civil Society Participation in Africa* (OSSREA African Book Collective 2009) 72. Zambia's copper mining sector specifically has been described as 'the engine that will drive [economic] diversification'. See Sikamo, Mwanza, and Mweemba (n 99) 494. In South Africa, the mining industry has been described as 'the backbone' of its economy. Lorraine Kearney, 'Mining and Minerals in South Africa' *Brand South Africa* (16 August 2012) <https://www.brandsouthafrica.com/investments-immigration/business/economy/mining-and-minerals-in-south-africa> accessed 28 February 2019. President Cyril Ramaphosa, 'State of the Nation Address 2018' <https://www.gov.za/speeches/state-nation-address-2018#> accessed 28 February 2021 refers to it as the 'sunrise industry', even though the contribution of the South African mining industry to the GDP has shrunk from 21 per cent in 1970 to 7.3 per cent in 2018. Compare eg 'A Debate that will Persist; Nationalisation in South Africa' *The Economist* 401(8762) (3 December 2011) 6. <https://link.gale.com/apps/doc/A273833856/AONE?u=unict&sid=bookmark-AONE&xid=6ea6864b> accessed 12 November 2021; Jacqueline Holman, 'Mining's Contribution to SA's GDP Expands' *Mining Journal* (2019) <https://www.mining-journal.com/events-coverage/news/1355683/minings-contribution-to-sas-gdp-expands> accessed 23 February 2021.

corruption, persistent inequality, and intractable underdevelopment.[246] As Field remarks, this tension forces states into the dual role of being both the promoters of mining and the protectors against it.[247]

In resource-dependent states or regions, the propensity for economic development is correlated with states' control over resource wealth.[248] Where a country's economy depends on such resource extraction, its economic policies must, logically, be geared towards its extractives sector. But where such a state's economic strategies and policies are inherently contradictory, they will affect the optimal and sustainable exploitation of resources.[249]

A shared element of African resource narratives across state boundaries is the apparently widespread consensus[250] about the influence that resource extraction exerts on a country's political and economic choices and the design of its laws. These narratives often highlight the correlation between political and economic failures within the states, the absence of important regulatory frameworks for foreign investment and resource extraction, and the prevalence of outdated business practices.[251]

Commentators often emphasize the link between economic prosperity and 'prudent resource governance'.[252] They point out that, in the absence of such an approach, the negative effects are felt far beyond the mining sector: weak policies and strategies regarding resource extraction affect, inter alia, the mineral sector's potential to contribute to eradicating poverty and underdevelopment. Lack of clear direction on how to turn an abundant resource (such as mineral wealth) into a sustainable development opportunity can also hamper productivity, economic diversification, and quality of life.[253] Understanding this tension is crucial when envisioning African futures freed from the constraints of ideological or political modalities that, over many decades, have not served the African context well.

Neither privatized nor nationalized resource holding has proven capable of enabling resource-dependent states to rise above historical challenges that hamper economic development. Resorting to notions of custodial resource holding, and including references to popular benefit and fiduciary duties in mining statutes or codes around the African continent, represent more recent attempts to pre-empt the resource curse. However, to ensure that the concept of resource holding does not become vulnerable to manipulation, it needs a clearly articulated meaning.

As such, the lack of a direct constitutional expression of resource sovereignty in many African countries (as highlighted in Table 9.1) may contribute to difficulties in conceptualizing a resource-holding model sufficiently robust to withstand

---

[246] See Africa Progress Panel Report 2013 (n 49) 14; Heilbrunn (n 70) 2; Jensen and Wantchekon (n 55) 816–18.
[247] Field (n 124) 1.
[248] Flomenhoft (n 33).
[249] Funa Moyo and Clifford Mabhena, 'Harnessing Mineral Resources in Gwanda District of Zimbabwe: A Myth or a Reality?' (2014) 38 International Letters of Social and Humanistic Sciences 1–21.
[250] See eg Karolina Werner, 'Zambia: Governance and Natural Resources' (2016) 13(2) Revue Gouvernance 32, 49.
[251] See eg Jefferies (n 202) 62; United Nations, 'United Nations Conference on Trade and Development: Report on the Implementation of the Investment Policy Review: Kenya' United Nations (2013) <https://unctad.org/sys tem/files/official-document/diaepcb2012d6_en.pdf> accessed 23 February 2021; Murtala Chindo, 'An Extensive Analysis of the Mining in Nigeria Using a GIS' (2011) 3(1) Journal of Geography and Geology 3, 4 and 7.
[252] See eg Mupfumi and Masiya (n 222) 3.
[253] See eg the commentary of Miles Larmer, 'Historical Perspectives on Zambia's Mining Booms and Busts' in Fraser and Larmer (n 101) 7 and 33ff.

nationalization–privatization cycles on the economic and political planes. Legislative expression of the same principle allows for more flexibility of conceptualization; but it does not address weaknesses in the constitutional systems pertaining to faltering institutions, vulnerability to corruption, or transgressions of the rule of law. It seems, indeed, that many of Africa's constitutions lack real anchors for achieving better dispensations of mineral custodianship.

This survey of holding clauses, and the highlighted examples of countries, should demonstrate at least that different expressions of the principle of resource sovereignty are possible. Still, they all confirm that natural resources are assets of national interest. They have also come to epitomize the idea of regulated property: in other words, custodial resource holding requires that the state ensures that benefits derived from mineral resource extraction are equitably shared among the people of a particular state. Custodial resource holding requires, furthermore, that resources should be extracted in socially and environmentally sustainable ways. Appropriate regulatory frameworks that are properly implemented and enforced will be a key facilitating factor in reviving Africa's mining sector—especially so if economic approaches continue to place increasing reliance on a hybridization of political ideologies, as other chapters in this volume demonstrate.

Bibliography

'A Debate that Will Persist; Nationalisation in South Africa' *The Economist* 401(8762) (3 December 2011) <https://link.gale.com/apps/doc/A273833856/AONE?u=unict&sid=bookmark-AONE&xid=6ea6864b> accessed 12 November 2021

Abada IM and Ngwu EC, 'Corruption, Governance, and Nigeria's Uncivil Society, 1999–2019' (2019)

Ades A and Di Tella R, 'Rents, Competition, and Corruption' (1999) 89(4) American Economic Review 982

Africa Progress Panel in Africa, Progress Report 2013, 'Equity in Extractives: Stewarding Africa's Natural Resources for All' https://reliefweb.int/sites/reliefweb.int/files/resources/relatorio-africa-progress-report-2013-pdf-20130511-125153.pdf accessed 23 February 2021

African Development Bank and the African Union, *Oil and Gas in Africa* (OUP 2009)

African Union, 'Africa Mining Vision' (February 2009) <https://docs.igihe.com/IMG/pdf/africa_mining_vision_english.pdf> accessed 14 February 2021

Al Faruque A, 'Transparency in Extractive Revenues in Developing Countries and Economies in Transition: A Review of Emerging Best Practices' (2006) 24(1) Journal of Energy and Natural Resources 66

Auty RM, *Sustaining Development in Mineral Economies: The Resource Curse Thesis* (Routledge 1993)

Auty RM, 'Introduction and Overview' in Auty R (ed), *Resource Abundance and Economic Development* (Oxford University Press 2001)

Badeeb R and others, 'The Evolution of the Natural Resource Curse Thesis: A Critical Literature Survey' (2017) 51(C) Resources Policy 123

Badenhorst PJ and Mostert H, 'Artikel 3(1) en (2) van die Mineral and Petroleum Development Act 28 of 2002: 'n herbeskouing' [2007] TSAR 469

Badenhorst PJ and Mostert H, *Mineral and Petroleum Law of South Africa* (Juta 2004)

Bagabo P and others, 'Contract Transparency in Uganda's Petroleum and Mining Sectors' (2019) ACODE Policy Research Paper Series No 94

Banya N, 'About the Missing $15 Billion Diamond Revenue …' *Zimfact* (16 March 2018) <https://zimfact.org/did-zimbabwe-lose-15-billion-in-diamond-revenue-zimbabwes-15-billion-diamond-question/> accessed 28 February 2021

Barberis D, *Negotiating Mining Agreements: Past, Present and Future Trends* (Kluwer Law International 1998)

Bastos FL, 'A Southern African Approach to the Permanent Sovereignty over Natural Resources and Common Resource Management' in Bungenberg M and Hobe S (eds), *Permanent Sovereignty over Natural Resources* (Springer 2015)

Bebbington A and others, 'Contention and Ambiguity: Mining and the Possibilities of Development' (2008) 39(6) Development and Change 965

Besson S, 'Sovereignty' (Max Planck Encyclopaedias of International Law [MPIL], Max Planck Encyclopaedia of Public International Law [MPEPIL]) (April 2011) <https://opil.ouplaw.com/view/10.1093/law:epil/9780199231690/law-9780199231690-e1472?prd=MPIL> accessed 14 February 2021

Bhorat H and others, 'Resource Dependence and Inequality in Africa: Impacts, Consequences and Potential Solutions' in Odusola A and others (eds), *Income Inequality Trends in Sub-Saharan Africa: Divergence, Determinants and Consequences* (United Nations Development Programme 2019)

Botlhale E, 'Infusing Value for Money (VfM) into the Public Procurement System in Botswana' (2017) 17(3) Journal of Public Procurement 281

Bridge G, 'Global Production Networks and the Extractive Sector: Governing Resource-Based Development' (2008) 8 Journal of Economic Geography 389

Brinčiková Z, 'The Dutch Disease: An Overview' (2016) 12(10) European Scientific Journal, Special Edition 95

Butler A, 'Resource Nationalism and the African National Congress' (2013) 113 The Journal of the Southern African Institute of Mining and Metallurgy 11

Campbell Jr NJ, 'Principles of Mineral Ownership in the Civil Law and Common Law Systems' (1956) (31) Tulane Law Review 303

Campbell B, 'Revisiting the Reform Process of African Mining Regimes' (2010) 30(1–2) Canadian Journal of Development Studies 197

Carmignani F and Chowdhury A, 'Why are Natural Resources a Curse in Africa, but not Elsewhere?' (2010)

Casey JP, 'Mining in Zimbabwe: Time to Use It or Lose It' *Mining Technology* (4 March 2020) <https://www.mining-technology.com/features/mining-in-zimbabwe-time-to-use-it-or-lose-it/> accessed 27 February 2021

Charlesworth H, 'Democracy' in D'Aspremont J and Singh S (eds), *Concepts for International Law—Contributions to Disciplinary Thought* (Edward Elgar 2019)

Chindo M, 'An Extensive Analysis of the Mining in Nigeria Using a GIS' (2011) 3(1) Journal of Geography and Geology 3

Chiwandamira S and Majoko T, 'South Africa: The Evil Triplets and the Mining Industry' *Modise* (2 February 2012) <https://www.mondaq.com/southafrica/mining/163204/the-evil-triplets-and-the-mining-industry> accessed 17 December 2020

Chiwandamira S and Majoko T, 'The Evil Triplets and the Mining Industry' (2011) 11 Without Prejudice 53

Chua AL, 'The Privatization–Nationalization Cycle: The Link between Markets and Ethnicity in Developing Countries' (1995) 95(2) Columbia Law Review 223

Curry Jr RL, 'Poverty and Mass Unemployment in Mineral-Rich Botswana' (1987) 46(1) The American Journal of Economics and Sociology 71

Dale MO and others, *South African Mineral and Petroleum Law* (LexisNexis Butterworth 2005)

Dassah MO, 'Theoretical Analysis of State Capture and its Manifestation as a Governance Problem in South Africa' (2018) 14(1) The Journal for Transdisciplinary Research in Southern Africa 1

Dell M, 'The Devil's Excrement: The Negative Effect of Natural Resources on Development (2004) 26(3) Harvard International Review 38

Duruigbo E, 'Permanent Sovereignty and Peoples' Ownership of Natural Resources in International Law' (2006) 38(1) George Washington International Law Review 33

Duruigbo E, 'The World Bank, Multinational Oil Corporations, and the Resource Curse in Africa' (2005) 26 U Pa J Int'l L 1

Emel J and others, 'Extracting Sovereignty: Capital, Territory and Gold Mining in Tanzania' (2011) 30(2) Political Geography 70

Endoh FT, 'Democratic Constitutionalism in Post-apartheid South Africa: The Interim Constitution Revisited' (2015) 7(1) Africa Review 67

Extractive Industries Transparency Initiative, 'EITI in Africa' *EITI* (October 2018) <https://eiti.org/files/documents/eiti_africa_brief_en.pdf> accessed 11 February 2021

Extractive Industries Transparency Initiative, 'The Global Standard for Good Governance of Oil, Gas And Mineral Resources' *EITI* (October 2020) <https://eiti.org/files/documents/en_eiti_factsheet_2020.pdf> accessed 22 February 2021

Extractive Industries Transparency Initiative, 'Zambia Declared EITI Compliant' <http://eiti.org/news-events/zambia-declared-eiti-compliant> accessed 23 February 2021

Field T, *State Governance of Mining, Development and Sustainability* (Edward Elgar 2019)

Flomenhoft G, 'Historical and Empirical Basis for Communal Title in Minerals at the National Level: Does Ownership Matter for Human Development?' (2018) 10(6) Sustainability

Fombad CM and Steytler N (eds), *Corruption and Constitutionalism in Africa* (Oxford University Press 2020)

Fombad CM, 'Corruption and the Crisis of Constitutionalism in Africa' in Fombad CM and Steytler N (eds), *Corruption and Constitutionalism in Africa* (Oxford University Press 2020)

Fox-Decent E, 'The Fiduciary Nature of State Legal Authority' (2005) 31 Queen's Law Journal 259

Fraser A and Larmer M (eds), *Zambia, Mining, and Neoliberalism: Boom and Bust on the Globalized Copperbelt* (Palgrave Macmillan 2010)

Freudenburg WR and Gramling R, 'Linked to What? Economic Linkages in an Extractive Economy' (1998) 11(6) Society & Natural Resources 569

Gapa A, 'Strategic Partner or Shot Caller? The De Beers Factor in Botswana's Development' (2016) 33(1) Journal of Global South Studies 49

Garrett N, 'The Extractive Industries Transparency Initiative (EITI) & Artisanal and Small-Scale Mining (ASM): Preliminary Observations from the Democratic Republic of the Congo (DRC)' (2007)

Glazewski J, *Environmental Law in South Africa* (2nd edn, LexisNexis South Africa 2005)

Guldbrandsen C, 'Why Poverty? Stealing Africa', Denmark: Guldbrandsen Film, 2012. HD, 58 min. <https://www.youtube.com/watch?v=WNYemuiAOfU> accessed 25 September 2021

Gümplová P, 'Sovereignty over Natural Resources—A Normative Reinterpretation' (2020) 9 Global Constitutionalism 7

Gylfason T, 'Natural Resources, Education and Economic Development' (2001) 45 European Economic Review 847

Hansen MW, 'From Enclave to Linkage Economies? A Review of the Literature on Linkages between Extractive Multinational Corporations and Local Industry in Africa' (2014) DIIS Working Paper

Hanson KT, D'Alessandro C, and Owusu F (eds), *Managing Africa's Natural Resources: Capacities for Development* (Palgrave Macmillan 2014)

Harris D, *Cases and Materials on International Law* (7th edn, Sweet & Maxwell 2010)

Heilbrunn JR, *Oil, Democracy and Development in Africa* (Cambridge University Press 2014)

Hillbom E, 'Diamonds or Development? A Structural Assessment of Botswana's Forty Years of Success' (2008) 46(2) Journal of Modern African Studies 191

Hilson G, 'The Africa Mining Vision: A Manifesto for More Inclusive Extractive Industry-led Development?' (2020) 41 Canadian Journal of Development Studies/Revue canadienne d'études du développement 417

Hoexter C, *Administrative Law in South Africa* (2nd edn, Juta 2012)

Hogan W, Sturzenegger F, and Tai L, 'Contracts and Investment in Natural Resources' in Hogan W and Sturzenegger F (eds), *The Natural Resources Trap: Private Investment without Public Commitment* (MIT Press 2010)

Holman J, 'Mining's Contribution to SA's GDP Expands' *Mining Journal* (2019) <https://www.mining-journal.com/events-coverage/news/1355683/minings-contribution-to-sas-gdp-expands> accessed 23 February 2021

Hood C, 'Accountability and Transparency: Siamese Twins, Matching Parts, Awkward Couple?' (2010) 33(5) West European Politics 989

Humphreys M, Sachs JD, and Stiglitz JE, 'Introduction: What is the Problem with Natural Resource Wealth?' in Humphreys M and others (eds), *Escaping the Resource Curse* (Columbia University Press 2007)

Ince OU, 'Development' in D'Aspremont J and Singh S (eds), *Concepts for International Law— Contributions to Disciplinary Thought* (Edward Elgar 2019)

Jacob T and Pedersen RH, 'New Resource Nationalism? Continuity and Change in Tanzania's Extractive Industry' (2018) 5(2) The Extractive Industries and Society 287

Jefferies K, 'The Role of TNCs in the Extractive Industry of Botswana' (2009) 18(1) Transnational Corporation 62

Jensen N and Wantchekon L, 'Resource Wealth and Political Regimes in Africa' (2004) 37(7) Comparative Political Studies 816

Jerome A and others, 'Addressing Oil Related Corruption in Africa: Is the Push for Transparency Enough? (2005) 11(1) Review of Human Factor Studies Special Edition 7

Kearney L, 'Mining and Minerals in South Africa' *Brand South Africa* (16 August 2012) <https://www.brandsouthafrica.com/investments-immigration/business/economy/mining-and-minerals-in-south-africa> accessed 28 February 2019

Kofele-Kale N, 'Patrimonicide: The International Economic Crime of Indigenous Spoliation' (1995) 28(1) Vanderbilt Journal of Transnational Law 45

Kohn L and Corder H, 'Judicial Regulation of Administration Action' in Murray C and Kirkby C (eds), *South African Monograph on Constitutional Law* (Suppl. 108, International Encyclopaedia of Laws (IEL) 2014)

Kopiński D and others, 'Resource Curse or Resource Disease? Oil in Ghana' (2013) 112 African Affairs 583

Krueger AO, 'The Political Economy of the Rent-Seeking Society' (1974) 64(3) American Economic Review 291

Kurečić P and Seba M, 'The Resource Curse in Sub-Saharan Africa: A Reality Corroborated by the Empirical Evidence' (Conference paper for the 15th International Scientific Conference on Economic and Social Development—Human Resources Development, Varazdin. Vol 1, June 2016) <https://bib.irb.hr/datoteka/820620.The_Resource_Curse_in_Sub-Saharan_Africa.pdf> accessed 15 February 2021

Langa PN, 'The Role of the Constitution in the Struggle Against Poverty' (2011) 22(3) Stellenbosch Law Review 446

Lange S and Kinyondo A, 'Local Content in the Tanzanian Mining Sector' (2016) 15(3) CMI Brief 2

Latham B, 'Zimbabwe Eyes Taking Back Unused Mining Licences to Boost Output' *Business Day* (19 May 2017) <https://www.businesslive.co.za/bd/world/africa/2017-05-19-zimbabwe-eyes-taking-back-unused-mining-licences-to-boost-output/> accessed 22 February 2021

Leite C and Weidmann J, 'Does Mother Nature Corrupt? Natural Resources, Corruption, and Economic Growth' (1999) IMF Working Paper No 99/85

Luhende B, 'Towards a Legal Framework for Preventing Tax Revenue Leakage in the Upstream Oil and Gas Industry in Tanzania: An Analysis of the Concepts, Methods and Options Available in a Public Trusteeship Model of Natural Resource Holding' (PhD thesis, University of Cape Town 2017)

Lundgren CJ, Thomas AH, and York RC, *Boom, Bust, or Prosperity? Managing Sub-Saharan Africa's Natural Resource Wealth* (International Monetary Fund 2013)

Luong PJ and Weinthal E, 'Rethinking the Resource Curse: Ownership Structure, Institutional Capacity and Domestic Constraints' (2006) 9 Annual Review of Political Science 241

Madonsela S, 'Critical Reflections on State Capture in South Africa' (2019) 11(1) Insight on Africa 113

Mailey JR, *The Anatomy of the Resource Curse: Predatory Investment in Africa's Extractive Industries ACSS Special Report No 3* (Africa Center for Strategic Studies 2015)

Matshediso IB, 'A Review of Mineral Development and Investment Policies of Botswana' (2005) 30(3) Resource Policy 203

Mayer CP and Meadowcroft SA, 'Selling Public Assets: Techniques and Financial Implications' (1985) 6(4) Fiscal Studies 42

Mehlum H, Moene K, and Torvik R, 'Cursed by Resources or Institutions?' (2006) 29(8) The World Economy 1117

Mikesell RF, 'Explaining the Resource Curse, with Special Reference to Mineral Exporting Countries' (1997) 23(4) Resources Policy 191

Mosala SJ, Venter JCM, and Bain EG, 'South Africa's Economic Transformation since 1994: What Influence has the National Democratic Revolution (NDR) Had? (2017) 44(3–4) The Review of Black Political Economy 327

Mostert H and Van den Berg M, 'Expressing Local Content through Black Economic Empowerment in the South African Petroleum Industry' in Oluwayi DS (ed), *Local Content, Sustainable Development and Treaty Implementation in Global Energy Markets* (Cambridge University Press 2021)

Mostert H and Young C, 'Natural Resources as "Regulated Property": The Challenges of Resource Stewardship in South Africa' in Godt C (ed), *Regulatory Property Rights: The Transforming Notion of Property in Transnational Business Regulation* (Brill Nijhoff 2016)

Moyo F and Mabhena C, 'Harnessing Mineral Resources in Gwanda District of Zimbabwe: A Myth or a Reality?' (2014) 38 International Letters of Social and Humanistic Sciences 1.

Mupfumi J and Masiya T, 'An Analysis of Zimbabwe's Mines and Minerals Amendment Bill' (2016) 1 (1) Policy Analysis 1

Namibian Ministry of Mines and Energy, 'Mission and Vision' <http://www.mme.gov.na/about-us/mission/> accessed 19 February 2021

Natural Resource Governance Institute, '2017 Resource Governance Index: Measuring the Quality of Governance in the Oil, Gas and Mining Sectors of 81 Countries' <https://resourcegovernanceindex.org> accessed 22 February 2021

Natural Resource Governance Institute, 'Tanzania's 2015 Extractive Industry Legislation: Recommendations for Implementation' *NRGI Briefing* (November 2016)

Ndulo M, 'Mining Legislation and Mineral Development in Zambia' (1986) 19(1) Cornell International Law Journal 1

Ndulo M, 'The Ownership of Base Minerals in Zambia' (1980) 13(1) The Comparative and International Journal of Southern Africa 78

Ng'ambi SP, 'Permanent Sovereignty Over Natural Resources and the Sanctity of Contracts, from the Angle of Lucrum Cessans' (2015) 12(2) Loyola University Chicago International Law Review 153

Ngocho B and Magai S, 'Mining in Tanzania: Effects of the Mining Legal Framework Overhaul' *DLA Piper* (11 August 2020) <https://www.dlapiper.com/nl/global/insights/publications/2020/08/africa-connected-issue-4/6tanzania-mining-legal-framework-overhaul/> accessed 22 February 2021

Nussbaum MC, *Anger and Forgiveness: Resentment, Generosity, Justice* (Oxford University Press 2016)

Ocheni S and Nwankwo BC, 'Analysis of Colonialism and Its Impact in Africa' (2012) 8(3) Cross-Cultural Communication 48

Papyrakis E and Gerlagh R, 'The Resource Curse Hypothesis and Its Transmission Channels' (2004) 32(1) Journal of Comparative Economics 181

Pereira R and Gough O, 'Permanent Sovereignty over Natural Resources in the 21st Century: Natural Resource Governance and the Right to Self-Determination of Indigenous Peoples under International Law' (2013) 14(2) Melbourne Journal of International Law 451

Pessoa A, 'Natural Resources and Institutions: The "Natural Resources Curse" Revisited' (2008) MPRA Paper No. 8640

Pinielo I, 'PPADB Battles to Stamp Out Tender Corruption' *MmegiOnline* (7 July 2017) <https://www.mmegi.bw/index.php?aid=70113&dir=2017/july/07> accessed 22 February 2021

Poncian J and Kigodi H, 'Transparency Initiatives and Tanzania's Extractive Industry Governance' (2018) 5(1) Development Studies Research 106

Pritchard R, 'Safeguards for Foreign Investment in Mining' in Bastida M, Wälde T, and Warden-Fernández J (eds), *International and Comparative Mineral Law and Policy: Trends and Prospects* (Kluwer Law International 2005)

Ramaphosa C, 'State of the Nation Address 2018' <https://www.gov.za/speeches/state-nation-address-2018#> accessed 28 February 2021

Ramírez-Cendrero JM and Wirth E, 'Is the Norwegian Model Exportable to Combat Dutch Disease' (2016) 48 Resource Policy 85

Report of the International Council on Mining & Metals (ICMM), 'Social Progress in Mining-Dependant Countries: Analysis through the Lens of the SDGs' (ICMM 2018)

Reuters Staff, 'Zambian Ex-Mines Minister Found Guilty of Corruption' *Reuters* (2015) <https://www.reuters.com/article/us-zambia-mining-corruption/zambian-ex-mines-minister-found-guilty-of-corruption-idUSKBN0LT1X420150225> accessed 22 February 2021

Rodney W, *How Europe Underdeveloped Africa* (Bogle-L'Ouverture Publications with the Tanzanian Publishing House 1972)

Rønne A, 'Public and Private Rights to Natural Resources and Differences in Their Protection?' in McHarg A and others (eds), *Property and the Law in Energy and Natural Resources* (9th edn, Oxford University Press 2010)

Ross ML, *The Oil Curse: How Petroleum Wealth Shapes the Development of Nations* (Princeton University Press 2012)

Ross ML, 'The Political Economy of the Resource Curse' (1999) 51 World Politics 297

Rosser A, 'The Political Economy of the Resource Curse: A Literature Review' (2006) Institute of Development Studies Working Paper 268

Rwomire A, 'Economic Growth, Poverty and Governance: The Case of Botswana' in Organization for Social Science Research in Eastern and Southern Africa (OSSREA), *Good Governance and Civil Society Participation in Africa* (OSSREA African Book Collective 2009)

Sachs JD and Warner AM, 'Natural Resource Abundance and Economic Growth' (1995) National Bureau of Economic Research Working Paper 5398

Sachs JD and Warner AM, 'The Curse of Natural Resources' (2001) 45 European Economic Review 827

Schrijver N, 'Self-determination of Peoples and Sovereignty over Natural Wealth and Resources' in United Nations Human Rights Office of High Commissioner, *Realizing the Right to Development* (United Nations Publication 2013)

Schrijver NJ, 'Permanent Sovereignty over Natural Resources versus Common Heritage of Mankind: Complementary or Contradictory Principles of International Economic Law' (1987) 21 Series: Development & Security 1

Sebudubudu D, 'Corruption and its Control in Botswana' (2003) 35 Botswana Notes and Records 125

Sikamo J, Mwanza A, and Mweemba C, 'Copper Mining in Zambia—History and Future' (2016) 116(6) The Journal of the Southern African Institute of Mining and Metallurgy 491

Sovacool BK and Andrews N, 'Does Transparency Matter? Evaluating the Governance Impacts of the Extractive Industries Transparency Initiative (EITI) in Azerbaijan and Liberia' (2015) 45 Resources Policy 183

Statistics South Africa, 'SA Economy Sheds 2,2 Million Jobs in Q2 but Unemployment Levels Drop' (29 September 2020) <http://www.statssa.gov.za/?p=13633> accessed 15 February 2021

Stevens P and Dietsche E, 'Resource Curse: An Analysis of Causes, Experiences and Possible Ways Forward' (2008) 36 Energy Policy 56

Stiglitz JE, 'What Is the Role of the State?' in Humphreys M and others (eds), *Escaping the Resource Curse* (Columbia University Press 2007)

Sulla V and Zikhali P, *Overcoming Poverty and Inequality in South Africa: An Assessment of Drivers, Constraints and Opportunities* (The World Bank 2018)

Taylor I, 'As Good as It Gets? Botswana's "Democratic Development"' (2003) 21(2) Journal of Contemporary African Studies 225

Taylor I, 'Botswana's "Developmental State" and the Politics of Legitimacy' (Conference Paper: 'Towards a New Political Economy of Development: Globalisation and Governance', University of Sheffield, United Kingdom, 4–6 July 2002)

Todd F, 'DRC Mining Becoming More Transparent but Lacks Accountability, says EITI, 2019' *Extractive Industries Transparency* (17 October 2019)

Torvik R, 'Natural Resource, Rent Seeking and Welfare' (2002) 67(2) Journal of Development Economics 455

Torvik R, 'Why do Some Resource-Abundant Countries Succeed While Others Do Not? (2009) 25(2) Oxford Review of Economic Policy 241

Trading Economics, 'South Africa Unemployment Rate' (2020) <https://tradingeconomics.com/south-africa/unemployment-rate> accessed 15 February 2021

UNCTAD *World Investment Report 2007: Transnational Corporations, Extractive Industries and Development* (2007)

United Nations, 'United Nations Conference on Trade and Development: Report on the Implementation of the Investment Policy Review: Kenya' United Nations (2013) <https://unctad.org/system/files/official-document/diaepcb2012d6_en.pdf> accessed 23 February 2021

Van Dalsen A and Simkins C, 'Does Gini Index Really Show SA as Most Unequal Society in the World?' *Politics Web* (13 June 2019) <https://www.politicsweb.co.za/opinion/does-the-gini-index-show-that-sa-is-the-most-unequ> accessed 17 February 2021

Van den Berg HM, 'Ownership of Minerals Under the New Legislative Framework for Mineral Resources' (2009) 20 Stellenbosch Law Review 139

Van den Berg HM, 'Regulation of the Upstream Petroleum Industry: A Comparative Analysis and Evaluation of Regulatory Frameworks of South Africa and Namibia' (PhD thesis, University of Cape Town 2014)

Van der Ploeg F and Poelhekke S, 'Volatility and the Natural Resource Curse' (2009) 61(4) Oxford Economic Papers 727.

Van der Schyff E, 'Who "Owns" the Country's Mineral Resources? The Possible Incorporation of the Public Trust Doctrine through the Mineral and Petroleum Resources Development Act' (2008) 4 TSAR 757

Van der Schyff E, *Property in Minerals and Petroleum* (Juta 2016)

Van der Vyver JD, 'Nationalisation of Mineral Rights in South Africa' (2012) 45(1) De Jure 125

Van Niekerk H, 'Towards a New Understanding of Mineral Tenure Security: The Demise of the Property-Law Paradigm' (PhD thesis, University of Cape Town 2016)

Van Wyk D, 'Policy Gap 5 SADC Research: Corporate Social Responsibility in the Diamond Mining Industry in Botswana', 22 Bench Marks Foundation (2009)

Venables AJ, 'Using Natural Resources for Development: Why Has it Proven So Difficult' (2016) 30(1) Journal of Economic Perspective 161

Venter F, 'State Capture, Corruption, and Constitutionalism in South Africa' in Fombad CM and Steytler N (eds), *Corruption and Constitutionalism in Africa* (Oxford University Press 2020)

Viñuales JE, 'The "Resource Curse"—A Legal Perspective' (2011) 17(2) Global Governance 197

Visser F, 'The Principle of Permanent Sovereignty over Natural Resources and the Nationalization of Foreign Interests' (1988) 21(1) Comparative and International Law Journal of Southern Africa 76

Wälde T, 'Permanent Sovereignty over Natural Resources Recent Developments in the Mineral Sector' (1993) 7(3) National Research Forum 240

Weinthal E and Luong PJ, 'Combating the Resource Curse: An Alternative Solution to Managing Mineral Wealth' (2006) 4(1) Perspectives on Politics 35

Wenar L, 'Property Rights and the Resource Curse' (2008) 36(1) Philosophy & Public Affairs 2

Werner K, 'Zambia: Governance and Natural Resources' (2016) 13(2) Revue Gouvernance 32

Williams A, 'Shining a Light on the Resource Curse: An Empirical Analysis of the Relationship Between Natural Resources, Transparency, and Economic Growth' (2011) 39(4) World Development 490

Wolf L, 'The Remedial Action of the "State of Capture" Report in Perspective' (2017) 20 PER/PELJ 2

World Bank, 'Gini Index (World Bank Estimate)—South Africa' (2000–2021) <https://data.worldbank.org/indicator/SI.POV.GINI?locations=ZA> accessed 15 February 2021

World Bank, 'Poverty headcount ratio at national poverty lines (% of population)—South Africa' (1985–2020) <https://data.worldbank.org/indicator/SI.POV.NAHC?locations=ZA> accessed 15 February 2021

10

Namibia's Resource-Based Economy

Protection versus Exploitation of Nature

*Henning Melber**

1. Introduction

This chapter seeks to assess to what extent the Namibian government and state authorities, operating as they do within a resource-based economy, give preference to either the protection or the exploitation of the country's natural resources. By doing so, it offers some evidence about how Namibia navigates between environmental protection and economic interests. Reconciling the implicit tension between a social and intergenerational contract and the exploitation of resources poses a tough challenge to good governance: the risk of lasting environmental damage through decisions motivated by short-term economic gains could be strongly at variance with the essentials of sustainable development. A precarious balancing act is thus involved in weighing up economic priorities against their potentially damaging consequences for the ecology and environment.

The chapter examines the dilemmas facing a government that inherited a colonial economic structure and regulates an economy dependent, through its primary sector, on the world market. The chapter's focus is on recent controversies surrounding the exploitation of (unprocessed) natural resources. In an introductory overview, it describes Namibia's fragile socio-economic context and thereafter summarizes the constitutional and legal provisions regarding environmental sustainability and the protection of the natural habitat. Particular reference is then made to marine phosphate mining, the harvesting of timber, and the establishment of a tobacco plantation. The concluding section highlights the ambiguities of navigating through conflicting demands and expectations that stem from, on the one hand, economic interests and, on the other, the need for environmental protection and sustainable management of natural resources.

2. Namibia's Socio-economic Challenges

After more than a century of colonial occupation, first by Germany and then South Africa, Namibia became a sovereign state on 21 March 1990. The liberation movement South West Africa People's Organization (SWAPO), following a long struggle that included armed resistance, became the legitimately elected government. Since then it has been the party in political control of a large territory more than 824,000 km^2 in area and, in 2020, home to

* I am grateful for the constructive advice of my anonymous reviewers, and also thank the editors for their guidance.

Henning Melber, *Namibia's Resource-Based Economy* In: *Constitutionalism and the Economy in Africa*. Edited by: Charles M Fombad and Nico Steytler, Oxford University Press. © Henning Melber 2022. DOI: 10.1093/oso/9780192886439.003.0012

an estimated 2.5 million people. Namibia is one of the driest and most sparsely populated countries on earth. Environmental degradation and the other effects of climate change (not least of them the increasing shortage of water) have created high vulnerabilities for social and economic reproduction. For the majority of people, commercial and communal agriculture remain, directly or indirectly, the most important sectors.[1]

There is, nonetheless, rapid rural-urban migration, with an increasing concentration of people at the margins of a few urban centres. Almost half of the country's population live in what is euphemistically called 'informal settlements'. The structural legacy of colonial rule is perpetuated in an export economy rooted in the primary sector and lacking any meaningful local value addition. This is accompanied by gross socio-economic inequalities and social disparities; moreover, efforts to transform the economy have displayed features of a rent-seeking strategy. As argued elsewhere, limited redistribution of income and wealth were to a considerable extent guided by strategies of a new elite in party, government, and public administration seeking more access to the resources under state control. Despite the rhetoric, the country's proclaimed pro-poor policy has not translated into serious implementation.[2]

For many years, the export of mainly unprocessed raw material from mining, fishing, and agriculture provided steady economic growth, turning Namibia statistically into an upper middle-income country. In addition, with a Human Development Index (HDI) value of 0.645 for 2018, it ranked in 130th position out of 189 countries and fell into the medium human development category.[3] Its gross national income per capita increased by about two-thirds between 1990 and 2018, peaking in 2016 at USD 10,171 (in 2011 PPP$, ie purchasing power rates of 2011). Due to a recession since 2016, this figure declined to USD 9,779 in 2017 and USD 9,683 in 2018, even though it remains way above the average for sub-Saharan Africa of USD 3,443.

Namibia's average, however, does not reflect the fundamental socio-economic disparities that exist in a country with one of the world's highest Gini coefficients and hence one of its most unequal distributions of income. As such, when the inequality-adjusted HDI (IHDI) is calculated and the value 'is discounted for inequality, the HDI falls to 0.417, a loss of 35.3 percent due to inequality'.[4] Based on 2013 survey data, the Multidimensional Poverty Index (MPI), which assesses deprivation beyond income poverty by including health, education and/or standard-of-living dimensions, classifies 38 per cent of Namibia's population as multidimensionally poor and another 20.3 per cent as vulnerable to multidimensional poverty. It has been concluded therefore that Namibia is 'a rich country with poor people'.[5]

Namibia has no lack of programmatic documents and strategic plans. In 2004, Vision 2030 was published as a blueprint under the country's first president, Sam Nujoma. Its ambitious aims include full industrialization, food self-sufficiency, and equal opportunities for all in a high-income country, goals which were to be achieved through 'the development

---

[1] See Henning Melber, 'Colonialism, Land, Ethnicity, and Class: Namibia after the Second National Land Conference' (2019) 1(54) Africa Spectrum 73.

[2] See Henning Melber (ed), *Transitions in Namibia: Which Changes for Whom?* (Nordic Africa Institute 2007); Henning Melber, *Understanding Namibia: The Trials of Independence* (Hurst and Jacana 2014, OUP 2015).

[3] For this and the following data, see UNDP, 'Briefing Note on Namibia for 2019 Human Development Report' <http://hdr.undp.org/sites/all/themes/hdr_theme/country-notes/NAM.pdf> accessed 22 January 2020.

[4] ibid 5.

[5] Herbert Jauch, Lucy Edwards, and Bram Cupido, *A Rich Country with Poor People* (Labour Resource and Research Institute 2009); see also Herbert Jauch, *Poverty, Unemployment and Inequality in Namibia* (International Union for the Conservation of Nature and Commission on Environmental, Economic and Social Policies 2012).

of Namibia's "natural capital" and its sustainable utilization, for the benefit of the country's social, economic and ecological well-being'.[6] Furthermore, a year into his first term in office, President Hage Geingob in 2016 released the Harambee Prosperity Plan (HPP). It reinforces the ambitious goals of Vision 2030, 'targeting a growth rate of seven per cent and higher' for the years to come. 'Growth must promote value addition, diversification and result in the creation of industries and jobs'.[7] In 2017, a fifth five-year National Development Plan (NDP5) elaborated on strategies for achieving the goals and aspirations outlined in the other two documents.[8] Yet while broadly compatible and overlapping, these blueprints were to differing degrees out of touch with socio-economic realities and based on wishful thinking.

During the many 'fat years' when the country enjoyed economic growth rates of 5 per cent and above, the state made no provision for the lean years. Since 2015, drought and a decline in world market prices of commodities such as diamonds, copper, and uranium oxide reduced economic performance. The decline of the Angolan and South African economies added to the constraints. As a result, the government faced serious liquidity problems. Instead of opting for fiscal prudence, however, it sought to resolve the financial impasse by a marked increase in borrowing.

Between 2008 and 2015, 'fiscal policy went into a super-expansionary mode', swinging from a 6.6 per cent surplus to a 8.6 per cent current account deficit.[9] In late 2016, the government faced serious fiscal constraints that resulted in massive borrowing to secure continued liquidity. As the Finance Minister declared at the time in his Mid-Year Budget Review Policy Statement in the National Assembly, 'The Namibian economy has never before been in such a precarious situation.'[10] Public debt tripled from NAD 30.9 billion in the financial year 2013/14 (24.3 per cent of GDP) to NAD 96.9 billion for 2019/20 (49.0 per cent of GDP), while interest payments almost quadrupled during the same period from NAD 1.8 billion (4.3 per cent of GDP) to NAD 7.0 billion (11.9 per cent of GDP).[11]

As a result of the deteriorating economic situation and the growing debt spiral, which went along with a recession starting in 2016, the country lost its earlier singular lead position among sub-Saharan countries as a creditworthy economy. The two credit rating agencies Fitch and Moody's between 2016 and 2020 downgraded their outlooks five and four times, respectively, to junk status.[12] A diagnosis published by a leading local think tank on the occasion of the national budget for 2018/19 concluded that 'the government remains

[6] Republic of Namibia, *Namibia Vision 2030: Prosperity, Harmony, Peace and Political Stability. Policy Framework for Long-Term National Development* (Office of the President 2004) 41.

[7] Republic of Namibia, *Harambee Prosperity Plan 2016/17–2019/20. Namibian Government's Action Plan towards Prosperity for All* 13

[8] Republic of Namibia, *Namibia's 5th National Development Plan (NDP5): Working Together towards Prosperity 2017/18–2021/22.*

[9] The Growth Lab at Harvard University, 'The Challenge of Sustained and Inclusive Prosperity in Namibia' (PowerPoint presentation, 9 November 2019) <http://www.slideshare.net/miguelangelsantos/namibia-the-challenge-of-sustained-and-inclusive-growth> accessed 25 July 2020.

[10] 'Financial Year 2016/17 Mid-Year Budget Review Policy Statement'. Presented by Calle Schlettwein, MP, Minister of Finance (27 October 2016) <http://www.parliament.na/phocadownload/media/2016/mtr.pdf> accessed 24 July 2020.

[11] Institute for Public Policy Research, *Namibia Quarterly Economic Review* (October–December 2019) <https://ippr.org.na/publication/namibia-qer-quarter-4-2019/> accessed 22 January 2020.

[12] 'Namibia Credit Rating' *World Government Bonds* (nd) <http://www.worldgovernmentbonds.com/credit-rating/namibia/> accessed 24 July 2020.

on an expenditure tightrope, with too much and too little expenditure both likely to cause major long-term economic damage in the country'.[13]

Owing to the economic decline, the employment situation deteriorated too. In a population of 1.5 million people 15 years of age and older, the National Labour Survey in 2018 described one-third as 'broad[ly]' and one-fifth as 'strict[ly]' unemployed, with agriculture, forestry, and fishing by far the biggest employment sector (167,242), followed by accommodation and food service (83,056) and private households (72,185). While mining and quarrying make an important contribution to GDP, they employed only 12,087 people.[14] However, the definition applied is one of 'informality' and registers all as 'employed' who worked for at least an hour for pay, profit, or family gain during the previous seven days. If employment is understood as formal employment, including with the provision of some form of social protection, the picture changes dramatically: the number then declines from 365,703 in 2013 to 307,067 in 2018. If government employment (86,864) and employment in state-owned enterprises (30,654) are subtracted, the number of people formally employed in the private sector drops to 189,549.[15]

According to a survey in late 2019, 80.6 per cent of the respondents thought the country was going in the wrong direction; 72.6 per cent described the economic condition as very or fairly bad; 58.2 per cent believed the conditions were worse or much worse than a year before; and 47.3 per cent expected them to become even worse or much worse in twelve months' time.[16] Sentiments like these exert additional pressure on the government and affected the results of the presidential and National Assembly elections at the end of November 2019. For the first time, SWAPO and its presidential candidate suffered considerable losses among the electorate.[17] Given the growing frustration of the population, the country's medium-term economic policy is confronted with massive demands for improving the situation of the common people. This makes the SWAPO government's balancing act—weighing the protection of public goods such as facets of the natural environmental against economic gains through resource extraction—all the more precarious.

3. The Constitutional and Legal Framework

In the decades since independence, Namibia has sought to establish not only an independent judiciary and give anchorage to the rule of law, but also to create a legal framework applicable to matters of environmental concern. The Constitution was drafted and accepted by a constituent assembly elected under United Nations supervision during the first weeks of 1990 as the last step towards the country's independence. It was considered a pioneering document for Namibia as well as a general showpiece for the advancement

---

[13] Rowland Brown and Cheryl Emvula, 'The National Budget 2018–19: Walking the Fiscal Tightrope' (IPPR Democracy Report, Special Briefing Report No 23, April 2018) 12 <https://ippr.org.na/wp-content/uploads/2018/04/23_Budget_WEB.pdf> accessed 24 July 2020.

[14] Institute for Public Policy Research (n 11) 15.

[15] ibid 17.

[16] Survey Warehouse, 'Summary of Results: Afrobarometer Round 8 survey in Namibia, 2019' (Survey Warehouse 2019).

[17] Henning Melber, 'Namibia's Parliamentary and Presidential Elections: The Honeymoon is over' (2020) 1(109) The Round Table 13.

of civil liberties.[18] In chapter 11 ('Principles of State Policy'), article 95 ('Promotion of the Welfare of the People'), the Constitution declares:

> The State shall actively promote and maintain the welfare of the people by adopting, inter alia, policies aimed at the following:
>
> ...
>
> (l) maintenance of ecosystems, essential ecological processes and biological diversity of Namibia and utilization of living natural resources on a sustainable basis for the benefit of all Namibians, both present and future; in particular, the Government shall provide measures against the dumping or recycling of foreign nuclear and toxic waste on Namibian territory.

Notably, article 100 stresses sovereign ownership of natural resources: 'Land, water and natural resources below and above the surface of the land and in the continental shelf and within the territorial waters and the exclusive economic zone of Namibia shall belong to the State if they are not otherwise lawfully owned.' Article 101 ('Application of Principles contained in this Chapter') then concludes:

> The principles of state policy contained in this Chapter shall not of and by themselves be legally enforceable by any Court, but shall nevertheless guide the Government in making and applying laws to give effect to the fundamental objectives of the said principles. The Courts are entitled to have regard to the said principles in interpreting any laws based on them.

While the principles as laid down in chapter 11 of the Constitution are not legally enforceable, they anchor a concept of custodianship by the state over natural resources, a concept which since then has also been confirmed in court rulings.[19]

Subsequent laws have to some extent translated the commitment into a binding obligation by making it clearly justiciable. These include the Minerals (Prospecting and Mining) Act of 1992,[20] which vests all rights (including the granting of licences) in the state. The Minerals Policy defined by the Ministry of Mines and Energy in 2004 ends the list of objectives as specified in section 1.6 with the obligation to 'ensure compliance with national environmental policy'. This underlines an existing awareness to view resource exploitation in line with the protection of the environment and natural habitat. The latter was formulated as a binding commitment in the Environmental Management Act of 2007,[21] which seeks to

---

[18] See various contributions in Anton Bösl, Nico Horn, and André du Pisani (eds), *Constitutional Democracy in Namibia: A Critical Analysis after Two Decades* (Konrad Adenauer Foundation 2010).

[19] See Willem Odendaal and Paul Hebinck, 'Mining on Communal Land as a New Frontier: A Case Study of the Kunene Region, Namibia' (2019) 2-3(15) Journal of Land Use Science 457, 464. The authors refer to *Agnes Kahimbi Kashela v Katima Mulilo Town Council and Others* (SA 15/2017) (2018), NASC 409 in confirmation of this understanding.

[20] Act 33 of 1992.

[21] Act 7 of 2007, which came into force with Government Notice No 28, Government Gazette No 4878 of 6 February 2012. For its practical meaning, see Dianne Hubbard, *Guide to the Environmental Management Act No. 7 of 2007* (Ministry of Environment and Tourism 2008).

promote the sustainable management of the environment and the use of natural resources by establishing principles for decision making on matters affecting the environment; to establish the Sustainable Development Advisory Council; to provide for the appointment of the Environmental Commissioner and environmental officers; to provide for a process of assessment and control of activities which may have significant effects on the environment; and to provide for incidental matters.

According to article 3(2) of the Act, the principles of environmental management include the following:

(a) renewable resources must be used on a sustainable basis for the benefit of present and future generations;

...

(d) equitable access to environmental resources must be promoted and the functional integrity of ecological systems must be taken into account to ensure the sustainability of the systems and to prevent harmful effects;

...

(g) Namibia's cultural and natural heritage including, its biological diversity, must be protected and respected for the benefit of present and future generations;

(h) the option that provides the most benefit or causes the least damage to the environment as a whole, at a cost acceptable to society, in the long term as well as in the short term must be adopted to reduce the generation of waste and polluting substances at source;

...

(k) where there is sufficient evidence which establishes that there are threats of serious or irreversible damage to the environment, lack of full scientific certainty may not be used as a reason for postponing cost-effective measures to prevent environmental degradation; and

(l) damage to the environment must be prevented and activities which cause such damage must be reduced, limited or controlled.

As stated by the Ministry of Environment and Tourism with regard to the stipulated environmental impact assessment:

All Government institutions, companies, other organisations and individuals that are involved in planning or undertaking listed activities must apply the principles outlined ... Therefore, before starting any operations that might likely cause a significant effect on the environment, an Environmental Impact Assessment (EIA) must be undertaken.

The principles of the Act 'provide a high potential for decision-makers and for courts to develop a foundation for good environmental governance'.[22] However, given the Act's relatively brief history, 'the body of cases giving practical meaning to the Act by decision-makers and courts is thus still relatively limited'.[23] The legal framework in place empowers

[22] K Ruppel-Schlichting, 'General Principles of Environmental Management in Namibia' in OC Ruppel and K Ruppel-Schlichting (eds), *Environmental Law and Policy in Namibia: Towards Making Africa the Tree of Life* (3rd fully revised edn, Hanns Seidel Foundation 2016) 116.
[23] Katharina Ruppel-Schlichting, 'General Principles of Environmental Management in Namibia' in Oliver C Ruppel and Katharina Ruppel-Schlichting (eds), *Environmental Law and Policy in Namibia. Towards Making Africa the Tree of Life* (3rd fully revised edn, Hanns Seidel Foundation 2016) 121.

the judiciary to settle disputes over the protection and promotion of environmental human rights if brought to the attention of courts.[24] But as Ruppel argues:

> A legal culture upholding environmental rights is still in the initial phase of being created. On paper, a broad variety of laws directed at environmental protection exists; and in principle, these laws also provide for effective mechanisms to ensure compliance with and enforcement of these environmental laws. What, however, remains a challenge is the full implementation of these provisions.[25]

What compounds the challenge is that policy-makers and civil society organizations lack a shared, articulated awareness of how best the obligations to protect Namibia's natural environment could be met. This is apparent in the following three case studies, which bring to light some of the divisions and lines of conflict among policy-makers in government and within the public discourse in regard to how 'development' is understood.

4. Resource Exploitation Versus Environmental Protection

Large parts of Namibia are desert or semi-desert. This creates a fragile environment for human reproduction. But the country is rich in mineral resources. Since the discovery of diamonds in the Namib Desert along the coast of the Atlantic Ocean during German colonialism in the early twentieth century, these have been an attractive prey for foreign interests. Copper, gold, strategic minerals, and uranium oxide have given rise to multiple engagements by international mining companies. In addition, the cold Benguela current along the coast has been one of the world's best habitats for a wealth of fish and other biomass, estimated to be the biggest in African waters and, according to a 2007 FAO Fishery Country Profile, 'one of the most productive fishing grounds in the world'.[26] This asset was systematically depleted since the late 1940s by South African and Western fishing companies, and by the mid-1980s was already declared a 'disaster zone'.[27] During the border war of the 1970s and 1980s between the South African army and the People's Liberation Army of SWAPO, the few forests with rare precious woods along the northern sub-tropical belt with boundaries to Angola and Zambia in the west and Botswana to the east were another object of desire and ruthless plundering.

Resource extraction did not end with sovereign rule at independence. Instead, it continued much as before, with international companies gradually replacing or joining the various South African and Western enterprises which had originally benefited from the country's occupation by the apartheid state. These have seen some degree of (rather passive) local co-ownership, mainly with members of the new black elite as the frontmen and women providing the formal window-dressing of Namibianization of economic activity.

---

[24] Oliver C Ruppel, 'Environmental Justice, Compliance and Enforcement' in OC Ruppel and K Ruppel-Schlichting (eds), *Environmental Law and Policy in Namibia: Towards Making Africa the Tree of Life* (3rd fully revised edn, Hanns Seidel Foundation 2016) 497.

[25] ibid 507–8.

[26] FAO, The Republic of Namibia 2007 <http://www.fao.org/fi/oldsite/fcp/en/nam/profile.htm> accessed 28 March 2021.

[27] Richard Moorsom, *Exploiting the Sea* (Catholic Institute for International Relations 1984) 70.

But, at a closer look, this tokenism of Namibian representation in the boards of companies—in popular parlance referred to as 'sightholders' in contrast to 'rightholders'—has brought little change to the nature of economic activities in the resource-based sectors, with raw materials as well as profits continuing to be transferred to other countries and the local population enjoying few gains.

The ongoing over-exploitation of the biomass along the Namibian coast is a prominent example.[28] Under the proclaimed policy of 'Namibianization', individual local beneficiaries received fishing quotas that were sold in turn to international companies. As facilitators, they received money that was not invested in the development of a locally owned fishing industry or other productive economic activities but used mainly for purposes of individual consumption. A major act of fraud that went unnoticed for years involved the organized misappropriation of fishing quotas by a foreign company in return for massive bribes. Investigative journalists brought the case to light in 2018,[29] but it was only in late 2019 that reports disclosed details of bribery of hitherto unknown proportions. The dealings involved the biggest Icelandic fishing company, two Namibian ministers, and several other high-ranking officials in state institutions.[30] The large-scale fraud made international headlines.[31] Dubbed #*Fishrot*, files disclosed massive illegal transactions. A documentary broadcast by Al Jazeera on 1 December 2019[32] revealed further intricate details.[33]

Of late, the growing presence of Chinese-owned operations, mainly in the construction and mining (in particular uranium) sectors, has brought further evidence of the presence of foreign beneficiaries in key sectors of the economy. This has become a notable and much-discussed new tendency.[34] While celebrated by the Namibian and Chinese governments as an 'all-weather friendship' and win-win situation, the economic impact has neither transformed the pattern of unequal foreign trade, nor created new employment for ordinary Namibians. As before, natural resources are transferred without value addition to other parts of the world, while local employment in the construction sector has suffered from the dominance of Chinese companies now receiving the bulk of state tenders for public works. Neither Chinese nor other foreign direct investment has had any meaningful impact on the country's economic diversification, and as a result, the colonial nature of the economy—exporting raw materials in exchange for importing manufactured goods and

---

[28] See Henning Melber, 'Of Big Fish & Small Fry: The Fishing Industry in Namibia' (2003) 95(30) Review of African Political Economy 142.

[29] Ndapewoshali Shapwanale and Shinovene Immanuel, 'Namibian Fishing Industry Cries Foul as Quota Handed to International Interests' *Daily Maverick* (14 May 2018) <http://www.dailymaverick.co.za/article/2018-05-14-amabhungane-namibian-fishing-industry-cries-foul-as-quota-handed-to-international-interests/> accessed 26 July 2020.

[30] Shinovene Immanuel and Sakeus Iikela, 'Kickback Kings fall' *The Namibian* (15 November 2019) <http://www.namibian.com.na/85501/read/Kickback-Kings-fall> accessed 15 November 2019.

[31] James Kleinfeld, 'Two Namibian Ministers Resign Following Al Jazeera Investigation' *Al Jazeera* (14 November 2019) <http://www.aljazeera.com/news/2019/11/namibian-ministers-resign-al-jazeera-investigation-191113161947877.html> accessed 18 November 2019.

[32] Al Jazeera Investigations, Anatomy of a Bribe, 1 December 2019 <https://www.youtube.com/watch?v=_FJ1TB0nwHs> accessed 28 March 2021.

[33] James Kleinfeld, 'Two Namibian Ministers Resign Following Al Jazeera Investigation' *Al Jazeera* (14 November 2019). <http://www.aljazeera.com/news/2019/11/namibian-ministers-resign-al-jazeera-investigation-191113161947877.html> accessed 18 November 2019.

[34] See Meredith J De Boom, 'Nuclear (Geo)Political Ecologies: A Hybrid Geography of Chinese Investment in Namibia's Uranium Sector' (2017) 3 Journal of Current Chinese Affairs 46; Henning Melber, 'Looking East/Going South: The Namibian-Chinese "All Weather Friendship"' (2018) 35(18) Stichproben: Vienna Journal of African Studies 25.

commodities—has not changed fundamentally. Likewise, due to a higher degree of capital-intensive resource extraction, there has been no significant employment creation.

The following section discusses a few exemplary cases in which concerns for environmental protection and the interest in economic exploitation of the country's natural resources clash, or at any rate exist in tension with each other.

4.1 Marine Phosphate Mining

As documented above, article 100 of Namibia's Constitution mandates the government as the custodian of natural resources not privately or 'otherwise lawfully owned'. The catchphrase of the 'blue economy', one gaining ground internationally and entailing the utilization of oceanic resources without damage to the ecosystem, has therefore found a receptive ear with the Namibian government. As Prime Minister Saara Kuugongelwa-Amadhila declared at the Sustainable Blue Economy Conference (SBEC) in late 2018, her government plans 'to develop sustainable seabed mining (including mineral and fossil fuels)'.[35] NDP5 points to the potential of a blue economy for transforming the economy through key industries such as fishing, tourism, and seabed mining. As a desired outcome, it aims by 2022 to have 'implemented a Blue Economy governance and management system that sustainably maximizes economic benefits from marine resources and ensures equitable marine wealth distribution to all Namibians'.

The challenge which NDP5 identifies is a 'lack of coordination and integration between sectors due to the lack of a regulatory and legal framework which ensures appropriate planning, management, and governance'.[36] However, as Carver observes,

the disparate global definitions of the blue economy have led to an absence of clarity over what this agenda means to Namibia and how it will be consolidated within policy … [T]he lack of understanding of the blue economy within Namibia itself highlights that African states' ownership of the marine domain is not antagonistic to external actors. Rather, the agenda and associated rhetoric are being transposed over the marine sphere including by non-state and external actors.[37]

Marine phosphate mining is a prominent example of how private conglomerates of international and local companies seek to enter the blue economy, and illustrates how fears of environmental damage, on the one hand, and potential investment in resource extraction for profit generation, on the other, are clashing. While there were two licences issued for such marine phosphate activities, the case of LL Namibia Phosphates (Pty) Ltd (LLNP) as a second operation has remained largely ignored, also due to its lower profile. It obtained a licence for an area 185 km north of Lüderitz and 80 km offshore.[38] Owned by the Israeli

---

[35] SBEC, *Report on the Global Sustainable Blue Economy Conference*, 26–28 November 2018, Nairobi, Kenya <http://www.blueeconomyconference.go.ke/wp-content/uploads/2018/12/SBEC-FINAL-REPORT-8-DECEMBER-2018-rev-2-1-2-PDF2-3-compressed.pdf> accessed 28 March 2021.
[36] Namibia's 5th National Development Plan (n 8) 24.
[37] Rosanna Carver, 'Lessons for Blue Degrowth from Namibia's Emerging Blue Economy' (2020) 15 Sustainability Science 131.
[38] LL Namibia Phosphates (Pty) Ltd, Marine Phosphate Project Namibia. Windhoek Mining Expo—April 2016 <https://www.miningexponamibia.com/assets/docs/2015/4_Marine_Phosphate.pdf> accessed 28 March 2021.

company Lev Leviev Diamonds, it has so far largely restricted its activities to establishing a processing plant for marine phosphate at Lüderitz.[39]

In contrast, Namibian Marine Phosphate (Pty) Ltd (NMP) is registered as a local joint venture company owned 85 per cent by Mawarid Mining LLC from Oman and 15 per cent by the Namibian-registered Havana Investments. It was established in 2008 to obtain a mineral exploration licence to develop the offshore 'Sandpiper' marine phosphate project. Located some 60 km off the coast, the latter 'covers a total area of approximately 7000 km^2 in the regional phosphate-enriched province to the south of Walvis Bay in water depths of 180–300 m'.[40] The project is the first of its kind worldwide.[41] It promised capital expenditure to the tune of NAD 4 billion (since then adjusted to some NAD 5.2 billion),[42] annual revenue of NAD 3 billion, and the creation of an estimated 150 direct and 200 indirect jobs (via subcontractors, suppliers, and the like).[43]

An exploration licence was issued in 2009, and a mining licence (ML 170) followed in July 2011. But in September 2013, the government placed an eighteen-month moratorium on bulk seabed mining activities for industrial minerals, base, and rare minerals. This included the planned marine phosphate mining on the basis that no environmental clearance had yet been issued.[44] On 5 September 2016, the Environmental Commissioner in the Ministry of Environment and Tourism (MET) informed the company that the project has been cleared.[45] On 2 November 2016, however, MET Minister Pohamba Shifeta set aside the Environmental Clearance Certificate (ECC) because there were no adequate consultations by the Commissioner with the concerned public and other stakeholders. An NMP appeal to the High Court was heard on 10 August 2017 and judgment was delivered on 11 May 2018.[46] The court ruled that the procedure did not follow the required formal regulations, to the disadvantage of the appellant, and therefore declared the original decision 'to be no decision'. The Minister might, however, conduct an appeal hearing de novo. This took place on 18 June 2018.[47] Three days later, Minister Shifeta reaffirmed his decision to set aside the ECC. He announced that the consultation process should continue for another six months.

In the absence of any follow-up, the NMP in mid-July 2019 sued the minister, the environmental commissioner, and the deputy environmental commissioner of the MET to force them to grant the ECC.[48] In parallel, the case was pending in the High Court: three

[39] Eveline de Klerk, 'Marine Phosphate Mining Misconstrued' New Era (19 June 2014) <https://neweralive.na/posts/marine-phosphate-mining-misconstrued> accessed 27 July 2019.

[40] Namibian Marine Phosphate (Pty) Ltd, Sandpiper Marine Phosphate Project <http://www.namphos.com/project/sandpiper.html> accessed 28 March 2021.

[41] As critics maintain, similar plans in Australia and Mexico were put on hold by the governments due to the unknown harm operations like these could have on marine ecosystems.

[42] The Namibian dollar is pegged to the South African rand.

[43] For this and other of the company's own information, see <http://www.namphos.com> and <http://www.mawaridmining.com/namibia.html> accessed 25 July 2019.

[44] Chamre Kaira, 'Phosphate Mining Banned' The Namibian (19 September 2013)<http://www.namibian.com.na/index.php?page=archive-read&id=114235> accessed 26 July 2019.

[45] Shinovene Immanuel, 'Phosphate Mining Approved' The Namibian (19 October 2016) <http://www.namibian.com.na/157079/archive-read/Phosphate-mining-approved> accessed 26 July 2019.

[46] Namibian Marine Phosphate (Proprietary) Limited v Minister of Environment and Tourism and Others (CA 119/2016) [2018] NAHCMD 122 (11 May 2018).

[47] Sakeus Ikela, 'D-Day for Phosphate Mining' The Namibian (19 June 2018) <http://www.namibian.com.na/178589/archive-read/D-Day-for-phosphate-mining> accessed 27 July 2019.

[48] Werner Menges, 'Phosphate Company Seeks Sea Mining Go-Ahead' The Namibian (19 July 2019) <http://www.namibian.com.na/80987/read/Phosphate-company-seeks-sea-mining-go-ahead> accessed 26 July 2019.

umbrella agencies representing the Namibian fishing industry, plus an individual fishing company, were

> asking the court to declare that a mining licence issued to NMP in July 2011 has expired or lapsed because the company failed to undertake an environmental impact assessment and apply for an environmental clearance certificate within the time limits stipulated in the law.[49]

In the case's first hearing in early September 2019, the Judge concluded that he would require additional scientific background information to be submitted by mid-October. The court proceedings were announced for early 2020.[50]

Due to the unknown effects of such an enterprise, concerns remain among the fishing industry, conservationists, and local residents. Beyond the potential impacts on the marine habitat there is also a fear of the toxic effects triggered by phosphate once refined onshore. The use of a considerable amount of water in the processing could negatively affect local communities, flora, and fauna. As critics maintain, phosphate mining is a relatively short-term, non-renewable activity. If it indeed has negative impacts on fisheries and the environment, these are longer-lasting than the claimed benefits of the operation. While the focus of attention has been on the potential effects of seabed mining on the marine ecosystem, phosphate processing takes place on land when the mineral is separated from the ground brought onshore. This separation process is, according to the plans, supposed to take place seven kilometres inland, but so far has not been part of an EIA. However, the devastating effects of such processing are well known from similar operations along the coast in Tunisia.[51] Critics suspect that NMP deliberately refrained from opening such a can of worms so as to avoid fuelling even greater concerns among the local population.

Differences in opinion among policy-makers at cabinet level suggest that constitutional and legal provisions remain open to interpretation and do not resolve the tension between economic and environmental imperatives. The conflict of interest between mining and fisheries with regard to seabed mining came to the fore with the introduction of offshore diamond mining along the coast of southern Namibia, which highlighted another dilemma:

> [A]ctor's preferred definitions are often dependent on the industry that they represent(ed), or are/were otherwise involved with. For example, mining industry representatives spoke of economic potential and explained that the blue economy had been introduced to them as means of 'getting resources out of the sea'. However, representatives of the fishing industry spoke of a blue economy that prioritises sustainability and protection of Namibia's EEZ [Exclusive Economic Zone]—a prioritisation that they view as incongruous with activities such as seabed mining.[52]

[49] ibid.

[50] Clemens von Alten, 'Phosphat-Gegner gewinnen Zeit' *Allgemeine Zeitung* (11 September 2019) <http://www.az.com.na/nachrichten/phosphat-gegner-gewinnen-zeit2019-09-11> accessed 26 January 2020.

[51] See inter alia Simon Speakman Cordall, ' "Inside, the Fish are Black": The Pollution Tainting Tunisian Beaches' *The Guardian* (9 July 2019) <http://www.theguardian.com/environment/2019/jul/09/pollution-taint-tunisia-beaches> accessed 26 January 2020.

[52] Carver (n 37).

While a 'blue economy presents opportunities for new forms of capitalist accumulation', this 'has resulted in struggles over who can accumulate in the marine sphere' and thereby '[brought] to the fore political and economic realities that are shaping these contentions, particularly with regards to Namibia's fishing industry'.[53] The case of seabed mining illustrates precisely such contestation: the marine environment and seabed mining have emerged as a major 'battlefront' in Namibia's resource management. It also points to the importance of the ways in which those with the power of definition conceive of the notion of the blue economy: 'Several key actors stated that they had little interest in the concept, comparing it to the green economy and arguing that it was "another buzzword", coined externally, with little substance or reflection of Namibian agendas.'[54]

4.2 Timber and Tobacco: Up in Smoke?

As following subsections will show, conflicts of interest among local and external agencies over access to resources with business potential are also playing out in the exploitation of natural resources on the land surface—conflicts in which constitutional and legal principles are not the necessary point of reference and orientation (as well as basis of implementation) that they ought to be.

It is estimated that about 10 per cent of Namibia's vegetation is composed of woody plants greater than 1 metre in height and that less than 10 per cent of the country's land area is covered by trees higher than 5 metres. As mentioned in the introduction, precious timber in the forests along the border area in the north-east of the territory (previously called the Caprivi Strip) was an attractive prey for the colonial power and consequently looted by the South African army during the border war.[55] Deforestation has continued apace since then: at independence in 1990, Namibia had some 8.7 million hectares of forests, but by 2015 they had been depleted by one-fifth to 7 million hectares.[56]

Responsibility for the management of this resource falls to the Ministry of Agriculture, Water and Forestry (MAWF). The legal and policy frameworks are defined by the Forest Act[57] and a national Forest Policy Statement.[58] Most forests in Namibia are under the responsibility of local communities, which are involved in land use management. Community forestry also hands influence over decisions to the traditional authorities, or local chiefs. But, notably so, in terms of the Forest Act, anybody who harvests, transports, and exports or markets forest resources first has to acquire a valid permit issued by the nearest forestry office.

---

[53] Rosanna Carver, 'Resource Sovereignty and Accumulation in the Blue Economy: The Case of Seabed Mining in Namibia' (2019) 26 Journal of Political Ecology 381, 398.

[54] Carver (n 37).

[55] On the special history of this region, see Henning Melber, 'One Namibia, One Nation? The Caprivi as a Contested Territory' (2009) 4(27) Journal of Contemporary African Studies 463.

[56] Data taken from Oliver C Ruppel and Katharina Ruppel-Schlichting, 'Namibia's Constitution in the Context of Environmental Protection and Combatting Climate Change' in Nico Horn and Manfred O Hinz (eds), *Beyond a Quarter of a Century of Constitutional Democracy: Process and Progress in Namibia* (Konrad Adenauer Stiftung 2017) 131.

[57] Act 12 of 2001, as amended by the Forest Amendment Act 13 of 2005.

[58] Ministry of Agriculture, Water and Forestry, Forestry Policy Statement <http://www.mawf.gov.na/documents/37726/186033/National+Forestry+Policy/59a90e4e-b01d-45c7-a99a-acdba399420d> accessed 28 March 2021.

4.2.1 Harvesting trees

The management of forests and their culling emerged as a matter of wider public interest and concern in 2017 when large volumes of timber (mainly species of African rosewood, teak, and bloodwood trees) from the Democratic Republic of the Congo (DRC), Angola, and, in particular, Zambia began to be transported through Namibia to the port of Walvis Bay. Extraction in Namibia concerns mainly rosewood trees.[59] The chief destination of the shipments is China, where they are used in furniture manufacturing. The rapid increase in volumes captured worldwide attention and raised questions about its legality. On several occasions, customs authorities at Walvis Bay and elsewhere confiscated transport vehicles; subsequent evidence pointed to looting, due to a legal loophole, in Namibia's Caprivi State Forest near the border town of Katima Mulilo, the capital of the Zambezi region, and later in the Kavango East and Kavango West regions, with Rundu as their centre. A Chinese businessman operating through various businesses, including New Force Logistics CC, played a central role in the networks that were established.[60]

According to official figures by the Namibian Ports Authority, exports of Namibian timber through Walvis Bay harbour increased tenfold in three years. The total amount of timber exported between 2013 and early 2019, including wood from Zambia, but so too Angola and the DRC, amounted to 430,700 tonnes.[61] Answering an inquiry in the National Assembly, the Minister of the MAWF disclosed that all felling and transportation of timber until 26 November 2018 had taken place without ECCs. Due to confusion between the MAWF and MET, so he explained, logging had been allowed without consulting the Environmental Management Act, which makes an ECC compulsory before issuing a logging permit. When it became aware of the loophole, the ministry suspended logging at the date mentioned.[62] The Minister admitted that as yet there was no obligation for trees to be planted to replace the ones that had been harvested.[63]

In early 2019, a leaked government document listed '231 politicians, traditional leaders, MPs, business people, church leaders and others who, after the ban was imposed, applied for clearance from the environment ministry to cut down nearly 200,000 trees over five

---

[59] Some species take over 100 years to mature, and among the logged trees were some older than 400 years. For the value of rosewood trees and the dimensions of its Zambian–Chinese trade, see Paolo Omar Cerutti and Davison Gumbo, 'Why Zambia Has Not Benefitted from its Rosewood Trade with China' *The Conversation* (25 June 2018) <https://theconversation.com/why-zambia-has-not-benefitted-from-its-rosewood-trade-with-china-98092> accessed 28 July 2019. See also for the case of Madagascar, Annah Zhu, 'Rosewood Occidentalism and Orientalism in Madagascar' (2017) 86 Geoforum 1; Annah Zhu 'Hot Money, Cold Beer: Navigating the Vanilla and Rosewood Export Economies in Northeastern Madagascar' (2018) 2(45) American Ethnologist 253.

[60] John Grobler, 'Chinese "Mafia Boss" Turns to Timber in Namibia' *Oxpeckers* (7 February 2017) <https://oxpeckers.org/2017/02/xuecheng-hou-and-timber/> accessed 28 July 2019; John Grobler, 'Felling Namibia's Ancient Giants' *Organized Crime and Corruption Reporting Project* (13 October 2017) <http://www.occrp.org/en/28-ccwatch/cc-watch-indepth/7125-felling-namibia-s-ancient-giants> accessed 28 July 2019. See also Shinovene Immanuel, 'Chief Trades Timber for Offices' *The Namibian* (3 August 2018) <http://www.namibian.com.na/180130/archive-read/Chief-trades-timber-for-offices> accessed 28 July 2019; Catherine Sasman, 'Spotlight on Hou' *Namibian Sun* (15 March 2019) <http://www.namibiansun.com/news/spotlight-on-hou2019-03-15> accessed 17 March 2019).

[61] Shinovene Immanuel, 'Timber Exports to China Escalate' *The Namibian* (6 March 2019) <http://www.namibian.com.na/186354/archive-read/Timber-exports-to-China-escalate> accessed 28 July 2019.

[62] Nghinomenwa Erastus, 'Govt Accepts Blunder on Timber Harvest' *The Namibian* (25 June 2019) <http://www.namibian.com.na/189992/archive-read/Govt-accepts-blunder-on-timber-harvest> accessed 28 July 2019.

[63] Edgar Brandt, 'N$ 94m Worth of Timber Exported in First Two Months of 2019' *New Era* (17 June 2019) <https://bit.ly/3cgm2db> accessed 24 June 2019.

years'.[64] The politically influential lobby group sought to reverse the decision, thereby triggering an internal conflict in cabinet between the environment and agriculture ministers over the granting of applications. The inter-ministerial dispute, as well as the lack of proper control on the ground to ensure that the moratorium was adhered to, resulted in further illegal logging. It was reported that New Force Logistics CC proceeded unabated by using concessions issued before the moratorium was announced; to speed up the process, trucks were allegedly overloaded and the freight limit of 20 tonnes was doubled.[65] Local farmers complained that the overloaded trucks, operating day and night, destroyed privately constructed and maintained rural roads and thereby affected their livelihoods.[66]

Despite such evidence to the contrary, Minister Pohamba Shifeta of the MET stressed in the National Assembly in mid-March 2019 that no commercial harvesting of timber had taken place since the moratorium was introduced. He also reported, though, that an estimated 390 permits without ECC had been issued locally in Kavango East, with some 68,000 trees exported. This included randomly cut, non-marked trees, since controls were difficult due to the high volumes of trucks and timber.[67] As he stated further:

> The scientific projection is that if timber harvests had to be permitted at such high scale and rate as it happened until last year when it was suspended, it will take less than 20 years to bid farewell to the only forest zones we have.[68]

In an interview, the minister then pointed to another neglected legal prerequisite contained in the Forest Act of 2001, one in terms of which 'a person may not export any unprocessed forest produce, including semi-processed planks, unless authorised by the director for special purposes such as research, education, cultural and disease identification, for which relevant documents are to be provided as a prerequisite'.[69] Namibian wood has, however—as numerous media reports attest—been exported almost exclusively as semi-processed timber.

In marked contrast to the environmental minister, Alpheus !Naruseb, the Minister of the MAWF, remained silent. The chief executive of the Namibian Chamber of Environment, a previously long-serving, high-ranking public servant and internationally renowned environmental expert and ecologist nicknamed 'Dr Green', criticized this as double standards: 'It is cynical to expect the global community to support our climate change adaptation and mitigation plans if we do not have the political will to do something as simple as protecting our woodlands.' Because of the 'inherently unsustainable' nature of a timber industry in

---

[64] Shinovene Immanuel, Okeri Ngutjinazo, and Nghinomenwa Erastus, 'Rare Namibian Hardwood Trees Face the Chop' *Daily Maverick* (12 March 2019) <http://www.dailymaverick.co.za/article/2019-03-12-rare-namibian-hardwood-trees-face-the-chop/> accessed 28 July 2019.

[65] Catherine Sasman and Frank Steffen, 'Raubbau in Wäldern dauert an' *Allgemeine Zeitung* (13 March 2019) <http://www.az.com.na/nachrichten/raubbau-in-wldern-dauert-an2019-03-13/> accessed 28 July 2019.

[66] Kenya Kambowe, 'Timber Trucks Destroy Rural Roads' *Namibian Sun* (27 March 2019) <http://www.namibiansun.com/news/timber-trucks-destroy-rural-roads2019-03-27> accessed 27 March 2019.

[67] Catherine Sasman, '"There's No Timber Harvesting"' *Namibian Sun* (18 March 2019) <http://www.namibiansun.com/news/theres-no-timber-harvesting2019-03-18> accessed 18 March 2019.

[68] Shinovene Immanuel, 'Namibia's Forests Could Disappear in 20 Years' *The Namibian* (18 March 2019) <http://www.namibian.com.na/186697/archive-read/Namibias-forests-could-disappear-in-20-years> accessed 18 March 2019.

[69] Shinovene Immanuel, 'Raw Timber Exports Illegal' *The Namibian* (10 April 2019) <http://www.namibian.com.na/187453/archive-read/Raw-timber-exports-illegal> accessed 10 April 2019.

Namibia, he maintained, this situation equates to 'practically giving away precious timber in return for the long-term destruction of woodlands that provide essential ecosystem and climate mitigation services'.[70] Since then, the agriculture and environment ministries agreed to lift the ban on the transportation of already harvested timber,[71] but introduced regulations to eliminate the export of unprocessed wood.[72] Following discussion in the cabinet, it was announced in January 2020 that 'no new or fresh timber may be harvested'.[73]

The new state has—as in the case of phosphate mining—gradually introduced appropriate legislative references that would allow regulation of a precarious environment to preserve it for future generations in recognition of a social contract which is also an intergenerational obligation; however, colliding interests, along with an at times inefficient local administration which is either not always conversant with the regulatory framework or simply unwilling to comply with it, are factors that weaken this framework.

4.2.2 Tobacco or food?

The current timber exploitation at times uses the clearing of land for agricultural purposes as a pretext and smokescreen. This has been the agenda in the case of a proposal by the locally registered company Namibia Oriental Tobacco CC. A subsidiary of the Chinese state-owned Hongyunhonghe Tobacco Group of Companies (the fifth-largest tobacco company in the world), it applied for 10,000 hectares of land on the outskirts of Katima Mulilo for the primary purpose of establishing a tobacco plantation. The plan promised investment of NAD 14 billion, the operations of which were to include steps by New Force Logistic CC to clear 1,000 trees from the area. This was endorsed by the local Mafwe traditional authority, which in return was promised the building of new office headquarters;[74] moreover, the tobacco plantation was advocated by the SWAPO regional coordinator of the Oshikoto region. It received an ECC by the MET, dated 19 December 2014 and valid for three years.[75]

However, the decision was criticized by, among others, the then outgoing Minister of Health (whose successor criticized the project just as vehemently), local conservationists, and grassroots activists, all of whom argued in essence that the fertile land in question should be used for food production and not to produce drugs. A Zambezi Integrated Regional Land Use Plan (IRLUP), drafted in close collaboration with the local communities, declared:

> The state forest is reserved for protection of natural resources and the clearing of 10,000 hectares of land will be against this principle. The state forest is also an important wildlife

[70] Shinovene Immanuel, '!Naruseb's Efforts on Timber Questioned' *The Namibian* (14 April 2019) <http://www.namibian.com.na/187554/archive-read/Narusebs-efforts-on-timber-questioned> accessed 14 April 2019. See also the quoted expert's own article: Chris Brown, 'Harvesting Timber in Namibia is Unsustainable' *Observer Connect* (Windhoek, May/June 2019) 50–51.

[71] Ellanie Smit, 'Timber Transport Ban Lifted' *Namibian Sun* (23 September 2019) <http://www.namibiansun.com/news/timber-transport-ban-lifted2019-09-23> accessed 26 January 2020.

[72] Charmaine Ngatjiheue, 'Govt Puts Stringent Measures on Timber Exports' *The Namibian* (11 December 2019) <http://www.namibian.com.na/196253/archive-read/Govt-puts-stringent-measures-on--timber-exports> accessed 26 January 2020.

[73] Ellanie Smit, 'No New Timber may be Harvested' *Namibian Sun* (15 January 2020) <http://www.namibiansun.com/news/no-new-timber-may-be-harvested2020-01-15> accessed 26 January 2020.

[74] Immanuel (n 60).

[75] Tuyeimo Haidula, 'Environment Clears Tobacco Project' *The Namibian* (13 April 2015) <http://www.namibian.com.na/135778/archive-read/Environment-clears-tobacco-project#> accessed 29 July 2019.

corridor and any such large project will have an impact on the wildlife movement. The project needs to find an alternative area within the irrigation area proposed by the IRLUP. The size of the project is quite extensive and it is proposed that for a first phase the project be allocated 3,000 hectares of land until they have proved their capability to make this project work.[76]

Due to its controversial nature, the project was put on hold by the new government that took office on 21 March 2015. Approval by cabinet was announced officially only on 13 June 2019, following the recommendation of a technical committee. The announcement drew widespread criticism from organizations and individuals in Namibian civil society.[77] The Health Minister described the decision as a collective one by cabinet and refused to give further comment.[78] His predecessor, however, did not mince his words. Commenting on the decision in a public panel debate, he remarked:

> Some people say if it makes money, it is good. What would you decide if you had power? Are we responsible if we allow our land to produce poison to kill other people? ... Some say a tobacco plantation will bring employment or development, but the value chain is not at growing the tobacco, but at processing it and its distribution. And where tobacco grows, it leaves destruction, including child labour and environmental issues; fumes and chemicals. We cannot look at the N$ 14 billion and fool ourselves. This planet is all we have, and we must protect this environment.[79]

Such public criticism gives voice to sentiments that are common in civil society, but—as in the case of the looting of scarce forests—it should not be assumed that simply because there is voluble public discourse it has much influence on political decision-making; indeed, the government's decisions seem to have far more to do with the exigencies of the day. In this instance, crony connections appear to outweigh any other factors, including considerations of short-term economic gain that otherwise might take priority over environmental concerns. As was revealed, in its initial stages Namibia Oriental Tobacco CC employed only seven Namibians, while it was awarded as one of nineteen special companies the status of an Export Processing Zone (EPZ) in recognition of creating meaningful employment opportunities. Namibia's EPZ regime was introduced in 1995 as an incentive to attract foreign investment. The EPZ status includes exemption from paying a variety of taxes.[80] Since then, the policy has been criticized for offering benefits in return for nothing but extra profits for foreign investors.[81]

---

[76] Ministry of Lands and Resettlement, *Integrated Regional Land Use Plan for the Zambezi Region (Volume 2)* (2015) <https://bit.ly/3ccg3WD> accessed 28 July 2019.

[77] Ndanki Kahiurika, 'Tobacco Plant Approval Draws Criticism' *The Namibian* (19 June 2019) <http://www.namibian.com.na/189733/archive-read/Tobacco-plant-approval-draws-criticism> accessed 19 June 2019.

[78] Kenya Kambowe, 'Tobacco Critics "Misinformed"' *Namibian Sun* (18 June 2019) <http://www.namibiansun.com/news/tobacco-critics-misinformed2019-06-17> accessed 24 June 2019.

[79] Ndanki Kahiurika, 'Haufiku Condemns Tobacco Plantation Approval' *The Namibian* (9 July 2019) <http://www.namibian.com.na/80563/read/Haufiku-condemns-tobacco-plantation-approval> accessed 9 July 2019.

[80] Shinovene Immanuel, 'Tobacco Project Will Not Pay Tax' *The Namibian* (25 September 2019) <http://www.namibian.com.na/193457/archive-read/Tobacco-project-will-not-pay-tax> accessed 26 January 2020.

[81] Herbert Jauch, 'Export Processing Zones and the Quest for Sustainable Development: A Southern African Perspective' (2002) 1(14) Environment & Urbanization 101; Volker Winterfeldt, 'Liberated Economy? The Case of Ramatex Textiles Namibia' in Henning Melber (ed), *Transitions in Namibia: Which Changes for Whom?* (Nordic Africa Institute 2007).

5. Conclusion

Two decades after independence, an assessment of environmental rights declared that 'Namibia is at the dawn of environmental advocacy, which refers to the act of speaking out in favour of, supporting, and defending the environment with the aim of having an impact on a decision or policy'.[82] As this chapter has suggested, though, a legal culture that protects and promotes environmental rights as human rights, and that defines and gives effect to the substance of these rights, still has to be consolidated in Namibia.

The cases presented in this chapter document steps towards a more aware and active advocacy of such rights and the application of legal provisions. They show that 'a legal culture upholding environmental rights is in the process of being created' and that 'the existing legal framework provides for a variety of mechanisms to ensure compliance with and enforcement of environmental laws'.[83] But implementation remains a challenge. Significantly, NDP5 identified 'weak institutional capacity and governance mechanisms' as obstacles to the country's environmental management and response to climate change: 'This is evident in the implementation and enforcement of existing legislation, particularly the Environmental Management Act, which requires close inter-sectoral collaboration. It further leads to lack of resources for environmental management.'[84]

Administrative capacity and the know-how to apply the legal framework efficiently and effectively are at times insufficient. What is also lacking is the visible, declared political will among policy-makers to ensure that the extant legal and constitutional provisions are applied. The normative relevance of these provisions to policy-making is limited and their translation into substantive governance practices is a mission unaccomplished.[85] The potential tension between the economy and the ecology is scarcely acknowledged in any political strategy or programmatic orientation, be it by SWAPO, as the dominant party, or by any of the country's other political parties. Explicit links between economic challenges and the ecology are also largely absent in statements made by leading office-holders in national politics.

With regard to the contestations over seabed mining, it had been suggested that 'Namibia's top leadership should be busy forging a national vision for the future ... striving for broad social and political consensus'.[86] But such an initiative is nowhere in sight. While the notion of a blue economy entered the official vocabulary via the NDP5 in 2017, it has been subject to conflicting interpretations, '[with] its uneven and ambiguous definitions resulting in the agenda being understood in multiple ways'.[87]

The Environmental Management Act provides for the precautionary principle, which is the injunction to avoid serious or irreversible harm in cases where there is uncertainty about the potential impact of interventions on the natural habitat. The Act, however, is weak inasmuch as it 'obligates decision-makers to only consider precautionary measures (as

---

[82] Oliver C Ruppel, 'Environmental Rights and Justice under the Namibian Constitution' in A Bösl, N Horn, and A Du Pisani (eds), *Constitutional Democracy in Namibia: A Critical Analysis after Two Decades* (Macmillan Education Namibia 2010) 353.
[83] Ruppel and Ruppel-Schlichting (n 56) 133.
[84] Namibia's 5th National Development Plan (n 8) 85.
[85] See the instructive analysis by Carver (n 53).
[86] Nicholas N Kimani, 'Seabed Mining in Namibia: Quo Vadis?' (2015) 17 Journal of Namibian Studies 7, 23.
[87] Carver (n 37).

opposed to precautionary action)'.[88] The relevant decision-makers nevertheless have sufficient authority vested in their offices for preventative measures of theirs to be justifiable. In one of the rare cases so far in this regard, the company Black Range Mining (Pty) Ltd appealed a High Court decision of 2010 which had dismissed the company's appeal against a ministerial notice that nuclear energy prospecting licences in certain areas would not be granted. The Supreme Court upheld the High Court decision, and the appellant's case was dismissed with costs.

According to the Supreme Court, the appellant would have been successful if the minister had no statutory powers to issue the notice, or if the process were unprocedural. However, the minister indeed had such powers under section 122(1) of the Mineral (Prospecting and Mining) Act of 1992. Consequently, the court held that it could not order the minister to issue the licence if the notice was still in existence. The court also held that the constitutional provision on the right to work does not mean that people can conduct mining activities without being regulated, given the environmental challenges.[89]

As the case underlines, there is room for legally endorsed interventions. Although these are applied occasionally, the need remains for establishing a wider Namibian ethic against which governance could and should be measured. As an opinion article concluded, 'There are moral counterpoints to the nihilistic extractive ideology that currently permeates our society. It takes human agency to achieve this. The debate is too important to be left to self-serving politicians alone.'[90]

In times when economic recession puts pressure on policy-makers and creates the temptation to adopt quick-fix solutions, the danger is that long-term perspectives opposed to a 'nihilistic extractive ideology' will be neglected in favour of perceived short-term gains. When ethics come at a cost, their attractiveness dwindles; likewise, in a society where members of the local and national elite consider resource extraction as an opportunity to garner material benefits for themselves, ethics are (con)tested even further. As I have argued elsewhere,[91] a constitution and the laws adopted subsequent to it are living documents only so long as they are not shelved. An independent judiciary is essential for upholding the rule of law, but government and civil society play a decisive role too: courts can only but react to interventions seeking judgments, rather than take the initiative by themselves. By implication, even the best constitutional and legal provisions remain irrelevant so long as they are not serving as reference points to be interpreted and applied.

---

[88] Stanley L Kambonde, 'Marine Phosphate: Prevention is Better than Cure' *The Namibian* (23 August 2019) <http://www.namibian.com.na/192272/archive-read/Marine-Phosphate-Prevention-is-Better-than-Cure> accessed 26 January 2020.

[89] *Black Range Mining (Pty) Ltd v Minister of Mines and Energy NO and Others* (SA 09/2011) [2014] NASC 4 (26 March 2014).

[90] André du Pisani, 'How Might We Live: Ethics in Namibia?' *The Namibian* (23 July 2019) <http://www.namibian.com.na/81112/read/How-Might-we-Live-Ethics-in-Namibia> accessed 23 July 2019.

[91] See Henning Melber, 'The Impact of the Constitution on State- and Nation-Building' in A Bösl, N Horn, and A Du Pisani (eds), *Constitutional Democracy in Namibia: A Critical Analysis after Two Decades* (Macmillan Education Namibia 2010); 'Constitutionalism in Democratic South Africa: Celebrations, Contestations and Challenges' (2014) 2(36) Strategic Review for Southern Africa 203; 'Why We Need a Constitution—and Those Bringing Constitutional Democracy to Life' in N Horn and MO Hinz (eds), *Beyond a Quarter Century of Constitutional Democracy: Process and Progress in Namibia* (Konrad Adenauer Stiftung 2017).

Bibliography

'Namibia Credit Rating' *World Government Bonds* (nd) <http://www.worldgovernmentbonds.com/credit-rating/namibia/> accessed 24 July 2020)

Al Jazeera Investigations, Anatomy of a Bribe, 1 December 2019 <https://www.youtube.com/watch?v=_FJ1TB0nwHs> accessed 28 March 2021.

Brandt E, 'N$ 94m Worth of Timber Exported in First Two Months of 2019' *New Era* (17 June 2019) <https://bit.ly/3cgm2db> accessed 24 June 2019

Brown C, 'Harvesting Timber in Namibia is Unsustainable' *Observer Connect* (Windhoek, May/June 2019) 50–51

Brown R and Emvula C, 'The National Budget 2018-19: Walking the Fiscal Tightrope' (IPPR Democracy Report, Special Briefing Report No 23, April 2018) <https://ippr.org.na/wp-content/uploads/2018/04/23_Budget_WEB.pdf>accessed 24 July 2020)

Carver R, 'Chinese "Mafia Boss" Turns to Timber in Namibia' *Oxpeckers* (7 February 2017) <https://oxpeckers.org/2017/02/xuecheng-hou-and-timber/> accessed 28 July 2019

Carver R, 'Felling Namibia's Ancient Giants' *Organized Crime and Corruption Reporting Project* (13 October 2017) <http://www.occrp.org/en/28-ccwatch/cc-watch-indepth/7125-felling-namibia-s-ancient-giants> accessed 28 July 2019

Carver R, 'Resource Sovereignty and Accumulation in the Blue Economy: The Case of Seabed Mining in Namibia' (2019) 26 Journal of Political Ecology 381

Carver R, 'Lessons for Blue Degrowth from Namibia's Emerging Blue Economy' (2020) 15 Sustainability Science 131

Cerutti PO and Gumbo D, 'Why Zambia Has Not Benefitted from its Rosewood Trade with China' *The Conversation* (25 June 2018) <https://theconversation.com/why-zambia-has-not-benefitted-from-its-rosewood-trade-with-china-98092> accessed 28 July 2019

Cordall SS, '"Inside, the Fish are Black": The Pollution Tainting Tunisian Beaches' *The Guardian* (9 July 2019) <http://www.theguardian.com/environment/2019/jul/09/pollution-taint-tunisia-beaches> accessed 26 January 2020

De Boom MJ, 'Nuclear (Geo)Political Ecologies: A Hybrid Geography of Chinese Investment in Namibia's Uranium Sector' (2017) 3(46) Journal of Current Chinese Affairs 53

De Klerk E, 'Marine Phosphate Mining Misconstrued' *New Era* (19 June 2014) <https://neweralive.na/posts/marine-phosphate-mining-misconstrued> accessed 27 July 2019

Du Pisani A, 'How Might We Live: Ethics in Namibia?' *The Namibian* (23 July 2019) <http://www.namibian.com.na/81112/read/How-Might-we-Live-Ethics-in-Namibia> accessed 23 July 2019

Erastus N, 'Govt Accepts Blunder on Timber Harvest' *The Namibian*, 25 June 2019 <http://www.namibian.com.na/189992/archive-read/Govt-accepts-blunder-on-timber-harvest> accessed 28 July 2019

FAO, The Republic of Namibia 2007 <http://www.fao.org/fi/oldsite/fcp/en/nam/profile.htm> accessed 28 March 2021

The Growth Lab at Harvard University, 'The Challenge of Sustained and Inclusive Prosperity in Namibia' (PowerPoint presentation, 9 November, 2019) <http://www.slideshare.net/miguelangelsantos/namibia-the-challenge-of-sustained-and-inclusive-growth> accessed 25 July 2020

Haidula T, 'Environment Clears Tobacco Project' *The Namibian* (13 April 2015) <http://www.namibian.com.na/135778/archive-read/Environment-clears-tobacco-project#> accessed 29 July 2019

Hubbard D, 'Guide to the Environmental Management Act No 7 of 2007' (Ministry of Environment and Tourism 2008)

Immanuel S, 'Chief Trades Timber for Offices' *The Namibian* (3 August 2018) <http://www.namibian.com.na/180130/archive-read/Chief-trades-timber-for-offices> accessed 28 July 2019

Immanuel S 'Timber Exports to China Escalate' *The Namibian* (6 March 2019) <http://www.namibian.com.na/186354/archive-read/Timber-exports-to-China-escalate> accessed 28 July 2019

Immanuel S 'Namibia's Forests Could Disappear in 20 Years' *The Namibian* (18 March 2019) <http://www.namibian.com.na/186697/archive-read/Namibias-forests-could-disappear-in-20-years> accessed 18 March 2019

Immanuel S 'Raw Timber Exports Illegal' *The Namibian* (10 April 2019) <http://www.namibian.com.na/187453/archive-read/Raw-timber-exports-illegal> accessed 10 April 2019

Immanuel S '!Naruseb's Efforts on Timber Questioned' *The Namibian* (14 April 2019) <http://www.namibian.com.na/187554/archive-read/Narusebs-efforts-on-timber-questioned> accessed 14 April 2019

Immanuel S 'Tobacco Project Will Not Pay Tax' *The Namibian* (25 September 2019) <http://www.namibian.com.na/193457/archive-read/Tobacco-project-will-not-pay-tax> accessed 26 January 2020

Immanuel S and Iikela S, 'Kickback Kings Fall' *The Namibian* (15 November 2019) <http://www.namibian.com.na/85501/read/Kickback-Kings-fall> accessed 15 November 2019

Immanuel S, Ngutjinazo O, and Erastus N, 'Rare Namibian Hardwood Trees Face the Chop' *Daily Maverick* (12 March 2019) <http://www.dailymaverick.co.za/article/2019-03-12-rare-namibian-hardwood-trees-face-the-chop/> accessed 28 July 2019

Institute for Public Policy Research, *Namibia Quarterly Economic Review* (October–December 2019 <https://ippr.org.na/publication/namibia-qer-quarter-4-2019/> accessed 22 January 2020

Jauch H, 'Export Processing Zones and the Quest for Sustainable Development: A Southern African Perspective' (2002) 1(14) Environment & Urbanization 101

Jauch H, *Poverty, Unemployment and Inequality in Namibia* (International Union for the Conservation of Nature and Commission on Environmental, Economic and Social Policies 2012)

Jauch H, Edwards L, and Cupido B, *A Rich Country with Poor People* (Labour Resource and Research Institute 2009)

Kahiurika N, 'Tobacco Plant Approval Draws Criticism' *The Namibian* (19 June 2019) <http://www.namibian.com.na/189733/archive-read/Tobacco-plant-approval-draws-criticism> accessed 19 June 2019

Kahiurika N, 'Haufiku Condemns Tobacco Plantation Approval' *The Namibian* (9 July 2019) <http://www.namibian.com.na/80563/read/Haufiku-condemns-tobacco-plantation-approval> accessed 9 July 2019

Kambonde SL, 'Marine Phosphate: Prevention is Better than Cure' *The Namibian* (23 August 2019) <http://www.namibian.com.na/192272/archive-read/Marine-Phosphate-Prevention-is-Better-than-Cure> accessed 26 January 2020

Kambowe K, 'Timber Trucks Destroy Rural Roads' *Namibian Sun* (27 March 2019) <http://www.namibiansun.com/news/timber-trucks-destroy-rural-roads2019-03-27> accessed 27 March 2019

Kambowe K, 'Tobacco Critics "Misinformed"' *Namibian Sun* (18 June 2019) <http://www.namibiansun.com/news/tobacco-critics-misinformed2019-06-17> accessed 24 June 2019

Kaira C, 'Phosphate Mining Banned' *The Namibian* (19 September 2013) <http://www.namibian.com.na/index.php?page=archive-read&id=114235> accessed 26 July 2019

Kimani NN, 'Seabed Mining in Namibia: Quo Vadis?' (2015) 17 Journal of Namibian Studies 7

Kleinfeld J, 'Two Namibian Ministers Resign Following Al Jazeera Investigation' *Al Jazeera* (14 November 2019) <http://www.aljazeera.com/news/2019/11/namibian-ministers-resign-al-jazeera-investigation-191113161947877.html> accessed 18 November 2019

Kleinfeld J, 'Former Namibian Ministers Arrested in Fisheries Corruption Scandal' *Daily Maverick* (2 December 2019) <http://www.dailymaverick.co.za/article/2019-12-02-former-namibian-ministers-arrested-in-fisheries-corruption-scandal> accessed 12 January 2020

LL Namibia Phosphates (Pty) Ltd, Marine Phosphate Project Namibia. Windhoek Mining Expo—April 2016 <https://www.miningexponamibia.com/assets/docs/2015/4_Marine_Phosphate.pdf> accessed 28 March 2021

Melber H, 'Of Big Fish & Small Fry: The Fishing Industry in Namibia' (2003) 95(30) Review of African Political Economy 142

Melber H (ed), *Transitions in Namibia: Which Changes for Whom?* (Nordic Africa Institute 2007)

Melber H, 'One Namibia, One Nation? The Caprivi as a Contested Territory' (2009) 4(27) Journal of Contemporary African Studies 463

Melber H, 'The Impact of the Constitution on State—and Nation-Building' in Bösl A, Horn N, and Du Pisani A (eds), *Constitutional Democracy in Namibia: A Critical Analysis after Two Decades* (Macmillan Education Namibia 2010)

Melber H, 'Constitutionalism in Democratic South Africa: Celebrations, Contestations and Challenges' (2014) 2(36) Strategic Review for Southern Africa 203

Melber H, *Understanding Namibia: The Trials of Independence* (Hurst and Jacana 2014, OUP 2015)

Melber H, 'Why We Need a Constitution—and Those Bringing Constitutional Democracy to Life' in Horn N and Hinz MO (eds), *Beyond a Quarter Century of Constitutional Democracy: Process and Progress in Namibia* (Konrad Adenauer Stiftung 2017) 17–25

Melber H, 'Looking East/Going South: The Namibian-Chinese "All Weather Friendship" ' (2018) 35(18) Stichproben: Vienna Journal of African Studies 25

Melber H, 'Colonialism, Land, Ethnicity, and Class: Namibia after the Second National Land Conference' (2019) 1(54) Africa Spectrum 73

Melber H, 'Namibia's Parliamentary and Presidential Elections: The Honeymoon is over', (2020) 1(109) The Round Table 13

Minister of Finance, 'Financial Year 2016/17 Mid-Year Budget Review Policy Statement'. Presented by Calle Schlettwein, MP, Minister of Finance (27 October 2016) <http://www.parliament.na/phocad ownload/media/2016/mtr.pdf> accessed 24 July 2020

Ministry of Agriculture, Water and Forestry, Forestry Policy Statement (n.d.) <http://www.mawf.gov. na/documents/37726/186033/National+Forestry+Policy/59a90e4e-b01d-45c7-a99a-acdba3994 20d> accessed 28 March 2021

Ministry of Lands and Resettlement, *Integrated Regional Land Use Plan for the Zambezi Region (Volume 2)* (2015) <https://bit.ly/3ccg3WD> accessed 28 July 2019

Moorsom R, *Exploiting the Sea* (Catholic Institute for International Relations 1984)

Namibian Marine Phosphate (Pty) Ltd, Sandpiper Marine Phosphate Project (n.d.) <http://www. namphos.com/project/sandpiper.html> accessed 28 March 2021

Ngatjiheue C, 'Govt Puts Stringent Measures on Timber Exports' *The Namibian* (11 December 2019) <http://www.namibian.com.na/196253/archive-read/Govt-puts-stringent-measures-on--timber-exports> accessed 26 January 2020

Odendaal W and Hebinck P, 'Mining on Communal Land as a New Frontier: A Case Study of the Kunene Region, Namibia' (2019) 2–3(15) Journal of Land Use Science 457

Republic of Namibia, *Namibian Government's Action Plan towards Prosperity for All* (Office of the President 2016)

Republic of Namibia, *Namibia Vision 2030: Prosperity, Harmony, Peace and Political Stability. Policy Framework for Long-term National Development* (Office of the President 2004)

Republic of Namibia, *Namibia's 5th National Development Plan (NDP5): Working Together towards Prosperity 2017/18–2021/22* (National Planning Commission 2016)

Ruppel OC, 'Environmental Rights and Justice under the Namibian Constitution' in Bösl A, Horn N, and Du Pisani A (eds), *Constitutional Democracy in Namibia: A Critical Analysis after Two Decades* (Macmillan Education Namibia 2010) 323–60

Ruppel OC, 'Environmental Justice, Compliance and Enforcement' in Ruppel OC and Ruppel-Schlichting K (eds), *Environmental Law and Policy in Namibia: Towards Making Africa the Tree of Life* (3rd fully revised edn, Hanns Seidel Foundation 2016) 471–76

Ruppel OC, 'Human Rights and the Environment' in Ruppel OC and Ruppel-Schlichting K (eds), *Environmental Law and Policy in Namibia: Towards Making Africa the Tree of Life* (3rd fully revised edn, Hanns Seidel Foundation 2016) 401–20

Ruppel OC and Ruppel-Schlichting K, 'Namibia's Constitution in the Context of Environmental Protection and Combatting Climate Change' in Horn N and Hinz MO (eds), *Beyond a Quarter Century of Constitutional Democracy: Process and Progress in Namibia* (Konrad Adenauer Stiftung 2017) 103–33

Ruppel-Schlichting K, 'General Principles of Environmental Management in Namibia' in Ruppel OC and Ruppel-Schlichting K (eds), *Environmental Law and Policy in Namibia: Towards Making Africa the Tree of Life* (3rd fully revised edn, Hanns Seidel Foundation 2016) 191–208

Sasman C and Steffen F, 'Raubbau in Wäldern dauert an' *Allgemeine Zeitung* (13 March 2019) <http://www.az.com.na/nachrichten/raubbau-in-wldern-dauert-an2019-03-13/> accessed 28 July 2019

Sasman C, 'Spotlight on Hou' *Namibian Sun* (15 March 2019) <http://www.namibiansun.com/news/spotlight-on-hou2019-03-15> accessed 17 March 2019

Sasman C, ' "There's No Timber Harvesting" ' *Namibian Sun* (18 March 2019) <http://www.namibian sun.com/news/theres-no-timber-harvesting2019-03-18> accessed 18 March 2019

SBEC, *Report on the Global Sustainable Blue Economy Conference*, 26th–28th November 2018, Nairobi, Kenya <http://www.blueeconomyconference.go.ke/wp-content/uploads/2018/12/SBEC-FINAL-REPORT-8-DECEMBER-2018-rev-2-1-2-PDF2-3-compressed.pdf> accessed 28 March 2021

Shapwanale H and Immanuel S, 'Namibian Fishing Industry Cries Foul as Quota Handed to International Interests' *Daily Maverick* (14 May 2018) <http://www.dailymaverick.co.za/article/2018-05-14-amabhungane-namibian-fishing-industry-cries-foul-as-quota-handed-to-internatio nal-interests/> accessed 26 July 2020

Smit E, 'Timber Transport Ban Lifted' *Namibian Sun* (23 September 2019) <http://www.namibian sun.com/news/timber-transport-ban-lifted2019-09-23> accessed 26 January 2020

Smit E, 'No New Timber may be Harvested' *Namibian Sun* (15 January 2020) <http://www.namibian sun.com/news/no-new-timber-may-be-harvested2020-01-15> accessed 26 January 2020

Survey Warehouse, 'Summary of Results: Afrobarometer Round 8 Survey in Namibia, 2019' (Survey Warehouse 2019)

UNDP, 'Briefing Note on Namibia for 2019 Human Development Report' <http://hdr.undp.org/sites/all/themes/hdr_theme/country-notes/NAM.pdf> accessed 22 January 2020

Von Alten C, 'Phosphat-Gegner gewinnen Zeit' *Allgemeine Zeitung* (11 September 2019) <http://www.az.com.na/nachrichten/phosphat-gegner-gewinnen-zeit2019-09-11> accessed 26 January 2020

Winterfeldt V, 'Liberated Economy? The Case of Ramatex Textiles Namibia' in Melber H (ed), *Transitions in Namibia: Which Changes for Whom?* (Nordic Africa Institute 2007) 65–93

Zhu A, 'Rosewood Occidentalism and Orientalism in Madagascar' (2017) 86 Geoforum 1

Zhu A, 'Hot Money, Cold Beer: Navigating the Vanilla and Rosewood Export Economies in Northeastern Madagascar' (2018) 2(45) American Ethnologist 253

PART IV

THE CONSTITUTIONAL FRAMEWORK FOR THE STATE'S ROLE IN THE ECONOMY

11

The New Economic Empire of the Egyptian Military

A Lesson in Blurred Lines and Constitutional Transgression

Sherif Elgebeily

1. Introduction

Egypt is the third largest economy in Africa, with a nation of more than 100 million inhabitants and a gross domestic product (GDP) of USD 298.15 billion.[1] Though officially a non-aligned state during the Cold War, under the leadership of its first president, Gamal Abdel Nasser, it functioned as a socialist state with a commensurate command economy. Later, under President Sadat, capitalism was welcomed through an 'open door' policy, and a shift began to take place towards a free-market economy. Under President Mubarak, alongside its heavy emphasis on foreign investment, tourism, and international trade, the government proclaimed—at least publicly—a belief in Adam Smith's 'invisible hand' theory in which supply and demand organically create economic equilibrium; in reality, economic mismanagement, rampant inequality, and pervasive corruption widened the chasm between rich and poor, paving the way for grassroots organizations like the Muslim Brotherhood to fill the political gap.

Egypt is one of only a handful of developing countries to have transitioned from a capitalist to planned economy before returning to a more capitalistic economy. This chapter begins by briefly exploring the development of the Egyptian economy in five stages: the Nasser era (1956–70); Sadat era (1970–81); Mubarak era (1981–2011); Egyptian Revolution (2011–15); and Sisi era (2014–present). Today, the 2014 Constitution does not explicitly outline which type of economy Egypt has; rather, it enumerates certain responsibilities that the state has to public and private enterprise and the protections it must ensure for them. Egypt's Constitution protects three kinds of ownership: public, private, and cooperative.[2]

The chapter argues that the creation of a new economic empire under the control of the military, coupled with the political controls that President Sisi has assumed as head of state, places at his discretion control over both the economic and political levers of Egypt. Ultimately, this chapter shows how the principles of constitutionalism in Egypt in regard to economic protections have been undermined by a private military sector that blurs the line between public provision and private gain.

---

[1] IMF Datamapper <https://bit.ly/2MaVzQP> accessed 30 November 2020.
[2] Egyptian Constitution of 2014, art 33.

Sherif Elgebeily, *The New Economic Empire of the Egyptian Military* In: *Constitutionalism and the Economy in Africa*. Edited by: Charles M Fombad and Nico Steytler, Oxford University Press. © Sherif Elgebeily 2022. DOI: 10.1093/oso/9780192886439.003.0013

2. The Five Stages of the Egyptian Economy

2.1 The Nasser Era (1956–1970)

Prior to the revolution of 1952, Egypt was ruled by the westernized monarch King Farouk. After an interim government between 1952 and 1954, and against the backdrop of growing East–West tensions during the Cold War, socialist thought took root in Egypt thanks to the revolutionary leader Gamal Abdel Nasser. Driven by notions of Arab nationalism, self-sufficiency, and re-boosting national industry, Nasser began to establish the Egyptian military as an economic entity. Alongside this, he nationalized numerous businesses and started a process of industrialization under the aegis of the military, with such initiatives including the Suez Canal and Aswan Dam. This policy was enshrined in the 1964 Constitution, which stipulated that 'the people control all the means of production'.[3]

Not long after his ascent to formal power in 1956, Nasser began granting the armed forces special exemptions from civilian oversight and payments to the state, arrangements that have stayed in place since then. Nasser's permissions for the Ministry of Defence to assume responsibility from the Ministry of Finance and Economy for auditing military stores[4] and to purchase and import armaments, both without tax and outside typical financial regulations, are examples of laws that have lasted to this day.[5]

2.2 The Sadat Era (1970–1981)

After the death of Nasser, another military officer filled the role of president—Anwar Sadat. In contrast to the statism and command-economy focus of the Nasser era,[6] Sadat introduced a policy of *al-Infitah aliqtisadi* ('economic opening') which encouraged private investment in the market economy,[7] a development marking a shift from proximity to the Soviet Union towards the United States.[8] This shift was not immediate, however, and the Constitution continued to assert the socialism synonymous with Nasser. Article 4 of the Egyptian Constitution of 1971 reads:

> The economic foundation of the Arab Republic of Egypt is a socialist democratic system based on sufficiency and justice in a manner preventing exploitation, conducive to liquidation of income differences, protecting legitimate earnings, and guaranteeing the equity of the distribution of public duties and responsibilities.

---

[3] الاقتصاد المدني للجيش المصري من عهد عبد الناصر إلى مابعد ثورة 25 يناير

[4] Decree 263 of 1956 (Excluding Ministry of Defense Stores of a Secret Nature from Inspection by the Accounting Department and the Ministry of Finance and Economy).

[5] Law 204 of 1957 (on Exempting Armament Contracts from Taxes, Fees, and Financial Regulations).

[6] Angela Joya, *The Roots of Revolt: A Political Economy of Egypt from Nasser to Mubarak* (Cambridge University Press 2020) 114.

[7] Marvin G Weinbaum, 'Egypt's "Infitah" and the Politics of US Economic Assistance' (1985) 21(2) Middle Eastern Studies 206.

[8] RA Hinnebusch, 'Egypt under Sadat: Elites, Power Structure, and Political Change in a Post-Populist State' (1981) 28(4) Social Problems 442, 457.

To effect this 'economic opening', the distribution of public resources to the military was reduced and military officers removed from key positions, paving the way for more foreign investors. Whereas joining the military Free Officers had been a pathway to the elite under Nasser, Sadat dissolved them in the late 1970s and ended military domination of senior roles.[9] Nonetheless, he ensured that the military maintained a coveted position in the economy and offered it increased economic autonomy in order to alleviate the burden upon the state.

This he did by doubling down on the establishment of so-called 'authorities', organizations which Nasser had introduced to little effect and which had the dual aim of producing foodstuffs for the army and selling any surplus on the local market. In a bid to alleviate state expenditure on the military—a significant budgetary concern following the war in 1973 with Israel—the National Service Projects Organization (NSPO) was launched[10] with the aim of liberating the armed forces from dependence on the private sector. It was also under Sadat that the Arab Organization for Industrialization (AOI) was established, its primary purpose being to manufacture military aircraft. One of the lucrative industries which the military began entering was the ownership and sale of land to investors.

Against the backdrop of the newly adopted 1971 Constitution, which would remain valid subject to amendments for forty years and granted the president new powers of intervention over the military, Sadat relieved these authorities of tax and accountability burdens. Sadat expanded upon Nasser's 1957 exemption of the Ministry of Defence from customs duties to include these new authorities and removed government procurement and auditing obligations from the NSPO created in 1979. In 1981, another presidential decree[11] granted control of access to all land not registered as owned—an estimated 95 per cent of the territory of Egypt—to the Ministry of Defence. Sadat then established the Land Projects Agency,[12] an arm of the Ministry of Defence, to generate revenue from these lands. In this sense, the military not only holds overwhelming sway in the economic and therefore political spheres, but also literally controls the vast majority of Egypt.

2.3 The Mubarak Era (1981–2011)

After the assassination of Sadat, Hosni Mubarak—another military man—took up on the wave of privatization that his predecessor had started and continued with it throughout the 1990s. For most of the Mubarak era, constitutional protection of the country's economic foundations remained the same as under Sadat. It was only in 2007, when constitutional reform was undertaken, that article 4 of the Constitution—relating to the national economy—was amended to provide that '[t]he national economy is based on the development of economic activity, social justice, the guarantee of the different forms of property and the preservation of workers' rights'.[13] The amendment, coming amidst a raft of others,

---

[9] Raymond Hinnebusch, 'From Nasir to Sadat, Elite Transformation in Egypt' (1983) 7(1) Journal of South Asian and Middle Eastern Studies 24, 27–8.

[10] Presidential Decree No 32 of 1979 (on the National Service Projects Organization).

[11] Presidential Decree 143 of 1981 (on Rules of Disposal of Lands and Real Estate Vacated by the Armed Forces and Assignment of Return to Construct Replacement Military Cities and Areas).

[12] Law 531 of 1981 (on Regulations for Disposing of Lands and Real Estate Vacated by the Armed Forces and Allocating the Revenue to Establish Replacement Military Cities and Zones).

[13] Egyptian Constitution of 1971, art 4.

simply inserted into the Constitution the free-market realities that for many years already had been the hallmark of the Mubarak era.

Under Mubarak, the military consolidated its central position among the business and political elite, with several laws being passed to increase its power in the economy. In 1986, Mubarak extended Nasser's original customs exemption on the Ministry of Defence by removing tax burdens on non-military items such as medicine and food destined for civilian markets.[14] From 1991 onwards, the newly appointed Minister of Defence and later head of the Supreme Council of Armed Forces (SCAF), Field Marshal Mohammed Hussein Tantawi, oversaw expansion of the armed forces' intervention in civilian areas, including the construction of public schools, affordable housing, stadiums, utility plants, and factories.[15] The armed forces also took control of many privatized government companies or acted in a coordinated fashion and led them through influential positions on boards.[16] Companies tended to 'hire officers, for example as deputy heads of boards, so as to have a "hot line" to officers in other agencies or in the military command and facilitate getting permissions'.[17]

2.4 The Egyptian Revolution (2011–2015)

After the ousting of Mubarak in 2011, the armed forces and the newly elected Muslim Brotherhood entered a mutually fruitful alliance: while the armed forces facilitated the Muslim Brotherhood's entry onto the political stage through the presidency of Mohammed Morsi, the Muslim Brotherhood supported the SCAF's constitutional amendments.[18] However, this relationship soon soured due to steps taken on both sides to maintain control for themselves—in a context in which 70 per cent of Egypt's parliamentary seats were held by Islamist parties,[19] the military aimed to keep control. In an attempt to maintain the military's oversight and power in the constitution-drafting process, the 2011 Selmi Principles[20] granted it greater autonomy,[21] but drew strong opposition from the Muslim Brotherhood and were withdrawn. When Morsi announced, without consultation, that the army would support Syrian rebels against the Assad regime,[22] a final line was crossed.

The military played a key role in Morsi's ousting in 2013, doing so against its own best interests,[23] and seized the opportunity to cement its control of the Egyptian economy.

[14] Law 186 of 1986 (on Publication of Law Regulating Customs Exemptions).

[15] Zeinab Abul-Magd, *Militarizing the Nation: The Army, Business, and Revolution in Egypt* (Columbia University Press 2017) 11–38.

[16] Shana Marshall, *The Egyptian Armed Forces and the Remaking of an Economic Empire* (Carnegie Endowment for International Peace 2015) 8; Yezid Sayigh, *Owners of the Republic: An Anatomy of Egypt's Military Economy* (Carnegie Middle East Center 2019) 192.

[17] Sayigh (n 16) 191.

[18] Stephan Roll, 'Managing Change: How Egypt's Military Leadership Shaped the Transformation' (2016) 21(1) Mediterranean Politics 23, 28.

[19] Daniela Pioppi, 'Playing with Fire: The Muslim Brotherhood and the Egyptian Leviathan' (2013) 48(4) The International Spectator 51.

[20] 'Declaration of the Fundamental Principles of the New Egyptian State', written by deputy Prime Minister Ali al-Selmy but almost certainly in consultation with the SCAF.

[21] Yezid Sayigh, 'The Specter of "Protected Democracy" in Egypt' *Carnegie Middle East Center* (15 December 2011)   <https://carnegie-mec.org/2011/12/15/specter-of-protected-democracy-in-egypt>   accessed   30 November 2020.

[22] محمد حسان يناشد مرسي ألا يفتح باب مصر أمام «رافضة» إيران Basem Ramadan, 15 June 2013.

[23] Zeinab Abul-Magd, 'The Egyptian Military in Politics and the Economy: Recent History and Current Transition Status' [2013] CMI Insight 4.

Echoing Tantawi two decades earlier, General Mahmoud Nasr of the Ministry of Defence declared outright in 2012 that the military would 'never surrender to any other authority the military-controlled projects ... [which resulted from] the seat of the Ministry of Defence and its own special projects'.[24]

Further legislation favourable to military enterprises came into effect. A 2013 decree by interim president Adly Mansour allowed the government to sidestep tender procedure and select contractors at will in urgent cases: in essence, transparent tender-award processes could be ignored in event of emergency,[25] the definition and parameters of which would be specified by the military. In addition, infrastructure projects worth an estimated EGP 7 billion (USD 1 billion) were awarded to the armed forces between September and November 2013: EGP 4.7 billion for the construction and maintenance of twenty-seven bridges and a tunnel; EGP 2.2 billion over the financial year 2013/14 for the Sinai investment plan; EGP 357 million for 132 buildings as part of a housing project in El Alrish; and EGP 170 million for 62 buildings in a housing project in Ras Sedr.[26] The military was also authorized to collect toll revenue on numerous key roads, including the busiest in Egypt— the Cairo-Alexandria desert road—and the high-traffic Cairo ring road.[27]

Although some commentators initially suggested that the 'military's [post-revolutionary] economic involvement does not imply a general reversal of liberalization in Egypt',[28] there are indications that the expansion of the Egyptian military into the private sector is likely to be a long-term affair and motivated by not only economic but political aims.

2.5 The Sisi Era (2014—Present)

Almost immediately upon taking office in 2014, Sisi began expanding the military's economic empire. The first of several planned 'mega-projects'—the expansion of the Suez Canal—was announced barely a month after his oath of office and has had direct military involvement. The National Fish Farming Project[29]—the largest fish farm in the Middle East—and the construction of a New Administrative Capital are further examples. Under Sisi and the SCAF interim government that preceded him, economic rhetoric has focused on the improvement and expansion of public services, as well as the affordability and availability of basic commodities.[30]

Under Sisi, however, the military empire has expanded to serve not only national interests but those of the individuals serving within the military. A 2015 law permitted officers in the military to start private security agencies,[31] with the result that many retired military

---

[24] Wael Gamal, 'Al-'Askarai: Mashru'atuna 'Araq Wazarat al-Difa'..wa lan Nasmah li-l-Dawla bi-l-Tadakhkhul Fiha' Al-Shorouk (27 March 2012).

[25] Presidential Decree 82 of 2013.

[26] 'The Egyptian Army Collects Billions in Government Contracts' Eldahshan.com (3 January 2014) <http://eldahshan.com/2014/01/03/army-contracts> accessed 30 November 2020; Marshall (n 16).

[27] Amr Adly, 'The Future of Big Business in the New Egypt' Carnegie Middle East Center (19 November 2014) https://carnegie-mec.org/2014/11/19/future-of-big-business-in-new-egypt-pub-57269> accessed 30 November 2020.

[28] ibid.

[29] Al-Masry Al-Youm, 'Egypt to Build Largest Fish Farm in Middle East' Egypt Independent (17 November 2017) <http://www.egyptindependent.com/egypt-to-build-largest-fish-farm-in-middle-east> accessed 30 November 2020.

[30] Tom Perry, 'Egypt Restores Ex-Generals' Role in Provinces' Reuters (13 August 2013).

[31] Law 86 of 2015, as amended by Presidential Decree 126 of 2015.

personnel now lead private companies to which the military subcontracts its projects; by some counts this reaches 10–15 per cent of the workforce.[32] Numerous anecdotal examples attest to the practice. For instance, Major-General Samir Fathi's firm, Egyptian Tracking Services and Information Technology Company (ETIT), provides web-based vehicle-tracking services geared toward commercial banks and tour operators through a partnership with Vodafone Egypt.[33] The same also seems true of non-profits, which have hired ex-military personnel to ensure that any potential business obstacles such as permits or approvals are eliminated.[34]

3. The Rise of a Military Private Sector

Since 1952, the military has held a valued place in society—and its constitutions—as the liberator of the people and a catalyst in the transition from kingdom to republic. The special position of the military sector is a unique facet of the modern Egyptian economy that blurs the lines between the public and private sector. This section argues that the allowances granted by law to the military have had immensely damaging effects on the constitutional protection of private business in Egypt, with these effects including impacts on the prohibition of monopolistic practices and on the pillars of competitiveness.[35]

3.1 Constitutional Protections

As mentioned, the 2014 Egyptian Constitution does not outline which type of economy Egypt has; instead it enumerates the responsibilities that the state has to public and private enterprise and protections it must ensure for them. As also noted, the Constitution protects three kinds of ownership: public, private, and cooperative.[36]

Certain socialist elements are heavily protected under the 2014 Constitution, including workers' shares of management and profits, and minimum thresholds of 50 per cent worker representation on public boards of directors, as well as farmer and craftsmen representation of 80 per cent in agricultural and industrial enterprise boards of directors.[37] Private properties are to be protected[38] and special attention must be paid by the state to small, medium, and micro enterprises in all fields;[39] notably, the state is constitutionally obliged—'shall', rather than 'may', is the term used—to 'motivate' the private sector to shoulder a responsibility to serve society and the economy.[40] At the same time, while the Suez Canal is an international waterway owned by the state,[41] natural resources belong to the people and are to be

---

[32] Sayigh (n 16) 191.

[33] Samer Atallah, 'Seeking Wealth, Taking Power' *Carnegie Endowment for International Peace* (18 November 2014) <https://carnegieendowment.org/sada/57252> accessed 30 November 2020.

[34] International Crisis Group, 'Popular Protest in North Africa and the Middle East (I): Egypt Victorious?' (24 February 2011) Middle East/North Africa Report No 101, 17 <http://bit.ly/2liVUrB> accessed 30 November 2020.

[35] Egyptian Constitution of 2014, art 27.

[36] ibid art 33.

[37] ibid art 42.

[38] ibid art 35

[39] ibid art 28.

[40] ibid art 36.

[41] ibid art 43.

safeguarded by the state.[42] Nonetheless, military influence in the economy has continued to grow through a variety of means, with the armed forces having played a significant role in the drafting of successive constitutions.[43]

3.2 The Current Situation

Egyptian private businesses are generally found in the service rather than goods sector—that is, in trade, banking, insurance, tourism, communication, and education. Conversely, goods sectors, such as food and medicine, tend to be viewed by the government as having greater strategic importance than service sectors and are hence less likely to be forums for private participation. The speed and depth of the military's encroachment on these areas has been staggering—the military today owns business enterprises that span the breadth of the economy's sectors, ranging from cement[44] and steel[45] to pasta,[46] marble,[47] tourism,[48] and many more.[49]

In addition, ex-generals sit in high-ranking positions in administrative departments of government, with powers to sign contracts with military-linked or -owned companies in sectors such as energy, water and sewage, public transportation, social housing, and internet supply.[50] The military's reach extends so far into the private sector that some call Egypt an 'officers' republic'.[51] A military-linked production company has even taken charge of several of the biggest television shows, using this power to dictate the content of *mosalsalaat*—the fictional series shown during Ramadan—and some of the country's most widely viewed entertainment. Nor, indeed, is this the first time the Egyptian military has used mass communication as a political tool. The Arab Organization for Industrialization is a stakeholder in the Egyptian Satellite Company, better known as Nilesat. During the unrest that took place in 2013, the military used its influence to block Al Jazeera from using a Nilesat satellite, claiming it was broadcasting false news about a crisis in Egypt.[52]

There are at least four main institutions that form the military empire in Egypt: the NSPO; the National Organization for Military Production (NOMP); the AOI; and the Armed Forces Engineering Authority (AFEA).

---

[42] ibid art 32.

[43] Nirmala Pillay, 'The Rule of Law and the New Egyptian Constitution' (2014) 35 Liverpool Law Rev 135.

[44] Patrick Werr and Amina Ismail, 'Egypt's $1.1 Billion Cement Plant in Beni Suef to Start Up in Days' *Reuters* (31 January 2018) <https://reut.rs/2q0oU9i> accessed 30 November 2020.

[45] Maha Salem, 'Details of President Sisi's Inauguration of a Number of Service and Development Projects in Suez and in Central and South Sinai' *al-Ahram Online* (5 November 2019) <https://bit.ly/2WOARvh> accessed 30 November 2020.

[46] Mohamed Ibrahim, 'The National Service Projects Organization: 13 Companies Serving Development in Egypt and Providing Army Needs' *Sada el-Balad* (5 January 2018) <https://bit.ly/2MR58WY> accessed 30 November 2020.

[47] Ayat Al Tawy, 'Sisi Inaugurates Mega Industrial Complex in Upper Egypt's Beni Suef' *al-Ahram Online* (15 August 2018) <https://bit.ly/2p8hotb> accessed 30 November 2020.

[48] Military-owned Tolip hotels are listed at <http://www.tolip-eg.com> and Masah hotels, at <http://www.almasa-hotels.com>.

[49] Bruce Rutherford, 'Egypt's New Authoritarianism under Sisi' (2018) 72(2) The Middle East Journal 185; Marshall (n 16); Sayigh (n 16) 16–17.

[50] Zeinab Abul-Magd, 'The Egyptian Republic of Retired Generals' *Foreign Policy* (8 May 2012) <https://foreignpolicy.com/2012/05/08/the-egyptian-republic-of-retired-generals> accessed 30 November 2020.

[51] Sayigh (n 16).

[52] Lisa O'Carroll, 'Egypt Accused of Jamming Al Jazeera' *The Guardian* (7 September 2013).

3.2.1 The National Services Projects Organisation[53]

The most prolific of these key organizations, the NPSO, consists of at least twenty-one companies in the agricultural, food, industrial, engineering, mining, and services sectors. It was established under Presidential Decree No 32 of 1979 in the wake of the Camp David accords, under Sadat, and is affiliated with the Ministry of Defence. Foodstuffs produced include bottled water, pasta, dairy, fish, meat, poultry, honey, tomato paste, jam, juice, and olive oil. Its companies manufacture its own refrigerated trucks, run its own petrol stations, and have constructed utilities, roads, hospitals, and water-pump stations. The organization was created to make the military self-sufficient in meeting its needs and funnel surplus into local markets to be sold at subsidized prices to the general public.

3.2.2 The National Organization for Military Production

The NOMP, affiliated with the Ministry of Military Production, produces civilian goods and military products. It oversees at least twenty military factories, including major missile development hubs, as well as holding shares in other companies, such as the Petroleum Wealth Company, the International Pipe Industry Company (IPIC)—the largest oil and gas pipeline producer in the Middle East—and the Arab Company for Computer Manufacturing (ACCM), an electronics manufacturer of motherboards, PCs, and TVs. Over and above this, it has a host of civilian companies that encroach on the private sector, among them the Egyptian National Company for Pharmaceuticals, founded in 2017.[54]

3.2.3 The Arab Organization for Industrialization

The original aim of the AOI was to meet the defence-equipment needs of the Egyptian armed forces, but its scope was broadened to include civil projects in addition to existing military ones. With at least eleven factories and companies that specialize in military and civilian industries and produced motor and aircraft parts, rail cars, electronics, renewable energy, and fertilizers, the AOI is a major player in the economy. Internationally, it also holds partnerships with civil manufacturing companies such as GE, Lockheed Martin, and Mitsubishi.

3.2.4 The Armed Forces Engineering Authority

One of the most important arms of the Egyptian military-industrial complex is the AFEA. Affiliated with the Ministry of Defence and specializing in both military and civilian infrastructure and construction, it was awarded tenders for two of Sisi's signature megaprojects: the extension of the Suez Canal[55] and the New Cairo capital project.[56] Given that elements of such large projects are inevitably subcontracted to local businesses, the AFEA has the capacity to carry out much of such work thanks to its departments of Military Works, Military Engineering, Military Surveys, Water, and Management of Major Projects. Its wide field of expertise, as well as its status as a military organization, allows it to participate in a

---

[53] National Service Projects Organization website at <http://www.nspo.com.eg>.

[54] Ahmed Aboulenein and Mark Potter, 'Egypt's Military to Enter Pharmaceutical Industry' *Reuters* (22 January 2017) <https://reut.rs/37sQ4YH> accessed 30 November 2020.

[55] Asma Alsharif and others, 'Egypt Awards Ambitious Suez Project to Army-Linked Gulf Firm' *Reuters* (19 August 2014) <https://reut.rs/3qlSIrY> accessed 30 November 2020.

[56] Eric Knecht, 'Egypt's Capital Project Hits Latest Snag as Chinese Pull Out' *Reuters* (8 February 2017) <https://reut.rs/3obuZsq> accessed 30 November 2020.

range of development projects in Egypt, including the construction of bridges, roads, and fields, schools, and sports facilities.

3.3 A Shift from Military to Civilian Production

Although these four organizations were originally created to support military capacity, even under Mubarak their gaze had begun to turn towards the civilian sphere. Throughout the 1990s, the Ministry of Military Production converted 40 per cent of production lines to civilian commodities, while the AOI—originally a conglomerate of nine defence factories—turned 70 per cent of the production of it arms factories into civilian lines.[57] Rather than manufacturing only missiles, aircraft, or rockets, military factories were now deeply entrenched in producing consumer goods such as washing machines, auto parts, fridges, TVs, fans, and kitchenware. Shortly after 2000, Mubarak awarded the military numerous high-value privatized state-owned enterprises, such as the SEMAF Railway Factory, Alexandria Shipyard, and El-Nasr Automotive Manufacturing Company.[58]

Today, through its four main commercial venture bodies, the military owns or controls at least seventy-five companies active in the civilian sector and ranging in area from agriculture and fisheries to pharmaceuticals, construction, real estate, wind and solar energy, industrial manufacturing, and petrol retail. In addition, President Sisi has hand-selected the AFEA to implement all mega-projects since assuming power—namely, the construction of 1 million housing units, announced in 2014; the extension of the Suez Canal, completed in 2016; and the construction of the New Administrative Capital, due for completion in 2022.

3.4 The Military outside of Constitution

The Egyptian Constitution provides that 'the economic system is committed to the criteria of transparency and governance'.[59] However, the government has sought actively to obscure public awareness of the extent of the armed forces' holdings, the extent to which the military is involved in the private sector, and the means through which it is awarded contracts. The full relationship between the armed forces and the Egyptian economy is unclear—the military has been referred to as a 'black box',[60] not only because of its unwillingness to share this information openly, but also as a result of the long-standing Law 313,[61] which prohibits the publication of any information about the armed forces without the prior authorization of the Director of Military Intelligence.

---

[57] Zeinab Abul-Magd, 'Egypt's Military Business: The Need for Change' *Middle East Institute* (19 November 2015) <https://www.mei.edu/publications/egypts-military-business-need-change> accessed 30 November 2020.

[58] Abul-Magd (n 15).

[59] Egyptian Constitution of 2014, art 27.

[60] Ingy Salama, 'A Military Empire' *Qantara* (13 February 2018) <https://en.qantara.de/content/the-role-of-egy pts-armed-forces-a-military-empire> accessed 30 November 2020.

[61] Law 313 of 1956: 'It is prohibited to publish or broadcast any information or news regarding the armed forces, its formations, movements, artillery, or members and generally anything that is related to military or strategic affairs in any way through publishing or broadcasting except after obtaining a written permission by the director of military intelligence, or his deputy in case of the latter's absence, whether by the publisher of the published or broadcasted material or the person responsible for its publishing or broadcast.'

There have, however, been glints of information, notably after the fall of Mubarak. During a 2012 SCAF press conference, Major-General Mahmoud Nasr—the then Assistant Minister of Defence for Financial Affairs—announced that military-owned businesses had a revenue of USD 198 million and that 4.2 per cent of the state's budget was allocated to the military. This, he continued, justified diversification of the military's portfolio into food-stuffs and garments.[62] These estimates are significantly less than those provided only three years earlier by Sayed Mishaal, the former Minister of Military Production, who gave a figure of USD 345 million in revenue.[63]

In a rare admission, President Sisi asserted in 2016 that the military accounts for be-tween 1.5 and 2 per cent of Egypt's total EGP 3–4 trillion (USD 160–213 billion) economic output,[64] which would put the military's share at between USD 2.39 billion and USD 4.26 billion. While even this seems like a large amount, the real figure has been estimated by commentators as up to 60 per cent,[65] which seems more likely in the light of the vast range of areas in which military-owned businesses operate. At the same press conference in which Nasr announced these figures, he also revealed that the military gave EGP 12.2 billion from its own budget, of which EGP 1 billion went to the Central Bank, EGP 350 million to the Radio and Television Union, and EGP 150 million to the Ministry of Electricity.[66] There is a clear disparity between the financial capacity to which the military admits and its likely full holdings.

Indeed, many of the policies pursued by the government post-2011, such as cuts to fuel subsidies for industrial manufacturers, had no impact on the military, since the subsidies they received were unaccounted for and would not be affected by the policy.[67] Because military budgets, spending, and holdings are all secret, the caretaker military government, the SCAF, placed a disproportionate financial burden on non-military competitors under the guise of fiscal responsibility. Moreover, from a constitutional standpoint, the SCAF successfully maintained the military's immunity from any parliamentary oversight in its negotiations with political parties and stewardship of the nation's trajectory. There is no parliamentary oversight of the budget or scope of military activity, as this is exclusively the remit of the National Defence Council.[68]

Furthermore, military officials are constitutionally protected from civilian trial for any alleged offences committed while a member of the serving military,[69] meaning that only military courts may investigate even where the matter has a civilian element.[70] Law 25 of 1966 was amended in 2012 to allow for military courts to try such crimes only upon retire-ment of the officer in question. Alongside this, the 2018 Law Concerning the Treatment of

[62] Al-Masry Al-Youm, 'Army Gets 4.2% of State Budget, Says SCAF Member' *Egypt Independent* (27 March 2012) <http://www.egyptindependent.com/army-gets-42-state-budget-says-scaf-member> accessed 30 November 2020.

[63] Nimrod Raphaeli, 'Egyptian Army's Pervasive Role in National Economy' *MEMRI* (29 July 2013) <http://www.memri.org/reports/egyptian-armys-pervasive-role-national-economy> accessed 30 November 2020.

[64] Ahmed Aboulenein and others, 'Egypt's Sisi Says Military Accounts for 1.5–2 Percent of Economy' *Reuters* (24 December 2016) <https://reut.rs/37qsXOj> accessed 30 November 2020.

[65] Abigail Hauslohner, 'Egypt's "Military Inc" Expands Its Control of the Economy' *The Guardian* (18 March 2014) <https://bit.ly/2VqBBHc> accessed 30 November 2020.

[66] Al-Youm (n 62).

[67] Sayigh (n 16) 32–33.

[68] Egyptian Constitution of 2014, art 203

[69] ibid art 204.

[70] Maged Mandour, 'The Military's Immunity in Egypt' *Carnegie Endowment* (24 July 2018) <https://carnegieendowment.org/sada/76904> accessed 30 November 2020.

Some Senior Officers of the Armed Forces[71] allows for members of the military to be viewed legally as members of the military so long as they have been called upon by the president. Taken together, this paves the way for perpetual immunity even after having left service. In essence, trial and prosecution of military personnel accused of, say, embezzlement or corruption when leading a military-controlled private company falls within the exclusive jurisdiction of the military courts; however, prosecution can be postponed indefinitely owing to a combination of the 2018 Law Concerning the Treatment of Some Senior Officers of the Armed Forces and Law 25 of 1966.

For instance, in the early aftermath of the 25 January revolution, the military was able to maintain this lack of parliamentary oversight by playing off the prosecution of *felool*—or Mubarak-era cronies—against reigning in the military under any future civilian government and convincing the incoming political actors that they could pursue only one or the other. As Marshall notes, 'Despite some early demands for accountability, Egypt's Illicit Gains Authority was unable to secure jurisdiction over military officers, in part because many influential legal scholars prioritized prosecuting Mubarak's business cronies over bringing the military under civilian legal authority.'[72]

In April 2019, twenty-four constitutional amendments were approved by the pro-Sisi Parliament[73] and put to a popular referendum, among them extensions to presidential terms and new powers for the president over judicial appointments. Among these amendments were several that consolidated the powers of the military by declaring the country's military the 'guardian and protector' of the Egyptian state, democracy, and the Constitution; underlining the civil nature of the state; granting military courts wider jurisdiction in trying civilians; enshrining veto power for Egypt's Supreme Council of the Armed Forces over choice of defence minister, which previously had been set to expire after Sisi's second term; and guaranteeing a lasting political role for the military in state policies.[74] Despite reports of irregularities and misconduct—including bribery, lack of oversight, and pro-Sisi Future Party members showing up at polling stations[75]—the amendments were approved by an 89 per cent majority vote.[76]

3.5 Benefits for the Military

Since 2014—following the ousting of the first democratically elected leader in Egypt's history—the military has tightened its grip on the nation's private sector by squeezing out local and foreign business through anti-competitive devices that in the US or Europe would

---

[71] <https://bit.ly/2KRrXcK>. المسلحة القوات قادة كبار معاملة قانون حول البرلمان لجان تقرير <ننشر
[72] Marshall (n 16) 9–10.
[73] Nour Ali and Noura Fakhri <https://bit.ly/2V3mC7h>. نص التعديلات الدستورية بعد موافقة البرلمان عليها بأغلبية 531 نائبا
[74] 'A Look at Proposed Amendments to Egypt's Constitution' *AP News* (14 February 2019) <http://www.apnews.com/0496eac8134840e89295dabbfbf50bfa> accessed 30 November 2020.
[75] 'Judge Overseeing Polling Station Recounts Troubling Incidents in Constitutional Referendum' *Mada Masr* (1 May 2019) <https://bit.ly/2VnZO0H> accessed 30 November 2020.
[76] 'Egypt's Constitutional Amendments Passed by 88.83% in Referendum—National Elections Authority' *Ahram Online* (23 Apr 2019) <https://bit.ly/33yDMNo> accessed 30 November 2020.

almost certainly fall foul of competition or anti-trust legislation. Indeed, military companies have a number of advantages over their civilian counterparts due to their privileged status.

First, the Constitution itself has been used to justify expansion of the military's control of Egyptian land and exploitation of the associated financial opportunities. It confers jurisdiction over military installations and infrastructure on the military alone.[77] Using this as a springboard, Sisi decreed in 2016 that any roads built by the armed forces were security relevant, as were the adjacent lands.[78] This gave the military permanent control of the land and consolidated existing opportunities to generate revenue through roadside advertising billboards and hoardings and military-owned Al-Watan petrol stations set up in prime locations.

Secondly, military factories and companies are entirely exempt from paying taxes and customs. This not only allows them to undercut competitors on goods and services but violates the constitutional stipulation that tax must be paid by all.[79] On the basis of legislation passed in 2016, the military has paid no value-added tax on goods, equipment, machinery, services, and raw materials needed for armaments, defence, and national security; as with all defence-related matters, the scope for deciding what falls within this remit is reserved for the Ministry of Defence alone. Since 2015, hotels owned by the Ministry of Defence have been exempted from real estate taxes,[80] and since 1986 and 2005, from import[81] and income[82] taxes, respectively; conversely, value-added taxes in the civilian sector have risen by 14 per cent since 2016,[83] while the import tax on hundreds of products was increased, in some cases by as much as 60 per cent,[84] thus doubly affecting the cost of doing business in Egypt.

Thirdly, revisions in government procurement laws now mean that key government budget-holders can award contracts for purchases, studies, and construction directly and without resort to a tender process.[85] In practice, it translates to a facilitation of contract awards to military or military-owned companies. Given that Egypt suffers from an endemic corruption problem, this legitimizes the arm's-length award of major contracts, exemplified by the mega-projects that Sisi has pursued in recent years. In 2015, a USD 4.9 billion stimulus package, financed principally by the United Arab Emirates, funded major infrastructure contracts awarded to companies that are, perhaps unsurprisingly, affiliated with the military.[86] Large portions of public investment have been channelled to military firms and their partners, sometimes with notable controversy,[87] but usually—due to the legal

---

[77] Egyptian Constitution of 2014, art 204.

[78] Presidential Decree 233 of 2016 (on Allocating Desert Lands to the Ministry of Defense and Regarding Them as Strategic Zones of Military Importance).

[79] ibid art 38.

[80] Minister of Defense and Military Production Decree 68 of 2015 (on Exempting Certain Units Belonging to the Armed Forces From the Tax on Built-Up Plots).

[81] Law 186 of 1986 (on Publication of Law Regulating Customs Exemptions).

[82] Law 91 of 2005 (on Income Tax).

[83] Eric Knecht and Ahmed Aboulenein, 'Egyptian Parliament Approves Value-Added Tax at 13 Percent' *Reuters* (26 August 2016) <https://reut.rs/37mvXLO> accessed 30 November 2020.

[84] Lin Noueihed and Ehab Farouk, 'Egypt Sharply Increases Customs Duties as It Seeks to Curb Imports' *Reuters* (4 December 2016) <https://reut.rs/37nhSxz> accessed 30 November 2020.

[85] Law 89 of 1998 on bids and tenders.

[86] Eldahshan (n 26).

[87] 'Egyptian-Saudi Engineering Venture Wins General Contract' *Al-Akhbar* (20 August 2014) <http://www.al-akhbar.com/node/213809> accessed 30 November 2020.

amendments—with little fanfare at all. In late 2014, more than USD 1 billion of no-bid government contracts were issued to the military.[88]

Fourthly, military companies benefit from secret subsidies that fall outside budgetary oversight or constraint under Egypt's Constitution. The budget of the military is controlled by the National Defence Council and 'is incorporated as a single figure in the state budget'.[89] This lack of civilian oversight extends to instances of alleged corruption. A 2011 amendment to the Military Justice Act, pushed through under the interim rule of the SCAF, provided the military prosecution and judges alone with the right to investigate the illegal gain of military officers, even after their retirement and assumption of civil positions.[90] Even the Administrative Control Authority, the most powerful of Egypt's anti-corruption bodies, with the power to audit and investigate illegal gains in state and public administrative bodies, is headed[91] and staffed by former military officers.

Fifthly, the military owns vast swathes of undeveloped land, which it is able to exploit for economic gain without concern over paying even below-market prices for its acquisition. In recent years, Sisi has added to what had been granted already by Sadat—in 2015 the military obtained 10,000 acres for land reclamation and commercial farming.[92] This position has enabled military companies to benefit from significant income. For instance, in August 2016, the Ministry of Military Production sold 4,200 hectares of land in Kafr al-Sheikh to investors as part of a government effort to launch an investment hub in the governorate.[93] In November 2015, Sisi amended the powers of the Armed Forces Land Projects Agency,[94] a Sadat-era organization established to oversee the sale of military land no longer required. The amendment added to the existing powers of the agency, empowering it to engage in commercial activity 'to develop its resources, for which purpose it may form companies in all their guises, whether on its own or jointly with national and foreign capital'.[95]

Sixthly, through the use of military conscripts for armed forces-led projects, the military has at its disposal an unending roster of almost free labour for construction, production, and distribution. Military service is a constitutional obligation[96] for those aged 18–30 and lasts between one to three years depending on the individual's level of education. While some conscripts are sent to defend Egypt against the Islamic State in Sinai or from pockets of armed resistance in the desert, others are mandated to work in service industries, factories, clubs, bakeries, and other army projects, including as production line workers.[97] The average wage of an Egyptian soldier is about EGP 300 per month, and though additional state costs are incurred for expenses such as food, accommodation, and basic medical care, the salary of a conscript is significantly less than that of the average non-skilled Egyptian

---

[88] Adly (n 27).

[89] Egyptian Constitution of 2014, art 203.

[90] Sayigh (n 16) 18.

[91] Current Minister Sherif Seif Eldien Hussain Khalil is a decorated former infantry commander and defence attaché to Germany.

[92] Muhammad Hasan, 'Ra'is al-Hay'a al-Handasiyya li-l-Ahram: 850 Mashru' Tusharik Fiha al-Quwwat al-Musallaha li-Khidamt al-Sha'b al-Misri' al-Ahram (20 August 2014); Mahir Abu Nur, 'Mihlib Yatafaqqad 10 Alaf Faddan bi-l-Farafira Tastalimhum al-Quwwat al-Musallaha' al-Youm al-Sabi' (14 September 2014).

[93] ‹https://bit.ly/2VqEveZ› «الأوقاف» تفوض «الإنتاج الحربي» لطرح 10 آلاف فدان من أراضيها على المستثمرين»

[94] Presidential Decree 446 of 2015.

[95] ibid.

[96] Egyptian Constitution of 2014, art 84.

[97] Jamal Boukhari, 'Egypt's Conscripts Serving the Army's Economic Empire' The New Arab (5 September 2017) ‹https://bit.ly/2Jt2W8N› accessed 30 November 2020.

worker. Moreover, the advantage of a perpetually young, able, and cheap labour force should not be underestimated.

Finally, it is clear that conducting large-scale business in Egypt faces security risks, risks which the military is able to contain to a higher standard than any private party. This, in turn, makes working with the armed forces appealing to foreign investors. In one example, the Egyptian military provided forces, reinforced with tanks, to protect the Kharafi Group's major power sites in Al Shabab and Damietta and escort large pieces of its equipment. Shortly thereafter, the Kharafi Group announced USD 80 million of additional investment in Egyptian industrial infrastructure.[98]

4. The Impact of the Military on the Economy

The increasingly broad product spectrum of military enterprise—covering everything from arms and electrical goods to pasta—is regarded as a competitive threat. There are also conspicuously blurred lines in the way in which military organizations conduct their business, with a significant relationship existing between them and government policy and legislation.

In June 2016, for instance, the NOMP signed a partnership agreement with the Chinese group Galanz to manufacture domestic air-conditioning units. Three months later, in September 2016, the Egyptian government began placing restrictions on the importation of air-conditioning units.[99] Several similar case studies show how the Egyptian military is undermining economic advancement within Egypt by stifling industry, artificially supporting production through free labour and existing access to land and resources, and damaging the potential for a thriving, developed economy. This stands in stark contrast to article 28 of the 2014 Constitution, which guarantees a level field of opportunity:

> Economic production, service-based and information-based activities are *key components of the national economy*. The state commits to protecting them, *increasing their competitiveness*, providing an environment that attracts investment, and works on increasing production, encouraging exports, and regulating imports.[100]

4.1 Monopolies and Unfair Practices

In its enumeration of the proposed economic system, the Egyptian Constitution explicitly aims at 'preventing monopolistic practices',[101] and since 2013, the military has engaged more extensively in the type of public-private partnerships and international joint ventures that have existed since the 1990s. However, it has also clearly dominated economic sectors that should be open to free and fair competition and undermined the competitiveness the Constitution seeks to create.[102] An entrepreneur is reported to have said in response:

---

[98] 'Commitments Delivered Despite Severe Pressures' *Transmissions* [Kharafi National corporate newsletter] No 28 (May 2011), 6.
[99] Boukhari (n 97).
[100] Emphases added.
[101] Egyptian Constitution of 2014, art 27.
[102] ibid.

If a company is importing a product and the army comes in as an importer, the company can't compete … Despite having some justifications, we now have a new reality; there is direct competition between the army and some companies across various sectors.[103]

In 2016, the Ministry of Military Production signed a protocol with the Holding Company for Drinking Water and Sanitation, affiliated with the Ministry of Housing and Urban Development, stipulating that it would take charge of manufacturing three million water meters over a five-year period; the deal took place without a tender process.[104] In the same year, responsibility for the 'smart card' food subsidy scheme—which allows Egyptians to purchase low-cost bread and other items—was transferred entirely from the Ministry of Planning to the Ministry of Military Production.[105]

Again in 2016, the High Universities Council made the decision to end all tenders for medicines and medicinal utilities in preparation for its purchase by the Medical Services Department of the Armed Forces.[106] Shortly afterwards, in 2017, the Egyptian Ministry of Health signed an agreement to purchase all medical supplies through the Ministry for Defence, stressing that military control of the medical-supplies market came by direct order 'for the benefit of the citizen'.[107] Similarly, a 2018 cooperation agreement with Al-Falah Ready Mix Company saw the NOMP 'produce ready-mix concrete to supply all projects currently under construction in Egypt'.[108]

Many other examples are available to highlight the improper intervention of the military and its companies in the private sector.[109]

4.1.1 Pharmaceuticals

The establishment of the Egyptian National Company for Pharmaceuticals in 2017 was welcomed as a solution to the shortage of medicines in the country. However, as the vice-president of the Pharmaceutical Chamber at the Egyptian Industrial Federation noted, 'If the same privileges that will be given to the military are instead given to the existing 154 drug factories and the 55 under construction, this would solve the crisis and there would be no need for creating a new company'.[110]

[103] Quoted in Heba Saleh, 'President Sisi Deploys Army to Tackle Egypt's Economic Woes' *Financial Times* (5 October 2016) <https://www.ft.com/content/00ea1c04-8a14-11e6-8cb7-e7ada1d123b1> accessed 30 November 2020.

[104] بروتوكول تصنيع 3 ملايين عداد مياه ذكى بين الإنتاج الحربى والإسكان *Alahram* <http://www.masress.com/ahram/1545048>.

[105] Ahmed Aboulenein and Mark Potter, 'Egypt's Military Takes Over Running of Smart Card Subsidy System' *Reuters* (9 November 2016) <https://reut.rs/2JDohN2> accessed 30 November 2020.

[106] Rabee Assaadany, الجيش يسيطر على سوق المستلزمات الطبية بالأمر المباشر.. والصحة: «لصالح المواطن» *Altahrir* (26 July 2016) <https://bit.ly/3eXfCiZ> accessed 30 November 2020.

[107] Noura Ali, 'Egypt's Military Extends Its Domination to Pharmaceutical Industry' *Middle East Observer* (23 Jan 2017) <https://bit.ly/2JzoZ9m> accessed 30 November 2020.

[108] Sam Rifki, 'National Organization for Military Production (NOMP) in Egypt Signed a Cooperation Agreement with Al Falah Ready Mix, A UAE-Based Company' *LinkedIn* (17 June 2018) <https://bit.ly/33xo5WH> accessed 30 November 2020.

[109] Lina Attalah and Mohamed Hamama, 'The Armed Forces and Business: Economic Expansion in the Last 12 Months' *Mada Masr* (9 September 2016) <https://bit.ly/3qsWdwK> accessed 30 November 2020.

[110] Sonia Farid, 'Why is Egypt's Military Entering the Pharmaceutical Industry?' *Al Arabiyah* (2 February 2017) <https://bit.ly/3ql9Q0E> accessed 30 November 2020.

4.1.2 Baby formula

In 2016, when Egypt suffered a shortage of baby formula, the military was on hand to assist, importing 30 million units of it and selling them at half the price of traditional retailers. Army trucks rolled out to distribute the product, emerging from a military hub in Alexandria. The logic proposed by Armed Forces spokesperson Mohamed Samir was that in buying formula in collaboration with the Ministry of Health at a cost of EGP 60 per unit and selling it at EGP 30 per unit, 'the Armed Forces has landed a blow against the greedy monopoly of traders and companies working in the milk industry'.[111] This was a clear swipe at the Egyptian Pharmaceutical Trading Company (Egydrug), previously the only importer of baby formula; indeed, the Egydrug spokesperson, Karim Karm, described the military's entry into the baby-formula market as a 'fatal blow'.[112]

Shortly afterwards, the NSPO took over the importation of all infant milk formula,[113] moving from undercutting competitors to assuming a full monopoly. In essence, the military replaced one monopoly with another—its own.

4.1.3 Mining

Since a presidential decree in 2014,[114] the military has also held an almost total monopoly of the country's mines by way of the Egyptian Mineral Resources Authority—its first move was to treble the price of the right to mine. Although this does not violate constitutional provisions in regard to 'granting a concession to a public utility',[115] it is noteworthy that the public utility is itself part of the military empire and exhibits a clear conflict of interest— something which a tender process would have helped prevent.

In 2017, the NSPO moved more deeply into the marble-production industry, adding four production facilities to its existing three factories and aiming to produce 1 million m^2 marble—80 per cent of Egypt's total output. Once again, the military financed the project and provided conscript labour to ensure its speedy completion. The military's entry into the marble industry meant thousands of job losses.

4.2 Economic Impact

Despite a stark warning in 2017 from the International Monetary Fund (IMF) that '[p]rivate sector development and job creation ... might be hindered by involvement of entities under the Ministry of Defense',[116] the Egyptian armed forces have pressed ahead with their agenda. Appointments of ex-military officers to key positions within the Sisi administration, along with the wide-ranging privileges granted to military-owned and -controlled businesses, undermine the potential for meaningful reform in Egypt and the constitutional aims of a mixed market. Ex-generals are appointed to lead public authorities

---

[111] Facebook posting on the official page of the Military Spokesperson for the Armed Forces, available at <http://www.facebook.com/Egy.Army.Spox/posts/889559114508405> accessed 30 November 2020.

[112] Boukhari (n 97).

[113] See video clip at <http://www.youtube.com/watch?v=lQAJvISqqL8> accessed 30 November 2020.

[114] Law 198 of 2014.

[115] Egyptian Constitution of 2014, art 32.

[116] 'First Review Under the Extended Arrangement under the Extended Fund Facility and Requests for Waivers for Nonobservance and Applicability of Performance Criteria—Press Release; Staff Report; and Statement by the Executive Director for the Arab Republic of Egypt', IMF Country Report No. 17/290, para 24 (September 2017).

in industrial development, agricultural development, import and export control, maritime transport, railways, sea and Nile ports, and the Suez Canal. Similarly, key positions such as Minister of Transportation, Chairman of the State Telecommunication Holding Company, and Chairman of the Maritime and Land Transport Holding Company are all occupied by ex-military personnel.

The youth population of Egypt today—aged 18–29 years—is estimated at 20.2 million people,[117] about half of whom[118] will be conscripted into the army for at least a year. Meanwhile, in recent years, unemployment among 15–29-year-olds has reached 79 per cent.[119] Conscripts are brought in to work for the military, following which they are released to a job market which is flailing due—in part—to the military's model of using conscripts to carry out work: it is a vicious cycle. This model, along with restrictions on business through tax hikes and bureaucratic burdens, not only hinders efforts to boost job creation, which may be beneficial for short-term infrastructure projects, but severely limits the potential in the first place for any such new jobs to be created.

Sisi's aims may be noble in their attempt to provide basic and vital goods to a population struggling with rampant poverty and wealth inequality. However, measures such as providing 95 per cent of cancer medicines through military organizations[120] are stop-gaps that fail to address the country's underlying economic issues. Rather than directly tackling chronic economic obstacles such as the growing income gap, inflation, or youth unemployment, mega-projects like those being built through the AFEA aim at making Egypt more attractive externally. This is a flawed plan.

The Sisi administration appears to be borrowing from both Mubarak's centralized security state of the 1990s and 2000s and the mega-projects for which Nasser is celebrated. In this fashion, it is able to deregulate industries while bolstering patriotism through the increased role and visibility of the military as saviour, builder, and backbone of the nation. While it may produce short-term results, its longer-term impact is that it is 'unlikely to inspire confidence among local or international investors, who would like to see a vibrant private sector'.[121]

4.2.1 Wider constitutional implications

The military's entry into the civilian market also has far-reaching consequences for the constitutional rights of workers. The Egyptian Constitution prohibits civilian trials in military courts 'except for crimes that represent a direct assault against military facilities, military barracks, or whatever falls under their authority'.[122] Given the wide expansion of the military's economic empire, this now includes hotels, resorts, factories, farms, and a range of public properties and institutions. While 'striking peacefully is a right which is organised by law',[123] civilian workers on military-owned premises have been tried recently in military

---

[117] MENA, 'CAPMAS: Youths Constitute 21% of Egypt's Population' *Egypt Today* (12 August 2018) <http://www.egypttoday.com/Article/1/55806/CAPMAS-youths-constitute-21-of-Egypt-s-population> accessed 30 November 2020.

[118] Military service is mandatory only for men.

[119] Boukhari (n 97).

[120] ibid.

[121] Mohamed Elmeshad, 'Egypt's Ad Hoc Economy' *Carnegie Endowment for International Peace* (20 July 2016) <https://carnegieendowment.org/sada/64140> accessed 30 November 2020.

[122] Egyptian Constitution of 2014, art 204.

[123] ibid art 15.

rather than civilian courts for instigating a labour strike and disrupting the company's operations.[124] Strikes are banned under the current protest laws in Egypt and any infractions are supposed to be tried in civilian courts; the fact that the premises of the strike were military owned—the Alexandria Shipyard—meant that individuals could be tried in a military court instead.

Nor, indeed, is this the first time such a situation has arisen. Of the four instances since 1952 where civilian workers have been tried before a military court, three have occurred in the last decade during a period in which the military has been consolidating its position in the private sector: Helwan Engineering Industries Company in 2010; the Petrojet Company in 2011; and the Alexandria Shipyard Company in 2016.[125] In the case of the Alexandria Shipyard protesters, 1,000 members of the 2,300-strong workforce were dismissed; unsurprisingly, the project, which involved building three French Corvettes, was completed by army personnel.[126]

4.2.2 The role of constitutionalism in Egypt

There are, to be sure, elements of the Constitution that the military strongly upholds, notably those to do with its protections from parliamentary oversight and the civilian judicial system. The constitutional referendum in 2019 allowed the military to tighten its grip on the country through the inclusion of vague and ambiguous language the remit for definition of which lies with the military itself. Article 200 once stated that the duty of the armed forces was to 'protect the country, and preserve its security and territories'; after the constitutional amendments of 2019, their duty is 'safeguarding the constitution and democracy, maintaining the foundations of the state and its civilian nature, the gains of the people, and the rights and freedoms of the individual'.[127]

Interpreting where the limits of 'safeguarding' and 'maintaining' lie, what constitutes 'the gains of the people', which 'rights and freedoms' are inviolable, and a range of other matters is the responsibility of the Constitutional Court should the military exceed its mandate under the amended constitutional provision. However, interestingly, another of the 2019 amendments granted a new power to the president to choose the president of the Constitutional Court from among the five oldest vice-presidents of the court; previously, this position was appointed by the Constitutional Court's General Assembly. It is not hard to imagine that a court led by a presidentially appointed president would side with the military in cases such as those above.

5. Conclusion

The military stronghold on the economy shows no signs of abating; rather, since consolidating their position, Sisi's administration and the wider military empire have sought to expand their reach into new sectors. At the same time, the lack of transparency surrounding

---

[124] 'Military Trial of Alexandria Shipyard Workers Adjourned Again' *Mada Masr* (20 December 2016) <https://bit.ly/2VnkxSr> accessed 30 November 2020.

[125] Jano Charbel, 'The 4 Times in Egyptian History Civilian Workers Were Tried by Military Courts' *Mada Masr* (20 June 2016) <https://bit.ly/3ojRNq9> accessed 30 November 2020.

[126] Boukhari (n 97).

[127] Ali and Fakhri (n 73).

the full extent of the military's impact on the economy—including its holdings, its budgets, and its influence in private companies—makes accountability a nigh-impossible feat. A campaign demanding the release of information about military business enterprises arose in the post-revolutionary era; shortly afterwards, the founders of the *manhouba* ('looted') campaign were arrested while attempting to distribute documentary evidence of the military's economic operations.

From a constitutional perspective, the armed forces' involvement in the private sector undermines a variety of protections. The military has established monopolies, engaged in anti-competitive practices, undermined economic freedoms, reduced job opportunities, increased unemployment, and flouted any notion of a fair tax system; by the same token, the economy has seen the re-emergence of the statism of the Sadat and Nasser eras. As for the Constitution, it facilitates rather than constrains the military. The military, duly empowered in this way, has come to occupy a central role in the economy, but due to a lack of constitutionalism (no transparency, limited accountability, and no respect for the 'mixed economy'), this has had a dire impact on the same economy.

Bibliography

'Commitments Delivered Despite Severe Pressures' *Transmissions* [Kharafi National corporate newsletter] No 28 (May 2011), 6

'The Egyptian Army Collects Billions in Government Contracts' *Eldahshan.com* (3 January 2014) <http://eldahshan.com/2014/01/03/army-contracts> accessed 30 November 2020

'Egyptian-Saudi Engineering Venture Wins General Contract' *Al-Akhbar* (20 August 2014) <http://www.al-akhbar.com/node/213809> accessed 30 November 2020

'Egypt's Constitutional Amendments Passed by 88.83% in Referendum—National Elections Authority' *Ahram Online* (23 Apr 2019) <https://bit.ly/33yDMNo> accessed 30 November 2020

'Judge Overseeing Polling Station Recounts Troubling Incidents in Constitutional Referendum' *Mada Masr* (1 May 2019) <https://bit.ly/2VnZO0H> accessed 30 November 2020

'A Look at Proposed Amendments to Egypt's Constitution' *AP News* (14 February 2019) <http://www.apnews.com/0496eac8134840e89295dabbfbf50bfa> accessed 30 November 2020

'Military Trial of Alexandria Shipyard Workers Adjourned Again' *Mada Masr* (20 December 2016) <https://bit.ly/2VnkxSr> accessed 30 November 2020

Aboulenein A and Potter M, 'Egypt's Military Takes Over Running of Smart Card Subsidy System' *Reuters* (9 November 2016) <https://reut.rs/2JDohN2> accessed 30 November 2020

Aboulenein A and Potter M, 'Egypt's Military to Enter Pharmaceutical Industry' *Reuters* (22 January 2017) <https://reut.rs/37sQ4YH> accessed 30 November 2020

Aboulenein A and others, 'Egypt's Sisi Says Military Accounts for 1.5–2 Percent of Economy' *Reuters* (24 December 2016) <https://reut.rs/37qsXOj> accessed 30 November 2020

Abul-Magd Z, 'The Egyptian Republic of Retired Generals' *Foreign Policy* (8 May 2012) <https://foreignpolicy.com/2012/05/08/the-egyptian-republic-of-retired-generals> accessed 30 November 2020

Abul-Magd Z, 'The Egyptian Military in Politics and the Economy: Recent History and Current Transition Status' (October 2013) (2) CMI Insight 4

Abul-Magd Z, 'Egypt's Military Business: The Need for Change' *Middle East Institute* (19 November 2015) <https://www.mei.edu/publications/egypts-military-business-need-change> accessed 30 November 2020

Abul-Magd Z, Militarizing the Nation: The Army, Business, and Revolution in Egypt (Columbia University Press 2017)

Adly A, 'The Future of Big Business in the New Egypt' *Carnegie Middle East Center* (19 November 2014) <https://carnegie-mec.org/2014/11/19/future-of-big-business-in-new-egypt-pub-57269> accessed 30 November 2020

Ali N, 'Egypt's Military Extends Its Domination to Pharmaceutical Industry' *Middle East Observer* (23 January 2017) <https://bit.ly/2Jzo79m> accessed 30 November 2020

Alsharif A and others, 'Egypt Awards Ambitious Suez Project to Army-Linked Gulf Firm' *Reuters* (19 August 2014) <https://reut.rs/3qlSIrY> accessed 30 November 2020

Al Waqa' M, 'Through Sole-Sourcing, Armed Forces Control the Implementation of Government Contracts and Collection of Road Tolls' *Yanair* (29 March 2014) <http://yanair.net/archives/31896> accessed 30 November 2020

Al-Youm A-M, 'Army Gets 4.2% of State Budget, Says SCAF Member' *Egypt Independent* (27 March 2012) <http://www.egyptindependent.com/army-gets-42-state-budget-says-scaf-member> accessed 30 November 2020

Al-Youm A-M, 'Egypt to Build Largest Fish Farm in Middle East' *Egypt Independent* (17 November 2017) <http://www.egyptindependent.com/egypt-to-build-largest-fish-farm-in-middle-east> accessed 30 November 2020

Assaadany R, الجيش يسيطر على سوق المستلزمات الطبية بالأمر المباشر.. والصحة: «لصالح المواطن» *Altahrir* (26 July 2016) <https://bit.ly/3eXfCiZ accessed 30 November 2020

Atallah S, 'Seeking Wealth, Taking Power' *Carnegie Endowment for International Peace* (18 November 2014) <https://carnegieendowment.org/sada/57252> accessed 30 November 2020

Attalah L and Hamama M, 'The Armed Forces and Business: Economic Expansion in the Last 12 Months' *Mada Masr* (9 September 2016) <https://bit.ly/3qsWdwK> accessed 30 November 2020

Boukhari J, 'Egypt's Conscripts Serving the Army's Economic Empire' *The New Arab* (5 September 2017) <https://bit.ly/2Jt2W8N> accessed 30 November 2020

Charbel J, 'The 4 Times in Egyptian History Civilian Workers Were Tried by Military Courts' *Mada Masr* (20 June 2016) <https://bit.ly/3ojRNq9> accessed 30 November 2020

Elmeshad M, 'Egypt's Ad Hoc Economy' *Carnegie Endowment for International Peace* (20 July 2016) <https://carnegieendowment.org/sada/64140> accessed 30 November 2020

Farid S, 'Why is Egypt's Military Entering the Pharmaceutical Industry?' *Al Arabiyah* (2 February 2017) <https://bit.ly/3ql9Q0E> accessed 30 November 2020

Gamal W, *'Al-'Askarai: Mashru'atuna 'Araq Wazarat al-Difa'..wa lan Nasmah li-l-Dawla bi-l-Tadakhkhul Fiha'* Al-Shorouk (27 March 2012)

Hasan M, 'Ra'is al-Hay'a al-Handasiyya li-l-Ahram: 850 Mashru' Tusharik Fiha al-Quwwat al-Musallaha li-Khidamt al-Sha'b al-Misri' al-Ahram (20 August 2014)

Hauslohner A, 'Egypt's "Military Inc" Expands Its Control of the Economy' *The Guardian* (18 March 2014) <https://bit.ly/2VqBBHc> accessed 30 November 2020

Hinnebusch R, 'Egypt under Sadat: Elites, Power Structure, and Political Change in a Post-Populist State' (1981) 28(4) Social Problems 442

Hinnebusch R, 'From Nasir to Sadat, Elite Transformation in Egypt' (1983) 7(1) Journal of South Asian and Middle Eastern Studies 24

Ibrahim M, 'The National Service Projects Organization: 13 Companies Serving Development in Egypt and Providing Army Needs' *Sada el-Balad* (5 January 2018) <https://bit.ly/2MR58WY> accessed 30 November 2020

International Crisis Group, 'Popular Protest in North Africa and the Middle East (I): Egypt Victorious?' (24 February 2011) Middle East/North Africa Report No 101, 17, <http://bit.ly/2liVUrB> accessed 30 November 2020

Joya A, *The Roots of Revolt: A Political Economy of Egypt from Nasser to Mubarak* (Cambridge University Press 2020)

Knecht E and Aboulenein A, 'Egyptian Parliament Approves Value-Added Tax at 13 Percent' *Reuters* (26 August 2016) <https://reut.rs/37mvXLO> accessed 30 November 2020

Knecht E, 'Egypt's Capital Project Hits Latest Snag as Chinese Pull Out' *Reuters* (8 February 2017) <https://reut.rs/3obuZsq> accessed 30 November 2020

Mandour M, 'The Military's Immunity in Egypt' *Carnegie Endowment* (24 July 2018) <https://carnegieendowment.org/sada/76904> accessed 30 November 2020

Marshall S, *The Egyptian Armed Forces and the Remaking of an Economic Empire* (Carnegie Endowment for International Peace 2015)

MENA, 'CAPMAS: Youths Constitute 21% of Egypt's Population' *Egypt Today* (12 August 2018) <http://www.egypttoday.com/Article/1/55806/CAPMAS-youths-constitute-21-of-Egypt-s-pop ulation> accessed 30 November 2020

Noueihed L and Farouk E, 'Egypt Sharply Increases Customs Duties as It Seeks to Curb Imports' *Reuters* (4 December 2016) <https://reut.rs/37nhSxz> accessed 30 November 2020

Nur MA, 'Mihlib Yatafaqqad 10 Alaf Faddan bi-l-Farafira Tastalimhum al-Quwwat al-Musallaha' al-Youm al-Sabi' (14 September 2014)

O'Carroll L, 'Egypt Accused of Jamming Al Jazeera' *The Guardian* (7 September 2013)

Perry T, 'Egypt Restores Ex-Generals' Role in Provinces' *Reuters* (13 August 2013)

Pillay N, 'The Rule of Law and the New Egyptian Constitution' (2014) 35 Liverpool Law Rev 135

Pioppi D, 'Playing with Fire: The Muslim Brotherhood and the Egyptian Leviathan' (2013) 48(4) The International Spectator 51

Raphaeli N, 'Egyptian Army's Pervasive Role in National Economy' *MEMRI* (29 July 2013) <www. memri.org/reports/egyptian-armys-pervasive-role-national-econom accessed 30 November 2020

Rifki S, 'National Organization for Military Production (NOMP) in Egypt Signed a Cooperation Agreement with Al Falah Ready Mix, A UAE-Based Company' *LinkedIn* (17 June 2018) <https:// bit.ly/33xo5WH> accessed 30 November2020

Roll S, 'Managing Change: How Egypt's Military Leadership Shaped the Transformation' (2016) 21(1) Mediterranean Politics 23

Rutherford B, 'Egypt's New Authoritarianism under Sisi' (2018) 72(2) The Middle East Journal 185

Salama I, 'A Military Empire' *Qantara* (13 February 2018) <https://en.qantara.de/content/the-role-of-egypts-armed-forces-a-military-empire> accessed 30 November 2020

Saleh H, 'President Sisi Deploys Army to Tackle Egypt's Economic Woes' *Financial Times* (5 October 2016) <https://www.ft.com/content/00ea1c04-8a14-11e6-8cb7-e7ada1d123b1> accessed 30 November 2020

Salem M, 'Details of President Sisi's Inauguration of a Number of Service and Development Projects in Suez and in Central and South Sinai' *al-Ahram Online* (5 November 2019) <https://bit.ly/2WOA Rvh> accessed 30 November 2020

Sayigh Y, 'The Specter of "Protected Democracy" in Egypt' *Carnegie Middle East Center* 15 (December 2011) <https://carnegie-mec.org/2011/12/15/specter-of-protected-democracy-in-egypt> accessed 30 November 2020

Sayigh Y, *Owners of the Republic: An Anatomy of Egypt's Military Economy* (Carnegie Middle East Center 2019)

Tawy AA, 'Sisi Inaugurates Mega Industrial Complex in Upper Egypt's Beni Suef' *al-Ahram Online* (15 August 2018) <https://bit.ly/2p8hotb> accessed 30 November 2020

Weinbaum MG, 'Egypt's "Infitah" and the Politics of US Economic Assistance' (1985) 21(2) Middle Eastern Studies 206

Werr P and Ismail A, 'Egypt's $1.1 Billion Cement Plant in Beni Suef to Start Up in Days' *Reuters* (31 January 2018) <https://reut.rs/2q0oU9i> accessed 30 November 2020

12

Determining the Jurisdiction of Regional States in Promoting Investment in Ethiopia

A Constitutional and Practical Inventory

Solomon Negussie

1. Introduction

Ethiopia[1] is hailed as one of the fastest-growing economies in Africa, having enjoyed an average growth of 10 per cent per annum for ten consecutive years. It has ambitious plans to become a middle-income country by 2025, further to which it has introduced policies, strategies, and institutional arrangements to make itself as a destination for foreign direct investment (FDI). The World Investment Report[2] lists Ethiopia as one of Africa's best-performing countries, registering USD 4.1 billion in FDI in 2017 and attracting investors in key industries and sectors. Investment and development activities are guided by a federal constitution, which determines the powers and functions of the federal government and regional states, and by investment laws and regulations, as well as institutions mandated to facilitate investment.

However, despite its economic growth and its policies geared towards inclusive development, the country has faced political unrest since 2015, with investments having been targeted by protesters where some industries and commercial farming were burnt down. Regional governments also challenged federal investment decisions on the ground that regions are not benefiting from shared investment revenue, and want to attract FDI and domestic investment directly themselves.

This chapter examines the jurisdiction of Ethiopia's regional states in matters of investment and considers whether investment decisions are guided by the principles of constitutionalism. It reviews the constitutional and legal framework and analyses practical issues in determining states' investment jurisdiction. In so doing, the chapter identifies what states can and cannot do in promoting investment; it also defines the relationship between the federal and regional governments in their respective efforts to promote investment that uses resources efficiently and accountably.

The chapter is organized into six sections, including this introduction. The next section deals with general issues to do with investment in a developmental state and considers the role of these issues in recent political developments in Ethiopia. The third section looks at

---

[1] The Federal Democratic Republic of Ethiopia (FDRE) has nine member states—also known as regions, states, or national regional self-governments—and a capital city with self-administrative autonomy.

[2] UNCTAD, *World Investment Report 2018: Investment and New Industrial Policies* (United Nations 2018) <https://unctad.org/en/publicationsLibrary/wir2018_en.pdf> accessed 10 April 2019.

Solomon Negussie, *Determining the Jurisdiction of Regional States in Promoting Investment in Ethiopia* In: *Constitutionalism and the Economy in Africa*. Edited by: Charles M Fombad and Nico Steytler, Oxford University Press. © Solomon Negussie 2022.
DOI: 10.1093/oso/9780192886439.003.0014

the constitutional division of powers, focusing on investment, natural resource management, agriculture, and environment, and examines the specific roles that states may play in promoting investment. The fourth section analyses institutionalized federal-state relations in promoting investment—relations which are especially important in view of the increasing assertiveness shown by regional governments. Section 5 explores investment and fiscal policy under the FDRE Constitution and focuses on efforts to broaden state-level fiscal capacity through concurrent taxes on investments. Finally, recommendations are made.

2. Investment, the Developmental State, and Political Unrest

One may wonder why determining the investment jurisdiction of a state under Ethiopian federalism is a matter worth considering, or, even more succinctly, why investment is a contested issue. It could be argued that, in spite of its political unrest, Ethiopia remains one of Africa's fastest-growing non-oil economies,[3] a fact due in part to the investment policy of the government led by the EPRDF (Ethiopian People's Revolutionary Democratic Front). Indeed, reports indicate that over the years the country has made considerable economic, social, and cultural progress. The government declared that it had fulfilled most of the Millennial Development Goals (MDGs) by 2015[4] in terms of improving primary health-care coverage, securing universal access to primary education, improving maternal health care, and reducing child mortality. In terms of expansion of services and infrastructures, the country has shown remarkable improvements in road infrastructure, the energy sector, and telecommunications.[5] Moreover, to promote domestic and foreign investment, the Ethiopian Investment Commission (EIC) has identified investment priorities in large and rapidly growing sectors, developed investor-friendly policies for these sectors,[6] and established a total of ten industrial parks in various parts of the country.

Abraham Tekeste, former Minister of Finance and Economic Cooperation, has argued[7] that the government's development strategies have been geared towards achieving sustainable development by reducing poverty and promoting regional equity through a policy of inclusiveness.[8] Tekeste said that by having pursued the model of a 'democratic

---

[3] Although the World Bank projects that growth will decline to 7.5 per cent in 2018, it still considers Ethiopia the fastest-growing non-oil-producing economy in Africa. World Bank, 'Ethiopia Country Overview' (World Bank n.d.) <http://bit.ly/3bp9HUA> accessed 30 March 2019

[4] See eg Ministry of Finance and Economic Development (MoFED), 'Ethiopia's Progress towards Eradicating Poverty: An Interim Report on Poverty Analysis Study 2010/11' (2012).

[5] According to a 2015 government report, Ethiopian road infrastructure has increased over the years from 18,000 km to 78,000 km. In the telecom sector, the number of mobile subscribers increased from several thousand in 2001 to more than 20 million in 2013. In the energy sector, the country significantly increased production and distribution, and construction of the Great Renaissance Dam has commenced. The government also increased its revenue collection capacity to more than a hundred billion ETB. In addition, it claims to have achieved significant improvements in food security, with the number of people living below the poverty line decreasing from 38.7 per cent in 2004 to 29.6 per cent in 2011. See Government Communication Office, 'Ethiopia Country Report 2012' (2012).

[6] See Ethiopian Investment Commission, 'Ethiopian Investment Report 2017' (2017).

[7] Abraham Tekeste, 'Fiscal Resource Allocation and Inclusive Development in Federal Ethiopia' (June 2018), paper presented at the Symposium on Federalism and Development in Ethiopia, Addis Ababa.

[8] The arguments have been supported through the successive development strategies reflected in the Agricultural Development Led Industrialization (ADLI) 1993–2002, Sustainable Development and Poverty Reduction Program (SDPRP), PASDEP (Plan for Accelerated and Sustained Development to End Poverty) (2006–10), GTP I (2011–15), and GTP II (2016–20).

developmental state' since 2002, the government ensured accelerated and sustained growth by means of a centrally controlled approach. With this in mind, it had 'poured its resources [into] infrastructure investments, building industrial parks and factories, dams for hydro-electricity production, powerlines and real-estate development, [and] building road networks, etc.'[9]

Similarly, on previous occasions Meles Zenawi and Arkebe Okubay[10] characterized Ethiopia as a developmental state.[11] In the aftermath of the 2005 election, the government often declared itself a 'democratic developmental state', a model held to underlie the success of East Asia. Certain scholars, such as Clapham, have also classified Ethiopia as a developmental state and attributed its economic growth to the adoption of this model; Clapham nevertheless argued that there is a tension between the developmental state and the federal structure.[12]

In line with Clapham's argument, Jebena[13] and Zemenu[14] have highlighted the inherent contradiction between Ethiopia's ethnic-based federalism and the developmental state. For his part, A. Fiseha counter-argues that there cannot be any inherent contradiction between federalism and developmental state, but observes all the same that Ethiopia's record of economic growth is coupled with a poor human rights record.[15] Others have compared and contrasted Ethiopia's economic growth with that of East Asian developmental states, while shying away from describing it as a developmental state.[16] Others yet argued that the country's problems are rooted in the ideology of the developmental state, which focuses on centrally designed state-led economic growth that compromises the autonomy of regional states.[17]

The present study does not pretend to give a comprehensive analysis of the developmental state and the question of whether Ethiopia can be classified as such. Rather, its objective in this section is to indicate that recent political developments (at least until 2018) revealed that, under a 'democratic developmental state' model, it is difficult to manage competing

---

[9] However, there is a less salutary side to these successes. The UNDP Human Development Index (HDI 2013) ranks Ethiopia at the bottom of the list (173 out of 186 countries); other discrepancies are the gap between the rich and poor, ethnic fragmentation, and the country's political unrest. Ethiopia is a country of contrasting stories—economic growth is combined with poverty and conflict.

[10] Meles Zenawi, 'African Development: Dead Ends and New Beginnings' (n.d.) <http://www.ethiopiantreasures.co.uk/meleszenawi/pdf/zenawi_dead_ends_and_new_beginnings.pdf> accessed 10 January 2015; Arkebe Oqubay, *Made in Africa: Industrial Policy in Ethiopia* (OUP 2015). Oqubay, the former mayor of Addis Ababa, was a senior adviser to the Prime Minister at the time of this writing.

[11] There is no universally agreed-upon definition of a developmental state. AK Bagcht, 'The Past and the Future of the Developmental State' 2000 11(2) Journal of World-systems Research 398, defines it as 'a state that puts economic development as the top priority of government policy and is able to design effective instruments to promote such goals'. According to him, the formal and informal institutions of the developmental state trace back to the introduction of capitalism. For others, the developmental state is a political-cum-ideological construction that emerged from the experience of Japan and other East Asian countries.

[12] Christopher Clapham, 'The Political Economy of Ethiopia from the Imperial Period to the Present' in Cheru F, Cramer C, and Oqubay A (eds), *Oxford Handbook of the Ethiopian Economy* (OUP 2019).

[13] BA Jebena, 'Ethnic Federalism and Democratic Developmental State in Ethiopia: Some Points of Contradiction' (2015) 3(7) International Journal of Political Science and Development 291.

[14] Y Zemenu, 'The Developmental State and Ethnic Federalism in Ethiopia: Issues to Worry about' (2017) 1 Hawassa University Journal of Law 1.

[15] A Fiseha, 'Ethiopia—Development with or without Freedom?' in Brems E, Van der Beken C, and Yimer SA (eds), *Human Rights and Development: Legal Perspectives from and for Ethiopia* (Brill Nijhoff 2015).

[16] J Hague and H Chang, 'The Concept of a "Developmental State" in Ethiopia' in Cheru F, Cramer C, and Oqubay A (eds), *Oxford Handbook of the Ethiopian Economy* (OUP 2019).

[17] A Fiseha, 'Ethiopia's Experiment in Accommodating Diversity: 20 Years' Balance Sheet' (2012) 22(4) Regional & Federal Studies 435.

economic, political, social, and development concerns. This difficulty can be linked to the deficits of the developmental state approach which the EPRDF followed. In terms of this approach, which its architects claim was inspired by the East Asian model, state-led economic development aspired to achieve agricultural transformation and industrialization, as was reflected in the country's Growth and Transformation Plans (GTPs). However, there are questions as to whether Ethiopia's approach lived up to the notion of the developmental state. Some of the reasons for the apparent discrepancy relate to weak and corrupt institutions, the disregard of meritocracy, the strong overlap between party and government structure, the lack of institutional checks and balances, and limited regard for human rights and political pluralism. Ethiopia's approach led ultimately to the complete centralization of key decision-making power at the federal-government or party-leadership level.

Further problems arose from constraints on the private sector and the lack of a competitively level playing field, lack of transparency about the flow of foreign currency into the economy, and lack of proper regulation. In particular, with the government placing a heavy hand on every aspect of the economy, it wielded a monopoly of regulatory power, in addition to which the investment decisions of state-owned enterprises had not been legally and financially accountable. The government's investment in infrastructure and mega-projects had regularly consumed more than half of its annual budget, yet project awards, contracts, and access to foreign currency and imports had been systematically closed to the competitive private sector.

As a result, there is a widespread public perception that the multi-billion-dollar unaudited spending of state-owned endeavours such as METEC (Metal and Engineering Technology Company), the Sugar Corporation, and the Renaissance Dam project has benefited certain ethnic groups to the detriment of others. The public has lost trust in these much-vaunted government projects due to '[perceived] corruption in the political system and lack of equal economic benefits'.[18] This is arguably one of the factors that has led to ethnic fragmentation and undermined the government's legitimacy. Furthermore, the impact of real or perceived ethno-regional inequalities, a narrowing space for political pluralism, and the undermining of civil liberties and human rights, cannot be doubted. These trends demonstrate the incompatibility of democracy and the developmental agenda, with the resultant challenges aggravated by high unemployment, urban poverty, persistent rural vulnerability, and the mismanagement and unfair distribution of resources.

In this regard, the ruling EPRDF party admitted that one of the factors in the country's unrest is unfair distribution of resources and lack of economic opportunities for the youth. Likewise, parties governing the two larger regional states of Oromia and Amhara asserted that political marginalization, rising youth unemployment, and unfair distribution of resources are the major causes of discontent and political crisis. These two regional governments argued for an 'economic revolution' that would ensure their fair share of resources, tap their natural endowments, increase local revenue capacity, attract investment to their regions, and utilize available financial resources efficiently and effectively.

One has to be cautious about recent moves by regional governments to reject decisions of the federal government made within the ambits of its constitutional power: despite the criticism made of the federal government, both spheres of government have to respect the

---

18 Hague and Chang (n 16) 834.

constitutional design and its division of power. Nevertheless, the government's focus on economic growth and its neglect of other political, social, and legal limitations set by the Constitution have not served to advance constitutionalism, a situation compounded by a lack of transparency, accountability, checks and balances, and equality of partnership between the federal and state governments. Some of these deficits may require a complete overhaul of the Constitution, with new political, economic, and institutional choices, while others may require scrutiny of the constitutional-legal framework in order to define the powers and function of regional states properly.

In the spirit of the latter, this study examines the FDRE Constitution to identify factors that may enhance the role of regional states in investment opportunities and activities by respecting the limitations set by the Constitution, making governmental institutions effective, and promoting constitutionalism, the latter being a normative ideal in terms of which the exercise of political authority is limited and constrained.[19]

3. Division of Powers and Functions

3.1 A Centralized Approach?

A constitutional division of power between the federal government and the states is the essence of federalism. The division results in powers that are exclusive to the centre and states respectively, albeit that the dividing line between the two levels is never entirely clear—concurrent and residual powers are thus common in federal constitutions. Accordingly, in article 50, the FDRE Constitution divides governmental functions between the federal government and the states, with each having their own legislative, executive, and judicial powers. Article 51 in turn contains a list of exclusive federal competences, while other such powers are distributed throughout the text of the Constitution.[20] The latter article provides that all residual powers (ie those which are neither exclusive to the federal government nor concurrent state–federal competences) are exclusively assigned to the regional states. Concurrent powers of the federal government and states can be found in different parts of the Constitution.

Some of the powers concurrently attributed to both levels of government relate to economic, social, and development matters. While the federal government has the power to 'formulate and implement the country's policies, strategies and plans in respect of overall economic, social and development matters',[21] the Constitution also explicitly authorizes the regional states to formulate and execute policies on regional economic, social, and development matters. The Constitution provides no further detail as to whether and to what extent federal laws give space for the state policies and laws to become effective—for instance, it is unclear how the federal investment commission can solely regulate and administer all investment activities in the country. Concurrency of power entails at least two consequences. First, federal laws and policies should serve as framework laws and leave enough space for the states to provide their own detailed laws; and, secondly, in the federal law-making

---

[19] For further discussion, see NW Barber, *The Principles of Constitutionalism* (OUP 2018).
[20] See eg arts 55(3), (4), (5), and (13).
[21] Art 51(2).

process there should be meaningful consultation with and participation by citizens and subnational governments.

In looking into the powers of the states mentioned throughout the Constitution, one may argue that the regions have significant functions except for fiscal matters. In this regard, many areas are not in the list of federal competences over which the states may exercise legislative power. These include issues that do not have extra-territorial effects. There is agreement, though, that the Constitution is generous to the regional states as far as matters pertaining to ethnic and cultural identity are concerned; in addition, its article 52 author-izes the regions to administer land and other natural resources.

In practice, however, the federal government has played a dominant role. It did make excessive use of its power to formulate policies on matters of social and economic devel-opment, with these policies and strategies being so detailed that they leave little room for regional action. Numerous empirical studies[22] found that this centralization of policy for-mulation stems from the ruling party's centralized structure and operations. The federal government's dominant role in policy-making has had visible impacts on regional and local governments. In this regard, Fiseha concludes that most of its policy papers 'originate[d]' as 'party documents', and, after being discussed by party leaders at the federal and state gov-ernment levels, were tabled for approval by Parliament and published as government policy papers.[23] This has been the process for more than two decades, and run contrary to the de-centralized and participatory federalism envisaged in the Constitution.

3.2 State Powers in Investment

A common feature of federations is, on the one hand, the existence of a powerful motive to be united for certain purposes, and, on the other, a well-established set of motives for au-tonomy in respect of other purposes. Accordingly, in most mature federations, the federal government is vested with those powers that are shared in common and which symbolize the people of the country as a whole, while constituent units retain powers considered vital for the full exercise of regional autonomy and self-governance. Such a combination of unity and diversity, shared rule and self-rule, epitomizes federalism, with the power of states re-flecting the dimension of self-rule. With this in mind, the section below discusses various investment-related state powers in Ethiopia.

3.2.1 Investment promotion

Promoting investment is often seen as one of the primary engines of an economy's growth; for the same reason, it is an issue of contention in federal arrangements because it is the major source of revenue for the central as well as subnational governments. Its effectiveness, though, rests on several factors, among the most important of which is diversifying invest-ment activity; more generally, they include 'a favourable macro-economic policy environ-ment, specific policies and institutions aimed at encouraging savings and attracting and directing investment to key sectors in the economy, thereby enhancing the contributions of

---

[22] See eg Fiseha (n 17); E Andreas, 'Ethnic Federalism: New Frontiers', First National Conference on Federalism, Conflict, and Peace Building Addis Ababa: Ministry of Federal Affairs (2003) 167; see also Tekeste (n 7).

[23] Fiseha (n 17).

investment to skills formation, technological change, competition and economic growth'.[24] As such, the question is whether promoting investment falls under the jurisdiction of the federal government, the states, or both the federal and state governments; if it is the latter, the mode of division or interaction between them should be spelt out explicitly.

In the FDRE Constitution, it is clear that formulating and executing policy that promotes foreign investment is assigned to the federal government.[25] Empowering the centre in this regard implies that promoting such investment is one of the areas where uniform laws are required for its regulation; further to this, what is required is a national strategy to encourage investment inflow to the country by making it an environment conducive to this. Mapping out all the necessary factors to attract foreign investment, and identifying policy responses to serve an effective investment promotion strategy, is the role of the federal government, as is often the case in federations.

In analysing the constitutional provision that refers specifically to 'formulating foreign investment policies and strategies', one should not jump to the conclusion that, by contrast, all domestic investment policies and strategies are left to the states. This has to be investigated in relation to other constitutional powers related to domestic or local investment. The law-making power of the federal government extends to aspects of domestic or local investment since it has the power 'to enact laws for the utilization and conservation of land and other natural resources, historical sites and objects'.[26] Furthermore, if domestic investment targets air, rail, waterways, and the utilization of rivers or lakes linking two or more states, the federal government again assumes responsibility for the development, administration, and regulation of these sectors.[27] The federal power that refers to 'regulating inter-state and foreign commerce'[28] may also involve dictating the local investment policies of the states.

Having looked at federal powers, there are two issues to be addressed. First, under articles 51(2) and (3) and 52(2)(c), both levels of government are respectively empowered 'to formulate and execute economic, social and development policies, strategies and plans'. There is obviously considerable overlap, or 'concurrency of power', but it is not clear what is exercised by the centre and what is left to the states. For instance, to what extent could the states formulate economic, social, and development policies? Federal experiences have shown that certain matters cannot be dealt with exhaustively by the centre; in such cases, states may have to take the initiative to come up with laws of their own in matters not addressed or covered by federal laws.

The second issue concerns the power to administer and follow up on the execution of federally designed policies.[29] The states are conferred with the power to execute 'land utilization and conservation law' issued by the federal parliament. Taking into account the policy directions from the centre, they are entitled to endorse implementation legislation; as such, federal powers cannot be enforced properly unless the states are willing or legally bound to cooperate with the centre.

---

[24] A Tesfaye, *State and Economic Development in Africa: The Case of Ethiopia* (Palgrave Macmillan 2017) vi.
[25] Art 51(4).
[26] Art 51(5).
[27] Art 51(9) and (11).
[28] Art 51(12). See also Solomon Negussie, *Fiscal Federalism in the Ethiopian Ethnic-based Federal System* (Wolf Legal Publishers 2008).
[29] Art 51(5) and 52(2)(d).

The analysis in the two scenarios above shows that there is constitutional space for regional states to design their own policies, regulations, and detailed implementation guidelines in line with the federal investment policy and framework legislations. Apart from ensuring timely allocation of land to investors, a regional government can play a role in monitoring the implementation of investment projects, giving policy input to federal institutions about local investment priorities, and collating, analysing, and disseminating information about investment opportunities in the regions. Various federal legal instruments dealing with investment should be activated to promote both domestic and foreign investment. However, it ought to be noted that an effective and efficient regulatory scheme in the area of investment is strongly linked to the availability of ethical and competent persons who serve in institutions governing investment.

3.2.2 Natural resource management

In exploiting natural resources such as minerals, oil, and gas and bringing them to market, the role of central and regional governments is immense. Before delving into determining the functions of each level of government, though, it is necessary to understand the framework provided by the FDRE Constitution. According to its article 40(3),

> The right to ownership of rural and urban land, as well as of all natural resources, is exclusively vested in the State and in the peoples of Ethiopia. Land is a common property of the nations, nationalities and peoples (NNP) of Ethiopia and shall not be subject to sale or to other means of exchange.[30]

The Constitution imposes a general obligation upon federal and state governments to hold land and other natural resources for the common benefit and development of the people.[31] Both levels of government also have the duty to protect the country's natural endowment,[32] utilize them for the common benefit and development of the people,[33] provide equal opportunities to improve their economic condition,[34] and ensure equitable distribution of national wealth among the people.[35] Yet these statements leave the legal regime governing the ownership and administration of land far from clear. It is open to debate as to how land is attributed to the state, on the one hand, and to each NNP, on the other.

Another point of argument is whether common ownership of land by the NNP and administration of land by each state imply different meanings. Land is neither subject to private ownership, nor subject to sale or some form of exchange, even though the particulars regarding utilization, administration, and the determination of the rights of rural

---

[30] This principle is the cornerstone of land policy in Ethiopia, but complications arise from constitutional phrasing that refers to the right as 'vested in the State and in the peoples of Ethiopia' and to land as 'a common property of the Nations, Nationalities and Peoples of Ethiopia'. The right to natural resources is also part and parcel of the right to self-determination, by virtue of which people are entitled to utilize their resources. Many scholars contend that while each group has a constitutional right to self-determination up to secession, what the right 'vested in the State and in the peoples of Ethiopia' implies remains subject to discussion. It should be noted too that the Constitution neither defines nor provides criteria to define which ethnic group is a nation, nationality, or people.

[31] Art 89(5).
[32] Art 92(1).
[33] Art 89(2).
[34] Art 41(8).
[35] Arts 41(8) and 89(2).

landholders, pastoralists, investors, and urban dwellers have significant implications for economic decision-making in general and for regulating investment in particular. For instance, how could regional governments make land available for investment unless they are clear in their minds about the right attributed to them and the economic benefit they derive from their role?[36]

The Constitution also addresses the division of power with respect to the management, utilization, and taxation of natural resources. It allocates the legislative and the executive power separately to the federal government and the states, respectively. However, to gain a picture of the power of states, one has to look at the constitutional allocation of taxation power (discussed in detail below). Under the Constitution, regional states have the power to enact laws pertaining to the collection of royalties for the use of forest resources (article 97(10)) and to income taxes, royalties, and land rentals on mining operations other than 'large-scale' ones (article 97(8)).

The Ethiopian Mining Law (Proclamation No 678/2010) divides mining activities into the artisanal, small-scale, and large-scale. Of the three types, regional governments have the power to license and control artisanal and small-scale mining, as well as the power to levy and collect royalties, income tax, and fees from them. According to the Constitution, royalties, income tax, and other charges to be paid by small-scale and artisanal mining are paid to the states based on state laws; however, holders of large-scale mining licences have to pay royalties, value-added tax (VAT), excise, and profit taxes based on federal laws. The federal government has the power to levy and collect revenue from these concurrent tax sources,[37] but has to share the revenue with states on a formula basis. Since states are the ultimate beneficiaries of these taxes, the assessment and sharing of revenue requires that states play a role in ensuring proper valuation of mining activities and their profits.

With regard to determining the regulatory jurisdiction of states, it has to be noted that natural resource management calls for strong collaboration between federal and regional governments. Irrespective of whether a mining operation is large- or small-scale, there are cases where similar mining activities are subject to different licences issued by the federal and regional mining authorities.[38] There are also concerns that inspections, supervisions, and control are not conducted effectively by federal and regional agencies. Although federal and regional licensing authorities are expected to 'ensure that mining operations are carried out by licenced investor, environmentally sustainable and are beneficial to the community in the mining areas, both agencies have serious capacity problems [in] discharg[ing] their responsibilities'.[39]

---

[36] Menberetsehai and Belachew argued that land is a common property of all NNP, which is distinguished from their exclusive task of land administration. However, the political rhetoric and the practice in Ethiopia do not seem to be in line with their argument. In fact, each NNP claims sole 'ownership' of land within its territory. See T Menberetsehai and M Belachew, 'Ethiopia's Constitutional Framework and Legal Institutions for Development' in F Cheru, C Cramer, and A Oqubay (eds), *Oxford Handbook of the Ethiopian Economy* (OUP 2019).

[37] The HoF has repeatedly asserted that the constitutional provision on concurrent power of taxation (art 98) was amended to give levying and collecting power to the federal government while guaranteeing the states' entitlement to share revenue. However, the amended text has not been published yet, and the validity of the current practice may be challenged by states.

[38] Interview with experts at the Amhara investment office, 8 February 2019.

[39] ibid.

3.2.3 Agriculture

The constitutional dispensation confers considerable autonomy on regional states in different matters, including the administration of land. According to articles 51(5) and 52(d) of the Constitution, the federal government retains legislative power over the conservation and utilization of land, whereas regional states administer it on the basis of federal laws. Regions may also enact laws provided these do not contradict federal laws—for instance, the Amhara regional state enacted the Rural Land Administration and Use Proclamation (No 133/2006), which was crafted in line with the federal law (specifically Proclamation No 456/2005).

In contrast to this constitutional design, however, the federal government had taken measures that recentralized the administration of land in regional states, the intention being to expedite approval of large-scale agricultural investments. Thus, instead of enabling the regions themselves to allocate agriculture, centralization resulted in land being administered on behalf of the states. Although the practice had been widely observed in the emerging lowland regions, there were certain cases too in the Oromia region that led to the federal agency allocating land for agricultural investment.[40]

As part of the adoption of Ethiopia's GTP,[41] large-scale agricultural investment was given strong emphasis in a bid to attract private individuals and companies, whether domestic or foreign. The plan was aimed at 'intensifying production of marketable farm products for domestic and export markets [and] thereby reduce the level of extreme poverty in Ethiopia'. Given that there was a rush to allocate farm land to foreign investors, the plan ultimately failed,[42] but even at its inception, concerns were raised about 'lack of adequate consultation with affected communities, lack of adequate environmental impact assessment, and lack of clarity about the communal land tenure system relating to such land deals'.[43] Another criticism of the large-scale agricultural investment envisaged in the GTP was that it failed to stimulate revenue flow to regions and local governments in the form of land use fees or sales or profit taxes. As the government later reported, there was failure on the part of the investors too: not only did they do little to contribute to agricultural productivity, but investors abused the financial system, with more that ETB 4 million in public loans written off as bad debts.[44]

In short, legal analysis and the record of experience show that the centralization of agricultural land administration contravened the Constitution, in terms of which such land should be administered autonomously by regional states, subject to the guidance of federal framework legislation. The practice instead clearly demonstrated that the rule of law was undermined by the centre's usurpation of state power.

---

[40] While the FDRE Constitution provides mechanisms whereby the federal government may delegate its mandate to regional states, it does not explicitly provide for delegating the mandates of regional states to the federal government. Even if one argues that delegation is possible, delegation was not sought at the time of the government decision.

[41] FDRE, GTP I (MoFED 2010).

[42] For a general assessment, see Dessalegn Rahmato, 'Large-Scale Land Investments Revisited' in D Rahmato and others (eds), *Reflections on Development in Ethiopia* (Forum for Social Studies 2014).

[43] Martha Belete and Zeray Yihdego, 'The Law and Policy of Foreign Investment Promotion and Protection in Ethiopia' in *The Ethiopian Yearbook of International Law* 1(1) (Springer 2017).

[44] The Development Bank reported in September 2018 that its non-performing loan reached 40 per cent.

3.2.4 Regional investment

In a discussion of the powers and functions of states, one of the issues is whether regional states can engage in investment activities by establishing enterprises. The establishment of state enterprises depends on the economic policy of the country, the roles of the private sector, and the financial capacity of regional governments. However, an examination of the constitutional provisions reveals that, as is the case with the federal government and 'federal public enterprises', a regional state may establish 'state public enterprises' and engage in investment or business activities in Ethiopia.[45] For instance, articles 97(1), (6), (7), and 98(1) of the Constitution envisage the establishment of enterprises by the federal government, the states, or jointly by the federal and state governments. Proclamation No 769/2012 defines the term 'enterprise' as an entity owned wholly or partially by the federal or regional government and established to engage in production, distribution, and service-rendering, or related economic activities, in the form of commerce.[46] The Commercial Registration and Business Licensing Proclamation[47] and the Trade Practice and Consumers' Protection Proclamation[48] likewise subcategorize public enterprises as federal or regional.

Despite the new Prime Minister's commitment to privatizing federal public enterprises fully or partially, establishing state enterprises has become one of the development and investment-promotion strategies adopted by some regional governments.[49] Investment through public–private partnership is another approach to boosting investment in the regions. Of course, regionally owned public enterprises could be established to facilitate balanced sub-regional development if the state is able to finance large development programmes. However, the existing federal investment laws and regulations, the tax regime, the commercial law, and relevant provisions dispersed in various statutes would have to be reviewed to take into account all issues pertaining to management, financing, accountability, and auditing of public enterprises. Furthermore, the distinction between public enterprises and endowments[50] and the separation between party and business should also be examined.

More widely, the importance of regional or federal public enterprises in the economy, as well as the efficiency of the private sector, has to be considered before public enterprises are established. Regional investments could focus on improving the quality of infrastructure for the private sector by introducing 'regional industrial zones' or 'investment corridors' with a view to enabling efficient provision of infrastructure, to managing interrelated industries properly, or facilitating incentive packages.[51] Above all, it has to be borne in mind that investment decisions by regional governments have a direct impact on the public. This is particularly so in cases involving expropriation, which may result in displacement of

---

[45] Art 96 of the FDRE Constitution also refers to revenue collected through taxes on federal public enterprises.

[46] However, the new investment law defines an enterprise as 'an undertaking established for profit-making' (art 2(1) of Investment Proclamation No 1180 /2020).

[47] Proclamation No 685/2010. There is no justification for why the new Trade Competition and Consumers Protection Proclamation No 813/2013, which repealed Proclamation No 685/2010, omitted the definition.

[48] Proclamation No 686/2010.

[49] Examples are the establishment of Abay Industrial Sh Co in Amhara and Gada Company in Oromia region.

[50] The so-called endowment companies affiliated to EPRDF (in particular TPLF's Efforts) had been a major causes of public discontent in general and complaints in the private sector in particular. Similar concerns had also been raised against Tiret companies, which are affiliated to Amhara regional state.

[51] See Proclamation No 769/2012 Art 2 (17); see also the regulatory functions provided in Industrial Parks Proclamation No 889/2015 and Regulation No 326/2014.

people, lack of adequate valuation and compensation packages, administrative inefficiency, or abuse of discretionary power.[52]

In regard to promoting investment in the regions, at least three issues should be addressed by the regional and federal governments. The first is to do with incentives, importation of goods, access to foreign currency, and related administrative matters.[53] The areas of investment eligible for incentives, the type and extent of entitlements of the incentive packages, and exemptions from custom duties and other dues are clearly defined in laws and regulations issued by the federal government.[54] However, the implementation of these laws in some regions affected investment activities due to reasons attributed to lack of clear implementation guidelines and due to corrupt practices. These kind of practices inherently impact upon the intended uniform application of laws in the country.

Secondly, the lack of transparency in the sharing of revenue collected through the concurrent power of taxation has compromised government accountability. The issue is discussed in detail below, but the practice so far has been regarded as a disincentive to investment promotion by regional governments. Informants argued that this is due to lack of clarity about the returns on investment that flow to regions and local communities; in turn, this is due to obscurity in the process of determining and transferring the revenue shared between the federal government and the regional states.[55]

Thirdly, the benefits of investment are often expected to accrue to local communities in the form of job opportunities, technology transfers, and other incidental benefits relating to ease of access to local products, services, and infrastructure. But these expectations are not sufficient to ensure a transfer of benefits from an investor to the local public: there should be an effective regulatory framework in this regard. The Ministry of Mines, Petroleum, and Natural Gas recently mentioned that it aims to introduce a law that forces mining companies to allocate 2 per cent of their profits to community development works.[56] The details are yet to be seen in respect of how the law is to be implemented and how the contribution is to be utilized. Nonetheless, there is a need to build a relationship between natural resource investment and the local community not only in terms of direct social or economic benefits but in terms of trust between the two. A report by the Ethiopian Extractive Industry Transparency Initiative (EEITI) has emphasized the need both to build relations with local communities and other stakeholders and to act responsibly. The report underscored that this 'is good for the country as it contributes to transparency, allows a full understanding of who is benefiting from exploitation of Ethiopia's resources, enhances governance and ultimately should contribute to increased foreign investment in the sector.'[57]

---

[52] For an analysis of rural or urban allocation and expropriation decisions, see Daniel W Ambaye, *Land Rights and Expropriation in Ethiopia* (Springer Thesis 2015).

[53] Fiscal and non-fiscal benefits are provided to investors under the Regulation (No 270/2012 and 312/2014) for investment incentives and investment areas reserved for domestic investors.

[54] It is obvious that the law-making procedure does not give space to regional governments to influence federal laws, given that under the Constitution such laws are passed only by the Lower House.

[55] The revenue-sharing mechanism determines the share of the regional governments, but regional governments for their part have not designed a sharing formula to determine the share of local governments.

[56] K Bekele, 'Ministry Aims at Introducing Local Tax' *Ethiopian Reporter Newspaper* (17 February 2018) Vol 23, No 1859.

[57] M Barron and T Law, 'Ethiopia's Beneficial Ownership Scoping Study' (2017) 5 <https://eiti.org/sites/defa ult/files/documents/170330_ethiopia_beneficial_ownership_scoping_study.pdf> accessed 20 April 2019. See also EITI, 'Ethiopia's Extractive Industries Transparency Initiative' (EITI, June 2018) <https://eiti.org/document/2017-eeiti-annual-progress-report> accessed 1 May 2019.

3.2.5 Environmental regulation

Global experience shows that environmental regulatory policies and laws are usually issued by central governments, while most of the responsibility for implementing them is delegated to or shared with regional and local governments.[58] As such, federal and regional (and sub-regional) institutions are responsible for regulating the environment.

Proclamation No 295/2002 for the establishment of environmental protection organs established the federal environmental protection authority, regional environmental agencies, and sectoral environmental units. The main objective of this law is to ensure that no individual or corporate investor commences the implementation of a project that requires an environmental impact assessment until the project has been approved by federal or regional environmental agencies. The environmental protection authority is responsible for formulating policies, strategies, laws, and standards to ensure the social and economic development activities of the country and for sustainably enhancing human welfare and the safety of the environment.[59] The law requires regional states to establish their own agencies for coordinating the formulation, implementation, review, and revision of regional conservation strategies and for conducting environmental monitoring, protection, and regulation.[60] Regional agencies are also responsible for evaluating environmental impact assessment reports on projects that are licensed, executed, or supervised by regional states, and for auditing and regulating the implementation of such projects. In addition, regional states may establish sectoral environmental units at regional sector-office level for coordination and follow-up of activities in different sectors.

4. Investment and Federal–State Relations

As we saw in the preceding section, there are gaps in the provisions of the Constitution that should be addressed through federal–state relations. Even in cases of clarity of division of power, there are also various aspects of interactions beginning with the implementation of federal investment laws at state level and proceeding to federal-level regulation of regional investment. Above all, be it in the fulfilment of responsibilities or in managing inter-jurisdictional differences, federal–state relations are a vital component of federal systems. This is particularly evident in federations where the constituent units of government deliver on many of the federally enacted laws and policies; where there is joint responsibility in functional areas; where there is a need for technical or knowledge support; or where states rely heavily on revenue-sharing or federally transferred grants.[61]

While intergovernmental relations (commonly known as IGR) are a fact of life in federations, the nature of these relationships varies considerably. As in many of the examples above, their importance can be considered from the perspective of efficiency and effectiveness. Thus, where the relationship between the federal and state governments is harmonious, the effectiveness of the relationship is taken for granted; when disagreements

---

[58] MR Shannon, 'Federalism and Local Environmental Regulation' (2015) 48 UC Davis Law Review 1111.

[59] Proclamation No 295/2002, art 6.

[60] ibid art 15.

[61] Peter Meekison, 'Intergovernmental Relations in Federal Countries' (Forum of Federations 2007). For a comparative assessment of IGR, see J Poirier, C Saunders, and J Kincaid (eds), *Intergovernmental Relations in Federal Systems: Comparative Structures and Dynamics* (Forum of Federations, OUP 2015).

arise, the reality of the relationship may differ from what it is imagined or expected to be. Common sources of intergovernmental disagreement include disputes over jurisdiction, disagreements relating to revenue-sharing mechanisms, on causes of fiscal imbalances, and disputes on natural resource revenues.[62] Disputes also arise over federal spending in regard to which region benefits the most from it, as they do as well when the absence of collaboration in matters of common concern results in one or the other level of government taking unilateral action. For regional states, the relations can be a forum for bargaining with the federal government on matters of common interest; if they are conducted on the basis of a sense of partnership between the two governments, then the relations become a forum for attaining common goals through cooperation.[63]

In the Ethiopian context, preliminary researches have shown that most of the activities that could be regarded as IGR have taken place behind closed doors and through party channels inappropriately used as instruments of centralization.[64] The centralization was manifested through unilateral policy initiative in commonly shared areas. Some forums of interactions had also served as a means to use it as a 'command and control' approach. IGR is becoming ever more important given the likelihood of different political parties controlling different spheres of government following the upcoming election in 2021.

If one anticipates a post-election scenario with different political actors, there is a need for an urgent action to design policies, institutions, and accountability mechanisms to regulate vertical as well as horizontal relations for a meaningful federal governance. This is especially so in the case of investment regulation (both foreign and domestic), since it is difficult for the federal government to establish agencies in each and every territory where investments are in operation. Furthermore, according to the Constitution, land and natural resources have to be administered by the states. How, then, can a state administer land and undertake other natural resource management on the basis of federal laws without being able to interact satisfactorily with the relevant federal agencies? IGR is a missing link in investment administration.

It is important to note that the need for a strong collaboration between federal and regional governments to address investment issues appears to have been heeded in the form of the new Investment Proclamation No 1180/2020, which came into effect on 2 April 2020. The Proclamation recognized the importance of IGR to tackle issues of administration of investment in a cooperative and coordinated approach between the federal government and regional states. The proclamation establishes an Investment Council whose members are the prime minister and presidents of regional states and to be chaired by the former. It is commendable that the new proclamation gives emphasis to IGR as an important forum to deliberate on and put forward recommended solutions to issues of investment administration and resolve hindrances to investment promotion in the country.

The establishment of the federal government and regional states investment council[65] as one of Ethiopia's investment administration organs is commendable; however, its effectiveness is yet to be seen since the council did not start its formal meeting until a year after the coming into effect of the proclamation. Nonetheless, the council as an IGR forum can

---

[62] Meekison (n 61).

[63] Assefa Fiseha, 'The System of Intergovernmental Relations (IGR) in Ethiopia: In Search of Institutions and Guidelines' (2009) 23(1) Journal of Ethiopian Law 96.

[64] ibid.

[65] See arts 44–49 of the new Investment Proclamation No 1180/2020.

be expected to address various investment-related issues. For instance, with respect to land administration, the Federal Rural Land Administration and Use Proclamation expects regional governments to provide detail in their laws to control the degradation of land and the environment.[66] Similarly, in order for a mining company to pay royalties, there should be clarity as to who assesses the company's production. Further, there are issues as to who monitors an environmental impact of a mining activity, and as to who manages disputes between a mining company and local communities. To ensure that investors have a long-term commitment to a region, the economic constraints on them have to be identified and addressed through federal–state relations within the framework of the investment council. Some of these constraints may concern access to foreign currency, tax benefits, access to local or international market, and ensuring transparency and accountability of governance at federal and local levels. Furthermore, the powers and duties of the federal investment commission and other government agencies can not been meaningfully implemented in the absence of well-structured IGR between federal and regional investment commissions and other government agencies.[67] Thus, IGR may serve as a forum to forge close cooperation between the federal government and state investment administration organs 'with a view to creating a uniform, coordinated and efficient national investment administration system'.[68]

5. Investment and Fiscal Policy

Promoting investment is primarily intended to attract domestic and foreign capital, increase employment opportunities, boost public revenue, and improve socio-economic services, among other things. It is through investment that a government can generate revenue and spend it on expanded provision of socio-economic services; in turn, government spending is itself expected to create jobs, increase individual income, and fuel economic growth. Therefore, it is important to understand how investment is intertwined with the Ethiopian fiscal system. In general, fiscal federalism[69] in Ethiopia is concerned with the distribution of expenditure responsibilities, the allocation of taxation power, intergovernmental transfers for adjusting fiscal imbalances, the management of regional borrowing, and institutional mechanisms for maintaining fiscal relations between different levels of government.

The division of taxation power is a principal aspect of the Constitution that provides the legal foundation for the Ethiopian federation. The tax power is divided into three categories, namely 'the federal power of taxation',[70] 'the state power of taxation',[71] and 'concurrent

---

[66] See Rural Land Administration and Use Proclamation No 456/2005.

[67] See eg the powers and duties of states in the provision of land for investment and investment-related information under arts 51 and 52 of Investment Proclamation No 1180/202.

[68] See art 50(1) of the new Investment Proclamation No 1180/2020.

[69] 'Fiscal federalism' concerns the fiscal implications of a decentralized system of multilevel government.

[70] Federal government tax sources (art 96) include customs duties, taxes, and other charges on imports and exports; personal income tax on employees of the federal government and international organizations; personal income tax, profit tax, sales, and excise taxes on enterprises owned by the federal government; taxes on income from national lotteries and other games of chance; taxes on the income of air, rail, and sea transport services; tax on rental of houses and properties owned by the federal government; federal stamp duties and tax on monopolies; and collecting fees and charges related to licences issued and services rendered by the federal government.

[71] The revenue sources allocated to the states (art 97) include personal income tax collected from employees of the state and private enterprises; rural land use fee, and tax on income of private farmers and cooperative associations; profit and sales tax on individual traders; tax on income from inland water transportation; taxes on income

power of taxation.[72] The Constitution also prescribes the conditions under which regional governments may acquire revenue through grant subsidies. In terms of the assignment of taxation, exclusive revenue sources are allocated to each level of government, whereas concurrent sources of revenue are jointly owned. Nevertheless, although the title of article 98 of the Constitution appears to give both levels of government access to the same tax base or to apply a kind of 'piggyback' taxation, in practice the regional states retain only the right to share revenue levied and collected by the federal government.[73]

When it comes to fiscal imbalances, the extent of vertical as well as horizontal imbalance is considerable in Ethiopia. The reason is that major revenue sources are assigned to the centre; in the case of the states, they have widely divergent revenue-raising capacity. To illustrate the point, in the 2015/16 fiscal year the federal government collected the lion's share of tax revenue, with the nine regional states and two chartered cities accounting for only 25 per cent of the total. Of the latter proportion, the largest share was collected by Addis Ababa (11.5 per cent of the total), followed by Oromia (4.57 per cent), Amhara (2.71 per cent), and Southern Nations, Nationalities, and Peoples (SNNP) (2.37 per cent), with the remaining six regional States and Dire Dawa city administration accounting for less than 4 per cent of total tax revenue.[74]

The tax revenue received by regional states is insufficient to meet their expenditure needs, with the result that all of the subnational governments—with the exception of Addis Ababa city administration—rely on central government transfers to cover the bulk of their spending. For example, again in 2015/16, federal subsidies to regions accounted for 49 per cent of federal total revenue and 59 per cent of federal tax revenues. In that year, Tigray, Amhara, Oromia, and SNNP regional states covered about 30 to 40 per cent of their expenditure with local revenues, with the remaining states relying to a greater extent on central government transfers.[75]

5.1 Taxing Investment

As mentioned, one of the major factors in political unrest in Ethiopia is the lack of proportionality in the benefits that accrue to local people from investment taxation. It is thus important to analyse the types of taxes that exist and how they relate to investment. Accordingly, in this section we examine the assignment of taxation and the levying,

---

derived from rent of houses and other properties in the states; personal income tax, profit, sales, and excise taxes on enterprises owned by the states; income tax, royalties, and rent of land levied on small- and medium-scale mining activities; royalties for use of forest resources; and charges and fees on licences and services issued by state governments.

[72] Types of taxes and sources listed under the 'concurrent power' of taxation (art 98) include profit, sales, excise, and personal income taxes levied on enterprises jointly established by the federal and state governments; profit, sales, and excise taxes on companies, and tax on dividends due to shareholders; profit tax and royalties on large-scale mining and all petroleum and gas operations.

[73] Formulas for allocating grants and revenue-sharing are decided by the second chamber, the House of Federation.

[74] Computations from data in the 2015/16 fiscal year report of the Ministry of Finance and Economic Cooperation.

[75] ibid.

administration, collection, and distribution of revenue generated from investment and consider how the system affects investment promotion in regional states.

Investors in Ethiopia are classified as sole entrepreneurs, companies (foreign or domestic), or public enterprises, be they federal enterprises, state enterprises, or enterprises jointly established by federal and state governments. In general, the assignment of taxation powers goes with the nature of the tax sources and tax bases. Tax sources are specified according to type of ownership and the nature of business organizations, while tax bases are specified by the type of taxes collected (direct, indirect, payroll, and the like). Accordingly, excises and taxes on the income, profit, and sales of individual traders are assigned to regional states in terms of article 97 of the Constitutions; taxes levied on enterprises owned by the federal government or states are assigned respectively to the federal government or the states; and taxes levied on companies are joint federal and state revenue subject to 'concurrent taxation'. The revenue-sharing scheme allows regional states to access a specific share of revenue derived from concurrent taxes levied and collected by the federal government.

5.2 Revenue-Sharing Formula

Taxes levied on investment or business activities in different parts of the country are subject primarily to concurrent taxation (discussed above). As such, the way in which the revenue collected from concurrent taxes is divided has to be addressed so that a regional government can promote investment in its jurisdiction and thereby maximize its share of investment returns.

While the definition of power of taxation has been dealt with in the above provisions, the division of revenue collected from concurrent sources is carried out in accordance with article 62(7) of the Constitution. In this regard, the House of Federation (HoF), the upper house of Ethiopia's federal parliament, prepared a formula for sharing the concurrent revenue based on a derivation principle.[76] The contents of the formula adopted by the HoF[77] are all relevant to understand, to review the existing arrangement, to determine the share of each regional state, and to ensure transparency with the active involvement of regions. The formula specifies the shares of federal and state governments from tax sources and types as set out in Table 12.1.

The joint taxes are broadly categorized in the formula document into direct tax, indirect tax, and royalties. The sharing arrangement that was effective from 2003–19 divided revenue from concurrent taxes between the federal and regional governments respectively as follows: direct taxes from companies in the proportion of 50:50, and indirect taxes in the proportion of 70:30; similarly, direct taxes from large-scale mining and petroleum operations are divided 50:50, while royalties are divided in the proportion of 60:40.[78] As Table 12.1 indicates in its last column, a new sharing arrangement was implemented for five years beginning in the 2020/21 fiscal year. The HoF revised the original formula in a move to increase fiscal capacity and maximize the revenue return from investment to regional

---

[76] However, it did not clarify how the derivative principle is compatible with the country's existing tax system.

[77] In Regulation No 28/2002, issued by the Council of Ministers, and Directives No 22/2001, issued by the Ministry of Revenue.

[78] Although the formula was prepared in 1996, the decision to put it into effect was made by the HoF on 13 March 2003 (Minutes of the 2nd ordinary meeting of the HoF).

Table 12.1 Joint revenue distribution formula

Tax sources	Types of tax	2003 Share of federal and regional governments[a]	New formula effective in 2020/21 fiscal year[b]
1. Enterprises jointly established by the federal and regional governments	a. Profit taxes	Share relates to capital contribution	Share as per contributions of capital (75%) and derivation for hosts (25%)
	b. Personal income tax from employees	50% to the federal government and 50% to states	75% to the particular hosting region and 25% to federal government
	c. ales tax (VAT), service and excise taxes	70% to the federal government and 30% to states	50% to federal and 50% to all regions
2. Private companies (corporations)	a. Profit tax	50% to the federal and 50% to states	50% to all hosting states where the enterprises have branches, and 50% to federal government
	b. ales tax (VAT), service and excise taxes	70% to the federal government and 30% to states	50% to federal and 50% to all regions on equalization basis
	c. Taxes from dividends due to shareholders	50% to the federal government and 50% to states	50% to all hosting states where the enterprises have branches, and 50% to federal government
3. Large-scale mining and petroleum and gas operations	a. Profit tax	50% to the federal government and 50% to states	50% to producing regional states and 50% federal
	b. Royalties	60% to federal government and 40% to states	20% to producing region; 10% to producing local government; 30% to the federal government; 40% to all non-producing regions on equalization basis

Source: House of Federation
[a] Formula effective since 2003.
[b] The new formula adopted by the HoF to be effective starting 2020/21 fiscal year.

governments. This decision can be seen as reflecting the regions' increasing assertiveness at the federal level.

5.3 Administration of Concurrent Taxes

Self-evidently, effective implementation of revenue-sharing depends on the institutions responsible for the administration, allocation, and disbursement of joint revenue. The federal bodies tasked with this responsibility are the Ministry of Finance and Economic Development and the Ministry of Revenue (the latter recently took over this responsibility from the Ethiopian Revenue and Customs Authority). The administration of joint taxes raises several concerns. Should regional institutions also collect the revenue? Is it important to determine the costs of administration by federal or regional tax authority? Which institution should audit the administration and disbursement of the proceeds from such tax sources? How and by whom should data about joint revenues be collected, organized, analysed, and made available to concerned bodies? What are the mechanisms for ensuring transparency in the administration, collection, and disbursement of concurrent taxes? How do federal and state institutions interact and collaborate with each other?

Answering these questions paves the way to determining the total revenue generated from investment or business activities on a state-by-state basis. But, it is not easy for regional governments to get full and correct information about concurrent taxes such as VAT.[79] In addition, there is lack of clarity about whether the disbursement of revenue has been on the basis of the derivative or equity principle.[80] Although the federal government claims efficiency in the administration of concurrent taxes uniformly, weaknesses have been observed in the administration of these taxes. In sum, from the perspective of regional governments, federal tax administration of shared taxes is characterized by uncertainty and a lack of transparency, both of which are contrary to the rule of law. The above issues were raised and included as one of the reform agenda during the national workshop organized by the HoF to discuss the revision of the revenue sharing formula in 2019.

6. Conclusion and Recommendations

Ethiopia is again in a political transition. The factors that led to this transition and the country's unrest relate to lack of good governance and an apparent departure from constitutionalism and the rule of law. Arguably, the absence of constitutionalism has caused instability in that the values and benefits of the federal system have not been fairly realized— this is particularly the case in the field of the economy and investment, as the present study demonstrates. The chapter has examined the application of the constitutional principle of the division of powers between the centre and the regions, in the course of which it

---

[79] For further details, see Solomon Negussie, 'Intergovernmental Fiscal Arrangement in Ethiopia: Some Basic Issues' in Assefa Fiseha and Asnake Kefale (eds), *Federalism and Local Government in Ethiopia* (AAU Center for Federal Studies 2015)

[80] By derivate principle is meant that each state receives a share based on the amount of revenue collected in that specific state. An equity principle entitles every state a share of revenue irrespective of the amount of revenue collected in a particular state.

considered issues to do with making governments effective in discharging their responsibilities. The study has highlighted Ethiopia's lack of transparency, accountability, and rule of law. Furthermore, it argued that constitutional supremacy has not been enforced effectively against the centre. This is partly due to the ambiguity of the constitutional provisions and partly due to the centre's unconstitutional usurpation of state powers.

On the basis of these findings, several legal interventions and policy measures are recommended above under section 3.2 in order to strengthen the role that regional governments can play in building regional investment. First, there is a need for a better clarity of the legal framework that defines states' jurisdiction. The applicable federal and state constitutions stipulate that investment laws, policies, and strategies are developed by the federal government. Federal laws serve primarily as a framework for promoting investment in regional states, but the powers and functions of the Federal Investment Commission cannot be exercised meaningfully without the involvement of relevant regional institutions and without reference to local and regional policies and implementation guidelines.[81] In regard to this, regional states have the mandate to set guidelines for the implementation of federal laws and to provide policy choices and guidelines for the allocation of land to investors.[82] Further policy direction can be provided for specific investment sectors and areas of attraction; similarly, policy direction can be provided in regard to the nature of benefits to local communities in the region as well as the nature of the promotional activities that a regional government carries out. These are some of the issues that the newly introduced Investment Council may grapple with.

Secondly, clarity is needed on the governance aspects relating to compensation granted to people displaced due to expropriation of land, and incentive packages to investors. What is clear is that the allocation of urban or rural land for foreign or domestic investment falls under the jurisdiction of the regional state. This process of allocation of land will have its own impact on the relationship between investment projects and local communities (in particular) and on overall investment governance (in general). Ethiopia's lack of transparency and accountability in investment governance, and its top-down, centralized approach, have contributed to public resentment and political unrest. Though land-related legislation falls under the mandate of the federal government, important policy choices are left to the states, as is the implementation of such legislation. Accordingly, states have to examine their laws governing expropriation, valuation, and compensation, examine their resettlement and rehabilitation programmes for managing displaced persons, and consider the impact of land allocation on sustainable development in the region. Similarly, they have to ensure peace and security to investment activities in the regions and build institutions to promote transparency and accountability within their jurisdictions.

Thirdly, revenue-sharing and fiscal transparency require attention. Companies engaged in foreign or domestic investment activities are expected to be the major sources of state revenue collected through states' concurrent taxing power. Therefore, although the HoF is assumed to protect states, there should be adequate links between federal institutions engaged in administering concurrent taxes and institutions of the regional government

---

[81] See Investment Proclamation No 769/2012, part 7; FDRE Constitution, art 52(2)(c).

[82] FDRE Constitution, art 52(2)(d), Investment Proclamation No 769/2012, Industrial Park Proclamation No 886/2015, and Agricultural Investment Proclamations all provide for the allocation of land by subnational governments.

concerning the administration and sharing of revenue. Regional states should have a role in setting clear guidelines on the collection and reporting of revenue generated from concurrent tax sources such as VAT, profit tax, royalties, and excises levied on companies. This requires analysing the legal framework governing the sharing of revenue generated under the concurrent power of taxation.

Currently, there are no laws or guidelines that determine the share of local governments (*woredas*) from all concurrent taxes except a royalty of 10 per cent which has been proposed in the new HoF revenue-sharing formula. As such, legal, institutional, and administrative reforms should be undertaken to ensure transparency and accountability in determining the respective shares of local, regional, and federal governments. Determining the share due to local governments would improve the relationships between local communities and investors, and, in the case of mining investments, the share could be used in rehabilitating environmental damage.

Fourthly, federal-state relations should be improved. Investment in Ethiopia is governed primarily by federal laws, but—particularly in mining, manufacturing, and large-scale agriculture—it depends on the implementation power of the states. It also necessitates strong interaction between levels of government to ensure timely allocation of land as well as proper follow-up, monitoring, and supervision of investment activities. Moreover, regional states need to address various gaps in federal laws, a situation that requires effective IGR. IGR is also important for ensuring the transparency and equitability of federal spending. The federal government is expected to spend its resources partly to address regional disparities and partly to promote investment in the regions, but the process of allocating federal spending becomes a source of dispute when certain regions manoeuvre federal power to maximize benefits to investments in their territories in terms of availing infrastructure, foreign currency, and tax benefits. Consequently, IGR forums for policy initiation, law-making, executive interaction, and federal spending programmes should be reviewed in order to enhance their equitability in promoting regional investment.

Bibliography

Anderson G, *Federalism: An Introduction* (Forum of Federations, OUP 2008)

Andreas E, 'Ethnic Federalism: New Frontiers' *First National Conference on Federalism, Conflict, and Peace Building* Addis Ababa: Ministry of Federal Affairs (2003)

Bagcht AK, 'The Past and the Future of the Developmental State' 2000 11(2) Journal of World-Systems Research 398

Barber NW, *The Principles of Constitutionalism* (OUP 2018)

Barron M and Law T, 'Ethiopia's Beneficial Ownership Scoping Study' (2017) <https://eiti.org/sites/default/files/documents/170330_ethiopia_beneficial_ownership_scoping_study.pdf> accessed 20 April 2019

Bekele K, 'Ministry Aims at Introducing Local Tax', *Ethiopian Reporter Newspaper* (17 February 2018) Vol 23, No 1859

Bizuayehu D and Mulu F, 'Incorporating "Democratic Developmental State Ideology" into Ethiopia's Ethnic Federalism—A Contradiction?' (2017) 6(1) Üniversitepark Bulletin 109

Central Statistical Authority, '2007 Population and Housing Census of Ethiopia' (CSA 2012) in Cheru F, Cramer C, and Oqubay A (eds), *Oxford Handbook of the Ethiopian Economy* (OUP 2019)

Clapham C, 'The Political Economy of Ethiopia from the Imperial Period to the Present' in Cheru F, Cramer C, and Oqubay A (eds), *Oxford Handbook of the Ethiopian Economy* (OUP 2019)

Daniel WA, *Land Rights and Expropriation in Ethiopia* (Springer Thesis 2015)

De Villiers B and Sindane J, 'Cooperative Government: The Oil of the Engine' (Policy Paper No 6 KAS, SA 2011)

Edigheji O, *Constructing a Developmental State in South Africa: Potentials and Challenges* (Human Sciences Research Council 2010)

EITI, 'Ethiopia's Extractive Industries Transparency Initiative' *EITI* (June 2018) <https://eiti.org/document/2017-eeiti-annual-progress-report> accessed 1 May 2019

Ethiopian Investment Commission, 'Ethiopian Investment Report 2017' (2017)

Fessha Y, *Ethnic Diversity and Federalism: Constitution-Making in South Africa and Ethiopia* (Ashgate 2010)

Fiseha A, 'Ethiopia's Experiment in Accommodating Diversity: 20 Years' Balance Sheet', (2012) 22(4) Regional & Federal Studies 435

Fiseha A, 'The System of Intergovernmental Relations (IGR) in Ethiopia: In Search of Institutions and Guidelines' (2009) 23(1) Journal of Ethiopian Law 96

Fiseha A, Ethiopia—Development with or without Freedom?' in Brems E, Van der Beken C, and Yimer SA (eds), *Human Rights and Development: Legal Perspectives from and for Ethiopia* (Brill Nijhoff 2015)

Fiseha A and Fiseha HG, 'The Interface between Federalism and Development in Ethiopia' in Cheru F, Cramer C, and Oqubay A (eds), *Oxford Handbook of the Ethiopian Economy* (OUP 2019)

Government Communication Office, 'Ethiopia Country Report 2012' (2012)

Hague J and Chang H, 'The Concept of a "Developmental State" in Ethiopia' in Cheru F, Cramer C, and Oqubay A (eds), *Oxford Handbook of the Ethiopian Economy* (OUP 2019)

Hailu MB and Yihdego Z, 'The Law and Policy of Foreign Investment Promotion and Protection in Ethiopia' in Z. Yihdego (ed.), *The Ethiopian Yearbook of International Law* 1(1) (Springer 2017)

Jebena BA, 'Ethnic Federalism and Democratic Developmental State in Ethiopia: Some Points of Contradiction' (2015) 3(7) International Journal of Political Science and Development 291

Meekison P, 'Intergovernmental Relations in Federal Countries' (Forum of Federations 2007)

Menberetsehai T and Belachew M, 'Ethiopia's Constitutional Framework and Legal Institutions for Development' in Cheru F, Cramer C, and Oqubay A (eds), *Oxford Handbook of the Ethiopian Economy* (OUP 2019)

Ministry of Finance and Economic Development (MoFED), 'Growth and Transformation Plan (GTP) I, Ethiopia' (2010)

Ministry of Finance and Economic Development (MoFED), 'Ethiopia's Progress towards Eradicating Poverty: An Interim Report on Poverty Analysis Study 2010/11' (2012)

Negussie S, 'Intergovernmental Fiscal Arrangement in Ethiopia: Some Basic Issues' in Assefa Fiseha and Asnake Kefale (eds), *Federalism and Local Government in Ethiopia* (AAU Center for Federal Studies, 2015)

Negussie S, *Fiscal Federalism in the Ethiopian Ethnic-Based Federal System* (Wolf Legal Publishers 2008)

Oqubay A., *Made in Africa: Industrial Policy in Ethiopia* (OUP 2015)

Poirier J, Saunders C, and Kincaid J (eds), *Intergovernmental Relations in Federal Systems: Comparative Structures and Dynamics* (Forum of Federations, OUP 2015)

Rahmato D, 'Large-Scale Land Investments Revisited' in Rahmato D and others (eds), *Reflections on Development in Ethiopia* (Forum for Social Studies 2014)

Shannon MR, 'Federalism and Local Environmental Regulation' (2015) 48 UC Davis Law Review 1111

Takagi Y and others (eds), *Developmental State Building: The Politics of Emerging Economies* (Economy State and International Policy Studies, Springer open, 2019)

Tekeste A, 'Fiscal Resource Allocation and Inclusive Development in Federal Ethiopia' (June 2018) Paper presented at the Symposium on Federalism and Development in Ethiopia, Addis Ababa

Tesfaye A, *State and Economic Development in Africa: The Case of Ethiopia* (Palgrave Macmillan 2017)

UNCTAD, *World Investment Report 2018: Investment and New Industrial Policies* (United Nations 2018) <https://unctad.org/en/publicationsLibrary/wir2018_en.pdf> accessed 10 April 2019

World Bank, 'Ethiopia towards the Competitive Frontier Strategies for Improving Ethiopia's Investment Climate: Finance and Private Sector Development' (2009) Africa Region Report No 48472-ET

World Bank, 'Policy and Legislative Options Report Ethiopia Mining Sector Development' (2016) Report No 7175163

World Bank, 'Ethiopia Country Overview' (World Bank n.d.) <http://bit.ly/3bp9HUA> accessed 30 March 2019

Zemenu Y, 'The Developmental State and Ethnic Federalism in Ethiopia: Issues to Worry about' (2017) 1 Hawassa University Journal of Law 1

Zenawi M, 'African Development: Dead Ends and New Beginnings' (n.d.) <http://www.ethiopiantr easures.co.uk/meleszenawi/pdf/zenawi_dead_ends_and_new_beginnings.pdf>   accessed   10 January 2015

PART V

IMPACT OF GLOBALIZATION ON THE ECONOMY AND CONSTITUTIONALISM

13

Taming the Spectre of Unsustainable Public Debt in Africa

A Heightened Role for Constitutions

Adem Kassie Abebe

1. Introduction

In June 2019, the Constitutional Council of Mozambique invalidated a government guarantee worth hundreds of millions of euros over a loan raised by a state-owned tuna-fishing company.[1] The case was submitted to the Council by a non-governmental organization that seeks to promote public financial transparency and which challenged the secrecy in the raising of the loan, along with other legal and constitutional violations. The Council found in particular that the absence of parliamentary approval of the guarantee and the failure to register it as part of the approved budget violated the Mozambican constitution. Although Mozambique continued a debt-restructuring process after the decision,[2] and the government confirmed that it would honour its international obligations regarding the debt,[3] the decision established a critical precedent that constitutional regulations on public debt are important, binding, and legally enforceable.

Constitutional regulation provides a useful control on debt. Indeed, the Zambian government, one of the most indebted in Africa,[4] pursued a failed constitutional amendment that would have weakened the oversight role of Parliament in the debt acquisition process.[5] Had the amendment succeeded, the government would have had a free hand potentially to resort to cumbersome commercial loans without need for parliamentary approval, as

---

[1] Borges Nhamire and Mathew Hill, 'Mozambique Nullifies State Guarantee on Loan Linked to Eurobonds' *Bloomberg* (5 June 2019) <http://www.bloomberg.com/news/articles/2019-06-05/mozambique-nullifies-state-guarantee-on-loan-linked-to-eurobond> accessed 4 December 2019.

[2] 'Mozambique to Continue Debt Restructuring Talks Despite "Tuna Bond" Court Ruling' *Club of Mozambique* (12 September 2019) <https://clubofmozambique.com/news/mozambique-to-continue-debt-restructuring-talks-despite-tuna-bond-court-ruling-141826/> accessed 4 December 2019.

[3] Catarina Demony, 'Mozambique Committed to International Law after "Tuna Bond" Ruling' *Reuters* (4 July 2019) <https://af.reuters.com/article/investingNews/idAFKCN1TZ0MN-OZABS> accessed 4 December 2019.

[4] Siphilisiwe Ncube, 'Zambia Needs Strong Fiscal Intervention—ActionAid' *News Diggers* (27 November 2019) <https://diggers.news/local/2019/11/27/zambia-needs-strong-fiscal-intervention-actionaid/> accessed 4 December 2019.

[5] Cephas Lumina, 'Zambia's Proposed Constitutional Amendments: Sowing the Seeds of Crisis?' *ConstitutionNet* (16 September 2019) <http://constitutionnet.org/news/zambias-proposed-constitutional-amendments-sowing-seeds-crisis> accessed 4 December 2019. The proposed amendment was defeated in October 2020—Kizzi Asala, 'Zambian President's Bid to Amend Constitution Fails' *Africa News* (30 October 2020) <https://www.africanews.com/2020/10/30/zambia-s-ruling-party-s-controversial-bid-to-pass-bill-10-fails//> accessed 6 November 2020.

Adem Kassie Abebe, *Taming the Spectre of Unsustainable Public Debt in Africa* In: *Constitutionalism and the Economy in Africa*. Edited by: Charles M Fombad and Nico Steytler, Oxford University Press. © Adem Kassie Abebe 2022. DOI: 10.1093/oso/9780192886439.003.0015

traditional multilateral institutions offering concessional loans are reluctant to provide more funding due to already stressful debt levels.[6]

This chapter explores the importance of constitutional regulation of public debt in Africa at a time when the debt levels of African countries are rising and concerns abound over their long-term impact on the economy and even sovereignty of African countries. As at May 2020, African countries owed almost half a trillion US dollars to foreign official and commercial creditors.[7] In particular, due to the COVID-19 pandemic, African countries have been forced to take in even more debt to tackle its horrific impact on health and livelihood, ballooning already high levels of debt while their economies shrink and tax revenues drop, crippling their ability to pay mature debts.[8] The COVID-19 pandemic arrived at a time when African countries were already paying more in interest on their debts than they allocated to their dilapidated health sectors.[9] Constitutions can play an important role in determining key aspects of the debt process, such as the authority to borrow, outlining the objectives of public loans, and enhancing transparency and democratic accountability in the debt acquisition, management, and repayment process.

Accordingly, section 13.2 provides a brief discussion of public debt generally and the increasing role of constitutions in regulating public debt. Sections 13.3 and 13.4 consider the impact of debt on the economy and on democracy, respectively, while section 13.5 argues that constitutions should play a critical role in managing and regulating debt: at a minimum, they can guarantee transparency and oversight procedures, which, if accompanied with robust enforcement mechanisms, including efforts by opposition groups and non-state actors to seek judicial and political accountability, can go a long way in laying the groundwork to tame the spectre of unsustainable debt. Section 13.6 provides examples of the constitutional regulation of debt in African constitutions. Section 13.7 concludes the chapter.

2. Growing Debt Levels in Africa

Public debt, alongside external assistance, is a principal tool to finance budget and foreign currency deficits, undertake long-term development projects, and tackle short-term fluctuations in economic performance due to a slump in commodity prices and emergency expenditure. States may borrow from internal as well as external sources.[10] In addition to increasingly borrowing from commercial banks and loans raised through bonds, the main sources of external debt in Africa, which vary from country to country, include bilateral loans from other states, notably China, which is owed more than half of the state-to-state

---

[6] 'Zambia's Path Very Narrow—Outlook Already Subdued' *The Mast* (25 November 2019) <http://www.themas tonline.com/2019/11/25/zambias-path-very-narrow-outlook-already-subdued-imf/> accessed 4 December 2019.

[7] Danny Bradlow, 'Vultures, Doves and African Debt: Here's a Way out' *The Conversation* (5 May 2020) <https://theconversation.com/vultures-doves-and-african-debt-heres-a-way-out-137643> accessed 16 May 2020. The figure does not include debts from internal sources. Moreover, not all debts are officially declared, so the actual level may be higher.

[8] 'African Governments Face a Wall of Debt Repayments' *The Economist* (6 June 2020) <http://www.econom ist.com/middle-east-and-africa/2020/06/06/african-governments-face-a-wall-of-debt-repayments> accessed 16 June 2020.

[9] Bradlow (n 7).

[10] In federations, the rules regulating borrowing may be different in relation to the various spheres of government. In particular, subnational levels of government may be allowed little to no access to external loans, as is the case eg in South Africa.

debt in Africa,[11] and multilateral funders, notably the World Bank, International Monetary Fund (IMF), and the African Development Bank. The loans may be *concessional*, where states borrow at below market interest rates with extended repayment arrangements, or *commercially* at the market interest rate, which often depends on the credit rating of the country.

Borrowing helps to raise funds when the ability to mobilize domestic resources is insufficient to cover needed budget and investment. If used strategically and with integrity, debt enables governments to raise funds without unduly reducing the wealth of private citizens through taxation. Productive debts can be used to kick-start and stimulate an ailing or receding economy, build basic infrastructure, and provide needed public services. As investments made today benefit future generations, funding productive infrastructure through debt, which is repaid over time, ensures intergenerational sharing of both the burden and benefits of debt.

Nevertheless, when debt reaches unsustainable levels, debt repayment would swallow a significant chunk of the annual budget, thereby limiting the resources available for investment and educational, health, and other social programmes, which are necessary to sustain the economic growth cycle. High levels of debt also negatively affect the credit rating of states and reduce the chances of further borrowing as the need may arise, or may necessitate the acquisition of commercial loans with unfavourable terms, thus inhibiting the mobilization of needed resources. High levels of debt could also discourage investment, as investors may anticipate the prospect of higher tax rates to service the debt, which affects their spending power and profit margins.

Particularly following the 2008 economic crisis, which exposed many countries to unsustainable debt, debates on managing and regularizing public debt have resurfaced. In Africa, public debt is steadily climbing and has emerged as one of the principal structural macroeconomic vulnerabilities.[12] The lack of transparency in the debt acquisition process and the purposes and conditions of debt have created situations where it can be difficult to know exactly the level of public debt. In this regard, the Mozambican debt crisis, which forced the country to default on its foreign debt in 2017 and is expected to last until 2023, was related to huge undisclosed debt incurred with little transparency and without the approval of Parliament.[13]

Moreover, with trade and economic relations growing between China and Africa, Western governments in particular have expressed concern that African countries may be falling into a 'debt trap' that could force them to hand over strategic assets to repay their unsustainable loans, claims which China has dismissed as alarmist and biased.[14]

---

[11] 'Africa's Growing Debt Crisis: Who Is the Debt Owed to?' *Jubilee Debt Campaign* (October 2018) <https://jubileedebt.org.uk/wp/wp-content/uploads/2018/10/Who-is-Africa-debt-owed-to_10.18.pdf> accessed 16 June 2020.

[12] 'IMF Warns African Countries against Spiraling Levels of Public Debt' *iAfrica News Agency* (11 October 2018) <http://www.engineeringnews.co.za/article/imf-warns-african-countries-against-spiraling-levels-of-public-debt-2018-10-11> accessed 4 December 2019.

[13] Mathew Hill and Borges Nhamire, 'IMF Expects Mozambique to Default on Foreign Debt until 2023' *Bloomberg* (28 February 2019) <http://www.bloomberg.com/news/articles/2018-02-28/imf-expects-mozambique-to-default-on-external-debt-until-2023> accessed 18 December 2019; Tom Collins, '"Most African Countries Have Debt Levels That Are Manageable": IMF African Head' *Africa Business Magazine* (6 July 2018) <https://africanbusinessmagazine.com/interviews/most-african-countries-have-debt-levels-that-are-manageable-imf-africa-head/> accessed 4 December 2019.

[14] 'China Counters "Debt Trap" Claims over African Loans' *Africa Times* (23 May 2019) <https://africatimes.com/2019/05/23/china-counters-debt-trap-claims-over-african-loans/> accessed 4 December 2019.

This accusation was made with especial vociferousness after the unveiling of the Trump administration's strategy for Africa, one which saw competition with China (and Russia), rather than terrorism and security, as the principal US foreign policy priorities.[15]

The foreign policy clashes of the big powers and accuracy of alarmist reports aside, as long as African economies continue to grow,[16] there is no systemic risk of debt crisis.[17] Nevertheless, while some countries in Africa have manageable debt levels,[18] there is clear evidence that public debt is rising and threatening, or likely to threaten, the economies of some African states.[19] Moreover, the way debt is contracted and accumulated leaves a lot to be desired.

It therefore calls for sober analysis and engagement to ensure that African countries contract and manage their debts in a manner that serves their long-term public interest and enhances, rather than undermines, democratic accountability, transparency, and economic performance. Indeed, the African Charter on Democracy, Elections, and Governance requires state parties to institutionalize sound economic and corporate government through, inter alia, the 'efficient management of public debt'.[20]

In this regard, the establishment of clear and robust legal regimes is central to, and a precondition for, effective debt management.[21] While political and economic factors will affect the level of debt and the quality of its management, proper legal frameworks can engender discipline, transparency, and accountability in debt raising and repayment. In particular, constitutions traditionally provided minimal guidance regarding public debt, with regulations detailed in subsidiary legislation, including broad public finance management frameworks. Nevertheless, there is significant advantage to anchoring the debt management regime in a constitutional framework.

Indeed, several countries, including Germany, where a 2009 amendment required a balanced budget without 'revenue from credits',[22] have revised their constitutions to provide for basic rules on public debt, but with defined procedures for exceptions, for instance in relation to higher borrowing in response to the economic impact of the COVID-19 pandemic.[23] The constitutionalization of the basic rules ensures that transient political

---

[15] Micheal Khorommbi, 'How Africa Should Treat the Trump Administration's Strategy for the Continent' *Daily Maverick* (13 January 2019) <http://www.dailymaverick.co.za/opinionista/2019-01-13-how-africa-should-treat-the-trump-administrations-strategy-for-the-continent/> accessed 10 January 2020.

[16] According to the economic outlook of the African Development Bank, Africa's economy was expected to grow by 4 per cent in 2019 and 4.2 per cent in 2020, but even this level may be insufficient to address 'persistent fiscal and current account deficits and unsustainable debt'—see 'African Economic Outlook 2019', <http://www.afdb.org/en/knowledge/publications/african-economic-outlook/> accessed 4 December 2019.

[17] ibid xiv. According to a related report, '[b]y the end of 2017, the gross government debt-to-GDP ratio reached 53 percent in Africa, but with significant heterogeneity across countries. Of 52 countries with data, 16 countries—among them Algeria, Botswana, Burkina Faso, and Mali —have a debt-to-GDP ratio below 40 percent; while 6 countries—Cabo Verde, Congo, Egypt, Eritrea, Mozambique, and Sudan—have a debt-to-GDP ratio above 100 percent. The traditional approach to estimating debt sustainability classifies 16 countries in Africa at high risk of debt distress or in debt distress'—<http://www.afdb.org/fileadmin/uploads/afdb/Documents/Publications/2019AEO/AEO_2019-EN.pdf> accessed 4 December 2019.

[18] Collins (n 13).

[19] Indermit Gill, Kenan Karakulah, and Shanta Devarajan, 'Stressful Speculations about Public Debt in Africa' *Brookings* (19 June 2019) <http://www.brookings.edu/blog/future-development/2019/06/19/stressful-speculations-about-public-debt-in-africa/> accessed 4 December 2019.

[20] African Charter on Democracy, Elections and Governance, art 33(4).

[21] Elsie Addo Awadzi, 'Designing Legal Frameworks for Public Debt Management' (2015) IMF Working Paper, WP/15/147 4.

[22] Eckhard Janeba, 'Germany's New Debt Brake: A Blueprint for Europe?' (2012) 68(4) *FinanzArchiv/Public Finance Analysis* 383.

[23] 'Germany Opens the Money Tap' *The Economist* (11 June 2020) <http://www.economist.com/europe/2020/06/11/germany-opens-the-money-tap> accessed 16 June 2020.

majorities do not alter the debt management framework to serve their short-term interests. In addition, it allows opposition groups and civil society organizations to monitor and even challenge, including in courts, debt acquisition, management, and repayment. Indeed, as noted above, the case against the illegal and non-transparent Mozambican debt was submitted to the Constitutional Council by a civil society organization.

Political actors and advocates of sustainable public finance should explore how constitutions can enable sound public debt management. However, it is important to note that even when there are no specific provisions dealing with the management of debt, the broader constitutional division of powers, both horizontal and vertical, has implications for public debt. For instance, provisions for transparency of public undertakings,[24] auditing,[25] and reporting would have implications for debt. Accordingly, even without a robust constitutional regulation on debt, stakeholders can and should still anchor arguments aimed at working towards sustainable debt in constitutional values and frameworks in the struggle to create transparent and accountable public debt. In the absence of a robust implementation mechanism and effective state and non-state institutions ensuring compliance with fundamental constitutional values, their impact would be minimal. Indeed, despite the constitutional requirement for transparency in relation to debt in Zimbabwe, there is little publicly and easily accessible information about the exact level of the country's debt.

3. Indebtedness and the Economy

States have for centuries relied on debt to fight wars, respond to emergencies, complement transient budgetary fluctuations, invest in infrastructure, and stimulate economic growth. There are hardly any modern states that do not to some extent rely on public debt. The proper functioning of economies may at times require debt to fund productive long-term investment. Debt allows states to think long-term and engage in productive projects to inject a cycle of economic productivity and government revenue, including in times of economic slowdown or recession. Without debt, such investments would be infeasible or would require significant domestic resource mobilization that the economy may be unable to generate.

Moreover, large-scale investments often benefit generations of people. Because debt arrangements allow the payment of debt obligations for such investments over a long time, they advance intergenerational equity in offsetting the benefits and costs of debt among taxpayers across generations.[26] Nevertheless, debt incurred to cover recurrent costs may impose more costs than benefits on future generations. Even debt to cover productive investments may not be growth-enhancing if the general public debt is too high.[27]

Despite its benefits, when debt reaches unsustainable levels, as determined in specific contexts, it could burden the economy and induce an economic and financial crisis.[28] States

---

[24] Eg Constitution of Seychelles of 1993, arts 153 and 154; Constitution of Zimbabwe of 2013, art 288(1)(f).

[25] Eg Constitution of Kenya of 2010, art 299(4).

[26] F. Modigliani, 'Long-Run Implications of Alternative Fiscal Policies and the Burden of the National Debt' (1961) 71 *Economic Journal* 730.

[27] CS Adam and DL Bevan, 'Fiscal Deficits and Growth in Developing Countries' (2005) 4 *Journal of Public Economics* 571.

[28] The IMF has a debt sustainability framework that seeks to assist low income countries in assessing their needs, ability to repay debt, and the overall economic impact of debt—see <http://www.imf.org/en/About/Factsheets/Sheets/2016/08/01/16/39/Debt-Sustainability-Framework-for-Low-Income-Countries> accessed 16 June 2020.

under heavy debt have at times been forced to take severe austerity measures that stagnate economic growth and destine millions of people to lower levels of livelihood. The 2008 economic crisis and the high level of debt of the Eurozone and other developed economies triggered a flurry of research on the link between debt and growth. While the exact level at which debt is considered unsustainable is controversial, according to a 2010 European Central Bank study debt levels of between 90 and 100 per cent of gross domestic product (GDP) may have a deleterious impact on long-term economic growth, while the negative-growth effect of high debt may start already from levels of about 70–80 per cent of GDP.[29] In the context of Africa, increasing debt levels have been found to be inversely related to economic growth and positively related to high inflation.[30]

More recent research has found a similar negative correlation between high public debt and economic growth, with some indicating that public debt level above 50 per cent of GDP is risky.[31] Nonetheless, the correlation between debt and the economy may be weak once one considers endogenous factors unique to each country, such as fiscal and other economic policies and structural features—that is, the debt–growth correlation is heterogeneous across countries,[32] affecting current borrowing risks.[33] The slowing of economic growth could in turn cause increases in the burden of government debt. The increase in interest rates on public borrowing due to debt burden also leads to an increase in borrowing costs for the private sector, which is why business entities pressure governments to keep borrowing at manageable levels. In short, debt sustainability is a complicated and controversial issue that may defy specific legal limits or regulations. Nevertheless, in all cases, debt management should be transparent and subject to appropriate mechanisms of accountability and oversight.

In particular, high and growing external debt has been linked to a negative impact on economic growth and could lead to 'debt overhang', where a country's ability to pay external debt falls below the contractual value of the debt.[34] Foreign debt accumulation can promote investment 'up to a certain threshold', beyond which the debt overhang will start adding negative pressure on investors' willingness to provide capital.[35] In the context of developing countries, the negative impact of external public debt on the economy may start from debt levels above 35–40 per cent of GDP,[36] and may go as low as 20–25 per cent for low-income

---

[29] Cristina Checcherita and Philipp Rother, 'The Impact of High and Growing Government Debt on Economic Growth: An Empirical Investigation for the EURO Area' (August 2010) European Central Bank, Working Paper Series No 1237 <http://www.ecb.europa.eu/pub/pdf/scpwps/ecbwp1237.pdf> accessed 17 April 2019. See also M Gomez-Puig and S Sosvilla-Rivero, 'Public Debt and Economic Growth: Further Evidence for the Euro Area', Research Institute of Applied Economics, Working Paper 2017/15 <http://www.ub.edu/irea/working_papers/2017/201715.pdf> accessed 17 April 2019.

[30] Lopes da Veiga, Alexandra Ferreira-Lopes, and Tiago Neves Sequeira, 'Public Debt, Economic Growth, and Inflation in African Economies' (2014) Munich Personal RePEc Archive <ttps://mpra.ub.uni-muenchen.de/57377/1/MPRA_paper_57377.pdf> accessed 4 December 2019.

[31] Gill, Karakulah, and Devaraja (n 19).

[32] Ugo Panizza and Andrea F Presbitero, 'Public Debt and Economic Growth: Is There a Causal Link?' (2014) 41 Journal of Macroeconomics 21; Markus Eberhardt and Andrea F Presbitero, 'Public Debt and Growth: Heterogeneity and Non-linearity' (2015) 97(1) Journal of International Economics 45.

[33] Yi-Bin Chiu and Chien-Chiang Lee, 'On the Impact of Public Debt on Economic Growth: Does Country Risk Matter?' (2017) 35(4) Contemporary Economic Policy 751.

[34] P Krugman, 'Financing vs. Forgiving a Debt Overhang: Some Analytical Issues' (1988) NBER Working Paper No 2486.

[35] Checcherita and Rother (n 29).

[36] C Pattillo, H Poirson, and L Ricci, 'External Debt and Growth' (2002) IMF Working Paper 02/69.

countries.[37] A recent study focusing on Nigeria has found that external debt 'negatively impacts the economy', while internal debt has a positive correlation with economic growth.[38]

Overall, there is evidence that high public debt can negatively affect economic growth. This is particularly the case in countries with structural deficiencies and high borrowing costs due to their low credit rating and inefficiencies in the use of borrowed resources, factors that are common in many African countries.

4. Public Debt and Democracy

Public debt has a direct and significant effect on the rights, responsibilities, and livelihood of the people of the borrowing country, both positive and negative. It is therefore directly related to democracy. There is some evidence linking high external public debt with difficulties in democratic transitions.[39] The management of debt, from its raising to its repayment, should therefore be subject to democratic principles of responsiveness, transparency, and accountability. In particular, elected political representatives in the legislature can play a critical role in approving borrowing transactions,[40] establishing the broader framework for borrowing, and overseeing the latter's implementation, notably through accounting or auditing and reporting requirements.

Given the expertise and resources of the executive, the negotiation of borrowing transactions is often left to the entities in charge of finance, such as finance ministries and central banks, subject to a level of oversight and control from cabinet. Nevertheless, this need not entail the absence of legislative approval of public borrowing. While parliamentary approval requirements could make the process more cumbersome, as it would require negotiation and compromise with a broader range of actors, and possibly increase transactional costs, this could be a useful trade-off for ensuring democratic control, considering the difficulty of trusting executive self-control in debt management, which is often mired in irresponsible borrowing. At the same time, economic decisions often require a level of efficiency that the executive is equipped to deliver. Accordingly, regulations must seek a balance between screening potential abuse and efficient and effective raising and use of debt.

The prior legislative approval of public debt can ensure better transparency, oversight, and representation of the views of wider political forces. Executives often represent single political groups that won elections, while parliaments provide formal and legitimate representation and platforms for opposition voices. In this regard, the provision of opportunities for opposition groups, such as through leadership of parliamentary financial committees,[41]

---

[37] B Clements, R Bhattacharya, and TQ Nguyen, 'External Debt, Public Investment, and Growth in Low-Income Countries' (2003) IMF Working paper 03/249.

[38] Isibor Areghan Akhanolu and others, 'The Effects of Public Debt on Economic Growth in Nigeria: An Empirical Investigation' (2018) 12(6) International Business Management 436.

[39] Jean-Louise Combes and Rasmane Ouedraogo, 'How Does External Debt Impact Democratisation? Evidence from Developing Countries' (2014) <https://halshs.archives-ouvertes.fr/halshs-00969172v2/document> accessed 19 April 2019. However, the authors indicate that external debt may 'incite governments to improve [their] investment profile and therefore [improve the] business climate' and that international support programmes, such as from the IMF, could 'dampen the negative effect of debt on democratic transitions'.

[40] Legislative approval requirements may apply to all loan transitions or only to some (eg based on the amount of transaction in each case, or by setting annual loan ceilings), or they could take the form of standard terms and conditions for public loans with which the executive would have to comply.

[41] Eg art 60 of the 2014 Constitution of Tunisia provides that the opposition must chair the parliamentary Finance Committee and be the Rapporteur of the External Relations Committee. These platforms create important

with access to loan negotiation proceedings, could ensure that loans are contracted in the public interest rather than merely to advance the interests of the governing party. Similarly, opposition representation may be required in other critical institutions, such as the debt management offices or departments that are established in many countries to provide a centralized point for consolidated debt management as well as maintaining and reporting on all debt liabilities.

Democracy also requires transparency in the raising and settling of public debt. It is critical to ensure government accountability and consideration of the views of the public, opposition groups, the media, and interested civil society groups in relation to debt undertakings. Transparency enables the proper and continuing monitoring and evaluation of public debt. The publication, regular updating, and accessibility of the status of public debt of all relevant government entities is therefore necessary. Moreover, regular reporting mechanisms, particularly to parliament, are necessary for ensuring continuous transparency and auditing. Overall, transparency can nurture a productive cycle of feedback, criticism, and justification.

As noted above, public debt has intergenerational implications that require the representation and consideration of the interests of future generations. It has been argued sometimes that current voters and politicians are likely to think short-term and run budget deficits, that is, spend more money than they raise.[42] Voters may prefer politicians that promise either lower taxes or higher spending. The combination of low taxes and high public expenditure creates a perennial budget deficit. In order not to alienate voters, politicians may be tempted to fill the deficit through more borrowing rather than taxes. Such myopic borrowing habits benefit the current generation at the expense of the future generation who cannot yet vote. Intergenerational equity therefore requires protection against inequitable borrowing temptations and habits in the form of constitutional or legislative restrictions on borrowing.[43]

In the African context, governments with questionable legitimacy that rely on extensive patrimonial structures may find it easier to fund these networks through debt rather than more cumbersome taxation efforts, which could trigger public protests and demands for accountability.

5. Constitutions and Debt

Constitutions outline the fundamental values, objectives, processes, and institutions of a state. As public debt is an issue with significant democratic and economic implications, constitutions should engage with it to ensure transparency, accountability, government discipline, and protect the interests of the public and future generations. While ordinary legislation can provide important safeguards, it is ultimately subject to fleeting majoritarian review and adjustments. Effective protection may therefore require the constitutional regulation of fundamental aspects of public debt, including guarantees of transparency,

---

opportunities for the opposition to oversee public debt acquisition and other financial proceedings, which creates better transparency and accountability.

[42] Mark Crain and Robert Ekelund, 'Deficits and Democracy' (1978) 44(4) Southern Economic Journal 813.

[43] Schragger has argued, however, that constitutional limits are undesirable and that distrust of ordinary political processes is unwarranted. See Richard Schragger, 'Democracy and Debt' (2012) 121 Yale Law Journal 860.

accountability, and the interests of future generations. In practice, many modern constitutions contain provisions dealing with public debt in varying degrees of detail.[44]

While constitutional regulation is necessary, debt management is a complex issue that cannot be comprehensively regulated in a constitution; since public debt is a financial tool, there is also need for a degree of flexibility, which is something that constitutions might hamper unnecessarily. Accordingly, constitutions should limit themselves to outlining broad issues related to the authority to borrow and repay debt on behalf of the state (such as whether that authority can be delegated); to the debt-raising process, particularly with reference to parliamentary approval, any crucial limits, and borrowing purposes; and to issues of transparency and accountability, including by setting out publication, reporting, and auditing requirements. Detailed rules and institutional structures may be provided for in laws dealing with public finance, central banks, and the management of public debt.

A number of aspects of public debt are amenable to constitutional regulation. First, constitutions should bestow the legal mandate to borrow, that is, they should determine the entity that exercises borrowing authority on behalf of the state. When the borrowing power is conferred on parliament, it may for practical reasons authorize executive entities to borrow on its behalf, subject to any conditions and/or its subsequent approval. The legal mandate would include clarification of the process of debt approval, but this could also be expanded upon in ordinary legislation.

Constitutions and other laws may also outline regulations touching on the purpose of public borrowing as well as its sources for the various levels of government. While some countries allow borrowing to defray any legal expense (eg Tanzania allows general purpose loans),[45] others anticipate borrowing only in relation to certain costs (specific-purpose loans). For instance, in Nigeria, borrowing is allowed only to cover costs for capital investment and human development.[46] South Africa allows borrowing for a wide but circumscribed range of purposes (limited-purpose loans), and restricts provincial loans to cases of capital expenditure, while current expenditure may be procured only for purposes of bridging during a fiscal year.[47]

The rules governing public borrowing may also vary depending on the source of the debt. In general, the rules are stricter in relation to external borrowing than internal borrowing. For instance, in Sierra Leone, Parliament must approve all external borrowing, while there is no similar requirement for borrowing from domestic sources.[48] In some federations and devolved systems, while the federal government may be allowed to borrow from any source, lower-level governments may not be allowed to borrow or be limited to raising loans only from domestic sources; even when they can raise external sources, it may be subject to the supervision and approval of the federal government. For instance, in Kenya county governments may borrow only with the guarantee of the national government and with the approval of county assemblies,[49] while in South Africa provinces need the consent of the

---

[44] See eg the Constitution of Angola of 2010, art 162(d); Constitution of Kenya of 2010, arts 214, 220, and 229; Constitution of Zambia of 1991 (revised 2016), art 208; Constitution of Finland, art 82; Constitution of Mexico, art 73(8).

[45] Constitution of Tanzania of 1977, art 141; Government Loans, Guarantees and Grants Act of 1974; and Government Loans, Guarantees and Grants (Amendment) Act of 2003, art 3.

[46] Nigeria Fiscal Responsibility Act 31 of 2007, art 41.

[47] South African Public Finance Management Act 1 of 1999 (as amended), art 71, and Constitution of South Africa 1996, art 230.

[48] Sierra Leone's Public Debt Management Act of 2011, arts 9(2) and 10.

[49] Constitution of Kenya 2010, art 212.

relevant national minister to raise loans[50] and may not raise loans from foreign sources or otherwise denominated in a foreign currency.[51]

Some countries have established binding limits on the amount of public debt through debt ceilings measured as a share of their total GDP. At the European Union level, the 1992 Maastricht Treaty and 1997 Stability and Growth Pact (SGP) require member states to achieve public debt-to-GDP ratios of below 60 per cent by 2020.[52] Nevertheless, states have wide discretion in this regard and many still have debt levels that far exceed the limit. The West African Economic and Monetary Union (WAEMU) and Central African Economic and Monetary Community (CEMAC) similarly establish debt ceilings of 70 per cent of GDP.[53] However, the sub-regional entities have not established procedures and institutions to monitor and ensure compliance with the ceiling.

In addition to these supranational standards, which are highly flexible and lack serious enforcement mechanisms, increasingly there are countries that impose debt ceilings through their domestic constitutional and/or legislative frameworks. For instance, the Hungarian Constitution imposes a 50 per cent debt ceiling,[54] while the Polish Constitution follows the European Union model and sets a 60 per cent limit.[55] A 2009 amendment to the Constitution of Germany requires a balanced budget without 'revenue from credits', subject to certain exceptions such as recession or emergencies.[56]

While constitutional establishment of debt ceilings precludes arbitrary changes, it could also undermine flexibilities that are needed to respond to critical economic changes—contingencies that are by nature difficult to predict.[57] Constitutional regulation of debt ceilings should therefore include cautiously designed flexibilities. While critical economic situations could be assumed to induce broad political consensus that can enable constitutional reforms, political agreement may not always be forthcoming. Parliamentary approval requirements and the establishment of exceptions through extraordinary approval procedures, such as supermajority approval, could provide the needed flexibility.

For debt ceilings to be effective, there must be clear procedures to correct excesses and hold those responsible accountable (civilly and criminally). In some countries, loans raised in excess of the debt ceiling are not legally recognized (eg South Africa and Nigeria).[58] Creditors should therefore have a duty to ascertain the level of public debt. For this to be effective, the existence of publicly available information on the level of debt is critical.

Although no constitution in Africa appears to impose debt ceilings,[59] some countries have established such limits through legislation. For instance, the Mauritian Public Debt

---

[50] Borrowing Powers of Provincial Governments Act 48 of 1996, art 3.

[51] South African Public Finance Management Act 1 of 1999 (as amended), art 67.

[52] See Andrea Schaechter and others, 'Fiscal Rules in Response to the Crisis—Toward the "Next-Generation" Rules. A New Dataset' (2012) IMF Working Paper WP/12/187.

[53] International Monetary Fund, 'Country Report No 19/90: West African Economic and Monetary Union' (March 2019) <http://www.imf.org/~/media/Files/Publications/CR/2019/1WAUEA2019001.ashx> accessed 18 December 2019.

[54] Constitution of Hungary, art 36(4).

[55] Constitution of Poland, art 216(5).

[56] Constitution of Germany, art 109(3).

[57] Elsie Addo Awadzi, 'Designing Legal Frameworks for Public Debt Management' (2015) IMF Working Paper WP/15/147 25.

[58] South Africa Public Finance Management Act of 1999 (as amended), s 68; Nigerian Fiscal Responsibility Act of 2007, s 45(2).

[59] Art 300(1) of the Constitution of Zimbabwe of 2013 requires Parliament to enact legislation setting limits on state borrowing and public debt.

Management Act establishes a 50 per cent limit from December 2018.[60] Under the Act, the limit may be crossed only in cases of natural disaster or other emergency, serious economic slowdown requiring fiscal stimulus, and where cabinet decides that borrowing is necessary to fund a large investment project which is considered timely and prudent. In cases where exceptional borrowing in excess of the ceiling is found to be necessary, the Ministry of Finance is required to provide for plans to ensure that the increase in debt level under these exceptional circumstances will be reduced to the ceiling within three fiscal years and take measures to ensure that such plan is made public.

6. Constitutional Regulation of Public Debt in Africa

Many African constitutions contain provisions dealing with aspects of public debt. Even so, such reference is often minimal and does not provide a sufficient framework to ensure that public debt serves the general interest and is contracted in a democratic, accountable, and transparent manner. While the light level of constitutional regulation may reflect a decision by constitutional drafters that public debt management is more appropriate for subsidiary policy and the legislative framework, it is not clear if public debt attracts significant attention in times of constitutional transformation.

In practice, several countries, among them Ghana, Nigeria, Tanzania, and South Africa, have adopted legislation on public debt management that outlines the process of undertaking debt-related activities on behalf of the state, sets possible limits on borrowing, and addresses issues of oversight, accountability, transparency, and reporting. This section focuses on the level of constitutional regulation of aspects of public debt management. It is important to note that there may be statutory frameworks expounding upon and covering various aspects of public debt.

A look at African constitutions reveals some crucial provisions outlining the process of incurring debt and establishing oversight, accountability, and transparency. These provisions could provide useful guidance for decision-makers as well as those seeking possibilities to tame the heavy and growing debt burdens of some African countries. As noted in relation to Mozambique, courts can play a significant role in ensuring compliance with constitutional provisions on public debt.

6.1 Oversight and Justification of Public Debt

Some constitutions establish procedures for incurring public debt in a manner that ensures oversight of the loan process, notably through parliamentary approval requirements. The constitutions of some African countries, mainly from the anglophone tradition, require that loan agreements cannot come into effect without the approval of parliament. Egypt,[61] Ghana,[62] Liberia,[63] Gambia,[64] and Zambia[65] follow this approach. While parliamentary

---

[60] The Act is available at <http://mof.govmu.org/English/Legislation/Documents/PubDebtManagementAct.pdf> accessed 14 December 2019.
[61] Constitution of Egypt of 2014, art 127.
[62] Constitution of Ghana of 1992, art 181(4).
[63] Constitution of Liberia, art 34(d)(iii).
[64] Constitution of The Gambia of 1997, art 155.
[65] Constitution of Zambia of 1991 (revised 2016), art 114(1)(e).

consideration and approval of loan agreements may make the process appear tedious and economically inefficient, they may be legitimate in view of the potential burden the loans impose. In particular, keeping in mind that legislatures in many African countries are largely extensions of the executive with mere rubberstamping roles, the formality of parliamentary approval may be seen simply as an inconvenience. Nevertheless, even in such cases, parliamentary processes are likely to create opportunities for oversight and transparency and to allow opposition groups to access the content of agreements and put forward their views.

In some countries, parliament may through law outline the loan process as well as any conditions. The borrowing authority is then exercised by the government in line with the parliamentary legislative framework, without the need for specific consideration and approval of each loan agreement and its terms by parliament. This approach is common in many francophone countries, for example, Congo,[66] Gabon,[67] and Madagascar.[68] The establishment of a generally applicable legislative framework could allow for the efficient conduct of loan negotiation agreements. Nevertheless, while such legislative frameworks can provide some guidance and control, they might not allow opposition groups and the broader public sufficient opportunities to oversee the loan process and seek justification for such undertakings. Parliamentary consideration of each loan agreement can thus lead to better deliberation on and transparency of loan agreements.

The constitutions of some countries confer the power of borrowing on the executive and do not specifically anticipate legislative approval requirements. For instance, the Ethiopian Constitution grants the power of raising loans to the council of ministers.[69] Even in such cases, though, Parliament has the plenary legislative authority to regulate public debt. Accordingly, the Ethiopian parliament has adopted a law outlining the purpose and process of raising loans as well as the attendant reporting requirements. The failed Zambian government attempt to amend the constitution would have removed the power of Parliament to approve loans negotiated by the executive, thereby giving the executive the final say.[70] The absence of parliamentary oversight increases the chances of impropriety and unsustainable loans and guarantees.

6.2 Transparency and Accountability in Public Debt Transactions

While parliamentary approval requirements can in themselves ensure relatively transparent public debt acquisition and management and a level of accountability, some constitutions recognize specific procedures to ensure that information about public debt is made publicly available. Such transparency and knowledge in turn strengthen mechanisms of enabling accountability for decisions related to public debt. The constitutional regulation may take the form of a duty to provide regular updates to parliament and/or the public on debt levels.

The Zimbabwean Constitution specifically requires that 'all transactions involving the national debt must be carried out transparently and in the best interests of Zimbabwe'.[71]

---

[66] Constitution of Congo of 2015, art 125.
[67] Constitution of Gabon of 2011, art 47.
[68] Constitution of Madagascar of 2010, art 90.
[69] Constitution of Ethiopia of 1995, art 77(4).
[70] Lumina (n 5).
[71] Constitution of Zimbabwe, art 288(1)(f).

Accordingly, the minister responsible for finance must ensure that the terms of all loan agreements as well as guarantees by the state are published in the official gazette within sixty days of the agreement. In Kenya, the Auditor-General is required to audit and report on public debt within six months of the end of each financial year.[72] In addition, the minister responsible for finance is required to submit information on any specific loan undertaking within seven days of a resolution of one of the two houses of parliament.[73]

Similarly, in Mozambique, the administrative court is given the authority to supervise the use of resources obtained through loans and other foreign sources.[74] The Constitution of Seychelles requires the minister responsible for finance to present at the beginning of each financial year a report before Parliament indicating, among other matters, the expected level of public debt, and, at the end of the financial year, the actual level of public debt.[75] In South Africa[76] and Zambia,[77] the budget must specifically indicate borrowing intentions.

In addition, or alternatively, to regular reporting requirements, information on public debt may be required at irregular intervals at the request of Parliament or other actors. This is, for instance, the case in Uganda[78] and The Gambia.[79] When the submission of reports upon request is in addition to regular reporting responsibilities, it can provide useful platforms to demand timely explanation as loan transactions unfold. Nevertheless, in the absence of regular reporting duties, parliamentary requests for information about public debt may not be forthcoming, considering the dominance of the executive in many African countries. In such cases, parliaments may not have sufficient independence from the executive to hold it to account. Regular reporting requirements may therefore provide useful channels of enhancing the transparency of the general debt level as well as specific debt transactions.

6.3 Upper Limits on Public Debt

As noted above, the author is not aware of any African constitution that imposes a debt ceiling, albeit that some states provide for such ceiling in public debt management legislation. Nevertheless, the Zimbabwean Constitution empowers Parliament to set limits on state borrowing and the public debt.[80] Such limits can take the form of debt ceilings. The constitutions of Mozambique[81] and Cape Verde[82] anticipate the possibility for Parliament to establish an upper limit on the maximum state guarantee for non-public loans, which counts as a form of public debt, that the state can provide. There is no similar provision for public debt in general.

While constitutional debt ceilings are not common in Africa, this is not necessarily reflective of their undesirability. Although legislative ceilings may achieve similar goals while

---

[72] Constitution of Kenya, art 299(4).
[73] ibid art 211(2).
[74] Constitution of Mozambique of 2004, art 230(2)(d).
[75] Constitution of Seychelles, art 154(3).
[76] Constitution of South Africa, art 215(3)(c).
[77] Constitution of Zambia, art 202(2).
[78] Constitution of Uganda of 1995, art 159(4)(a).
[79] Constitution of The Gambia, art 155(6).
[80] Constitution of Zimbabwe, art 300(1).
[81] Constitution of Mozambique, art 179(2)(p).
[82] Constitution of Cape Verde of 1992, art 191(2)(e).

retaining flexibility, they may be less effective, as governments may seek to bypass them through simple legislative procedures. An alternative could be to establish ceilings in the constitution while recognizing exceptional instances that may justify short-term deviations. While constitutional ceilings may be relatively inflexible, it could be assumed that exceptional circumstances warranting deviations are likely to garner broad political consensus, which could enable constitutional adjustments whenever they are found necessary.

7. Conclusion

As debt increasingly becomes a critical aspect of African economies and politics, a more deliberate and reflective approach is needed. Public debt has not received the level of attention from constitutional designers and experts that it deserves. For instance, the general trends in terms of parliamentary approval requirements for public debt agreements in anglophone countries, where prior parliamentary approval is often required, and in francophone countries, where parliament merely has the power to establish legal frameworks for executive management of debt, show the impact of historical contingency and path dependency on the constitutional framework on public debt rather than reflecting deliberate decision-making.

As supreme laws laying the foundation for the values and structure of state and public governance, constitutions have a potentially prominent role to play in the regulation of public debt. At a minimum, constitutional regulation of core aspects of public debt could enhance the political salience and visibility of the issue, which is necessary to keep it continually on the agenda of political parties, the media, civil society organizations, academics, and the broader public. Such interest and engagement would establish the conditions for and contribute to more justification, oversight, transparency, caution, and discipline in public debt management. It is hoped that this preliminary contribution will trigger political and intellectual engagement that leads both to better understanding of the utility and limits of constitutional regulation of public debt as one of the critical issues of our time as well as to improved compliance with constitutional provisions on debt management.

Partly as a result of the insufficient constitutional regulation of public debt in practice, African constitutions have not contributed to taming the spectre of debt, which continues to rise in all countries. In fact, the growing discourse on public debt in Africa has been led principally by external competitors for influence and economic advantage in Africa, notably the US and China. Despite their potential, parliaments have served largely as rubber-stamp institutions in the process of debt acquisition, acquisition which has been steadily increasing in all countries and has reached unsustainable levels in some. Considering public debt's impact on democracy and the economy, it is critical to enhance the capacity of parliaments to oversee debt processes. In addition, procedures to ensure opposition oversight, such as through control of parliamentary finance committees, can provide the needed monitoring and publicity regarding public debt. Constitutional provisions on transparency in relation to debt management have also not been effective.

Accordingly, in addition to pursuing constitutional reforms to ensure better constitutional regulation of key aspects of public debt, stakeholders should seek to popularize and enforce existing constitutional and legal standards, including through the judiciary. The

Mozambican experience provides a hopeful example that stakeholders in other countries should seek to emulate.

Bibliography

'African Economic Outlook 2019' <http://www.afdb.org/en/knowledge/publications/african-econo mic-outlook/> accessed 4 December 2019

'African Governments Face a Wall of Debt Repayments' *The Economist* (6 June 2020) <http://www.economist.com/middle-east-and-africa/2020/06/06/african-governments-face-a-wall-of-debt-repayments> accessed 16 June 2020

'Africa's Growing Debt Crisis: Who Is the Debt Owed to?' *Jubilee Debt Campaign* (October 2018) <https://jubileedebt.org.uk/wp/wp-content/uploads/2018/10/Who-is-Africa-debt-owed-to_10.18.pdf> accessed 16 June 2020

'China Counters "Debt Trap" Claims over African Loans' *Africa Times* (23 May 2019) <https://afri catimes.com/2019/05/23/china-counters-debt-trap-claims-over-african-loans/> accessed 4 December 2019

'Germany Opens the Money Tap' *The Economist* (11 June 2020) <http://www.economist.com/europe/2020/06/11/germany-opens-the-money-tap> accessed 16 June 2020

'IMF Warns African Countries against Spiraling Levels of Public Debt' *iAfrica News Agency* (11 October 2018) <http://www.engineeringnews.co.za/article/imf-warns-african-countries-against-spiraling-levels-of-public-debt-2018-10-11> accessed 4 December 2019

'Mozambique to Continue Debt Restructuring Talks Despite "Tuna Bond" Court Ruling' *Club of Mozambique* (12 September 2019) <https://clubofmozambique.com/news/mozambique-to-conti nue-debt-restructuring-talks-despite-tuna-bond-court-ruling-141826/> accessed 4 December 2019Adam C and Bevan D, 'Fiscal Deficits and Growth in Developing Countries' (2005) 4 Journal of Public Economics 571

'Zambia's Path Very Narrow—Outlook Already Subdued' *The Mast* (25 November 2019) <http://www.themastonline.com/2019/11/25/zambias-path-very-narrow-outlook-already-subdued-imf/> accessed 4 December 2019

Akhanolu I and others, 'The Effects of Public Debt on Economic Growth in Nigeria: An Empirical Investigation' (2018) 12(6) International Business Management 436

Awadzi E, 'Designing Legal Frameworks for Public Debt Management' (2015) IMF Working Paper WP/15/147

Bradlow D, 'Vultures, Doves and African Debt: Here's a Way Out' *The Conversation* (5 May 2020) <https://theconversation.com/vultures-doves-and-african-debt-heres-a-way-out-137643> accessed 16 May 2020

Checherita C and Rother P, 'The Impact of High and Growing Government Debt on Economic Growth: An Empirical Investigation for the EURO area' (August 2010) European Central Bank, Working Paper Series No 1237 <http://www.ecb.europa.eu/pub/pdf/scpwps/ecbwp1237.pdf> accessed 17 April 2019

Chiu Y and Lee C, 'On the Impact of Public Debt on Economic Growth: Does Country Risk Matter?' (2017) 35(4) Contemporary Economic Policy 751

Clements B, Bhattacharya R, and Nguyen T, 'External Debt, Public Investment, and Growth in Low-income Countries' (2003) IMF Working paper 03/249

Collins T, '"Most African Countries Have Debt Levels That Are Manageable": IMF African Head' *Africa Business Magazine* (6 July 2018) <https://africanbusinessmagazine.com/interviews/most-african-countries-have-debt-levels-that-are-manageable-imf-africa-head/> accessed 4 December 2019

Combes J and Ouedraogo R, 'How Does External Debt Impact Democratisation? Evidence from Developing Countries' (2014) <https://halshs.archives-ouvertes.fr/halshs-00969172v2/docum ent> accessed 19 April 2019

Crain M and Ekelund R, 'Deficits and Democracy' (1978) 44(4) Southern Economic Journal 813

Da Veiga L, Ferreira-Lopes A, and Sequeira T, 'Public Debt, Economic Growth, and Inflation in African Economies' (2014) Munich Personal RePEc Archive <https://mpra.ub.uni-muenchen.de/57377/1/MPRA_paper_57377.pdf> accessed 4 December 2019

Demony C, 'Mozambique Committed to International Law after "Tuna Bond" Ruling' *Reuters* (4 July 2019) <https://af.reuters.com/article/investingNews/idAFKCN1TZ0MN-OZABS> accessed 4 December 2019

Eberhardt M and Presbitero A, 'Public Debt and Growth: Heterogeneity and Non-linearity' (2015) 97(1) Journal of International Economics 45

Gill I, Karakulah K, and Devarajan S, 'Stressful Speculations about Public Debt in Africa' *Brookings* (19 June 2019) <http://www.brookings.edu/blog/future-development/2019/06/19/stressful-speculations-about-public-debt-in-africa/> accessed 4 December 2019

Gomez-Puig M and Sosvilla-Rivero S, 'Public Debt and Economic Growth: Further Evidence for the Euro Area' (2017) Research Institute of Applied Economics Working Paper 2017 <http://www.ub.edu/irea/working_papers/2017/201715.pdf> accessed 17 April 2019

Hill M and Nhamire B, 'IMF Expects Mozambique to Default on Foreign Debt until 2023' *Bloomberg* (28 February 2019) <http://www.bloomberg.com/news/articles/2018-02-28/imf-expects-mozambique-to-default-on-external-debt-until-2023> accessed 18 December 2019

Janeba E, 'Germany's New Debt Brake: A Blueprint for Europe?' (2012) 68(4) FinanzArchiv/Public Finance Analysis 383

Khorommbi M, 'How Africa Should Treat the Trump Administration's Strategy for the Continent' *Daily Maverick* (13 January 2019) <http://www.dailymaverick.co.za/opinionista/2019-01-13-how-africa-should-treat-the-trump-administrations-strategy-for-the-continent/> accessed 10 January 2020

Krugman P, 'Financing vs. Forgiving a Debt Overhang: Some Analytical Issues' (1988) NBER Working Paper No 2486

Lumina C, 'Zambia's Proposed Constitutional Amendments: Sowing the Seeds of Crisis?' *ConstitutionNet* (16 September 2019) |<http://constitutionnet.org/news/zambias-proposed-constitutional-amendments-sowing-seeds-crisis> accessed 4 December 2019

Modigliani F, 'Long-Run Implications of Alternative Fiscal Policies and the Burden of the National Debt' (1961) 71 Economic Journal 730

Ncube S, 'Zambia Needs Strong Fiscal Intervention—ActionAid' *News Diggers* (27 November 2019) <https://diggers.news/local/2019/11/27/zambia-needs-strong-fiscal-intervention-actionaid/> accessed 4 December 2019

Nhamire B and Hill M, 'Mozambique Nullifies State Guarantee on Loan Linked to Eurobonds' *Bloomberg* (5 June 2019) <http://www.bloomberg.com/news/articles/2019-06-05/mozambique-nullifies-state-guarantee-on-loan-linked-to-eurobond> accessed 4 December 2019

Panizza U and Presbitero A, 'Public Debt and Economic Growth: Is There a Causal Link?' (2014) 41 Journal of Macroeconomics 21

Pattillo C, Poirson H, and Ricci L, 'External Debt and Growth' (2002) IMF Working Paper 02/69

Schaechter A and others, 'Fiscal Rules in Response to the Crisis—Toward the "Next-Generation" Rules: A New Dataset' (2012) IMF Working Paper WP/12/187

Schragger R, 'Democracy and Debt' (2012) 121 Yale Law Journal 860

14

The Turn to Global Constitutionalism at the WTO and Its Impact on African Constitutionalism

Eva Maria Belser*

1. Introduction

The verticalization and pluralization of public authority in recent decades has changed public law profoundly.[1] Numerous public matters that in the past were dealt with exclusively by national legislators and governments are nowadays negotiated between states or decided by international organizations. Significant areas of legislative competence have shifted upwards, in addition to which verticalized public authority has been pluralized—a large number of public international and private actors have become the source of an evolving international legal regime, a phenomenon that impacts on states and individuals and their scope of action.

These important changes in international law affect public authority, states, and individuals, in the process raising 'the age-old problem of constitutionalism'.[2] What is the basis and legitimacy of the power exercised by public and hybrid actors in the international sphere? How is the use of power limited and effectively constrained by law, and how are abuses of power prevented? Are the rights and freedoms of individuals and the autonomy (or sovereignty) of states properly protected, or are they exposed to the whims of uncontrolled actors?

While the global 'constitutionalist question' has been debated with great zeal, no uniform 'constitutionalist response' has yet been given. Currently, there is still no agreement about how to engage with constitutional issues in the global sphere, nor a common understanding of what global constitutionalism actually is or would entail.[3] Representatives of normative approaches highlight significant dysfunctionalities at the international level, perceived largely as a lack of constitutional features, and postulate the constitutionalization of global governance. These authors emphasize that verticalization and pluralization of power lead to disturbing democratic deficits, and call for compensatory democratic structures and mechanisms at the international level, such as the establishment of a global parliament and a

* The author is grateful to Simon Mazidi (MLaw) for his invaluable support in the drafting of this chapter.
[1] Jan Klabbers, 'Setting the Scene' in Jan Klabbers, Anne Peters, and Geir Ulfstein (eds), *The Constitutionalization of International Law* (OUP 2009) 11ff.
[2] Philip Allot, 'The Emerging Universal Legal System' (2001) 3(1) International Law FORUM Du Droit International 12, 16.
[3] Klabbers (n 1) 16 and 25.

Eva Maria Belser, *The Turn to Global Constitutionalism at the WTO and Its Impact on African Constitutionalism* In: *Constitutionalism and the Economy in Africa*. Edited by: Charles M Fombad and Nico Steytler, Oxford University Press. © Eva Maria Belser 2022. DOI: 10.1093/oso/9780192886439.003.0016

global court, or the putting into effect of a global social treaty making up for the weakening of national constitutionalism.[4]

Conversely, representatives of empirical approaches apply constitutional terminology to describe existing features of global governance that resemble functions typically fulfilled by national constitutions. By referring to an increasing consensus on fundamental values, an evolving hierarchy of international norms, and some general norms about rule-making, application, and adjudication, they claim that global constitutionalism already exists.[5] In this way, proponents of global constitutionalism borrow constitutional language 'to capture, name and also promote the fundamental changes in the international legal order which we all are witnessing but cannot easily express in the language of (international) law we learned'.[6]

The predominant area in which a consolidation of a global order can be observed is the protection of human rights. Most advocates of global constitutionalism thus associate the phenomenon with worldwide pledges to human rights,[7] going to great lengths to plead for the global relevance of fundamental values and the duty of all states to endorse them. There are indeed sound arguments for seeing the UN Charter as part of an international constitution and for qualifying the main UN treaties as an international bill of human rights binding on all states. But while it is an easy task to illuminate the presence of individual rights and freedoms in the global sphere, documenting their primacy and capacity to limit the use of public authority—which is what constitutionalism would imply—is not.

International institutions such as UN treaty bodies lack the power of imposing respect for globally constitutionalized human rights law on actors unwilling to comply with their duties. They are also short of mechanisms to adjudicate international human rights cases authoritatively and enforce their decisions.[8] In the event of conflict with other international norms and domestic principles or practices, international human rights have the worse hand. Hence, the advocates of a turn to global constitutionalism who, as such, claim to describe the constitutional value of international human rights refer, indeed, to what ought to be rather than what is actually the case. They argue, rightly, that constitutionalism is endangered if new and newly empowered international actors escape the legal corsets entrenched by national constitutions and use unconstrained, unchecked, and unbalanced power in the international sphere; but it is a *normative claim* that human rights ought to be the fundamental values and yardstick against which government action at all levels, from the local to the international, is evaluated.[9]

This is entirely different in the field of global trade, where, surprisingly, the turn to constitutionalism has been much more pronounced.[10] Advocates of a turn to global

---

[4] Anne Peters, 'Compensatory Constitutionalism: The Function and Potential of Fundamental International Norms and Structures' (2006) 19 Leiden Journal of International Law 579, 592.

[5] Wouter Werner, 'The Never-ending Closure: Constitutionalism and International Law' in Nicholas Tsagourias (ed), *Transnational Constitutionalism: International and European Perspectives* (Cambridge University Press 2007) 330.

[6] Bardo Fassbender, 'We the Peoples of the United Nations' in Martin Loughlin and Neil Walker (eds), *The Paradox of Constitutionalism: Constituent Power and Constitutional Form* (OUP 2008) 274.

[7] See eg the research description of the Center for Global Constitutionalism <http://www.wzb.eu/en/research/trans-sectoral-research/center-for-global-constitutionalism> accessed 22 July 2019.

[8] cf Jack Donnelly, *Universal Human Rights in Theory and Practice* (2nd edn, Cornell University Press 2003) 173ff.

[9] Neil Walker, 'The Shaping of Global Law' (2017) 8(3) Transnational Legal Theory 360, 364.

[10] Jeffrey L Dunoff, 'Constitutional Conceits: The WTO's "Constitution" and the Discipline of International Law' (2006) 17(3) EJIL 647, 648.

constitutionalism at the WTO typically follow a *positivist claim* and state that international trade rules take primacy over international non-trade and domestic rules in case of conflict. They argue that the binding dispute-resolution mechanisms of the WTO operate like an international court and allow for economic retaliation when international trade rules are violated.[11] They also claim that a rule-based global trading system fulfils crucial constitutional functions, such as preventing national governments from arbitrarily opting for protectionist policies or adopting other harmful trade policies.

They argue, moreover, that a global trade system offers stability conducive to trade and development and to the fundamental value of equality of all states. In the absence of binding global trade rules, the argument goes, there is a great risk that unilateral or bilateral trade policies are determined by short-sighted governments, influenced by national lobbies, or orchestrated by powerful multilateral enterprises. Finally, it is argued that binding global trade rules offer better protection from geopolitical moods of the moment and the effects of unequal bargaining power among the trading partners.[12]

It is true that some recent developments, including the inability to bring about reform, the crisis of the appellate body, and the spread of bilateral and regional trade treaties, curb enthusiasm for constitutionalized WTO law. The political mood of the moment seems to have changed and numerous countries doubt the advantages of global trade rules, opt for unilateral actions, or negotiate bilateral or regional arrangements.[13] But while many observers have turned their attention away from the WTO, its rules continue to shape global trade, which is why the turn to global constitutionalism at the WTO has not lost its relevance. The fact that the reform process is stuck preserves the current trade rules. Bilateral and multilateral trade arrangements do not replace but complement global rules.[14]

The constitutionalist question at the WTO also remains a crucial issue because the rules for which the supporters of global trade constitutionalism claim special entrenchment are very different from the ones of the UN regime and regional human rights organizations. While global human rights aim at constraining the power of states in order to guarantee respect for and protection of individual rights and freedoms, constitutionalized global trade rules assert the primacy of the state's obligations to follow tariff concessions, to eliminate trade barriers, to respect the principle of non-discrimination, to protect intellectual property and, overall, to guarantee private parties a right to trade freely across borders. In contrast to the international bill of human rights, these rules are not aligned with domestic

---

[11] At the international level, the primacy of international (trade) rules over national rules is supported by art 27 of the Vienna Convention on the Law of Treaties (VCLT), which obliges states to comply with their international obligations ('*pacta sunt servanda*'). It is, however, an entirely different question how to resolve conflicts between different international legal obligations, such as trade rules and international human rights obligations. Apart from *jus cogens*, there is no clear normative hierarchy in international law, while VCLT art 27 is of no use in such constellations as it does not address the question of the relationship between treaties. For other provisions in the Vienna Convention dealing with the resolution of conflicts between different treaties, see Seyed Ali Sadat-Akhavi, *Methods of Resolving Conflicts between Treaties* (Nijhoff 2003) 47ff.

[12] For reasons why the WTO stands for a successful cooperative regime, see Eric A Posner and Alan O Sykes, 'International Law and the Limits of Macroeconomic Cooperation' (2013) 86(5) Southern California Law Review 1025, 1030ff.

[13] cf Vinicius Rodrigues Vieira, 'Beyond the Market: The Global South and the WTO's Normative Dimension' (2016) 21(2) International Negotiation: A Journal of Theory and Practice 267, 270ff, who emphasizes the material and symbolic factors that underpin the WTO as a multilateral system.

[14] For further information on this topic, see Stephen W Hartman, 'The WTO, the Doha Round Impasse, PTAs, and FTAs/RTAs' (2013) 27(5) The International Trade Journal 411; Talitha Bertelsmann-Scott and others, 'The Impact of Plurilateral Trade Agreements on Developing Countries: To Participate or Not to Participate?' (2018) 25(2) South African Journal of International Affairs 177.

constitutional rules, which instead highlight democracy, human rights, and development and are silent on free trade.

The question this paper addresses is what the turn to constitutionalism at the WTO signifies for its African member states and their constitutional law and practice, in particular their aim of constituting state authorities as active actors of human rights fulfilment and development. I argue that the constitutionalization of global trade rules, as currently advocated for, is worrisome from an African perspective.

First, constitutionalizing global trade rules would be advantageous only if these rules had been made with the active participation of African states and favour their development. While the first was not the case, the second is a highly controversial matter. African states have contributed only marginally to the global trade regime, which has been negotiated predominantly by countries of the North. The WTO trade rules thus lack procedural legitimacy. The flaws of the 'constitution'-making process, I will argue, have had an adverse outcome for the rules themselves: they favour those who made them.

The lack of substantive legitimacy of some of the global rules, it is argued, also stands in the way of recognizing their constitutional value. It is true that the extent to which African states benefit from the global trade regime is a contentious matter. While it is clear that increased trade liberalization generally leads to greater wealth, it is a fact too that the gains do not flow proportionally.[15] Given that African states mostly export natural resources and play only a marginal role in the global trade in goods,[16] claims are made that WTO law is unfavourable to African countries, continues colonial trade patterns between the North and South, and limits the opportunities to reduce poverty.[17] If these arguments are valid, constitutionalizing WTO law has the effect of further entrenching rules biased in favour of highly industrialized states and thereby works to the detriment of developing countries.[18] The turn to constitutionalism at the WTO then has the potential to harm the interests of the forty-four African states which are currently WTO members as well as those of the seven African observer states preparing accession.

Secondly, this chapter demonstrates that the rule-based trading regime is not rule-based when it comes to development. Under WTO law, developed states may foresee special and differential treatment for developing states but are not obliged to do so.[19] African states thus cannot rely on the stability of the regime applicable to them, or enforce limited government on others, but remain delivered to the discretionary powers of their trading partners.

Thirdly, the elevation of global trade rules to constitutional rules signifies the priority of free trade over non-trade rules and constitutes a risk for human rights and development. It is, of course, welcome that entrenched trade rules help to constrain the influence of short-sighted governments and of powerful lobby groups seeking to push through their narrow agendas at the cost of general welfare. The primacy of free trade, however, increases the imbalance of the international legal system. Global human rights—in line with most African

---

[15] Joost Pauwelyn, Andrew Guzman, and Jennifer Hillman, *International Trade Law* (3rd edn, Kluwer 2016) 25.

[16] cf UNCTAD, 'Economic Development in Africa, Report 2019, Made in Africa—Rules of Origin for Enhanced Intra-African Trade' UN Doc UNCTAD/ALDC/AFRICA/2019, 19.

[17] cf Olu Fasan, 'Global Trade Law: Challenges and Options for Africa' (2003) 47(2) Journal of African Law 143, 161.

[18] For a description of the term 'developing countries' in the WTO, see Charlotte Sieber-Gasser, *Developing Countries and Preferential Services Trade* (Cambridge University Press 2016) 4ff.

[19] For an overview of special and differential treatment provisions within the WTO legal framework, see ibid 20ff.

constitutions—oblige states to promote human rights actively by using trade and numerous other mechanisms; global trade law—in contrast to most African constitutions—indulges states to rely on the forces of markets passively. While the human rights canon remains flexible and its enforcement pliable, the global trade regime constitutes an uncompromising package which is rigidly enforced. Where the legal hierarchy is reversed and free trade placed above other fundamental constitutional values, entrenched trade rules run the risk of crushing human rights initiatives affecting trade.

In assessing the impact of constitutionalized WTO law, the chapter begins by briefly presenting the liberal claim to global constitutionalism at the WTO and discussing the making of the international trading regime and its main pillars. Thereafter it turns to human rights and shows that, while these values are central in African constitutionalism, they are merely exceptions to free trade at the WTO: where African constitutionalism clashes with liberal trade, human rights therefore run the risk of being compromised, as certain cases illustrate. Before concluding, the chapter argues in favour of a plural approach to global constitutionalism in which liberal trade is one value amongst others and open to contestation by domestic constitutions.

2. The Liberal Turn to Constitutionalism at the WTO

Despite the fact that the WTO lacks the political will to make a constitution and has no constitutional court, no constitutional convention, no constitutional drafting process, and no identifiable constitutional moment to claim as its own, constitutional discourse has moved to the centre of academic writing about the WTO.[20] More than elsewhere in international law, the invocation of constitutional rhetoric and constitutional imaginary in regard to the WTO has become a habit in global trade law—in spite of its current crisis.

According to the liberal turn to constitutionalism, the WTO law entrenches fundamental trade rules that take primacy over conflicting rules. The advocates of the liberal approach, dominant in foreign trade policy and scholarship, claim that the WTO trade regime is constitutionalized in that it serves as a legitimate and effective legal instrument to prevent national governments from interfering in liberal and non-discriminatory trade regulation and to allow private actors to freely develop their economic activities across borders. Constitutionalized trade rules fulfil the constitutional function of limiting government and inhibiting abuses of power. Accordingly, the principal aim of liberal constitutional theories is to uncouple international trade from the interference of national politics and globally entrench the right of private actors, mostly corporate entities, to import and export goods and services freely.[21] The turn to constitutionalism at the WTO, in other words, endows the right to free trade with the aura of supreme law and keeps international rules and national politics at bay from limiting trade.[22]

---

[20] For the different leading conceptions about the qualification of the WTO as a constitution, see Joel P Trachtman, 'The Constitutions of the WTO' (2006) 17(3) EJIL 623; Jeffrey L Dunoff, 'The Politics of International Constitutions: The Curious Case of the World Trade Organization' in Jeffrey L Dunoff and Joel P Trachtman (eds), *Ruling the World? Constitutionalism, International Law, and Global Governance* (Cambridge University Press 2009) 184ff.

[21] Armin von Bogdandy, 'Verfassungsrechtliche Dimensionen der Welthandelsorganisation 2. Teil: Neue Wege globaler Demokratie?' (2001) 34(4) Kritische Justiz 425, 425ff.

[22] cf Robert Howse and Kalypso Nicolaidis, 'Enhancing WTO Legitimacy: Constitutionalization or Global Subsidiarity?' (2003) 16(1) Governance: An International Journal of Policy, Administration, and Institutions 73,

According to Jackson, the fundamental purpose of the General Agreement on Tariffs and Trade (GATT) is 'to constrain governments from imposing or continuing a variety of measures that restrain or distort international trade' and 'to prevent member states from abusing their national powers when those would damage the operation of world markets'.[23] To support their claim, advocates of constitutionalized trade law often recall the making of the GATT 1947 in the wake of the Second World War. By adopting this agreement, signatory states agreed not to raise tariffs and trade barriers and not to discriminate against foreign goods even in situations where they would wish to do so. The underlying assumption is that states are tempted to adopt economic policies harming themselves and others, and that international handcuffs are necessary to prevent governments from falling prey to popular claims or rent-seeking actors.[24]

The liberal theory takes it for granted that liberal markets maximize public goods and serve enterprises and consumers in all countries participating in the system. Conversely, it qualifies trade-restricting measures as protectionist and harmful.[25] Governments interfering with the right to trade freely across borders for economic or non-economic motives thus impede growth and development and should not be allowed to do so. According to the liberal theory, the WTO and its treaties oblige states to follow a liberal trade policy externally as well as internally. States restraining international trade are suspected of 'abusing their national powers'. Preventing them from doing so thus forces them to behave in an economically rational manner and not to interfere with the 'invisible hand' of international markets which, if undisturbed, maximizes wealth.

Authors such as Petersmann argue in favour of the constitutionalization at the WTO by claiming that the international trade rules protect enterprises and consumers more effectively from harmful trade policies than national constitutions do.[26] His presumption is that national constitutions can fall victim easily to selfish elites and greedy private actors. As a powerful global actor, the WTO provides more reliable instruments to entrench the right to free trade and offers unfailing enforcement mechanisms that enterprises and consumers, harmed by their governments, do not necessarily have at hand domestically.

3. The Making of the WTO Rules

The global trade rules have been designed by developed states to serve their economic interests and since then have not overcome their birth defects. These issues must be considered before evaluating the turn to constitutionalism at the WTO.

74, who point out that constitutionalizing the WTO accords it 'the legitimacy of higher law—irreversible, irresistible, and comprehensive'. The quotation can also be found in Dunoff (n 20) 201.

[23] John H Jackson, *The World Trade Organization: Constitution and Jurisprudence* (The Royal Institute of International Affairs 1998) 22–23 and 102.

[24] cf Joost Pauwelyn, 'The Transformation of World Trade' (2005) 104(1) Michigan Law Review 1, 3–4; Jeff Waincymer, 'The Trade and Human Rights Debate: Introduction to an Interdisciplinary Analysis' in Sarah Joseph, David Kinley, and Jeff Waincymer (eds), *The World Trade Organization and Human Rights: Interdisciplinary Perspectives* (Elgar 2009) 8–9.

[25] See also Bogdandy (n 21) 429.

[26] Ernst-Ulrich Petersmann, *Constitutional Functions and Constitutional Problems of International Economic Law* (1st edn, Routledge 1991) 210ff; Ernst-Ulrich Petersmann, 'The WTO Constitution and Human Rights' (2000) 3(1) Journal of International Economic Law 19, 19 and 24.

3.1 The Flawed Beginnings of the Global Trade Regime

The making of the modern global trade system started after the First World War with the establishment of the International Labour Organization (ILO), mandated to provide minimum labour standards to ensure the fairness of global competition.[27] States, however, failed to agree on an obligation in terms of which all member states would endorse ILO labour standards, as a result of which they were allowed to cherry-pick the conventions of their liking ('ILO à la carte').[28] They were also unsuccessful in equipping the ILO with enforcement mechanisms. When the United Nations (UN) came into being after the Second World War, it suffered from similar shortcomings. Member states are free to ratify or not human rights conventions, and risk no more than shaming-and-blaming if they fail to implement human rights obligations. Hence, the ILO and the UN guarantee rights and freedoms and codify global constitutional values for all but fail to endow them with primacy.

After the Second World War, the international community planned to create an International Trade Organization (ITO) to deal with international trade and ensure that it contributes to general welfare and development. However, the comprehensive approach of the ITO, agreed upon in the Havana Charter, was stillborn. Only its chapter IV on the reduction of tariffs and the elimination of quantitative restrictions and subsidies survived, entering into force as the GATT in 1947. Thereafter, the international trading system would take an entirely different turn. While the liberalization of the trading regime provided for in chapter IV started to imprint its features on international trade relations, the regulation of the trading regime, its institutions and processes, and all plans to design a trading regime in line with development needs and human rights, as envisaged in the other chapters, ended in a cul de sac. With the entering into force of the GATT 1947, the liberalization leg started to walk; the regulation leg remained paralysed.

The limping global trading system thus opened up transnational markets without providing for rules on labour and human rights, development, commodities, or competition. Since the GATT 1947 is only a multilateral treaty, the trade regime also lacked an international organization, rules of decision-making, conflict resolution, and enforcement. While it could have considered itself a complement to the international rules established by the ILO and the UN, it evolved separately from these institutions and with no mechanism to ensure coherence.[29]

When the WTO was finally established in 1995, it did not take up the ambitions of the ITO. The WTO still merely liberalizes but—with the exception of intellectual property— fails to regulate international trade; it also continues to operate outside UN frameworks. The mandate of the organization is limited to constituting an umbrella for the sixty treaties dealing with trade in goods, services, and intellectual property and providing a mandatory dispute-resolution mechanism. By adopting a single-package approach, the WTO obliges member states to accept the global trade regime as a whole and puts an end to the 'à la carte-model' dominant in all other fields of international law. As far as trade in goods is

---

[27] The Constitution of the International Labour Organization, adopted by the Peace Conference in April 1919, became Part XIII of the Treaty of Versailles (28 June 1919).

[28] Eva Maria Belser, *The White Man's Burden: Arbeit und Menschenrechte in der globalisierten Welt* (Stämpfli 2007) 35–36.

[29] Belser (n 28) 52ff.

concerned, the WTO transforms the GATT 1947 into an enforceable global commercial code for the member countries without changing its original focus.[30]

3.2 From Uruguay to Doha: 'Business as Usual'

When the GATT 1947 was signed, only two of the twenty-three signatory states were African countries: Southern Rhodesia, then a British crown colony and later ruled by a white-minority government, and South Africa, entering the period of National Party rule and heightened segregation. Despite having a considerable number of developing states from other continents amongst its founding states,[31] the GATT 1947 system does not reflect the needs and priorities of developing countries.[32]

In 1944, when the global economy was in shambles, the United States and Britain were the driving forces in the making of a new international economic order consisting of the Bretton Woods institutions—the World Bank and International Monetary Fund—and the GATT. Rapid decolonization created the fear that the newly independent countries would redirect their resources into building their own economies by allocating them to their developing domestic industries, which would restrict the free flow of commodities to war-ravaged Europe.[33] The GATT 1947 was overwhelmingly designed to assuage this fear. Given that the drafters were 'mainly guided by the vested idea of securing resources for industries in Europe and America and opening market across the globe for their merchandise',[34] its approach is strikingly mercantilist. The purpose of GATT 1947 was less to increase global welfare than 'to protect domestic interests, often prompted by the interests of powerful corporate lobbies'.[35]

As the powerful states of the time embarked on designing an international regime, 'the role of the developing countries was predominantly reduced to that of a compliant eye-witness of the legitimization process of the international order'.[36] India, Guatemala, and Middle Eastern countries complained about the colonial approach to international trade, but their impact was minimal.[37] Their strategy thus shifted to advocating for special and differential treatment and carving out exemptions for the South.[38]

Numerous African countries joined the GATT 1947 shortly after gaining independence: the interests of northern states in securing access to resources and markets would have made little sense without the newly independent states joining in. Ghana thus became a signatory state in 1957, Nigeria in 1960, Sierra Leone and Tanzania in 1961, and

---

[30] For an analysis of how the international trade regime developed, see Pauwelyn (n 24) 9ff.

[31] Brazil, Burma, Ceylon, Chile, China, Cuba, India, Lebanon, Pakistan, and Syria.

[32] Hunter Nottage, 'Trade and Development' in Daniel Bethlehem and others (eds), *The Oxford Handbook of International Trade Law* (OUP 2009) 484.

[33] Surendra R Bhandari, *Global Constitutionalism and the Path of International Law* (Brill 2016) 146: 'Consequently, the UK was primarily concerned with designing a mechanism in the GATT to obtain raw materials from former colonies and developing countries in general ...'.

[34] ibid 133.

[35] ibid 132.

[36] ibid 143.

[37] ibid 135ff; Ngaire Woods, 'Order, Globalization, and Inequality in World Politics' in Andrew Hurrell and Ngaire Woods (eds), *Inequality, Globalization, and World Politics* (OUP 1999).

[38] Bhandari (n 33) 136; Nottage (n 32) 485–86; cf Frank J Garcia, 'Beyond Special and Differential Treatment' (2004) 27(2) Boston College International and Comparative Law Review 291, 296ff.

Uganda in 1962. In 1963, a large number of African states simultaneously joined the GATT 1947: Benin, Burkina Faso, Cameroon, Central African Republic, Chad, the Republic of Congo, Ivory Coast, Gabon, Madagascar, Malawi, Mauritania, Niger, and Senegal. Togo followed in 1964, Burundi and Gambia in 1965, Rwanda in 1966, Egypt in 1970, Democratic Republic of the Congo in 1971, and Zambia in 1982.

When the negotiation of the Uruguay Round started in 1986, twenty-seven of the sixty-five signatory states were African. During the negotiation round, Botswana, Morocco, Lesotho, Tunisia, Mozambique, Namibia, Mali, and Swaziland joined, and, when it ended, Angola, Djibouti, Guinea and Guinea Bissau, and Kenya.[39] In 1996, Angola, Benin, Chad, and The Gambia became members of the WTO.[40]

Despite the impressive number of African countries, their participation in the GATT 1994 negotiation, including the Uruguay Round, was scant or close to non-existent. For most African states, engaging in years and years of negotiation and evaluating the effects of thousands of rules and regulations on their economies pose an insurmountable challenge. On the coming into force of the WTO in 1995, African WTO members were obliged to give primacy to rules 'to which they had become bound regardless of their level of participation or whether they had fully understood the commitments they had undertaken.'[41] Indeed, at the time, only half of them had representations in Geneva—it is only recently that most African member states are physically present at the organization's headquarters.

However, there is still a great discrepancy between the efforts African countries invest in the pursuit of national economic reforms and their 'minimal, nominal and largely ineffectual participation at the WTO.'[42] National economic reform plans are often disengaged from global trade rules and in conflict with free trade obligations or frustrated by them. African priorities have not changed the asymmetric structure of the WTO, which does not make 'optimal use of trade policy as an engine for growth, development and poverty reduction.'[43]

For these reasons, the Uruguay Round was fraught with tension between developing and developed countries. Most of the concerns of the countries of the South remained unaddressed, however.[44] The extension of multilateral trade discipline to services (GATS), mainly serving the interests of developed states undergoing deindustrialization, was agreed upon in the face of pronounced resistance from developing countries, which were obliged to open up their markets to foreign banking, insurance, and tourism companies. With the adoption of the Treaty on Trade-Related Aspects of Intellectual Property Rights (TRIPS), also part of the Uruguay package, the adoption of common trade standards (positive harmonization) started to complement the unmaking of national rules impeding free trade

[39] WTO, 'The 128 Countries that Had Signed GATT by 1994' <http://www.wto.org/english/thewto_e/gattme m_e.htm> accessed 22 July 2019.

[40] Cape Verde joined much later (23 July 2008); see also WTO, 'Members and Observers' <http://www.wto.org/ english/thewto_e/whatis_e/tif_e/org6_e.htm> accessed 22 July 2019. In short, more than two-thirds of all WTO member states are developing or least-developed countries (LDCs); cf Nottage (n 32) 482.

[41] Joan Apecu, 'The Level of African Engagement at the World Trade Organization from 1995 to 2010' (2013) 4(2) International Development Policy 29, 41.

[42] Apecu (n 41) 30. Minimal participation also applies to the use of the dispute settlement system. cf Nottage (n 32) 491ff; Lorand Bartels, 'Making WTO Dispute Settlement Work for African Countries: An Evaluation of Current Proposals for Reforming the DSU' (2013) 6(2) Law and Development Review 47; Jan Bohanes and Fernanda Garza, 'Going Beyond Stereotypes: Participation of Developing Countries in WTO Dispute Settlement' (2012) 4(1) Trade, Law and Development 45; Ka Zeng, 'Legal Capacity and Developing Country Performance in the Panel Stage of the WTO Dispute Settlement System' (2013) 47(1) Journal of World Trade 187.

[43] Apecu (n 41) 30.

[44] Bhandari (n 33) 142.

(negative harmonization). The regulatory framework remains limited, however, to the protection of intellectual property, and adds extra costs to numerous products that Southern countries purchase from Northern countries, such as technology and drugs.

Finally, the Dispute Settlement Understanding (DSU) was introduced, equipping the WTO with a mandatory (and costly) enforcement mechanism.[45] Since WTO dispute settlement bodies have the power to assess domestic laws and policies in the light of global trade rules, their establishment is crucial for the turn to constitutionalism. The same is true for the single-package approach, which obliges member states to accept all WTO treaties and excludes a variable geometry allowing states to opt in or out of trade obligations according to their economic interests or constitutional obligations.[46]

As GATT 1994 and its exemptions (in the field of agriculture and textiles and clothing), GATS and TRIPS, operated mostly as international mechanisms transferring wealth from the global South to the North, the 1999 ministerial conference in Seattle occasioned high expectation.[47] The poor countries had made significant commitments to open their markets and enforce intellectual property protection, while the rich had not substantially increased market access to their products, especially in agriculture, textiles and clothing, but had used quotas and export subsidies, consequently distorting international markets to the disadvantage of more competitive developing countries. Developing countries also claimed that their developed trading partners had not implemented the vague provisions promising special and differential treatment and were using anti-dumping measures to harass competitive exporters in the South and dispute-settlement procedures to attack legitimate development policies.[48]

The developed countries had no open ears for these requests and instead insisted on putting investment, competition, environment, and labour on the agenda, priorities that raised little enthusiasm among African countries, which saw ecological and social clauses as new protectionist devices for marginalizing their products. During the conference, the anti-globalization movement transformed the streets of Seattle into warlike zones; inside the venues, the negotiations failed.

The next, and still ongoing, Round was finally launched in 2001. The negotiators met in the desert of Qatar (and not on a Titanic-like luxury-cruise ship, as had been considered) to deal with an increasingly vocal civil society, and named the new negotiations the Doha Development Round to end the marginalization of poorer members. According to the Doha Development Agenda, states commit themselves to transform the WTO in profound ways and turn it into an organization that no longer disadvantages the developing countries but enhances their access to global markets. African WTO members, despite their considerable

---

[45]   See Nottage (n 32) 482, who notes that the introduction of binding dispute settlement procedures has been hailed as a 'paradigm shift from a system based on economic power and politics to one based on the rule of law'.

[46]   The single-package rule applies to all Multilateral Trade Agreements (WTO Agreement, art 1 para 2). There are only very few Plurilateral Trade Agreements that WTO member states can ratify or not (WTO Agreement, art 1 para 2). Among them is the Agreement on Trade-Related Investment Measures (TRIMs), which also emerged from the Uruguay Round. The TRIMs was the result of long and controversial negotiations, with predominantly developing countries opposing such measures. cf Paul Civello, 'The TRIMs Agreement: A Failed Attempt at Investment Liberalization' (1999) 8 Minnesota Journal of International Law 97. For a detailed description of the negotiations, see Willian A Fennell and Joseph W Tyler, 'Trade-Related Investment Measures' in Terance P Stewart (ed), *The GATT Uruguay Round: A Negotiating History 1986–1992, Volume II: Commentary* (Kluwer 1993) 2072ff.

[47]   See Susan K Sell and Aseem Prakash, 'Using Ideas Strategically: The Contest between Business and NGO Networks in Intellectual Property Rights' (2004) 48(1) International Studies Quarterly 143.

[48]   Belser (n 28) 380–81.

differences in economy and interest, sought to play a more active and united role in the Doha Round.[49]

They concluded that the Doha Development Agenda as it stands is likely to benefit the strong players and further harm small and vulnerable economies.[50] On the export side, most African countries do not benefit from further tariff cuts as long as these do not include agriculture. In other fields, the least developed among them currently enjoy preferential access to Northern markets; general tariff cuts would erode this advantage. On the import side, African states would find it more difficult to develop their own industries when forced to reduce tariffs further.[51]

In 2014, the Bali Ministerial Conference set out to change the fact that most developing countries were more likely to lose than to win from the Doha Agenda, and took a number of decisions relating to LDCs. However, the endeavours to develop more non-reciprocal trade rules produced no binding results. The highly acclaimed decision on duty-free and quota-free market access for LDCs, for instance, simply asks developed countries (but not developing ones) 'to seek to improve' the coverage of their existing preference system.[52] Such an open space, not regulated by binding rules but subject to the political choices of developed states, adversely affects global constitutionalism. The vagueness of the commitment and the lack of a binding character 'permit the powerful countries to play with the LDC's expectations by making them constantly dependent on the discretion of the North'.[53]

The Bali Ministerial Conference thus partly excludes LDCs from the rule-based trading system. The most likely outcome is that developing countries will continue to offer duty-free and quota-free market access to goods, commodities in particular, not harming but benefiting the countries of the North. Some observers therefore concluded that the old-world order was still in good shape after Bali[54] and that the Declaration was 'business as usual', as it was likely to bring greater advantage to industrial states than developing and least-developed ones.[55]

For the time being, there is still no agreement on most of the issues of the Development Agenda. As the round currently gives no tangible sign of making progress, it is unclear if the lengthiest of the international trade negotiations will ever succeed. Doha might not be dead, but it is 'scrambling on its last legs'.[56] Despite its severe shortcomings, the fate of the round remains of crucial interest to African constitutionalism: failure would retain a trade system that was made without relevant participation by African states, that enforces biased trade rules, and which gives up on rules when the interests of developing countries are at stake.

---

[49] Many declarations and decisions were adopted, with the Kigali (2004), Cairo (2005), and Addis Ababa (2014) declarations best capturing the common African Group positions in the Doha Round. Joan Apecu Laker, *African Participation at the World Trade Organization: Legal and Institutional Aspects, 1995–2010* (Nijhoff 2014) 66.

[50] See Kevin P Gallagher, 'Understanding Developing Country Resistance to the Doha Round' (2007) 15(1) Review of International Political Economy 62.

[51] Christopher Stevens, 'The WTO Doha Round Impasse: Implications for Africa' ODI (19 November 2008) <http://www.odi.org/events/313-wto-doha-round-impasse-implications-africa> accessed 22 July 2019.

[52] WTO Ministerial Conference, *Duty-Free and Quota-Free Market Access for Least-Developed Countries*, WTO Doc WT/L/919; WT/MIN(13)/44 (Ministerial decision of 7 December 2013).

[53] Bhandari (n 33) 150.

[54] Badar A Iqbal and Sibghatullah Farooqi, 'WTO's Global Trade Summit at Bali: Pre and Post Bali Scenario' (2014) 6(1) Transnational Corporations Review 1, 13.

[55] Rorden Wilkinson, Erin Hannah, and James Scott, 'The WTO in Bali: What MC9 Means for the Doha Development Agenda and Why It Matters' (2014) 35(6) Third World Quarterly 1032, 1032.

[56] Bhandari (n 33) 94.

4. Pushing back the Ladder: Domestic Development Policies versus Global Liberalism

International trade law has the potential to strengthen African constitutionalism and support the pursuit of democracy, human rights, and development. Entrenched liberal trade rules offer prospects for economic growth, mitigate against the capriciousness and short-sightedness of governments, and assist in constraining the effects of government corruption and reckless private enterprise. This section argues, however, that the current WTO only partially fulfils these functions. This is so, first, because the rules claiming primacy tend to liberalize trade only when open borders benefit the North but it in other situations; it is so, secondly, because the WTO fails to discipline the behaviour of governments whenever developmental issues are at stake.

The conclusion reached is that, for these reasons, constitutionalizing international trade rules does not fulfil the promise of freeing developing countries from the discretionary power of their developed trading partners. Since the WTO rules reflect the unequal bargaining power of its members, both of the WTO's main principles—the obligation to liberalize, and the prohibition of discrimination—affect rich and poor countries unequally. Furthermore, these two pillars have only minor cracks for accommodating developing countries, but major ones when it comes to empowering rich countries to break the rules imposed on others.

4.1 The Inconsistent Obligation to Liberalize

The first principle of GATT, later incorporated into the WTO regime, is that states make binding and enforceable commitments to liberalize trade. The agreement sets limits on quantitative restrictions to trade and obliges them to reduce tariffs and other non-tariff barriers.[57] The tariff commitments made by each member, often the result of lengthy multilateral bargaining, are enumerated in schedules of concessions establishing binding ceilings the country may not exceed.[58] African states participated only marginally in the first negotiation rounds of the GATT 1947,[59] which focused on tariff commitments.[60] They lowered their tariffs for products in which influential exporting states had an interest and retained comparatively high tariffs for other products. Hence, African states are often relatively open for trade with Northern countries and comparatively protective vis-à-vis their neighbours—leaving great potential for inner-African trade fallow cooperation.[61]

By enforcing a transparent system of trade regulation and improving predictability and stability, the tariff commitments strengthen constitutionalism at the global and domestic level. The obligation to open up borders exposes domestic enterprises to international competition and disadvantages less competitive trading partners. While this can be effective in transforming the economy, reallocating resources and capitalizing on comparative advantages, unrestrained international competition can harm countries in development. The

---

[57] GATT 1994, arts 11 and 13.
[58] GATT 1994, arts 2 and 11.
[59] Geneva Round: 1955–56; Dillon Round: 1960–62; Kennedy Round: 1964–67; and Tokyo Round: 1973–79.
[60] cf Nottage (n 32) 484ff.
[61] In regard to regional cooperation, see Apecu (n 41).

obligation to open borders for imports (of manufactured goods) and unlimited exports (of raw materials) has therefore been described as a mechanism which is 'pushing back the ladder'. After all, all industrial states developed their industries behind high protectionist walls and accepted free trade only when their economies were globally competitive.[62] By imposing liberalized trade, they prevent developing countries from doing the same and moving up the economic ladder as they did.

In reaction to reproaches that the GATT 1947 lacked a level playing field, part IV on trade and development was included in the agreement in 1965. It formally introduced the concept of special and differential treatment into the global trade system, mostly by affording developing countries longer transition periods and allowing them to protect infant industries for limited timeframes. Part IV thus did not fundamentally change the asymmetrical structure of the trade system or give prominence to non-trade issues; it merely offered developing countries the opportunity to delay adjustment to the system.[63] Similarly, the TRIPS agreement includes special and differential treatment measures by providing for longer transitional periods[64] and technical assistance.[65] Special and differential treatment thus allows for delaying the implementation of global trade rules, but does not question their overall design.

The same is true for the Trade Facilitation Agreement (TFA), which entered into force on 22 February 2017 and aims at reducing the time and cost of trade by simplifying, modernizing, and harmonizing export and import processes. While the TFA constitutes a new and more dynamic approach to special and differential treatment provisions, the system largely remains and operates within the old logic of the global trade regime.

The agreement offers the advantage of differentiation:[66] while provisions under Category A must be implemented when the agreement enters into force,[67] Category B allows for transitional periods,[68] and Category C for assistance and support.[69] Each developing country can decide individually which provision it agrees to implement under categories A and B, with the result that the provisions are no longer treated as a single group.[70] In addition, any developing country may declare that a provision under the TFA will not be implemented until the country has received technical assistance and capacity-building support under Category C through the Trade Facilitation Agreement Facility (TFAF).[71] Further flexibility

---

[62] Bhandari (n 33) 146. Moreover, success stories among developing countries such as China, India, and Vietnam also present a compelling case for high tariff walls and other protectionist measures; see Bhandari (n 33) 159.

[63] Bhandari (n 33) 136ff (with further references) and 158–59. cf also Frank J Garcia, 'Global Justice and the Bretton Woods Institutions' (2007) 10(3) Journal of International Economic Law 461, 469, who raises the criticism that preferential market access will not benefit the least-advantaged partners so long as it is not made binding, non-exclusive, and unconditional.

[64] TRIPS, arts 65 and 66.

[65] TRIPS, art 67. See further BN Pandey and Prabhat Kumar Saha, 'Technical Cooperation under TRIPS Agreement: Flexibilities and Options for Developing Countries' (2011) 53(4) Journal of the Indian Law Institute 652.

[66] TFA, art 14.

[67] TFA, art 15.

[68] TFA, art 16.

[69] ibid.

[70] cf Joost Pauwelyn, 'The End of Differential Treatment?' (2013) 22(1) Review of European, Comparative and International Environmental Law 29, who also argues for a shift away from differential treatment for developing countries as a group towards individualized differentiation between countries.

[71] For a general overview, see Hsing-Hao Wu, 'Refining the WTO Trade Facilitation Agreement in the Face of an Uncertain Trade Environment: Challenges and Opportunities' (2019) 11(1) Trade Law and Development 132, 138–39.

comes from the fact that there is an early-warning mechanism,[72] as well as support for expert groups,[73] the possibility of switching between categories B and C,[74] and a grace period.[75] This highlights that ensuring compliance through dispute resolution is not at the core of the TFA.

Against the backdrop of multilevel constitutionalism, the TFA can be welcomed as it strengthens self-determination and does not implement global rules without regard to national conditions and priorities or obligations provided for by national constitutions. However, greater self-determination is granted only with regard to timing and support. By adopting a longer transitional period, on the one hand, and provisions for technical assistance, on the other, the TFA applies two conventional categories of special and differential treatment measures. Consequently, it neither changes the asymmetrical structure of the trade system, nor gives prominence to non-trade issues. Furthermore, focusing only on a more flexible implementation system does not help resolve conflicts that could arise when implementation of treaty obligations requires a change of existing custom, law, or regulation and clashes with important public interests such as public health or environmental issues.[76]

In the absence of any mechanism allowing for the balancing of conflicting interests, the global trade regime continues to fail to live up to its claim to be a constitutionalized order.

In addition to these exemptions for developing countries, the free-trade agreement accepts exceptions accommodating developed countries. The most important one empowers the US, Europe, Japan and other industrial states to exclude agriculture, fisheries, textiles, and clothes from multilateral trade discipline.[77] These carve-outs legitimize interventions, such as tariffs, quotas, and subsidies, which rich countries adopt to protect their non-competitive industries, and permit flagrant derogations from trade liberalization where open markets are mostly likely to profit the global South. By *regulating* trade where free trade would harm rich countries, and *liberalizing* trade where poor countries are likely to lose, the current global trade regime impairs the prospects for development.

Because the trade regime allows for quotas and import licensing in agriculture and textiles, the advantages of global constitutionalism are further undermined. The discretion given to developed states permits them to 'dangle a carrot before poor countries while threatening them with a stick'.[78] Frequently, quotas and licences are offered to countries that cooperate in any field of interest to the importing state, for instance in the fight against terrorism or drug control, and expose developing countries to un-transparent political considerations that an effective constitutional system would prevent.[79]

Anti-dumping measures have similar effects on constitutionalism. The GATT 1994 allows member states negatively affected by dumping (or what they consider as such) to impose trade barriers to protect domestic industries from harm. Mechanisms permitting states to suspend liberalization duties are used extensively by rich states and hardly disciplined by

---

[72] TFA, art 17.
[73] TFA, art 18.
[74] TFA, art 19.
[75] TFA, art 20.
[76] Hsing-Hao Wu (n 71) 141ff.
[77] GATT 1994, art 11(2)(C).
[78] Bhandari (n 33) 148.
[79] See Appellate Body Report European Communities—Conditions for the Granting of Tariff Preferences to Developing Countries, WTO Doc WT/DS246/AB/R (adopted 7 April 2004).

the trade system.[80] A developing state successfully competing in manufactured goods is thus likely to see foreign borders closing up to these goods and to be prevented in effect from profiting from price advantages.[81]

Countervailing duties operate in equally problematic ways. Such anti-subsidy duties can be imposed to neutralize the negative effects of subsidies on importing countries.[82] Again, there is little constitutionalism in the field, as importing countries can launch their own investigations, qualify state interventions as subsidies, and decide to charge extra duties when they believe their domestic producers are being harmed by imports (often doing so at the request of domestic industries). National trade policies supporting new industries in African countries are hence usually in line with the constitutional vision of a developmental state but run the risk of failure: if national development plans are successful to the point that they allow for increased market share, this success can easily be counteracted by the imposition of countervailing duties.[83]

The fact that economic sanctions against dumping and subsidies are imposed not by the WTO but by individual member states compounds the inequality of the system: whenever affluent countries impose extra duties, they in effect prevent imports from the South to important markets and protect their industries at the expense of Southern competitors. Developing countries find it much harder to act in the same way. This is due to the fact that the process of imposing anti-dumping or anti-subsidy duties is complex and demands a high level of technical expertise; what is more, few developing countries have the economic strength to harm developed countries even by successfully imposing extra charges. In sum, the cracks in the pillar of trade liberalization illustrate 'how deeply derogations and asymmetries have been institutionalized in the GATT legal structure, which is bequeathed to the WTO'.[84]

4.2 The Ambiguous Prohibition of Discrimination

The second principle of the WTO trading system, non-discrimination, has two major components.[85] According to the most-favoured-nation rule, states must apply to all WTO member states the same conditions they grant to their most favoured trading partners. The first component of the non-discrimination principle thus works partly in favour of developing countries, as it allows them to free-ride on trade liberalization commitments negotiated by more powerful states. At the same time, the rule originally prevented developed states from offering developing countries preferential access to their markets. To overcome this obstacle, the Enabling Clause was introduced in 1979: it 'enables' developed countries to introduce a General System of Preferences and apply tariffs lower than the ones in the country's schedule to developing countries and to them only.[86]

[80] Robert E Hudec, *Enforcing International Trade Law: The Evolution of the Modern GATT Legal System* (Butterworth Legal Publisher 1993) 357.

[81] Belser (n 28) 379ff.

[82] Belser (n 28) 390ff. cf for subsidies, GATT 1994, art 15.

[83] GATT 1994, art 6; see also Agreement on Subsidies and Countervailing Measures (SCM Agreement).

[84] Bhandari (n 33) 148. In regard to fear of political and economic retaliation, see Nottage (n 32) 497.

[85] GATT 1994, arts 1 and 3.

[86] Ramesh Adhikari and Prema-chandra Athukorala, 'Developing Countries in the World Trading System: An Overview' in Ramesh Adhikari and Prema-chandra Athukorala (eds), *Developing Countries in the World Trading System: The Uruguay Round and Beyond* (Elgar 2002) 2.

By allowing for the fragmentation of markets, the clause has made unilateral initiatives, such as the US African Growth and Opportunity Act and the Everything But Arms Initiative of the European Union (EU), compatible with non-discriminatory trade. It has abstained, however, from constitutionalizing special and differential treatment for developing states: as the clause only enables, rather than requires, preferential market access, developing countries remain exposed to the whims of their developed trading partners.[87] Consequently, the effects of part IV and the enabling clause on global constitutionalism are equivocal:[88] they recognize that unequal trading partners must be treated unequally, but fail to constitutionalize or even regulate this approach.

The second component of the non-discrimination principle, the national treatment clause, requires states to treat imported goods no less favourably than domestic products that are alike to them. The principle aims to prevent states from bypassing liberalization commitments by using taxes and regulations and other non-tariff barriers. By doing so, it subjugates all domestic laws and policies affecting the economy to WTO review. States adopting economic measures to enforce social and economic rights or support development are thus suspected of illegally favouring national products. Local initiatives in the vein of the Proudly Buy South African campaign have proliferated and become a popular tool for governments to stimulate domestic industries. None of these policies has been formally challenged yet for violating the national treatment principle, but trade scholars have concluded that few of them can be considered compatible with WTO law.[89]

The Italian Agricultural Machinery Case, decided by a GATT panel in 1958, first illustrated the effect of the non-discrimination principle on domestic policies. The Italian government had adopted an agricultural development programme offering special credit terms to farmers purchasing agricultural machinery if it had been made in Italy. When the United Kingdom complained that Italy was discriminating against British goods, the Italian government argued that prohibiting domestic development programmes would unduly limit the possibility for states to formulate domestic economic policies aiming at equality; Italy, it declared, had not contemplated being handcuffed in such a way when it accepted the GATT 1947. Nonetheless, the GATT panel held that Italy had violated the national treatment rule.[90]

This broad interpretation of the national treatment clause dramatically limits the policy space available to governments. The fact that the Italian agriculture development programme, designed to support the impoverished southern parts of the country, also profited the more industrialized north of the country, was crucial for its democratic adoption. Using tax income to transfer national resources to a poorer part of the country, thereby

---

[87] See Appellate Body Report, *European Communities—Regime for the Importation, Sale and Distribution of Bananas*, WTO Doc WT/DS27/AB/RW/USA; WT/DS27/AB/RW2/ECU (adopted 26 November 2008); Appellate Body Report *European Communities—Conditions for the Granting of Tariff Preferences to Developing Countries*, WTO Doc WT/DS246/AB/R (adopted 7 April 2004). See also Bhandari (n 33) 140: 'Among others, the fragmented mechanisms introduced in the form of S&D and GSP are legally misconstrued and flawed, since they cannot impose an obligation on developed countries.' Similarly, Nottage (n 32) 498–99 points out that the fact that preferential treatment is not part of enforceable WTO law leads to a lack of legal security and predictability if trading takes place under such a scheme.

[88] Bhandari (n 33) 139, with further references.

[89] Holger P Hestermeyer, 'The Legality of Local Content Measures under WTO Law' (2014) 48(3) Journal of World Trade 553, with references.

[90] Report of the Panel, Italian Discrimination against Imported Agricultural Machinery, L/833—7S/60 (23 October 1958).

strengthening substantive equality, is less acceptable when the preferences end up bene-fiting foreign producers. The national treatment clause thus can make it difficult for states to strike national deals and implement constitutional mandates to fight poverty and develop domestic industries.

The WTO system permits further derogations from the principle of non-discrimination by allowing bilateral or regional customs unions and free-trade areas to persist or be es-tablished provided that they apply to a substantial part of the trade.[91] These regional trade agreements have recently increased in number, reach, and relevance. Since they establish reciprocal preferential trade agreements between two or more partners, they constitute an exception to the WTO non-discrimination principle. If it is true that the future belongs to such trade agreements with varying geometries,[92] the WTO equality principle—and the very idea of global constitutionalism—will be further compromised. As the making of re-gional trade agreements does not follow rules, national and geopolitical interests are likely to harm those countries with limited bargaining power. While it is true that regional trade agreements in Africa present opportunities for cooperation in the economic sphere and elsewhere, regional trade agreements between the North and the South tend to follow old and asymmetrical patterns.[93]

Put differently, intercontinental African trade agreements offer the chance of compen-sating for some of the shortcomings of the global trade regime. The African Continental Free Trade Area, outlined in an agreement among fifty-four African Union member states, entered into force in May 2019.[94] It requires the state parties to progressively eliminate tar-iffs and non-tariff barriers to trade in goods, to gradually liberalize trade in services, and to cooperate in all trade-related areas.[95] The agreement establishing the African Continental Free Trade Area abstains from using constitutional rhetoric and recognizes consensus, vari-able geometry, flexibility, and special and differential treatment as its basic principles.[96] It thus constitutes an international agreement aiming at the creation of a single continental market without affecting domestic constitutional values.

5. Disagreeing on Priorities: Human Rights versus Free Trade

African states are particularly concerned by the tensions between national development plans and global trade rules. Their constitutions share an interest in limiting governments and preventing them from adopting harmful economic practices;[97] however, they do not

---

[91] GATT 1994, art 24.

[92] See the speech of the deputy director-general Alan W Wolff, 'The Future Belongs to Trade Agreements of Varying Geometries' WTO (11 August 2020) <http://www.wto.org/english/news_e/news20_e/ddgaw_11aug20_e.htm> accessed 23 September 2020.

[93] See Jaime de Melo, 'Regional Trade Agreements in Africa: Success or Failure?' IGC (3 December 2013) <http://www.theigc.org/blog/regional-trade-agreements-in-africa-success-or-failure/> accessed 23 September 2020; cf for further information the analytical notes from The South Centre at <http://www.southcentre.int/categ ory/issues/trade-and-investment/regional-trade-agreements/page/2/> accessed 23 September 2020.

[94] The African Continental Free Trade Area is the largest free-trade area since the formation of WTO in terms of the number of participating countries. See UNCTAD (n 16) 16.

[95] Agreement establishing the African Continental Free Trade Area, art 4.

[96] ibid art 5.

[97] cf Charles M Fombad, 'An Overview of Separation of Powers under Modern African Constitutions' in Charles M Fombad (ed), Separation of Powers in African Constitutionalism (OUP 2016) 58.

entrench liberal trade policies with a view to giving them priority over laws and policies implementing non-trade aims. While the constitutionalization of international human rights is in line with most African constitutions and regional commitments, this is not the case with binding international rules for liberalizing trade across borders and abstaining from interference in markets.

A general overview of African constitutions shows a decided tendency to give human rights, social justice, and development the highest priority in constitutional law. In contrast, the WTO agreements do not refer to human rights, and require member states to implement their domestic constitution only insofar as the measures taken are compatible with free trade. This tension tends to weaken African constitutionalism, as countries can be bound to choose between the respect of global trade rules and the implementation of their respective constitutions.

5.1 Human Rights as a Priority in African Constitutionalism

Numerous African constitutions emphasize social justice, equality, and development, as well as prominently codifying rights and freedoms that are largely co-substantial with the international bill of human rights. The constitutions also tend to endow states with an active role and a mandate to help the invisible hand of the market to operate for all, including for marginalized territories and vulnerable communities.[98] Many of the post-1990 constitutions of the continent incorporate international human rights instruments or explicitly refer to them.[99] In the last few decades, a large number of African states have undergone profound constitutional changes and strengthened democracy and participation, horizontal and vertical power-sharing, human rights, and the rule of law.[100]

However, while entrenching the principle of limited government with a view to the control and limitation of public power, numerous African constitutions have also mandated state authorities to play an active role and use their power to promote development and transform the economy as well as wider society.[101] African constitutionalism is hence not limited to handcuffing governments but seeks to turn them into transformative actors eradicating poverty and guaranteeing substantial equality. The 'third wave'[102] of African

---

[98]   See Belser (n 28) 608ff.

[99]   cf Charles M Fombad, 'Internationalization of Constitutional Law and Constitutionalism in Africa' (2012) 60(2) The American Journal of Comparative Law 439, 445ff, who refers to the preamble of the Constitution of Cameroon; arts 7 and 40 of the Constitution of Benin; arts 26 and 27 of the Constitution of Angola; art 2(5) and (6) of the Constitution of Kenya; art 39(1) of the Constitution of South Africa; art 17(3) of the Constitution of Cape Verde; and s 11(2) of the Constitution of Malawi. See also Magnus Killander, 'The Effects of International Law Norms on Constitutional Adjudication in Africa' in Charles M Fombad (ed), *Constitutional Adjudication in Africa* (OUP 2017) 212ff. For a discussion of domestic fundamental or human rights in different African constitutions, see Christof Heyns and Waruguru Kaguongo, 'Constitutional Human Rights Law in Africa: Current Developments' (2006) 22(4) South African Journal on Human Rights 673.

[100]   Charles M Fombad, 'Constitutional Reforms and Constitutionalism in Africa: Reflections on Some Current Challenges and Future Prospects' (2011) 59(4) Buffalo Law Review 1007, 1008–09.

[101]   cf Heyns and Kaguongo (n 99) 710, who note that in 2006 '[t]wenty-four African constitutions recognise the right to development or related rights. Fourteen countries refer to this right in terms of the free development of the person, thus an individual right, while nine others protect it as a collective right.'

[102]   The term was coined by Samuel P Huntington, *The Third Wave: Democratization in the Late Twentieth Century* (University of Oklahoma Press 1991). For a detailed overview of the different generations of African constitutions, see Charles M Fombad, 'The Evolution of Modern African Constitutions' in Charles M Fombad (ed), *Separation of Powers in African Constitutionalism* (OUP 2016) 14ff.

constitutionalism, that is to say, does not envisage the role of the state as passively trusting the invisible hand of free markets but as using the visible hand of accountable governments wherever it is needed to actualize the social and economic rights of all citizens.[103]

According to the constitution of Tunisia, for instance, the state must seek 'to achieve social justice, sustainable development and a balance between regions based on development indicators and the principle of positive discrimination'.[104] Rwanda commits itself in its constitution to eradicating discrimination, building a state committed to promoting social welfare, and establishing appropriate mechanisms for equal opportunity to social justice.[105] South Africa is founded on the values of human dignity, the achievement of equality, and the advancement of human rights and freedoms,[106] and places strong emphasis on the guarantee of socio-economic rights for all citizens.

The priority of human rights and development for all—and potential conflicts with free trade—are also present in Kenya's Constitution of 2010. The national values and principles of governance include equity, social justice, equality, human rights, non-discrimination, protection of the marginalized, and sustainable development.[107] The Bill of Rights—and not free trade—constitutes the binding framework for all social, economic, and cultural policies, the overall purpose of which is to preserve the dignity of individuals and communities and to promote social justice.[108]

The constitution of the youngest African state, coming into force as a transitional constitution in 2011, recognizes 'justice, equality, respect for human dignity and advancement of human rights and fundamental freedoms' as the fundamental values on which South Sudan is founded.[109] All rights and freedoms enshrined in international human rights conventions ratified by South Sudan are an integral part of the constitutional Bill of Rights, and together constitute the 'cornerstone of social justice, equality and democracy'.[110]

While the central values of the South Sudanese Constitution are in line with international human rights obligations, other fundamental objectives and principles enshrined in it are, in contrast, potentially in conflict with international duties in the field of trade. To eradicate poverty and attain the Millennium Development Goals, the Constitution obliges the government to develop and regulate the economy' so as to increase production, create an efficient and self-reliant economy, encourage free markets, facilitate the development of the private sector, particularly so of indigenous entrepreneurs, and promote agricultural, industrial, and technological development. The Constitution mandates the government to adopt all appropriate measures to achieve these goals and 'to bring about balanced, integrated and equitable development'.[111]

---

[103] In regard to the colonial, ideological, religious, and indigenous influences on African constitutions, see Fombad (n 102) 22ff. Many constitutions enshrine, for example, a right to work and rights in work, a right to a healthy environment, a right to social security, a right to development, and a right to an adequate standard of living. See in detail Heyns and Kaguongo (n 99) 698ff.

[104] Constitution of Tunisia, art 12.

[105] Constitution of Rwanda, art 10.

[106] Constitution of South Africa, s 1.

[107] Constitution of Kenya, art 10.

[108] ibid art 19(1) and (2).

[109] Transitional Constitution of the Republic of South Sudan of 2011, art 1 para 5.

[110] ibid art 9.

[111] ibid art 37.

In 2019, South Sudan and the WTO commenced membership negotiations.[112] While WTO membership offers prospects for development, it simultaneously renders the implementation of domestic measures aiming at the strengthening of a self-reliant economy and indigenous enterprises more challenging.

The African Charter on Human and Peoples' Rights (ACHPR), currently ratified by fifty-three African states, confirms the conviction of states that human rights constitute essential obligations of states and override conflicting laws and policies. The ACHPR underscores that governments are bound to respect, protect, and fulfil human rights and that these obligations are no longer in the sphere of free political choices but constitute binding international obligations monitored by supra-national mechanisms. The fact that the ACHPR establishes an African Commission on Human and Peoples' Rights further emphasizes the binding character of human rights obligations on all member states. In 1998, these states approved a protocol creating an African Court on Human and Peoples' Rights. By agreeing that domestic laws and decisions should be the object of supra-national judicial review, the states recognized the primacy of individual rights and freedoms throughout the continent.

5.2 Human Rights as an Exception in WTO Constitutionalism

In contrast to African constitutions and regional instruments, the WTO system is silent on international and national human rights. It is true that some of the agreements refer in their preambles to the aim of raising living standards or ensuring full employment and provide for certain exceptions, thus leaving a degree of space for human rights considerations (such as the protection of public morals).[113] Generally, though, the global trade rules are not concerned with human rights. None of the trade agreements explicitly guarantees human rights or refers to the duty of states to respect and protect individual rights and freedoms. The Singapore Declaration of 1998 is the only document that at the least mentions labour standards, but only to defer them to the ILO.[114] At first sight, the global trade system is blind to non-trade issues.[115] At second sight, constitutionalized trade rules dethrone human rights from the top of the legal hierarchy in that they can enter the scene of international trade law only via the back door of exception clauses.[116]

In African constitutionalism, human rights are the yardstick against which economic and social policies must be measured, whereas free trade is the fundamental value at the WTO. WTO obligations imposing open borders, prohibiting domestic subsidies, and requiring the protection of intellectual property rights can harm the rights to work, health, and food.[117] A significant body of GATT and WTO case-law examines government policies

[112] See WTO, 'South Sudan Kicks off WTO Membership Negotiations' (21 March 2019) <http://www.wto.org/english/news_e/news19_e/acc__21mar19_e.htm> accessed 23 September 2020.

[113] GATT 1994, art 20 lit 1; Belser (n 28) 398ff.

[114] Singapore Ministerial Declaration, para 4; see also Thomas Cottier, 'The Implications of EC—Seal Products for the Protection of Core Labour Standards in WTO Law' in Henner Gött (ed), *Labour Standards in International Economic Law* (Springer 2018) 71–73.

[115] Peter-Tobias Stoll, 'International Economic and Social Dimensions: Divided or Connected?' in Henner Gött (ed), *Labour Standards in International Economic Law* (Springer 2018) 19 and 26–27.

[116] GATT 1994, arts 20 and 21.

[117] Robert Howse and Ruti G Teitel, 'Beyond the Divide: The International Covenant on Economic, Social and Political Rights and the World Trade Organization' in Sarah Joseph, David Kinley, and Jeff Waincymer (eds), *The World Trade Organization and Human Rights: Interdisciplinary Perspectives* (Elgar 2009).

aimed at or justified by the protection of human rights. In most cases, the states seeking policy space to attain non-economic objectives lost their case in the WTO rulings.[118] The latter make it clear that states using the exceptions have a considerable burden of proof to demonstrate that trade restrictions are necessary and that less trade-restrictive means are not available. Domestic measures aiming at the protection of human rights thus can easily fall prey to overriding obligations to liberalize trade. In addition, the outcomes in these decisions are likely to have a chilling effect: they can cause states to abstain from human rights-oriented regulations for fear of having to defend them, at significant cost, in front of the WTO.[119]

Under the current system, those 'seeking to protect policy space for the right reasons—human rights and not protectionism per se—will need to remain vigilant'.[120] The WTO dispute settlement bodies, composed of international trade experts, are not ideally equipped to strike a balance between free trade and conflicting but overriding values. They generally lack expertise in human rights law as well as African members.[121] Overall, the WTO does not strengthen African member states in their pursuit of constitutionalism but rather incentives them to follow global trade rules even if these clash with constitutional aims and obligations.

6. Fighting for the Throne: Human Rights versus Free Trade in Practice

The general exceptions to the GATT 1994 principles, articles 20 and 21, do not mention domestic constitutions, human rights, or development.[122] States taking adequate measures to promote equality and social justice, for example by protecting local small and medium-sized enterprises, providing jobs, interfering with agriculture, supporting marginalized regions or vulnerable groups, therefore run the risk of violating WTO obligations. Conversely, the respect of WTO rules, such as importing subsidized agricultural goods from Northern countries, treating like products equally, or protecting patents on drugs, can clash with a state's obligation to promote development as well as respect and protect human rights.

The cases presented below show that the turn to constitutionalism at the WTO gives priority to free trade—at the price of degrading human rights to mere exceptions from the rule. They also illustrate that the current WTO regime largely fails in its attempt to constrain the powers of developed states.

---

[118] Eg Appellate Body Report European Communities—EC Measures Concerning Meat and Meat Products (Hormones), WTO Doc WT/DS26/AB/R; WT/DS48/AB/R (adopted 16 January 1998); Panel Report, European Communities—Measures Affecting the Approval and Marketing of Biotech Products, WTO Doc WT/DS291/R; WT/DS292/R; WT/DS293/R (adopted 29 September 2006); Appellate Body Report, Brazil—Measures Affecting Imports of Retreaded Tyres, WTO Doc WT/DS332/AB/R (adopted 3 December 2007); or Appellate Body Report, United States—Measures Affecting the Production and Sale of Clove Cigarettes, WTO Doc WT/DS406/AB/R (adopted 4 April 2012).

[119] Steven R Ratner, *The Thin Justice of International Law: A Moral Reckoning of the Law of Nations* (OUP 2015) 335–36; Gabrielle Marceau, 'WTO Dispute Settlement and Human Rights' (2002) 13(4) EJIL 753.

[120] Ratner (n 119) 337.

[121] See Ratner (n 119) 339: 'The paucity of expertise on human rights law within the DSB panels and AB may well explain not only their reluctance to address human rights obligations in their rulings but the restrictions on policy space as well.'

[122] Rachel Harris and Gillian Moon, 'GATT Article XX and Human Rights: What Do We Know from the First 20 Years?' (2015) 16(2) Melbourne Journal of International Law 432.

6.1 Development and Trade in Agriculture

Trade in agriculture has become one of the most important and controversial issues at the WTO. Soon after the GATT 1994 came into being, most developed states waived obligations to liberalize trade in agriculture. After the Uruguay Round of trade negotiations, the average bound tariff on manufactured goods fell to 4 per cent, while the average bound tariff on agricultural goods remained at 40 per cent. Tariffs as high as 500 per cent are sometimes imposed by the US, EU, and Canada on products that include beef, dairy products, vegetables, fresh and dried fruit, cereals, sugar, and tobacco, as well as prepared fruit and vegetables.[123]

At the end of the Uruguay Round, when developing countries had to accept a trade package favouring the countries of the North, the developed states agreed to bring agriculture back under multilateral trade discipline. However, this commitment was not implemented.[124] The current system hence largely prevents African states from using their comparative advantage in agriculture. Although most developing countries stand to gain substantial benefits from free trade, these do not materialize. Even special agreements between developed and developing nations discriminate against agricultural products. For instance, the African Growth and Opportunity Act (AGOA), a preferential trade agreement between the US and countries from Africa, excludes dairy products, cocoa, coffee, tea, tobacco, nuts, and certain fabrics.[125]

The lack of international trade discipline under the current WTO Agreement on Agriculture also relates to subsidies. Currently, rich countries pay about USD 1 billion a day to their farmers in agricultural subsidies. That is more than four times all development assistance going to poor nations.[126] By way of domestic subsidies, Northern states support their non-competitive agricultural sectors; by way of export subsidies, they distort international markets and harm foreign producers. African states are particularly concerned at the bias of the trade regime.[127] Agriculture is a crucial source of income and provides food and a means of living to the roughly 70 per cent of the continent's population that lives in rural areas.

In addition, these states' own markets are harmed by subsidized import products. As the WTO allows Northern countries to dump excess products on the international market, African markets are often, but unreliably, flooded with subsidized US and European agricultural products. These have a negative effect on price stability, weaken the livelihoods of farmers, and endanger food security.[128]

The controversy about trade in agriculture illustrates the reversal of fundamental values in global trade law. The asymmetrical implementation of the free trade regime violates the principles of equality, social justice, and development. The Doha negotiation mandate, vaguely promising the phasing-out of export subsidies and reduction of trade-distorting domestic farm support,[129] makes it clear that the turn to constitutionalism at the WTO does

---

[123] Reddy Karunanidhi, 'Developing Africa: Trade Barriers, Liberalization and Inequality in the World Trade Organisation' (2011) 5(22) African Journal of Business Management 8686.

[124] Adhikari and Athukorala (n 86) 2.

[125] Karunanidhi (n 123).

[126] Mike Moore, 'Globalisation: The Impact of the Doha Development Agenda on the Free Market Process' *WTO* (February 2002) <http://www.wto.org/english/news_e/spmm_e/spmm77_e.htm> accessed 23 September 2020.

[127] Bhandari (n 33) 159.

[128] Ratner (n 119) 342.

[129] Moore (n 126).

not enforce equal trade roles for all and fails to prevent governments from selfish and rent-seeking behaviour.

6.2 The Right to Life and the Kimberly Process

The controversies relating to the Kimberly Process further illustrate that African and WTO constitutionalism can clash. Since the mid-1990s, civil war in parts of Africa has been fuelled by armed groups' practice of raising funds through the international sale of diamonds mined in areas they control. In 2000, a group of African states, joined by diamond-importing states and diamond companies, came together to stop this fundraising strategy by creating an international certification regime, the Kimberley Process, with the aim of keeping conflict diamonds out of the international market. In 2003, the UN Security Council endorsed the system.

By obliging states to allow only the export and import of diamonds accompanied by a certificate that guarantees they are not conflict diamonds, the Kimberly Process affects international trade. Hence, it immediately triggered concerns that it would violate WTO rules, in particular the elimination of quantitative restrictions and the duty to apply the most-favoured-nation rule: when a country bans the export or import of uncertified diamonds, it treats 'like products' unequally and thus abstains from implementing the non-discrimination principle. After much debate whether blood diamonds were like other diamonds, the WTO's General Council in 2003 issued a formal waiver of the GATT 1994 articles that might be violated by the Kimberly Process. In doing so, it recognized 'the extraordinary humanitarian nature of the issue and the devastating impact of conflicts fuelled by the trade in conflict diamonds on the peace, safety and security of people in affected countries'.[130]

From the perspective of African constitutionalism, the waiver is highly problematic. By issuing it, the General Council affirmed the view that member states adopting measures to protect the right to life of their citizens violate international trade law and need an exemption.[131] That is to say, even when a state in extraordinary circumstances takes appropriate measures to prevent or stop systematic and gross human rights violations, their compatibility with the WTO regime is not a given but in need of a waiver. The Kimberley Process thus illustrates that the turn to constitutionalism at the WTO reverses the hierarchy of values and places free trade above human rights. The waiver merely expresses a political agreement to accept the Kimberly Process, not a commitment to give primacy to human rights over trade obligations.[132]

---

[130] WTO General Council, Waiver Concerning Kimberley Process Certification Scheme for Rough Diamonds, WTO Doc WT/L/518 (Decision of 15 May 2003).
[131] See Krista Nadakavukaren Schefer, 'Stopping Trade in Conflict Diamonds: Exploring the Trade and Human Rights Interface with the WTO Waiver for the Kimberley Process' in Thomas Cottier, Joost Pauwelyn, and Elisabeth Bürgi (eds), *Human Rights and International Trade* (OUP 2005) 420–40.
[132] Ratner (n 119) 328–29.

6.3 The Right to Health and Trade in Generics

African and WTO constitutionalism also clash in the field of health. International and domestic human rights law obliges states to adopt all appropriate measures to ensure access to health care for all.[133] In contrast, the WTO forces them to respect patents and to accept that the respect of intellectual property rights renders drugs more expensive and unaffordable to poor patients.

The victims of HIV/AIDS in particular, who live predominantly in developing countries, are often unable to buy medicines developed and patented by Northern pharmaceutical companies. The original TRIPS agreement allowed governments of developing countries confronted with national health emergencies to produce generic medicines for their domestic markets without the patent owners' consent.[134] The so-called 'compulsory licensing' arrangements still meant that poorer countries without manufacturing capacity could not access generic drugs.[135] After long negotiations, WTO members in 2001 issued the Doha Declaration, which affirmed that TRIPS 'can and should be interpreted and implemented in a manner supportive of WTO members' rights to protect public health and, in particular, to promote access to medicines for all'.[136] In 2003, WTO members agreed to give developing countries a temporary waiver to export and import generic drugs. Two years later, the waiver was made permanent under the TRIPS agreement.[137]

By waiving key obligations of the TRIPS, the WTO member states managed to invalidate the accusation that the treaty prevented developing states from solving national health crises and fulfilling human rights obligations. However, the trade system did not give in to the primacy of human rights but merely accepted a limited exception to the obligation to protect intellectual property rights. The WTO trade rules thus continue to take primacy and only yield to human rights in exceptional cases.[138] The ad hoc solution of the WTO, adopted under enormous public pressure, falls short in other key ways.

First, some developing countries lack the technical capacity to amend their trade laws to reflect the Doha flexibility and thus struggle to grant licences. Secondly, pharmaceutical companies are pressuring developing states not to accept compulsory licences, and do not shy away from pursuing developing countries for manufacturing generics.[139] Thirdly, Europe and the US, the home of many powerful pharmaceutical companies, circumvent Doha flexibilities through different strategies, including by requiring greater intellectual property protection ('TRIPS-plus') in regional and bilateral trade agreements.[140] These realities suggest that the substance of the Doha solution belies its form; in fact, the global trade system is not able to avoid interference by trade law in the right to health.[141]

---

[133] See eg Ruling of the Constitutional Court of South Africa, *Minister of Health v Treatment Action Campaign (TAC)* (2002) 5 SA 721 (CC).

[134] TRIPS, art 31(b).

[135] WTO Ministerial Conference, *Declaration on the TRIPS Agreement on Public Health*, WTO Doc WT/MIN(01)/DEC/2 (adopted 14 November 2001), para 4.

[136] WTO (n 135) paras 4–6.

[137] See Ratner (n 119) 332.

[138] Ratner (n 119) 332.

[139] See Joseph E Stiglitz and Arjun Jayadev, 'India's Patently Wise Decision' *Project Syndicate* (8 April 2013) <https://bit.ly/3o9jUIr> accessed 23 September 2020.

[140] Ratner (n 119) 332–33.

[141] Ratner (n 119) 333.

7. The Plural Turn to Global Constitutionalism: The Way Forward

The liberal turn to constitutionalism at the WTO insists on the primacy of free trade but overlooks the numerous exceptions to free trade, in particular in agriculture and textiles. It promotes convergence amongst states and, by streamlining laws and policies in the interest of open borders, substantially reduces the regulatory space of states. Under such a regime, states limiting trade by fulfilling human rights mandates find themselves in the same position as states distorting markets in the interest of powerful elites and rent-seeking enterprises. The liberal approach to global constitutionalism thus comes at the risk of compromising human rights.

In contrast, a plural model of global constitutionalism recognizes a variety of constitutional values and actors determining them. While the liberal approach tends to crush domestic constitutional values incompatible with free trade, the plural approach aims at identifying and accommodating different constitutional values. The international system for the protection of human rights, for example, shows much greater flexibility in this respect. International human rights are an integral part of most domestic constitutions, entrenching largely co-substantial duties on governments. National courts increasingly frequently interpret national fundamental rights in accordance with international and supra-national human rights obligations and enter into a transnational dialogue with international courts and other adjudication or implementation bodies. The same is true for international bodies. They meticulously follow national developments, take inspiration from local innovation, and observe and contribute to the making of an international consensus.

There is intense communication between the different tiers of constitutionalism, an interaction involving top-down as well as bottom-up learning and feedback loops. These complex human rights networks, in which public, hybrid, and private actors such as non-governmental organizations play important roles, ultimately contribute to the emergence of an international (or at least regional) human rights system characterized by common features and standards of protection.[142] Furthermore, most states have subscribed to regional charters and enforcement mechanisms, such as the ACHPR and the African Commission on Human and Peoples' Rights.[143] They have thus declared their international commitment to human rights and accepted that they should limit the national policy space accordingly.

Instead of establishing a rigid hierarchy between global and national constitutionalism, a plural model of global constitutionalism focuses on the protection of common values and on agreements on common methods for resolving differences both between and within political communities. Hence, plural global constitutionalism emphasizes principles which are shared between different tiers and fragments of constitutionalism, but recognizes differences and their legitimacy. Its focus thus lies on rules of mutual recognition, conflict rules, proportionality tests, and other ways of dealing with differences. It puts less emphasis on

---

[142] Matthias Klatt, *Die Praktische Konkordanz von Kompetenzen, Entwickelt anhand der Jurisdiktionskonflikte im Europäischen Grundrechtsschutz* (Mohr Siebeck 2014) 28; Laurence R Helfer and Anne-Marie Slaughter, 'Toward a Theory of Effective Supranational Adjudication' (1997) 107(2) The Yale Law Journal 273, 276–77; Jörg Paul Müller, 'Koordination des Grundrechtsschutzes in Europa' (2005) 124(2) Zeitschrift für Schweizerisches Recht 9.

[143] cf Mumba Malila, 'Individuals' Duties in the African Human Rights Protection System' in Stephan Parmentier, Hand Werdmölder, and Michaël Merrigan (eds), *Between Rights and Responsibilities: A Fundamental Debate* (Intersentia 2016) 188 ff; Fatsah Ouguergouz, *La Charte Africaine des Droits de l'Homme et des Peuples: une approche juridique des droits de l'homme entre tradition et modernité* (Presses universitaires de France 1993) 41ff.

global normative warrants limiting governments and greater emphasis on mechanisms balancing interests and making different laws and policies compatible with each other.

Plural constitutionalism limits the reach of global trade law. According to von Bogdandy, one of the most prominent supporters of 'the plural turn', the aim of the WTO is limited to organizing economic interdependence. Global trade law neither imposes free trade nor forces member states to follow liberal policies domestically.[144] According to the preamble of the Marrakesh Agreement Establishing the World Trade Organization, states should conduct their trade relations 'with a view to raising standards of living, ensuring full employment and a large and steadily growing volume of real income and effective demand'. The expansion of production of and trade in goods and services is to be achieved 'in accordance with the objective of sustainable development'. The preamble expresses the desire of contributing to these objectives 'by entering into reciprocal and mutually advantageous arrangements directed to the substantial reduction of tariffs and other barriers to trade'. The 'substantial reduction of tariffs and other barriers to trade', not their elimination, thus appears as a means to achieve the aim of raising living standards and sustaining development. While tariffs and other trade barriers at borders are to be reduced, other national economic policies may persist as long as they are applied non-discriminatorily towards all trading partners.

In sharp but often overlooked contrast to the law of the EU, the law of the WTO does not aim at the harmonization of national laws or the creation of an ever-closer union.[145] While the EU has many institutional mechanisms by which to negotiate trade-offs between liberalization and other policy aims, the WTO lacks such instruments; it thus must leave more space for international organizations and to member states to protect and promote conflicting constitutional values, and cannot crush national decision-making without weakening human rights.

The plural model recognizes the absence of an all-encompassing source of final global authority and holds that this leads to a 'dialectic of challenge, resistance and creative adjustment within a framework of competitive universalism'.[146] In such a system of competing values and interests, the generative power of dissent is crucial. Despite increasing interconnectedness, states thus remain important actors allowing for democratic dissent and the primacy of human rights. Global constitutionalism hence cannot come at the price of weakening domestic constitutionalism, since otherwise the creative adjustment of international norms would be at risk.[147]

8. Conclusion

African states are particularly concerned by the liberal turn to WTO constitutionalism. As the global trade rules have been designed to serve their interests, developed countries find it easier to comply with a global commercial code and to accept its primacy over their domestic constitutions.[148] In contrast, African states see themselves confronted with

---

[144] Bogdandy (n 21) 430.
[145] Bogdandy (n 21) 432.
[146] Walker (n 9) 364
[147] Walker (n 9) 367.
[148] For harsh criticism, see Thomas Pogge, *World Poverty and Human Rights: Cosmopolitan Responsibilities and Reforms* (Polity Press 2007) 18–20.

overriding trade rules that do not promote development and sometimes even hinder it. While it can be useful to limit the power of governments to deal with international trade at will, forcing them to apply biased rules is not.

Another shortcoming of the turn to global constitutionalism at the WTO is that the rule-based system fails to be rule-based when development issues are at stake. The only rules which are enforced are those based on the formal equality of all states; those relating to the differences in development and wealth amongst the states, and providing special and differential treatment with a view of achieving substantive equality, are not binding. These imbalances must be addressed before WTO trade rules can legitimately claim primacy. The Doha Development Round, promising a profound transformation of the WTO in the interests of development, is floundering, however. Against this background, the agenda to constitutionalize the existing, development-unfriendly rules comes as a mockery of the African continent.

In contrast to the liberal turn to constitutionalism at the WTO, the plural approach to global constitutionalism offers avenues that are more promising. If human rights and development are recognized as the fundamental constitutional norms to which all laws and policies, including international agreements, must conform, the turn to global constitutionalism would be of great interest to African countries. Domestic measures, as well as free and differential trade, would then have to stand the test of whether or not they are contributing to general well-being.[149]

In such a system, a comprehensive national development programme such as the one at the origin of the Italian agricultural machinery case would not violate WTO duties, as it serves the aims of poverty reduction and national coherence. The fact that the programme had a negative impact on British machinery manufacturers would have had to be assessed against the background of not only free-trade regulations but human rights guarantees and development strategies. Under such a general welfare constitutionalism, agricultural policies in the North and South would be assessed in view of their effects on the right to food, food security, and development.

Consequently, domestic measures affecting trade in developing countries would often appear in a different light from those applied in developed countries. While the former often serve the interests of the impoverished rural population, the latter comply with the interests of industrial farms. Under a general welfare constitutionalism, mechanisms like the Kimberly Process would no longer need a waiver but comply perfectly with overriding norms.

Overall, moving the debate of global constitutionalism away from the WTO and bringing it closer to human rights, social justice, and development opens new avenues for a transnational constitutionalism which is not based on strict hierarchies between domestic and global constitutions but leaves room for contestation and opportunities for improving a system that has yet to become fair.

---

[149] See Frank J Garcia, *Trade, Inequality, and Justice: Towards a Liberal Theory of Just Trade* (Transnational Publishers 2003); Margot E Salomon, *Global Responsibility for Human Rights* (OUP 2007).

Bibliography

Adhikari R and Athukorala P, 'Developing Countries in the World Trading System: An Overview' in Adhikari R and Athukorala P (eds), *Developing Countries in the World Trading System: The Uruguay Round and Beyond* (Elgar 2002)

Allot P, 'The Emerging Universal Legal System' (2001) 3(1) International Law FORUM Du Droit International 12

Apecu J, 'The Level of African Engagement at the World Trade Organization from 1995 to 2010' (2013) 4(2) International Development Policy 29

Apecu J, *African Participation at the World Trade Organization: Legal and Institutional Aspects, 1995–2010* (Nijhoff 2014)

Bartels L, 'Making WTO Dispute Settlement Work for African Countries: An Evaluation of Current Proposals for Reforming the DSU', 2013 6(2) Law and Development Review 47

Belser EM, *The White Man's Burden: Arbeit und Menschenrechte in der globalisierten Welt* (Stämpfli 2007)

Bertelsmann-Scott T and others, 'The Impact of Plurilateral Trade Agreements on Developing Countries: To Participate or Not to Participate?' (2018) 25(2) South African Journal of International Affairs 177

Bhandari SR, *Global Constitutionalism and the Path of International Law* (Brill 2016)

Bogdandy A von, 'Verfassungsrechtliche Dimensionen der Welthandelsorganisation 2. Teil: Neue Wege Globaler Demokratie?' (2001) 34(4) Kritische Justiz 425

Bohanes J and Garza F, 'Going Beyond Stereotypes: Participation of Developing Countries in WTO Dispute Settlement' (2012) 4(1) Trade, Law and Development 45

Civello P, 'The TRIMs Agreement: A Failed Attempt at Investment Liberalization' (1999) 8 Minnesota Journal of International Law 97

Cottier T, 'The Implications of EC—Seal Products for the Protection of Core Labour Standards in WTO Law' in Henner Gött (ed), *Labour Standards in International Economic Law* (Springer 2018)

Donnelly J, *Universal Human Rights in Theory and Practice* (2nd edn, Cornell University Press 2003)

Dunoff JL, 'Constitutional Conceits: The WTO's "Constitution" and the Discipline of International Law' (2006) 17(3) EJIL 647

Dunoff JL, 'The Politics of International Constitutions: The Curious Case of the World Trade Organization' in Dunoff JL and Trachtman JP (eds), *Ruling the World? Constitutionalism, International Law, and Global Governance* (Cambridge University Press 2009)

Fasan O, 'Global Trade Law: Challenges and Options for Africa' (2003) 47(2) Journal of African Law 143

Fassbender B, 'We the Peoples of the United Nations' in Loughlin M and Walker N (eds), *The Paradox of Constitutionalism: Constituent Power and Constitutional Form* (OUP 2008)

Fennell WA and Tyler JW, 'Trade-Related Investment Measures' in Stewart TP (ed), *The GATT Uruguay Round: A Negotiating History 1986–1992, Volume II: Commentary* (Kluwer 1993)

Fombad CM, 'Constitutional Reforms and Constitutionalism in Africa: Reflections on Some Current Challenges and Future Prospects' (2011) 59(4) Buffalo Law Review 1007

Fombad CM, 'Internationalization of Constitutional Law and Constitutionalism in Africa' (2012) 60(2) The American Journal of Comparative Law 439

Fombad CM, 'An Overview of Separation of Powers under Modern African Constitutions' in Fombad CM (ed), *Separation of Powers in African Constitutionalism* (OUP 2016)

Fombad CM, 'The Evolution of Modern African Constitutions' in Fombad CM (ed), *Separation of Powers in African Constitutionalism* (OUP 2016)

Gallagher KP, 'Understanding Developing Country Resistance to the Doha Round' (2007) 15(1) Review of International Political Economy 62

Garcia FJ, *Trade, Inequality, and Justice: Towards a Liberal Theory of Just Trade* (Transnational Publishers 2003)

Garcia FJ, 'Beyond Special and Differential Treatment' (2004) 27(2) Boston College International and Comparative Law Review 291

Garcia FJ, 'Global Justice and the Bretton Woods Institutions' (2007) 10(3) Journal of International Economic Law 461

Harris R and Moon G, 'GATT Article XX and Human Rights: What Do We Know from the First 20 Years?' (2015) 16(2) Melbourne Journal of International Law 432

Hartman SW, 'The WTO, the Doha Round Impasse, PTAs, and FTAs/RTAs' (2013) 27(5) The International Trade Journal 411

Helfer LR and Slaughter AM, 'Toward a Theory of Effective Supranational Adjudication' (1997) 107(2) The Yale Law Journal 273

Hestermeyer HP, 'The Legality of Local Content Measures under WTO Law' (2014) 48(3) Journal of World Trade 553

Heyns C and Kaguongo W, 'Constitutional Human Rights Law in Africa: Current Developments' (2006) 22(4) South African Journal on Human Rights 673

Howse R and Teitel RG, 'Beyond the Divide: The International Covenant on Economic, Social and Political Rights and the World Trade Organization' in Joseph S, Kinley D, and Waincymer J (eds), *The World Trade Organization and Human Rights: Interdisciplinary Perspectives* (Elgar 2009)

Howse R and Nicolaidis K, 'Enhancing WTO Legitimacy: Constitutionalization or Global Subsidiarity?' (2003) 16(1) Governance: An International Journal of Policy, Administration, and Institutions 73

Hudec RE, *Enforcing International Trade Law: The Evolution of the Modern GATT Legal System* (Butterworth Legal Publisher 1993)

Huntington SP, *The Third Wave: Democratization in the Late Twentieth Century* (University of Oklahoma Press 1991)

Iqbal BA and Farooqi S, 'WTO's Global Trade Summit at Bali: Pre and Post Bali Scenario' (2014) 6(1) Transnational Corporations Review 1

Jackson JH, *The World Trade Organization: Constitution and Jurisprudence* (The Royal Institute of International Affairs 1998)

Karunanidhi R, 'Developing Africa: Trade Barriers, Liberalization and Inequality in the World Trade Organisation' (2011) 5(22) African Journal of Business Management 8686

Killander M, 'The Effects of International Law Norms on Constitutional Adjudication in Africa' in Fombad CM (ed), *Constitutional Adjudication in Africa* (OUP 2017)

Klabbers J, 'Setting the Scene' in Klabbers J, Peters A, and Ulfstein G (eds), *The Constitutionalization of International Law* (OUP 2009)

Klatt M, *Die Praktische Konkordanz von Kompetenzen, Entwickelt anhand der Jurisdiktionskonflikte im Europäischen Grundrechtsschutz* (Mohr Siebeck 2014)

Malila M, 'Individuals' Duties in the African Human Rights Protection System' in Parmentier S, Werdmölder H, and Merrigan M (eds), *Between Rights and Responsibilities: A Fundamental Debate* (Intersentia 2016)

Marceau G, 'WTO Dispute Settlement and Human Rights' (2002) 13(4) EJIL 753

Melo J de, 'Regional Trade Agreements in Africa: Success or Failure?' *IGC* (3 December 2013) <http://www.theigc.org/blog/regional-trade-agreements-in-africa-success-or-failure/> accessed 23 September 2020

Moore M, 'Globalisation: The Impact of the Doha Development Agenda on the Free Market Process' *WTO* (February 2002) <http://www.wto.org/english/news_e/spmm_e/spmm77_e.htm accessed 23 September 2020)

Müller JP, 'Koordination des Grundrechtsschutzes in Europa' (2005) 124(2) Zeitschrift für Schweizerisches Recht 9

Nadakavukaren Schefer K, 'Stopping Trade in Conflict Diamonds: Exploring the Trade and Human Rights Interface with the WTO Waiver for the Kimberley Process' in Cottier T, Pauwelyn J, and Bürgi E (eds), *Human Rights and International Trade* (OUP 2005)

Nottage H, 'Trade and Development' in Bethlehem D and others (eds), *The Oxford Handbook of International Trade Law* (OUP 2009)

Ouguergouz F, *La Charte Africaine des Droits de l'Homme et des Peuples: une approche juridique des droits de l'homme entre tradition et modernité* (Presses universitaires de France 1993)

Pandey BN and Saha PK, 'Technical Cooperation under TRIPS Agreement: Flexibilities and Options for Developing Countries' (2011) 53(4) Journal of the Indian Law Institute 652

Pauwelyn J, 'The Transformation of World Trade' (2005) 104(1) Michigan Law Review 1

Pauwelyn J, 'The End of Differential Treatment?' (2013) 22(1) Review of European, Comparative and International Environmental Law 29

Pauwelyn J, Guzman A, and Hillman J, *International Trade Law* (3rd edn, Kluwer 2016)

Peters A, 'Compensatory Constitutionalism: The Function and Potential of Fundamental International Norms and Structures' (2006) 19 Leiden Journal of International Law 579

Petersmann E-U, *Constitutional Functions and Constitutional Problems of International Economic Law* (1st edn, Routledge 1991)

Petersmann E-U, 'The WTO Constitution and Human Rights' (2000) 3(1) Journal of International Economic Law 19

Pogge T, *World Poverty and Human Rights: Cosmopolitan Responsibilities and Reforms* (Polity Press 2007)

Posner EA and Sykes AO, 'International Law and the Limits of Macroeconomic Cooperation' (2013) 86(5) Southern California Law Review 1025

Ratner SR, *The Thin Justice of International Law: A Moral Reckoning of the Law of Nations* (OUP 2015)

Sadat-Akhavi SA, *Methods of Resolving Conflicts between Treaties* (Nijhoff 2003)

Salomon ME, *Global Responsibility for Human Rights* (OUP 2007)

Sell SK and Prakash A, 'Using Ideas Strategically: The Contest between Business and NGO Networks in Intellectual Property Rights' (2004) 48(1) International Studies Quarterly 143

Sieber-Gasser C, *Developing Countries and Preferential Services Trade* (Cambridge University Press 2016)

Stevens C, 'The WTO Doha Round Impasse: Implications for Africa' *ODI* (19 November 2008) <http://www.odi.org/events/313-wto-doha-round-impasse-implications-africa> accessed 22 July 2019

Stiglitz JE and Jayadev A, 'India's Patently Wise Decision' *Project Syndicate* (8 April 2013) <https://bit.ly/3o9jUIr> accessed 23 September 2020

Stoll PT, 'International Economic and Social Dimensions: Divided or Connected?' in Gött H (ed), *Labour Standards in International Economic Law* (Springer 2018).

Trachtman JP, 'The Constitutions of the WTO' (2006) 17(3) EJIL 623

UNCTAD, 'Economic Development in Africa, Report 2019, Made in Africa—Rules of Origin for Enhanced Intra-African Trade' UN Doc UNCTAD/ALDC/AFRICA/2019

Vieira VR, 'Beyond the Market: The Global South and the WTO's Normative Dimension' (2016) 21(2) International Negotiation: A Journal of Theory and Practice 267

Waincymer J, 'The Trade and Human Rights Debate: Introduction to an Interdisciplinary Analysis' in Joseph S, Kinley D, and Waincymer J (eds), *The World Trade Organization and Human Rights: Interdisciplinary Perspectives* (Elgar 2009)

Walker N, 'The Shaping of Global Law' (2017) 8(3) Transnational Legal Theory 360

Werner W, 'The Never-ending Closure: Constitutionalism and International Law' in Tsagourias N (ed), *Transnational Constitutionalism: International and European Perspectives* (Cambridge University Press 2007)

Wilkinson R, Hannah E, and Scott J, 'The WTO in Bali: What MC9 Means for the Doha Development Agenda and Why it Matters' (2014) 35(6) Third World Quarterly 1032

Woods N, 'Order, Globalization, and Inequality in World Politics' in Hurrell A and Woods N (eds), *Inequality, Globalization, and World Politics* (OUP 1999)

Wu HH, 'Refining the WTO Trade Facilitation Agreement in the Face of an Uncertain Trade Environment: Challenges and Opportunities' (2019) 11(1) Trade Law and Development 132

Zeng K, 'Legal Capacity and Developing Country Performance in the Panel Stage of the WTO Dispute Settlement System' (2013) 47(1) Journal of World Trade 187

PART VI
GENERAL CONCLUSION

15

Constitutionalizing the Market Economy and the Quest for Constitutionalism

Nico Steytler

1. Introduction

This volume seeks to understand the relationship between constitutions, constitutionalism, and the economy. This relationship has been broken down into five interrelated lines of enquiry:

- The first line of enquiry engages with the constitutional backdrop provided by thirty years of socialism experienced across the continent and asks whether (and if so, how) a market economy has been constitutionalized in Africa since the second wave of democratization.
- The second line of enquiry concerns the centrality of land and natural resources to many African economies, and asks whether (and if so, how) the control and management of these resources has been constitutionalized. Is there, for example, a constitutional framework for determining who 'owns' such wealth and how the revenue derived from such wealth is to be distributed among the inhabitants of a country?
- The third line of enquiry asks whether the relationship between the state and the economy is constitutionally regulated, and if so, how? In other words, what is the constitutional scope allowed to the state for direct intervention in the economy?
  - o The first aspect of this line of enquiry concerns the state's regulatory role. Is there a set of guiding principles? In systems of multilevel government, who performs the regulatory function? Have central banks been constitutionalized, thereby imposing a substantive limit on the executive's regulatory role with regard to monetary policy?
  - o The second aspect focuses on the state's actual participation in the economy, often under the rubric of its being a 'developmental state'.
  - o The third probes the role of the state as a provider of services, that is, as the 'social state'.
  - o The fourth aspect concerns the protection of the state from over-indebtedness.
  - o The last relates to the protection of the state against the market's predatory elements.
- The fourth line of enquiry concerns the impact that global economic integration could have on constitutionalism in Africa. What is the impact of international and regional trade liberalization on democratic sovereignty and thus on constitutional governance?
- The final set of questions probes the dynamic between constitutionalism and economic growth. Where the basic elements of constitutionalism—the practice of democracy, limited government, and the rule of law—are present, what impact, if any, do

Nico Steytler, *Constitutionalizing the Market Economy and the Quest for Constitutionalism* In: *Constitutionalism and the Economy in Africa*. Edited by: Charles M Fombad and Nico Steytler, Oxford University Press. © Nico Steytler 2022. DOI: 10.1093/oso/9780192886439.003.0017

they have on the economy? Conversely, does the absence of constitutionalism impact adversely on the economy?

The contributions to this volume show that the return to multiparty democracy in the 1990s was accompanied by the explicit or implicit constitutionalization of a market economy, principally through the protection of property and the insistence on freedom of contract. Although land and other natural resources are crucial to the economy of many countries, the constitutionalization of the guardianship role which the state should have over such resources is uneven. Affording protection to a market economy did not mean that the state withdrew from the marketplace: the notion of the 'developmental state' has seen the state playing the role both of a dominant regulator of the economy and a full participant in it, this by way of state-owned enterprises. However, despite the state's quest for control of the domestic market, its powers are curtailed through a globalization of the economy powered by the international trading system. Finally, while constitutionalism might be a necessary element for a growing economy, it is far from a sufficient condition for it. There is, nonetheless, a strong correlation between the absence of constitutionalism and negative economic growth.

2. The Constitutionalization of the Market Economy

For the first thirty years of independence, many, if not most, African regimes proclaimed a Marxist or African socialist utopia. Whether it was due to something in Marxist ideology itself or to the reality of the play of underlying social forces, the various attempts to create egalitarian and communitarian societies ended in dystopias of misrule, corruption, and military or civilian dictatorship. As Ramos Mabugu notes in Chapter 2, the economies of African countries south of the Sahara virtually collapsed in the 1980s, with only a few countries reporting positive economic growth (and even then from very low initial baselines). He points out, however, that external as well as domestic factors contributed to this poor overall economic performance. External factors included rising import prices, declining export prices, and severe droughts. Domestic factors centred on poor economic policies and poor governance, with the latter including corruption in the management of natural resources. As a result, most countries became highly indebted to the World Bank and International Monetary Fund (IMF), both of which then imposed structural adjustment programmes.

These dystopian results led to revolt among the general population. When the Cold War ended and spelt the demise of propped-up tyrants and thieves, a new governance paradigm of democracy and constitutionalism came to the fore—and with it, the market economy and its entrenchment in constitutions across Africa. The link between democracy and the market was occasionally made explicit, as for example in the Preamble of the Angolan Constitution of 2010, which emphasizes that

the present Constitution represents the culmination of the constitutional transition initiated in 1991, following the passing of Law no. 12/91 by the Assembly of the People, enshrining multi-party democracy, guarantees of the fundamental rights and freedoms of citizens and a market economy, changes extended later by Constitutional Revision Law no. 23/92.

However, such apparently firm commitments to the essentials of a market economy, democracy, and constitutionalism have proved in practice to be just as hollow as the promises made by the socialist rhetoric of the previous era. The next thirty years in Africa continued to be marked by maladministration, corruption, and the existence of self-serving patrimonial states that seek to control and exploit the economy while the majority of the people eat the bitter bread of the state's failure to serve them.

2.1 The African Socialist Dystopia

After the achievement of political independence in the 1960s, the focus of the new African governments turned to their economies—still largely in the hands of their former colonial masters. Following Kwame Nkrumah's call for an African Socialism for Ghana, the idea of an indigenous, non-exploitative economic system as a necessary part of the process of decolonialization gained ground in most of sub-Sahara Africa. As Charles Fombad points out in Chapter 4, most countries (including Benin, Congo, Ghana, Tanzania, and Zambia) flirted with socialism, at least as an idea, and this interest in socialism fitted perfectly into the categories of a Cold War paradigm in which the West's market economy was set against the command economy of the Soviet Union. Come the 1970s, the liberation of the Portuguese colonies (Angola, Cape Verde, Guinea-Bissau, Mozambique, and São Tomé) and of Zimbabwe with the help of military and financial assistance from the Soviet Union and/or Communist China made the adoption of a Marxist-Leninist economic model a foregone conclusion in these countries.

Given the centrality of the economy to the new political dispensation, it featured prominently in the new constitutions, often as a declaration of intent. The Benin Constitution of 1977 illustrates the approach well: 'In the People's Republic of Benin the development path is socialism. Its foundation is Marxism-Leninism, which should be applied in a living and creative way to Beninois realities.'[1] Only one country on the continent did not follow the usual independence path and change its economic course: Botswana. However, as explained by Stephan Ollick in Chapter 3, while Botswana's independence constitution made no overt mention of the market economy, it did protect property rights, thus falling under the Western constitutional tradition.

In the political sphere, the constitutions adopted at independence favoured the multi-party system of democracy. But these soon shifted towards support for a one-party system, eventually placing centralized state power in the hands of the president (or military leader after a coup). In these now authoritarian (or totalitarian) regimes, the centralization of power also applied to the economy. Nationalization of assets, state corporations, and the patrimonial state allowed little scope for an economy to develop at arm's length from the executive. After all, wasn't the state the real engine for economic growth?

---

[1] Art 4, which was omitted in the Constitution of the People's Republic of Benin of 1990.

When, instead of economic growth, there was deterioration, African governments had to go cap in hand to the ugliest embodiments of Western capitalism: the World Bank and IMF. They were forced to ask for loans to keep their fragile regimes and crumbling economies afloat. The loans came with a hefty price, and not only an economic one: this was the loss of sovereignty entailed by accepting the structural adjustment programmes of the two institutions. The collapse of the Soviet Union and the fall of the Berlin Wall meant the demise of both political centralism and the accompanying idea of the command economy; socialism, African or otherwise, failed to take root. As Charles Fombad reminds us: 'In spite of the continent's traditional communitarian approach to life, the core principles of Marxist-Leninism had never penetrated deeply and could be discarded at the least opportunity.'[2] The political sea-change of the 1990s meant exactly that. No longer was the one-party state regarded as an acceptable mode of governance by either the people or the international community. And as support for multiparty democracy grew, along with it came—hand in glove—the idea of a market economy based on the protection of private property and the call for limited government with respect to the economy.

2.2 Constitutionalizing the Market

In the 1990s, most African constitutions adhered to the model provided by Botswana, and little effort was made to directly constitutionalize the market economy as the appropriate economic model. Such direct modelling had been the style of the old socialist constitutions. The new method was rather to shield the market from state interference as far as possible, though further developments have seen the emergence of some protection for workers and citizens against the excesses of market behaviour.

2.2.1 Projecting economic models of the market
Generally speaking, with regard to constitutions, the places to find the ideological moorings of the economy are the preambles or general statements of policy intent, such as Directive Principles of State Policy. They can be found both in constitutions that formerly contained flourishes of socialist ideology (such as those of the lusophone countries) but so too in those of anglophone countries such as Ghana, Nigeria, and Namibia.

Take, for instance, the Ghanaian Constitution of 1992. This has a chapter on Directive Principles of State Policy, and the economy figures here. After the statement that it is the state's general responsibility to manage the economy to the benefit of all, article 36(2) contains the following ambiguous directive:

> The State shall, in particular, take all necessary steps to establish a sound and healthy economy whose underlying principles shall include—... (b) affording ample opportunity for individual initiative and creativity in economic activities and fostering an enabling environment for a pronounced role of the private sector in the economy.

---

[2] Chapter 4, this volume, 99.

This policy does not posit the private sector as the driver of the economy, but assigns it a more modest role: a 'pronounced role', to be sure, though this is decidedly less than a leading role.

Meanwhile, in the chapter on Directive Principles of State Policy, the Nigerian Constitution of 1999 still maintains that the state will be the driver of the economy: the *state must* 'without prejudice to its right to operate or participate in areas of the economy, other than the major sectors of the economy, *manage and operate the major sectors of the economy*'.[3] Furthermore, the state must 'direct its policy towards ensuring: the promotion of a planned and balanced economic development'.[4] The Namibian Constitution of 1990 also foresees a mixed economy: 'The economic order of Namibia shall be based on the principles of a mixed economy with the objective of securing economic growth, prosperity and a life of human dignity for all Namibians.'[5]

Fombad notes that in francophone Africa 'very few provisions deal with the country's economic orientation and, when they do, usually only in a vague and indirect manner'.[6] In contrast, in lusophone countries the matter is spelt out with some specificity. For example, the Angolan Constitution states as a fundamental principle that '[t]he state shall respect and protect the private property of individuals and corporate bodies and free economic and entrepreneurial initiatives exercised within the terms of the Constitution and the law'.[7] Likewise, the Mozambican Constitution of 2007 declares that economic policy will be based, among other factors, 'on market forces; ... [and] on the co-existence of the public sector, the private sector and the social and co-operative sector'.[8]

In a 2007 amendment to the Egyptian Constitution of 1971 (as Sherif Elgebeily points out), a general mixed approach to the economy is followed.[9] In the opening chapter it is declared: 'The national economy is based on the development of economic activity, social justice, the guarantee of the different forms of property and the preservation of workers' rights.'[10] After the Arab Spring Revolution of 2011, the 2014 Constitution prescribes no economic objects but maintains its mixed approach by protecting ownership of three types: public, private, and cooperative.[11]

These policy commitments to a full or partial market economy are an infrequent constitutional feature and, in any event, do not provide a secure basis for market development. The real protection for the market and the private sector is to be found in the bills of rights.

2.2.2 Protecting the market from the state
At the core of the market lies the right to private property, supported by the freedom of contract, and with these enforceable by an independent judiciary. Further elements include the freedom of enterprise and competition. Since the 1990s most of these elements have been included in bills of rights, but with varying degrees of enforceability.

---

[3] Nigerian Constitution (1999), art 16(1)(c), emphasis added.
[4] Nigerian Constitution (1999), art 16(2)(a).
[5] Section 98(1).
[6] Chapter 4, this volume, 99.
[7] Angolan Constitution (2010), art 14.
[8] Mozambican Constitution (2007), art 97(b).
[9] Chapter 11, this volume.
[10] Egyptian Constitution (1971, amended), art 4.
[11] Egyptian Constitution (2014), art 33.

(a) Property rights

Although some constitutions explicitly recognize various kinds of property—state, private, and communal/cooperative property are distinguished in Egypt[12] and Mozambique[13]—it is the protection of private property that lies at the heart of a market economy. In most constitutions, the arbitrary deprivation of property is prohibited, though expropriation in the public interest is permitted against compensation. There is significant variation with regard to the question of whether compensation is to be calculated at market value or not. In Ghana, market value determines compensation, whereas in the 1996 South African Constitution it is just one of a number of factors to be taken into consideration (and if a proposed constitutional amendment is accepted, market value will cease entirely to be a consideration in certain circumstances).[14]

Fombad notes that protection of private property is weak in the francophone and lusophone constitutions when compared to the elaborate protections provided by the anglophone constitutions.[15] He also argues that the protection of private property is only as good as the legal system that enforces it. While constitutional entrenchment is the first and necessary step, it is the detailed statutory rules and the independent courts enforcing them that really matter. Even where there is no explicit constitutional protection for private property, a well-entrenched legal culture which favours its protection, if expressed in legislation and in practice, may actually achieve better results.

(b) Freedom of contract

Freedom of contract is generally understood as a key component of the market, but it does not per se receive explicit protection in either Western or African constitutions.[16] It is seen rather as an aspect of the right to freedom. This is illustrated by South African jurisprudence. In the pre-constitutionalism era, freedom of contract was based on the common law principle of *pacta sunt servanda* (the freedom of contract and the enforceability of such), but has now found a new basis in the constitutional values of 'freedom and dignity'.[17]

(c) Freedom of enterprise—competition

The explicit recognition of competition as the driving force of a market economy is rare in Africa. In the 2010 Angolan Constitution, we find: 'The state shall respect and protect the private property of individuals and corporate bodies and *free economic and entrepreneurial initiatives* exercised within the terms of the Constitution and the law'.[18] Similarly, the Ghanaian Constitution refers to competition only indirectly, in the Directive Principles of State Policy. These assert that the state must take the necessary steps 'to establish a sound and healthy economy' the underlying principles of which include 'affording ample opportunity for individual initiative and creativity in economic activities and fostering an enabling environment for a pronounced role of the private sector in the economy'.[19] In the

---

[12] ibid.
[13] Mozambique Constitution, title III, ch V, art 82(2) provides that '[e]xpropriation may take place only for reasons of public necessity, utility, or interest, as defined in the terms of the law, and subject to payment of fair compensation'.
[14] Section 25(3). See Klug, Chapter 7, this volume.
[15] Chapter 4, this volume.
[16] See Ollick, Chapter 3, this volume.
[17] See Steytler, Chapter 5, this volume.
[18] Art 14.
[19] Art 36(2)(b).

South African Constitution, this general principle is transformed into a right (albeit a weak one): 'Every citizen has the right to choose their trade, occupation or profession freely [but] [t]he practice of a trade, occupation or profession may be regulated by law.'[20]

At the other end of the spectrum are constitutional provisions that exclude competition in particular areas. A directive principle in the Nigerian Constitution is that the state must 'manage and operate the major sectors of the economy' and to that end, must 'protect the right of every citizen to engage in any economic activities *outside* the major sectors of the economy.'[21] This provision allows for state monopolies in key economic sectors.

2.2.3 Protecting the people from the market

At the same time as protecting the market from the state, bills of rights also contain provisions seeking to protect people—in particular workers and consumers—from the most damaging market forces. Prior to the articulation of specific workers' rights, the general political freedom of association was regarded as the basis for the formation of trade unions and collective action in pursuit of workers' interests. The explicit protection of workers' rights to the formation of trade unions and collective bargaining, including, in the case of South Africa, the right to strike, is a new phenomenon.[22] The South African constitution is also unique in protecting the rights of employers to organize collectively (but the right to lockout workers is not included in this).[23]

Seeking to provide protection against the excesses of a *laissez-faire* economy for the broader public, consumer protection is a novel right that has been added to bills of rights. As Fombad finds, only the 2010 Angolan Constitution and the 2010 Kenyan Constitution explicitly provide for such protection.[24] The right is then made contingent on legislation to give effect thereto.

2.2.4 Enforcement of rights

There is little evidence to show that the rights listed above are routinely or consistently honoured, and the mechanisms necessary to realizing these rights are often missing. In Mozambique, for example, possible claimants of rights violations do not have standing in court to challenge any such violations.[25] Meanwhile, the courts which hear challenges do not always have the necessary powers to vindicate the aggrieved rights (as is the case in Zimbabwe, where the court's jurisdiction over land matters has been removed).[26] All too often, courts lack the independence to find against the state, while executives simply will not abide by court rulings.

In short, a bill of rights has meaning only when it operates within a pervasive ethos of constitutionalism. As we shall see below, this is a commodity in short supply in most African countries.

---

[20] Constitution of the Republic of South Africa, 1996, s 22.
[21] Art 16(1)(c) and (d), emphasis added.
[22] Section 23(2)(c).
[23] Section 23(3).
[24] Chapter 4, this volume.
[25] Fombad, Chapter 4, this volume.
[26] Makonese, Chapter 8, this volume.

3. Constitutionalizing Ownership and Control of Land and Natural Resources

3.1 Overview

Land and natural resources play crucial roles in the economies of most African countries. Given the low levels of urbanization, agriculture remains central to most people's economic activity. It also constitutes an important component of the gross domestic product (GDP) of most countries and remains (in some cases) a significant source of foreign exchange. In Zimbabwe, for example, the majority of the rural population depend for their livelihood on subsistence farming, while tobacco alone constituted almost a fifth of export earnings (after gold) in 2019.[27] Underpinning agriculture is, of course, access to land. Non-renewable natural resources—oil, gas, and minerals—are the largest export earners in resource-endowed countries and make up the main source of state revenue. Meanwhile, renewable natural resources (such as forestry and fisheries) are also an important trading commodity, though these can, through over-exploitation, all too easily become exhausted beyond repair.

Inequitable access to land and natural resources and the skewed and limited distribution of the latter's revenue have lain at the core of many (if not most) conflicts in Africa after independence. As John Hursh notes, the post-colonial constitutional orders of Kenya, Sudan, and South Sudan

> distributed resources unjustly and inequitably, typically along politicized ethnic group status. Constitutional provisions and subsequent legislation allowed for the over-concentration of executive power and the centralization of decision-making, which in turn undermined economic opportunity and denied citizens their basic rights and freedoms.[28]

Furthermore, the exploitation of land and natural resources often serves immediate economic goals in an unsustainable manner, leading eventually to the destruction of renewable resources and the loss of their economic value.

Did the constitutional reforms of the 1990s and beyond bring any positive changes? Were any attempts made to use constitutions as constraints on the ways governments managed land and natural resources, or as a means for assisting with the advancement of the national interest of the countries concerned?

3.2 Land

A distinction is often drawn between land and property, with the former understood as a distinct type of property, one which requires greater protection. Not only is land regarded as a valuable commercial commodity for agriculture, it also represents, as Makanatsa Makonese points out, a deeply spiritual element that connects communities to a particular territory.[29] Thus, in Zimbabwe, while there is extensive legal protection for property (including private

---

[27] Makonese, Chapter 8, this volume.
[28] Chapter 6, this volume, 118.
[29] Chapter 8, this volume.

property), agricultural land is explicitly exempted from that protection, and, in the case of expropriation (crucial to the history of land dispossession), only improvements on land have been deemed subject to compensation.[30]

The dispossession of land during the colonial and apartheid eras (and even after independence) has given rise to severe conflicts. Demands for equitable access to land often formed part of peace-making deals and were consequently enshrined in constitutions. A part of Sudan's Comprehensive Peace Agreement of 2005 was the commitment to address the inequitable allocation of resources and skewed regional development policies which had fuelled protracted civil war between the South and the central government.[31] In Kenya, one dimension of the ethnic conflict which burst open after the rigged 2007 presidential elections was the long-running contestation over land. South Africa is just one example where the question of land was directly addressed in a constitution promising land restitution and redistribution.

The constitutional relationship between the state and land varies from one country to another. Landownership may be vested in the state alone, with the state taking on the role of a guardian: in Mozambique, the Constitution of 2012 holds that '[a]ll ownership of land shall vest in the State' and '[l]and may not be sold or otherwise disposed of, nor may it be mortgaged or subject to attachment'.[32] Landownership can reside in both the state and the people, with the former exercising ownership on the latter's behalf. The Ethiopian Constitution of 1995, for example, provides that '[t]he right to ownership of rural and urban land, as well as of all natural resources, is exclusively vested in the State and in the peoples of Ethiopia'.[33] More specifically, given Ethiopia's federal dispensation, land is regarded as 'a common property of the Nations, Nationalities and Peoples of Ethiopia and shall not be subjected to sale or to other means of exchange'.[34] In addition, a number of constitutions recognize state, communal (or collective), or private land, as is the case with Kenya,[35] South Sudan,[36] and Egypt.[37] In South Africa, the Constitution makes no assertion regarding the state ownership of land, but the state is mandated to effect the restitution of dispossessed land.[38]

Although a constitution may prohibit foreign ownership, this does not necessarily mean that foreign property interests are entirely excluded. In Ethiopia, where land is owned by the state but under the control of the regions, the federal government has nonetheless centralized ownership. Eager to attract foreign investment, it has made large tracts of land available to foreign companies and governments on lengthy leasehold agreements for the undertaking of large-scale agricultural projects. Solomon Negussie notes in Chapter 12 that the proceeds of land use fees or any sales or profit taxes do not make their way back to the regions and local authorities, providing another cause of friction. Thus, where the state is the owner in terms of the constitution, the latter often facilitates, rather than constrains, the sale (or leasing) of land.

---

[30] Zimbabwean Constitution, 2013, art 73(3)(a). See Klug, Chapter 7, this volume.
[31] Hursh, Chapter 6, this volume.
[32] Art 109(1) and (2).
[33] Art 40(3) first sentence.
[34] Art 40(3) second sentence.
[35] Constitution of Kenya, 2010, art 61(2).
[36] South Sudanese Constitution 2011, art 170(2).
[37] Egyptian Constitution (2014), art 33.
[38] South African Constitution, s 25(7).

Given the history of the exploitation of landholdings by state executives (usually manipulated by 'imperial presidencies'), some limited attempts have been made to remove land questions entirely from the realm of political decision-making and place them under the jurisdiction of an independent land commission. However, the real independence of such bodies has rarely been safeguarded properly. In Kenya, the Land Commission (appointed by the President) has an ambiguous role. Its prime function is 'to manage public land on behalf of the national and country governments'.[39] However, in important questions of a national land policy (the registration of title programmes, and so on), it mainly plays only an investigatory and advisory role. Despite the existence of the Land Commission, as Hursh points out, there is still in practice an over-concentration of power in the executive, rather than in an independent authority that deals with this highly divisive and emotive issue.[40]

A similar situation prevails in the case of Sudan's National Land Commission, which is envisaged in the 2005 Constitution: the Commission is placed under the control of the President (in fact, the Commission was never formally established).[41] In South Sudan, the progeny of Sudan, little more has been achieved. The 2011 Transitional Constitution required an 'independent commission'—the Land Commission—made up of 'persons of proven competence, experience, integrity and impartiality',[42] but it is the President who has the sole power to make appointments.[43]

Given the extremely poor record of states in the performance of their allotted roles as impartial guardians of land affairs (not to speak of the fact of repeated acts of grabbing land from their own indigenous communities), the constitutional debate has moved towards the need for the protection of the land rights of communities from encroachment by the state. The first bills of rights in the new African constitutions focused on the protection of individual rights; a second wave of them is now moving towards the protection of community rights: providing necessary protection for indigenous communities against predation by their own states.

3.3 Non-renewable Natural Resources: Oil, Gas, and Minerals

Most African countries are regarded as economically dependent on their natural resources.[44] In terms of one test (that in a five-year period, 25 per cent or more of export revenue is derived from natural resources),[45] thirty-four sub-Saharan countries prove to be resource dependent. For the World Bank, South Sudan is regarded as one of the most oil-dependent countries in the world: all of its foreign exchange comes from oil exports, and oil accounts for 40 per cent of its GDP.[46] Nigeria is another extreme case: the government there is so reliant on oil revenue that it does not tax its citizens. This means, Mabugu argues,[47]

---

[39] Art 67(2)(a).
[40] Chapter 6, this volume.
[41] Hursh, Chapter 6, this volume.
[42] Art 172(1).
[43] Art 172(2).
[44] Mabugu, Chapter 2, this volume; Mostert, Chapter 9, this volume.
[45] Haroon Bhorat and others, 'Resource Dependence and Inequality in Africa: Impacts, Consequences and Potential Solutions' in Ayodele Odusola and others (eds), *Income Inequality Trends in Sub-Saharan Africa: Divergence, Determinants and Consequences* (United Nations Development Programme 2019).
[46] Hursh, Chapter 6, this volume.
[47] Chapter 2, this volume.

that there is little connection between the Nigerian state and its citizens, and a consequent lack of demand for state accountability from the citizenry. Indeed, having an abundance of natural resources may not necessarily be regarded as a boon, but rather as a curse. The so-called 'resource curse' thesis posits the following correlations: the more natural resources, the slower the growth, the higher the poverty, and the worse the political instability, corruption, and authoritarianism.[48]

Natural resources have also proved to be one of the most important sources of civil war.[49] The most recent example is South Sudan, where the civil war that began in 2013 was in part prolonged by contestation for control of oil-producing areas. The splitting-up of provinces effected by President Kirr's regime (in violation of a 2015 peace agreement) sought to ensure that the country's oil-producing areas remained under the control of the Dinka community and did not fall under the jurisdiction of provinces controlled by other ethnic groups.[50] Retracting the subdivision of the original eleven units became a necessary part of the 2018 peace agreement.

The exploitation of natural resources thus presents the following dilemma. Most economies are based on the extraction of natural resources for export, but conflict over ownership and control of these resources fuels social and political division; conflict and division ultimately damage the economy, but the economy is largely reliant on the exploitation of the natural resources that cause the conflict.[51]

Colonial history shows how foreign companies worked to exploit natural resources for their own enrichment with little benefit accruing to the local population. Following independence, this mode of colonial extraction was replaced by the nationalization of these resources. But, as Mostert remarks, such nationalization has usually done little to enhance domestic development in general, though it has worked to feather the nests of the ruling elites.[52] Did the post-1990 constitutions prove able to address this problem? Could natural resources be exploited in a way that brought the benefit directly to the people rather than being the occasion for serious social and political conflict?

In a number of modest ways, constitutions have attempted to do this, usually by nationalizing control of natural resources and investing the state (usually the executive) with a guardianship role over their exploitation to see that the benefits go to the people. The principle of national sovereignty over natural resources was recognized by the African Charter on Human and Peoples' Rights of 1986:

> All peoples shall freely dispose of their wealth and natural resources. This right shall be exercised in the exclusive interest of the people. In no case shall a people be deprived of it.
>
> ...
>
> State parties to the present Charter shall undertake to eliminate all forms of foreign exploitation particularly that practiced by international monopolies so as to enable their peoples to fully benefit from the advantages derived from their natural resources.[53]

---

[48] Mostert, Chapter 9, this volume.

[49] See Nicholas Haysom and Sean Kane, *Negotiating Natural Resources for Peace: Ownership, Control and Wealth Sharing*, Briefing Paper (UNDP October 2009) 20.

[50] See Zemelak Ayitenew Ayele, 'Constitutionalism: The Missing Element in South Sudan's Elusive Quest for Peace through Federalism?', in Charles Fombad and Nico Steytler (eds), *Decentralisation and Constitutionalism in Africa* (OUP 2019) 234-56.

[51] Hursh, Chapter 6, this volume.

[52] Chapter 9, this volume.

[53] Art 21(1) and (5).

This principle of linking national sovereignty directly to the exploitation of these resources for the benefit of the 'peoples' became a standard feature of the new wave of post-1990 constitutions. However, as Hanri Mostert notes, recognition of this principle rarely went beyond the mere assertion of national sovereignty, despite the importance of the issue.[54] In her survey of forty-five sub-Saharan constitutions, Mostert reports that in nearly half of them (49 per cent) there is a direct reference in the substantive provisions to natural resources, namely that natural resources are owned by the state or 'the people' or 'nation'. In a further 15 per cent, there is indirect reference in the preamble to the effect that natural resources belong to the people. At the same time, 36 per cent of these constitutions make no mention of natural resources at all, despite the fact that two-thirds of the countries can be classified as resource dependent.

Reference to state ownership of natural resources takes various forms. In the Namibian Constitution's Directive Principles of State Policy (which are not legally binding) it is stated:

> Land, water and natural resources below and above the surface of the land and in the continental shelf and within the territorial waters and the exclusive economic zone of Namibia shall belong to the State if they are not otherwise lawfully owned.[55]

In the Kenyan Constitution of 2010, 'all mineral and mineral oils as defined by law' are deemed to be 'public land', and thus fall under the regime described above.[56] The Egyptian Constitution of 2014 articulates the principle of custodianship as follows: 'Natural resources belong to the people. The state commits to preserving such resources, to their sound exploitation, to preventing their depletion, and to take into consideration the rights of future generations to them.'[57] Given that Egypt's natural resources are mainly renewable, the emphasis falls on their sustainable exploitation. With most of the country under military rule, there is little scope for the exercise of popular control over natural resources.[58]

The standard constitutional model is to vest natural resources in 'the people' and then bring in the national government to act as a guardian or to play a custodial role. On this basis, most African countries enacted legislation to give flesh to what Mostert calls a 'custodial resource-holding model', but only imperfectly so.[59] In a survey of the legislation of forty-five sub-Saharan countries, most of them vested ownership in the state, with only five explicitly stating that the resources should be used to the benefit of 'the people'. Even in countries lacking constitutional recognition of the 'holding model' (such as Tanzania and Botswana), a similar model is adopted in and through ordinary legislation. Mostert argues, however, that embedding the custodial holding model in a constitution may help give a more secure basis for such legislation.

Constitutions have little to say on any specific mechanisms for ensuring that non-renewable resources are exploited only to the benefit of the people. At best, there is a requirement that any state agreements with mining and exploration companies must be placed in the public domain. In Kenya, apart from the advisory role played by the Land

---

[54] Chapter 9, this volume.
[55] Namibian Constitution, 1990, s 100. The latter phrase thus allows for communal and private property.
[56] Art 62.
[57] Art 32.
[58] Elgebeily, Chapter 11, this volume.
[59] Chapter 9, this volume.

Commission, any agreement on the exploitation of natural resources requires parliamentary ratification.[60] This is also the case in Ghana.[61] The effectiveness of such a check on executive action is, of course, contingent on institutional transparency as well as the actions of a vigorous and attentive parliament. As we have seen, both of these are rare and the patrimonial state is the norm in most (if not all) African countries. The abundance of natural wealth has served only to increase the venality of the patrimonial state, resulting in the paradoxical 'resource curse' mentioned above.[62]

3.4 Renewable Natural Resources and Sustainable Development

Modern African constitutions are full of provisions exhorting the state to protect the environment and exploit natural resources within a sustainable-development framework that keeps a careful eye on the welfare of future generations. The 2010 Kenyan Constitution probably sets the gold standard on this score. Presenting an expansive definition of natural resources,[63] it requires that the state 'ensure sustainable exploitation, utilisation, management and conservation of the environment and natural resources, and ensure the equitable sharing of the accruing benefits'.[64] The 'equitable sharing' is even made explicit: the state must 'utilize the environment and natural resources for the benefit of the people of Kenya'.[65]

The mandates for sustainable development and environmental protection place governments under considerable pressure. To enhance fragile economies and boost employment, resources need to be exploited, and this may have an adverse impact on the environment, resulting in short-term gains at the expense of sustainable development. In addition, exploitation is usually, if not inevitably, mired in corruption. Namibia is a good example of this difficult dynamic.

In Chapter 10, Henning Melber focuses on the fishing and timber industries in Namibia. Although both resources are natural and naturally renewable, over-exploitation has resulted in their depletion and the threat of their ultimate destruction. Despite the aspirational goals set in legislation for preserving the environment, the inevitable trade-offs have tilted the scales in favour of over-exploitation in the short term. Melber notes that after thirty years of independence, the fact of continuing poverty in a land of natural riches has resulted in an increasingly restive population, one now more vocal than before in demanding a better life. The government is caught between exploiting resources for short-term gain and trying to protect the environment in the interests of long-term sustainability. Meanwhile, the ever-present spectre of corruption 'makes the SWAPO government's balancing act—weighing the protection of public goods such as facets of the natural environmental against economic gains through resource extraction—all the more precarious'.[66] As Melber observes,

---

[60] Kenyan Constitution, art 71(1)(a).

[61] Ghanaian Constitution, 1992, art 268.

[62] See Charles Fombad and Nico Steytler (eds), *Corruption and Constitutionalism in Africa: Revisiting Control Measures and Strategies* (OUP 2020).

[63] 'Natural resources' are defined as 'physical non-human factors and components, whether renewable or non-renewable, including (a) sunlight; (b) surface and ground water; (c) forests, biodiversity and genetic resources …' (art 260).

[64] Kenyan Constitution, art 69(1)(a).

[65] ibid, art 69(1)(h).

[66] Melber, Chapter 10, this volume 158.

concerns for the environment and sustainable development do not form part of the lexicon of the ruling elite.

3.5   Conclusion

What emerges from the country studies included in this volume? It is safe to say there is an abundance of constitutional statements to the effect that land and natural resources belong to the state (usually the executive), which is understood as performing a guardianship role on behalf of the people. While the prevention of foreign ownership and exploitation of natural resources has been readily obtained, the constitutional mandate that such resources must be used to the people's benefit is largely aspirational. Protection for the sustainable exploitation of renewable natural resources is similarly compromised. The constitutional texts have done little more than erect a flimsy fence around the national patrimony. Hursh argues that the experience of Sudan, South Sudan, and Kenya 'demonstrates that constitutional protections are necessary, but not sufficient to enact lasting reform, reshape economic relationships between the state and its citizens, and expand economic possibilities to include all citizens'.[67] Something else is needed to keep the fence upright and intact—something that should include the legal and political anchor wires of constitutionalism.

Because land is such an emotive issue, its effective management on behalf of the people by the state is important for a country's stability. As Klug observes (with respect to South Africa), the failure to build economic equality after the national democratic revolution has significant implications for this revolution's much-revered constitutional democracy:

> While [land] often serv[es] as a proxy for a more general claim for the redistribution of wealth, it is the continuing inequality in access to land, both urban and rural, that enables these claimants to question the legitimacy of the post-apartheid constitutional order.[68]

The failure to address the land question adequately places the entire project of constitutional democracy at risk. The same may well be true for other countries, as also with respect to other national resources. The centrality of equitable land and natural resource management to political stability and economic development is inescapable, and constitutions have a crucial role to play in this regard.

4.   The State's Role in the Economy

4.1   Overview

The first constitutional imprint on the economy is shielding the market from the state through the protection of the right to property and freedom of contract. The second constitutional imprint brings the state firmly back into the picture when it concerns land and natural resources: it is the owner or custodian of such resources on behalf of 'the people'.

---

[67] Chapter 6, this volume, 152.
[68] Klug, Chapter 7, this volume, 209.

This leads to the next area of enquiry—the regulation and participation of the state in the economy. Do constitutions provide any framework within which the state should perform this role?

This question can be broken down into four parts: the first asks whether there are any constitutional instructions or guidelines how the state should perform its regulatory function. The second concerns the role envisaged by the state (usually under the rubric 'developmental state') as an active participant in the economy. The third seeks clarification on what the role of the state is in the face of the market failure to feed and house the people. Does the state assume the role of a 'social state' responsible for providing the bare necessities of life? Moreover, given the usual lack of revenue, how is the state protected from over-indebtedness? The final question asks how the state is protected from the predatory elements of the market.

4.2 Regulating the Market-Oriented Economy

Economic regulation usually refers to the setting of frameworks or provision of guidelines within which a market economy must function in order to serve the pursuit of various social goals. Constitutionally, governments enjoy wide discretion in steering the economy, to which end they use a variety of mechanisms, some of which are at arm's length. In cases where a government faces a structurally biased economy with high inequality, poverty, and unemployment, the question is whether there is constitutional guidance on how these challenges can be addressed. Although this chapter focuses on the legal regulatory frameworks, the widespread informal nature of African economies should be borne in mind: people's survivalist economic activities operate in dimensions aside from or parallel to the formal institutions of law and government action, which tend to be weak at the best of times.[69]

4.2.1 Principles and guidelines for the economy

A number of aspirational goals that envisage the state playing the leading role in the economy for the benefit of its citizens run alongside constitutional statements of intent (discussed above) that favour a market-oriented economy.[70] For example, working within the same statist paradigm as its previous socialist constitutions, the Mozambican Constitution of 2004 sets the goals of the state's economic policy in the following terms:

> State economic policy shall be directed towards laying the fundamental bases for development, improving the living conditions of the people, strengthening the sovereignty of the State, and consolidating national unity, through the participation of citizens and the efficient use of human and material resources.[71]

Policy goals such as this are often to be found in non-binding Directive Principles of State Policy. The Nigerian Constitution's fine-sounding 'Fundamental Objectives and Directive Principles of State Policy' exhorts the state to

---

[69] Mabugu, Chapter 2, this volume.
[70] Section 2.1.
[71] Mozambique Constitution, art 96.

a) harness the resources of the nation and promote national prosperity and an efficient, a dynamic and self-reliant economy; [and]
b) control the national economy in such manner as to secure the maximum welfare, freedom and happiness of every citizen on the basis of social justice and equality of status and opportunity.[72]

Such lofty sentiments are often no more than pie in the sky. On the other end of the spectrum, as Klug shows, Botswana makes no explicit economic provisions other than the protection of property, and yet it actually achieves many of these people-oriented goals. As with Botswana, the constitutions of South Africa and Zimbabwe also have no specific constitutional provisions for defining the process of setting, forming, or directing economic policy.[73]

Despite either an explicit or implicit orientation in favour of the market economy, it is remarkable that in general the constitutions surveyed do not mandate the government to ensure competition within the marketplace so as to prevent monopolies; that function is usually left to legislation. The Nigerian Constitution provides one exception to this general rule. It directs the state to ensure 'that the economic system is not operated in such a manner as to permit the concentration of wealth or the means of production and exchange in the hands of few individuals or of a group', thereby serving both economic and political ends.[74]

Since the state is required to give effect to these economic goals, it is then often envisaged as a 'developmental state': that is, a state which is responsible not only for steering the economic boat, but also for being one of its rowers (a matter to which we will return below).

4.2.2 State actors in federal systems

While most constitutions remain silent on the precise regulatory role the government should play, in federal systems (which disperse powers among different levels of government) the constitutions under review are clear enough: the federal government should bear overall responsibility for the economy. The view is based on the notion of the economy as a unitary organism, one which should not be hindered or impeded in its workings by any internal political boundaries or the carving-up of economic regulation between the federal governments and constituent units.

In line with the federations of the United States and Germany, African federations or hybrid federations leave economic regulation exclusively in the hands of the federal or national governments.[75] In the Ethiopian Constitution, the federal government has the general mandate to 'formulate and implement the country's policies, strategies and plans in respect of the overall economic, social and development matters'.[76] As Solomon Negussie observes, the federal government makes excessive use of this power to formulate economic policies; the policies end up being so detailed that they leave little room for the regions'

---

[72] Art 16(1).
[73] In contrast to the national Constitution, the Western Cape Provincial Constitution, 1997, as a clear response to the national ruling party's left-leaning ideology, contains the following, unenforceable, Directive Principle of Provincial Policy: the government 'must adopt and implement policies to actively promote and maintain the welfare of the people of the Western Cape, including policies aimed at achieving the following ... the *promotion of a market-oriented economy*' (s 81(g), emphasis added).
[74] Art 16(2)(c).
[75] Ollick, Chapter 3, this volume.
[76] Art 51(2).

residual powers with regard to the economy.[77] The result is that investment decisions in Ethiopia are governed primarily by federal laws, much to the disadvantage of the regions.

In Nigeria, the wide range of federal powers (both exclusive and concurrent) enables the federal government to control most economic activities. In South Africa, although the Constitution lists the exclusive and concurrent powers of provinces and local government, and leaves the residual powers to the national government, the truth is that national legislation dominates economic policy. Nevertheless, in the exercise of their powers, including taxing powers, provinces and local governments are constrained to interfere with national economic unity and the free movement of persons, goods, and services.[78]

4.2.3 Arm's length regulation: the central bank

The regulation of the economy is customarily done by the government of the day; its health and condition (improving or worsening) is thus attributed to the government. The economic mandate is performed by a variety of government departments, with the Ministry of Finance (or the National Treasury) the *primus inter pares*. However, independent institutions have emerged which, standing at arm's length from the government, provide guidance on and control over key economic issues. Most notably, the world over,[79] central banks are mandated to protect monetary policy against the demands of short-term political expediency (by controlling the money supply and inflation, among other things).[80]

Although most African countries have a central bank, Fombad points out that very few of these enjoy constitutional protection of their independence.[81] Even when there is such protection, the degree of independence the banks enjoy varies considerably (as Klug observes with regard to the central banks in the constitutions of Zimbabwe, South Africa, and Mozambique). The Mozambican Constitution provides for a central bank established in terms of legislation with no clear reference to the bank's independence.[82] Zimbabwe is another such example, a fact no doubt linked to that country's runaway inflation. The Zambian Constitution of 2016 moves towards some degree of independence: it provides that the central bank (the Bank of Zambia) 'shall not be subject to the direction or control of a person or an authority in the performance of its functions'.[83] Nonetheless, in practice this meant little when Zambian President Edgar Lungu summarily dismissed the central bank governor in August 2020 and replaced him with a former deputy finance minister.[84] This act evoked a blistering rebuke from South Africa's Minister of Finance,[85] who is himself allowed only to hold regular consultations with the governor of the South African Reserve Bank.[86]

---

[77] Negussie, Chapter 12, this volume.

[78] See Steytler, Chapter 5, this volume.

[79] See Ollick, Chapter 3, this volume.

[80] See Nico Steytler, 'The "Financial Constitution" and the Prevention and Combating of Corruption: A Comparative Study of Nigeria, South Africa and Kenya' in Charles Fombad and Nico Steytler (eds), *Corruption and Constitutionalism: Revisiting Control Measures and Strategies* (OUP 2020) 386–416.

[81] See Chapter 4, this volume.

[82] Art 132.

[83] Art 213(5).

[84] Reuters, 'Zambian President Fires Central Bank Governor in Surprise Move', 22 August 2020, <https://www.reuters.com/article/us-zambia-cenbank-governor-idUSKBN25I0NV> accessed 3 May 2021. See also the dismissal of the Nigerian Central Bank's governor in 2014: Steytler (n 80) 410.

[85] Linda Ensor, 'Tito Mboweni Slams Dismissal of Zambian Central Banker' *Timeslive* (23 August 2020, <https://www.timeslive.co.za/sunday-times/business/2020-08-23-tito-mboweni-slams-dismissal-of-zambian-central-banker/> accessed 3 May 2021. Minister Tito Mboweni was previously the governor of the South African Reserve Bank.

[86] See Steytler, Chapter 5, this volume.

Francophone countries in West and Central Africa have also experienced, as Fombad alerts us, some independent monetary policy formulation. This not on account of any constitutional guarantee, but rather because these countries still use the CFA franc (African Financial Community franc) and a common central bank, whose monetary policy is in effect set by the French treasury.[87] He thus concludes that '[a]s a result of the continued use of the CFA in francophone Africa, France retains and exercises as much control over the financial policies of these countries as it did during the colonial period'.[88]

Overall, then, economic policies (including monetary policy) are firmly under the control of the executives, with little reliance on independent expertise.

4.3 The State Participating in the Market: The Developmental State

The failure of post-independence socialist experiments has not led inevitably to the state's withdrawal from active participation in the economy in the second wave of democratization and the assertion of market supremacy. In economies based mainly on extractive industries and agriculture, the market was perceived as not producing inclusive economic growth and equitable distribution of resources. The privatization of state-owned enterprises (SOEs) and imposition of structural adjustment programmes during the 1990s proved to be far from producing the desired results.

The state continued to be conceived of as the only vehicle to stimulate and produce economic growth, mainly through SOEs. It would not only steer the economic boat but also be the rower-in-chief. As Mabugu argues, SOEs were placed at the centre of national development strategies: they operated in virtually all aspects of economic activity, including infrastructure, oil, agriculture, transport, public utilities, telecommunications, finance/insurance, health, education, training, and more.[89] In effect, and without skipping a beat, the state-dominated economy returned with full force after democratization, though now in the guise of the 'developmental state'.

In some countries the leading role of the state was cemented in the constitution (as demonstrated above). In Nigeria, the Constitution unambiguously provides not only that the state must 'control the national economy' but also that it has to 'manage and operate the major sectors of the economy', which include, of course, the oil sector.[90] Meanwhile, in the admittedly extreme case of Egypt, a particular sector of the state (the military) is the key player in the economy. As Sherif Elgebeily explains, the military has occupied a privileged position there ever since Nasser's rise to power in 1956, and its intervention in the market continued throughout the 1990s. During the Arab Spring, the military helped the Morsi regime take power, but then, when its position was threatened, it staged a second revolution for President Sisi, who in turn expanded the military's economic role.[91] In addition to its substantial landholdings (see above), the military owns and operates a range of purely commercial enterprises. These produce (among other things) cement, steel, pasta, marble, tourism, and consumer goods. The blurring of lines between the public and private sector

---

[87] Fombad, Chapter 4, this volume.
[88] ibid 383.
[89] Mabugu, Chapter 2, this volume.
[90] Art 16(1)(c).
[91] Chapter 11, this volume.

has resulted in state monopolies and an uncompetitive market. Locating economic governance in the military added a layer of unaccountability—no transparency, no tender procedures, no taxes, and a conscripted workforce.

The success of a 'developmental state' depends on two main factors. The first is the problem of state incapacity and/or self-destructiveness through corruption. In South Africa the problem of uneven development prompted the National Development Planning Commission to promote the notion of the 'developmental state', despite being acutely aware that it could fail in the face of incapacity, maladministration, and corruption. These turned out to be very well-grounded concerns.[92] The dismal failure of the SOEs (almost without exception) has been the most significant reason for South Africa's fall into recession and the abandonment of any realistic hope for an economic turnaround. The existence of such a self-serving state, unconcerned with the economic advancement of its citizens, prepares the ground for significant political and social instability.

Secondly, even a capable and honest 'developmental state' may fail in the long term if the distribution of the benefits of development is not seen as equitable by all the communities that comprise 'the people'. The developmental state, which inevitably leads to centralization, may exhibit all the symptoms of a fragile state, with skewed development in favour of the ruling elite or ethnic group at the expense of minorities and the periphery. Even where a history of inequitable development (as in Ethiopia and Kenya) has led to a federal dispensation, the developmental centralized state might hollow out the promise of federalism through biased developmental investments that leave some group out in the cold.

For instance, although the development state in Ethiopia, under the guidance of Prime Minister Meles Zenawi, led to Ethiopia's posting the highest growth rate in Africa, it has not eased inter-communal tensions in the long run because of perceived inequitable outcomes. As Solomon Negussie shows, development planning which occurs without the participation of the regional governments and the equitable distribution of benefits can have tragic consequences: 'one of the major factors in political unrest in Ethiopia is the lack of proportionality in the benefits that accrue to local people from investment taxation'.[93] Even in unitary states, skewed or partisan development may lead to conflict. All in all, the developmental state may reveal the bias of the ruling elite more blatantly than ever.

4.4 The 'Social State'

However impressive a country's growth rate may be, the failure of the market to address poverty and unemployment has compelled the state to ensure a more equitable distribution of goods and services, giving rise to the 'social state'.[94] While the social state can be seen as an aspect of the developmental state, it is important to note that the social state focuses on the delivery of social services rather than on the growth of the economy as such.

Constitutionally speaking, social state commitments find expression in either the aspirational sentiments of Directive Principles of State Policy or in the enforceable socio-economic rights of a bill of rights. Most constitutions take the aspirational approach, with

---

[92] See Steytler, Chapter 5, this volume.
[93] Negussie, Chapter 12, this volume, 345.
[94] Ollick, Chapter 3, this volume.

just a few promoting the judicially enforceable route. The Nigerian Constitution deploys the (importantly) non-justiciable National Objectives and Directive Principles of State Policy to express a number of socio-economic 'rights'. At the other end of the spectrum, the South African Bill of Rights details its justiciable socio-economic rights (compare also Kenya). Ghana uses both: the right to education falls into the bill of rights, while other socio-economic rights are asserted as mere directive principles.

Where such rights are made justiciable, their actual enforcement is usually made subject to progressive realization within available state resources. This escape clause ties these rights to the performance of the economy and its ability to provide the necessary revenue. As Ollick notes, 'unconstitutional action or inaction could result not from lack of political will or respect for the law, but from the inadequate allocation of resources'.[95] As noted in Chapter 1, Piketty has generally argued that one cannot build a social state with low revenue; and low revenue is the common characteristic of most developing countries.[96] Although education, health, and housing are the major budget expenditure items across Africa, the successful social state in Africa is still very much in the making.[97]

4.5 Protecting the State from Over-Indebtedness

A part of the state's management of the economy, and certainly a part of being a 'developmental state', is incurring the debt necessary to the funding of long-term projects, in particular the funding of the infrastructure needed for economic development. However, more often than not, state borrowing is done to cover current expenditure, including meeting the immediate demands of the 'social state', when self-generated revenue is insufficient. Debt acquisition for infrastructure development is usually justified on the basis that such long-term projects would benefit future generations and thus they, too, must pay their share. Short-term debt for current expenditure may be necessary to deal with unexpected economic vicissitudes such as commodity price fluctuations. In the developmental state, it is not only the government that incurs debt. SOEs often run at huge losses, and then must borrow for both current expenditure and infrastructure development.

As Adem Abebe suggests, a more nefarious reason for debt is that borrowed money provides 'easy money' for patrimonial networks in government, much easier than that raised by the 'more cumbersome and accountable taxation efforts, which could trigger demands for accountability and public protests and opposition'.[98] Abebe finds that most African countries are swimming, if not drowning, in a sea of debt. The main lenders are China (which is currently owed more than half of all state-to-state debt in Africa); international development institutions (the IMF, World Bank, and African Development Bank); and a range of private banks, both local and foreign. There is little transparency around this massive debt burden, with no certainty about the real levels of indebtedness, or just who is owed exactly how much. As Abebe concludes, 'there is clear evidence that public debt is rising and threatening, or likely to threaten, the economies of some African states'.[99]

---

[95] Ollick, Chapter 3, this volume, 87.
[96] Thomas Piketty, *Capital in the Twenty-First Century* (Belknap Press of Harvard University Press 2014).
[97] Mabugu, Chapter 2, this volume.
[98] Abebe, Chapter 13, this volume, 370.
[99] ibid 357.

The consequences of such high levels of indebtedness are severe. Interest repayments compete with and tend to crowd out scarce revenue for funding social services. Abebe notes that, with the advent of the COVID-19 pandemic, debt repayments are higher than amounts spent on public health services.[100] Similarly, as he also notes, states enforce strict austerity measures to help reduce indebtedness, but these can stagnate economic growth, with dire consequences for the general population. In addition, future generations are not only required to pay back the loans for infrastructure development they enjoy, but are also saddled with repaying debts that should have been paid by earlier generations for their own benefits. If over-indebtedness leads to defaulting on repayments, the consequences can include the imposition of structural adjustment programmes on the countries concerned by the IMF or the actual loss of key state assets to China. In an already heavily indebted South Africa, an IMF loan for COVID-19-related expenditure was highly contested (but not defeated), as the spectre of structural adjustment programmes loomed large in the minds of political parties and labour unions.[101] Finally, in federal systems, unlimited borrowing by subnational governments and resultant defaulting on repayments may cause a contagion effect that damages the national economy, as the national government is either explicitly or implicitly the guarantor of subnational loans.

What has been done constitutionally to prevent or mitigate these consequences? On the continental level, the African Charter on Democracy, Elections, and Governance of 2007 already requires state parties to institutionalize sound economic and corporate government through, inter alia, the 'efficient management of public debt'.[102] The question follows as to whether constitutions have provided a suitable framework for ensuring sustainable borrowing.

Abebe's survey of African constitutions yields several findings. Very few constitutions even mention the national executive's borrowing power: usually, it is simply assumed as an implicit executive power. In others, the matter is dealt with only in a cursory manner (eg borrowing money is understood as part of the mandate of the Ethiopian executive).[103] The Nigerian Constitution empowers, rather than constrains, the federal government to borrow from internal and external sources.[104] In the Kenyan Constitution, the only requirement for borrowing is that legislation must regulate the terms on which the national government may borrow and the consequential reporting duties.[105]

By contrast, in federal systems, clear constitutional limits are placed on subnational borrowing. Nigeria bestows no borrowing powers on the states; the federal government has the exclusive power to do so on their behalf.[106] In South Africa, provinces and municipalities may borrow for both capital and current expenditure but only in terms of national legislation, while borrowing for current expenditure may be done only when necessary for bridging purposes during a financial year.[107] Kenya is even more restrained with regard to

---

[100] Chapter 13, this volume.
[101] Nico Steytler, Jaap de Visser, and Tinashe Chigwata, 'South Africa: Surfing towards Centralisation on the Covid-19 Waves' in Nico Steytler (ed), *Comparative Federalism and Covid-19: Combatting the Pandemic* (Routledge 2022) 349.
[102] Art 33(4).
[103] Ethiopian Constitution, 1995, art 77(4).
[104] Nigerian Constitution, 1999, second schedule, part I, item 7.
[105] Art 211(1).
[106] Nigerian Constitution, 1999, second schedule, part I, item 7.
[107] South African Constitution, ss 230 and 230A.

borrowing by its counties: a loan may be raised only if and when the national government guarantees it.[108]

In addition, although the placing of a debt ceiling is not to be found in constitutions, in some cases provision is made that such a ceiling may be imposed by legislation. The Zimbabwean Constitution obliges Parliament to adopt legislation that 'must set limits on— (a) borrowings by the State; [and] (b) the public debt'—limits that may not be exceeded without the approval of the National Assembly.[109]

A great deal of faith is placed in the national legislature's capacity to act as a check on executive borrowing. A popular measure is that any loan agreement must be ratified by parliament: this is found mainly in anglophone countries, including Ghana, Liberia, the Gambia, and Zambia. In the South African Constitution, the approval requirement is rather weak. Here the national budget 'must contain … an indication of intentions regarding borrowing and other forms of public liability that will increase public debt during the [fiscal] year'.[110] In the absence of parliamentary approval, transparency is often required, with parliaments playing an important oversight role in this. The Kenyan Constitution provides that legislation may impose reporting requirements, but once either of the houses of parliament requests information on any particular loan, the government must comply within seven days.[111] The oversight may go beyond Parliament to include other independent institutions. In Kenya, the Auditor-General is required to audit and report on public debt within six months of the end of each financial year.[112]

Although Abebe is sceptical of the value of parliamentary approval (legislatures tend simply to rubberstamp executive decisions), he sees great value in the transparency that the resulting disclosures bring. These can mobilize parliamentary opposition and empower civil society. Overall, Abebe argues, there is 'significant advantage to anchoring the debt management regime in a constitutional framework'.[113] However, the practice has also proved to be disappointing in many cases, and Abebe concludes that 'African constitutions have not contributed to taming the spectre of debt, which continues to rise in all countries'.[114]

4.6 Protecting the State from the Market: Anti-corruption Institutions

Given the dominant role that the state plays in the economy, the latter is, of course, subject to the omnipresent ethos of the patrimonial state, over and above being exploited by the predatory instincts of the market. Given the pervasiveness of corruption, there is no shortage of constitutionally enshrined anti-corruption institutions, ranging from auditors-general to ombudspersons, public protectors, and human rights commissions.[115] These serve, Klug suggests, democratic ends and also work as confidence-building institutions for external

---

[108] Kenyan Constitution, 2010, art 212(a). A further requirement is that the loan must be approved by the county assembly (art 212(b)).

[109] Zimbabwean Constitution 2013, art 300(1).

[110] Section 215(3)(c).

[111] Kenyan Constitution, art 211.

[112] Constitution of Kenya, art 299(4).

[113] Chapter 13, this volume, 357.

[114] Chapter 13, this volume, 368.

[115] Charles M Fombad and Nico Steytler (eds), *Corruption and Constitutionalism: Revisiting Control Measures and Strategies* (OUP 2020).

audiences such as foreign investors.[116] However, these constitutional endeavours have not amounted to much, either because the institutions are not independent enough from the executive they are supposed to police, or because their independence has been hollowed out through executive appointments. At the end of the day, the courts act as the last bastions against lawlessness, though they too may lose their independence and integrity.

5. Globalization, the African Economy, and Constitutionalism

As with the rest of the globalized world, African states are experiencing considerable pressures on their sovereignty (the cornerstone of any constitutional project), especially so in relation to the economy. As partners in many of Africa's trading blocs (and therefore subject to their regulations)—including the Common Market for Eastern and Southern Africa (COMESA), East Africa Community (EAC), Economic Community of West African States (ECOWAS), Southern African Customs Union (SACU), Southern African Development Community (SADC), West African Economic and Monetary Union (WAEMU), and most recently the African Continental Free Trade Area (AfCFTA) in 2019—the sovereignty of each state (particularly with regard to determining their own trade regimes) is being whittled away.

Even more far-reaching is the influence of the international trading system, in which the World Trade Organization provides significant sanctions for non-compliance with the rules of free trade. As Eva Maria Belser explains,

> [C]onstitutionalized global trade rules assert the primacy of the state's obligations to follow tariff concessions, to eliminate trade barriers, to respect the principle of non-discrimination, to protect intellectual property and, overall, to guarantee private parties a right to trade freely across borders.[117]

The enforceability of trade rules at the expense of domestic rules has given rise to the need for global trade constitutionalism limiting governments in their economic policy and legislative choices. Giving up complete sovereignty (in any event a sovereignty already compromised by the adoption of the legal frameworks provided by international human rights) has proved to be an easy trade-off in exchange for the promise of economic growth through free trade. In liberal theory, the aim is to keep governments out of trade and not to interfere with the invisible hand of international markets which, if undisturbed, maximizes wealth.[118] But, as Piketty remarks, trade liberalization 'is not a bad thing but only if it is not peremptorily imposed from without and only lost revenue can be replaced',[119] that is to say, if the loss in trade tariffs is offset by the economic advantages gained.

Belser argues in Chapter 14 that risks are incurred by shedding some national sovereignty; this may undermine a country's quest for constitutionalism. First of all, a country (or even a whole continent) may be left with no say in the drafting of the very rules that

---

[116] Klug, Chapter 7, this volume.
[117] Chapter 14, this volume, 373.
[118] Belser, Chapter 14, this volume.
[119] Piketty (n 96) 491–2.

limit its sovereignty. It has been argued that African countries played virtually no role in the drafting of the WTO rules: these were largely imposed on African countries by the world's major trading countries. So far, the attempt by African countries to influence the Doha Development Agenda has not borne any fruit. Indeed, the WTO agreements stand in sharp contrast to those of the AfCFTA and the other regional trading blocs that emerged through the agency of African countries themselves.

What is at stake is not merely the question of the legitimacy of the WTO rules for those who had no part in their drafting. Belser poses the significant question of whether the rules actually work in favour of each country and the continent as a whole.[120] The complaint here is that trade liberalization has increased the wealth of the developed economies that benefit from the trade, and less so the wealth of the African countries. As noted previously, African countries play a marginal role in international trade, and that role is confined largely to the export of their natural resources. In this sense, the trade regimes put in place by the WTO simply continue the old colonial patterns of trade, with the main share of profits going to the former colonizers.

A second risk is that trade agreements signed by national executives do not generally have popular support. As Fombad argues, parliamentary ratification of trade agreements is of particular importance given the latter's profound impact on economic policy.[121] This argument is as pertinent as with loan agreements: trade agreements are also long-term commitments that have a profound impact on economic policy.

Thirdly, international trade agreements may also disrupt the constitutional hierarchy of laws. In countries with a monist approach to the direct applicability of international treaties, these treatises always trump domestic laws. This, Fombad points out, is especially problematic in francophone and lusophone Africa, where, once ratified, an international agreement takes precedence over national legislation.[122]

Finally, the constitutionalized free-trade regime works to undermine a country's constitutional commitment to human rights and development. Belser argues that international human rights law aims at constraining the power of states in order to guarantee the respect and protection of individual rights and freedoms, and is thus compatible and supportive of the constitutional protection of domestic human rights. International trade law, in contrast, provides no comparable domestic constitutional values or rules. She thus states that 'the elevation of global trade rules to constitutional rules signifies the priority of free trade over non-trade rules and constitutes a risk for human rights and development'.[123] African countries may then be forced to choose between respecting global trade rules or pursuing a human rights-based development agenda, thus weakening their commitment to constitutionalism. This is particularly apparent in relation to agricultural policies. Northern states subsidize their non-competitive agriculture through a system of export subsidies, but these are in force at the expense of African states where agriculture is vital for the survival of the 70 per cent of the population who live in rural areas.

---

[120] Belser, Chapter 14, this volume.
[121] Chapter 4, this volume.
[122] Chapter 4, this volume.
[123] Belser, Chapter 14, this volume, 110.

The overall argument here is that the already limited work the constitution can do to mediate the clash of opposing interests in the economy may be undermined by the strong imposition of the international community on economic policy and conduct.

6. Constitutionalism and Economic Growth

Chapter 1 mapped the inconclusive links between economic growth and constitutionalism worldwide and raised the following question: do the African case studies in this volume suggest a positive, or any other, correlation between constitutionalism and economic growth?

Constitutionalism, understood as comprising three basic elements (democracy, limited government, and the rule of law) has only a small foothold in most African countries (as demonstrated in previous volumes in this series). Most constitutions do not fully embody these basic elements. When they do, it is usually clear that the democracy in question is often of the 'authoritarian' variety in which the separation of powers between the legislature, the executive, and the judiciary is weak, and in which the bills of rights pose few restraints. The rule of law—the observance of the constitution and legislation and their enforcement by an independent judiciary—is the exception rather than the rule. The main exceptions are Botswana, South Africa, Mauritius, Kenya, and Namibia; but these too are faltering in some respects. It is thus difficult to make any neat comparison between the rates of economic growth in constitution-abiding versus constitution-negating countries.

The focus of the volume is on constitutionalism in general; it is not on any specific constitutional features such as have been the interest of scholars such as Persson and Tabellini.[124] Their work seeks to find out whether, for example, the structure of government—presidential or parliamentary—creates different economic outcomes. Indeed, they found (on the basis of econometric analysis) that countries with parliamentary systems perform better than those with presidential systems. This is not a concern of constitutionalism because both systems are expressions of democracy, as long as, in practice, they allow free and fair competition. Our interest lies in the question of whether there is free and fair competitive democracy.

While the rest of the world may provide evidence of an equivocal relationship between the prevalence of constitutionalism and positive economic growth and prosperity, there is no doubt that the relationship between constitutionalism and economic growth in Africa is on the whole negative: more often than not, the absence of constitutionalism leads to economic decline. This conclusion can best be illustrated by reference to the three basic elements of constitutionalism.

6.1 Democracy

While the goal of democracy is not necessarily economic advancement, is there nevertheless a positive relation between democracy and economic growth in Africa?[125] The

---

[124] Torsten Persson and Guido Tabellini, *The Economic Effects of Constitutions: What do the Data Say?* (MIT 2003) 7.

[125] As Piketty (n 96) 570 notes, the goal of democracy is not simply economic growth which leads to greater levels of inequality, but larger societal goals.

constitutional reforms of the 1990s have meant that elections are no longer an issue in most African countries; they are routinely held (bar a few exceptions).[126] The focus is now on the quality of the elections, that is, whether they are free and fair or authoritarian (or, more specifically, engage in what has become known as 'competitive authoritarianism'). While Botswana, Mauritius, and South Africa have become known for holding free and fair elections, a strong authoritarian tendency has been gathering momentum in other African countries over the past thirty years.[127]

Free and fair elections have not guaranteed economic growth. In the touted examples of Botswana and Mauritius, such elections are just one of the factors that have contributed to the political stability which has proved to be an essential ingredient for generating investor confidence. Other factors (and more important ones) include sound economic policy and the efficient stewardship of SOEs. In South Africa, despite its proud record of democratic government since 1994 and an initial period of strong economic growth under President Mbeki (1999–2008), the next decade (under President Zuma) saw considerable dithering on economic policy as well as the wholesale looting of the state, resulting in a recession well before the global COVID-19 pandemic induced recession.[128]

The two most celebrated cases of economic growth are Ethiopia and Rwanda. Both of these countries are understood as representing 'developmental authoritarianism': that is, 'nominally democratic governments that provide significant public works and services while exerting control over nearly every facet of society'.[129] In the case of Ethiopia, the widescale protests since 2018 have undone the image of stability.[130] In the context of growing protests in the ethnic regions (with many of these claiming marginalization), the declaration of an emergency and the postponement of the 2020 national and regional elections under the sham cover of the COVID-19 pandemic[131] has led to civil war in the Tigray region.[132] As Paul Collier observes, civil war is extremely destructive for economic growth.[133] In hindsight, growth of the economy in Ethiopia under the rule of Prime Minister Meles was always built on insecure foundations.

Meanwhile, developmental authoritarianism continues to proceed without demur in Rwanda.[134] Time will tell whether the 'economic miracle' can continue and sustain the legitimacy of President Kagame's never-ending rule. What is clear is that authoritarian rule

---

[126] See Charles M Fombad, 'Democracy, Elections and Constitutionalism in Africa: Setting the Scene', in Charles M Fombad and Nico Steytler (eds), *Democracy, Elections and Constitutionalism in Africa* (OUP 2021) 1–35, 1.

[127] Charles M Fombad, 'Reversing the Surging Tide towards Authoritarian Democracy in Africa: Setting the Scene', in Charles M Fombad and Nico Steytler (eds), *Democracy, Elections and Constitutionalism in Africa* (OUP 2021) 463–517.

[128] Steytler, De Visser, and Chigwata (n 101).

[129] Hilary Matfess, 'Rwanda and Ethiopia: Developmental Authoritarianism and the New Politics of African Strong Men' (2015) 58(2) African Studies Review 181–204.

[130] Zemelak Ayitnew Ayele, 'Constitutionalism and Electoral Authoritarianism in Ethiopia', in Charles M Fombad and Nico Steytler (eds), *Democracy, Elections and Constitutionalism in Africa* (OUP 2021) 169–98.

[131] In a study of the reaction of eighteen federations to the COVID-19 pandemic, scheduled elections proceeded; only in Ethiopia were they postponed despite the lowest infection rate among the federations under comparison (Nico Steytler, 'Federalism under Pressure: Federal "Health" Factors and "Co-morbidities"' in Nico Steytler (ed), *Comparative Federalism and Covid-19: Combatting the Pandemic* (Routledge 2022) 396–422).

[132] Zemelak Ayitenew Ayele and Yonatan Tesfaye Fessha, 'Controlling Public Health Emergencies in Federal Systems: The Case of Ethiopia' in Nico Steytler (ed), *Comparative Federalism and Covid-19: Combatting the Pandemic* (Routledge 2022) 319–35.

[133] 'On the Economic Consequences of Civil War' (1999) 51 Oxford Economic Papers 168.

[134] Teresa Nogueira Pinto, 'Constitutionalism and Developmental Authoritarianism: Power, Law, and Legitimacy in Post-Genocide Rwanda', in Charles M Fombad and Nico Steytler (eds), *Democracy, Elections and Constitutionalism in Africa* (OUP 2021) 198–219.

per se does not produce good economic results, as for now Rwanda is an exception to the misrule of authoritarian rulers. Moreover, competitive authoritarian elections do not help in securing much-needed political stability.

6.3 Limited Government

Limited government is not usually associated with governance in most African countries. Each of the two main aspects of this—the separation of powers between the three branches of government and the protections offered by bills of rights—are weak.[135] The key question, then, is what effects do imperial presidencies with excessive and unconstrained concentrations of power have on economic performance? A weak separation between the executive and parliament can easily shrink its role to that of mere handmaiden to the executive. This makes nonsense of the confidence some constitutions place in legislatures to scrutinize and vet international loans, and so guard against reckless borrowing. A compliant parliament routinely fails to hold the executive to account. In South Africa, the Inquiry into State Capture heard from the Speaker of Parliament that the ruling party—the African National Congress (ANC)—knew all about the looting of the state during the Zuma presidency, but affirmed that their loyalty was to the party, not to the people of South Africa they purportedly represent.[136] State capture, it is commonly accepted, has resulted in untold damage to the country's economy. If not for the judiciary, it would have gone on unchecked.[137]

In Chapter 8, Makanatsa Makonese argues that the ousting of the Zimbabwean courts' jurisdiction over land distribution and evictions contributed significantly to the implosion of the Zimbabwean economy.[138] Starting in 1990, the courts' jurisdiction over determining what was fair compensation for landowners was removed. When land invasion and occupations occurred, the police refused to implement court orders, and the courts' jurisdiction over evictions was also removed. The government's reneging on its commitment to international treaty arbitration on land matters did not endear it to the international community. The collapse of the agricultural section which followed also impacted on the manufacturing sector and consequently on tax revenues, in effect leaving state coffers empty. Klug suggests that conflicts over landownership and the unregulated takeover of white farms (a process in which judicial review was excluded) were crucial to the economic implosion in Zimbabwe. Klug further argues that economic prosperity in Botswana has more to do with its overall political stability, rather than any constitutional provision (its Constitution has no provisions concerning landholding), though one should perhaps add to that the contribution made by its functioning judicial system.

The principle of 'limited government' is not to be understood as meaning the same thing as 'small government'. 'Small government' keeps out of the marketplace, leaving control of that to the private sector; the 'developmental state' (as discussed above) is entirely compatible with the limited government paradigm. SOEs represent an entirely legitimate

---

[135] See Charles M Fombad (ed), *Separation of Powers in African Constitutionalism* (OUP 2016).
[136] Siviwe Feketha, 'Modise Says ANC was Tardy on State Capture: South African Deserve Apology—National Assembly Speaker' *SowetanLive* (20 April 2021) <https://www.sowetanlive.co.za/news/south-africa/2021-04-20-modise-says-anc-was-tardy-on-state-capture/> accessed 12 May 2021.
[137] Steytler, Chapter 5. See also Steytler (n 80).
[138] See also Klug, Chapter 7, this volume.

exercise of state power. Their only problem is that—not being subject to the discipline of the market—they tend to operate ineffectually as monopolies. In addition, they are often governed outside the law, consequently defeating the ends of the developmental state rather than realizing them.

6.4 Rule of Law

The rule of law presupposes legal rules that are clear and governance which is performed according to these rules. When this is not done, the rules must be enforced by an independent judiciary and the state must comply with the judicial rulings. The rule of law can be breached either by neglect or by design: by neglect, when constitutional mandates are not translated into law and are thus not implemented (as with Namibia's environmental laws); by design, as in the most common form of challenge to the rule of law—corruption.[139]

One needs to go no further than South Africa for an example of how the collapse of the rule of law has disastrous consequences for the economy. As noted above, the new democratic government cast itself in the role of a 'developmental state' with the stated aim of rectifying the country's legacy of racial discrimination, high levels of poverty, and the inequality arising from that. The plan was that establishing SOEs in the key areas of electricity generation and transport (air and rail) would provide the necessary infrastructure for an expanding and inclusive economy. However, the widespread corruption engaged in by the Zuma presidency and the consequent looting of these SOEs achieved the exact opposite. In the end, only the courts were able to curb the looting spree.[140]

At a more general level, it is difficult for a self-proclaimed 'developmental state' truly to deliver on development when it is embedded in a patrimonial state in which a political elite governs not for the benefit of the population but the enrichment of the few. Indeed, it may be that the developmental state, due to its expansion into the economy, exacerbates corruption by providing more scope for politicians to feed at the ever-expanding trough of state money.[141]

7. Conclusion

Following the attempt at creating command economies in Africa in the immediate post-independence era, the 1990s saw the return on constitutional paper of the market as part of the democratization process. The revolt against the authoritarian and one-party regimes was not necessarily based solely on democratic concerns, but also on the ground of economic decline and devastation. If the authoritarian regimes had delivered on economic benefits, the revolts might not have occurred, as is amply evidenced elsewhere by the longevity authoritarian regimes enjoy on the back of ongoing economic performance.

---

[139] Melber, Chapter 10, this volume.
[140] See Steytler (n 80).
[141] Nico Steytler, 'Towards Understanding and Combating the Crime of Corruption in Africa', in Charles Fombad and Nico Steytler (eds), *Corruption and Constitutionalism: Revisiting Control Measures and Strategies* (OUP 2020) 457–98, 474.

The principal mechanism for the constitutional embedding of the market economy has been the inclusion of the protection of property rights and freedom of contract in a bill of rights (although the justiciability of these protections varies from one country to another). In Africa, however, the state did not retreat from the economy or become smaller, as neo-liberal theory dictated. Instead, African states continued to hold on to the levers of economic power, though often using them very badly indeed.

Constitutionally, the state was mostly allotted the guardianship of land and natural resources, the two mainstays of many African economies. The states, however, generally failed to perform their role to the advancement of the land toilers, and rarely used natural resources (minerals and oil) to benefit the citizenry at large. The abundance of natural resources paradoxically became a 'curse' and gave rise to major conflicts. As the helmsmen of the nation, state executives structured the economy to serve the ruling elite; as the dominant rower of the economic boat, the 'developmental state', captured by the pervasive 'patrimonial state', did not place the interest of the citizens as paramount.

In fact, the democratization of the 1990s did little to change significantly the centrist mode of governance in which power is concentrated in the executive and, ultimately, in the presidency itself. This remained unaffected by the formal political separation of powers or devolution of powers, and nor did this shift in relation to control of the economy. The aim, indeed, has been either to control or capture the private sector. The notion of non-centralism in the economy was as foreign as most of the major investment companies were.

At the same time as states sought to extend their control over the economy, larger, global forces were chipping away at that kind of control and autonomy. With its enforceable trade rules, the international trading regime worked to actively diminish and circumscribe the sovereignty of states, and not always to a country's benefit, or that of the continent as a whole.

While constitutions themselves articulated the terms of the relationship between states and economies quite loosely and in varying ways, it may be that it is the underlying practice of constitutionalism that mattered most. The absence of political stability through free and fair elections, the lack of checks and balances on self-serving executive action, and the disregard for the rule by law in favour of executive discretion, reveals a strong negative correlation with economic growth.

Although constitutionalism on its own does not secure economic growth and social development (sound economic policies do that), its absence holds them back. Building a political and social culture that actively supports constitutionalism is a necessary but not sufficient condition for economic and social advancement. The driver of the economy is likely to be the market, and even the harshest critics of capitalism acknowledge the creative energy that stems from the self-interest underlying the private sector (Collier wants to ameliorate its negative consequences through the social state; Piketty wants to reduce the inequality that the market creates and perpetuates). The role of the state, then, is to provide the environment, legal and otherwise, in which the economy can grow and harness the resultant productivity to the advancement of the population in general.

This stance also seems to be the one adopted as the collective agenda of the continent. The African Union (AU) Agenda 2063, formally adopted in March 2013, sets a strategic framework for the socio-economic transformation of the continent over the next fifty years. Amongst its main goals are effecting equitable and people-centred growth and development; eradicating poverty; and economic cooperation and integration. These goals connect to the AU's other main project: that of advancing constitutionalism on the continent. In advancing constitutionalism, the courts play an important role in mediating very different demands made by very different actors. In the words of Fombad: '[T]he role of courts in promoting economic constitutionalism will be determined by the way they are able to provide a proper balance between, for example, protecting property entitlements and promoting property redistribution.'[142] As Melber comments, '[a]n independent judiciary is essential for upholding the rule of law, but government and civil society play a decisive role too'.[143]

Embedding constitutionalism in government and civil society remains the major challenge of our time.

Bibliography

Ayele ZA, 'Constitutionalism: The Missing Element in South Sudan's Elusive Quest for Peace through Federalism?' in Fombad CM and Steytler N (eds), *Decentralisation and Constitutionalism in Africa* (OUP 2019).

Ayele ZA, 'Constitutionalism and Electoral Authoritarianism in Ethiopia' in Fombad CM and Steytler N (eds), *Democracy, Elections and Constitutionalism in Africa* (OUP 2021).

Ayele ZA and Fessha YT, 'Controlling Public Health Emergencies in Federal Systems: The Case of Ethiopia', in Steytler N (ed), *Comparative Federalism and Covid-19: Combatting the Pandemic* (Routledge 2022).

Bhorat H and others, 'Resource Dependence and Inequality in Africa: Impacts, Consequences and Potential Solutions' in Odusola A and others (eds), *Income Inequality Trends in Sub-Saharan Africa: Divergence, Determinants and Consequences* (United Nations Development Programme 2019).

Collier P, 'On the Economic Consequences of Civil War' (1999) 51 Oxford Economic Papers 168.

Ensor L, 'Tito Mboweni Slams Dismissal of Zambian Central Banker' *Timeslive* (23 August 2020) <https://www.timeslive.co.za/sunday-times/business/2020-08-23-tito-mboweni-slams-dismissal-of-zambian-central-banker/> accessed 3 May 2021.

Feketha S, 'Modise Says ANC was Tardy on State Capture: South African Deserve Apology—National Assembly Speaker' *SowetanLive* (20 April 2021) <https://www.sowetanlive.co.za/news/south-afr ica/2021-04-20-modise-says-anc-was-tardy-on-state-capture/> accessed 12 May 2021.

Fombad CM (ed), *Separation of Powers in African Constitutionalism* (OUP 2016).

Fombad CM, 'Democracy, Elections and Constitutionalism in Africa: Setting the Scene' in Fombad CM and Steytler N (eds), *Democracy, Elections and Constitutionalism in Africa* (OUP 2021).

Fombad CM, 'Reversing the Surging Tide towards Authoritarian Democracy in Africa: Setting the Scene' in Fombad CM and Steytler N (eds), *Democracy, Elections and Constitutionalism in Africa* (OUP 2021).

Fombad CM and Steytler N (eds), *Corruption and Constitutionalism in Africa: Revisiting Control Measures and Strategies* (OUP 2020).

Haysom N and Kane S, *Negotiating Natural Resources for Peace: Ownership, Control and Wealth Sharing*, Briefing Paper (UNDP October 2009).

Matfess H, 'Rwanda and Ethiopia: Developmental Authoritarianism and the New Politics of African Strong Men' (2015) 58(2) African Studies Review 181–204.

Persson T and Tabellini G, *The Economic Effects of Constitutions: What do the Data Say?* (MIT 2003) 7.

Piketty T, *Capital in the Twenty-First Century* (Belknap Press of Harvard University Press 2014).

Pinto TN, 'Constitutionalism and Developmental Authoritarianism: Power, Law, and Legitimacy in Post-Genocide Rwanda' in Fombad CM and Steytler N (eds), *Democracy, Elections and Constitutionalism in Africa* (OUP 2021).

---

[142] Chapter 4, this volume, 110.
[143] Chapter 10, this volume, 300.

Reuters, 'Zambian President Fires Central Bank Governor in Surprise Move' (22 August 2020) <https://www.reuters.com/article/us-zambia-cenbank-governor-idUSKBN25I0NV> accessed 3 May 2021

Steytler N, 'The "Financial Constitution" and the Prevention and Combating of Corruption: A Comparative Study of Nigeria, South Africa and Kenya' in Fombad CM and Steytler N (eds), *Corruption and Constitutionalism: Revisiting Control Measures and Strategies* (OUP 2020).

Steytler N, 'Towards Understanding and Combating the Crime of Corruption in Africa' in Fombad CM and Steytler N (eds), *Corruption and Constitutionalism: Revisiting Control Measures and Strategies* (OUP 2020).

Steytler N, 'Federalism under Pressure: Federal "Health" Factors and "Co-morbidities"' in Steytler N (ed), *Comparative Federalism and Covid-19: Combatting the Pandemic* (Routledge 2022).

Steytler N, de Visser J, and Chigwata T, 'South Africa: Surfing towards Centralization on the Covid-19 Waves' in Steytler N (ed), *Comparative Federalism and Covid-19: Combatting the Pandemic* (Routledge 2022).

Index